June 18–22, 2012
Delft, The Netherlands

I0028745

**Association for
Computing Machinery**

Advancing Computing as a Science & Profession

HPDC'12

Proceedings of the

21st ACM Symposium on High-Performance
Parallel and Distributed Computing

Sponsored by:
ACM SIGARCH & University of Arizona

Supported by:
**Delft University of Technology,
Netherlands Organization for Scientific Research,
NVIDIA, National Science Organization,
Netherlands eScience Center**

**Association for
Computing Machinery**

Advancing Computing as a Science & Profession

The Association for Computing Machinery
2 Penn Plaza, Suite 701
New York, New York 10121-0701

Notice to Past Authors of ACM-Published Articles

ISBN: 978-1-4503-0805-2 (Digital)

ISBN: 978-1-4503-1745-0 (Print)

Additional copies may be ordered prepaid from:

ACM Order Department
PO Box 30777
New York, NY 10087-0777, USA

Phone: 1-800-342-6626 (USA and Canada)
+1-212-626-0500 (Global)
Fax: +1-212-944-1318
E-mail: acmhelp@acm.org
Hours of Operation: 8:30 am – 4:30 pm ET

Printed in the USA

Welcome from the General Chair

On behalf of the organizing committee, welcome to the *21st ACM Symposium on High-Performance Parallel and Distributed Computing* (HPDC'12), to Delft University of Technology, the oldest and largest university of technology in the Netherlands, and to Delft, a city rich in history and old Dutch architecture with strong ties to the Dutch royal family! HPDC'12 follows the tradition set by previous versions of the conference by providing a high-quality, single-track forum for presenting new research results on all aspects of the design, the implementation, the evaluation, and the use of parallel and distributed systems for high-end computing, along with an interesting set of workshops on a range of infrastructure and application areas.

In addition to looking at current and new developments, this year HPDC also looks back. First, on the occasion of the 20th anniversary of the conference last year, a 20-year issue with the best HPDC papers of the last 20 years has been composed. PC members of previous editions of the conference were given the opportunity to nominate papers, and a committee under the guidance of the Chairman of the Steering Committee, Jon Weissman, made the final selection of the best papers. This 20-year issue will be presented at this year's conference. The list of the papers included in the issue can also be found at the website of the HPDC conference series at www.hpdc.org.

Secondly, a new element introduced into this year's HPDC is the establishment of an Annual Achievement Award. The purpose of this award is to recognize individuals who have made long-lasting, influential contributions to the foundations or practice of the field of high-performance parallel and distributed computing, to raise the awareness of these contributions, especially among the younger generation of researchers, and to improve the image and the public relations of the HPDC community. The first recipient of this award is Ian Foster of the University of Chicago and Argonne National Laboratory, USA, who will give an Achievement Award Talk at the conference.

There are a number of people who have put great effort into making HPDC'12 a success. First and foremost, we thank the Program Co-Chairs, Thilo Kielmann of the Vrije Universiteit in Amsterdam and Matei Ripeanu of The University of British Columbia in Vancouver, for assembling an excellent program committee, for expertly managing the paper reviewing and selection process, and for putting together a great conference program that will stimulate discussions in Delft and new research once you return home. In particular, we thank them for their efforts in putting into place a number of innovations in the reviewing process, which are all great improvements, and which they will discuss in their own welcome message. The HPDC community owes Matei and Thilo a great debt!

We also thank the Posters Chair, Ana Varbanescu, for her work on the Poster Session, which has a different structure this year. In addition to the usual posters based on full submitted papers that were just below the acceptance line for presentation, there are also posters for the accepted papers on display throughout the conference, and posters submitted in response to a separate call, for attendees of the conference to show their ongoing work. We hope that these additional two types of posters will foster lively discussions.

We greatly appreciate the work of the Workshops Chair, Alexandru Iosup, who has assembled a very interesting program of workshops. Three of these workshops deal with Application Domains (*Astro-HPC* on Astronomy applications, *ECMLS* on Life Sciences applications, and *Science Cloud* on scientific applications), one deals with Data-Intensive Computing (*DIDC*), and two deal with Infrastructure topics (*MapReduce*, and *VTDC* on Virtualization).

We acknowledge the help of Jack Lange as the Sponsorship Chair, the help of the Publicity Chairs, Gabriel Antoniu, Naoya Maruyama, and Ioan Raicu, in disseminating the different calls related to the conference, and the help of the staff of Delft University of Technology, in particular, Esther van Seters and Stephen van der Laan, with the local arrangements and with creating the conference website, respectively. We thank our sponsors, ACM SIGARCH and the University of Arizona, and our supporters, NWO (the Dutch National Science Foundation), the US National Science Foundation, the recently established Netherlands eScience Center (NLeSC), NVIDIA, and Delft University of Technology. Finally, we thank the General Chair and the Program Chair of the previous HPDC conference, Barney Maccabe and Douglas Thain, and the Chairman of the Steering Committee, Jon Weissman, for their advice along the way.

This year, as has been done a number of times in the past, the Open Grid Forum (OGF35) is co-located with HPDC. We hope that the two communities will mutually benefit from the co-location, and we have offered attendees of each of these two events free access to the sessions and the workshops of the other on the two days of overlap.

We hope that you will find the conference interesting and that you will enjoy your stay in Delft.

Dick Epema
HPDC'12 General Chair
Delft University of Technology
Delft, the Netherlands

Welcome from the Program Co-Chairs

Welcome to ACM HPDC 2012! This is the twenty-first year of HPDC and we are pleased to report that our community continues to grow in size, quality and reputation. The program consists of three days packed with presentations on the latest developments in high-performance parallel and distributed computing. Featured events include the ceremony to present the "Achievement Award" to Prof. Ian Foster followed by his keynote address reflecting on 20 years of Grid computing, as well as keynote talks by Dr. Mihai Budiu on "big-data" analytics, Prof. Ricardo Bianchini on leveraging renewable energy in data centers. Technical paper sessions focus on virtualization, high-performance storage, massively parallel processors, resource management, energy, data analytics, and networked systems. Awards for best paper, best talk, and best poster will be given in the concluding session on Friday.

This year we have introduced two major changes in the reviewing process: author rebuttals and a two-phase review process. Our goals were twofold: first to give authors the chance to respond to reviewer's comments to help identify the strongest submissions by a rigorous and balanced reviewing process focusing on quality as the most important criterion. A second, to provide additional feedback to the authors of the most promising submissions, to continue to raise the quality of the technical program and continue to make HPDC an attractive venue that will attract top quality submissions.

143 full papers were submitted for review this year. A program committee of 45 experts, assisted by 15 external reviewers considered the submissions and wrote a total of 623 reviews. All papers received at least three reviews, and most papers that have reached the second stage of the review process received six reviews. The program committee met in March at Vrije Universiteit Amsterdam to select the program, and chose 23 full papers for presentation, yielding an acceptance rate of 16.1 percent. In addition, seven papers were selected for poster presentation, and are accompanied by a two-page abstract in the proceedings. This was a large number of submissions; many truly good papers were declined. On the positive side, we are convinced you will enjoy a high-quality program!

On the two days preceding the main conference, six affiliated workshops will take place. Each of these workshops is a small conference by itself, and provides a venue for presenting work on focused and emerging topics. The workshops are:

- ⅄ ECMLS: The Third International Emerging Computational Methods for the Life Sciences Workshop
- ⅄ MapReduce: The Third International Workshop on MapReduce and its Applications
- ⅄ ScienceCloud: The Third Workshop on Scientific Cloud Computing
- ⅄ VTDC: The Sixth International Workshop on Virtual Technologies in Distributed Computing
- ⅄ DIDC: Fifth International Workshop on Data-Intensive Distributed Computing
- ⅄ Astro-HPC: The First Workshop on High-Performance Computing for Astronomy

The proceedings available at the conference contain 23 full papers and 7 poster abstracts from the main conference. These, along with papers from the affiliated workshops, will be incorporated into the ACM Digital Library.

This conference could not happen without the hard work of the many people involved. Thank you for all of your contributions. Enjoy the conference!

Thilo Kielmann
HPDC'12 Program Co-Chair
Vrije Universiteit, Amsterdam, The Netherlands

Matei Ripeanu
HPDC'12 Program Co-Chair
The University of British Columbia, Canada

Table of Contents

Session 3: GPUs

Posters

Keynote Address

Session 4: Applications and Resources

21st International ACM Symposium on High-Performance Parallel and Distributed Computing Organization

General Chair: Dick Epema *(Delft University of Technology and Eindhoven University of Technology, The Netherlands)*

Program Chairs: Thilo Kielmann *(Vrije Universiteit, The Netherlands)*
Matei Ripeanu *(The University of British Columbia, Canada)*

Posters Chair: Ana Varbanescu *(Delft University of Technology, The Netherlands)*

Workshops Chair: Alexandru Iosup *(Delft University of Technology, The Netherlands)*

Sponsorship Chair: John Lange *(University of Pittsburgh, USA)*

Publicity Chairs: Gabriel Antoniu *(INRIA, France)*
Naoya Maruyama *(RIKEN Advanced Institute for Computational Science, Japan)*
Ioan Raicu *(Illinois Institute of Technology & Argonne National Laboratory, USA)*

Web Master: Stephen van der Laan *(Delft University of Technology, The Netherlands)*

Local Arrangements: Esther van Seters *(Delft University of Technology, The Netherlands)*

Steering Committee Chair: Jon Weissman *(University of Minnesota, USA)*

Steering Committee: Henri Bal *(Vrije Universiteit, the Netherlands)*
Andrew A. Chien *(University of Chicago & Argonne National Laboratory, USA)*
Peter Dinda *(Northwestern University, USA)*
Ian Foster *(University of Chicago and Argonne National Laboratory, USA)*
Salim Hariri *(University of Arizona, USA)*
Dieter Kranzlmueller *(Ludwig-Maximilians-Universitaet Muenchen, Germany)*
Arthur "Barney" Maccabe *(Oak Ridge National Laboratory, USA)*
Satoshi Matsuoka *(Tokyo Institute of Technology, Japan)*
Manish Parashar *(Rutgers University, USA)*
Karsten Schwan *(Georgia Tech, USA)*
Doug Thain *(University of Notre Dame, USA)*

Program Committee: David Abramson *(Monash University, Australia)*
Kento Aida *(National Institute of Informatics, Japan)*
Gabriel Antoniu *(INRIA, France)*
Rosa Badia *(Barcelona Supercomputing Center, Spain)*
Henri Bal *(Vrije Universiteit, The Netherlands)*
Anne Benoit *(ENS Lyon, France)*
John Bent *(Los Alamos National Laboratory, USA)*

Program Committee:
(continued)

Dick Bulterman *(CWI, The Netherlands)*

Kirk Cameron *(VirginiaTech, USA)*

Franck Cappello *(INRIA, France and University of Illinois
   at Urbana-Champaign, USA)*

Abhishek Chandra *(University of Minnesota, USA)*

Andrew Chien *(University of Chicago and Argonne National Laboratory, USA)*

Paolo Costa *(Imperial College, UK)*

Marco Danelutto *(University of Pisa, Italy)*

Peter Dinda *(Northwestern University, USA)*

Gilles Fedak *(INRIA, France)*

Renato Figueiredo *(University of Florida, USA)*

Clemens Grelck *(University of Amsterdam, The Netherlands)*

Dean Hildebrand *(IBM Research, USA)*

Fabrice Huet *(INRIA, France)*

Adriana Iamnitchi *(University of South Florida, USA)*

Alexandru Iosup *(Delft University of Technology, The Netherlands)*

Emmanuel Jeannot *(INRIA, France)*

Kate Keahey *(Argonne National Laboratory, USA)*

Charles Kilian *(Purdue University, USA)*

John Lange *(University of Pittsburgh, USA)*

Arthur "Barney" Maccabe *(Oak Ridge National Laboratory, USA)*

Carlos Maltzahn *(University of California, Santa Cruz, USA)*

Naoya Maruyama *(RIKEN Advanced Institute for Computational Science, Japan)*

Satoshi Matsuoka *(Tokyo Institute of Technology, Japan)*

Manish Parashar *(Rutgers University, USA)*

Beth Plale *(Indiana University, USA)*

Ioan Raicu *(Illinois Institute of Technology and Argonne National
   Laboratory, USA)*

Philip Rhodes *(University of Mississippi, USA)*

John Romein *(ASTRON, the Netherlands)*

Prasenjit Sarkar *(IBM Research, USA)*

Martin Swany *(Indiana University, USA)*

Michela Taufer *(University of Delaware, USA)*

Kenjiro Taura *(University of Tokyo, Japan)*

Douglas Thain *(University of Notre Dame, USA)*

Cristian Ungureanu *(NEC Research, USA)*

Ana Varbanescu *(Delft University of Technology, The Netherlands)*

Jon Weissman *(University of Minnesota, USA)*

Chuliang Weng *(Shanghai Jiao Tong University, China)*

Dongyan Xu *(Purdue University, USA)*

Additional reviewers:

Leonardo Arturo
Chang Bae
Erik Bodzsar
George Bosilca
Niels Drost
Trilce Estrada
Ana Gainaru
Abdullah Gharaibeh
Bautista Gomez
Sathish Gopalakrishnan
Apala Guha
Kyle Hale

Arnaud Legrand
Bogdan Nicolae
Rob van Nieuwpoort
Akira Nukada
Ana-Maria Oprescu
Karthik Pattabiraman
Kaveh Razavi
Kees van Reeuwijk
Kento Sato
Kees Verstoep
Lei Xia

Achievement Award Committee:

Dick Epema *(Delft University of Technology and Eindhoven University of Technology, The Netherlands)*
Thilo Kielmann *(Vrije Universiteit, The Netherlands)*
Arthur "Barney" Maccabe *(Oak Ridge National Laboratory, USA)*
Matei Ripeanu *(The University of British Columbia, Canada)*
Karsten Schwan *(Georgia Tech, USA)*

21st International ACM Symposium on High-Performance Parallel and Distributed Computing

2012 Sponsors & Supporters

Sponsors:

Supporters:

Delft University of Technology

Netherlands Organisation for Scientific Research

Putting A "Big-Data" Platform to Good Use: Training Kinect

Mihai Budiu
Microsoft Research SVC
Mihai.Budiu@microsoft.com

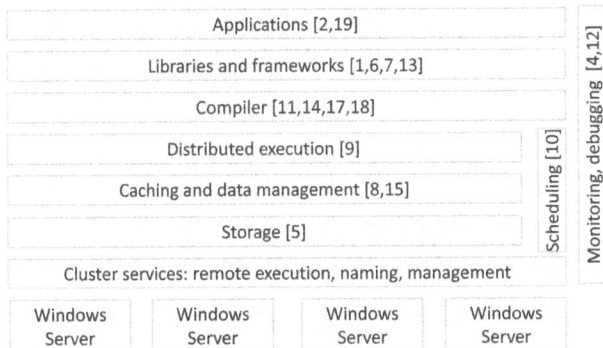

Figure 1: DryadLINQ software stack.

Categories and Subject Descriptors

C.5.m [**Computer Systems Organization**]: Miscellaneous

1. THE DRYADLINQ PLATFORM

In the last 7 years at Microsoft Research in Silicon Valley we have constructed the DryadLINQ software stack for large-scale data-parallel cluster computations. The architecture of the ensemble is depicted in Figure 1. The goal of the DryadLINQ project is to make writing parallel programs manipulating large amounts of data (terabytes to petabytes) as easy as programming a single machine. DryadLINQ is a batch computation model[1], optimized for throughput; since it is targets large clusters of commodity computers fault-tolerance is a primary concern. A primary tenet is that moving computation close to the data is much cheaper than moving the data itself. Here we discuss briefly the current architecture of the system (but more research is ongoing).

---

[1]Our system does not address interactive computation, wide-area (grid) computing, in-memory computation (e.g., HPC) or streaming.

Our software runs on relatively inexpensive computer clusters, using unmodified Windows Server. Our software makes minimal assumptions about the underlying cluster, and has been ported to several platforms: the Cosmos cluster runtime (built and used internally by Bing), Windows HPC Server and Windows Azure.

We have built a simple distributed filesystem, **TidyFS** [5][2]. All cluster machines have local disks, providing persistent storage; these disks are aggregated by TidyFS into a global filesystem. We assume that files can be very large, append-only, and thus partitioned into multiple pieces, each piece being replicated on several machines for fault-tolerance. Essentially, TidyFS is a reliable metadata service, allowing cluster applications to locate the actual data, which is stored as raw files on the local filesystem of each machine.

Dryad [9] is a distributed execution engine. Dryad programs (jobs) are coarse-grain, acyclic dataflow graphs. Each *vertex* in the job graph is an arbitrary computation, and vertices communicate with each other using point-to-point *channels*. The job graph is "virtualized," i.e., it is not tied to the available resources, and it can be executed by time-sharing these resources for the job vertices. For providing application-independent fault-tolerance Dryad assumes that job vertices are idempotent, computing a deterministic function of the contents of their input channels. Each channel contains a finite set of abstract records. Dryad is currently deployed by Bing for large-scale analytics, using many tens of thousands of machines and analyzing tens of petabytes of data every day.

In practice all Dryad computations are synthesized automatically from high-level languages. **DryadLINQ** [17, 11] is our compiler[3] The input language of DryadLINQ is .Net. DryadLINQ takes advantage of the LINQ (Language-Integrated Query) extensions to .Net to generate parallel computations. LINQ is a small declarative and functional language embedded in .Net that operates on collections of values. LINQ is similar to the database relational algebra, but has a much richer data model, since LINQ collections can contain arbitrary .Net objects. LINQ computations are compiled into dataflow graphs using sophisticated optimizations [14, 16]. DryadLINQ takes advantage of the strong typing of .Net to generate efficient serialization code for doing data I/O. DryadLINQ not only parallelizes the compu-

---

[2]DryadLINQ also interoperates with several other storage layers, such as Cosmos, the Distributed Storage Catalog, SQL Server, and even raw files exposed through remote file access protocols.

[3]Other compilers that target Dryad exist, such as Scope [3].

tation across machines, it also parallelizes the computation on each machine across CPU cores. By leveraging the native support for LINQ in the Visual Studio IDE, DryadLINQ provides a seamless experience writing programs that span multiple jobs (workflows).

Many large-scale computations are performed on data sets that grow constantly (e.g., search logs). **DryadInc** [15] rewrites such computations to be incremental by rewriting Dryad graphs. the incrementalization effort can be automated with knowledge about program semantics, as done by the **Nectar** [8] system, which unifies storage, computation and incrementalization. Storage is treated as a cache of computation results, enabling a simple trade-off between (re)computation and persisting (partial) results.

In batch computing systems big jobs can impede the timely progress of other computations. The **Quincy** [10] scheduler attempts to provide a compromise between fairness and efficiency by optimizing resource assignment using a distributed max-flow model. Quincy takes advantage of the fault-tolerance mechanisms of Dryad to perform preemptive vertex-level scheduling, dramatically improving the interactive user experience of sharing a large cluster.

While DryadLINQ provides the illusion of programming a computer cluster as a single machine, the presence of bugs and failures may reveal the complexity of the underlying system. We have built tools such as **Artemis** [4] for profiling and visualizing the performance of distributed computations, and **Daphne** [12] for job introspection and debugging.

On these foundations we have built various domain-specific libraries: e.g., branch-and-bound search in **DryadOpt** [1], information retrieval [6], machine learning [7] and **PINQ** for privacy-preserving computations [13].

2. TRAINING KINECT

The reliability and usability of DryadLINQ were instrumental in overcoming some difficulties encountered when building the Kinect body tracking pipeline [2]. Kinect is a device designed to complement the Xbox 360 games console, enabling users to control the console using only body gestures and voice control. The hardware device provides a *depth* image, where each pixel is labeled with the distance to the sensor. The Kinect SDK computes a skeletal representation of the players in the device field of view, which is used by games and applications to control interaction. The most computationally-intensive stage of the Kinect body tracking pipeline recognizes and labels each pixel in the input scene with a (set of) likely body parts. This stage uses a decision forest classifier. This classifier has been built using supervised learning, by analyzing a large number of labeled images. Training the classifier requires a very large number of calculations, and has been implemented in DryadLINQ.

DryadLINQ provided several advantages compared with MPI: (1) a high-level parallel programming language for building distributed computations instead of a simple low-level messaging API, (2) automatic and efficient serialization of complex data types for transport on the network, (3) resource virtualization, which allowed the manipulation of datasets much larger than the collective memory of the available machines, (4) built-in fault-tolerance and checkpointing, and (5) strong integration with C#, which enabled us to reuse the libraries developed by the computer vision experts, and orchestrate the many parallel and sequential phases of the training in a single program.

3. REFERENCES

[1] M. Budiu, D. Delling, and R. Werneck. DryadOpt: Branch-and-bound on distributed data-parallel execution engines. In *International Parallel and Distributed Processing Symposium (IPDPS)*, 2011.

[2] M. Budiu, J. Shotton, D. G. Murray, and M. Finocchio. Parallelizing the training of the Kinect body parts labeling algorithm. In *Big Learning: Algorithms, Systems and Tools for Learning at Scale*, 2011.

[3] R. Chaiken, P. L. Bob Jenkins, B. Ramsey, D. Shakib, S. Weaver, and J. Zhou. SCOPE: Easy and efficient parallel processing of massive data sets. In *International Conference of Very Large Data Bases (VLDB)*, 2008.

[4] G. F. Creţu-Ciocârlie, M. Budiu, and M. Goldszmidt. Hunting for problems with Artemis. In *USENIX Workshop on the Analysis of System Logs*, 2008.

[5] D. Fetterly, M. Haridasan, M. Isard, and S. Sundararaman. TidyFS: a simple and small distributed file system. In *USENIX Annual Technical Conference*, 2011.

[6] D. Fetterly and F. McSherry. A data-parallel toolkit for information retrieval. In *SIGIR Conference*, 2010.

[7] D. Fetterly, Y. Yu, M. Budiu, F. McSherry, and M. Isard. *Scaling Up Machine Learning*, chapter Large-scale Machine Learning using DryadLINQ. Cambridge University Press, 2010.

[8] P. K. Gunda, L. Ravindranath, C. A. Thekkath, Y. Yu, and L. Zhuang. Nectar: Automatic management of data and computation in datacenters. In *Symposium on Operating System Design and Implementation (OSDI)*, 2010.

[9] M. Isard, M. Budiu, Y. Yu, A. Birrell, and D. Fetterly. Dryad: Distributed data-parallel programs from sequential building blocks. In *European Conference on Computer Systems (EuroSys)*, 2007.

[10] M. Isard, V. Prabhakaran, J. Currey, U. Wieder, K. Talwar, and A. Goldberg. Quincy: fair scheduling for distributed computing clusters. In *Symposium on Operating Systems Principles (SOSP)*, 2009.

[11] M. Isard and Y. Yu. Distributed data-parallel computing using a high-level programming language. In *SIGMOD International conference on Management of data*, 2009.

[12] V. Jagannath, Z. Yin, and M. Budiu. Monitoring and debugging dryadlinq applications with Daphne. In *Workshop on High-Level Parallel Programming Models and Supportive Environments (HIPS)*, 2011.

[13] F. McSherry. Privacy integrated queries: an extensible platform for privacy-preserving data analysis. In *SIGMOD International conference on Management of data*, 2009.

[14] D. G. Murray, M. Isard, and Y. Yu. Steno: automatic optimization of declarative queries. In *ACM SIGPLAN Conference on Programming Language Design and Implementation (PLDI)*, 2011.

[15] L. Popa, M. Budiu, Y. Yu, and M. Isard. DryadInc: Reusing work in large-scale computations. In *Workshop on Hot Topics in Cloud Computing (HotCloud)*, 2009.

[16] Y. Yu, P. K. Gunda, and M. Isard. Distributed aggregation for data-parallel computing: interfaces and implementations. In *Symposium on Operating Systems Principles (SOSP)*, 2009.

[17] Y. Yu, M. Isard, D. Fetterly, M. Budiu, Ú. Erlingsson, P. K. Gunda, and J. Currey. DryadLINQ: A system for general-purpose distributed data-parallel computing using a high-level language. In *Symposium on Operating System Design and Implementation (OSDI)*, 2008.

vSlicer: Latency-Aware Virtual Machine Scheduling via Differentiated-Frequency CPU Slicing

Cong Xu, Sahan Gamage, Pawan N. Rao, Ardalan Kangarlou,
Ramana Rao Kompella, Dongyan Xu

Department of Computer Science
Purdue University
West Lafayette, Indiana 47907, USA
{xu172,sgamage,phosakot,ardalan,kompella,dxu}@cs.purdue.edu

ABSTRACT

Recent advances in virtualization technologies have made it
feasible to host multiple virtual machines (VMs) in the same
physical host and even the same CPU core, with fair share
of the physical resources among the VMs. However, as more
VMs share the same core/CPU, the CPU access latency experienced by each VM increases substantially, which translates into longer I/O processing latency perceived by I/O-
bound applications. To mitigate such impact while retaining
the benefit of CPU sharing, we introduce a new class of VMs
called *latency-sensitive VMs (LSVMs)*, which achieve better performance for I/O-bound applications while maintaining the same resource share (and thus cost) as other CPU-
sharing VMs. LSVMs are enabled by *vSlicer*, a hypervisor-
level technique that schedules each LSVM more frequently
but with a smaller micro time slice. vSlicer enables more
timely processing of I/O events by LSVMs, without violating the CPU share fairness among all sharing VMs. Our
evaluation of a vSlicer prototype in Xen shows that vSlicer
substantially reduces network packet round-trip times and
jitter and improves application-level performance. For example, vSlicer *doubles* both the connection rate and request
processing throughput of an Apache web server; reduces a
VoIP server's upstream jitter *by 62%*; and shortens the execution times of Intel MPI benchmark programs *by half or
more*.

Categories and Subject Descriptors

D.4.1 [**OPERATING SYSTEMS**]: Process Management—
Scheduling

General Terms

Design, Performance, Measurement

Keywords

Virtualization, Scheduler, Cloud Computing

1. INTRODUCTION

The advent of the cloud computing paradigm has allowed
enterprises and users to reduce their capital and operational
expenditures significantly, because they can simply lease
cloud resources to host their applications with a simple pay-
as-you-go charging model. A key approach that powers
cloud-based hosting is virtual machine (VM) consolidation,
where a single physical machine is "sliced" into multiple
VMs each assigned virtual core(s) for their execution. While
each VM is typically assigned at least one virtual core (e.g.,
vCPU in Xen [13] parlance), the mapping between virtual
and physical cores is not always one-to-one. For example,
in commercial cloud offerings such as Amazon EC2 [1], the
compute instances (VMs) are allocated in the units of EC2
compute units (ECU), each of which is roughly equivalent of
a 1GHz machine, with the smallest EC2 instance allocated 1
ECU. In a 3 GHz physical machine, there may be three VMs
sharing a physical CPU (pCPU). In such cases, the CPU
scheduler in the underlying hypervisor (e.g., Xen's default
credit scheduler) schedules the runnable VMs in a round-
robin fashion, with each VM given access to the physical
CPU for the same amount of time, ensuring fairness among
the CPU-sharing VMs.

Unfortunately, recent research [36, 19, 25, 35, 34] has discovered a serious downside of CPU sharing among multiple VMs: It leads to significant negative impact on I/O-
bound applications running in those VMs. In this paper,
we especially address a key aspect of the impact: *I/O processing latency perceived by applications*. More specifically,
a VM with a pending I/O event will have to wait for its
turn to access the CPU before processing the I/O event.
Because of the multiple sharing VMs, the CPU access latency tends to be a *multiple* of the default CPU time slice
for each VM (e.g., 30ms in Xen); and such latency cannot
be hidden from the corresponding application. This impact
is particularly harmful to I/O-bound applications, which in
this paper refer to applications *involving both I/O and computation, with I/O dominating computation*. For example,
consider a simple VoIP gateway server which basically establishes and maintains connections between clients. For
fast call setup and traffic relay, the gateway's network I/O
dominates its computation (e.g., audio transcoding). With
default CPU slices for the sharing VMs, the VM that hosts
the gateway may not be able to access the CPU in time to
process requests for new calls or traffic from ongoing calls.
Another example is a low-volume web server that needs to

quickly respond to client requests, yet its overall CPU usage is relatively lower.

To avoid the impact on I/O processing latency, one could choose to request a non-sharing VM that exclusively occupies a physical CPU. However, that would incur higher cost which may not be desirable for cost-sensitive customers. In this paper, we propose to mitigate such impact *with the presence of CPU-sharing VMs* (e.g., small- or micro-instances of EC2). More specifically, we introduce a new (sub)class of VM instances called *latency-sensitive VMs* (LSVMs), which will achieve better performance for I/O-bound applications. Contrary to LSVMs, we also define non-latency-sensitive VMs (NLSVMs) for the execution of *CPU-bound applications that do not have stringent timing/latency requirement.* LSVMs and NLSVMs will share the same CPU with fair share and similar cost; whereas the LSVMs will achieve lower I/O processing latency.

One way to enable LSVMs, as advocated by existing work [21, 26, 29, 22], is to modify the hypervisor's CPU scheduler to prioritize certain I/O-bound VMs over the CPU-bound ones. For example, [21] preferentially schedules communication oriented applications over their CPU-intensive counterparts. Unfortunately, it introduces short-term unfairness in CPU shares. Similarly, partial boost is used in [26] to help I/O-bound tasks to preempt a running vCPU in response to an incoming event. However, such a system is hard to configure for preserving fairness among the sharing VMs, which is undesirable for a VM-hosting cloud. The credit scheduler is extended in [29] to support soft real-time applications. But it may give more CPU time to latency-sensitive VMs thus breaking the fairness among VMs.

In this paper, we propose our solution named *vSlicer* to realize LSVMs. vSlicer is based on a simple idea which we call *differentiated-frequency microslicing*. Traditional VM schedulers such as Xen's credit scheduler "slice up" a CPU in relatively large time slices. Under vSlicer, we further divide a CPU slice (e.g., 30ms) of a given LSVM into several *microslices* (e.g., 5ms) and schedule the LSVM at a higher frequency (e.g., 6 times) compared to an NLSVM (one time) in each scheduling round. Therefore, both the LSVMs and NLSVMs sharing a physical core will still obtain the same amount of CPU time thus ensuring fairness; but an LSVM will be scheduled more frequently albeit with a smaller time slice, resulting in shorter CPU access latency for the LSVM. Consequently, for an I/O-bound application, vSlicer gives the corresponding LSVM more frequent CPU accesses – each for a shorter duration – to process its pending I/O activities, resulting in better application-level performance.

Since the overall CPU share is the same for both LSVMs and NLSVMs, their charging model does not need any change and can be priced the same. At first glance, it may appear that every cost-sensitive customer (namely, one who is unwilling to upgrade to VMs with exclusive CPUs) would request only LSVMs. This is not true for the simple reason that LSVMs may not help all applications across the board. In particular, running a CPU-bound application in an LSVM may actually be worse than running it in an NLSVM, because of the more frequent context switches and subsequently more frequent cache flushes. Therefore, customers running CPU-bound applications will be motivated to choose NLSVMs over LSVMs. Consequently, we are likely to see a mix of LSVMs and NLSVMs sharing the physical machines.

The main contributions of this paper are as follows:

- We propose a new class of CPU-sharing VMs called LSVMs to mitigate the impact of VM consolidation on I/O processing latency in VM-hosting clouds. LSVMs achieve much better performance for I/O-bound applications while maintaining the same cost benefit and CPU-share fairness across all sharing VMs.

- We develop a simple, effective technique called vSlicer to realize LSVMs. Based on the idea of differentiated-frequency microslicing, vSlicer enhances the CPU scheduler of the hypervisor by scheduling LSVMs with smaller microslices but with higher frequency while scheduling NLSVMs with regular (larger) slices, giving I/O-bound VMs more timely access to the CPU for I/O processing without penalizing the NLSVMs' CPU shares.

- We have implemented a prototype of vSlicer in the Xen hypervisor and conducted extensive evaluation with both micro-benchmarks and application benchmarks. Our micro-benchmark evaluation shows that vSlicer significantly reduces network packet round-trip times (RTTs) and packet jitter (by 70% compared to the vanilla Xen scheduler). Our evaluation with application benchmarks shows substantial improvement in application-specific performance metrics. For example, in our experiments, vSlicer *doubles* both the connection rate and request processing throughput of an Apache web server; reduces a VoIP server's upstream jitter *by 62%*; and shortens the execution times of Intel MPI benchmark programs *by half or more*.

The rest of the paper is organized as follows. We explain our motivation in detail in Section 2 followed by the design of vSlicer in Section 3. Section 4 describes the Xen based prototype of vSlicer. Then we present our evaluation results in Section 5. We discuss some possible extensions in Section 6 followed by related work and conclusions in Section 7 and Section 8.

2. MOTIVATION

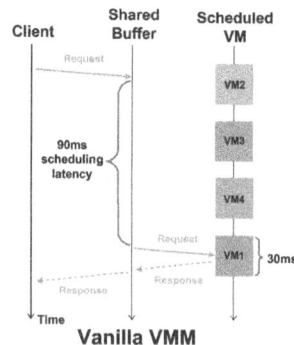

Figure 1: Application responsiveness with credit scheduler

In this section, we motivate the problem by demonstrating the impact of VMs' CPU sharing on I/O processing latency. We then discuss the inadequacy of existing solutions.

2.1 Impact of CPU Sharing

To understand the negative impact of VM CPU sharing on the latency of I/O processing, consider the example shown in Figure 1. In this example, 4 VMs are sharing a physical CPU. VM1 is hosting an I/O-bound application while

4

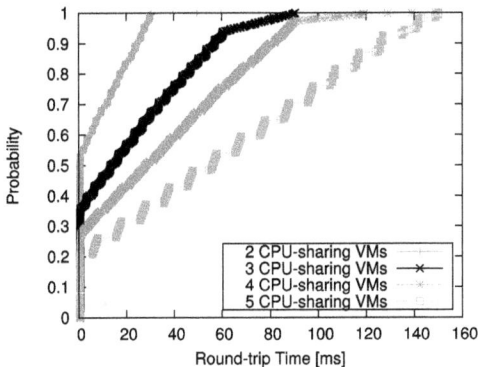
Figure 2: CDF of *ping* round-trip time

VM2-VM4 are hosting CPU-bound applications. The application in VM1 waits for client requests and then responds to the requests with data or control messages. This simple communication pattern can be found in many applications such as web servers, VoIP proxies, and MPI jobs. We assume that the VM scheduler in the hypervisor uses a proportional-share scheduling policy adopted by many commercial VM platforms (e.g., Xen, that is used in Amazon EC2 [1], RackSpace [10] and GoGrid [2] commercial clouds). Since each VM has a runnable task in it, it occupies the entire CPU slice allotted to it. As shown in the figure, when a request for VM1 arrives at the physical host, it needs to be buffered outside VM1 (e.g., in the VMM or in the privileged driver domain not shown in the figure), until VM1 is scheduled to run. When VM1 gets scheduled, it will process the request and generate a response. Assuming a CPU slice of 30ms, the request response latency can be as high as 90ms (i.e. *(Number of sharing VMs -1) × Time Slice*). Such a high latency hampers the responsiveness (and consequently, request processing rate) of the application in VM1.

We perform a simple experiment to demonstrate this increase in latency empirically. Figure 2 shows the CDF of the round-trip time (RTT) by "pinging" VM1. In our measurement experiments, we vary the number of non-idle, CPU-sharing VMs from 2 to 5 (including VM1). Our results clearly show that the ping RTT increases with the number of CPU-sharing VMs; and the worst-case RTT is proportional to *(Number of sharing VMs -1) × Time Slice*.

2.2 Problems with Alternative Solutions

We now examine several alternative solutions and argue why they do not work well in our setting.

Prioritize I/O-Bound VMs The first option to reduce the above I/O processing latency is to prioritize the VMs running the I/O-intensive applications. In fact, Xen's credit scheduler uses *BOOST* mechanism to shorten the I/O response time by temporarily boosting (i.e. assigning a higher priority to) the I/O bound VMs. This mechanism works quite well for pure I/O bound VMs. However, in the presence of heterogeneous workloads, once the VM gets scheduled to process the I/O request by the BOOST mechanism, it will consume its CPU share (i.e. credits in Xen terms) due to the CPU bound segment of the workload. This will effectively disable the BOOST mechanism for the rest of this scheduling cycle resulting in higher I/O latency. In other words, while BOOST can temporarily cede the CPU to I/O-bound VMs, it can often lead to exhausting the VM's credits early and, as a result, the VM may starve for the rest of

the scheduling round (since the credit scheduler is CPU-fair across VMs).

A naive workaround to this would be to aggressively boost the I/O bound VMs without considering its CPU share. Unfortunately, this prioritization will break the overall CPU fairness in the system. We demonstrate such an unfairness in Figure 3, where VM1 is hosting an I/O-bound application with a network-intensive task and a computation task whereas other VMs are hosting computation-intensive applications. The incoming packets to VM1 trigger the boosting of VM1 so that it can process the packets. However, since the hypervisor does not preempt a scheduled VM as long as the VM has runnable tasks, the computation portion of the application in VM1 will consume the rest of the time slice after the packet processing is done. This causes CPU-time deprivation of other VMs, as long as packets destined to VM1 keep arriving, compromising the CPU fairness of the overall system.

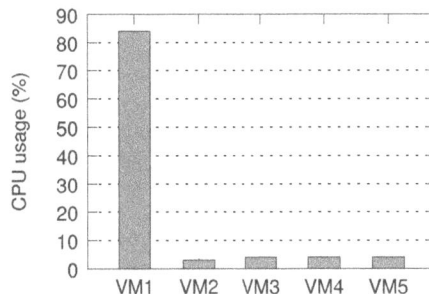
Figure 3: Unfair CPU allocation under aggressive boost

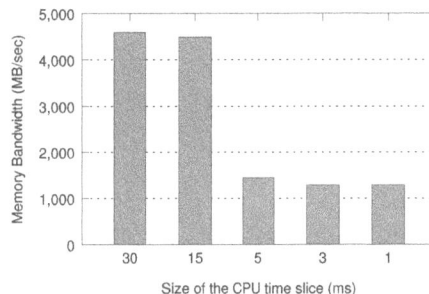
Figure 4: STREAM benchmark performance under credit scheduler with various time slice sizes

Soft Real-Time Scheduler The second option is to adopt a soft real-time scheduler such as Xen's former scheduler – Simple Earliest-Deadline First (SEDF) scheduler [17]. SEDF is based on a preemptive, deadline-driven real-time scheduling algorithm to achieve latency guarantees. However, such a scheduler requires complex configuration and careful parameter tuning and selection – per-VM – to achieve the latency guarantees desired, which may not be possible in a cloud environment with dynamic placement and migration of VMs. In addition, and perhaps more importantly, extending SEDF to perform global load-balancing on multicore systems is non-trivial, making it not attractive on multicore platforms. Because of these reasons, SEDF has been replaced by the credit scheduler as Xen's default scheduler. Another low-latency scheduler available in Xen is based on Borrowed Virtual Time (BVT) scheduling scheme [18]. BVT achieves low latency by making use of virtual-time warping. However, lack of a non-work-conserving mode in BVT

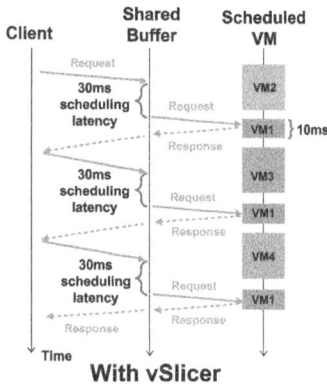

Figure 5: Application responsiveness with vSlicer

severely limits its usability in a number of environments, leading to its retirement from Xen's latest version.

Reducing Slice Size for all VMs The third option is to uniformly reduce the time slice size of the credit scheduler so that all the sharing VMs will get scheduled in and out more frequently, resulting in shorter CPU access latency. However, such an option would increase the number of context switches (and cache flushes) in the system, degrading the performance of CPU-bound applications running in the NLSVMs. To demonstrate the problem with this option, we measure the *memory bandwidth* of VMs running the STREAM benchmarks [6], scheduled by the credit scheduler under various time slice sizes (30ms to 1ms). The STREAM benchmarks measure memory bandwidth for large array operations such as copy, addition, scalar multiplication, and triad. Here we only present the "STREAM-copy" results in Figure 4. (We obtain similar results from the other 3 benchmarks.) The results indicate that reducing the time slice size uniformly is clearly not desirable as it degrades the memory access efficiency and consequently application performance of the VMs.

3. DESIGN

The previous section suggests that, if the CPU-sharing VMs are scheduled in a strictly round-robin fashion, it will be difficult to reduce the I/O processing latency without hurting the performance of CPU-bound NLSVMs. On the other hand, prioritizing the LSVMs may violate the CPU share fairness among all VMs. To address this dilemma, we come up with the following key idea behind vSlicer: Within one scheduling round, the CPU time for an LSVM does not have to be allocated in one single time slice. Instead, it can be allocated "in installment" as long as the sum of the installments (i.e., microslices) is equal to a standard CPU time slice. Such a high-frequency microslicing will give more opportunities to the LSVM to process pending I/O events; yet it does not affect/preempt the regular time slices allocated to the NLSVMs. This ensures timely processing of I/O events while maintaining fair share of the CPU among all VMs. We illustrate this idea in Figure 5 for the same application scenario as in Figure 1. In one scheduling round, the LSVM (VM1) will be scheduled three times (instead of once), each for a microslice of 10ms (instead of 30ms). As a result, it can process three requests (instead of one) in the same time period, improving the application's responsiveness.

For the purely CPU-bound applications, as demonstrated in Section 2, there is a strong incentive *not* to run them in

LSVMs because the higher-frequency microslicing will cause more frequent cache flushes which will hurt application performance. Fortunately, the NLSVMs under vSlicer will give these applications the same performance as if running them in round-robin-scheduled VMs with the default time slice.

3.1 vSlicer Scheduling Model

The idea of CPU microslicing itself is quite general; one could pick any size for the microslice and simply derive the scheduling frequency. There are two main concerns one needs to keep in mind though. First, setting the microslice too small will excessively increase the context switch overhead; so it is important to keep it to a reasonable duration (e.g., at least 5ms). Second, the best schedule one can come up with, in terms of latency for LSVMs, depends on the number of LSVMs and NLSVMs sharing a core. In practice, we expect only a small number (≤ 5) that share a core, and even among these, the number of LSVMs is going to be very small (≤ 3).

We use the following approach to determine the scheduling order in one scheduling round. Assume m LSVMs and n NLSVMs are sharing a single CPU core. We denote the scheduling period (i.e., scheduling round) by T_P and the total time an LSVM executes during a scheduling period as T_{LSVM}. Similarly, the total time an NLSVM executes during a scheduling period is T_{NLSVM}. We want T_{NLSVM} to be a fairly large value to allow each CPU-bound VM to execute sufficiently long. (In our implementation we use Xen credit scheduler's default time slice 30ms as T_{NLSVM}.) Since we aim to fairly allocate the CPU among all the VMs (both LSVMs and NLSVMs), we want the following to hold:

$$T_{LSVM} = T_{NLSVM} \quad (1)$$

Let us denote the time period where one (micro-)round of LSVMs are scheduled after scheduling an NLSVM as T_S. vSlicer runs all the LSVMs during T_S in round robin fashion. We want to further divide T_S into micro time slices T_m (refer to Figure 6b for illustration of T_S and T_m; here subscript m indicates "micro" rather than the number of LSVMs). The selection of T_m depends on the scheduling latency we intend to achieve. We will further discuss the scheduling latency achieved by the vSlicer later in this section. Depending on the selection of T_m, an LSVM can run one or more times during a single time slice T_S. Let us denote the total time the ith LSVM runs during T_S as T_{n_i}.

$$\sum_{i=1}^{m} T_{n_i} = T_S \quad (2)$$

Suppose the ith LSVM can get scheduled r_i times during T_S. We have:

$$T_{n_i} = r_i \times T_m \text{ where } r_i \geq 1 \quad (3)$$

In this paper, we assume all the LSVMs have the same latency requirement and hence, for any $i, j \in \{1, m\}$ we have $T_{n_i} = T_{n_j} = T_n$ and $r_i = r_j = r$. Equation 3 becomes

$$T_n = r \times T_m \text{ where } r \geq 1 \quad (4)$$

and

$$T_S = m \times T_n \quad (5)$$

Given vSlicer's alternating scheduling of LSVMs and NLSVMs (i.e., it schedules a round of all LSVMs followed by one of the NLSVMs), the total time that an LSVM executes during a scheduling period T_P is equal to the number of NLSVMs multiplied by the time an LSVM executes during a time slice T_S (i.e. T_n). That is:

$$T_{LSVM} = n \times T_n \qquad (6)$$

A scheduling period consists of running times of all LSVMs and NLSVMs and therefore we get:

$$
\begin{aligned}
T_P &= mT_{LSVM} + nT_{NLSVM} & (7) \\
&= m \times (n \times T_n) + nT_{NLSVM} & (8)
\end{aligned}
$$

Rearranging the first term of RHS of Equation (8) and substituting from Equation (5) gives us:

$$T_P = nT_S + nT_{NLSVM} \qquad (9)$$

Also substituting for T_{LSVM} from (1) to (7) we get :

$$
\begin{aligned}
T_P &= mT_{NLSVM} + nT_{NLSVM} \\
&= (m+n)T_{NLSVM} & (10)
\end{aligned}
$$

Combining Equations (9) and (10) gives us an important invariant we maintain in the system:

$$nT_S + nT_{NLSVM} = (m+n)T_{NLSVM} \qquad (11)$$

That is, maintaining this invariant ensures that we are not violating CPU share fairness while scheduling LSVMs more frequently. Moreover, Equation (11) allows us to define T_S, T_n in terms of T_{NLSVM}. That is :

$$
\begin{aligned}
T_S &= \frac{mT_{NLSVM}}{n} \\
T_n &= \frac{T_{NLSVM}}{n} \\
T_m r &= \frac{T_{NLSVM}}{n} & (12)
\end{aligned}
$$

As mentioned earlier, the selection of T_m depends on the desired scheduling latency of the LSVM. Equation (12) defines the product of T_m and r in terms of T_{NLSVM} and n. The only restriction for the selection of T_m is, it should be a whole divisor of $\frac{T_{NLSVM}}{n}$. However, selecting a too small value for T_m will increase the number of context switches during T_S, affecting the performance of the all LSVMs.

Let us denote the required latency for an LSVM during T_S as T_l. To achieve this scheduling latency we should schedule the ith VM within T_l. Since we schedule all the LSVMs in a round-robin order, all the other $(m-1)$ LSVMs should be executed in less than T_l. That is:

$$(m-1)T_m \leq T_l$$

which gives us the upper bound for T_m:

$$T_m \leq \lfloor \frac{T_l}{(m-1)} \rfloor$$

If we consider the influence of NLSVMs, the scheduling latency curve for a specific LSVM looks like a *continuous wavy line*. The wave crest is $T_{NLSVM} + (m-1)T_m$.

Examples We now show two examples of scheduling sequence under two different settings. Figure 6 illustrates two

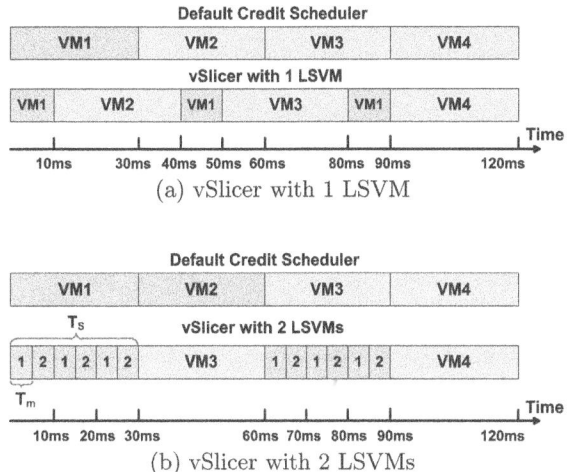

(a) vSlicer with 1 LSVM

(b) vSlicer with 2 LSVMs

Figure 6: vSlicer scheduling sequence (The green block indicates LSVM)

scheduling sequences for a system running four VMs. In Figure 6a, we have one LSVM and three NLSVMs. If all these VMs were scheduled by the default credit scheduler, any of them would experience a 90ms scheduling latency. Under vSlicer, by dividing the time slice of the LSVM (i.e. VM1) to multiple microslices and scheduling it three times during the scheduling round, the latency drops to 30ms. In Figure 6b, there are two LSVMs and two NLSVMs in the system. By dividing the time slice into 5ms microslices, vSlicer can achieve a best-case latency of 5ms and a worst-case latency of 35ms.

In our discussion towards the end of Section 2, we emphasized that reducing the time slice uniformly for all sharing VMs is not a desirable option, primarily due to the increased context switches between the VMs. Now that we have discussed the details of vSlicer, let us quantitatively compare the credit scheduler – with uniformly reduced time slice – with vSlicer using a system with two LSVMs and two NLSVMs. With the credit scheduler having the default time slice, the CPU access latency of each LSVM is $(m+n-1)T_{NLSVM}$. Here it is $(4-1)T_{NLSVM} = 3 \times 30 = 90ms$. In order to reduce the latency to 15ms, we need to reduce the time slice from 30ms to 5ms, which will make the context switch rate increase by $6\times$. With vSlicer, however, setting $T_m = 5ms$ – to achieve 15ms average latency – would increase the number of context switches only by $3\times$.

4. IMPLEMENTATION

vSlicer only requires a simple modification to the VM scheduler in the hypervisor. The VMs in the physical host are grouped at two levels. First, vSlicer maintains a list of VMs that are executing in a physical CPU. Second, within this group vSlicer divides these VMs into LSVMs and NLSVMs. Decision on whether a particular VM is LSVM or NLSVM is left to the user (or the cloud administrator) and vSlicer provides an interface to the administrative tools (such as *xm tools* in Xen) to configure that. If dynamic VM characterization is preferred, existing methods using virtual interrupt counters or pending packet counters can be applied to infer VM's type dynamically. However, the grouping of VMs per physical CPU is done by the global load balancing algorithm of the VM scheduler.

While the design of vSlicer is generic and hence applicable

to many VMMs (e.g., Xen, VMware [12]), we implement a prototype of vSlicer in Xen 3.4.2. In our implementation, we add a new scheduler type in Xen, called sched_vSlicer by extending the credit scheduler. The vSlicer code is in the critical path of the scheduler code which is frequently executed. Therefore we keep the modifications to the critical path of the credit scheduler to a minimum, with only 250 lines of additional code. The user-level utilities add another 400 lines of code which is executed only when the user configures the system using the Xen management tools. vSlicer does not depend on para-virtualization for its scheduling function. So our prototype can support Xen HVM guests without modifications or performance degradation.

Since vSlicer is based on the credit scheduler, vSlicer inherits its proportional fairness policy and multi-core support. We maintain the credit scheduler's existing set of controls, *weight* and *cap*, that decide the proportional share of the VM, and the maximum amount of CPU a domain will be able to consume even if the host system has idle CPU cycles respectively. We add a new control in addition to these two to specify the micro time slice. Initially vSlicer treats all the VMs as NLSVMs, which have their micoslices set to zero. When a user configures a particular VM to be LSVM, the microslice of that VM will be set to the specified value. This action will trigger vSlicer configuration functions, which will in turn recalculate the global parameters such as T_S. Starting from the next scheduling interrupt, vSlicer will schedule that VM as an LSVM.

Algorithm 1 Scheduling Algorithm for vSlicer

Require: $num\_nlsvm \geq 1$
Require: $num\_lsvm + num\_nlsvm \geq 3$
Ensure: $schedule\_time = now$
Ensure: $time\_slice = T_{NLSVM}$
Ensure: $micro\_slice = T_m$
 1: $burn\_credit(curr\_vm.schedule\_time, now)$
 2: **if** $curr\_vm$ is $nlsvm$ **then**
 3:    $insert\_tail(curr\_vm, runq)$;
 4: **else** $\{curr\_vm$ is $lsvm\}$
 5:    $burn\_micro(curr\_vm.micro\_credits, micro\_slice)$
 6:    **if** $curr\_vm.credits > 0$ **then**
 7:       **if** $curr\_vm.micro\_credits > 0$ **then**
 8:          $insert\_before\_nlsvm(curr\_vm, runq)$;
 9:       **else** $\{curr\_vm.micro\_credits \leq 0\}$
10:          $insert\_after\_nlsvm(curr\_vm, runq)$;
11:       **end if**
12:    **else** $\{curr\_vm.credits \leq 0\}$
13:       $insert\_tail(curr\_vm, runq)$;
14:    **end if**
15: **end if**
16: $next\_vm \Leftarrow get\_first\_elem(runq)$;
17: **if** $next\_vm$ is $nlsvm$ **then**
18:    $next\_vm.runtime \Leftarrow time\_slice$;
19: **else** $\{next\_vm$ is $lsvm\}$
20:    $next\_vm.runtime \Leftarrow micro\_slice$;
21: **end if**
22: $run(next\_vm)$;

Scheduling Algorithm The most important function that we modify is *do_schedule*, which is executed in the critical path and responsible for selecting the next vCPU for pCPU from the run queue. We show the pseudo-code of the algorithm in Algorithm 1.

We assign *micro credits* to each LSVM in addition to the credits assigned by the original algorithm of Xen credit scheduler. vSlicer algorithm uses the micro credits to schedule LSVMs during T_S in a round-robin order. We initialize the algorithm by initializing T_{NLSVM}, T_S, and T_m. T_{NLSVM} is defined by the implementation (in our implementation we used Xen's default 30ms). T_S and T_m can be calculated using T_{NLSVM}, m, n, and equations in Section 3.1. This initialization has to be done in the event of: a vCPU migration (for load balance on multi-core), a VM initialization, a VM shutting down or any other event that changes the number of VMs running on the particular CPU core.

vSlicer algorithm is executed whenever the time slice of the currently running VM expires. First the algorithm checks the VM type. If it is an NLSVM, the time slice of it has expired and hence the VM is inserted to the back of the *run queue*. In vSlicer both NLSVMs and LSVMs share a single run queue. If the the current VM is an LSVM, depending on how much credits and *micro credits* the VM has, it will be scheduled to run in the same T_S, in the same T_P, or in the next scheduling period. Then the algorithm picks the next VM to run from the head of the run queue. If it is an NLSVM, it will be assigned a regular time slice (T_{NLSVM}). If it is an LSVM, it will be assigned a microslice.

5. EVALUATION

In this section, we present our detailed evaluation of vSlicer using the Xen-based prototype. We use both micro-benchmarks and application-level benchmarks to evaluate the effectiveness of vSlicer. Our experiments evaluate three key aspects: (a) transport-level latency reduction achieved by vSlicer; (b) overall CPU-sharing fairness with vSlicer; and (c) application-level performance improvement by vSlicer.

Experimental Setup Our experiments involve physical machines (desktops as clients and servers as VM hosts) connected by a Gigabit Ethernet network. Each physical server hosts multiple VMs and has a dual-core 3GHz Intel Xeon CPU with 4GB of RAM and a Broadcom NetXtreme 5752 Gigabit Ethernet card. These hosts run Xen 3.4.2 with Linux 2.6.18 running in the driver domain (dom0). The VMs share one core of the host, whereas the driver domain is pinned to the other core. Each VM in this host is allocated 512MB of RAM and a single vCPU, except the VM that hosts the MyConnection media server (Section 5.2) which is allocated 1GB RAM following the requirement of the MyConnection benchmarks. The physical client machine has a 2.4GHz Intel Core 2 Duo CPU with 4GB of RAM and an Intel Pro Gigabit network card and runs Linux 2.6.35.

5.1 Evaluation with Micro-benchmarks

This section presents improvement of network I/O performance achieved by vSlicer using micro-benchmarks. In each experiment we vary the number of VMs sharing the same core from 3 to 5 and measure the same transport-level metrics under vSlicer and Xen's default credit scheduler, respectively. We keep the CPU utilization of each VM to 40% using the *lookbusy* tool [7].

Ping RTT Recall the experiment presented in Section 2 that measures the RTTs of ping packets to a non-idle VM

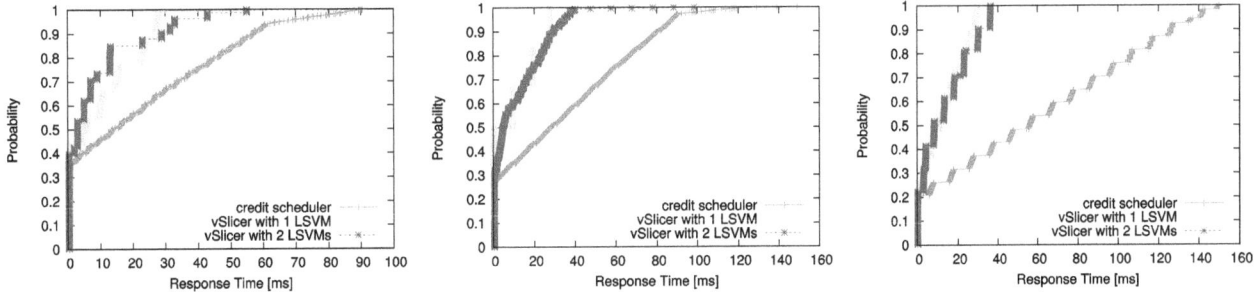

(a) 3 non-idle VMs sharing a core (b) 4 non-idle VMs sharing a core (c) 5 non-idle VMs sharing a core

Figure 7: CDFs for RTTs of 100 *ping* packets under default credit scheduler and vSlicer

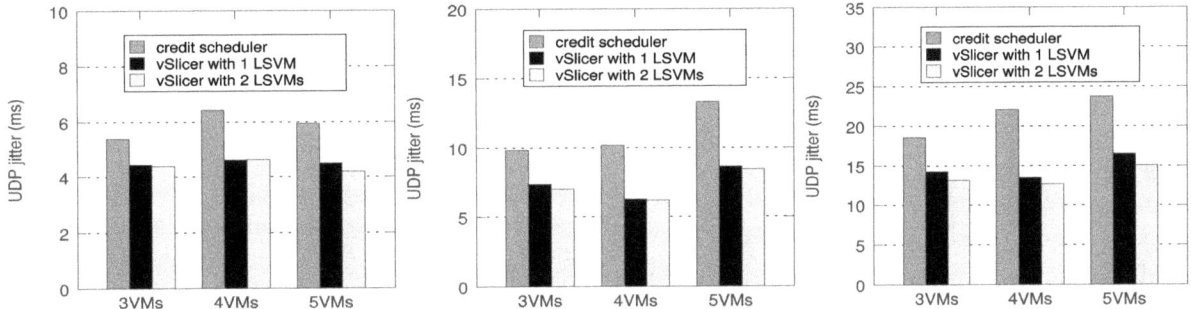

(a) Jitter for 256 bytes datagrams (b) Jitter for 512 bytes datagrams (c) Jitter for 1024 bytes datagrams

Figure 8: Effect of vSlicer on UDP jitter

from another physical machine in the same LAN. We repeat the same experiment, but use vSlicer as the VM scheduler and compare the results with those achieved by the default scheduler. Figure 7 shows the CDFs of RTTs of 100 *ping* packets, with 3, 4, and 5 CPU-sharing VMs, respectively. For each setup, we show the CDFs under the credit scheduler, vSlicer with 1 LSVM (the ping receiver), and vSlicer with 2 LSVMs (one being the ping receiver), respectively. These results show that vSlicer consistently reduces the ping RTTs in all setups. For example, in the 4-VMs scenario (Figure 7b), vSlicer reduces the average RTT from 35ms to 10ms with 1 LSVM (the other three are NLSVMs), a 71% reduction. With 5 CPU-sharing VMs (Figure 7b), the average ping RTT is shortened by about 80% under vSlicer. More importantly, we find that, under vSlicer, the RTT towards an LSVM *does not increase linearly with the number of sharing VMs*. With vSlicer, the average RTT we observe across our experiments remains about 12ms with 1 LSVM; and 14ms with 2 LSVMs; whereas a near-linear increase in average RTT is observed under the default scheduler.

UDP Jitter UDP is a simpler transport protocol with no reliable, in-order packet deliver guarantee. Yet UDP is popular in audio/video streaming, online gaming and other latency-sensitive applications. We measure the jitter of UDP datagrams, which will translate into user-level QoS of the aforementioned applications. We use Iperf [5] to generate a stream of UDP datagrams and vary the datagram size in each setup. The UDP receiver runs in a non-idle VM (an LSVM when running on vSlicer) and the UDP sender is a different physical machine in the same LAN. We also vary the number of CPU-sharing VMs from 3 to 5. The average UDP jitter observed on the receiver side is shown in Figure 8. The results under different datagram sizes all show UDP jitter reduction. The reason for the jitter reduction is that an LSVM has multiple opportunities to run during

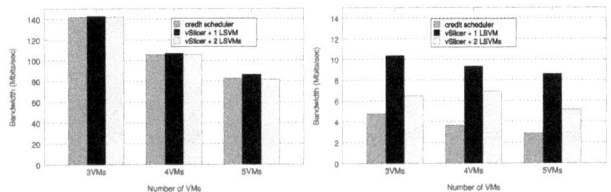

(a) In LAN (b) For high RTT setting

Figure 9: Effect of vSlicer on TCP throughput

one scheduling round under vSlicer (vs. only one under the default scheduler), leading to more timely and more evenly timed processing of UDP datagrams.

TCP Throughput Our measurement of TCP throughput generates some interesting (and somewhat surprising) results. Since vSlicer reduces a VM's CPU access latency and benefits latency-sensitive applications, we first thought that vSlicer would also improve TCP throughput to/from a VM. We use Iperf to measure the TCP bandwidth between a physical machine and a VM in the same LAN. The Iperf server runs in a non-idle (40% CPU load) VM sharing the CPU core with 2-4 other non-idle VMs. Interestingly, as shown in Figure 9a, vSlicer does not improve TCP throughput within a LAN. The reason, after a closer examination, is the following: First, even with vSlicer, LSVMs experience longer latencies periodically when the NLSVMs are getting scheduled. This delay would be less compared to the delay with the default credit scheduler (30ms compared to the 60ms in 3 VM scenario). However, this is still high compared to the sub-millisecond latencies in the LAN environment. Second, when we microslice the time slice of the LSVM (in this case from 30ms to 15ms), we also reduce the amount of packets that can be processed during a single micro time slice by some fraction (by 50% in this case), which means

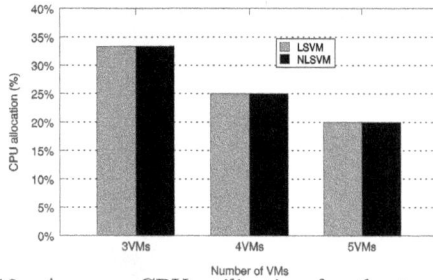

Figure 10: Average CPU utilization for the two types of VMs under vSlicer

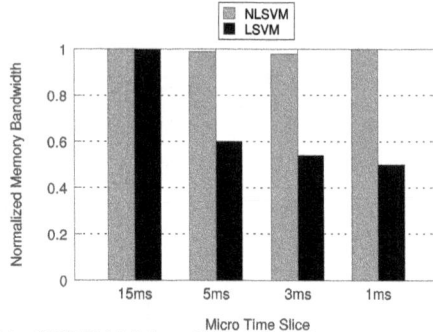

Figure 11: STREAM benchmark performance under different configurations

that the rest of the packets have to wait one full NLSVM execution time slice until they get processed, which makes throughput of the connection similar to that achieved by the credit scheduler.

However, the results are different when we look at a WAN environment. We simulate higher RTTs in a WAN by adding 30ms of network delay between the TCP sender and receiver using Linux *netem* module. The 30ms additional delay is based on average RTTs between our lab and well-known services (e.g. Google, AmazonEC2 and Microsoft Azure). This time we observe that vSlicer improves TCP throughput by up to 3×, as shown in Figure 9b. When we add 30ms network delay, this delay will effectively mask the execution period of the NLSVM. Recall that our VM scheduling pattern from Section 3 – an execution of an NLSVM is always followed by an execution period of all the LSVMs. So if we consider 3 VM case with one LSVM, once LSVM acknowledges a set of TCP packets and schedule out, it will take another 30ms time for the arrival of another batch of TCP data segments due to the added network delay. Now, during this 30ms in the receiving host, one NLSVM will be executed and the LSVM will be scheduled by the time of the arrival of TCP data packets, which can be immediately processed. On the other hand, if we consider the default credit scheduler, adding 30ms network delay will mask the execution time of just one VM. Since the credit scheduler schedules VMs in a round-robin fashion, in the 3 VM scenario, packets still have to wait one more time slice until the receiving VM gets scheduled. With the same experiment setting, we confirm that vSlicer can improve wide-area TCP throughput under varying additional delays (20ms-100ms) for the same reason.

Fairness of CPU Sharing After evaluating vSlicer's improvement of network I/O, we now evaluate the fairness of CPU sharing among all sharing VMs (LSVMs and NLSVMs). We use *xentop* to monitor the CPU utilization of each VM while running lookbusy and sysbench benchmark in each

VM. We observe that, regardless of its type (LSVM or NLSVM), each VM has an equal share of the CPU as the other VMs. Figure 10 shows the average CPU utilization (reported by *xentop* over a period of 30 seconds) of one LSVM and one NLSVM (out of a total of 3, 4, or 5 VMs) under vSlicer. The results show that vSlicer maintains CPU sharing fairness between the two types of VMs.

We then measure the performance of a CPU/memory-bound application running in an NLSVM under vSlicer. We use the STREAM benchmarks as in Section 2 and run 4 VMs – two LSVMs and two NLSVMs in a physical host. We run the STREAM benchmark in one of the NLSVMs, each getting one regular 30ms time slice in a scheduling round, while we vary the microslice size (from 15ms to 1ms) of the sharing LSVMs. Figure 11 shows the results in terms of memory bandwidth achieved by the benchmark. For comparison, we normalize the memory bandwidth relative to the one achieved by the default credit scheduler with the same 4 VMs and same workloads. The results show that the performance of STREAM running in the NLSVM (the red bars) is not affected by the more frequent scheduling of the LSVMs under vSlicer, maintaining (almost) the same performance as under the credit scheduler. To demonstrate the unsuitability of LSVMs for CPU-bound applications, we also run the STREAM benchmark in an LSVM and the results are shown by the black bars in Figure 11. This time the STREAM performance degrades with the decrease of microslice size (i.e., with the increase of LSVM scheduling frequency).

5.2 Evaluation of Application Performance

Experiment with Apache Web Server We first use the Apache web server along with httperf [3] to evaluate the effectiveness of vSlicer for I/O-bound applications. While not a soft-real-time application, the Apache web server is sensitive to (network and disk) I/O processing latency, which will cause delay in both connection establishment and data transmission stages and thus affect the web server's response time and request handling throughput.

In this experiment the physical server hosts four core-sharing VMs. Two of the VMs are LSVMs, with one of them running the Apache web server. A physical client machine generates requests for a 5KB web page with httperf to measure the web server's performance. To simulate the WAN environment, a random delay between 20ms to 40ms using the Linux *netem* is added. For comparison, we perform the experiment under the default credit scheduler and under vSlicer. We measure the following metrics: (a) connection rate, (b) connection time, (c) response time, and (d) net I/O (average network throughput), with the corresponding results shown in the four sub-figures of Figure 12. Under the credit scheduler, the connection rate saturates at 90 connections/sec and the net I/O throughput saturates at 450 KB/s. Under vSlicer, Apache can sustain up to a 180 connections/sec connection rate and achieve up to 900 KB/s throughput. Moreover, the connection time and response time are much shorter and more stable under vSlicer; whereas under the credit scheduler, these two metrics increase rapidly once the request rate goes beyond 100 requests/sec.

To understand the root cause for the saturated connection rate of 90 connections/sec under the credit scheduler, we first traced packets using *tcpdump* at multiple points: (1) in the client host, (2) in the driver domain of the phys-

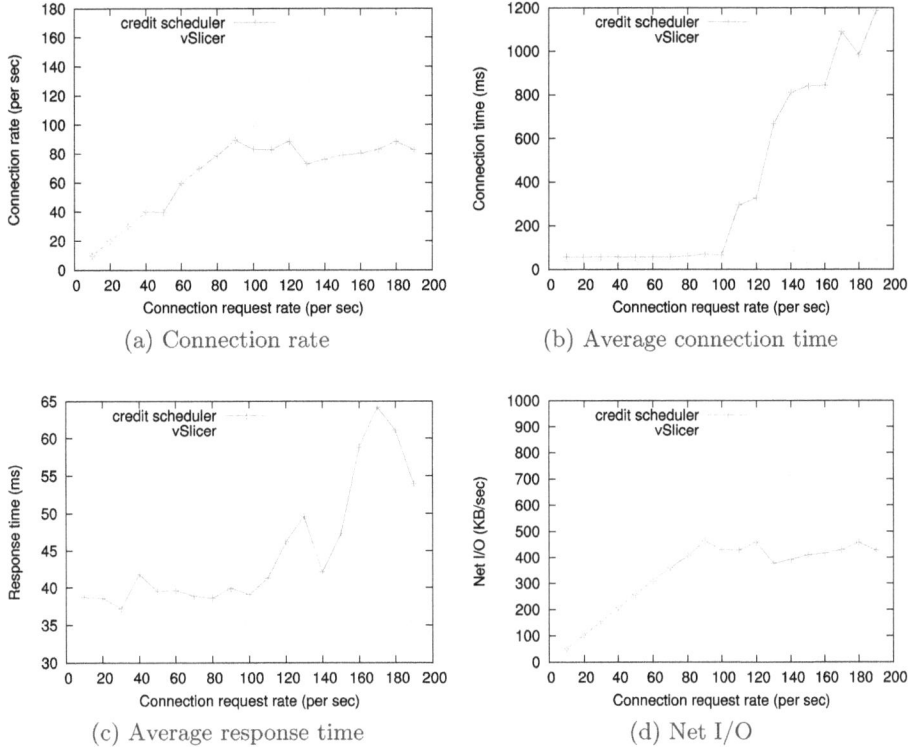

(a) Connection rate

(b) Average connection time

(c) Average response time

(d) Net I/O

Figure 12: Apache web server experiment results

ical server, and (3) in the LSVM where the Apache server runs. We make two interesting observations: First, when the connection rate goes beyond 90 connections/sec, packet retransmissions start to appear in the trace. Second, our further analysis of flows with packet retransmissions shows that almost all of the retransmissions happen due to the packets dropped at the driver domain (by comparing the traces from the driver domain and from the VM).

To identify the main culprit of the dropped packets inside the driver domain, we inserted tracing points along the path taken by the packets inside the driver domain from physical NIC (*peth*) to the VMs virtual interface (*vif*). We found out that the I/O ring buffer, which connects the driver domain and the VM, gets full when the request rate exceeds 90 connections/sec while the VM is waiting in the run queue. This in turn back-pressures the packet processing *tasklets* in the driver domain causing packet drops. On the other hand, with vSlicer, the LSVM running the Apache server gets scheduled more frequently and hence, it empties the ring buffer more often hence eliminating the back-pressure. Compared with the maximum CPU access latency (90ms) under the credit scheduler, the maximum latency for the LSVM is 40ms under vSlicer. This translates into a higher connection rate (up to 180 connections/sec) of the web server without packet drops and retransmissions in the driver domain.

Experiments with MPI Benchmarks We next evaluate the effectiveness of vSlicer for reducing the execution time of MPI communication primitives using the Intel MPI Benchmark (IMB) [4]. Our setup consists of 4 VMs each with MPICH2 [8] libraries installed. We host these 4 VMs in two physical hosts with 2 VMs sharing a single CPU core. We also run 2 other VMs per core with CPU-bound tasks.

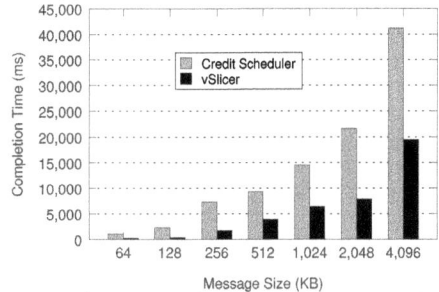

Figure 13: Performance of Intel MPI benchmark: *Alltoall*

When experimenting with vSlicer, we mark the VMs running the IMB as LSVMs and the VMs running CPU-bound tasks as NLSVMs. We measure the execution time of two MPI communications primitives from IMB suite: *Sendrecv* and *Alltoall*.

In the IMB *Alltoall* benchmark, each MPI process sends a distinct message to each process in the system. A process executing this communication pattern usually sends messages to all other processes using non-blocking *sends* and waits for the receipt messages from all other processes. When vSlicer is used, each LSVM gets scheduled frequently for a micro time slice period (of 5ms), leading to more timely processing of send/receive messages to/from other processes and hence faster process of the entire MPI job. Figure 13 shows that, under various message sizes, vSlicer reduces the execution time by half or more, compared with the credit scheduler.

In the IMB *Sendrecv* benchmark, the MPI processes form a periodic communication chain. Each process sends a message to its right neighbor in the chain and receives a message from its left neighbor. Figure 14 shows the results for this benchmark. vSlicer leads to significant reduction in the execution time (up to 4.5 × improvement when the message

11

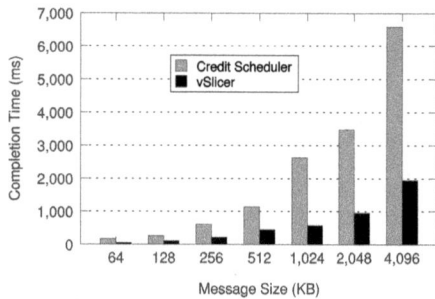

Figure 14: Performance of Intel MPI benchmark: *Sendrecv*

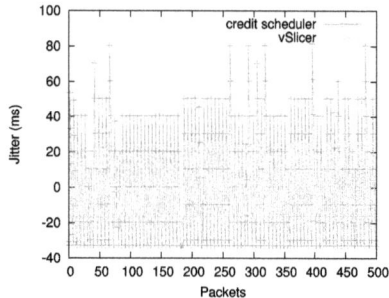

Figure 15: Single line VoIP upstream jitter

size is 1024KB). The reduction is even higher than in the *Alltoall* case. The main reason lies in the chain of dependencies imposed by this particular communication pattern. Each process depends on its left neighbor to receive and acknowledge the message being sent; and each process depends on its right neighbor to send a complete message. The longer message processing delays incurred by the credit scheduler causes the entire messaging chain to take longer time in a *cascading* way. When vSlicer is used, each LSVM has multiple opportunities in one scheduling round to process those incoming/outgoing messages, leading to faster progress of messaging chain.

Experiments with MyConnection Server Finally, we evaluate the effectiveness of vSlicer with latency-sensitive, soft real-time applications such as streaming media servers and VoIP gateways. We use MyConnection Server (MCS) [9] as our benchmark application. MCS is a suite of benchmarks for assessing the performance and quality of networking and computing infrastructures for hosting soft real-time applications such as VoIP, video streaming, IPTV, and video conferencing. We use the *VoIP* test and the *streaming video* test of MCS for our evaluation of vSlicer. We run MCS in a VM which shares the same CPU core with 3 other non-idle VMs. Two of these VMs are LSVMs, including the VM that runs the MCS tests. The VoIP/media streaming clients

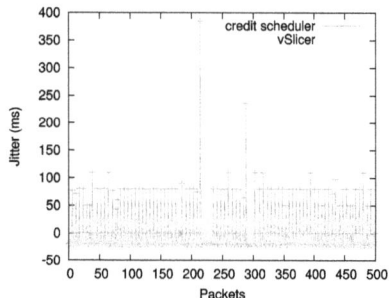

Figure 16: Single line VoIP downstream jitter

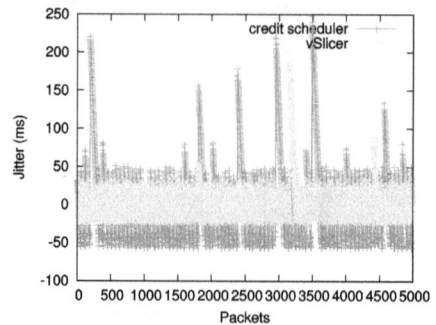

Figure 17: Multi-line VoIP upstream jitter

run in another physical machine in the same LAN, but we simulate remote clients in the real world by introducing a random delay between 20ms to 40ms using the Linux *netem* module.

The VoIP test generates voice traffic of one or more active VoIP sessions with a selected audio compression algorithm. In this test, a VoIP client connects to the MCS via the SIP protocol, emulates one or more voice conversations using G.711 codec, and measures QoS metrics such as jitter, packet loss, and the discarded packet percentage. Figure 15 and Figure 16 show the upstream and downstream jitter for the *single line* VoIP test (i.e. when only one VoIP session is active), respectively. Figure 17 shows the upstream jitter for the *multi-line* VoIP test (i.e. when multiple VoIP sessions are active simultaneously). Table 1 and Table 2 summarize the results of the VoIP test. Compared with the credit scheduler, vSlicer achieves a 16.6ms (62%) reduction in upstream jitter and 11ms (43%) reduction in downstream jitter in the single line VoIP test. In the case of multi-line VoIP test, vSlicer achieves a 23.7ms (65%) reduction in downstream jitter and 29.2% reduction in downstream packet loss. Under the credit scheduler, we could not even obtain meaningful downstream jitter results for the multi-line VoIP test, due to the heavy packet loss.

Scheduler	Upstream Jitter	Downstream Jitter	Packets Discard
Credit scheduler	26.7ms	25.8ms	1.2%
vSlicer	10.1ms	14.8ms	0%

Table 1: Single line VoIP test results under credit scheduler and vSlicer

Scheduler	Upstream Jitter	Downstream Packet Loss	Packets Discarded
Credit scheduler	36.7ms	44.5%	6.0%
vSlicer	13.0ms	15.3%	1.5%

Table 2: Multi-line VoIP test results under credit scheduler and vSlicer

The *streaming video* test involves video streaming sessions from the MCS to the clients via TCP based on the Real Time Streaming Protocol (RTSP) [11]. The streaming video server sends a series of audio and video packets at a fixed rate to the client. The client will measure the packet jitter and the server will measure the trip time, which is the application-level round-trip time. The test also measures the time to perform different RTSP commands such as SETUP, DESCRIBE, and PLAY. In this experiment, the payload of each audio packet is 32 bytes and the payload of each video packet is 160 bytes. The media transmission rate is 20 packets per second (for both audio and video packets). Table 3

Scheduler	Video Jitter (ms)	Audio Jitter (ms)	Trip Time (ms)	SETUP Time (ms)	DESCRIBE Time (ms)	PLAY Time (ms)
Credit	46.2	41.2	110	361	480	509
vSlicer	16.6	15.8	51	176	262	243

Table 3: Streaming video test results under credit scheduler and vSlicer

shows the results of the test. Compared with the credit scheduler, vSlicer reduces the video jitter by 29.6ms (64%) and reduces the audio jitter by 25.4ms (62%). Furthermore, vSlicer achieves significant improvements (time reduction) for all the other streaming video metrics measured.

6. DISCUSSION

Non-uniform Microslice Size In this paper, we assume that all LSVMs sharing the same CPU have the same microslice size. In fact, vSlicer can be fairly easily generalized to support different microslice sizes for LSVMs in the same system. The change to the scheduling model (Section 3.1) is that, instead of scheduling LSVMs in a round-robin order, different microslices will need to be accommodated within T_S. One possible approach would be to use the earliest-deadline-first [30] policy within T_S. Another possibility would be to devise a frequency-based policy where the number of times an LSVM gets scheduled within T_S is inversely proportional to its microslice (T_m).

Determining VM Type As we pointed out in Section 4, the decision on whether a particular VM is an LSVM or an NLSVM is left up to the user/administrator. However, it may be possible to infer the type of a VM by dynamically monitoring its I/O and computation behavior. Moreover, since an application or an entire VM may change its behavior (e.g., from I/O-bound to CPU-bound) at runtime, it is desirable to allow a VM to *switch* between LSVM and NLSVM dynamically. We leave such capability as future work.

Effectiveness towards Other Types of I/O In our evaluation we mainly focus on the effectiveness of vSlicer in reducing network I/O processing latency. However, we point out that, by design, vSlicer is *not* specific to network I/O and can effectively reduce the processing latency of other types of I/O (e.g., disk I/O). For example, in Xen, disk I/O is handled similarly to network I/O: When an application requests a disk I/O, the request will go through the driver domain. However, if the requesting VM is not running when the disk I/O is completed, the VM may have to wait for multiple time slices before getting the CPU to process the I/O. vSlicer will give the VM more timely access to the CPU for processing the disk I/O.

7. RELATED WORK

Existing work that is most related to vSlicer has been discussed in Section 1. We now discuss other related efforts that belong to the general area of I/O performance improvement for virtualized environments. They fall into two broad categories: (1) reducing/analyzing virtualization overheads along the I/O path and (2) VM scheduling.

Reducing/Analyzing Virtualization Overheads In recent years, researchers have proposed various solutions to measure and alleviate virtualization-induced overheads along the I/O path. For instance, Chadha et al. present an execution-driven, simulation-based analysis methodology with symbol annotation to evaluate the performance of I/O virtualization [16]. Their methodology provides detailed architecture-level profiling information which will allow designers to evaluate the effectiveness of hardware-level enhancement for more efficient virtualized I/O. Menon et al. have proposed several optimizations to improve network device virtualization using techniques such as packet coalescing [33], scatter/gather I/O, checksum offload, segmentation offload [31], and offloading device driver functionality [32]. vSlicer is complementary to these techniques. The offloading technique improves network *throughput* but does not reduce the *application-perceived latency*. Packet coalescing may even increase the response time of a VM when sending one interrupt for several arriving packets. vSlicer alleviates this problem by differentiating the VMs as LSVMs and NLSVMs and satisfying their corresponding requirements for CPU time. XenSocket [39], XenLoop [37], Fido [15], and Xway [27] specialize in improving inter-VM communication within the same physical host. vFlood [19] and vSnoop [25] improve TCP *throughput* between VMs in a datacenter. However they *cannot* reduce the end-to-end *latency* perceived by applications. IVC [23] is another effort in this direction that targets high-performance computing platforms and applications. Lange et al. address how to minimize the overhead of virtualization for HPC via passthrough I/O [28], which enables direct guest/application access to a machine's specialized communication hardware. This in turn achieves both high bandwidth and low latency properties of that hardware.

VM Scheduling MRG [24] is a VM scheduler to improve the I/O performance of MapReduce on cloud servers. By exploiting the homogeneity of VM behaviors in MapReduce, MRG sorts the VMs in the CPU run queue based on their priorities as well as the pending I/O operations and batches the I/O operations from several VMs, hence reducing the context switch overhead. A two-level scheduling policy is proposed to achieve proportional fair sharing across both MapReduce clusters and individual VMs. MRG works well only when the guest VMs and the driver domain share the same CPU/core; and it is specific to MapReduce. On the other hand, vSlicer assumes that the driver domain is pinned to a *separate core* and it does not depend on specific applications' behaviors. Virtuoso's vSched [14] is a soft real-time scheduler based on a periodic real-time scheduling model; whereas vSlicer is adapted from Xen's credit scheduler based on the round-robin policy. vSched is a user-level program that runs on Linux and schedules type-II VMs [20] (e.g., VMware GSX) running as processes; whereas vSlicer is a hypervisor-level scheduler. The hybrid scheduling framework [38] combines two scheduling policies to meet the different requirements of high-throughput workload and concurrent processing workload. Its co-scheduling strategy may schedule all related vCPUs of a VM simultaneously to reduce the synchronization overhead and response time of multi-threaded applications. However, it requires that the number of vCPUs be no more than the number of physical CPUs.

8. CONCLUSION

We have presented vSlicer as a technique to support a new class of CPU-sharing VMs called LSVMs. LSVMs improve the performance of I/O-bound applications by reducing the I/O processing latency; yet they do not violate the CPU share fairness among all VMs sharing the same CPU. vSlicer is based on the idea of differentiated-frequency CPU microslicing, where the regular time slice for an LSVM is further divided into smaller microslices for scheduling the LSVM multiple times within each scheduling round. Therefore, the LSVM is given more frequent accesses to the CPU for timely processing of I/O events. vSlicer is simple and generic for implementation in various hypervisors. Our evaluation of a Xen-based vSlicer prototype demonstrates significant improvement at both network I/O and application levels over Xen's credit scheduler.

9. ACKNOWLEDGEMENTS

We thank the anonymous reviewers for their insightful comments. This work was supported in part by the US NSF under grants 0546173, 0720665, 1054788 and 1017898. Any opinions, findings, and conclusions or recommendations in this paper are those of the authors and do not necessarily reflect the views of the NSF.

10. REFERENCES

[1] Amazon Elastic Compute Cloud (Amazon EC2). http://aws.amazon.com/ec2/.

[2] Gogrid Cloud. http://www.gogrid.com.

[3] Httperf. http://www.hpl.hp.com/research/linux/httperf/.

[4] Intel MPI benchmark. http://software.intel.com/en-us/articles/intel-mpi-benchmarks/.

[5] The Iperf Benchmark. http://www.noc.ucf.edu/Tools/Iperf/.

[6] J. McCalpin. The STREAM benchmark. http://www.cs.virginia.edu/stream/.

[7] Lookbusy-a synthetic load generator. http://www.devin.com/lookbusy/.

[8] MPICH2. http://www.mcs.anl.gov/research/projects/mpich2/.

[9] Myconnection Server. http://www.myconnectionserver.com/.

[10] Rackspace Cloud. http://www.rackspace.com.

[11] RFC 2326:Real Time Streaming Protocol (RTSP). http://rfc-ref.org/RFC-TEXTS/2326/chapter10.html.

[12] VMware ESX. http://www.vmware.com/products/esx/.

[13] BARHAM, P., DRAGOVIC, B., FRASER, K., HAND, S., HARRIS, T., HO, A., NEUGEBAUER, R., PRATT, I., AND WARFIELD, A. Xen and the art of virtualization. In ACM SOSP (2003).

[14] BIN LI, P. A. D. Vsched: Mixing batch and interactive virtual machines using periodic real-time scheduling. In ACM SC'05 (2005).

[15] BURTSEV, A., SRINIVASAN, K., RADHAKRISHNAN, P., BAIRAVASUNDARAM, L. N., VORUGANTI, K., AND GOODSON, G. R. Fido: Fast inter-virtual-machine communication for enterprise appliances. In USENIX ATC (2009).

[16] CHADHA, V., ILLIKKAL, R., IYER, R., MOSES, J., NEWELL, D., AND FIGUEIREDO, R. I/O Processing in a Virtualized Platform: A Simulation-Driven Approach. In ACM VEE (2007).

[17] CHERKASOVA, L., GUPTA, D., AND VAHDAT, A. Comparison of the three cpu schedulers in xen. SIGMETRICS Performormance Evaluation Review 35, 2 (2007), 42–51.

[18] DUDA, K. J., AND CHERITON, D. R. Borrowed-virtual-time (BVT) scheduling: supporting latency-sensitive threads in a general-purpose scheduler. In ACM SOSP (1999).

[19] GAMAGE, S., KANGARLOU, A., KOMPELLA, R. R., AND XU, D. Opportunistic flooding to improve TCP transmit performance in virtualized clouds. In ACM SOCC (2011).

[20] GOLDBERG, R. Survey of virtual machine research. IEEE Computer (1974), 34–35.

[21] GOVINDAN, S., NATH, A. R., DAS, A., URGAONKAR, B., AND SIVASUBRAMANIAM, A. Xen and Co.: communication-aware CPU scheduling for consolidated Xen-based hosting platforms. In ACM VEE (2007).

[22] HU, Y., LONG, X., ZHANG, J., HE, J., AND XIA, L. I/O Scheduling Model of Virtual Machine Based on. In ACM HPDC (2010).

[23] HUANG, WEI, KOOP, J., M., GAO, QI, PANDA, AND K., D. Virtual machine aware communication libraries for high performance computing. In ACM/IEEE SC (2007).

[24] KANG, H., CHEN, Y., WONG, J. L., SION, R., AND WU, J. Enhancement of Xen's scheduler for MapReduce workloads. In ACM HPDC'11 (2011).

[25] KANGARLOU, A., GAMAGE, S., KOMPELLA, R. R., AND XU, D. vSnoop: Improving TCP throughput in virtualized environments via acknowledgement offload. In ACM/IEEE SC (2010).

[26] KIM, H., LIM, H., JEONG, J., JO, H., AND LEE, J. Task-aware virtual machine scheduling for i/o performance. In ACM VEE (2009).

[27] KIM, K., KIM, C., JUNG, S.-I., SHIN, H.-S., AND KIM, J.-S. Inter-domain socket communications supporting high performance and full binary compatibility on Xen. In ACM VEE (2008).

[28] LANGE, J. R., PEDRETTI, K., DINDA, P., BRIDGES, P. G., BAE, C., SOLTERO, P., AND MERRITT, A. Minimal-overhead virtualization of a large scale supercomputer. In ACM VEE (2011).

[29] LEE, M., KRISHNAKUMAR, A. S., KRISHNAN, P., SINGH, N., AND YAJNIK, S. Supporting soft real-time tasks in the Xen hypervisor. In ACM VEE (2010).

[30] LESLIE, I. M., D. MCAULEY, R. B., T. ROSCOE, P. T. B., D. EVERS, R. F., AND HYDEN, E. The design and implementation of an operating system to support distributed multimedia applications. In IEEE Journal of Selected Areas in Communications (1996).

[31] MENON, A., COX, A. L., AND ZWAENEPOEL, W. Optimizing network virtualization in Xen. In USENIX ATC (2006).

[32] MENON, A., SCHUBERT, S., AND ZWAENEPOEL, W. TwinDrivers: semi-automatic derivation of fast and safe hypervisor network drivers from guest OS drivers. In ACM ASPLOS (2009).

[33] MENON, A., AND ZWAENEPOEL, W. Optimizing TCP receive performance. In USENIX ATC (2008).

[34] NISHIGUCHI, N. Evaluation and consideration of the credit scheduler for client virtualization. In Xen Summit Asia 2008 (2008).

[35] PATNAIK, D., KRISHNAKUMAR, A., KRISHNAN, P., SINGH, N., AND YAJNIK, S. Performance implications of hosting enterprise telephony applications on virtualized multi-core platforms. Tech. rep., IPTComm, 2009.

[36] WALDSPURGER, C., AND ROSENBLUM, M. I/O virtualization. In Communications of the ACM (2012).

[37] WANG, J., WRIGHT, K.-L., AND GOPALAN, K. XenLoop: A transparent high performance inter-vm network loopback. In ACM HPDC (2008).

[38] WENG, C., WANG, Z., LI, M., AND LU, X. The hybrid scheduling framework for virtual machine systems. In ACM VEE (2009).

[39] ZHANG, X., MCINTOSH, S., ROHATGI, P., AND GRIFFIN, J. L. XenSocket: A high-throughput interdomain transport for virtual machines. In ACM/IFIP/USENIX Middleware (2007).

Singleton: System-wide Page Deduplication in Virtual Environments

Prateek Sharma   Purushottam Kulkarni

Department of Computer Science & Engineering
Indian Institute of Technology Bombay
{prateeks,puru}@cse.iitb.ac.in

ABSTRACT

We investigate memory-management in hypervisors and propose Singleton, a KVM-based system-wide page deduplication solution to increase memory usage efficiency. We address the problem of double-caching that occurs in KVM—the same disk blocks are cached at both the host(hypervisor) and the guest(VM) page caches. Singleton's main components are identical-page sharing across guest virtual machines and an implementation of an exclusive-cache for the host and guest page cache hierarchy. We use and improve KSM–Kernel SamePage Merging to identify and share pages across guest virtual machines. We utilize guest memory-snapshots to scrub the host page cache and maintain a single copy of a page across the host and the guests. Singleton operates on a completely black-box assumption—we do not modify the guest or assume anything about its behaviour. We show that conventional operating system cache management techniques are sub-optimal for virtual environments, and how Singleton supplements and improves the existing Linux kernel memory-management mechanisms. Singleton is able to improve the utilization of the host cache by reducing its size(by upto an order of magnitude), and increasing the cache-hit ratio(by factor of 2x). This translates into better VM performance(40% faster I/O). Singleton's unified page deduplication and host cache scrubbing is able to reclaim large amounts of memory and facilitates higher levels of memory overcommitment. The optimizations to page deduplication we have implemented keep the overhead down to less than 20% CPU utilization.

Categories and Subject Descriptors

D.4.2 [**OPERATING SYSTEMS**]: Storage Management—*Main memory, Storage hierarchies*; C.4 [**PERFORMANCE OF SYSTEMS**]: Performance attributes

General Terms

Performance

Keywords

Virtualization, Caching, Page-deduplication

1. INTRODUCTION

In virtual environments, physical resources are controlled and managed by multiple agents — the Virtual Machine Monitor(VMM), and the guest operating systems (running inside the virtual machines). Application performance depends on both the guest operating system and hypervisor, as well as the interaction between them. The multiple schedulers (CPU, I/O, Network), caches, and policies can potentially conflict with each other and result in sub-optimal performance for applications running in the guest virtual machines. An example of guest I/O performance being affected by the combination of I/O scheduling policies in the VMM and the guests is presented in [8].

In this paper we consider the effects of physical memory being managed by both the VMM(Virtual Machine Monitor) and the guest operating systems. Several approaches to memory management and multiplexing in VMMs like ballooning and guest-resizing exist [35]. We focus on techniques which do not require guest support(page-sharing) and consider system-wide memory requirements, including that of the *host* operating system.

The primary focus of our memory-management efforts is on the behaviour of the *page-cache*. The page-cache in modern operating systems like Linux, Solaris, FreeBSD etc. is primarily used for caching disk-blocks, and occupies a large fraction of physical memory. The virtualization environment we focus on is KVM(Kernel Virtual Machine) [18], which is a popular hypervisor for Linux, and allows unmodified operating systems to be run with high performance. KVM enables the Linux kernel to run multiple virtual machines, and in-effect turns the operating system(Linux) into a VMM(also called *hypervisors*). We consider the effectiveness of using conventional OS policies in environments where the OS also hosts virtual machines. We show that the existing operating system techniques for page-cache maintenance and page-evictions are inadequate for virtual environments.

In most KVM setups, there are two levels of the page-cache—the guests maintain their own cache, and the host maintains a page-cache which is shared by all guests. Guest I/O requests are serviced by their respective caches first, and upon a miss fall-through to the host page-cache. This leads to double-caching: same blocks are present in the guest as well as the host caches. Furthermore, the host-cache sees a low hit-ratio, because pages are serviced from the guest's

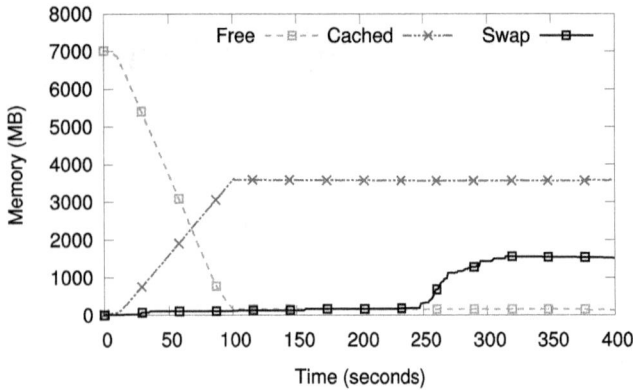

Figure 1: Memory usage graph for a sequential disk-read workload.

page-cache first. This double caching wastes precious physical memory and leads to increased memory-pressure, causing swapping and performance loss. In particular, the problem of swapping is detrimental for virtual setups. Figure 1 shows the memory-usage graph when guest VMs execute I/O intensive workloads, and illustrates that the host system starts swapping even in the presence of cached pages. Note that the guests maintain their own page-caches, and the host caching leads to swapping of pages belonging to VMs. While this unfortunate situation can be ameliorated with existing techniques like using direct I/O and `fadvise` for the guest VMs etc, we show that they adversely affect VM performance.

This paper addresses the problem of multiple levels of cache present in virtual environments, and we seek to implement an *exclusive-cache*. Exclusive caching entails not storing multiple copies of the same object in multiple locations in the cache hierarchy. While multi-level caching and exclusive caches are well studied in the context of network-storage systems [15, 11, 37] and CPU architectural caches, our work is the first to focus on exclusive caching in KVM-based environments. Furthermore, we implement a completely *black-box* approach—requiring no guest modifications or knowledge. We do not rely on graybox techniques like intercepting all guest I/O and page-table updates found in Geiger [17] and XRAY [5]. Another constraint we adhere to is that our solution must not cause performance regressions in non-virtualized environments, since the OS(Linux) serves both as a conventional OS running userspace processes and virtual machines. Thus, we do not change any critical kernel component. This prevents us from implementing specialized techniques for second-level cache-management which are found in [13, 37, 40, 41].

Page deduplication across Virtual Machines [35, 19, 20] is an effective mechanism to reclaim memory allocated to the VMs by the hypervisor in a completely guest-transparent manner. To implement the exclusive page-cache, we utilize content-based page deduplication, which collapses multiple pages with the same content into a single, copy-on-write protected page.

1.1 Contributions

As part of this work, we design and evaluate Singleton, a Kernel Samepage Merging (KSM) based system-wide page deduplication technique. Specifically, our contributions are the following:

- We optimize existing KSM duplicate-page detection mechanisms which reduce the overhead by a factor of 2 over the default KSM implementation.

- We implement an exclusive host page-cache for KVM using a completely black-box technique. We utilize the page deduplication infrastructure (KSM), and proactively evict redundant pages from the host cache.

- Through a series of workloads and micro-benchmarks, we show that Singleton delivers higher cache-hit ratios at the host, a drastic reduction in the size of the host-cache, and significantly improved I/O performance in the VMs.

- We show that proactive management of host cache provides higher levels of memory overcommitment for VM provisioning.

Our implementation is a non-intrusive addition to the host kernel, and supplements the existing memory-management tasks of the VMM (Linux), improves page-cache utilization and reduces system-load.

2. BACKGROUND

Singleton presents an exclusive cache solution for KVM, and uses the KSM page deduplication infrastructure. This section presents the relevant background which will help motivate our solution. Some of the optimizations which we have added to KSM to reduce the page-sharing overhead are also presented.

2.1 KVM architecture and operation

KVM(Kernel Virtual Machine) is a hardware-virtualization based hypervisor for the Linux kernel. The KVM kernel module runs virtual machines as processes in the host system, and multiplexes hardware among virtual machines by relying on the existing Linux resource-sharing mechanisms like its schedulers, file-systems, resource-accounting framework, etc. This allows the KVM module to be quite small and efficient.

The virtual machines are not explicitly created and managed by the KVM module, but instead by a userspace hypervisor helper. Usually, QEMU [6] is the userspace hypervisor used with KVM. QEMU performs tasks such as virtual machine creation, management and control. In addition, QEMU can also handle guest I/O and provides several emulated hardware devices for the VMs (such as disks, network-cards, BIOS, etc.). QEMU communicates with the KVM module using a well-defined API using the `ioctl` interface. An important point to note is that the virtual machines created by QEMU are ordinary user-space processes for the host. Similar to memory allocations for processes, QEMU makes a call to `malloc` to allocate and assign physical memory to each guest virtual machine. Thus, for the host kernel, there is no explicit VM, but instead a QEMU process which has allocated some memory for itself. This process can be scheduled, swapped out, or even killed.

16

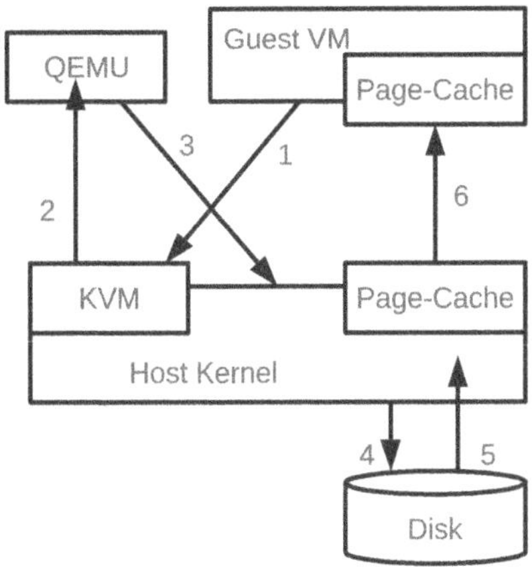

Figure 2: Sequence of messaages to fulfill an I/O operation by a guest VM.

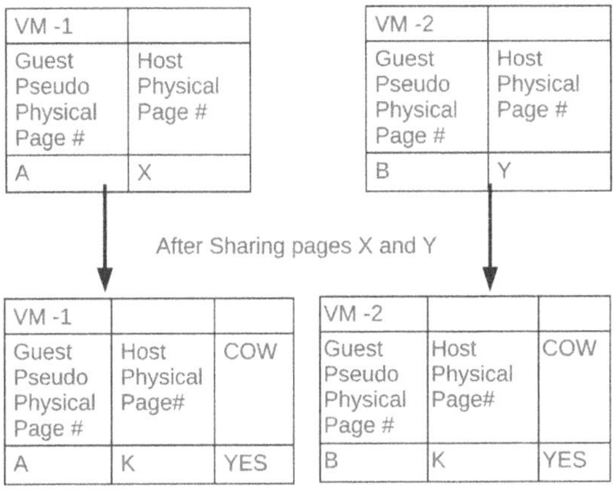

Figure 3: Copy-on-Write based hypervisor level page sharing.

2.2 Disk I/O in KVM/QEMU

The guest VM's "disk" is emulated in the host userspace by QEMU, and is frequently just a file on the physical disk's filesystem. Hence, the emulated disk's read/write are mapped to file-system read/write operations on the virtual-disk file. Figure 2 depicts the(simplified) control flow during a guest VM disk I/O operation. A disk I/O request by the guest VM causes a trap, on which KVM calls the QEMU userspace space process for handling. In the emulated disk case, QEMU performs the I/O operation through a disk I/O request to the host kernel. The host reads the disk block(s) from the device, which get cached in host-page-cache and passed on to the guest via KVM. For the guest, this is a conventional disk read, and hence disk blocks are cached at the guest as well.

2.3 Linux page-cache and page eviction

The Linux page-cache [25] is used for storing frequently accessed disk-blocks in memory. It is different from the conventional buffer-cache in that it also stores pages belonging to mmap'ed files, whereas traditional buffer-caches restricted themselves to read/write I/O on file-system buffers. In a bid to improve I/O performance, a significant amount of physical memory is utilized by the kernel as page-cache.

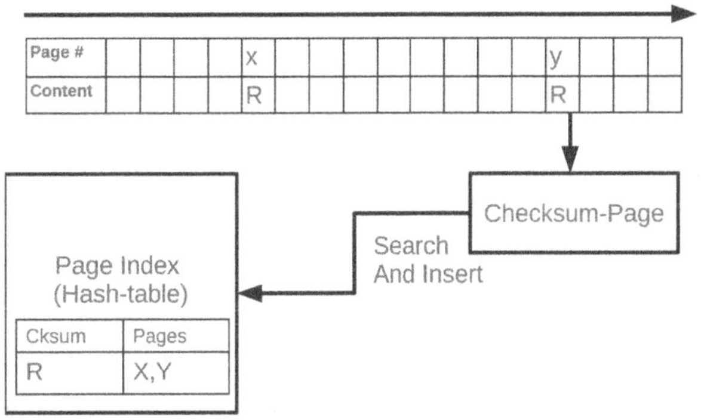

Figure 4: Basic KSM operation. Each page during a scan checksummed and inserted into the hash-table.

Linux uses an LRU variant (specifically, a variant of LRU/2 [27]) to evict pages when under memory pressure. All the pages are maintained in a global LRU list. Thus, page-cache pages as well as pages belonging to process' private address spaces are managed for evictions in a unified manner. This can cause the kernel to swap out process pages to disk inspite of storing cache pages. The page-cache grows and shrinks dynamically depending on memory pressure, file-usage patterns, etc.

2.4 Page Deduplication using KSM

KSM(Kernel Samepage Merging) [4] is a scanning based mechanism to detect and share pages having the same content. KSM is implemented in the Linux kernel as a kernel-thread which runs on the host system and periodically scans guest virtual machine memory-regions looking for identical pages. Page sharing is implemented by replacing the page-table-entries of the duplicate pages with a common KSM page.

As shown in Figure 3, two virtual machines have two copies of a page with the same content. KSM maps the guest-pseudo physical page of both machines A and B to the same merged host physical page K. The shared page is marked copy-on-write(COW) — any modifications to the shared page will generate a trap and the result in the sharing being broken. To detect page similarity, KSM builds a page-index periodically by scanning all pages belonging to all the virtual machines.

KSM originally used red-black binary-search trees as the page-index, and full-page comparisons to detect similarity. As part of Singleton, we have replaced the search-trees with hash-tables, and full-page comparisons with checksum(jhash2) comparisons. In each pass, a single checksum-computation is performed, and the page is inserted into a hash-table(Figure 4). Collisions are resolved by chaining. To reduce collisions, the number of slots in the hash-table is made equal to the total number of pages.

Due to volatility of the pages (page-contents can change any time) and the lack of a mechanism to detect changes, the page-index is created frequently. Periodically, the page-index(hash-table) is cleared, and fresh page-checksums are computed and inserted. The KSM scanning-based comparison process goes on repeatedly, and thus has a consistent impact on the performance of the system. KSM typically consumes between 10-20% CPU on a single CPU core for the default scanning-rate of 20MB/s. The checksumming and hash-tables implementation in Singleton reduces the overhead by about 50% compared to the original KSM implementation (with search-trees and full-page comparisons).

To see that KSM can really detect and share duplicate pages, the memory finger-print [38] of a VM is calculated and compared for similarity. The number of pages that KSM shares compared to the actual number of pages which are duplicate (which is obtained by the fingerprint) determines the sharing effectiveness of KSM. The memory fingerprint of a VM is simply a list of the hashes of each of its pages. By comparing fingerprint similarity, we have observed that KSM can share about 90% of the mergeable pages for a variety of workloads. For desktop workloads(KNOPPIX live-CD), KSM shares about 22,000 of the 25,000 mergeable pages. Ideal candidates for inter-VM page sharing are pages belonging to the kernel text-section, common applications, libraries, and files [20, 19, 35, 10]. These pages are often read-only, and thus once shared, the sharing is not broken.

At the end of a scan, KSM has indexed all guest pages by their recent content. The index contains the checksums of all guest pages, including the duplicate and the unique pages. Moreover, this index is created periodically (after every scan), so we are assured that the checksum corresponding to a page is fairly recent and an accurate representation of the page content. Thus, the KSM maintained page-index can be used as a snapshot of the VM memory contents.

3. SYSTEM-WIDE PAGE DEDUPLICATION

3.1 Motivation: Double caching

A pressing problem in KVM is the issue of double-caching. All I/O operations of guest virtual machines are serviced through the page cache at the host (Figure 2). Because all guest I/O is serviced from the guest's own page-cache first, the host cache sees a low hit-ratio, because "hot" pages are already cached by the guest. Since both caches are likely to be managed by the same cache eviction technique (least-recently-used, or some variant thereof), there is a possibility of a large number of common pages in the caches. This double-caching leads to a waste of memory. Further, the memory-pressure created by the inflated host cache might force the host to start swapping out guest pages. Swapping of pages by the host severely impacts the performance of the guest VMs. An illustration of how guest I/O impacts the host page cache is shown in Figure 5. A single VM writes to a file continuously, which causes a steady increase in the amount of host-page-cached memory and corresponding decrease in the free memory available at the host.

Double caching can be mitigated if we provide an exclusive-cache setup. In exclusive caching, lower levels of cache(the host page-cache in our case) do not store an object if it is present in the higher levels(the guest page-cache). Any solution to the exclusive caching problem must strive for a balance between size of the host page cache and performance of the guests. A host-cache has the potential to serve as a 'second-chance' cache for guest VMs and can improve I/O performance. At the same time, large host page-caches might force guest VM pages to be swapped out by the host kernel—leading to severely degraded performance. Singleton provides an efficient exclusive cache which improves guest I/O performance, and reduces host-cache size drastically.

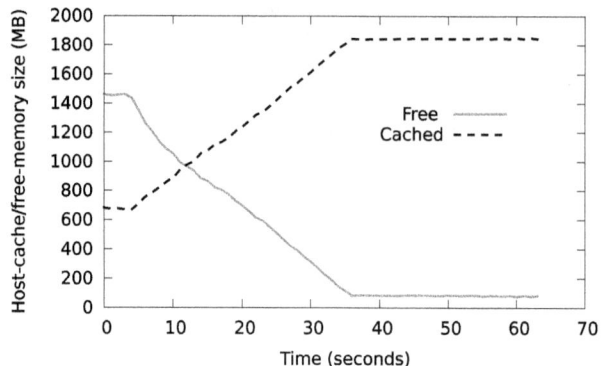

Figure 5: Host free and cached memory on a write-heavy guest workload.

The shared nature of the host-cache also makes it important to provide performance isolation among the virtual machines as well as the processes running on the host system. Disk I/O from an I/O intensive guest VM can fill-up the host-cache, to the detriment of the other VMs. Not only do other VMs get a smaller host cache, but also suffer in performance. The memory-pressure induced by one VM can force the host-kernel to put additional effort for page allocations and scanning pages for evictions, leading to increased system load.

3.2 Potential/Existing approaches

In the context of multi-level exclusive caching in storage systems [13, 37, 5], it has been shown that exclusive caches yield better cache utilization and performance. Exclusive caches are usually implemented using explicit co-ordination between various caches in a multi-level cache hierarchy. DE-MOTE [37] requires an additional SCSI command for demotion notifications. Gray-box techniques for inferring cache hits at higher levels in the cache hierarchy, like X-RAY [5] and Geiger [17] use file-system information to infer page-use by monitoring inode access-times.

In the host-guest cache setup that virtual systems deal with, notifications can cause a large overhead since the page cache sees high activity. Furthermore, the host/guest page-caches are present on a single system, unlike the distributed client/server storage caches. Solutions to exclusive caching require the lower-level(host) cache to explicitly read-in the items evicted from the higher-level(guest) cache. This is not desirable in our setup: VM performance would be impacted if the host does disk accesses for evicted items, leading to overall system-slowdown.

More pressing is the problem of actually generating the eviction notifications—modifications to both the host and the guest OS memory subsystems will be required. However, in spite of the benefits of exclusive caching, modifications to the operating system are not straight-forward. The first challenge is to get notifications of evictions—either by explicit notifications from the guest, or by using I/O-snooping techniques like those developed in Geiger [17]. The fundamental problem is that there is no easy way to map disk blocks in the host and the guest page cache. The hypervisor (QEMU) supports a large number of virtual disk formats (RAW, LVM, QCOW, QCOW2, QED, FVD [34]). The mapping from a virtual block number to a physical block

Operations	VM using Direct I/O	VM using host cache
putc	34,600	33,265
put_block	48,825	51,952
rewrite	14,737	24,525
getc	20,932	44,208
get_block	36,268	**197,328**

Table 1: Bonnie performance with and without caching at the host.

number (which the host file system sees) can be determined fairly easily in case of RAW images, but one would need explicit hypervisor support in other cases. The lack of a common API for these image formats results in a complex co-ordination problem between the host, the guest, and the hypervisor. Clearly, we need a better solution which does not need to contend with this three-way coordination and yet works with all the above mentioned setups and environments.

Direct IO: An existing mechanism to overcome the wastage of memory due double-caching is to bypass the host page-cache. This can be accomplished by mounting the QEMU disks with the `cache=none` option. This opens the disk-image file with the direct-IO mode (`O_DIRECT`). However, direct-I/O has an adverse impact on performance. Table 1 compares performance of file operations on two VMs running the Bonnie [2] file system benchmark. In one case, both Virtual Machines mount their respective (virtual) disks with `cache=writeback` option (QEMU default) set and in the other we use the `cache=none` option. Table 1 shows the Bonnie performance results of one of the VMs. Bypassing the host cache results in almost all operations with direct I/O to be slower than with caching. With direct I/O, the block read rates are 6x slower, the read-character rate 2x slower. Further, the average seek rate with Direct I/O was 2x slower than with host-page-caching—185 seeks per second with direct I/O and 329 seeks/second with caching. Clearly, the I/O performance penalty is too much to pay for a reduced memory usage at the host —host cache is not used with direct I/O. Additionally, using `O_DIRECT` turns off the clever I/O scheduling and batching at the host, since the I/O requests are immediately processed. Direct-I/O scales poorly with an increase in number of VMs, and we do not consider it to be a feasible solution to the double-caching problem.

Fadvise: Additionally, the hypervisor can instruct the host kernel to discard cached pages for the virtual disk-images. This can be accomplished by using the POSIX `fadvise` system-call and passing the `DONTNEED` flag. Fadvise needs to be invoked periodically by the hypervisor on the disk-image file for it to have the desired effect. All file data in the cache is indiscriminately dropped. While fadvise mitigates double-caching, it fails to provide any second-level caching for the guests. The `DONTNEED` advise can also potentially be ignored completely by some operating systems, including the previous versions of the Linux kernel.

3.3 The Singleton approach

To implement a guest-exclusive cache at the host, Singleton uses KSM and the page-index it maintains to search for pages present in the guests. As mentioned earlier (Section 2.4), KSM maintains a snapshot of contents of all pages in its search indexes (red-black trees in case of default KSM, hash-tables in Singleton).

Singleton's exclusive caching strategy is very simple and presented in Algorithm 1. We look-up all the *host* page-cache pages in the KSM maintained page-index of all the VMs to determine if a host-cache page is already present in the guest. The host page-cache pages are checksummed, and the checksum is searched in KSM's page-index. An occurrence in the guest page-index implies that the page is present in the guest, and we *drop* the page from the host's page-cache.

A page in the host's page cache is said to belong to VM V if an I/O request by V resulted that page being bought into the cache. Pages in the page-cache belong to files on disk, which are represented by inodes. We identify a page as belonging to a VM if it belongs to the file which acts as its virtual-disk. To identify which file corresponds to the virtual machine's disk, we pick the file opened by the QEMU process associated with the VM.

Algorithm 1 Singleton's cache-scrubbing algorithm implemented with ksm.

```
After scanning B pages of VM V:
    For each page in the host-cache belonging to V:
        If (page in KSM-Page-Index)
            drop_page(page);
```

Dropping duplicate pages from the host page-cache is referred to as *cache-scrubbing*. The cache scrubbing is performed periodically by the KSM thread—after KSM has scanned (checksummed and indexed) B guest pages. We refer to B as the *scrubbing-interval*.

After dropping pages from the host-cache during scrubbing, two kinds of pages remain in the host cache : pages not present in the guest, and pages which might be present in the guest but were not checksummed (false negatives due to stale checksums). Pages not present in the guest, but present in the host-cache can be further categorized thus: 1. Pages evicted from the guest. 2. Read-ahead pages which were not requested by the guest. The false-negatives do not affect correctness, and only increase the size of the host-cache. False negatives are reduced by increasing KSM's scanning rate.

Cache-utilization of the host's cache will improve if a large number of evicted pages are present(eviction based placement [37]). Keeping evicted pages in the host-cache increases the effective size of cache for the guests, and reducing the number of duplicates across the caches increases exclusivity. To reduce the multiplicative read-ahead [39] as well as to reduce cache size, read-ahead is disabled on the host. We treat the guest as a black-box and do not explicitly track guest evictions. Instead, we use the maxim that page-evictions are followed by page-replacement, hence a page replacement is a good indicator of eviction. Page replacement is inferred via checksum-changes. A similar technique is used in Geiger [17], which uses changes in disk-block addresses to infer replacement. To differentiate page-mutations(simple writes to a memory-address) from page-replacement, we use a very simple heuristic: a replacement is said to have occurred if the checksum and the first eight bytes of the page content have changed.

Singleton introduces cache-scrubbing functionality in KSM and runs in the KSM thread (ksmd) in the host-kernel. We take advantage of KSM's page-index and page-deduplication infrastructure to implement unified inter-VM page deduplication and cache-scrubbing. The cache-scrubbing functionality is implemented as an additional 1000 lines of code in KSM. The ksmd kernel thread runs in the background as a low-priority task (nice value of 5), consuming minimal CPU resources. Singleton extends the conventional inter-VM page deduplication to the entire system by also including the host's page-cache in the deduplication pool. While the memory reclaimed due to inter-VM page sharing depends on the number of duplicate pages between VMs, Singleton is effective even when the workloads are not amenable to sharing. Since all guest I/O passes through the host's cache, the number of duplicate pages in the host's cache is independent of the inter-VM page sharing. Singleton supplements the existing memory-management and page-replacement functionality of the hypervisor, and does not require intrusive hypervisor changes. While our implementation is restricted to KVM setups and not immediately applicable to other hypervisors, we believe that the ideas are relevant and useful to other hypervisors as well.

3.4 Scrubbing frequency control

The frequency of cache scrubbing dictates the average size of the host cache and the KSM overhead. To utilize system memory fully and keep scrubbing overhead to a minimum, a simple scrubbing frequency control-loop is implemented in Singleton. The basic motivation is to control the scrubbing frequency depending on system memory conditions (free and cached). A high-level algorithm outline is presented in Algorithm 2. The try_scrub function is called periodically (after KSM has scanned 1000 pages). We use two basic parameters: maximum amount of memory which can be cached (th_frac_cached) and minimum amount of memory which can be free (th_frac_free), both of which are fractions of the total memory available. The scrubbing frequency is governed by the time-period t, which decreases under memory pressure, and increases otherwise. With host cache getting filled up quickly, Singleton tries to increase scrubbing rate and decreases it otherwise. The time-period has minimum and maximum values between which it is allowed to vary(not shown in the algorithm). The time-period is also a function of number of pages dropped by the scrubber (scrub_host_cache).

4. EXPERIMENTAL ANALYSIS

Cache scrubbing works by proactively evicting pages from the host's page-cache. In this section we explore why additional cache management is required for the host's page cache, and why the existing Linux page eviction and reclaiming mechanisms are sub-optimal for virtual environments. We show how Singleton improves memory utilization and guest performance with a series of benchmarks. Our results indicate that significant reductions in the size of the host page-cache, an *increase* in the host page-cache hit-ratio, and improvement in guest performance can all be obtained with minimal overhead.

Algorithm 2 Singleton's frequency control algorithm.

```
try_scrub (th_frac_cached, th_frac_free) {
  Update_memory_usage_stats(&Cached, &Free, &Memory);
//Case1: Timer expires. t is current scrub interval
  if(cycle_count-- <= 0) {
    Dropped = scrub_host_cache() ;
    //returns num pages dropped
    prev_t = t ;
    t = prev_t*(Cached + Dropped)/Cached;
 }
//Case2: Memory pressure
 else if(Cached > Memory*th_frac_cached ||
            Free < Memory*th_frac_free) {
    Dropped=scrub_host_cache();
    prev_t = t ;
    t = prev_t*(Cached - Dropped)/Cached;
 }
  cycle_count=t;
}
```

4.1 Setup

Since scrubbing is a periodic activity and can have drastic impact on system performance when the scrubbing operation is in progress, all experiments conducted are of a sufficiently long duration (atleast 20 minutes). The workloads are described in Table 2. The scrubbing interval thresholds are between 100,000 and 200,000 pages scanned by KSM (scrubbing-interval algorithm presented in section 3.4), and is of the order of once every 30-60 seconds. The cache-threshold is set as 50% of the total memory and the free-threshold is 10%. For read-intensive benchmarks, the data is composed of blocks with random content, to prevent page deduplication from sharing the pages. For guest I/O, virtIO [30] is used as the I/O transport to provide faster disk accesses.The experiments have been conducted on an IBM x3250 blade server with 8GB memory, 2GB swap-space and one 150GB SAS hard-disk(ext4 file-system). In all the experiments otherwise stated, we run 4 VMs with 1 GB memory size each. The hosts and the guest VMs run the same kernel (Linux 3.0) and OS(Ubuntu 10.04 x86-64 server). To measure the performance on each of the metrics, a comparison is made for three configurations:

Default: The default KVM configuration is used with no KSM thread running.

Fadvise: This runs the page deduplication thread and calls fadvise(DONTNEED) periodically.

Singleton: Page deduplication and eviction based cache placement is used.

4.2 Host-cache utilization

The host cache sees a low hit-ratio, because "hot" pages are cached by the guest. Because of double-caching, if the host's cache is not large enough to accommodate the guest working set, it will see a low number of hits. Our primary strategy is to not keep pages which are present in the guest, and preserve pages which are *not* in the guest. This increases the effective cache size, since guest cache misses have a higher chance of being serviced from the host's page-cache. Presence of pages being present in the guest provides additional knowledge to Singleton about a cached page's use-

Workload	Description
Sequential Read	Iozone [26] is used to test the sequential read performance.
Random Read	Iozone is used to test random-read performance.
Zipf Read	Disk blocks are accessed in a Zipf distribution, mimicking many commonly occurring access patterns.
Kernel Compile	Linux kernel (3.0) is compiled with make allyesconfig with 3 threads.
Eclipse	The Eclipse workload in the Dacapo [7] suite is a memory-intensive benchmark, which simulates the Eclipse IDE [3].
Desktop	A desktop-session is run, with Gnome GUI, web-browsing, word-processor.

Table 2: Details of workloads run in the guest VMs.

fulness, which is not available to the access-frequency based page-eviction mechanism present in the host OS(Linux) kernel. We exploit this knowledge, and remove the duplicate page from the host cache.

Singleton's scrubbing strategy results in more effective caching. We run I/O intensive workloads in the guest VMs and measure the system-wide host cache hit-ratio. The hit-ratio also includes the hits/misses of files accessed by the host processes. Details of the workloads are in Table 2. The results from four VMs running sequential,random, and zipf I/O are presented in Figure 6. For four VMs running sequential read benchmark (Iozone) the cache-hit ratio is 65%, an improvement of about 4% compared to default case (vanilla KVM). A significant reduction in cache-hits is observed when using `fadvise(DONTNEED)` (16% less than Singleton). Calling `fadvise(DONTNEED)` simply drops all the file pages, in contrast to Singleton which keeps pages in the cache if they are not present in the guest. Thus, Singleton's eviction based placement strategy is more effective, and keeps pages to accommodate a larger guest working set.

Scrubbing impacts random-reads more, since the absence of locality hurts the default Linux page-eviction implementation. By contrast, keeping only evicted pages leads to a much better utilization of cache. The cache-hit ratio with Singleton is almost *2x* the default-case (Figure 6). For this experiment, the working set size of the Iozone random-read was kept at 2GB, and the VMs were allocated only 1 GB. Thus, the host-cache serves as the second-chance cache for the guests, and the entire working set can be accommodated even though it does not fit in the guest memory. For workloads whose working-sets aren't large enough, the host-cache sees a poor hit ratio : about 35% in case of the kernel-compile workload. In such cases, the scrubbing strategy only has a negligible impact on host cache utilization. We have observed similar results for other non I/O intensive workloads as well.

The increased cache utilization translates to a corresponding increase in the performance of the guest VMs. For the same setup mentioned above(four VMs executing the same workloads), sequential-reads show a small improvement of 2% (Table 3). In accordance with the higher cache-hit ratios, random-reads show an improvement of about 40% with Singleton over the default KVM setup. Similar gains are observed when compared to `fadvise(DONTNEED)`—indicating that by utilizing the host-cache more effectively, we can improve the I/O performance of guests. We believe this is important, since disk-I/O for virtual machine is significantly slower than bare-metal I/O performance, and one of the key bottlenecks in virtual machine performance.

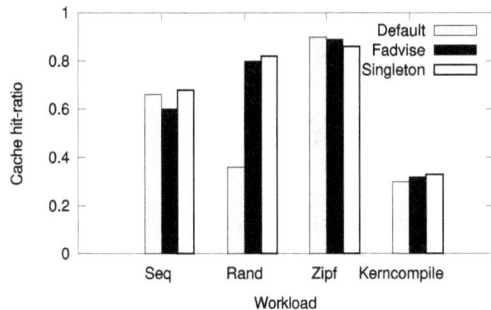

Figure 6: Host page-cache hit ratios.

	Sequential reads (KB/s)	Random reads (KB/s)	Zipf Reads (KB/s)
Default	4,920	**240**	265,000
Fadvise	4,800	280	260,000
Singleton	5,000	**360**	270,000

Table 3: Guest I/O performance for various access patterns.

4.3 Memory utilization

The Linux kernel keeps a unified LRU list containing both cache and anonymous(not backed by any file, belonging to process' address space) pages. Thus, under memory pressure, anonymous pages are swapped out to disk even in the presence of cached pages (Figure 1). Without the proactive cache-scrubbing, we see an increased swap traffic, as the host swaps pages belonging to the guest's physical memory. This swapping can be avoided with scrubbing. The preemptive evictions enforced by Singleton also reduce the number of pages in the global LRU page-eviction list in Linux. This leads to reduction in the kernel overhead of maintaining and processing the list of pages, which can be quite large (millions of pages on systems with 10s of gigabytes of memory). Scrubbing supplements the existing Linux memory-management by improving the efficiency of the page-eviction mechanism.

The periodic page evictions induced by scrubbing reduces the size of the cache in the host significantly. We ran I/O intensive benchmarks, which quickly fill-up the page-cache to observe Singleton's ability to reduce cache size. Figure 8a shows the average cache size over the workload-runs, when the workloads are running on four virtual machines. The host cache size with Singleton is **2-10x** smaller than the default KVM. Compared to the `fadvise(DONTNEED)` approach

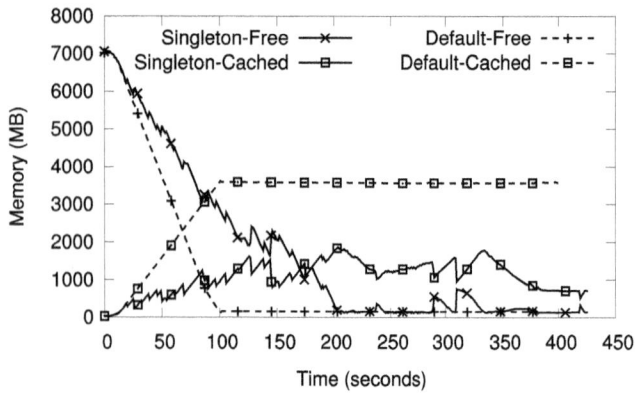

Figure 7: Memory usage graph for a sequential read workload with and without Singleton.

which drops all cache pages, Singleton has a larger cache size. The cache-size can be further reduced if needed by increasing the frequency of the cache-scrubbing. However, our scrubbing-frequency algorithm (presented in Section 3.4) enables us to make a more judicious use of available memory, and increases the scrubbing frequency only when under memory-pressure.

A lower average cache size increases the amount of free memory available, prevents swapping, and reduces memory pressure. In addition to scrubbing, Singleton also employs inter-VM page deduplication, which further decreases the memory usage. A reduction in the amount of swapping when different workloads are run in the guests can be seen in Figure 8b. Without scrubbing, the swap is utilized whenever the guests execute intensive workloads which fill-up the host page-cache. In contrast, using fadvise(DONTNEED) and Singleton results in no/minimal swap-space utilization.

As Figure 1 shows, pages are swapped to disk even though a significant amount of memory is being used by the page-cache. Scrubbing prevents this kind of behaviour, as illustrated in Figure 7. The periodic scrubbing results in sharp falls in the cache-size, and increases the amount of free-memory. This reduction in memory pressure and the reduced swapping reduces the system load and paging activity. In the kernel-compile and eclipse workloads, a further reduction in memory-usage is observed because of the inter-VM page-deduplication component of Singleton. When identical workloads are running in four guest VMs, we can see significant amount of pages being shared (seen in Table 8c). Out of a total 1 million pages (1 GB allocated to each of the 4 VMs with 4KB pages), the percentage of pages shared varied from 8% in the case of sequential read workload to 35% with the kernel-compile workload. The page-sharing is dependent on the workload—same files are used in the case of kernel compile, whereas only the guest kernel pages are shared with the sequential read workload.

An additional benefit of Singleton is that it helps provide a more accurate estimate of free memory, since unused cache pages are dropped. This can be used to make more informed decisions about virtual-machine provisioning and placement.

4.4 Memory overcommitment

The increased free memory provided by Singleton can be used to provide memory overcommitment. To measure the degree of overcommitment, the total amount of memory allocated to virtual machines is increased until the breaking-point. The breaking-point is the point at which the performance degradation is unacceptable(cannot SSH into the machine, kernel complains of a lock-up, etc) or the Linux Out-Of-Memory killer(OOM) kills one of the VMs. On a system with total 10GB virtual memory(8GB RAM + 2GB swap), 8 virtual machines(1 GB allocated to each) are able to run without crashing or being killed. Three kinds of VMs running different workloads(sequential-reads, kernel-compile, and desktop). The desktop VMs run the same OS (Ubuntu 10.04 Desktop), and benefit from the inter-VM page-deduplication, since the GUI libraries, application-binaries etc are shared across all the VMs. The number of desktop VMs were increased until the system crashed, and with Singleton we were able to run 7 desktop VMs in addition to 2 kernel-compile VMs and 2 sequential-I/O VMs (Table 4). A total of 11GB of memory was allocated to the VMs, with 1.5GB used by the host processes. Without Singleton, the number of VMs able to run is 8, after which the kernel initiates the Out-of-memory killing procedure, and kills one of the running VMs to reduce the memory pressure. Thus, the page deduplication and the cache-scrubbing provides a good combination for implementing memory overcommitment for virtual machines.

	Sequential	Kerncompile	Desktop	Total
Default	2	2	4	8
Fadvise	2	2	4	8
Singleton	2	2	7	**11**

Table 4: Number of running VMs till system crashes or runs out of memory.

4.5 Impact on host and guest performance

The improved cache utilization provides better performance for guest workloads. Performance for I/O intensive workloads running concurrently in four guest VMs is presented in Table 3. The overhead of building and maintaining a page-index periodically (done by the KSM thread) does not interfere with guest execution because of the minimal CPU resources it requires. The CPU utilization of Singleton and the system load-average during various workloads shown in Table 8. The CPU utilization stays below 20% on average for most scenarios. Due to the lower memory-pressure, the system load-average is significantly reduced. Most of the resource-utilization of Singleton is due to the cache-scrubbing, which needs to checksum and compare a large number of cache pages periodically. With the scrubbing turned off (only inter-VM page deduplication), our optimizations to KSM result in an average CPU utilization of just 6%, compared to 20% for the unmodified KSM.

Another important improvement is the reduction in the number of pages that the kernel page-eviction process has to scan to evict/drop a page from memory. As mentioned earlier, the kernel maintains a global LRU list for all the pages in memory, and this list can contain millions of entries(pages). Without any proactive cache scrubbing, the cache fills up this LRU list, and the kernel needs to evict

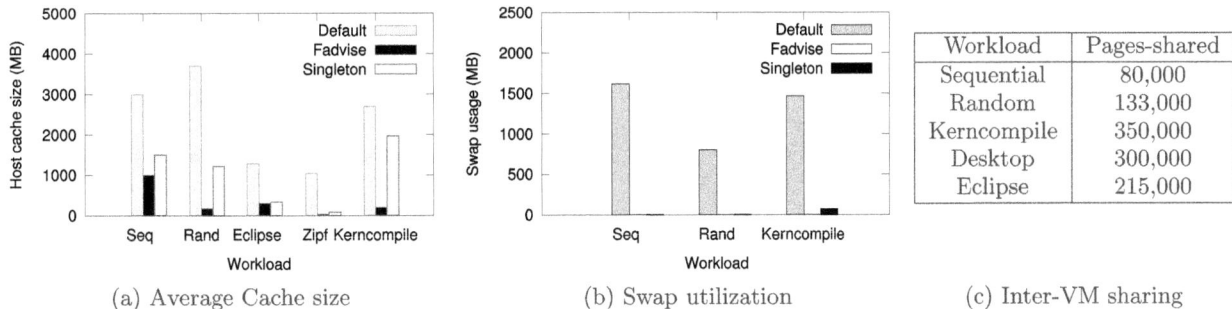

(a) Average Cache size   (b) Swap utilization   (c) Inter-VM sharing

Figure 8: Comparison of memory utilization with various workloads.

	Avg. pages scanned/s	Cache pages dropped/s	Scan efficiency
Default	1,839,267	1459	0.07 %
Singleton	7	109	99.87 %

Table 5: Page eviction statistics with and without Singleton.

	Sequential Read speed	Kernel compile time
Default	7,734 KB/s	3165 s
Fadvise	7,221 KB/s	3180 s
Singleton	7,432 KB/s	**2981 s**

Table 6: Impact of I/O interference on the kernel-compile workload.

	Eclipse benchmark time	Kernel compile time
Default	65 s	3300 s
Fadvise	62 s	3500 s
Singleton	**60 s**	3200 s

Table 7: Impact on host performance (Eclipse) due to kernel-compile workload running in VM.

some pages in order to meet page allocation demands. The overhead of scanning a large number of pages is significant, and is one of the causes of the system load. We show the average number of pages that the kernel scans (pgscand of sar tool) during VM workload execution, and also the *scan efficiency*. The scan efficiency is defined as the ratio of the number of pages dropped to the number of pages scanned, and a higher efficiency indicates lower overhead of the page eviction process. The results are presented in Table 5, which shows the average number of pages scanned and the scanning efficiency for the host system during an I/O intensive workload. Because singleton drops pages which are not going to be used (since they are present in the guests), the efficiency is very high (99%). This means that 99% of all the cache pages scanned by the kernel for dropping were actually dropped, and thus the overhead of scanning paid off. In contrast, we see very low efficiency (less than 1%) in the default case. The average number of pages scanned during the eviction process is also very high (1.8 million), which also explains the low efficiency. With cache-scrubbing, there are negligible number of pages which are scanned by the swap daemon (kswapd), partly because of the lower memory pressure, and also because of the guest cache-content aware eviction process which ensures that only pages which might be used in the future are kept in the cache.

Guest performance isolation: The host-cache is a shared resource among guests, and it can potentially benefit the VMs. However, the host-cache is not equally or proportionally distributed amongst the VMs. VMs doing heavy I/O will have more pages in the host-cache, and can potentially interfere with the operation of the other VMs. The memory pressure induced at the host can trigger swapping of guest pages and increased page-eviction activity, resulting in decreased guest performance. By scrubbing the host-cache, Singleton is able to provide increased performance isolation among guests. With two VMs doing heavy I/O and the other two running kernel-compile workload, the I/O activity floods the host page-cache, and reduces the kernel-compile perfor-

mance(Table 6). Scrubbing prevents this from happening, and the result is improved kernel-compile performance(6%).

In addition to providing isolation among guests, cache-scrubbing can also provide improved performance for applications running in the host system. Processes running on the host (along with the virtual machines) also share the page-cache with the VMs. Without scrubbing, the cache-size can increase, and the memory pressure can adversely affect the performance of the other host-processes/VMs. A common use-case of virtualization is running desktop operating systems in virtual machines. These VMs run along with existing host processes. On a desktop-class system (3GB memory), we run one VM(1 GB memory) running the kernel-compile workload, and run the Eclipse workload on the host. This mimics a common usage pattern. The workload executing in the VM results in performance degradation on the host. With Singleton, a 10% improvement in the workload running in the host(Eclipse) is observed(Table 7)

4.6 Summary of results

The important results based on our experimental evaluation are as follows:

- Singleton provides increased host-cache utilization due to system-wide page deduplication. In our case, upto **2x** increase in host cache hit-ratios was observed with random-read workload.

- The exclusive cache enables larger guest working sets to be present in memory, resulting in improved I/O

	Singleton CPU %	Singleton load average	Default load average
Sequential	17.74	5.6	**12.3**
Random	19.74	4.8	**10.3**
Kerncompile	11.7	5.3	6.0
Zipf	10.2	4.9	4.9

Table 8: Scrubbing overhead and host load averages.

performance in the guests, especially for random I/O, where we have observed a 40% improvement.

- Memory utilization with Singleton is significantly improved. Host cache sizes show **a 2-10x** decrease. The lower memory-pressure results in much lesser swapping—with 4 VMs and over different workloads, we observed close to no swap usage.

- Singleton's page deduplication and exclusive cache enable increased levels of memory overcommitment. In our setup, we were able to run 11 VMs instead of 8 VMs without Singleton.

5. RELATED WORK

Page deduplication : Transparent page sharing as a memory saving mechanism was pioneered by the Disco [9] project, although it requires explicit guest support. Inter-VM content based page sharing using scanning was first implemented in VMWare ESX Server [35]. While the probability of two random pages having exactly the same content is very small, the presence of a large number of common applications,libraries etc make the approach very feasible for a large variety of workload combinations [20, 19, 16, 21, 10]. Furthermore, page deduplication can also take advantage of presence of duplicate blocks across files (and file-systems). Storage deduplication for virtual environments is explored in [42, 29]. Page sharing in hypervisors can be broadly classified into two categories—scanning-based and paravirtualized-support. Scanning based approaches periodically scan the memory areas of all VMs and perform comparisons to detect identical pages. Usually, a hash based fingerprint is used to identify likely duplicates, and then the duplicate pages are unmapped from all the page tables they belong to, to be replaced by a single merged page. The VMWare ESX-Server [35] page sharing implementation, Difference Engine [14] (which performs very aggressive duplicate detection and even works at the sub-page level), and KSM [4] all detect duplicates by scanning VM memory regions. An alternative approach to scanning-based page sharing is detecting duplicate pages when they are being read-in from the (virtual) disks. Here, the virtual/emulated disk abstraction is used to implement page sharing at the device level itself. All VM read-requests are intercepted and pages having same content are shared among VMs. Examples of this approach are Satori [24] and Xenshare [19]. This approach is not possible with KVM because it does not primarily use paravirtualized I/O.

Cache Management: Page-cache management for virtual environments is covered in [33], however it requires changes to the guest OS. Ren et.al., [28] present a new buffer cache design for KVM hosts. Their 'Least Popularly Used' algorithm tracks disk blocks by recency of access and their contents. Duplicate blocks are detected by checksumming and eliminated from the cache. LPU does not provide a guest-host exclusive cache, nor does it implement any inter-VM page sharing. Instead, all VM I/O traffic goes through a custom LPU buffer-cache implementation. We believe that having a custom high-traffic page-cache would suffer for scalability and compatibility issues—the page-cache contains millions of pages which need to be tracked and maintained in an ordered list (by access time) for eviction purposes. This is not a trivial task: the Linux kernel has been able to achieve page-cache scalability (with memory sizes approaching 100s of GB and 100s of CPU cores conteding for the LRU list lock) only after several years of developers' efforts. Hence our goal with Singleton is to minimize the number of system components that need to be modified, and instead rely on proven Linux and KVM approaches, even though they may be sub-optimal.

Exclusive Caching : Several algorithms and techniques for implementing exclusive caching in a multi-level cache hierarchy exist. Second-level buffer management algorithms are presented in [41, 40]. Most work on exclusive caching is in the context of network storage systems— [13], DE-MOTE [37], XRAY [5].

An exclusive-cache mechanism for page-caches is presented in Geiger [17], which snoops on guest pagetable updates and all disk accesses to build a fairly accurate set of evicted pages. However it uses the paravirtualized drivers and shadow page-tables features of Xen, and its techniques are inapplicable in KVM and hardware-assisted two-dimensional paging like EPT and NPT [1].

Memory overcommitment : One way to provide memory overcommitment is to use conventional operating systems techniques of paging and swapping. In the context of VMMs, this is called host-swapping [35], where the VMM swaps out pages allocated to VMs to its own swap-area. Another approach is to dynamically change memory allocated to guests via a ballooning method [35, 31], which "steals" memory from the guests via a special driver. Several other strategies for managing memory in virtual environments, like transcendent memory [23], collaborative memory management [32] exist, but they require explicit guest support or heavy hypervisor modifications.

6. FUTURE WORK

To reduce the page deduplication and scrubbing overhead even further, we are in the process of implementing additional optimizations to KSM which we hope will bring down the overhead to negligible levels.

Scanning only dirtied pages: A fundamental limitation of KSM (and all other scanning-based page-deduplication mechanisms) is that page-dirty rates can be much higher than the scanning rate. Without incurring a large scanning overhead, it is not possible for a brute-force scanner to detect identical pages efficiently.

We are interested in reducing the scanning overhead by only checksumming dirtied pages—similar to VM Live Migration [12], where only dirtied pages are sent to the destination. Conventional techniques rely on write-protecting guest pages, and incur expensive faults on a guest access to that page. Instead, we intend to use a combination of techniques based on hardware-assisted page-dirty logging and random sampling. In some cases, like AMD's Nested Page Tables (NPT) implementation [1], it is possible to obtain a list of

24

dirtied pages without the expensive write-protect-trap approach seen in VM Live-migration. AMD's NPT implementation exposes dirty page information of the guests (pages in the guest virtual address space),which can be exploited to perform dirty-logging based scanning. Further, dirty logging overhead or scanning overhead can be reduced by sampling and subset of pages and by eliminating "hot" pages from the working set in the scan process.

Scrub pages in LRU order: Our current host cache scrubbing algorithm checksums and compares pages in the host's page cache in an arbitrary order which is determined by the kernel-maintained inode list. The overhead of scrubbing is equal to the number of pages in the page-cache which are checksummed but *not* dropped. To improve on this, we can look at the page-cache pages in the least-recently-used (LRU) order. We are exploring means to drop and scrub pages from the host page-cache by exploiting the LRU list and aggressively dropping the 'recent' pages, which have higher likelihood of being present in the guest VMs. Further, a heuristic to stop or reduce rate of scrubbing can be formulated based on the fraction of dropped host pages.

Estimating Working-Set-Size: As the cache scrubbing implementation shows, the page search index which KSM builds and maintains is a valuable resource. Below we describe a few other potential uses of the index for hypervisor memory management and other tasks. KSM's search index can be used to estimate the working set size (WSS) of a VM. Several approaches to estimating the WSS of VMs exist [17, 36, 35, 22], but we can exploit KSM's index to estimate the WSS with low overhead and implementation effort. Since page contents are recorded (checksummed), page evictions can be easily tracked, allowing us to use Geiger's [17] approach to estimate WSS by measuring page eviction rate. If the first few bytes of a page have changed since the last KSM scan, we can say that the page has been evicted, with a high probability. Strictly, a changed checksum and initial few bytes implies page *reuse*, but as Geiger [17] shows, it almost always implies page eviction.

7. CONCLUSION

By combining inter-VM page deduplication and host cache scrubbing, Singleton achieves unified redundancy elimination in KVM, and can reclaim massive amounts of memory. Through a series of workloads under varying degrees of memory-pressure, we have shown that host-cache scrubbing is a low-overhead way of implementing an host/guest exclusive-cache in KVM. Our exclusive cache implementation results in tiny host page-caches (of the order of a few megabytes, as compared to several gigabytes without the scrubbing), along with improved guest performance because of better cache utilization.

Singleton does not require any intrusive modification to either the hypervisor or the guest, and works in a wide variety of environments. We achieve significant guest performance gains (upto 40%) along with memory savings(2-4x reduction in cache sizes), despite being conservative about the components of the system we modify. By utilizing the existing page-sharing infrastructure, we have shown how to implement several memory management tasks like eviction-based placement, with minimal modifications and overhead. Further, our modifications to KSM have demonstrated that inter-VM page deduplication can save significant amount of memory with low overhead,

As remarked earlier, page-sharing is a guest-transparent technique to reclaim memory and allow for memory overcommitment. By demonstrating that page-sharing along with its associated benefits (like exclusive caching etc) increases guest-performance, we believe that it is a useful and viable memory overcommitment approach.

8. REFERENCES

[1] AMD-V Nested Paging. http://developer.amd.com/assets/NPT-WP-1%201-final-TM.pdf.
[2] Bonnie++ File System Benchmark. www.coker.com.au/bonnie++/.
[3] Eclipse IDE. http://eclipse.org/.
[4] A. Arcangeli, I. Eidus, and C. Wright. Increasing Memory Density by using KSM. In *Proceedings of the Linux Symposium*, pages 19–28, 2009.
[5] L.N. Bairavasundaram, M. Sivathanu, A.C. Arpaci-Dusseau, and R.H. Arpaci-Dusseau. X-ray: A Non-invasive Exclusive Caching Mechanism for Raids. In *31st Annual International Symposium on Computer Architecture.*, pages 176–187, 2004.
[6] F. Bellard. QEMU, a Fast and Portable Dynamic Translator. In *Proceedings of USENIX Annual Technical Conference, FREENIX Track*, pages 41–49, 2005.
[7] S.M. Blackburn, R. Garner, C. Hoffmann, A.M. Khang, K.S. McKinley, R. Bentzur, A. Diwan, D. Feinberg, D. Frampton, S.Z. Guyer, et al. The DaCapo Benchmarks: Java Benchmarking Development and Analysis. In *ACM SIGPLAN Notices*, volume 41, pages 169–190, 2006.
[8] D. Boutcher and A. Chandra. Does Virtualization Make Disk Scheduling Passé? *ACM SIGOPS Operating Systems Review*, 44(1):20–24, 2010.
[9] E. Bugnion, S. Devine, and M. Rosenblum. Disco: Running Commodity Operating Systems on Scalable Multiprocessors. *ACM SIGOPS Operating Systems Review*, 31(5):143–156, 1997.
[10] C.R. Chang, J.J. Wu, and P. Liu. An Empirical Study on Memory Sharing of Virtual Machines for Server Consolidation. In *IEEE Symposium Parallel and Distributed Processing with Applications (ISPA)*, pages 244–249, 2011.
[11] Z. Chen, Y. Zhou, and K. Li. Eviction-based Cache Placement for Storage Caches. In *Proceedings of USENIX Annual Technical Conference*, pages 269–282, 2003.
[12] C. Clark, K. Fraser, S. Hand, J.G. Hansen, E. Jul, C. Limpach, I. Pratt, and A. Warfield. Live Migration of Virtual Machines. In *USENIX Symposium on Networked Systems Design and Implementation (NSDI)*, pages 273–286, 2005.
[13] B.S. Gill. On Multi-level Exclusive Caching: Offline Optimality and why Promotions are Better than Demotions. In *Proceedings of the 6th USENIX Conference on File and Storage Technologies*, pages 1–17, 2008.
[14] D. Gupta, S. Lee, M. Vrable, S. Savage, A.C. Snoeren, G. Varghese, G.M. Voelker, and A. Vahdat. Difference engine: Harnessing Memory Redundancy in Virtual Machines. *Communications of the ACM*, pages 85–93, 2010.

[15] X. He, M.J. Kosa, S.L. Scott, and C. Engelmann. A Unified Multiple-level Cache for High Performance Storage Systems. *International Journal of High Performance Computing and Networking*, 5(1):97–109, 2007.

[16] M. Jeon, E. Seo, J. Kim, and J. Lee. Domain level Page Sharing in Xen Virtual Machine Systems. *Advanced Parallel Processing Technologies*, pages 590–599, 2007.

[17] S.T. Jones, A.C. Arpaci-Dusseau, and R.H. Arpaci-Dusseau. Geiger: Monitoring the Buffer Cache in a Virtual Machine Environment. In *Proceedings of ASPLOS*, pages 14–24, 2006.

[18] A. Kivity, Y. Kamay, D. Laor, U. Lublin, and A. Liguori. KVM: the Linux Virtual Machine Monitor. In *Proceedings of the Linux Symposium*, pages 225–230, 2007.

[19] J.F. Kloster, J. Kristensen, and A. Mejlholm. Efficient Memory Sharing in the Xen Virtual Machine Monitor. Technical report, Aalborg University, 2006.

[20] J.F. Kloster, J. Kristensen, and A. Mejlholm. On the Feasibility of Memory Sharing: Content-based Page Sharing in the Xen Virtual Machine Monitor. Technical report, Aalborg University, 2006.

[21] J.F. Kloster, J. Kristensen, and A. Mejlholm. Determining the use of Interdomain Shareable Pages using Kernel Introspection. Technical report, Aalborg University, 2007.

[22] P. Lu and K. Shen. Virtual Machine Memory Access Tracing with Hypervisor Exclusive Cache. In *Proceedings of the USENIX Annual Technical Conference*, 2007.

[23] D. Magenheimer, C. Mason, D. McCracken, and K. Hackel. Transcendent Memory and Linux. In *Proceedings of the Linux Symposium*, pages 191–200, 2009.

[24] G. Miłos, D.G. Murray, S. Hand, and M.A. Fetterman. Satori: Enlightened Page Sharing. In *Proceedings of USENIX Annual technical conference*, pages 1–14, 2009.

[25] Piggin Nick. A Lockless Page Cache in Linux. In *Proceedings of the Linux Symposium*, pages 241–250, 2006.

[26] W.D. Norcott and D. Capps. Iozone Filesystem Benchmark. www.iozone.org.

[27] E.J. O'neil, P.E. O'neil, and G. Weikum. The LRU-K page Replacement Algorithm for Database Disk Buffering. In *ACM SIGMOD Record*, volume 22, pages 297–306, 1993.

[28] J. Ren and Q. Yang. A New Buffer Cache Design Exploiting Both Temporal and Content Localities. In *2010 International Conference on Distributed Computing Systems*, 2010.

[29] S. Rhea, R. Cox, and A. Pesterev. Fast, Inexpensive Content-Addressed Storage in Foundation. In *USENIX Annual Technical Conference*, 2008.

[30] R. Russell. VirtIO: Towards a de-facto Standard for Virtual I/O Devices. *ACM SIGOPS Operating Systems Review*, 42(5):95–103, 2008.

[31] J.H. Schopp, K. Fraser, and M.J. Silbermann. Resizing Memory with Balloons and Hotplug. In *Proceedings of the Linux Symposium*, pages 313–319, 2006.

[32] M. Schwidefsky, H. Franke, R. Mansell, H. Raj, D. Osisek, and J.H. Choi. Collaborative Memory Management in Hosted Linux Environments. In *Proceedings of the Linux Symposium*, 2006.

[33] B. Singh. Page/slab Cache Control in a Virtualized Environment. In *Proceedings of the Linux Symposium*, pages 252–262, 2010.

[34] C. Tang. FVD: a High-Performance Virtual Machine Image Format for Cloud. In *Proceedings of the USENIX Annual Technical Conference*, pages 229–234, 2011.

[35] C.A. Waldspurger. Memory Resource Management in VMware ESX server. *ACM SIGOPS Operating Systems Review*, pages 181–194, 2002.

[36] R. West, P. Zaroo, C.A. Waldspurger, and X. Zhang. Online Cache Modeling for Commodity Multicore Processors. *Proceedings of the 19th international conference on Parallel architectures and compilation techniques*, pages 563–564, 2010.

[37] T.M. Wong and J. Wilkes. My cache or Yours? Making Storage More Exclusive. In *Proceedings of USENIX Annual Technical Conference*, pages 161–175, 2002.

[38] T. Wood, G. Tarasuk-Levin, P. Shenoy, P. Desnoyers, E. Cecchet, and M.D. Corner. Memory Buddies: Exploiting Page Sharing for Smart Colocation in Virtualized Data Centers. *ACM SIGOPS Operating Systems Review*, pages 31–40, 2009.

[39] Z. Zhang, A. Kulkarni, X. Ma, and Y. Zhou. Memory Resource Allocation for File System Prefetching: from a Supply Chain Management Perspective. In *Proceedings of the 4th ACM European conference on Computer systems*, pages 75–88, 2009.

[40] Y. Zhou, Z. Chen, and K. Li. Second-level Buffer Cache Management. *IEEE Transactions on Parallel and Distributed Systems*, pages 505–519, 2004.

[41] Y. Zhou, J.F. Philbin, and K. Li. The Multi-queue Replacement Algorithm for Second Level Buffer Caches. In *Proceedings of USENIX Annual Technical Conference*, pages 91–104, 2001.

[42] K. ÂŕJin and E.L. Miller. The Effectiveness of Deduplication on Virtual Machine Disk Images. In *Proceedings of SYSTOR 2009: The Israeli Experimental Systems Conference*. ACM, 2009.

Locality-Aware Dynamic VM Reconfiguration on MapReduce Clouds

Jongse Park, Daewoo Lee, Bokyeong Kim, Jaehyuk Huh, Seungryoul Maeng

Computer Science Department, KAIST
Daejeon, Korea

{jspark, dwlee, bokyeong, jhuh, and maeng}@calab.kaist.ac.kr

ABSTRACT

Cloud computing based on system virtualization, has been expanding its services to distributed data-intensive platforms such as MapReduce and Hadoop. Such a distributed platform on clouds runs in a virtual cluster consisting of a number of virtual machines. In the virtual cluster, demands on computing resources for each node may fluctuate, due to data locality and task behavior. However, current cloud services use a static cluster configuration, fixing or manually adjusting the computing capability of each virtual machine (VM). The fixed homogeneous VM configuration may not adapt to changing resource demands in individual nodes.

In this paper, we propose a dynamic VM reconfiguration technique for data-intensive computing on clouds, called *Dynamic Resource Reconfiguration (DRR)*. DRR can adjust the computing capability of individual VMs to maximize the utilization of resources. Among several factors causing resource imbalance in the Hadoop platforms, this paper focuses on data locality. Although assigning tasks on the nodes containing their input data can improve the overall performance of a job significantly, the fixed computing capability of each node may not allow such locality-aware scheduling. DRR dynamically increases or decreases the computing capability of each node to enhance locality-aware task scheduling. We evaluate the potential performance improvement of DRR on a 100-node cluster, and its detailed behavior on a small scale cluster with constrained network bandwidth. On the 100-node cluster, DRR can improve the throughput of Hadoop jobs by 15% on average, and 41% on the private cluster with the constrained network connection.

Categories and Subject Descriptors

D.4.7 [**Operating Systems**]: [Organization and Design] Distributed System; C.2.4 [**Computer-communication Networks**]: Distributed Systems

General Terms

Management, Design

Keywords

Cloud computing, virtual clusters, MapReduce

1. INTRODUCTION

Recently, cloud computing has been replacing traditional privately owned clusters, as it can provide high efficiency from the economies of scale and elastic resource provisioning. Such cloud computing has been expanding its services to data-intensive computing on distributed platforms such as MapReduce [10], Dryad [12], and Hadoop [2]. In such distributed platforms on clouds, physical machines are virtualized, and a large number of virtual machines (VMs) form a virtual cluster. A data-intensive platform runs on the virtual cluster instead of a traditional physical cluster. Such a virtual cluster can provide a highly flexible environment, which can scale up and down accommodating changing computation demands from various users. Cloud providers consolidate virtual clusters from different users into a physical data center, to maximize the utilization of resources.

Current virtual clusters for data-intensive computing can support the flexibility of selecting the type of computing nodes and the number of nodes in a cluster, when the cluster is configured. Users can choose the most appropriate virtual cluster configuration to meet their computational requirements. Although such a static configuration of each virtual machine in the cluster can still provide better flexibility than clusters with physical machines, the static configuration cannot satisfy dynamically changing computing demands during the life time of a virtual cluster. To adapt to changing demands on each VM in a virtual cluster, each VM may be dynamically reconfigured. Current virtualization techniques can support such a dynamic reconfiguration of each virtual machine using resource *hot-plugging*. As long as physical resources are available, each virtual machine can be assigned with more virtual CPUs and memory while the virtual machine is running. However, the currently available cloud services, such a dynamic reconfiguration of VM is not available,

In the distributed data-intensive computing platforms, resources required for each node may not be uniform. In such platforms, a user job is decomposed into many small tasks, and the tasks are distributed across computing nodes in the cluster. One of the most critical reasons for uneven resource usages is data locality. Input data are distributed across computing nodes using distributed file systems, such as Google File System (GFS)[9] or Hadoop File Systems (HDFS). Depending on whether a task is assigned to a node with its data (*local task or non-local task*), the execution time of the task may differ significantly. Prior studies showed that data locality affects the throughput of Hadoop jobs significantly, and they improve the locality by assigning tasks to the nodes with the corresponding data as much as possible [19]. However, to improve locality, when a task is scheduled, the computing node with the corresponding data must have available computing slots to process the task. If a computing slot is not available, the task must be scheduled to a remote node, which must transfer necessary data from another node for the task.

In this paper, we propose a dynamic VM reconfiguration technique, called *Dynamic Resource Reconfiguration (DRR)* for virtual clusters running the Hadoop platform. The technique can change the configuration of virtual computing nodes dynamically to maximize the data locality of tasks. The proposed technique increases the computing resource of a VM, if the next task has its data on the VM. Simultaneously, an idle virtual CPU is removed from another VM in the same virtual cluster, so that the size of the virtual cluster remains constant to provide a constant cost for the user. This dynamic reconfiguration of each VM improves the overall job throughput by improving data locality, while the total virtual CPUs in the cluster remain unchanged.

However, to add a virtual CPU to a VM for a newly scheduled local task, the physical system running the VM must have additional available CPU resources. Cloud providers may reserve some headroom for such a temporary increase of CPU demand in each physical system. Our first DRR scheduler, called *Synchronous DRR*, assumes the availability of such extra CPU resources in each physical system. Alternatively, we also propose a DRR scheduler, called *Queue-based DRR*, which can eliminate the CPU headroom completely. The scheduler coordinates the allocation and deallocation of virtual CPUs from different physical systems. Virtual clusters sharing the physical cluster, can exchange CPU resources, by deallocating virtual CPUs from a node without local tasks, and by allocating virtual CPUs to a node with pending local tasks. Our results show that such an exchange incurs only minor delays in executing tasks.

To the best of our knowledge, this paper is one of the first studies to dynamically reconfigure individual VMs in a virtual cluster running distributed data-intensive platforms. Each user may just limit the total resource size of a virtual cluster, while the configuration of each VM is dynamically determined by changing resource demands for the VM. Using a 100-node Amazon EC2 [1] cluster, we evaluate the potential performance improvement by locality-aware dynamic VM reconfiguration. With the Hive benchmark [5] running on the Hadoop and HDFS platforms, locality-aware reconfiguration can improve the overall throughput by 15% on average. On a small scale private cluster with a limited network bandwidth, dynamic reconfiguration can improve the throughput by 41% on average.

Another source for uneven data demands is that different jobs may have different resource usages. For example, some jobs require more CPU resources, while others need more memory or I/O bandwidth. Although this paper focuses only on mitigating load imbalance caused by data locality, DRR can be generalized to other dynamic resource imbal-

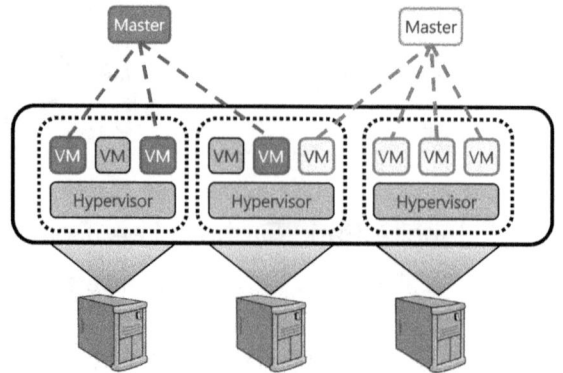

Figure 1: MapReduce on virtualized environments

ance among VMs, adjusting the configuration of each VM for changing demands.

The rest of this paper is organized as follows. Section 2 presents motivation for dynamic VM reconfiguration to improve data locality in data-intensive platforms. Section 3 describes the overall architecture of DRR and its reconfiguration policies. Section 4 evaluates the effectiveness of DRR with two different cluster environments. Section 5 presents prior work on VM reconfiguration and data-intensive platforms, and Section 6 concludes the paper.

2. MOTIVATION

2.1 Dynamic VM Reconfiguration

In cloud computing, system virtualization allows flexible resource management by allocating virtual machines, instead of physical systems, to cloud users. With virtualization, each user has an isolated secure computing environment, even though multiple users may share physical resources to improve the utilization of physical systems. System virtualization has been extended to a virtual cluster, which consists of multiple virtual machines, for distributed computing platforms. Instead of using physical systems directly, data and computation in such data-intensive platforms are distributed across a large number of virtual machines. Figure 1 depicts multiple virtual clusters running MapReduce platforms sharing the same physical cluster.

To configure virtual clusters, current public or private clouds use a homogeneous static configuration of virtual machines. When a virtual cluster is created, a user selects a type of virtual machines with a fixed number of virtual cores and a fixed memory size, and determines the number of virtual machines, by considering the overall cost of using the virtual cluster. One drawback of such a static configuration is that the resources required for each virtual machine may fluctuate during the life time of the virtual cluster. A virtual machine may require more CPU resources while another virtual machine needs more memory. Such a dynamic imbalance of resources in individual virtual machines, leads to the overall inefficiency of cluster resources.

In traditional data-intensive computing on physical clusters, it is not possible to change physical resources dynamically, as each physical system has a fixed amount of physical resources. In such physical clusters, numerous studies for data-intensive computing have tried to maximize the utilization of fixed physical resources by efficiently distributing loads on the nodes [10, 12, 2, 16, 4, 3]. A job is partitioned into small tasks, and evenly distributed to across computing nodes for load balancing. However, such a perfect load balancing may not be possible, as different jobs or tasks have different resource requirements. Furthermore, as will be discussed in the next section, data locality often makes a naive uniform distribution of tasks, inefficient for the overall throughput of the platform.

However, virtualization opens a novel opportunity to reconfigure virtual machines constituting a virtual cluster. Multiple virtual clusters share a set of physical machines, and within a physical system, multiple virtual machines for the same or different users co-exist. Exploiting the flexibility of virtualization, resources allocated for each virtual machine can be dynamically reconfigured by *resource hot-plugging*. For example, the number of virtual CPUs for a virtual machine can change while the virtual machine is running, or the size of allocated memory can also change with ballooning techniques[18].

The dynamic reconfiguration of virtual machines allows resources to be provisioned to demanding nodes. This can make traditional load balancing less critical in distributed platforms, as resources in each VM become flexible. This leads to a shift of cloud service from provisioning of a fixed set of virtual machines, to a cluster-level resource provisioning. Users just need to select the total amount of resources for a given cluster, and each virtual machine can be reconfigured during the runtime to maximize the performance of users' workloads.

There are two important factors causing unbalanced loads in distributed data-intensive platforms. Firstly, data locality requires flexible CPU resources in computing nodes. For load balancing, incoming task must be evenly distributed across different nodes. However, such a pure load-balanced scheduling of tasks can lead to the ignorance of data locality, causing expensive data transfer for non-local tasks. To maintain data locality, the virtual machine, which has data for an incoming task, may increase its computational capability temporarily to process the task.

Secondly, each MapReduce job or task has a different resource requirement. For example, certain tasks require more CPUs and others require more memory or I/O bandwidth. Users cannot predict the resource requirement precisely when a virtual cluster is configured. If virtual machines can be dynamically reconfigured for tasks, the cloud provider can relieve users from the burden of selecting the most efficient cluster configuration. In this paper, we focus on the data locality problem for VM reconfiguration, leaving the generalized VM reconfiguration as future work. In the next section, we elaborate the data locality problem in distributed data-intensive platforms.

2.2 Data Locality in MapReduce

The data locality problem occurs in MapReduce platforms since input data are distributed in computing nodes, using a distributed file system, such as Google File System [9] or Hadoop File System. A user job is partitioned to tasks which process a block of data. The block size is commonly configured to 64MB or 128MB. The entire data set is also partitioned at the block granularity and is distributed in the computing nodes. To improve the reliability and locality of

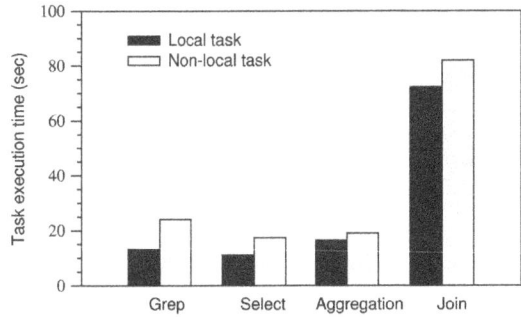

Figure 2: Task execution times for workloads at a 100-node cluster

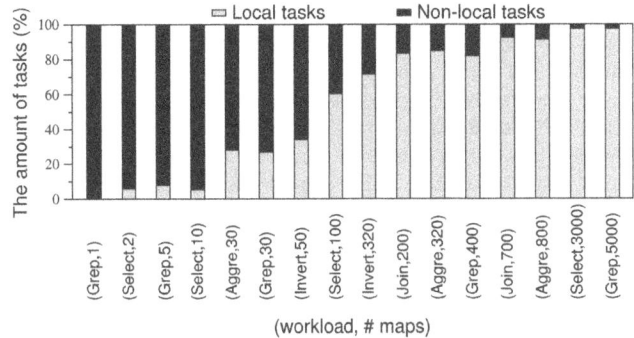

Figure 3: Data locality for various workloads with different numbers of map tasks at a 100-node cluster

input data, they are often replicated and stored in multiple computing nodes.

A MapReduce job is composed of three phases, map, shuffle, and reduce. The master schedules map and reduce tasks to free computing slots identified by heartbeats from slave nodes. Each slave sends a heartbeat every few seconds which announces that it can handle a new task if it has a free slot. Each slave node has a fixed number of map and reduce slots, which are proportional to the available computation capability, commonly one or two slots per core.

After receiving a heartbeat, the master assigns a new task to the slave node according to its scheduling policy. To improve data locality, the master scheduler attempts to assign a map task, which processes the data stored in the node with an available slot. However, it is not always possible to find such a *local* task to the node. As reduce tasks commonly receive data equally from all nodes, the data locality is less critical for reduce tasks than for map tasks.

If data locality is not satisfied in the node with a free slot, the node should read input data for computation through network, incurring significant network overheads. Such a remote data transfer for a map task, not only delay the execution time of the map task, but also increase network traffic in the cluster, negatively affecting other tasks running in the cluster. Although reduce tasks do not exhibit a significant data locality, as it receives intermediate data from all the nodes, the reduced network traffic from localized map tasks, can indirectly improve the performance for reduce tasks too. Therefore, it is critical to assign tasks to the nodes which have their input data, satisfying data locality.

Figure 2 shows the difference of execution times between *local* and *non-local* tasks. Local tasks get their input data from local disks during the map phase, while non-local tasks require data transfers from remote nodes. The results are measured from a 100-node cluster from Amazon EC2. The details of the methodology are described in Section 4.1. Depending on the locality of input data, task execution times can increase by as much as 53% in the **grep** workloads. The **select** workloads also exhibit a significant increase of execution times, if a map task must receive its input data from a remote node.

Figure 3 presents the ratios of local tasks for various sizes of MapReduce jobs. As the size of jobs, or the number of map tasks, increases, the chance to schedule map tasks to local VMs increases, since the scheduler has many candidate local map tasks when a slot becomes free in a VM. However, if a job consists of a small number of map tasks, scheduling the tasks to local VMs becomes very difficult. In commercial usage patterns as shown by Zaharia et al [19], such small jobs account for the majority of jobs running in Facebook. Their study showed that as a significant portion of real world workloads are small jobs, with low data locality, improving the data locality for such jobs is critical for the overall cluster performance. As the number of nodes increases, the locality problem for small jobs will become worse, as the data set is distributed in more nodes.

Fundamentally, the reason why the data locality issue becomes a critical problem on MapReduce is that a node of a MapReduce cluster has a dual role of computing node as well as data node. Load balancing for computation often conflicts with data locality. Dynamic VM reconfiguration mitigates such conflicts between computation load balancing and data locality, as the reconfiguration can transfer computational resources to the node with a pending task and the necessary data for the task. Virtualization enables such transfers of computation resources from a VM to another VM by dynamically adjusting virtual CPU resources in two VMs.

3. ARCHITECTURE

In this section, we describe a dynamic reconfiguration mechanism for virtual clusters to support locality-aware resource scheduling. We propose two schemes for the dynamic VM reconfiguration. The first scheme, synchronous DRR, can reconfigure VMs only when there are free CPU resources in physical systems. To support the first scheme, the cloud provider may need to reserve unassigned CPU slots in each physical system. The second scheme, queue-based DRR, does not require such headroom in CPU resources. We first describe the necessary modifications to virtual clusters to provide dynamic reconfiguration, and present the two schemes.

3.1 Overview

To support dynamic VM reconfiguration for Hadoop platforms, the cloud provider must offer cluster-level pricing options to allow users to choose the base VM configuration and the number of VMs. However, the configuration of a VM can be dynamically adjusted with more or less virtual CPUs than the base VM configuration, while the total cores assigned to the cluster does not change. The dynamic resource reconfiguration (DRR) architecture adds or removes virtual cores in VMs to maximize the data locality of the Hadoop platform.

To implement DRR, two new components must be added

Algorithm 1 Base Fair Hadoop Scheduler [19]
```
 1: when a heartbeat is received from node n:
 2:   if n has a free slot then
 3:     sort jobs in increasing order of the number of running tasks
 4:     for j in jobs do
 5:       if j has unlaunched task t with data on n then
 6:         launch t on n
 7:       else if j has unlaunched task t then
 8:         launch t on n
 9:       end if
10:     end for
11:   end if
```

---

to the current virtual cluster environments. The first component is *Reconfiguration Coordinator (RC)* which is a reconfiguration manager sending allocation and deallocation requests to the hypervisor running on each physical machine. A single RC is created for each virtual cluster and the master node of each virtual cluster runs the RC. If RC decides that a virtual machine in the cluster needs resource reconfiguration, RC sends an allocation or de-allocation request to *Machine Resource Manager (MRM)* running in the physical system, where the VM to be reconfigured is running on. After receiving requests from RC, MRM re-assigns the requested virtual CPUs to the VM. MRM makes requests to the hypervisor of the physical machine, to hot-plug or to un-plug virtual CPUs for VMs running on the system.

In this section, we propose two possible implementations of DRR, *Synchronous DRR* and *Queue-based DRR*. In the synchronous DRR, a task is assigned to a VM only when the physical system running the VM has an available core to allocate for the VM. Such synchronous reconfiguration requires free CPU resources in each system on the cloud. However, in the queue-based DRR, a task can be queued to a VM, even if the VM does not have an available virtual core immediately. The queue-based DRR increases the possibility of maintaining locality by waiting for a possibly short period time until the locality-matched VM has an available core. To support the queue-based DRR, MRM maintains two queues, allocation and deallocation queues (AQ and DQ). When the scheduler assigns a task to a VM, but the VM does not have an available slot, the task is appended to the allocation queue in MRM, waiting for an available core. If the VMs running the physical system have an idle core, MRM of the system appends the idle core to the deallocation queue.

Two proposed DRR implementations are both based on a naïve Hadoop scheduler for fairness [19]. The scheduler provides fairness among user jobs, while locality is also marginally supported. When the scheduler receives a heartbeat from a node (or VM in a virtual cluster) and the node has a free slot, it picks a job which has the lowest number of running tasks in the cluster, to guarantee the fairness among jobs. For locality, among the tasks in the picked job, the scheduler attempts to select a task, whose input data is in the newly freed node (local task for the node). If the scheduler cannot find a local task for the node, it attempts to find a task whose data is in the node of the same rack. Neither tasks are found for the picked job, the scheduler picks any task for the free node. Although the Hadoop scheduler distinguishes local and rack-local tasks, common cloud computing environments often do not support the distinction between local and rack-local tasks, as the cluster topology

Algorithm 2 Synchronous DRR Algorithm

1: when a heartbeat is received from node n:
2: **if** n has a free slot **then**
3:     sort *jobs* in increasing order of the number of running tasks
4:     **for** j in *jobs* **do**
5:         **if** j has unlaunched task t with data on n **then**
6:             launch t on n
7:         **else if** j has unlaunched task t **then**
8:             find node set s storing data of t
9:             pick a node m from s
10:            send resource allocation request to $MRM\{P_m\}$
11:            send resource de-allocation request to $MRM\{P_n\}$
12:            launch t on m
13:         **end if**
14:     **end for**
15: **end if**

is not revealed by the provider. Due to the limitation, this paper distinguishes a task only into either a local or remote task. Algorithm 1 describes the base fair scheduler, which guarantees jobs fairness with limited support for locality.

3.2 Synchronous DRR

Synchronous DRR can dynamically add a virtual core to a VM, if the VM has input data for a pending task. One restriction of the synchronous DRR is that it can add a core to a VM, only when there is a free CPU resource in the physical system (target system) the VM is running on. If the target does not have any available CPU resource, adding a virtual core to the VM will reduce the CPU shares assigned to the other virtual cores of the same VM or other VMs. Assigning more virtual cores than the available CPU resources can negatively affect other VMs and violate Service Level Agreement (SLA) for other users. Therefore, it should not be allowed to add a virtual core to a VM, if the physical system does not have an extra core to accommodate the virtual core to be added.

The synchronous DRR scheduler is based on the base fair scheduler to support both dynamic reconfiguration and fairness among user jobs. Algorithm 2 presents the synchronous DRR algorithm, extending the base fair scheduler discussed in the previous section. In the synchronous DRR algorithm, when a VM (*source VM*) has a free slot, the scheduler first picks a job for fairness, and attempts to pick a local task for the VM. If no local task is found for the VM, it picks any task and finds the VM (*target VM*) with the input data of the selected task. Once the target VM is selected, the scheduler in RC sends a CPU allocation request to the target system. At the same time, the scheduler also sends a CPU deallocation request to the source system, since the source VM, which has reported a free slot, does not have a task to schedule. The CPU allocation and deallocation requests are sent to MRMs in the source and target systems, and MRMs request the hypervisors to add or remove virtual cores. If no free core is available in the target system, the picked task is scheduled to the original source VM, violating the data locality of the task. By the coordination of RC and two MRMs in the source and target VMs, a core resource is transferred from the source VM to the target VM.

The limitation of the synchronous DRR algorithm is that it is effective only when the system running the target VM has an available core slot. The cloud provider can increase the chance of such a readily available CPU resource for temporary locality guarantee in various ways. The cloud

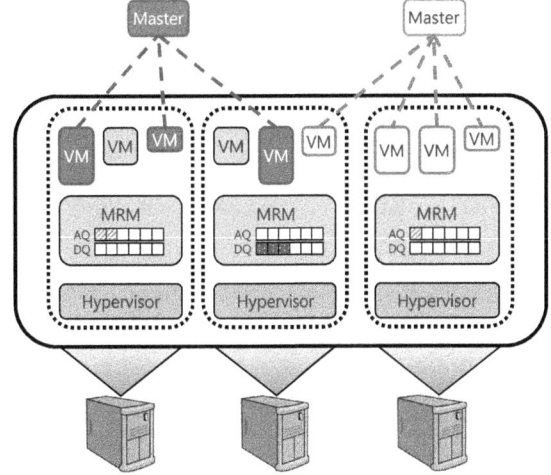

Figure 4: MapReduce with queue-based DRR

Algorithm 3 Queue-based DRR Algorithm

1: when a heartbeat is received from node n:
2: **if** n has a free slot **then**
3:     sort *jobs* in increasing order of number of running tasks
4:     **for** j in *jobs* **do**
5:         **if** j has unlaunched task t with data on n **then**
6:             launch t on n
7:         **else if** j has unlaunched task t **then**
8:             find node set s_d storing data of t which has entries on deallocation queue
9:             sort s_d in decreasing order of number of entries in deallocation queue
10:            **if** s_d is not $\emptyset$ **then**
11:                pick m at the top of sorted set s_d
12:            **else**
13:                find node set s_a storing data of t
14:                sort s_a in increasing order of number of entries in allocation queue
15:                pick m at the top of sorted set s_a
16:            **end if**
17:            send resource allocation request to $MRM\{P_m\}$
18:            send resource de-allocation request to $MRM\{P_n\}$
19:            launch t on m
20:         **end if**
21:     **end for**
22: **end if**

provider may leave a small portion of core resources as a headroom for dynamic CPU resource demands. As the number of cores in a system is expected to increase to tens of cores in future systems, reserving one or two cores for the headroom may not degrade the overall throughput. In the next section, we relax such a constraint of the synchronous DRR using per-system queues.

3.3 Queue-based DRR

Resource reconfiguration is composed of resource allocation to the target VM and de-allocation from the source VM. In the synchronous DRR, an allocation and deallocation of a core must occur in a coupled manner. An advantage of the synchronous DRR is that a task is never delayed, as it is always assigned to a local VM, if possible, but to a remote VM otherwise. If these two virtual machines locate on the same physical machine, resource reconfiguration between these virtual machines could be done immediately, but otherwise, allocating new resources in the physical machine of target VM may not be possible, if there is no available CPU resource.

However, to improve the chance to support locality, a task can be delayed until a core becomes available in the target node. Instead of synchronously deallocating and allocating cores in the source and target VMs, the queue-based DRR allows the decoupling of the two operations. If a VM has a free slot, it registers the free core to the deallocation queue (DQ) of the system. If a VM has a pending local task assigned by RC, the task is appended to the allocation queue (AQ) of the system. As soon as both the AQ and DQ of the same system (MRM) has at least an entry, VM reconfigurations occur in the system, deallocating a core from a VM, and allocating a core to another VM in the same system.

This delayed task scheduling occurs since the CPU resource cannot be transferred beyond the physical system boundary directly. Even if the system running the source VM has a free core, the computing resource cannot be directly available to the target VM. However, with multiple VMs sharing a physical system, the target system will soon have a free core, as a task finishes in one of the VMs, and a local task is not found for the VM.

In the queue-based DRR, such a queuing delay can be an important factor for cluster performance, as resource utilization might be degraded if handling request of the allocation and de-allocation queue is postponed due to a large queuing delay. In this paper, we use two schemes to reduce the queuing delay. For the schemes, RC must know the allocation and deallocation queue lengths in all MRMs. The first scheme attempts to schedule a task to the matching local VM in the system with the longest deallocation queue. Since the system has a pending deallocation request, the VM for the task can be reconfigured immediately. The second scheme, if there are no system with pending deallocation requests, schedules a task to the matching local VM with the shortest allocation queue. By selecting the system with the shortest allocation queue, the scheduler avoids increasing the allocation queues unnecessarily. In summary, task reconfiguration has to be done to the node with the largest number of deallocation entries, and the smallest number of allocation entries if there is no node with any deallocation entries.

Algorithm 3 describes the queue-based DRR algorithm. The algorithm checks the deallocation queue lengths of systems first (line 8 and 9), to assign a new task to the system with any available core. If not available, it checks the shortest allocation queue to spread tasks across systems in the cluster. This optimization reduces possible queue delays, and in Section 4.3, we evaluate the impact of such queue-aware schemes to improve the queue-based DRR.

The queue-based DRR mechanism overcomes the limitation of the synchronous DRR mechanism, eliminating the requirement for a CPU headroom in each physical system. Even with the queue-based DRR mechanism, the cloud provider can still add the CPU headroom in each machine, to further reduce possible short queue delays.

4. EVALUATION

In this section, we evaluate the locality and performance improvements by dynamic VM reconfiguration over the plain Hadoop platform. To evaluate the effectiveness of DRR in

Job Type	# jobs	# Maps	Intensity
Grep	30	1	I/O
Select	20	2	I/O
Grep	15	5	I/O
Select	10	10	I/O
Aggregation	5	32	Communication
Grep	5	35	I/O
Inverted Index	5	50	Communication
Select	5	100	I/O
Inverted Index	4	150	Communication
Join	2	200	I/O
Aggregation	2	300	Communication
Grep	2	400	I/O
Join	1	600	Communication
Aggregation	2	800	Communication
Select	1	3000	I/O
Grep	2	5000	I/O

Table 1: Benchmarks on Amazon EC2

a large scale cluster, we use a 100-node Amazon EC2 virtual cluster, in addition to a small private cluster for detailed experiments. Firstly, we evaluate the potential performance improvements by DRR in the setups where additional cores are always available in each system. We use such a pseudo-ideal setup, since large-scale experiments on EC2 do not allow system modifications necessary to run a real queue-based DRR implementation. Secondly, we evaluate the queue-based DRR on our small scale private cluster.

4.1 Evaluation Methodology

We evaluate our mechanisms in a cluster from Amazon Elastic Compute Cloud (EC2) as well as our private cluster with 6 physical machines. With Amazon EC2, we use 100 "High-CPU Extra Large" instances from the provider. It contains 8 virtual cores and 7GB memory, and supports high I/O performance. The topology information of the 100 nodes is not available. The 100-node EC2 cluster represents a relatively large scale virtual cluster, and we use the environment to show the potential performance and locality improvements by DRR. One drawback of the EC2 environment for our study is that it does not allow RC and MRM to run at the privileged level, as the controls over hypervisors are not available to guest users. Therefore, we configure our platform to use 6 cores per VM, and the rest two cores are reserved for dynamic reconfigurations to absorb temporary increases of core demands, as discussed in Section 3.2 for the synchronous DRR. However, the total number of virtual CPUs actually used for our workloads does not change, even if each node increases or decreases its core. The EC2 environment has the same effect as a synchronous DRR platform with two additional cores always available.

A physical machine included in the 6-node private cluster has an AMD Phenom 6-core processor, 16GB memory, and 1 disk. We allocate 5 virtual machines for each physical machine. Each virtual machine has 2 virtual cores, and 2GB memory. All of the physical machines are connected with a network switch, and we ran experiments on both 100Mbps and 1Gbps switches. The 100Mbps switch represents a constrained network bandwidth mimicking a constrained network bandwidth across multiple racks. A prior study use a similar 100Mbps switch to emulate the rack-to-rack network bandwidth [17]. With the small cluster size of 6 machines, the 1Gbps switch provides ample network bandwidth, and

Job Type	# jobs	# Maps	1Gbps	100Mbps
Grep	20	1	o	o
Select	15	2	o	o
Grep	10	5	o	o
Select	6	10	o	o
Grep	6	20	o	o
Aggregation	1	50	o	o
Select	2	100	o	o
Join	2	200	o	o
Aggregation	2	300	o	-
Grep	2	400	o	-

Table 2: Benchmarks on Private Cluster

thus data locality does not cause a significant performance difference. However, we evaluate our private cluster with the unrealistically large available network bandwidth too, in addition to the constrained 100Mbps switch.

We use Xen 4.0.1 to virtualize physical machines, and all the virtual machines can be reconfigured with the Xen credit scheduler[7], which supports virtual CPU hot-plugging. We implemented the features of dynamic resource reconfiguration on Hadoop 0.20.2.

The two environments, the EC2 cluster and private cluster, have different map and reduce slot configurations considering their core resources. A VM in the Amazon EC2 cluster has 5 map and 3 reduce slots while a VM in the private cluster has 2 map and 1 reduce slots. The input block size of both environments is 128MB, which is more commonly used than 64MB in the Hadoop default configuration. We modified the Hadoop Fair Scheduler [19] for the synchronous and queue-based DRR implementations.

The workloads we use with the EC2 cluster are described in the Table 1. Most of the workloads are from the Hive performance benchmark[5]. Among the workloads, "Grep" and "Select" are I/O intensive workloads, and "Aggregation" and "Join" are communication-intensive workloads. In addition, "Inverted Index" has been added as one of highly communication-intensive workloads [11]. We use a mixture of these workloads, and generate a random submission distribution similar to Zaharia et al [19], which is based on the Facebook trace. Workloads used in the private cluster are described on the Table 2. They are also from the same set of the benchmark, but they are scaled down to fit the resource capabilities of the small cluster.

4.2 Pseudo-ideal DRR Performance

In this section, we first evaluate the potential performance and locality improvements with DRR, by evaluating a single virtual cluster with additional available cores in each physical system. As additional cores are available in each system, a reconfiguration request to add a core to a VM is processed immediately. However, the total number of cores used by the cluster does not change, to assess the performance impact of DRR. To measure this pseudo-ideal DRR performance, we use both of the EC cluster and our private cluster. However, the additionally available cores are limited, so the performance gain can be slightly lower than that with the ideal configuration.

We use the synchronous DRR algorithm for the experiments in this section. A non-local VM (source VM) deallocates a core, while a local VM (target VM) allocates a core to handle an incoming task.

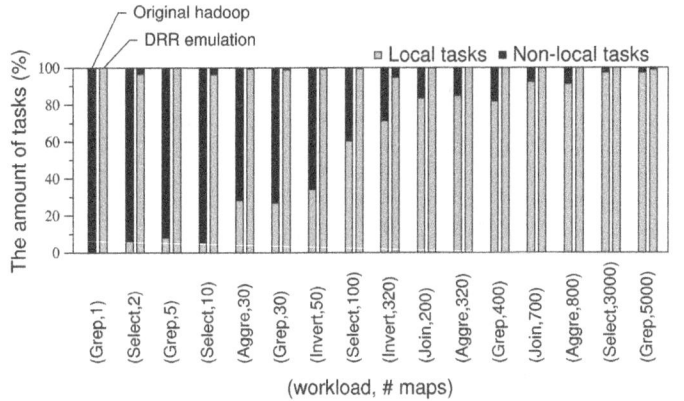

Figure 5: Locality improvements on the EC2 cluster

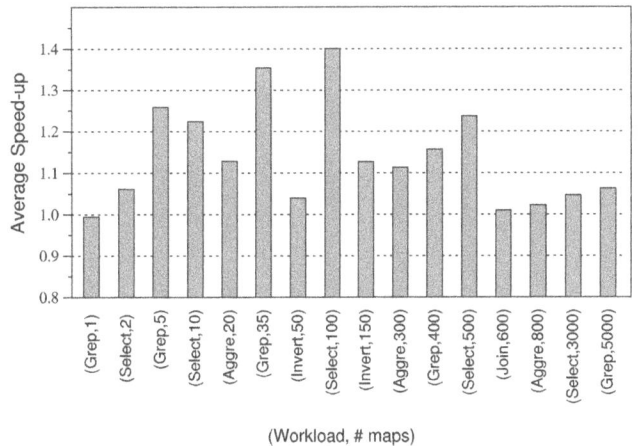

Figure 6: Speedups on the EC2 cluster: normalized to the default Hadoop

4.2.1 Large-scale Evaluation on the EC2 cluster

As modifying the hypervisor, or running DRR components at the privileged level in the EC2 cluster is impossible, we emulate the impact of DRR in the EC2 cluster. Firstly, we use a VM instance with eight cores, and initially turned off two CPUs from the VMs. We use the two additional cores to emulate VM reconfigurations to add a core or two to each VM. The total core count for the cluster is fixed to 600, and if an additional core is added to a node, another node must stop using a core to make the total core count fixed to 600. By emulating DRR in this way, we evaluate the performance improvement of the Hadoop cluster using the fixed total number of virtual cores of 600.

Figure 5 shows the locality improvement with the DRR emulation in the EC2 cluster over the plain Hadoop cluster. From the smallest to the biggest job, the data locality of the plain Hadoop jobs increases, because the input blocks of large jobs are broadly spread across all the nodes in the cluster. However, with the DRR emulation, almost all the tasks are executed at the local VMs with their input data. The results do not show 100% data locality with the DRR emulation, since infrequently, two additional cores are not enough for reconfiguration, making this emulation pseudo-ideal.

Due to the locality improvement, the Hadoop cluster with DRR has a significant performance improvement. Figure 6

33

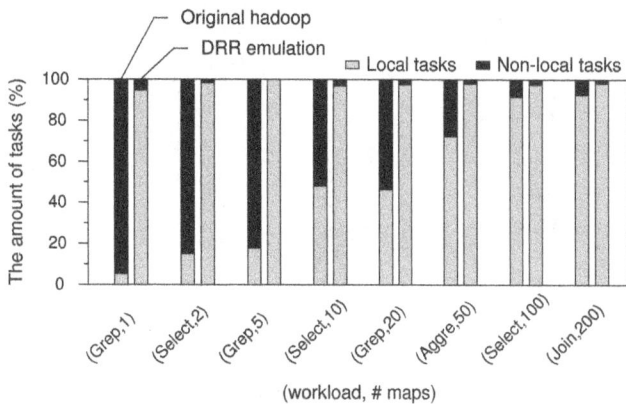

Figure 7: Locality improvements on the 100Mbps private cluster

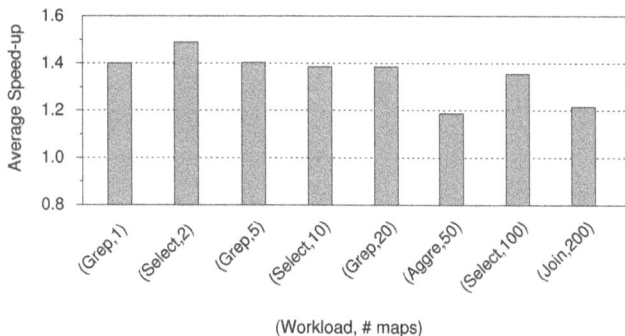

Figure 8: Speedups of synchronous DRR on the 100Mbps private cluster

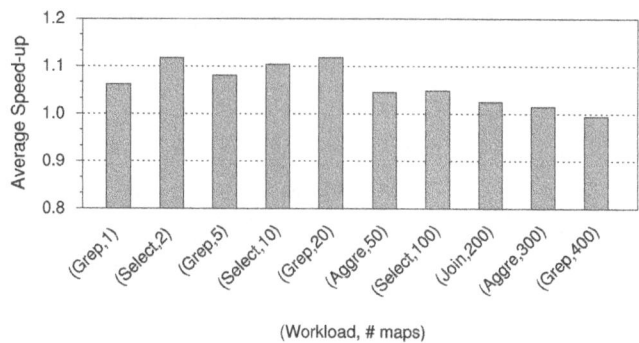

Figure 9: Speedups of synchronous DRR on the 1Gbps private cluster

shows the speedup of DRR on the EC2 cluster, compared to the default Hadoop scheduler. The I/O intensive workloads such as grep or select gain large performance benefits from DRR, but the inverted index workloads do not exhibit performance improvement since almost the entire run-time is spent during the reduce phase, which does not benefit from data locality. It is because this type of jobs needs many reduce tasks to compute a large amount of intermediate output data, whose size is more than three times of the map input data size. On average, DRR can potentially achieve nearly 15% performance improvement over the plain Hadoop.

The extra overheads for selecting a task and a VM for the task to implement DRR by the scheduler are negligible. We measured the scheduling overhead of task scheduling from DRR at the 100-node EC2 cluster. DRR adds about an extra 1 millisecond on average for scheduling, compared to the default Hadoop scheduler.

4.2.2 Evaluation on the Private Cluster

With the private cluster, we evaluate the pseudo-ideal DRR both with 1Gbps switch and 100Mbps switches. For these private cluster experiments, we use 2 vCPUs for each virtual machine initially, and each VM can use additional cores, if locality requires more cores for a VM. Figure 7 shows the locality difference between the base Hadoop and DRR on the private cluster. DRR allows the majority of tasks to run locally, although there are a small portion of non-local tasks, since additional core resources are limited.

Figure 8 shows the performance improvement with the

100Mbps switch. The overall performance improvement is 41% compared to the plain Hadoop on average. Figure 9 presents the performance improvement by DRR with the 1Gbps switch. Since a 1Gbps switch provides very high bandwidth for 6 systems, the potential performance improvements by DRR are much smaller than those with a 100Mbps switch, with about 5% improvement on average.

In this section, we showed the potential performance improvements by a pseudo-ideal synchronous DRR, when one or two additional cores are always available for each VM for reconfiguration. In the next section, we show a realistic setup, where virtual clusters use all the available cores without any headroom, to assess the true benefit of the queue-based DRR.

4.3 Queue-based DRR

In this section, we evaluate the queue-based DRR on the private cluster configuration, with one or more virtual clusters. We first show the performance improvement by the queue-based DRR, and evaluate how much delay the queue-based DRR incurs for the tasks pending in the queue. Since the quest-based DRR implementation cannot run in the EC2 cluster, we use only the private cluster for the experiments. In this setup, all the physical cores are assigned to virtual cores used by virtual clusters, without any free cores available for reconfiguration. Allocation of a core to a VM can occur only when there is a pending deallocation request for a core from the same system.

Figure 10 presents the performance improvement by the queue-based DRR with a 100Mbps switch. Compared to the ideal improvement shown in Figure 8, there is some reduction of performance improvement, since this realistic configuration cannot always provide additional cores immediately, unlike the pseudo-ideal runs. However, the performance improvement is still significant with 35% improvement on average, compared to 41% in the ideal setup.

We evaluate the queue delay of DRR with and without the queue-aware delay reduction schemes discussed in Section 3.3. Figure 11 presents the cumulative distributions of delays without and with the optimization schemes. On both cases, about 50% of allocation requests have zero delay, because there already exists a de-allocation request on the target MRM. However, when we do not apply the queue-aware schemes, a large portion of requests exhibit delays longer than tens of seconds, while the average task execution times are mostly less than 1 or 2 minutes. This is because allocation or de-allocation requests are not been widely spread to

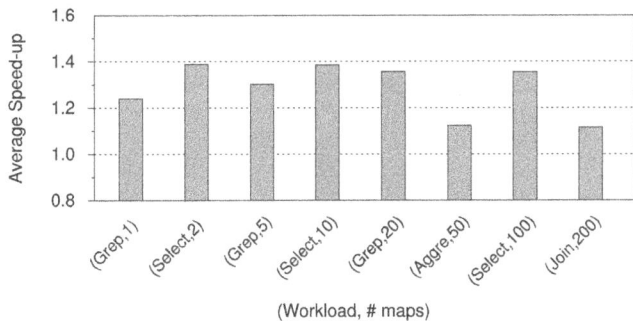

Figure 10: Speedups of queue-based DRR on the 100Mbps private cluster

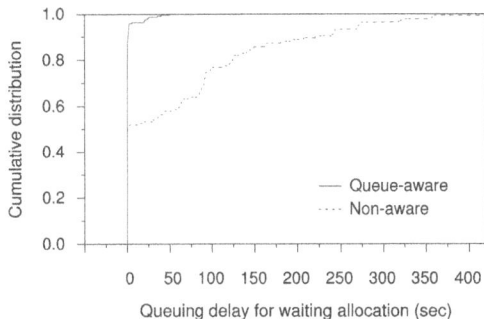

Figure 11: Queue delay distributions with or without queue-aware scheduling schemes

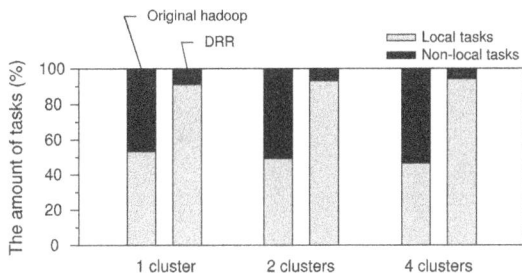

Figure 12: Locality improvements with multiple clusters

virtual machines, and some requests wait for a very long time at the allocation queue due to the skewed scheduling. However, the queue-aware schemes discussed in Section 3.3 for the queue-based DRR reduces the delay significantly, close to zero delay for more than 95% of reconfiguration requests as shown in Figure 11.

Multiple Cluster Evaluation: Multiple clusters can share physical systems and DRR mechanisms, improving the overall utilization of the systems. To evaluate the impact of running multiple virtual clusters, we run 1, 2, and 4 clusters composed of 30, 15, and 7 virtual machines respectively. With the three cluster configurations, we measure the locality improvement by the queue-based DRR. Figure 12 shows the locality improvements with different numbers of clusters sharing the physical cluster. The figure shows that regardless of the number of clusters, DRR can achieve similar locality improvements. Figure 13 presents the speedups of queue-based DRR with the three different numbers of clusters sharing the physical cluster, showing the effectiveness of DRR even with multiple virtual clusters on the same cloud.

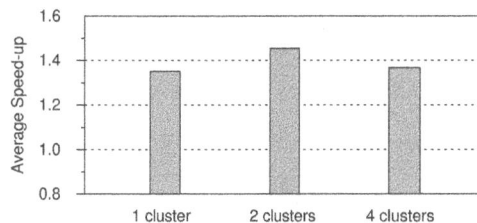

Figure 13: Speedups with Multiple Clusters

The results indicate that core exchanges by MRM across different virtual clusters work effectively.

5. RELATED WORK

Improving data locality, while providing fairness among jobs, has been critical for the performance of distributed data-intensive platforms. However, the two goals, locality and fairness, often conflict with each other in distributed platforms. As shown in Section 3.1, a fair scheduling can force a task to be scheduled to a remote node without its data. *Quincy* addressed such data locality and fairness problems on distributed data-intensive platforms by scheduling tasks for fine-grained resource sharing with graph-based workflow models [13]. *Delay Scheduling* proposed locality-aware scheduling policies to enhance data locality for Hadoop platforms [19]. The scheduler delays assigning a task to a node for a short period time until a node containing the input data for the task becomes free. The paper showed that the delays are relatively short in large scale Hadoop platforms, with negligible impacts on fairness.

Several prior studies have been improving MapReduce platforms on virtualized cluster environments. *Purlieus* improved the locality of map and reduce tasks in MapReduce platforms on the cloud by locality-aware VM placement [17]. The authors proposed that exploiting prior knowledge about the characteristics of MapReduce workloads before customers execute them, the cloud scheduler can place data to the proper physical machines using the workload information. Using the data layout, the VM scheduler places VMs to the physical systems with the corresponding input data. The approach differs from DRR, as DRR relies on dynamic VM reconfiguration without any prior information about the workloads.

Sandholm et al. proposed a dynamic VM reconfiguration mechanism with resource hot-plugging, to address skewed resource usages in MapReduce task executions. They assumed that multiple MapReduce clusters share physical resources, and a cluster can use more resources than another cluster, which may violate SLAs. In addition, resource sharing between virtual clusters should occur only within a single physical machine boundary. Kang et al. improved the performance of virtual MapReduce cluster by modifying the context-switching mechanism of the Xen credit scheduler for MapReduce platforms [14]. Zaharia et al. addressed the performance heterogeneity problem of MapReduce platforms on virtual clusters, where sharing I/O and network resources among customers cause performance interferences [20]. Using Amazon Web Service(AWS) such as EC2, S3, SimpleDB, and SQS, Liu and Orban proposed a new MapReduce computation model based the Hadoop platform [15].

There have been several recent studies to manage virtual resources efficiently in cloud systems [8]. Distributed

Resource Scheduler (DRS) proposed a cloud-scale resource management system [6]. The scheduler, from a large resource pool of physical systems, places VMs to maximize the utilization, and live-migrates VMs across physical systems to avoid resource conflicts in a system.

6. CONCLUSIONS

In this paper, we proposed and evaluated a dynamic VM reconfiguration mechanism for distributed data-intensive platforms on virtualized cloud environments, called Dynamic Resource Reconfiguration (DRR). DRR improves the input data locality of a virtual MapReduce cluster, by temporarily increasing cores to VMs to run local tasks. DRR schedules tasks based on data locality, and adjust the computational capability of the virtual nodes to accommodate the scheduled tasks. This approach differs from prior approaches assuming a cluster which always has a fixed amount of computational resource in each node. Using dynamic VM reconfiguration for distributed data-intensive platforms, can be extended to different types of load imbalance. Different resource requirements by different tasks or jobs may cause each virtual node to under-utilize its resource. With VM reconfiguration, each node can be adjusted to provide only the necessary amount of resource demanded for the node. Such a generalized framework with dynamic VM reconfiguration will be our future work. Such a generalized VM reconfiguration framework can lead to customer-friendly configuration methods for cloud resources. Each user may not need to fine-tune the configuration of each virtual machine, as the VM reconfiguration can adjust the individual VM configuration dynamically.

Acknowledgments

This work was partly supported by the IT R&D Program of MKE/KEIT [KI002090, Development of Technology Base for Trustworthy Computing]. It is also supported by the SW Computing R&D Program of KEIT(2011-10041313, UX-oriented Mobile SW Platform) funded by the Ministry of Knowledge Economy.

7. REFERENCES

[1] Amazon Elastic Compute Cloud (EC2). http://aws.amazon.com/ec2/.

[2] Apache Hadoop. http://hadoop.apache.org.

[3] Apache Hive. http://hadoop.apache.org/hive.

[4] Apache Pig. http://pig.apache.org.

[5] Hive Performance Benchmarks. https://issues.apache.org/jira/browse/HIVE-396.

[6] Resource management with VMware DRS. http://www.vmware.com/pdf/vmware_drs_wp.pdf.

[7] Xen credit scheduler. http://wiki.xen.org/wiki/Credit_Scheduler.

[8] I. A. Ajay Gulati, Ganesha Shanmuganathan. Cloud scale resource management: Challenges and techniques. In *Proceedings of the 2nd USENIX Workshop on Hot Topics in Cloud Computing (HotCloud)*, 2010.

[9] F. Chang, J. Dean, S. Ghemawat, W. C. Hsieh, D. A. Wallach, M. Burrows, T. Chandra, A. Fikes, and R. E. Gruber. Bigtable: A distributed storage system for structured data. *ACM Trans. Comput. Syst.*, 26:4:1–4:26, June 2008.

[10] J. Dean and S. Ghemawat. MapReduce: simplified data processing on large clusters. In *Proceedings of the 6th USENIX Symposium on Operating Systems Design and Implementation (OSDI)*, pages 137–150, 2004.

[11] S. L. Faraz Ahmad and T. V. Mithuna Thottethodi. MapReduce with communication overlap (marco). http://docs.lib.purdue.edu/cgi/viewcontent.cgi?article=1412&context=ecetr, 2007.

[12] M. Isard, M. Budiu, Y. Yu, A. Birrell, and D. Fetterly. Dryad: distributed data-parallel programs from sequential building blocks. In *Proceedings of the 2nd European Conference on Coputer Systems (EuroSys)*, 2007.

[13] M. Isard, V. Prabhakaran, J. Currey, U. Wieder, K. Talwar, and A. Goldberg. Quincy: fair scheduling for distributed computing clusters. In *Proceedings of the 22nd ACM Symposium on Operating Systems Principles (SOSP)*, 2009.

[14] H. Kang, Y. Chen, J. L. Wong, R. Sion, and J. Wu. Enhancement of xen's scheduler for MapReduce workloads. In *Proceedings of the 20th International Symposium on High Performance Distributed Computing (HPDC)*, 2011.

[15] H. Liu and D. Orban. Cloud MapReduce: A MapReduce implementation on top of a cloud operating system. In *Proceedings of the 11th International Symposium on Cluster, Cloud and Grid Computing (CCGrid)*, 2011.

[16] G. Malewicz, M. H. Austern, A. J. Bik, J. C. Dehnert, I. Horn, N. Leiser, and G. Czajkowski. Pregel: a system for large-scale graph processing. In *Proceedings of the 2010 international conference on Management of data (SIGMOD)*, 2010.

[17] B. Palanisamy, A. Singh, L. Liu, and B. Jain. Purlieus: locality-aware resource allocation for MapReduce in a cloud. In *Proceedings of 2011 International Conference for High Performance Computing, Networking, Storage and Analysis (SC)*, 2011.

[18] C. A. Waldspurger. Memory resource management in vmware esx server. In *Proceedings of the 5th Symposium on Operating Systems Design and Implementation (OSDI)*, 2002.

[19] M. Zaharia, D. Borthakur, J. Sen Sarma, K. Elmeleegy, S. Shenker, and I. Stoica. Delay scheduling: a simple technique for achieving locality and fairness in cluster scheduling. In *Proceedings of the 5th European Conference on Computer systems (EuroSys)*, 2010.

[20] M. Zaharia, A. Konwinski, A. D. Joseph, R. H. Katz, and I. Stoica. Improving MapReduce performance in heterogeneous environments. In *Proceedings of the 8th USENIX Symposium on Operating Systems Design and Implementation (OSDI)*, 2008.

Achieving Application-Centric Performance Targets via Consolidation on Multicores: Myth or Reality?

Lydia Y. Chen
IBM Zurich Lab
Switzerland
yic@zurich.ibm.com

Danilo Ansaloni
University of Lugano
Switzerland
danilo.ansaloni@usi.ch

Evgenia Smirni
College of William and Mary
USA
esmirni@cs.wm.edu

Akira Yokokawa
University of Lugano
Switzerland
akira.yokokawa@usi.ch

Walter Binder
University of Lugano
Switzerland
walter.binder@usi.ch

ABSTRACT

Consolidation of multiple applications with diverse and changing resource requirements is common in multicore systems as hardware resources are abundant and opportunities for better system usage are plenty. Can we maximize resource usage in such a system while respecting individual application performance targets or is it an oxymoron to simultaneously meet such conflicting measures? In this work we provide a solution to the above difficult problem by constructing a queueing-theory based tool that we use to accurately predict application scalability on multicores and that can also provide the optimal consolidation suggestions to maximize system resource usage while meeting simultaneously application performance targets. The proposed methodology is light-weight and relies on capturing application resource demands using standard tools, via non-intrusive low-level measurements. We evaluate our approach on an IBM Power7 system using the DaCapo and SPECjvm benchmark suites where each benchmark exhibits different patterns of parallelism. From 900 different consolidations of application instances, our tool accurately predicts the average iteration time of collocated applications with an average error below 10%.

Categories and Subject Descriptors

D.4.8 [**Operating Systems**]: Performance—*Modeling and Prediction*

Keywords

Performance modeling, consolidation, multicores.

1. INTRODUCTION

Multicore architectures hosting multi-threaded applications are the prevailing execution environments in today's data centers and cloud computing facilities. Modern multicore systems are characterized by large computational capacity, and deep memory hierarchies, and are well-equipped with hardware specific acceleration and optimization techniques. Various programming models are thus developed to optimize application execution on heterogeneous architectures. Often, a single application instance executing on such a powerful platform under-utilizes system resources [18, 23]. To increase resource efficiency, system providers resort to consolidation, i.e., packing multiple applications into a physical server, lowering the operating cost and augmenting system throughput [11, 20].

Typically, applications can be classified based on their concurrency level, intensity of resource demands, and performance level objectives. For example, certain applications may have stringent performance requirements especially if they are associated with higher service tiers [20], whereas some applications do not require any performance guarantees. In this paper, we consider two kinds of application consolidation: *homogeneous* consolidation, where multiple application instances of the same type are executed simultaneously and *heterogeneous* consolidation where different application instances are selected to execute simultaneously. Naturally, consolidation aims to avoid the perils of resource oversubscription under single instance execution and achieve a better utilization of resources [7]. This becomes a tough technical challenge, especially given the need of differentiated performance objectives per application.

In this paper, we aim to meet pre-set per application requirements in the form of average execution times while the instances of simultaneously executing applications are maximized. The challenge is to accurately *predict* performance interference among collocated applications on multicores [20, 15, 9], and based on this prediction to reach judicious decisions regarding this difficult problem. A posteriori, one could decide on the best consolidation if an exhaustive experimental search of all possible combinations is made. This may be a viable solution if only a small set of applications is executing on the system. Here, we advocate using a modeling-based methodology that can shed light on achieving a priori optimal consolidation, especially in terms of efficient and accurate predictions of performance objectives such as average application iteration time and system throughput. Central to the model's effectiveness is the ability to encapsulate the workload dynamics, executed over complex hardware and software stacks.

There are several related works [6, 22] that focus on models to capture low level end-to-end performance metrics, such as absolute or relative Instructions Per Cycle (IPC). Low-level models can provide a detailed overview of the resource demands of a single application execution at the cost of exploring a large number of hardware counters. Extracting the essential characteristics for application performance from state-of-the-art machines is a complex engineering task because of the multiple problem dimensions, including the execution of application threads on different cores, accesses to shared data structures, inter/intra thread communication, and runtime optimizations. In addition, low-level performance measures usually do not directly reflect application iteration time[1] among consolidated instances, neither can they convey information about the expected average iteration time.

In this paper, our objective is to identify optimal homogeneous or heterogeneous consolidations by accurately suggesting the maximum number of application instances to consolidate without violating target iteration times. We develop a model-driven approach that predicts iteration time under various consolidations and validate our results using the widely used DaCapo benchmark suite [5] on an IBM Power7 system. We first develop a light-weight and non-intrusive profiling methodology to compute application resource demands. The profiling methodology effectively captures the application concurrency level, the hardware parallelism, and the impact of resource runtime optimizations. We show that resource demands may vary according to the number of consolidated instances and that these variations are captured by the model. Performance interference among consolidated instances is captured via a surprisingly simple two station queueing model that is appropriately parameterized, thanks to the developed profiling methodology. We extend the mean value analysis algorithm for multi-class systems [17] to allow for load-dependent service demands and demonstrate the accuracy of the new model.

To summarize, our contributions are both theoretical and practical. On the theoretical side, we present an extension to the Mean-Value-Analysis (MVA) algorithm allowing for analytic computation in load dependent multi-class queueing networks that could only be solved via simulation. On the practical side, we present a light-weight profiling methodology that extracts vital resource demand information using standard profiling tools and use this information to parameterize the model. This model effectively captures performance interference, accurately predicts program execution time, and suggests ideal consolidations. From more than 500 experiments of homogeneous and heterogeneous consolidations of DaCapo benchmarks, the model achieves average prediction errors below 8%, further illustrating the model's robustness. We note that as our methodology is generic and platform independent, it can readily apply on different workloads and/or different platforms.

---

[1]Because the applications that we use to evaluate the methodology proposed in this paper are composed by a set of iterations, we use the average "iteration time" as a measure of the application end-to-end execution time. Effectively, a scaled iteration time (multiplied by the number of iterations) expresses the application execution time.

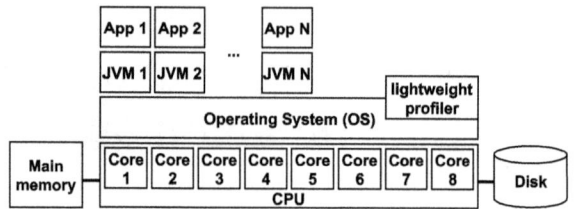

Figure 1: High-level view of the execution environment.

This paper is organized as follows. Section 2 gives an overview of homogeneous and heterogeneous consolidation. The proposed profiling methodology for capturing resource demands is described in Section 3. The queueing model and the extension of the mean value analysis algorithm is given in Section 4. Section 5 presents experimental results. Related work is given in Section 7, followed by the conclusion in Section 8.

2. CONSOLIDATION

The performance of an application depends not only on how application threads use the underlying hardware resources but also on the interference of collocated applications. In this section, we illustrate the complexity of consolidation using the DaCapo benchmark suite [5] on our target hardware platform, an IBM POWER7 server.

2.1 Reference System and Workload

The reference system is an IBM Power 750 Express server with a single POWER7 processor board hosting 8 cores running at 3.00 GHz, SMT set to 1, and 64 GB of RAM. The disk adapter is a PCI-X 266 Planar 3GB SAS and the disk is a Hitachi Ultrastar C10K300, 147 GB, 10000 RPM, with a 64 MB buffer. The system runs a logical partition with AIX 6.1 (64 bit) and IBM J9 JVM SR8-FP1 (64 bit) in server mode, with 2 GB heap size and default garbage collection algorithm. Figure 1 provides a high-level view of the system, omitting network components as we limit our observations to non-network intensive applications.

We first developed our methodology using a set of micro-benchmarks to test our predictions. This initial set of reference programs[2] included both Java and native workloads, giving us fined-grained control over the amount and the duration of CPU and disk operations. Due to the space limit, we skip the presentation of micro benchmark results.

In this paper, we mainly evaluate our methodology with workloads from the widely-used DaCapo 9.12 benchmark suite [5] and demonstrate the complexity of the workload dynamics. The Dacapo suite is representative of contemporary Java workloads and consists of fourteen benchmarks with various levels of parallelism. Here we focus on a selection of 10 benchmarks, excluding network intensive benchmarks (i.e., tomcat, tradebeans, and tradesoap) and benchmarks with high iteration time (i.e., eclipse). Extending the proposed technique to network intensive applications is subject of future work.

All empirical measurements presented in this paper are based on a warm-up time of 2 minutes and an observation

---

[2]Throughout this paper we use the terms "program", "benchmark" and "application" interchangeably.

Table 1: Concurrency in DaCapo benchmarks

Benchmark	total	no. of threads			
		alive		runnable	
		peak	average	peak	average
avrora	11	11	10.90	8	4.87
batik	13	8	6.93	6	3.00
fop	6	6	4.93	5	3.01
h2	8	7	5.65	5	3.22
jython	6	6	4.98	5	3.00
luindex	6	6	5.07	5	3.01
lusearch	6	6	5.96	5	3.01
pmd	14	13	8.90	12	4.04
sunflow	10	8	6.99	5	3.00
xalan	6	6	5.97	6	3.01

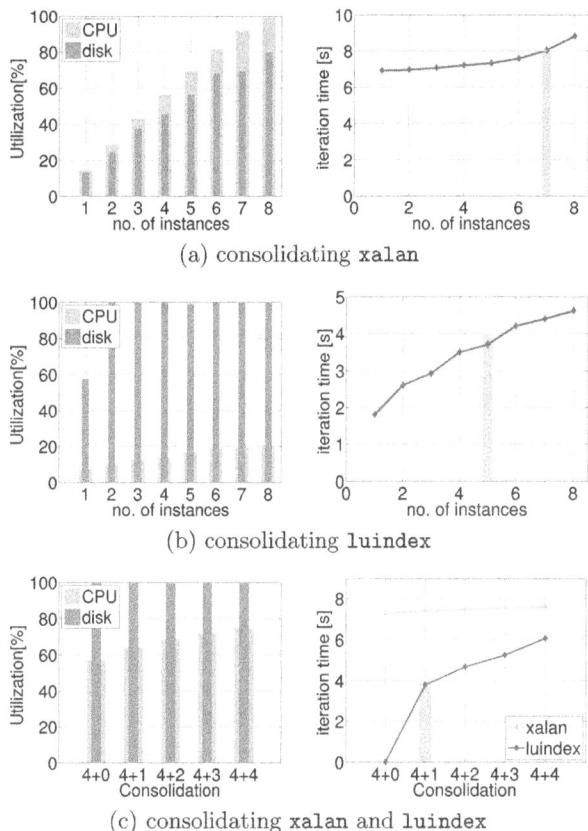

(a) consolidating `xalan`

(b) consolidating `luindex`

(c) consolidating `xalan` and `luindex`

Figure 2: Resource utilizations and iteration times under homogeneous and heterogeneous consolidation. For the heterogeneous consolidation (third row of graphs), we assume that there are 4 instances of xalan consolidated with 1, 2, 3, and 4 instances of luindex.

time of 3 minutes. To this end, we configure the benchmark harness to execute an infinite amount of iterations in the same JVM process[3]. We do not collect any metrics during the warm-up phase, as performance is affected by class-loading and just-in-time compilation. The average iteration time is computed as the average amount of time between consecutive benchmark iterations started after the beginning of the observation time. Garbage collection is not explicitly triggered between the iterations, the just-in-time compiler is always turned on, and we do not bind any process or thread to specific cores.

Table 1 summarizes the internal parallelism of each benchmark: total number of threads (including JVM threads), peak and average number of alive threads (including idle threads), and peak and average number of runnable threads (including running threads). The presented values are computed over an entire benchmark iteration using the Java Management and Monitoring API and a custom native agent.

The DaCapo benchmarks depict wide variability in their concurrency levels. Some benchmarks have a higher (lower) degree of concurrency, e.g. `pmd` (`luindex`), whereas some others have a higher (lower) volume of thread communications, e.g., `avrora` (`lusearch`). Each benchmark differs in hardware resource usage, i.e., some are CPU bound and some are disk bound. Due to the complexity of hardware architecture and applications, it is challenging to identify the key characteristics that dictate the iteration times per application, and even more challenging when consolidating multiple instances of applications. In the following, we illustrate the difficulties of finding effective consolidation of two DaCapo benchmarks: `xalan` and `luindex`.

2.2 Problem Statement with Examples

The problem addressed by this study is how to find the optimal (maximum) consolidation on multicore systems without violating target iteration times of individual applications. We consider two kinds of consolidations, homogeneous and heterogeneous, that raise several questions:

Homogeneous Consolidation: For a given application and hardware, what is the maximum number of instances one can simultaneously execute without violating the target iteration time? In particular, how does the concurrency pattern and underlying resource usage of the application affect this number? We illustrate this problem by consolidating multiple instances of `luindex` and `xalan`, see Figure 2(a) and 2(b).

---

[3]Throughout this paper we use the terms "JVM process" and "application instance" interchangeably.

Heterogeneous Consolidation: We consider that a system executes two heterogeneous applications, a primary and a secondary application. Given a fixed (required) number of execution instances and target iteration time for the primary application, what is the maximum number of consolidated instances of the secondary application so that the target iteration time of the primary application is not violated? How can an optimal consolidation leverage the complementary resource usage and concurrency patterns of both applications? We illustrate this problem by consolidating four instances of `xalan` (primary) with different instances of `luindex` (secondary) ranging from one to five.

To find the optimal consolidations for the above two problems we conduct exhaustive experiments. Figure 2 shows how CPU, disk utilization and the iteration times behave for several consolidations of `xalan`, `luindex`, and `xalan+luindex`. Let the target iteration times be 4 and 8 seconds for `luindex` and `xalan`, respectively. To meet the target iteration time, one can find that the optimal consolidation instances for `luindex`, `xalan` and `xalan+luindex` are 5, 7, and 4+1, respectively. As `xalan` and `luindex` are CPU- and disk intensive applications, their optimal homogeneous consolidation results in high CPU utilizations for `xalan` and high disk utilizations for `luindex`. The heterogeneous con-

Table 2: CPU related statistics under different consolidated instances of `batik` and `avrora`

instances	batik			avrora		
	T [s]	U_c [%]	U_{cs} [%]	T [s]	U_c [%]	U_{cs} [%]
1	2.08	13.6	93	7.47	33.2	92
2	2.09	26.9	97	7.88	49.4	93
4	2.09	53.3	98	11.00	60.8	95
6	2.09	77.6	99	12.38	74.8	97
8	2.15	96.4	100	14.29	85.2	100
10	2.65	99.6	100	16.39	91.2	100
12	3.14	99.9	100	18.85	94.9	100
14	3.70	100.0	100	21.55	97.0	100
16	4.23	100.0	100	24.19	98.2	100

solidation results instead in more "balanced" CPU and disk utilization levels.

Clearly, optimal consolidation depends on how the workload increases with each additional instance, how resource run-time optimizations are affected by collocation, and how strong performance interference is among competing applications. The prediction methodology should suggest a priori and without exhaustive experimentation the ideal consolidation. Prerequisite to the above target is the development of a methodology that can encapsulate the critical application characteristics. This is the subject of the following section.

3. CHARACTERIZING THE WORKLOAD

The concept of "resource demand", i.e., the time an application spends on CPU and disk resource, has been widely used in characterizing applications on multicore systems [6, 22] as well as on multi-tier and virtualized environments [25, 19, 18]. An application iteration completes by executing multiple threads, which can concurrently or sequentially access the system resources. The iteration time consists of the sum of execution times on the *distinct* resources, which are defined as resource demands, and the wait times on these resources due to contention caused by collocation. The aim here is to characterize the resource demands per application under consolidation scenarios. Note that we also refer to resource demands as execution times *without any consolidation*.

Most of the related studies focus on obtaining resource demands of a single application instance using very fine grained and detailed information, such as thread communication [6] and cache related statistics [11]. To this end, the standard approach is to explore a large number of hardware counters or even modify the application source code. Such a process is cumbersome, intrusive, and neither portable nor scalable. Using hardware performance counters is clearly the preferable approach but it is challenging to collapse such diverse information into a single value parameter such as the resource demand. In the following two subsections we illustrate how exactly we achieve the above target via a lightweight profiling methodology that can capture resource demands as a function of collocated workloads on different resources.

3.1 CPU Demand

On a single core system, the CPU demand can be obtained by the average CPU utilization, defined as the fraction of time the single core is busy during the execution. If there are multiple instances executing simultaneously and the CPU is not fully saturated, then one may assume that the CPU is shared equally among the competing instances. If the CPU

is saturated, waiting (queuing) time kicks in and contributes to the application iteration time. Therefore, CPU utilization is a good indicator of CPU demand per application instance, but not of the application iteration times.

For multicore systems, the CPU demand is not only defined by core utilization, but also by the time that *at least* one core is busy. To obtain the CPU demand of multi-threaded applications on multicores, we propose combining two performance counters: CPU utilization, U_c, which denotes the aggregate busy time of all cores and (CPU) system utilization U_{cs}, which denotes the fraction of time at least one thread is executing. On UNIX-like systems, those values can be collected using the `mpstat`, `sar`, and `vmstat` commands. Note that although the memory is another important resource, we encapsulate the time accessing the memory [11] simply within the CPU times, i.e., these two resources are coalesced as one.

We illustrate the CPU profiling using two DaCapo benchmarks, `batik` and `avrora`. Table 2 lists U_c, U_{cs}, and their iteration times, denoted by T, for different consolidated instances (homogeneous consolidations), with the number of instances ranging from 1 to 16. Looking at results for a single instance, a high difference between the two utilization values suggests that only a small set of cores are busy at a given moment in time, due to limited concurrency level within each application. When all cores are busy processing multiple instances, CPU utilization U_c is the same as the CPU system utilization U_{cs}. The minimum number of instances that keep all cores busy is considered the system *saturation point* for this specific homogeneous consolidation. In summary, U_c, U_{cs} and the saturation point are critical for our workload characterization as well as model development.

3.1.1 Linear Increment of U_c

From Table 2, one can observe that CPU utilization increases almost linearly and indicates that the CPU demand per additional instance is constant. From the constant iteration times, one can further infer that the additional CPU demand per instance is distributed to the idle cores.

In the case of linear demand increment, one can compute the CPU demand with respect to collocated instances as follows: When executing one instance of `batik`, CPU demand is $0.93 \cdot T$. When two instances are executing, the CPU demand is $0.93 \cdot T/2$. One can do similar calculations up to 8 instances. After that point the CPU approaches saturation and iteration times start increasing. In the `batik` case, we see that the value of such a point is roughly equal to the inverse of U_c of a single instance execution. In the following subsection we look at another typical case, that of `avrora`, where U_c does not increase linearly with the number of instances. In the following section we examine the reasons for this behavior.

3.1.2 Nonlinear Increment of U_c

In contrast to `batik`, the CPU utilization U_c of `avrora` grows non-linearly and its iteration times increase as the number of instances increases, even under a non-saturated situation, see Table 2. This behavior, observed also in `pmd`, is initially perplexing as it seems that the CPU demand contributed by each instance *decreases*, perhaps due to some run-time optimization. Extrapolating the saturation point from a single instance as we did successfully in `batik` would result in a significant error here, as the predicted saturation

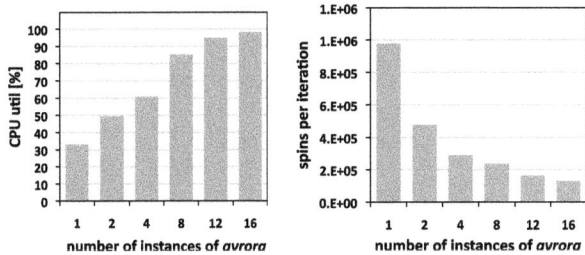

Figure 3: CPU utilization and number of spins depending on the number of instances of `avrora`.

point would be three instances, while in reality the saturation point is much larger. To obtain a good estimate of the saturation point, additional profiling is required.

`avrora` has a high number of threads, performing frequent, fine-grained interactions with each other. It intensively uses synchronization and spin locks, which are commonly used to protect specific code regions. Unlike standard locks, a thread that fails to acquire a spin lock does not get immediately descheduled, but it repeatedly tries to acquire the lock for some time, provided that computational resources are available. We conjecture that the CPU demand per instance can vary depending on the use of spin locks and idle cores.

Figure 3 presents the CPU utilization and number of spins with respect to different numbers of consolidated instances of `avrora`. The number of spins is collected via the Java Locking Monitor (JLM) tool. As the consolidated instances increase, the percentage of idle cores decreases, so do the spins per interaction. Such an observation confirms our conjecture that the CPU demand per instance decays due to a lower number of spins when fewer idle cores are available. Among the benchmarks considered in this study, `avrora` and `pmd` show non-linear increases in CPU utilization as consolidated instances increase due to the use of spin locks. We thus propose to monitor the number of spins and if this number is low, then we assume that we are in a "linear CPU demand increment" case as in `batik` and the saturation point is updated accordingly. If the number of spins is high, then we need more information to compute the saturation point. We address this issue in the following subsection.

3.1.3 Proposed Profiling for CPU Demand

Following analysis from previous subsection, we summarize the algorithmic description of CPU demand. Let $D_c(n)$ denote the CPU demand per iteration when n instances are consolidated. Let $U_c(n)$ and $U_{cs}(n)$ denote the CPU utilization and CPU system utilization respectively, given n consolidated instances. Moreover, we denote the saturation point as ξ, which represents the minimum number of instances that completely saturate the CPU. Depending on the number of spins, ξ can be decided as follows.

We estimate the per instance CPU demand under n consolidated instances, $D_c(n)$, by the product of iteration time $T(1)$ and CPU utilization $U_{cs}(1)$ under a single instance execution, divided by the minimum of the saturation point, ξ, and the number of instances, n:

$$D_c(n) = \frac{T \cdot U_{cs}(1)}{\min(n, \xi)} = \frac{D_c(1)}{\min(n, \xi)}. \qquad (1)$$

Both $T(1)$ and $U_{cs}(1)$ are measured via profiling the single instance execution. One can also view the denominator of Eq. 1 ($\min(n, \xi)$) as the maximum embedded parallelism.

To calculate the saturation point ξ, we first monitor the number of spins in a single instance execution. The saturation point $\xi(1)$, is estimated by the inverse of CPU utilization, i.e., $\frac{1}{U_c(1)}$. When the number of spins is below a threshold, we let $\xi = \xi(1)$; otherwise we re-estimate the new saturation point for non-linear demand increment, by executing $\lceil \xi(1) \rceil$ application instances. Note that the threshold for monitoring spins is obtained via prior empirical experiences. We then recompute the average CPU utilization per instance and take the inverse of such a value as the new estimate of the saturation point.

3.2 Profiling Disk Demand

Measuring the performance of the disk is particularly difficult due to the multiple buffers present at all storage levels, the high number of run time optimizations, e.g., out-of-order writes, and parallel writing across different disk platters. Profiling of disk demand must incorporate the inherent disk parallelism due to consolidation.

Here, we rely on disk operation statistics, instead of disk utilization, because the latter is a biased metric due to multiple I/O buffering [26]. To compute the disk demand under a single application instance $D_d(1)$, we need to obtain the disk parallelism and total disk execution time. We use the average service queue size, denoted by q, as an indicator of the disk parallelism. For the total disk execution time, we use the product of the average disk operations per second (i.e., the disk throughput), denoted by λ_d, and the average service time, denoted by s, which is obtained by the `iostat` tool. $D_d(1)$ is estimated as the total disk time divided by the disk parallelism

$$D_d(1) = \frac{\lambda_d s}{q + 1}. \qquad (2)$$

Similar to the CPU, various run time disk optimizations may affect the per instance disk operations, especially under consolidation. To verify this conjecture, we measure the disk throughput with synthetic benchmarks, which write and read files to disk with a controllable intensity. Our evaluation results confirm that indeed the disk throughput depends on the amount and intensities of IO operations. In general, our synthetic benchmarks confirm that the heavier the IO workload thanks to a high number of consolidated instances, the higher the disk throughput due to run time optimizations.[4]

As an example, we show how to calculate the disk demand of n consolidated instances, $D_d(n)$ of `luindex`, a disk-intensive benchmark. The disk operations of `luindex` that are optimized (or parallelized), can be inferred from the total number of disk operations per second, o_{td}, and disk queued operations per second, o_{qd}. When $\frac{o_{qd}}{o_{td}} \simeq 1$, it implies that there is a sufficiently high workload for the disk, whereas $\frac{o_{qd}}{o_{td}} \simeq 0$ implies a low disk workload. One can expect that $D_d(n)$ may decrease from $D_d(1)$ with respect to n, which in turn indicates parallelism.

After conducting extensive empirical fitting on both synthetic micro benchmarks and `luindex`, we conclude that

---

[4]We do not present these results here due to lack of space.

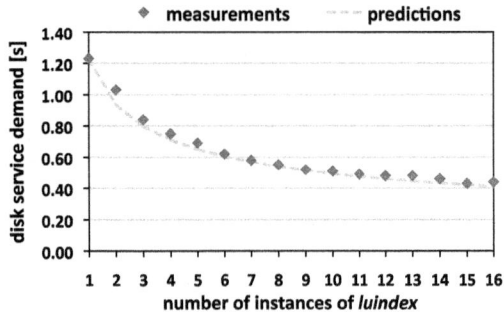

Figure 4: Disk service demand for `luindex`.

Table 3: Profiling of the DaCapo suite

benchmark	$D_c(1)$	ξ	$D_d(1)$	o_{qd}	o_{td}
avrora	6.88	5.52	0.12	0.0	1.9
batik	1.94	7.17	0.17	0.6	9.2
fop	0.52	5.62	0.06	0.0	18.7
h2	5.84	5.88	0.10	0.1	1.4
jython	6.01	4.30	0.65	4.7	9.4
luindex	1.27	8.79	1.23	63.7	161.1
lusearch	9.18	5.68	1.54	2.0	18.7
pmd	2.00	3.85	0.09	0.4	4.4
sunflow	15.19	6.21	0.63	0.5	5.1
xalan	6.09	6.49	1.05	0.6	28.2

$D_d(n)$ can be well captured by $D_d(1)$ divided by n to the power of $\frac{o_{qd}}{o_{td}}$,

$$D_d(n) = D_d(1)/n^{o_{qd}/o_{td}}. \qquad (3)$$

Following Eq. 2 and 3, Figure 4 shows the experimentally measured and predicted disk demand of `luindex` as a function of simultaneously executing `luindex` instances.

3.3 Profiling DaCapo Benchmarks

To profile CPU and disk demands of DaCapo suite, one needs to collect the statistics required in Eq. 1- 3 and calculate the CPU saturation point. Such statistics are collected non-intrusively by standard, open source profiling tools, including `mpstat`, `vmstat`, `sar`, and `iostat`. Table 3 summarizes CPU and disk demands for a single instance ($D_c(1)$ and $D_d(1)$), cpu saturation point (ξ), number of queued disk operations per second (o_{qd}), and total number of disk operations issued per second (o_{td}).

The relative difference between $D_c(1)$ and $D_d(1)$ indicate whether an application is CPU- or disk-bound. The table shows that `luindex` is a strong disk-bound workload. However, since $D_c(n)$ and $D_d(n)$ change with the number of consolidated instances, the distinction between CPU- and disk-bound also changes as a function of the degree of consolidation. Moreover, the saturation point serves as a good indicator of the application concurrency level. High saturation points indicate a low level of concurrency; low values of ξ indicate the contrary. For example, both `batik` and `pmd` are CPU-bound workloads for any consolidated instances, but they have very different saturation points, being 7.17 and 3.85 respectively. This is because `batik`, compared to `pmd`, has a lower internal concurrency. As reported in Section 3.1.2, `pmd` is affected by a nonlinear increment of CPU demand .

3.4 Resource Demands Under Heterogeneous Consolidation

Clearly, the CPU saturation point and disk related statistics depend on the total workload required by the collocated instances and resulting run-time optimizations. As a result, in the case of heterogeneous consolidation, one needs to adjust the estimation of the CPU saturation point and the average queued and total disk operations to consider *both* types of applications. We propose to update the values based on the average of both application classes, weighted by their number of instances.

In the heterogeneous consolidation, we let the primary (secondary) application associated with subscript $i = \{1, 2\}$.

The CPU saturation point under the consolidation is thus the average of ξ_1 and ξ_2 weighted by the number of instances of class 1 and 2, n_1 and n_2. Similar calculations are applied on o_{qd} and o_{td}. In the following, we summarize the proposed estimates , under consolidating n_1 and n_2 instances of class 1 (primary) and class 2 (secondary) applications.

$$\xi(n_1, n_2) = (\xi_1 \cdot n_1 + \xi_2 \cdot n_2)/(n_1 + n_2) \qquad (4)$$
$$o_{qd}(n_1, n_2) = (o_{qd1} \cdot n_1 + o_{qd2} \cdot n_2)/(n_1 + n_2) \qquad (5)$$
$$o_{td}(n_1, n_2) = (o_{td1} \cdot n_1 + o_{td2} \cdot n_2)/(n_1 + n_2). \qquad (6)$$

The CPU and disk demands can be conveniently adapted as the input for a queueing network model, which can then effectively capture the queueing and iteration times. As such, one can efficiently and accurately find the optimal consolidation for any given requirement of target iteration times. We validate our proposed profiling in conjunction with the proposed model described in the following section, by showing the difference between predicted and measured iteration times.

4. PREDICTION MODEL AND SOLVING ALGORITHM

To capture the performance interference and wait/queueing time of consolidated applications on multicores, we use a closed queueing network model which is parameterized by the proposed profiling on application CPU and disk demands. As resource demands vary according to the number of instances executed simultaneously, we develop a *load-dependent* queueing model [17]. In addition, depending on the collocated application instances being homogeneous or heterogeneous, the proposed model is correspondingly classified as single or multi-class load-dependent model.

MVA (Mean Value Analysis) [21] has been widely used to solve single and multi-class queueing networks[5]. MVA as an algorithm is quite powerful as it can provide analytical calculations of various performance metrics of interest, e.g., application throughput, iteration time, and resource utilization. To the best of our knowledge, there is no exact or approximate version of MVA that can solve a load-dependent queueing network where the resource demands depend on the collocated jobs in the system, instead the literature suggests to solve such models via simulation. Here, we enrich MVA with a new approximation algorithm that provides an analytic solution to such a load-dependent multi-class queueing networks with good accuracy.

---

[5]MVA provides the exact solution of product form queueing networks, whose solutions of the steady-state probabilities can be expressed as a product of factors describing the state of each queuing node.

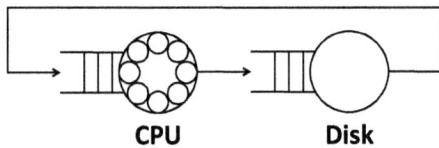

Figure 5: Two station closed queueing system. Station 1 corresponds to the aggregate of all cores and their memory, while station 2 corresponds to the disk.

4.1 Two Station Load-dependent Model

Resource demands characterize how application threads utilize the underlying resources. However, the queueing time due to performance interference among consolidated instances is yet to be predicted. Corresponding to the two most critical resources, CPU and disk, we propose a simple two station queueing system, depicted in Figure 5. Station one represents the aggregate computation capacity from available cores in the system, and station two represents a single disk. The number of consolidated application instances corresponds to the number of "jobs" in conventional closed queueing network terminology.

Assuming a closed queueing network structure as the one depicted in Figure 5, we solve the system for n simultaneous executing jobs (application instances, in our case) and estimate performance numbers for the various measures of interest. The main metric of interest here is the application iteration time, i.e., the time that one iteration completes after executing on both resources. We solve the proposed model by using multi-class load dependent MVA algorithm. The essential step is to update the resources demands according to the CPU saturation point and the disk total-queued operations according to consolidated instances.

4.2 Multi-class Load-Dependent MVA Algorithm

MVA is an algorithm that iterates through all possible states of consolidated instances that execute on resources and updates the corresponding job execution times and throughput in sequence. When homogenous consolidation is used, MVA iterates from one to n and calculates the average statistics. For the heterogeneous consolidation, MVA iterates through all possible number of jobs, $n = \{1 \ldots N\}$, in the system, and all possible combinations from jobs in each class. Furthermore, to incorporate the resource demands into the calculation of iteration times, the load-dependent MVA needs to compute the conditional probability that the CPU or the disk has j jobs of class i, provided that there are n jobs in the system. These probabilities are denoted by $P_{ki}(j|n)$, where $k = \{c, d\}$ stands for the CPU and disk respectively.

We depict a high level description of our approximated multi-class load-dependent MVA in Algorithm 1. A class is indexed by $i = \{1, 2\}$ and the resource is indexed by $k = \{c, d\}$. $T_{ci}(n_1, n_2)$ and $T_{di}(n_1, n_2)$ denote the iteration times of class i spent in CPU and disk, given n_1 and n_2 jobs in the system. The detailed description of resource demands given (n_1, n_2) consolidated instances, $D_{ci}(n_1, n_2)$ and $D_{di}(n_1, n_2)$, are described in Section 3. To ease the readability, we write $P_{ki}(j|n)$ in Algorithm 1 to encompass all the cases of $P_{ki}(j|(n_1, n_2))$ such that $n_1 + n_2 = n$. We direct

---

Algorithm 1 Proposed MVA Approximation Algorithm
1: **for** n=1 to N and all combinations such that $n_1 + n_2 = n$ **do**
2:    **for** class i=1,2 **do**
3:      **for** resource $k = c, d$ **do**
4:        Compute $D_{ki}(n_1, n_2)$ following Eq. (1)-(6)
5:        Compute $T_{ki}(n_1, n_2) = \sum_{j=1}^{n} D_{ki}(n_1, n_2) P_{ki}(j-1|n)$
6:      **end for**
7:      Compute $X(n_1, n_2) = \sum_i \frac{n_i}{\sum_k T_{ki}(n_1, n_2)}$
8:      **for** resource $k = c, d$ **do**
9:        **for** j= 1 to n jobs at resource k **do**
10:          Update $P_{ki}(j|n)$ [17]
11:        **end for**
12:      **end for**
13:    **end for**
14: **end for**

---

the interested reader to [17] for the detailed computation of $P_{ki}(j|n)$ in the standard Load dependent MVA algorithm. The critical step we propose here is to update the throughput $X(n_1, n_2)$ as the average of class throughput, weighted by the number of jobs in each class, i.e., $\sum_i \frac{n_i}{\sum_k T_{ki}(n_1, n_2)}$. We note that this approximation can capture the upper bound of performance measures as regulated by the bottleneck resource.

Finally, we point out that any variation in the workload/iteration time is captured via the MVA assumption that workload execution on each resource when run in isolation (i.e., no consolidation) results in exponentially distributed service demands. We will show in the following section that the exponential assumption is very effective and results in models with high prediction accuracy.

5. EVALUATION

In this section, we evaluate our proposed methodology to predict iteration times and to identify optimal homogeneous and heterogeneous consolidations. The detailed description of the DaCapo benchmarks and the reference system can be found in Section 2. The profiling interval has a duration of 5 minutes, including 2 minutes of warm-up phase, and the profiling results are summarized in Section 3.3.

5.1 Homogeneous Consolidation

In this subsection, we search for optimal homogeneous consolidations of 10 DaCapo benchmarks using the proposed methodology and validate our predictions with experimental data. We first summarize the predicted and measured iteration times in Figure 6. In more than half of the benchmarks, the iteration time increases very slowly until the number of consolidated instances reaches the saturation point ξ for the specific workload, as listed in Table 1. On the contrary, avrora and pmd show more increase in their iteration times, even for a small number of consolidated instances. This behavior is due to CPU run-time optimizations that we model via the load-dependent methodology. Also luindex exhibits a similar trend, due to disk run-time optimizations. Our predictions characterize those trends very well and capture the increments in iteration times, even the saturation point.

The average error computed from all consolidations is around 6%. The highest prediction errors are 21% for con-

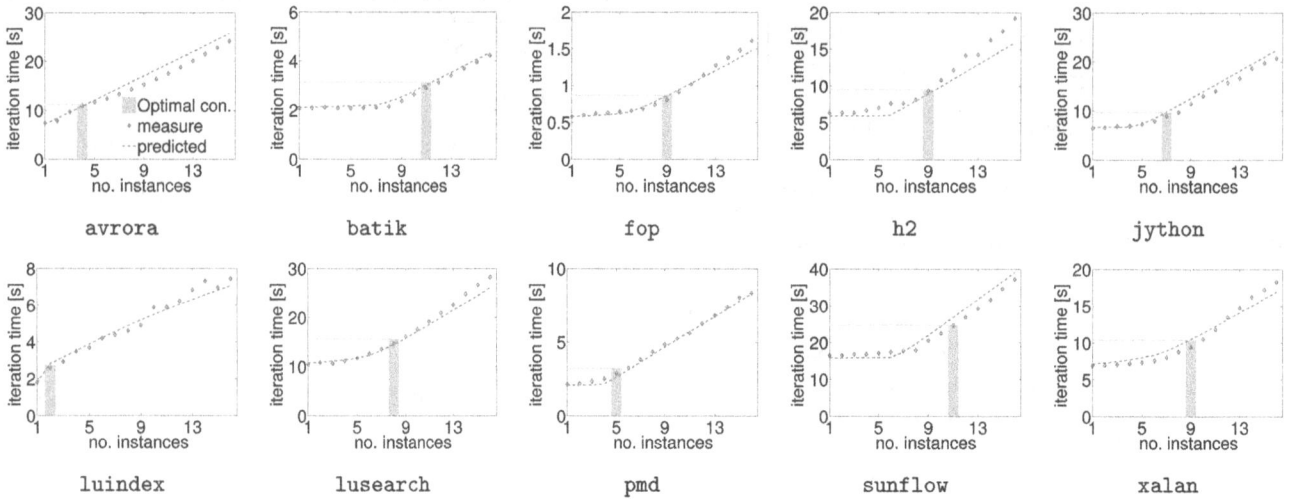

Figure 6: Prediction of iteration times for homogeneous consolidation of all DaCapo benchmarks.

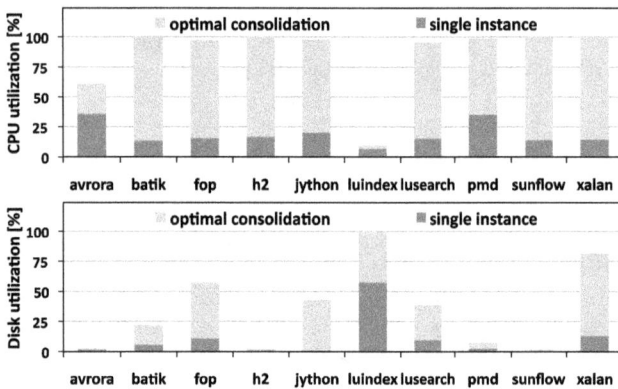

Figure 7: CPU and disk utilization of optimal homogeneous consolidations and single instance execution.

solidating 6 instances of **h2** and 17% when consolidating 16 instances of **h2**. Overall, when the number of consolidated instances is small, i.e., less than 10, prediction errors are small. These configurations are particularly interesting to service providers, as the system is not yet saturated. Our proposed methodology is particularly accurate in predicting iteration times for different consolidations, and also provides accurate results when the system is saturated. Overall, Figure 6 confirms the precision of our predictions for both CPU and disk intensive applications.

5.1.1 Optimal Consolidation of DaCapo

As benchmarks have a wide variety of resource demands, we define the target iteration time for all benchmarks as 1.5 times the iteration time of single instance, i.e., $1.5 \cdot T(1)$.[6] Using our predicted values and given a performance target for the average iteration, one can easily identify the optimal number of consolidated instances that achieve this performance target. In Figure 6 we highlight optimal instances and the corresponding target iteration times – see the gray

column and the corresponding target value (on the y-axis) on each graph. In many cases, increasing the number of consolidated instances does not have an impact on the iteration time. This is mainly due to the intrinsic parallelism offered by the CPU: as long as the CPU is not saturated, additional workload instances can be executed in parallel without affecting the iteration time. When the CPU saturates, the iteration time increases with the number of consolidated instances but there is no clear rule of thumb that one could use to project iteration times when more applications are consolidated. Overall, we see that the model consistently predicts the optimal consolidation given a target iteration time across workloads with very different characteristics.

Figure 7 summarizes CPU and disk utilization under the optimal consolidation and under single instance execution. For the optimal consolidation experiments, we used the target performance of $1.5 \cdot T(1)$ for iteration times. Resource utilization and system throughput are tremendously improved after consolidation. However, as most benchmarks are either CPU- or disk-intensive, optimal homogeneous consolidations often result in unbalanced resource utilizations. However, the degree of unbalance of CPU and disk usage in the single instance case does not necessarily carry in the consolidated cases, see **batik** and **xalan**.

5.1.2 SPECjvm2008 Benchmarks

To further test the applicability of our methodology on different workloads, i.e., beyond DaCapo benchmarks, we consider consolidations of benchmarks from the SPECjvm2008 suite[7]. In particular, we consider homogeneous consolidations of 2, 4, 8, and 16 instances of each benchmark in the suite, excluding only the benchmark **compiler** (due to runtime exceptions when multiple instances of **compiler** are concurrently executed on the same machine). Over a total of 76 considered consolidations, the average prediction error is 8.9%, comparable to the measured error for the DaCapo benchmark suite. Because of space limitations, we do not present the detailed results for the experiments with SPECjvm2008.

---

[6]Of course, any alternative definition of a "target" iteration would also work.

---

[7]See http://www.spec.org/jvm2008

Table 4: Prediction error [%] for iteration time under various heterogenous consolidations

		avrora				batik				fop				h2				jython			
		4;1	4;2	4;3	4;4	4;1	4;2	4;3	4;4	4;1	4;2	4;3	4;4	4;1	4;2	4;3	4;4	4;1	4;2	4;3	4;4
Secondary app.	avrora	3	7	9	10	16	15	19	23	13	7	11	14	22	14	12	15	5	18	30	32
	batik	6	12	18	24	4	4	5	9	6	6	5	7	12	13	9	8	1	6	11	13
	fop	5	6	11	14	4	4	5	7	5	2	3	5	10	12	9	4	4	6	6	6
	h2	6	7	11	10	3	3	7	5	8	8	6	4	16	21	9	2	1	1	7	8
	jython	3	8	20	37	5	3	10	12	7	6	7	9	13	5	8	8	1	8	10	15
	luindex	7	7	8	10	6	4	2	3	10	8	11	11	8	10	13	12	5	5	4	5
	lusearch	2	3	3	7	3	6	10	15	4	4	8	11	12	14	8	13	9	16	16	20
	pmd	4	15	25	35	2	3	3	3	9	5	9	13	16	6	8	8	4	4	4	8
	sunflow	7	8	11	14	3	6	8	8	7	6	5	4	16	16	10	2	6	7	5	13
	xalan	5	7	7	9	3	3	4	6	4	2	2	5	11	13	9	8	10	13	7	5

		luindex				lusearch				pmd				sunflow				xalan			
Secondary app.	avrora	6	8	6	6	9	7	6	8	8	22	31	38	17	14	12	15	11	8	7	9
	batik	4	2	4	4	2	4	10	14	5	5	3	2	6	6	8	8	6	6	5	6
	fop	3	5	6	8	3	6	8	11	6	6	8	12	7	9	4	6	4	3	3	4
	h2	1	6	6	12	4	10	10	10	6	8	4	11	8	12	6	4	3	5	7	10
	jython	12	2	8	8	8	11	18	20	3	3	4	6	10	6	9	14	3	6	8	6
	luindex	5	1	4	6	17	16	17	13	13	15	18	21	10	6	4	5	10	16	19	23
	lusearch	4	7	10	14	0	3	2	2	11	15	22	23	6	7	3	5	8	9	12	14
	pmd	5	9	13	19	11	16	22	22	9	4	5	5	12	8	9	7	7	17	22	19
	sunflow	2	0	2	2	1	4	4	7	6	7	8	6	7	9	2	9	5	4	4	5
	xalan	15	18	20	23	4	7	10	14	14	17	22	23	5	6	3	5	9	10	11	10

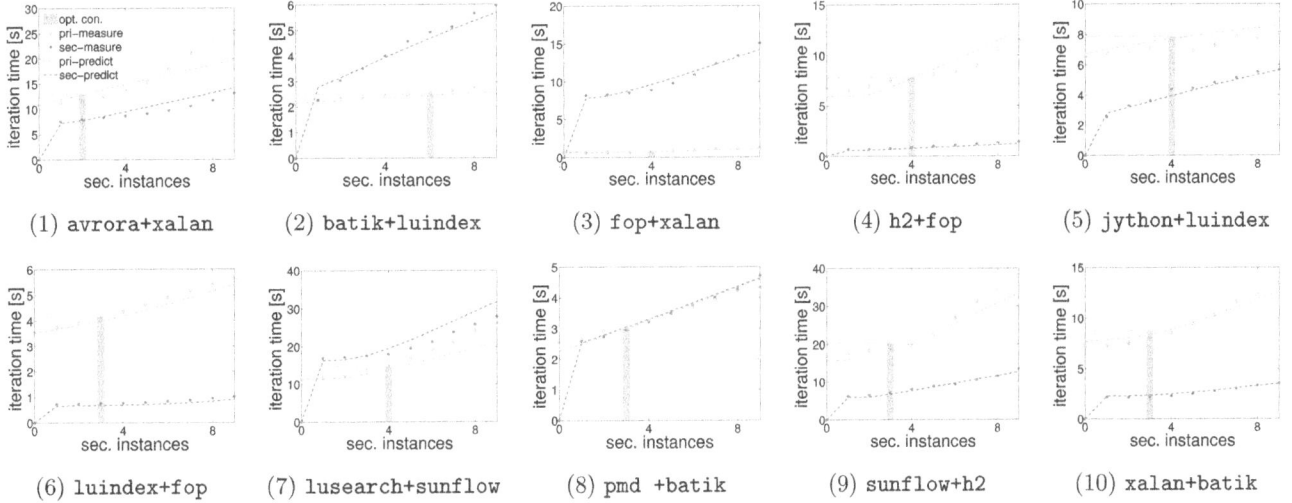

(1) avrora+xalan (2) batik+luindex (3) fop+xalan (4) h2+fop (5) jython+luindex

(6) luindex+fop (7) lusearch+sunflow (8) pmd +batik (9) sunflow+h2 (10) xalan+batik

Figure 8: Two-class heterogeneous consolidation (primary+secondary): iteration times when consolidating 4 primary application instances and a varying number of secondary application instances.

5.2 Two-Class Heterogeneous Consolidation

In this subsection, we evaluate the prediction errors of iteration times of primary and secondary applications in various two-class heterogeneous consolidations. We consider the following scenario: one application is considered to be of the primary type. For this application, four instances should be executing simultaneously.[8] The four primary applications are consolidated with a secondary application whose instances vary from 1 to 4.

For each of the 10 benchmarks, we select one as the primary application and pair it with all other nine benchmarks that are considered as the secondary one. Table 4 summarizes the relative prediction errors, presented as the average of prediction errors from the primary and the secondary applications. Overall, the average prediction error is only 8.1% across 400 possible heterogeneous consolidations. Note that this extensive experimentation to find the ideal pairing of primary and secondary applications can be very time consuming and could grow exponentially with the number and combination of consolidated instances. With our proposed methodology, we require only *a limited number* of profiling runs of single instances and achieve very accurate predictions across a large number of consolidations.

Prediction errors are generally higher for large numbers of secondary application instances, because either the CPU or disk is over-saturated. The pairing of applications with the highest errors are avrora and pmd. Recall the discussion in Section 3.1.2, both avrora and pmd make extensive use of spin locks and their performance highly depends on the number of collocated instances.

---

[8]Of course, this scenario can be changed and the number of primary execution instances can be any integer. We have done experiments that have varied this number from 1 to 10 but are not reported here due to lack of space. The selected number of four primary consolidated applications is representative of all experiments.

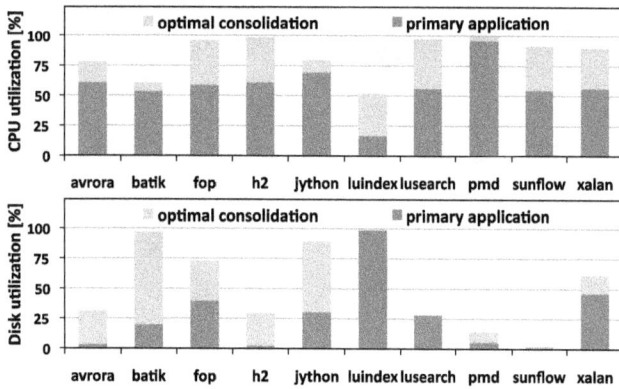

Figure 9: CPU and disk utilization of ten heterogeneous consolidations.

5.2.1 Optimal Consolidation

In this subsection, we define the goal that an optimal two-class heterogeneous consolidation corresponds to the maximum number of instances of the secondary application such that the overhead factor of the four primary application instances is less than factor 1.2.

In Figure 8, we illustrate the predicted and measured iteration times for ten cases of heterogeneous consolidation. With respect to the target iteration times, we identify the optimal number of instances of the secondary application using our prediction. We summarize the optimal heterogeneous consolidation in terms of the secondary application and the corresponding number of instances in Figure 8. The corresponding CPU and disk utilization values are also illustrated in Figure 9.

In case (2), `batik + luindex`, we can accurately predict iteration times for both benchmarks. The maximum number of consolidated instances of `luindex` without violating the target iteration time of `batik` is 6. As `luindex` is disk intensive and `batik` is CPU intensive, the optimal consolidation also increases both CPU and disk utilization. Case (5), `jython + luindex`, and case (6), `luindex + fop`, also benefit from complementary resource usage patterns. In most of the cases where two CPU-bound benchmarks are consolidated, the optimal number of secondary application instances is three or four, and the resulting CPU utilization is more than 95%.

5.3 Three-Class Heterogeneous Consolidation

In this subsection, we evaluate our predictions with various three-class heterogeneous consolidations. In particular, we consider only those cases in which the number of consolidated instances is the same for each class. A total of 360 three-class consolidation is evaluated. The aim here is to demonstrate our methodology can be applied on a higher degree of consolidation, i.e., three and even higher number of classes, and provide accurate prediction on iteration times of each class. Consequently, we do not stress the difference of target iteration times among primary and secondary applications, nor the optimal consolidation.

Figure 10 illustrates a small selection of the considered consolidations, in which the number of consolidated units goes from 1 to 3 for each class. As can be seen from the figures, our methodology accurately predicts the iteration

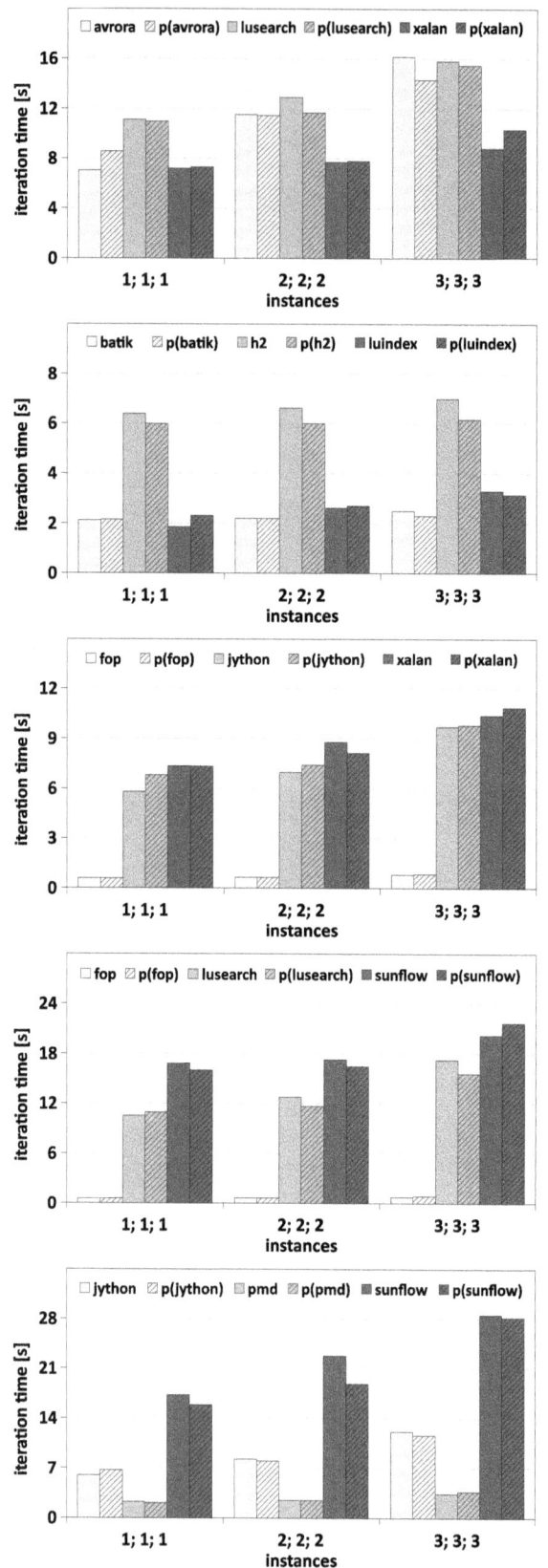

Figure 10: Three-class heterogeneous consolidation: measured v.s. predicted iteration times when consolidating different instances of applications. The notation "p" represents the predicted value.

time overhead for each class of consolidated applications. Over a total of 360 unique consolidations, the average error, computed from all three classes, is only 10.43%. This exhaustive evaluation confirms the stability of our results and suggests that our methodology can provide sufficiently accurate predictions for a higher number of consolidated classes of workloads.

6. DISCUSSION

Using our profiling and modeling methodology, we demonstrated that we can accurately predict iteration times for an extensive set of homogeneous or heterogeneous consolidations, and on a different benchmark suites, i.e., micro benchmarks, DaCapo and SPECjvm2008. Experiments show how our approach accurately predicts the target iteration times of a primary application. The same analysis and model can be used to predict the target iteration times of a secondary application. We stress that our model can be used to target different metrics, e.g., the minimal iteration slow-downs of the secondary application, to identify the optimal secondary application, to identify consolidations that meet certain system throughput or utilization levels.

In this paper, we mainly focused on a single example: how to best predict the iteration time of the primary application. Frequently, the optimal consolidation of primary with secondary applications is to achieve equal utilization across *all* system resources such that the system throughput and utilization are optimized. We would like to stress that the optimal heterogeneous consolidation indeed varies according to the definition of performance objectives. When the performance objective is to maintain a target weighted iteration time of two classes, it might be preferable to consolidate two CPU-bound applications with different concurrency levels. Such counter-intuitive solutions cannot be easily identified with existing profiling tools. Our solution not only captures the dynamics of consolidated workload but also provides a robust solution for performance prediction of a wide range of objectives.

7. RELATED WORK

Various simulation-based and model-based approaches have been developed to address workload performance interference on multicore systems. In particular, the performance metrics of interest are usually shared hardware counters, such as cycle per instruction (CPI) and L2/L3 cache misses. In [12], the authors use artificial neural networks to predict IPC for exploring the architecture design space and validate their results via simulation. Each benchmark is profiled, validated, and predicted in isolation. Chen et al. [6] estimate multi-resource demands, e.g., L2 cache size and memory bandwidth, of a single application, using ILP and MLP models, and validate their models via simulation. These models are not validated on consolidated workloads. In contrast, Lee et al. [16] propose composable regression models to predict CPI delay, considering consolidating multiple classes of application instances. METE [22] predicts the end-to-end IPC of collocating two benchmarks via simulation. The objective of METE is to dynamically provide sufficient on-chip resources to applications such that the target IPC is achieved via a feedback control approach.

The main focus of profiling single- and multi-threaded applications on multicore systems is to characterize the performance interference on hardware resources, e.g., cache misses and thread contention. Most characterization analysis considers a single instance of a single-threaded application and a few are applied on consolidated instances of applications [13, 8, 4]. The profiling approach can be non-intrusive using existing OS counters [14, 26, 27] or require modification of applications' source code or bytecode [10, 24]. Zhuravlev et al. [28] characterize resource contention of multi-threaded applications in the memory hierarchy, but their main focus is on comparing the systems while executing the application in isolation. In [4], the authors characterize the slow down of core interference, cache interference and virtual overhead, due to consolidating workloads on a multicore dual-processor Intel platform. Dey et al. [8] propose a general methodology to characterize any multi-threaded application for the last level cache contention, and private cache contention.

To summarize, existing methodologies combine model and simulation to address system-centric performance targets, whereas our proposed methodology can accurately and efficiently predict user-centric targets, i.e., iteration times, while maximizing performance targets, such as resource utilization, on a real system. In addition, our methodology predicts optimal consolidations by using only light-weight and non-intrusive profiling. We also stress that the proposed methodology can be used for consolidation predictions of any performance measure, we direct the interested reader to [2] for results that show optimal consolidations of even conflicting performance measures, and specifically when the target is the ratio of system throughput (that is aimed to be maximized) over the application execution time (that is aimed to be minimized).

8. CONCLUSION

In this paper, we develop a light-weight and non-intrusive methodology to achieve application-centric performance targets, for consolidating homogeneous and heterogeneous application instances on modern multicore systems. Using a very small number of profiling runs, our proposed profiling encapsulates crucial load dependent characteristics of applications, i.e., resource demands, application concurrency level, hardware parallelism, and the impact of run time optimization schemes. Furthermore, based on the resource demands profiled, we develop a load-dependent queueing model to predict various performance metrics. Our evaluation of consolidating multithreaded benchmarks with different concurrency levels on an IBM Power7 system shows a prediction error below 10 % over more than 900 consolidation cases.

Overall, our proposed methodology can accurately and efficiently achieve optimal consolidation, for any given combination of target iteration times of heterogeneous applications, in particular Java workloads. As our proposed methodology relies on low-level and easily-accessed performance counters, the methodology readily applies to more complex workloads. In our future work we intend to focus on network-intensive applications (i.e., extend the model by providing an additional queueing station) and on applying the methodology on different hardware platforms. We are also working on a prediction tool that focuses on automating the process of finding the best consolidation matches on multicores [1, 3].

Acknowledgments

This work has been supported by IBM and the Swiss National Science Foundation. Part of this work was conducted while Danilo Ansaloni was on an internship and Evgenia Smirni was on sabbatical leave at the IBM Zürich Research Laboratory. Evgenia Smirni is partially supported by NSF grants CCF-0811417 and CCF-0937925.

9. REFERENCES

[1] D. Ansaloni, L. Y. Chen, E. Smirni, and W. Binder. Towards autonomic consolidation of heterogeneous workloads. In *Workshop on Posters and Demos Track*, Middleware, pages 12:1–12:2, 2011.

[2] D. Ansaloni, L. Y. Chen, E. Smirni, and W. Binder. Model-driven Consolidation of Java Workloads on Multicores. In *Proceedings of DSN-PDS*, 2012.

[3] D. Ansaloni, L. Y. Chen, E. Smirni, A. Yokokawa, and W. Binder. Find Your Best Match: Predicting Performance of Consolidated Workloads. In *ICPE 2012 Posters/Demos Track*, ICPE, 2012.

[4] P. Apparao, R. Iyer, X. Zhang, D. Newell, and T. Adelmeyer. Characterization & Analysis of a Server Consolidation Benchmark. In *Proceedings of VEE*, pages 21–30, 2008.

[5] S. Blackburn, R. Garner, C. Hoffman, A. Khan, K. McKinley, R. Bentzur, A. Diwan, D. Feinberg, D. Frampton, S. Guyer, M. Hirzel, A. Hosking, M. Jump, H. Lee, J. Moss, A. Phansalkar, D. Stefanović, D. von Dincklage, and B. Wiedermann. The DaCapo Benchmarks: Java Benchmarking Development and Analysis. In *Proceedings of OOPSLA*, pages 169–190, 2006.

[6] J. Chen, L. John, and D. Kaseridis. Modeling Program Resource Demand Using Inherent Program Characteristics. In *Proceedings of SIGMETRICS*, pages 1–12, 2011.

[7] L. Y. Chen, A. Das, W. Qin, A. Sivasubramaniam, Q. Wang, R. Harper, and B. Morris. Consolidating Clients on Back-end Servers with Co-location and Frequency Control. *SIGMETRICS Perform. Eval. Rev.*, 34:383–384, June 2006.

[8] T. Dey, W. Wang, J. Davidson, and M. Soffa. Characterizing Multi-threaded Applications Based on Shared-resource Contention. In *Proceedings of ISPASS*, pages 76–86, 2011.

[9] S. Govindan, J. Liu, A. Kansal, and A. Sivasubramaniam. Cuanta: Quantifying Effects of Shared On-chip Resource Interference for Consolidated Virtual Machines. In *Proceedings of SOCC*, 2011.

[10] M. Hauswirth, P. Sweeney, A. Diwan, and M. Hind. Vertical Profiling: Understanding the Behavior of Object-oriented Applications. In *Proceedings of OOPSLA*, pages 251–269, 2004.

[11] M. R. Hines, A. Gordon, M. Silva, D. da Silva, K. D. Ryu, and M. Ben-Yehuda. Applications Know Best: Performance-Driven Memory Overcommit With Ginkgo. Technical report, IBM, 2011.

[12] E. Ïpek, S. McKee, R. Caruana, B. de Supinski, and M. Schulz. Efficiently Exploring Architectural Design Spaces via Predictive Modeling. In *Proceedings of ASPLOS*, pages 195–206, 2006.

[13] N. Jerger, D. Vantreaseand, and M. Lipast. An Evaluation of Server Consolidation Workloads for Multi-Core Designs. In *Proceedings of IISWC*, pages 47–56, 2007.

[14] R. Knauerhase, P. Brett, B. Hohlt, T. Li, and S. Hahn. Using OS Observations to Improve Performance in Multicore Systems. *IEEE Micro*, 28:54–66, 2008.

[15] Y. Koh, R. C. Knauerhase, P. Brett, M. Bowman, Z. Wen, and C. Pu. An Analysis of Performance Interference Effects in Virtual Environments. In *Proceedings of ISPASS*, pages 200–209, 2007.

[16] B. Lee, J. Collins, H. Wang, and D. Brooks. CPR: Composable Performance Regression for Scalable Multiprocessor Models. In *Proceedings of Micro*, pages 270–281, 2008.

[17] D. Menascé, V. Almeida, and L. Dowdy. *Capacity Planning and Performance Modeling: From Mainframes to Client-Server Systems*. Prentice Hall, 1994.

[18] X. Meng, C. Isci, J. Kephart, L. Zhang, E. Bouillet, and D. Pendarakis. Efficient Resource Provisioning in Compute Clouds via VM Multiplexing. In *Proceedings of ICAC*, pages 11–20, 2010.

[19] N. Mi, G. Casale, L. Cherkasova, and E. Smirni. Burstiness in Multi-tier Applications: Symptoms, Causes, and New Models. In *Proceedings of Middleware*, pages 265–286, 2008.

[20] R. Nathuji, A. Kansal, and A. Ghaffarkhah. Q-clouds: Managing Performance Interference Effects for QoS-aware Clouds. In *Proceedings of EuroSys*, pages 237–250, 2010.

[21] M. Reiser and S. S. Lavenberg. Mean-Value Analysis of Closed Multichain Queuing Networks. *J. ACM*, 27:313–322, 1980.

[22] A. Sharifi, S. Srikantaiah, A. Mishra, M. Kandemir, and C. Das. METE: Meeting End-to-end QoS in Multicores Through System-wide Resource Management. In *Proceedings of SIGMETRICS*.

[23] X. Song, H. Chen, R. Chen, Y. Wang, and B. Zang. A Case for Scaling Applications to Many-core with OS Clustering. In *Proceedings of EuroSys*, pages 61–76, 2011.

[24] N. Tallent and J. Mellor-Crummey. Effective Performance Measurement and Analysis of Multithreaded Applications. *SIGPLAN Not.*, 44:229–240, 2009.

[25] B. Urgaonkar, G. Pacifici, P. S. M. Spreitzer, and A. Tantawi. An Analytical Model for Multi-tier Internet Services and its Applications. In *Proceedings of SIGMETRICS*, pages 291–302, 2005.

[26] T. Wood, L. Cherkasova, K. Ozonat, and P. Shenoy. Profiling and Modeling Resource Usage of Virtualized Applications. In *Proceedings of Middleware*, pages 366–387, 2008.

[27] T. Wood, P. Shenoy, A. Venkataramani, and M. Yousif. Sandpiper: Black-box and Gray-box Resource Management for Virtual Machines. *Comput. Netw.*, 53:2923–2938, 2009.

[28] S. Zhuravlev, S. Blagodurov, and A. Fedorova. Addressing Shared Resource Contention in Multicore Processors via Scheduling. In *Proceedings of ASPLOS*, pages 129–142, 2010.

Enabling Event Tracing at Leadership-Class Scale through I/O Forwarding Middleware

Thomas Ilsche*‡, Joseph Schuchart*, Jason Cope†, Dries Kimpe†, Terry Jones‡,
Andreas Knüpfer*, Kamil Iskra†, Robert Ross†, Wolfgang E. Nagel*, Stephen Poole‡

*Technische Universität Dresden, ZIH 01062 Dresden, Germany
{thomas.ilsche,joseph.schuchart,andreas.knuepfer,wolfgang.nagel}@tu-dresden.de

†Argonne National Laboratory, 9700 South Cass Avenue, Argonne, IL 60439, USA
{copej,dkimpe,iskra,rross}@mcs.anl.gov

‡Oak Ridge National Laboratory, Mailstop 5164, Oak Ridge, TN 37831, USA
{trjones,spoole}@ornl.gov

ABSTRACT

Event tracing is an important tool for understanding the performance of parallel applications. As concurrency increases in leadership-class computing systems, the quantity of performance log data can overload the parallel file system, perturbing the application being observed. In this work we present a solution for event tracing at leadership scales. We enhance the I/O forwarding system software to aggregate and reorganize log data prior to writing to the storage system, significantly reducing the burden on the underlying file system for this type of traffic. Furthermore, we augment the I/O forwarding system with a write buffering capability to limit the impact of artificial perturbations from log data accesses on traced applications. To validate the approach, we modify the Vampir tracing toolset to take advantage of this new capability and show that the approach increases the maximum traced application size by a factor of 5x to more than 200,000 processes.

Categories and Subject Descriptors

D.2.5 [**Software Engineering**]: Testing and Debugging—
Tracing; D.4.3 [**Operating Systems**]: File Systems Management—*File organization*; D.4.4 [**Operating Systems**]:
Communications Management—*Input/output*

Keywords

event tracing, I/O forwarding, atomic append

1. INTRODUCTION

Performance analysis tools are a vital part of the HPC software ecosystem. They provide insight into the runtime behavior of parallel applications and guide performance optimization activities toward the most promising or urgent aspects. Porting and tuning performance measurement tools are essential since they must be efficient and must not perturb the runtime behavior of the analyzed application, even at full scale.

The rising levels of concurrency in leadership-class systems present a number of challenges to performance analysis tools. One challenge to scaling these tools is efficiently storing trace data. These tools often generate large amounts of data and must execute efficiently at full scale. Traditional access patterns for these tools, such as file per process, file per thread, and synchronous I/O, do not scale well past tens of thousands of processes. Such data access patterns require excessive use of file metadata operations and overwhelm leadership-class storage systems. Synchronous I/O may cause unnecessary delays in trace data collection and skew application execution. Alternative access patterns, such as a shared file pattern, may alleviate metadata bottlenecks but inject artificial synchronization into the application. Therefore, a unique data organization is desired that exploits the log like I/O behavior of performance analysis tools, allows for uncoordinated access to a shared file from multiple processes, and tolerates lazy I/O semantics.

To achieve and sustain application event trace recording at full leadership-class scale, we investigated several I/O optimizations to support high-performance, scalable, and unordinated access of event trace data generated by the Vampir toolset [17]. We observed that the uncoordinated I/O patterns generated by the VampirTrace and Open Trace Format (OTF) tools could be transparently optimized at an intermediate file I/O aggregation layer, known as the I/O forwarding layer. We integrated the I/O Forwarding Scalability Layer (IOFSL) [2, 23] with the VampirTrace/OTF toolset. Also as part of contributions of this paper, we implemented optimizations and new capabilities within IOFSL to reorganize and optimize the captured VampirTrace/OTF I/O patterns while preserving the independent I/O requirements of these tracing tools. These new features include a distributed atomic file append capability and a write buffering capability. By taking advantage of characteristics of the event trace workload and augmenting our HPC I/O stack to better support it, we have reduced the stress that the trace I/O workload places on HPC storage systems. Furthermore, we have reduced the impact of HPC I/O storage systems on the tracing tools.

Our investigation and evaluation resulted in significant improvements to the VampirTrace and OTF software stack. We increased the VampirTrace and OTF tracing infrastructure scalability by 5x (a 40,000 core to 200,000 core capability improvement), generated a trace containing 941 billion events at an average aggregate trace data storage rate of 13.3 billion events per second, and demonstrated that coupling IOFSL and the Vampir toolset yields a performance analysis framework suitable for end users on leadership-class computing systems. Overall, we have shown that the entire software stack including trace generation, middleware, post-processing, and analysis can be utilized to analyze a parallel application consisting of 200,448 processes.

The remainder of this paper is organized as follows. The general I/O requirements of performance analysis tools and the Vampir toolset I/O needs are described in Section 2. An overview of IOFSL and optimizations relevant to tracing is provided in Section 3. Section 4 describes the integration and scalability improvement efforts. The proposed concepts are evaluated on a leadership-class machine, and the resulting performance measurements are analyzed in Section 5. An overview of related work is given in Section 6. Conclusions and insights into future work are summarized in Section 7.

2. THE VAMPIR TOOLSET

The Vampir toolset is a sophisticated performance analysis infrastructure for parallel programs that use combinations of MPI, OpenMP, PThreads, CUDA, and OpenCL. It consists of the Vampir GUI for interactive post-mortem visualization, the VampirServer for parallel analysis, the VampirTrace instrumentation and runtime recording system, and the Open Trace Format as the file format and access library. The Vampir toolset relies on event trace recording, which allows the most detailed analysis of the parallel behavior of target applications. First, the Vampir toolset performs instrumentation of the target application using various techniques. During run time, the monitoring component collects the instrumented events together with significant properties. These include entry/exit events for user code subroutines, message send/receive events, collective communication events, shared memory synchronization, and I/O events. A single Vampir event needs approximately 10 to 50 bytes for its encoding in the buffer. Typically, event frequencies range from 100 to 100,000 per second (with proper settings). A parallel run with 10,000 processes or threads for 10 minutes results in data sizes of $6 \cdot 10^9$ to $3 \cdot 10^{13}$ bytes (approx. 5.6 GB to 27 TB[1]). The trace buffer size should not exceed the local main memory size minus the memory required by the target application; otherwise the application behavior will be severely distorted. Typical sizes are 10 MB to 1 GB per process or thread. The

---

[1]In this paper, we use $1\,\text{MB} = 2^{20}\text{B}$, $1\,\text{GB} = 2^{30}\text{B}$, and $1\,\text{TB} = 2^{40}\text{B}$.

event trace data is written to a set of OTF files and is then ready for post-mortem investigation with the Vampir GUI. By default, VampirTrace and OTF use a file-per-thread I/O pattern to store data to minimize coordination.

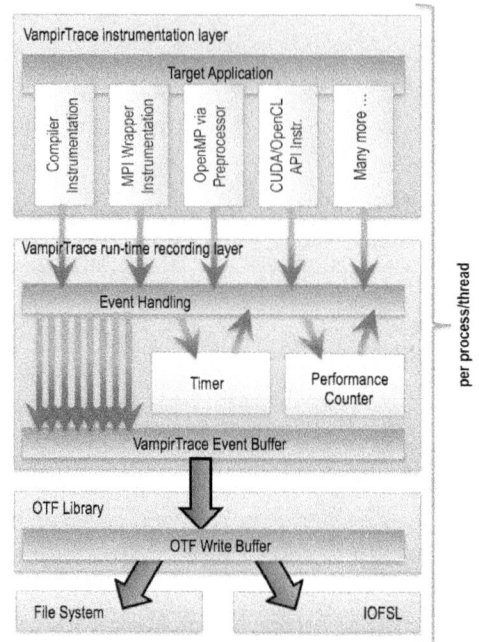

Figure 1: The VampirTrace data flow.

Figure 1 gives an overview of VampirTrace's data flow. Additional information about Vampir, VampirTrace, and OTF is provided in our prior work [17]. When the VampirTrace monitoring component captures the parallel runtime behavior of the target application, it strives to impose minimal perturbation. Triggered by events of interest, the runtime recording layer stores the event information together with vital properties (precise time stamp, event-specific properties, performance counter values if configured) to a preallocated memory buffer. The recording is performed independently for every process or thread into local buffers. In order to avoid artificial synchronization of the target application, buffers are never shared between processes or threads.

2.1 I/O Patterns in VampirTrace

The VampirTrace buffer can be written to an OTF file in several ways. The most general one is to flush the buffer as soon as it is filled. If the measurement library cannot ensure enough space for an event in the buffer, the application is delayed, and the data is written to a file through the OTF library. These buffer flush phases are clearly marked in the trace so that their effect is not mistaken for stray behavior of the target application. However, they can delay other processes waiting for messages or synchronization in the application, unless the buffer limit is reached at the same spot in the application for all processes (i.e., each process generated the same number of events). This becomes an issue for larger scale and tightly coupled applications.

Alternatively, VampirTrace can use collective MPI operations to trigger synchronized buffer flushes by piggybacking work on application collective operations. For each collective operation, the measurement environment communicates the maximum buffer level. Once a threshold is reached, all processes enter a flush phase. All synchronous flushes and synchronizations are captured in the trace and clearly marked for analysis. An additional barrier after the flush makes sure the processes resume simultaneously, avoiding an indirect impact on the application behavior.

Having a single flush at the end of the recording (typically during an `MPI_Finalize` wrapper) is preferred when possible because it removes trace I/O from the application execution. For this case, the event buffer must be able to hold all events generated during the application execution. This can be achieved by reducing the total event count, for example, by using filters or tracing only specific iterations of the application. In addition, transparent compression using zlib in the OTF layer helps reducing the file sizes. It is applied only to the output during a buffer flush to keep the perturbation minimal at the expense of the required memory buffer space.

In general, the number of buffer flushes per process can be limited to avoid uncontrolled use of storage space. The specialized cases for flushing largely improve the perturbation due to I/O, but it cannot be guaranteed that a collective operation triggers a buffer flush before the buffer is full. It is also difficult to choose appropriate settings that do not require buffer flushes. Therefore, VampirTrace may need to fall back to the general uncoordinated buffer flush that prevents loss of data at the cost of a performance impact. Traditional collective I/O optimizations and methods rely on implicit synchronization. This required synchronization distorts the measurement and is therefore not an appropriate solution for VampirTrace's data collection. Also, the possibility of processes or threads being created during runtime makes it impossible to know how many participants there might be for collective I/O at any point in time.

2.2 I/O Challenges and Solutions

The original configuration of VampirTrace imposed two I/O challenges that prevented it from tracing applications running at full-scale on leadership-class systems. First, the often nearly simultaneous buffer flushes of many processes or threads increase I/O bandwidth pressure on the I/O subsystem. This pressure can delay trace data storage and skew the application trace measurements. The storage targets can get overwhelmed with inefficient, nearly random workloads that can sap over 60% of their peak performance. Second, the metadata load for this configuration is high because of the creation of many individual files and the allocation of file system blocks for a large number of I/O operations. For example, ORNL's JaguarPF is in principle capable of opening one file per process even at the scale of 224,000 processes, taking around 45 seconds (David Dillow, personal communication, September 20, 2011). In production usage however, such operations have been observed to take five minutes [30]. Parallel file creation requests at a high rate will impact all other users and jobs on the machine. VampirTrace/OTF supports the use of node-local storage for the intermediate trace I/O. This involves copying the files from local to global directories after the measurement. However, node-local storage is not available on many current large-scale systems and the situation will not change on the next generation systems (Cray XK6, Blue Gene/Q) either.

To address these challenges, we identified several opportunities that allow VampirTrace to store its trace data col-

lections more efficiently while minimizing the overhead of the data accesses on the traced applications. We found that a shared file access pattern may be better suited for large-scale applications than is the file-per-thread access pattern. This approach significantly reduces the metadata load of the file-per-thread access pattern. Since writing to a shared file from many processes requires coordination among those processes, we opted to store trace data collections in multiple files, where the total number of files is far less than the number of traced processes or threads. For storing the trace data collections, we identified an append-only streaming access pattern that is easier for parallel file systems to handle than are random I/O patterns. To further reduce the impact of file system performance on trace data collection, we recognized that a write buffering strategy can isolate file system performance from the trace data collection storage.

The capabilities required by the improved VampirTrace I/O access pattern are not readily available or adequately supported by vendor-supplied I/O software stacks. The necessary capabilities missing from these stacks include transparent aggregation of uncoordinated I/O requests to a set of files, portable atomic append of file data, and write buffering. These capabilities can be implemented within I/O forwarding tools, such as IOFSL. Our I/O forwarding approach provides a convenient solution that integrates with the existing VampirTrace/OTF infrastructure and promises to scale much farther than today's high-end systems.

3. THE IOFSL I/O FORWARDING LAYER

The goal of I/O forwarding is to bridge computation and storage systems in leadership-class computers. Using this software, all application file I/O requests are shipped to dedicated resources that aggregate and execute the requests. This approach allows I/O forwarding layers to bridge compute nodes, networks, and storage systems that are physically disconnected, such as on the IBM Blue Gene systems [32]. I/O forwarding middleware aggregates file I/O requests from multiple distributed sources (I/O forwarding clients) to a smaller number of I/O handlers (the I/O forwarding servers). The I/O forwarding server delegates and executes the requests on behalf of the clients. Since the I/O forwarding layer has access to all the file I/O requests, one can implement file I/O optimizations on both coordinated and uncoordinated file access patterns. These optimizations include coalescing, merging, transforming, and buffering I/O requests.

IOFSL [2, 23] is a high-performance, portable I/O forwarding layer for leadership-class computing systems. For communication between the IOFSL clients and servers, the Buffered Message Interface (BMI) library [5] is used. BMI supports native access to the SeaStar2+ network used on the Cray XT platforms using the Portals API and to the IBM Blue Gene/P tree network using ZOID [14]. TCP is supported as a general transport. IOFSL provides a stateless I/O application programming interface called ZOIDFS that applications can use to directly communicate with IOFSL servers. It also provides compatibility layers for POSIX and MPI-IO programming interfaces.

IOFSL is an ideal location to prototype and evaluate new or existing HPC I/O capabilities. Figure 2 illustrates a typical HPC software stack on leadership-class systems and where I/O forwarding fits into it. IOFSL interacts directly with the parallel file system. Implementing our enhance-

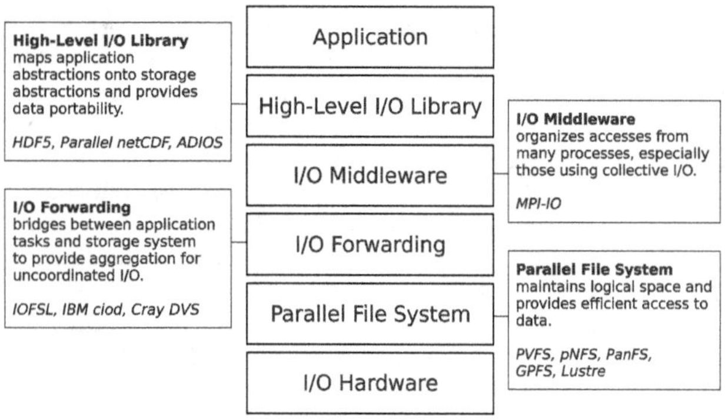

Application
High-Level I/O Library
I/O Middleware
I/O Forwarding
Parallel File System
I/O Hardware
High-Level I/O Library
maps application abstractions onto storage abstractions and provides data portability.
HDF5, Parallel netCDF, ADIOS
I/O Forwarding
bridges between application tasks and storage system to provide aggregation for uncoordinated I/O.
IOFSL, IBM ciod, Cray DVS
I/O Middleware
organizes accesses from many processes, especially those using collective I/O.
MPI-IO
Parallel File System
maintains logical space and provides efficient access to data.
PVFS, pNFS, PanFS, GPFS, Lustre

Figure 2: Overview of the HPC I/O software stack.

ments we present in this paper required no changes to vendor-supplied systems software; all of our I/O enhancements were implemented within IOFSL. Since IOFSL is positioned just above the file system, our enhancements to IOFSL can affect all applications using the I/O software stack.

In Section 2.2, we identified several file optimizations that can improve the performance and scalability of the trace data generation of VampirTrace. These improvements include a write buffering strategy to quickly offload trace data from the application compute nodes and an atomic file append capability to reduce random I/O workloads to the file system. In this section, we describe how we implemented these capabilities within IOFSL.

The IOFSL write buffering capability provides nonblocking file I/O enhancements to the IOFSL server and client. This capability transforms blocking I/O operations into nonblocking ones while requiring minimal changes to the application and no changes to the ZOIDFS API. It relaxes the data consistency semantics in order to achieve higher I/O throughputs for the application. To implement this, we modified the file write data path in the IOFSL server to signal operation completion to the client before initiating the file write operation. Once the I/O forwarding server receives the client data for a non-blocking operation, the data is buffered within the server and the client I/O operation is completed. The client is then free to release or reuse its transmitted data buffer since the server is now responsible for completing the I/O operation for the client. The I/O request will complete as soon as the server has resources to process the request or when the client forces all pending nonblocking I/O operations to complete using a commit operation. This behavior allows the IOFSL server to transparently manage nonblocking I/O operations initiated by clients.

IOFSL's atomic append capability allows multiple clients to share the same output file without client-side coordination and supports tools that exhibit log like data access patterns. This file append capability is a distributed and atomic I/O operation. We developed several new IOFSL features to support distributed atomic file append operations. IOFSL servers now provide a distributed hash table that is used to track the end-of-file offset for unique files. This data structure provides a fetch and update operation, so that the current file offset can be retrieved and updated. The distributed storage of file handles allows IOFSL to scatter and decentralize the file offset data. We also developed a mechanism for IOFSL servers to communicate with each other. Originally, IOFSL provided a client-server communication model. The server to sever communication capability allows an IOFSL server to query remote IOFSL servers and retrieve the end-of-file offset information. As a consequence, IOFSL clients are not required to contact multiple IOFSL servers to obtain and update file offset information. Additionally, the IOFSL server coalesces multiple atomic append requests to limit the amount of server to server traffic. The atomic append capability can be used by any number of IOFSL servers, including a local server mode when data files are not shared between IOFSL servers.

There are several benefits to our atomic append approach. Clients can append data to a file that is simultaneously being written to by other clients and I/O forwarding servers. IOFSL clients do not require prior knowledge of the end-of-file position and simply need to deliver the data to be written into the file to the server. This capability effectively allows applications to stream data to the IOFSL servers, which manage data placement within a file. The server returns to the client the file offset where the data was written. This capability is similar to MPI shared file pointers and the O_APPEND mode provided by the POSIX I/O API. The novelty of our approach is in supporting a distributed and portable append functionality — O_APPEND does not work in a multi node environment like a parallel computing system. Since this capability is implemented within IOFSL, it can be used on any system where IOFSL can run, regardless of the underlying file system, operating system, or network. For write buffering operations, the IOFSL server can also return the state of completed operations. The client and application can use this information to construct an index of the data accesses within the file and determine the state of pending nonblocking operations.

4. INTEGRATING OTF WITH IOFSL

The OTF layer provides a single integration point between the VampirTrace stack and IOFSL. Since all trace I/O happens in this layer, this permits a portable solution that is usable for other applications based on OTF. We chose to use the ZOIDFS API because it provides additional capabilities that are not present in the IOFSL POSIX translation layers.

The primary integration goal was to reduce the number of files generated by the Vampir tracing infrastructure. Instead of storing n OTF event streams in n files, we aggregate the streams into m files, where $m \ll n$. m can vary based on the tracing configuration. For example, m could be equal to the number of IOFSL servers (one file per IOFSL server) or be smaller (files shared between the servers). Figure 3 illustrates the file aggregation and integration of the used software layers.

To accomplish this, all ZOIDFS write operations use the novel atomic-append feature of IOFSL. This allows arbitrary subsets of event trace streams to share the same file without any coordination on the OTF side. IOFSL ensures that blocks from the same source stay in their original order but makes no guarantees with respect to global ordering; this approach enables additional optimizations.

The coordination of the blocks and their positions in the shared file is done by IOFSL and the results of this activity is reported to OTF. Every OTF stream[2] collects the file

[2]An OTF stream abstracts the events from a single thread or process.

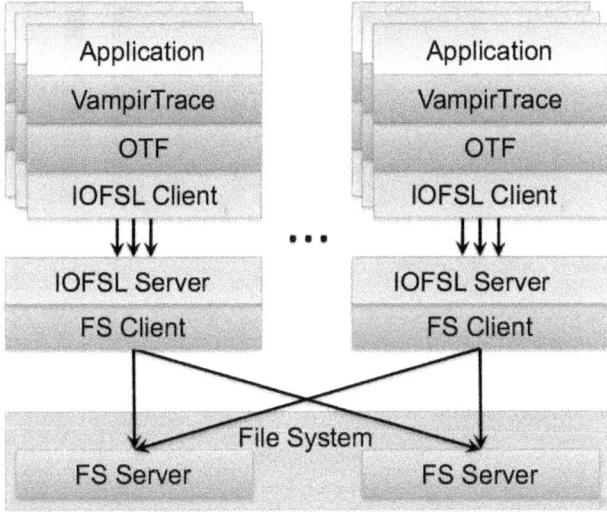

Figure 3: I/O aggregation provided by IOFSL for VampirTrace / OTF. One forwarding server serves multiple clients, usually many servers are used to provide high capacity.

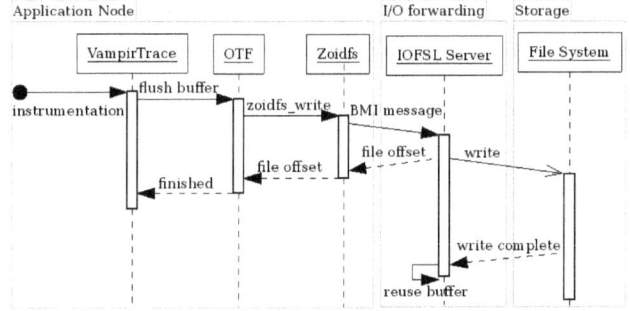

Figure 4: Sequence diagram of a flush that utilizes the buffered I/O capability of IOFSL. Vertical axis is time, increasing downward, not true to scale.

positions (returned by IOFSL) of its blocks individually in memory. As a final new step, all OTF streams write a list of file positions for their own blocks together with their stream identifier. This is sufficient to later extract all blocks from this stream in correct order during reading. The mapping is stored in a shared index file, which is also written via IOFSL using atomic append. The trace data files and index files can be read with or without the use of IOFSL.

The traditional OTF write scheme uses synchronous I/O calls to ensure that all I/O activities happen during the buffer flush phases, which are explicitly marked in the trace. While the flush phases are blocking and application buffers are reused, there can be buffering by the operating system, the standard library, or the file system itself. However, optimizations that just hide the transfer time can negatively affect the application when resources such as I/O bandwidth are used after the flush. The write buffering capability of IOFSL can also decrease the time spent in buffer flushes. Unlike local optimizations however, the trace data has been transferred from the application node to the I/O forwarding node after the completed flush. The file I/O is then initiated from the forwarding node, and no local resources are used after that, minimizing the application perturbation. The effects are similar to other jobs utilizing the shared network and I/O subsystem. In cases where this is undesirable — for example, if the target application's I/O is the subject of the analysis or if the machine's I/O network is not separate from the communication network — the nonblocking I/O capability may not be appropriate and can be disabled. Figure 4 displays the interaction between application, trace library, IOFSL, and the file system in a sequence diagram.

In addition to the improvements necessary to efficiently write the trace output, a number of other optimizations were performed to address scalability bottlenecks within the Vampir toolset. Trace post-processing with vtunify was previously parallelized using OpenMP and MPI. The master vtunify process serves as a global instance to unify the trace definitions (metadata about processes, functions, etc). In order to enable the handling of even larger traces, the serial workload in the master process has been significantly reduced. The remaining serial workload was optimized in time complexity with respect to the total number of application threads. A merge option was implemented in vtunify, where each unification worker writes only a single output file instead of one output file per processed stream. This can generate OTF files that are compatible with legacy OTF applications without running into the metadata issues from creating too many files. With these improvements, trace post-processing becomes feasible for large scales, as is documented in Section 5. A hierarchical unification scheme for definitions could further improve the scalability and eliminate the master process as a bottleneck.

As described in Section 2.1, a synchronized flush is beneficial for large-scale tracing scenarios that generate many events. For the required high watermark check, an MPI_Allreduce is injected into each global collective operation. At large scales this can result in more significant overhead, since the MPI_Allreduce operation is especially prone to high variability caused by operating system noise [16]. In order to reduce the total overhead, a configuration option has been introduced that specifies that the watermark should be checked only every n^{th} collective operation. This mitigates the overhead while still being able to reliably trigger collective synchronized flushes. The additional time used by the measurement library for the watermark check is still clearly marked in the trace file.

We also improved OTF's zlib compression capability. OTF provides zlib with a dedicated compression output buffer. During the OTF and IOFSL integration, the compression capability was updated to ensure that full compression output buffers were written to the file system. This modification ensured that most OTF writes have a fixed size and are stripe aligned, presenting a more efficient pattern to file systems. Unaligned OTF accesses can occur only at the end of the application's execution when the remaining contents of the compression buffer are flushed to the file system.

VampirTrace and the IOFSL integration presented in this paper was designed and tested with hybrid applications that use MPI in combination with OpenMP, threads, CUDA, or other node-local parallel paradigms. No restriction is imposed to when new threads can be created or when buffer flushes may happen.

5. EVALUATION AND ANALYSIS

JaguarPF [4] is a 2.3 petaflop Cray XT5 Supercomputer deployed at the Oak Ridge Leadership Computing Facility (OLCF) at Oak Ridge National Laboratory (ORNL). Data storage is provided by a Lustre-based center wide file system [28].

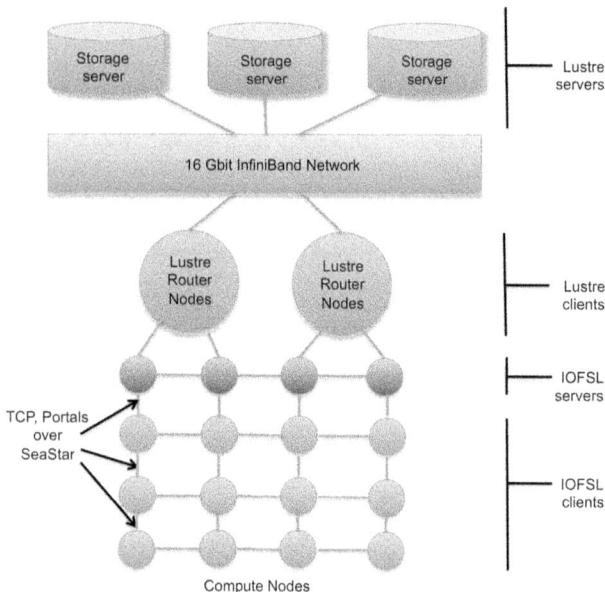

Figure 5: Deployment of application processes and IOFSL servers on JaguarPF.

User-level access to the I/O nodes or Lustre router nodes, which would be optimal locations for running IOFSL servers, is not possible on JaguarPF because of system administration policies. Therefore, we allocate additional compute nodes with each application launch, spawn IOFSL servers on these extra nodes, and proxy all application I/O requests through these nodes. Figure 5 illustrates this deployment strategy. On JaguarPF, the BMI Portals driver is used to leverage the performance of the XT5 SeaStar 2+ interconnect. Using the default IOFSL configuration (unbuffered I/O mode) and the IOR benchmark on JaguarPF when the system was in normal operation, we observed 10.8 GB/s to 11.5 GB/s aggregate sustained bandwidth writing to a single shared file for 1,920 to 192,000 IOFSL clients and when using at most 160 IOFSL servers. We also observed aggregate sustained bandwidths using 60 IOFSL clients per IOFSL server and when writing to unique files (one file per process) of 17.9 GB/s for 2,880 clients, 39.2 GB/s for 5,760 clients, and 42.5 GB/s for 11,520 clients.

To better understand the performance of the new IOFSL's write buffering capability when compared to the original IOFSL synchronous write behavior, we measured the performance of the new capability using a modified version of the IOR benchmark that invoked write buffering operations. These experiments focused on identifying the I/O throughput observed by the application, and the results ignore the cost of application-initiated flushes. Figure 6 illustrates the performance on Oak Ridge's JaguarPF Cray XT5 system. This data clearly indicates that IOFSL can significantly accelerate the sustained storage system bandwidth perceived

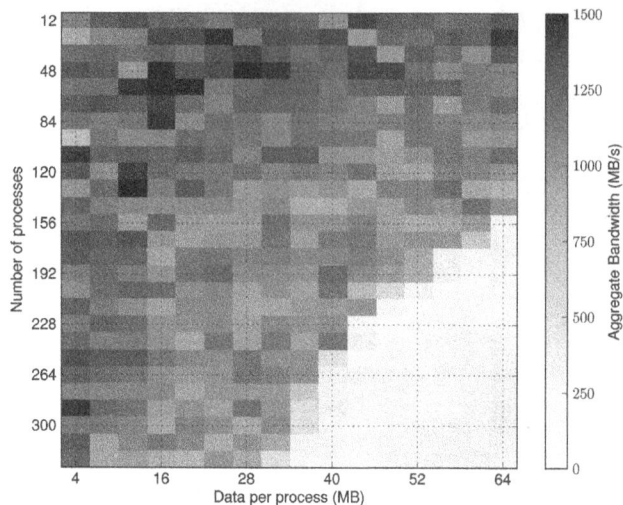

Figure 6: IOFSL write buffering performance on Cray XT5 system (OLCF's JaguarPF). For this experiment, we used a single IOFSL server, 12 to 324 IOFSL clients, and 4 MB to 64 MB of data per IOFSL client.

by the application when sufficient buffer space is available at the IOFSL server. The drop in performance at the bottom right corner of this figure occurs when the IOFSL server exceeds its write buffer space and forces nonblocking I/O operations to act like blocking ones. Therefore, the usefulness of this capability is constrained by the amount of write buffer available to an IOFSL server, the frequency of write buffering operations initiated by IOFSL clients, and the sustained bandwidth the IOFSL server can realize when transferring the buffered data to the storage system.

To demonstrate tracing at large scale, we instrumented the petascale application S3D with VampirTrace. S3D is a parallel direct numerical simulation code developed at Sandia National Laboratories [6]. We used a problem set that scales to the full JaguarPF system. It uses weak scaling to allow a wide range of process counts, from 768 to 200,448. In its role as a early petascale code, S3D is well understood and has been analyzed with TAU and Vampir at lower scales [15]. The purpose of our experiment was to investigate the scaling of trace recording rather than an analysis of the application. S3D provides a real-world instrumentation target for the measurement environment. In addition, the large number of MPI messages generated by S3D creates a high frequency of events (approximately 7,700 events per second per process). We have traced 60 application time steps during our experiments using a basic online function filter. Further improvements of the instrumentation, such as selective function instrumentation or manually tracing a limited number of time steps, were deliberately not applied in order to demonstrate a challenging situation for the measurement environment. The synchronous flush feature in VampirTrace was used with a total of three flushes during the application execution in addition to the final flush during the application shutdown.

Prior to our successful demonstration, the largest scale trace for VampirTrace was approximately 40,000 processes using POSIX I/O. In practice, achieving this level of parallelism is already difficult because of substantial overhead during file generation and the impact on other users of the file system.

In our demonstration we utilized the full stack that is involved in trace generation: application (S3D), VampirTrace, OTF, IOFSL, the BMI Portals driver for network transfers, and Lustre as a target file system. We have conducted multiple experiments tracing up to 200,448 application cores running S3D and using a set of 672 I/O forwarding nodes resulting in 2,688 files. The largest generated trace size was 4.2 TB of compressed data containing 941 billion events. The total time spent on trace I/O, including forwarding server connection setup, file creation, open, sync, and close, was 71 seconds with write buffering I/O, for a total application run time of 22 minutes. Trace I/O was synchronized among the MPI processes so this time includes the time spent in barriers when waiting for other processes to finish their writing. It therefore represents the total extension of application run time due to trace I/O. On average it took 5.5 seconds for each process to establish the connection to the forwarding server and to open the four shared output files (definitions file and events file, plus an index file for each). Some processes were delayed by up to 32 seconds because of the massive stress on I/O forwarding nodes resulting from write operations from other processes. The intermediate buffer flushes are not affected by connection initialization, file open times, and final commit and therefore show much better individual performance. With write buffering enabled, aggregated write rates of up to 154 GB/s or 33.5 billion events per second were observed, as recorded by the tracing measurement environment during individual flushes. We observed this high bandwidth because all trace data fit into the IOFSL servers' buffers. The cost for the client to flush this data was limited by the IOFSL server performance. This bandwidth result also includes the synchronization of all processes as well as the overhead of OTF and compression.

For comparison, we ran a full-scale experiment using the IOFSL enhancements and unbuffered I/O. The total trace I/O time was 122 seconds, yielding a sustained aggregate bandwidth of 35.3 GB/s. This further indicates that write buffering reduces the I/O overhead observed by the tracing infrastructure. The IOFSL capability buffers trace data at the IOFSL server and overlaps application tracing with trace data storage. In this test series, the trace size per process remains almost constant.

The post-processing (vtunify) for such a trace requires approximately 27 minutes but only a fraction of the resources of the application (10,752 workers). This is a required step, regardless of the use of IOFSL. In the post-processing, IOFSL was not utilized since only 10,754 files[3] are created in this step.

This large-scale demonstration shows that trace recording on full-scale leadership-class systems can be done with a well-manageable overhead, even with trace I/O phases during the application execution. We investigated the scaling behavior of our solution with a series of experiments in different configurations. Figure 7 shows the total application run times at different scales with and without tracing. While the overhead of both trace I/O and tracing in general increases

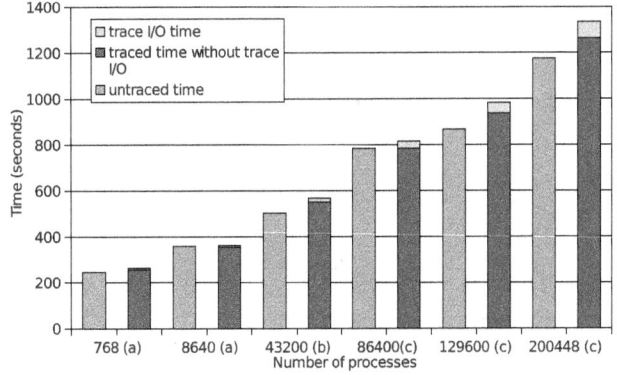

Figure 7: Run times of S3D with and without tracing for different process counts: (a) average of 11 experiments, (b) average of 7 experiments, (c) single test run during dedicated reservation.

with the number of processors, it remains below 15% even at full scale.

A comparison with POSIX I/O at different scales is shown in Figures 8 and 9. The POSIX I/O experiment with 86,400 cores was conducted during a dedicated system reservation. To avoid any potential impact to file system stability, we did not scale the POSIX I/O tests further. For all tests, the same software versions were used — this means that also POSIX I/O tests benefit from those improvements described in Section 4 that are not directly related to IOFSL. The event rate for IOFSL is limited mainly by the I/O throughput of the forwarding servers to the file system, while POSIX I/O is limited by the rate of file creation. The impact of file creation depends on total time, which in turn depends on trace size per process; it will be even more dominant with lower numbers of events.

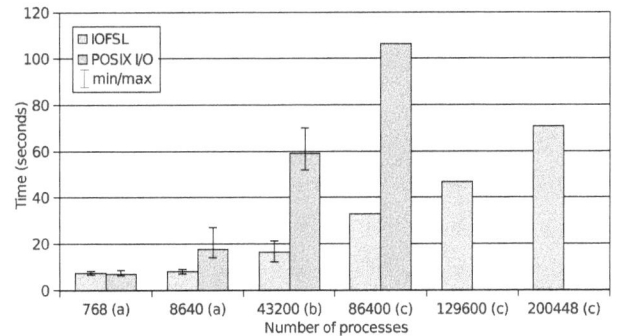

Figure 8: Total trace I/O times for different process counts: (a) average of 11 experiments with min/max, (b) average of 7 experiments with min/max, (c) single test run during dedicated reservation; no POSIX I/O data for 129600, 200448.

The experiments with lower process counts were repeated at different times during production use of the system. I/O in a shared system is always prone to variability, especially with a single metadata server being the bottleneck for any file metadata operation.

---

[3]10,752 event files, one definitions file, and one control file.

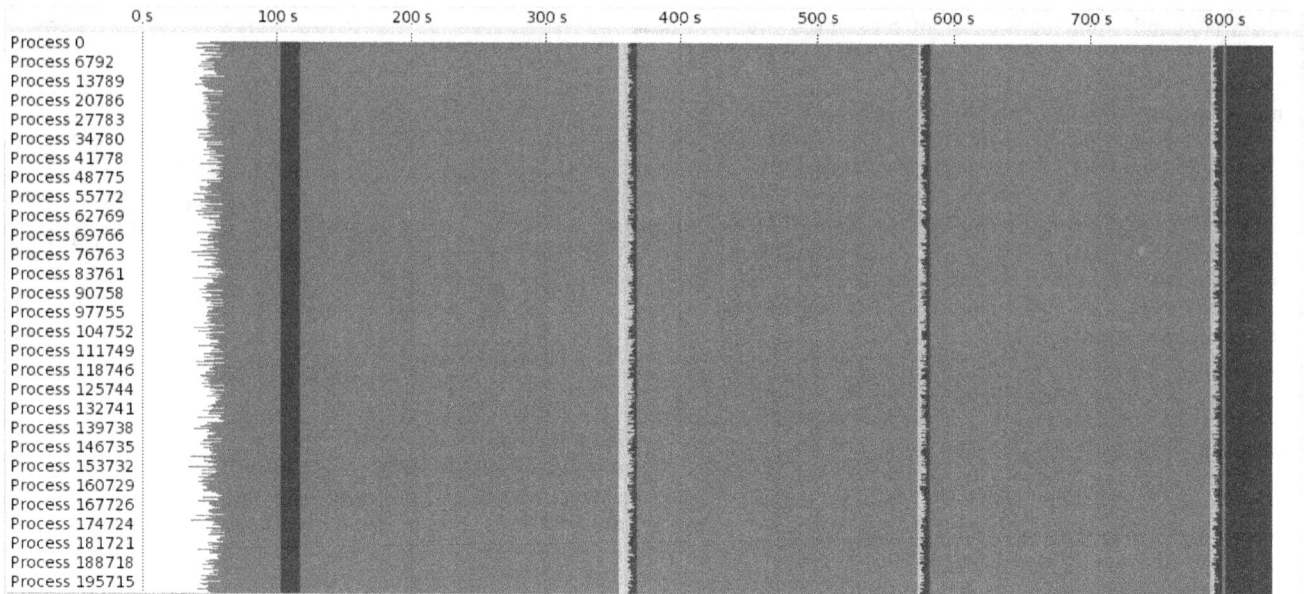

Figure 10: Screenshot of Vampir visualizing a trace of the S3D application using 200,448 cores on JaguarPF. User functions are shown in green, MPI operations in red, and activities of the measurement environment in yellow (file open), light blue (trace I/O) and dark blue (synchronization).

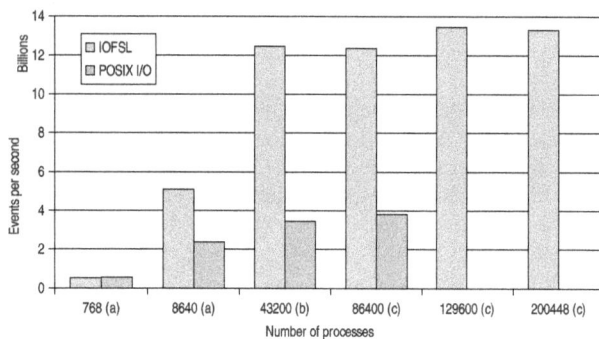

Figure 9: Aggregate event write rates for different process counts. Averages used as in Figure 7. The data includes the overheads of establishing the connection, file open, synchronization, commit, and close.

The trace files generated with IOFSL were validated by using the post-mortem analysis tool Vampir. Vampir was able to read valid trace files and display detailed graphics of measured events versus a timeline and various other displays. Figure 10 shows a trace of S3D with 200,448 processes opened in Vampir, using 21,516 processes for interactive visualization. All processes are visible in an overview showing user functions in green, MPI operations in red, and phases in which the application was suspended by the measurement environment in blue. In addition, file open operations in the first flush are presented in yellow, followed by the actual trace I/O colored light blue as in subsequent flushes. Dark blue represents synchronization phases at the end of each flush. The three flushes take place around 360 s, 580 s, and 790 s after the measurement start. Although being clearly visible, they are sufficiently short in relation to the overall run time of the application. Additionally, the figure shows VampirTrace's internal time synchronizations that extend the first and the last synchronization phase after 100 s and 800 s. This total overview serves as a starting point to further investigate the details by zooming into both the time and process axes.

At such large scales, visualization for analysis purposes becomes more challenging as the ratio between available pixels and displayed processes decreases. Vampir's ability to smoothly zoom and scroll into both the process and time dimension helps to navigate even in such large traces. However, new ways to highlight performance anomalies are required to help the user at those scales find the right spots to focus at. These topics are the subject of ongoing research; our solution lays a foundation for a comprehensive analysis at full scale by providing a feasible way to store event trace data.

We have also evaluated the integrated IOFSL and Vampir toolset on the Intrepid IBM Blue Gene/P (BG/P) leadership-class computing system deployed at the Argonne Leadership Computing Facility (ALCF). The purpose of this evaluation was to demonstrate the portability of our solution to other leadership-class computing platforms, runtime environments, storage systems, and applications.

Intrepid is a 557 teraflop IBM BG/P. It consists of 40,960 compute nodes and 640 I/O nodes, each node with one quad-core 850 MHz PowerPC 450 processor. Intrepid's compute nodes are interconnected by a torus network for point-to-point communication and a tree network for optimized collective operations. The tree network is also used for file I/O; each set of 64 compute nodes is connected over the tree to a dedicated I/O node. I/O nodes communicate via 10 Gigabit Ethernet with one another and with Intrepid's two high-performance storage systems: a 3 PB GPFS file system and a 512 TB PVFS file system.

Intrepid's system administration policies permit users to customize the runtime environment of the system. For our evaluation of IOFSL and VampirTrace/OTF, these policies allowed us to deploy the IOFSL servers on the I/O nodes. To do so, we had to replace IBM's ciod I/O forwarding software with the ZOID [14] BG/P tree network driver to facilitate high-throughput and low-latency communication between user-space processes on the compute and I/O nodes, and boot ZeptoOS [31] operating system on the BG/P compute nodes (replacing IBM's CNK). Additional information on how IOFSL is deployed on BG/P systems is provided in our prior work [23].

We successfully traced the Radix-k [26] image compositing algorithm on Intrepid at a variety of scales using the integrated IOFSL and VampirTrace/OTF toolset. Aside from small adjustments to the infrastructure deployment, the software stack required no additional changes to run on the system. Our evaluation on Intrepid demonstrates that we can trace additional applications, run our toolsets in different runtime environments and systems, and interact with different storage systems. Since our initial target platform was JaguarPF, assessing the performance and scalability of these tools on IBM BG/P systems is a work in progress.

6. RELATED WORK

The performance analysis toolset Scalasca faced similar problems to ours when handling large numbers of trace files. Recently, the scalability of Scalasca was improved up to 300,000 cores [30]. For tests on a large IBM BG/P system, the SIONlib library was used. It uses a special multifile format that contains additional metadata managing chunks of data from different processes within one file [9]. With SIONlib, multifile creation is a collective operation. This would pose a significant limitation to VampirTrace with respect to the dynamic threading model.

The POSIX I/O standard was designed before the advent of wide-scale parallelism. As such, it suffers from many fundamental characteristics that preclude it from scenarios such as multiple writers updating the same file — a common need for parallel I/O oriented activity [13].

New I/O research efforts within standards-oriented activities have recognized this fact and are actively working on APIs appropriate for extreme-scale parallelism [13, 25]. One such API is pNFS [12], an extension to NFSv4 designed to overcome NFS scalability and performance barriers.

MPI-IO [19] provides a more sophisticated I/O abstraction than POSIX. It includes collective operations and file views, which enable coordinated and concurrent access without locking [7]. It does not directly provide an "n-to-m" mapping from clients to output files. OTF's management of mixed blocks in shared files would be difficult to implement on top of MPI-IO, because most implementations (including the popular ROMIO) do not return accurate current file sizes unless a synchronizing collective is used.

The I/O Delegate Cache System (IODC) [22] is a caching mechanism for MPI-IO that resolves cache coherence issues and alleviates the lock contention of I/O servers. IOFSL offers similar capabilities but is located below MPI-IO in the I/O software stack, providing a dedicated abstract device driver enabling unmodified applications to take full advantage of its optimizations.

The I/O forwarding concept was introduced within the Sandia Cplant project [24], which used a forwarding framework based on an extended NFS protocol. IOFSL extends the target environment imagined by Cplant to much larger scales and higher performance through a more sophisticated protocol permitting additional optimizations.

Decoupled and Asynchronous Remote Transfers (DART) [8] and DataStager [1] achieve high-performance transfers on Cray XT5 using dedicated data staging nodes. Unlike our approach, which is transparent to the applications that use POSIX and MPI-IO interfaces, DART requires applications to use a custom API.

Similarly, Adaptable I/O System (ADIOS) [18] provides performance improvements through strategies such as prefetch and write-behind, based on application-specific configuration files read at startup; this information also helps ADIOS minimize the memory footprint during the course of the application run. In contrast, our approach requires no knowledge of the application behavior in advance, and it is situated at a lower level in the I/O software stack.

PLFS [3] is a file system translation layer developed for HPC environments to alleviate scaling problems associated with large numbers of clients writing to a single file. Like our solution, they interpose middleware between the client application and the underlying file system through the use of FUSE. Their solution, which is aimed at checkpointing and similar activities for architectures such as Los Alamos National Laboratory's Roadrunner (3,060 nodes), transparently creates a container structure consisting of subdirectories for each writer as well as index information and other metadata for each corresponding data file. Since our solution is focused on supporting hundreds of thousands of clients or more, we have chosen to aggregate I/O operations in the middleware, thus resulting in fewer metadata operations in the underlying parallel file system. Furthermore, our IOFSL-based solution focuses on transforming uncoordinated file accesses to many unique files, such as a file per process or thread I/O pattern, into a shared file per group of processes I/O pattern. Our solution reduces file system resource contention generated by shared file access patterns (such as file stripe lock contention or false sharing) and eliminates file system metadata overheads generated by I/O patterns with one file per process or thread (such as frequent file creation, stat, or attribute access operations) at extreme scales.

IOFSL work extends the earlier ZOID efforts [14]. ZOID is a Blue Gene-specific function call forwarding infrastructure that is part of the ZeptoOS project. The I/O forwarding protocol used by IOFSL was first prototyped in ZeptoOS. IOFSL is a mature, portable implementation that integrates with common HPC file systems and also works on the Cray XT series and Linux clusters.

While recent work has addressed the use of non-blocking I/O at the I/O forwarding layer [29], our work focuses on providing a portable and transparent to applications, write-buffering based, and high-performance non-blocking I/O capability in HPC environments. Furthermore, non-blocking file I/O capabilities are not provided by existing I/O forwarding tools, including IBM's ciod or Cray's DVS.

In other areas of computer science research, augmentations to existing I/O software that take advantage of specific workload characteristics have been shown effective in improving performance for important workloads. For example, in the Internet services domain, the Google File System provides specialized append operations that allow many tasks to contribute to an output file in an uncoordinated manner [10].

7. CONCLUSIONS AND FUTURE WORK

This paper described the use of I/O forwarding middleware for scalable event trace recording. Through an integration into the OTF library, the Vampir toolset benefits from a new atomic append capability that is provided by the IOFSL I/O forwarding layer. Using the Vampir tracing infrastructure, we demonstrated that this solution enables software tracing at full-scale on leadership-class systems (200,448 processes). A comprehensive trace-based analysis is now feasible for pattern recognition, post-processing, and visualization systems. Within the context of this paper, we have adressed the increasing trace data volumes at large scales at I/O level. Further ongoing work investigates advanced filtering, selective tracing and semantic runtime compression to provide additional benefits for tracing large application runs. We show that even at medium scales, tracing overhead can be significantly reduced with our solution. The benefit for scalability results from reducing the massive amount of metadata file system requests from all application processes to a much lower number. Further improvements on performance comes from utilizing write buffering, which, thanks to being implemented on separate I/O forwarding nodes, does not perturb the application processes. We improved the scalability of the Vampir toolset to leverage the entire performance analysis workflow.

While these results meet our immediate needs and objectives, this effort has led us to consider further related lines of inquiry. We will pursue more advanced aggregate memory footprint optimizations to yield more available memory to user applications. While we have addressed the data collection challenges in this paper and presented a solution to this problem, we do not address how to effectively visualize trace data for applications running at extreme scales. This information visualization challenge will be addressed as our work progresses. We plan to couple the data collection tools and techniques presented in this paper with recent MPI and I/O visualization tools that focus on extreme scale event and trace data collections [20, 21].

The capabilities described in this paper are also applicable to other use cases beyond improving VampirTrace's I/O and can be implemented within other I/O forwarding tools. The new IOFSL capabilities can improve the I/O performance of tools that generate per-process logs. Thus, these capabilities are applicable to massively parallel applications that exhibit log like data storage patterns (such as Qbox's [11] shared file pointer object capability), data-intensive stream processing tools (such as LOFAR's real-time signal processing pipeline [27]), and high-level I/O libraries that allow unlimited dimensionality or enlargement of variable data structures (such as chunked data storage in HDF5). While we limited our demonstration of these capabilities to IOFSL, the capabilities are sufficiently generic and can be implemented within other production-quality I/O forwarding layers, such as IBM's ciod and Cray's DVS. If these capabilities were implemented within these production tools, they could have a substantial impact on the HPC community's ability to understand applications running on leadership-class systems.

The OLCF and ALCF are in the process of upgrading their leadership-class computing resources. The new Titan Cray XK6 supercomputer at OLCF will consist of 299,008 CPU cores and 18,688 GPUs, whereas Mira, a 800,000 CPU core IBM Blue Gene/Q system, will be deployed at ALCF. Both centers will upgrade the storage systems that serve their leadership-class computing resources. While we are confident our toolsets will scale on these systems, we will re-evaluate the scalability and performance of our tools on these new platforms as they are deployed. Moreover, we plan to further investigate the IOFSL and OTF/VampirTrace configuration space on these systems so that we can identify optimal infrastructure configurations for performance analysis I/O workloads.

Acknowledgments

We thank Ramanan Sankaran (ORNL) for providing a working version of S3D as well as a benchmark problem set for JaguarPF. We are very grateful to Matthias Jurenz for his assistance on VampirTrace as well as Matthias Weber and Ronald Geisler for their support for Vampir. The IOFSL project is supported by the DOE Office of Science and National Nuclear Security Administration (NNSA). This research used resources of the Argonne Leadership Computing Facility at Argonne National Laboratory and the Oak Ridge Leadership Computing Facility at Oak Ridge National Laboratory, which are supported by the Office of Science of the U.S. Department of Energy under contracts DE-AC02-06CH11357 and DE-AC05-00OR22725, respectively.

The general enhancement of the VampirTrace and Vampir tools at TU Dresden for full-size runs on leadership-class HPC systems is supported with funding and cooperation by ORNL and UT-Battelle.

8. REFERENCES

[1] ABBASI, H., WOLF, M., EISENHAUER, G., KLASKY, S., SCHWAN, K., AND ZHENG, F. DataStager: Scalable data staging services for petascale applications. In *Proceedings of the 18th ACM International Symposium on High Performance Distributed Computing (HPDC)* (2009), pp. 39–48.

[2] ALI, N., CARNS, P., ISKRA, K., KIMPE, D., LANG, S., LATHAM, R., ROSS, R., WARD, L., AND SADAYAPPAN, P. Scalable I/O forwarding framework for high-performance computing systems. In *Proceedings of the 11th IEEE International Conference on Cluster Computing (CLUSTER)* (2009).

[3] BENT, J., GIBSON, G., GRIDER, G., McCLELLAND, B., NOWOCZYNSKI, P., NUNEZ, J., POLTE, M., AND WINGATE, M. PLFS: A checkpoint filesystem for parallel applications. In *Proceedings of 21st ACM/IEEE International Conference for High Performance Computing, Networking, Storage and Analysis (SC)* (2009).

[4] BLAND, A., KENDALL, R., KOTHE, D., ROGERS, J., AND SHIPMAN, G. Jaguar: The world's most powerful computer. In *Proceedings of the 51st Cray User Group Meeting (CUG)* (2009).

[5] CARNS, P., LIGON III, W., ROSS, R., AND WYCKOFF, P. BMI: A network abstraction layer for parallel I/O. In *Proceedings of the 19th IEEE International Parallel and Distributed Processing Symposium, Workshop on Communication Architecture for Clusters (CAC)* (2005).

[6] CHEN, J. H., CHOUDHARY, A., DE SUPINSKI, B., DEVRIES, M., HAWKES, E. R., KLASKY, S., LIAO, W. K., MA, K. L., MELLOR-CRUMMEY, J., PODHORSZKI, N., SANKARAN, R., SHENDE, S., AND YOO, C. S. Terascale direct numerical simulations of turbulent combustion using S3D. *Computational Science & Discovery 2*, 1 (2009), 015001.

[7] CHING, A., CHOUDHARY, A., COLOMA, K., LIAO, W., ROSS, R., AND GROPP, W. Noncontiguous I/O access through MPI-IO. In *Proceedings of the 3rd IEEE/ACM International Symposium on Cluster Computing and the Grid (CCGrid)* (2003), pp. 104–111.

[8] DOCAN, C., PARASHAR, M., AND KLASKY, S. DART: A substrate for high speed asynchronous data IO. In *Proceedings of the 17th International Symposium on High Performance Distributed Computing (HPDC)* (2008).

[9] FRINGS, W., WOLF, F., AND PETKOV, V. Scalable massively parallel I/O to task-local files. In *Proceedings of 21st ACM/IEEE International Conference for High Performance Computing, Networking, Storage and Analysis (SC)* (2009).

[10] GHEMAWAT, S., GOBIOFF, H., AND LEUNG, S. The Google File System. *SIGOPS Operating Systems Review 37* (Oct. 2003), 29–43.

[11] GYGI, F., DUCHEMIN, I., DONADIO, D., AND GALLI, G. Practical algorithms to facilitate large-scale first-principles molecular dynamics. *Journal of Physics: Conference Series 180*, 1 (2009).

[12] HILDEBRAND, D., AND HONEYMAN, P. Exporting storage systems in a scalable manner with pNFS. In *Proceedings of the 22nd IEEE / 13th NASA Goddard Conference on Mass Storage Systems and Technologies (MSST)* (2005), pp. 18–27.

[13] IEEE POSIX Standard 1003.1 2004 Edition. http://www.opengroup.org/onlinepubs/000095399/functions/write.html.

[14] ISKRA, K., ROMEIN, J. W., YOSHII, K., AND BECKMAN, P. ZOID: I/O-forwarding infrastructure for petascale architectures. In *Proceedings of the 13th ACM SIGPLAN Symposium on Principles and Practice of Parallel Programming (PPoPP)* (2008), pp. 153–162.

[15] JAGODE, H., DONGARRA, J., ALAM, S., VETTER, J., SPEAR, W., AND MALONY, A. D. A holistic approach for performance measurement and analysis for petascale applications. In *Proceedings of the 9th International Conference on Computational Science (ICCS)* (2009), vol. 2, pp. 686–695.

[16] JONES, T., DAWSON, S., NEELY, R., TUEL, W., BRENNER, L., FIER, J., BLACKMORE, R., CAFFREY, P., AND MASKELL, B. Improving the scalability of parallel jobs by adding parallel awareness. In *Proceedings of the 15th ACM/IEEE International Conference on High Performance Networking and Computing (SC)* (2003).

[17] KNÜPFER, A., BRUNST, H., DOLESCHAL, J., JURENZ, M., LIEBER, M., MICKLER, H., MÜLLER, M. S., AND NAGEL, W. E. The Vampir performance analysis tool-set. In *Tools for High Performance Computing* (2008), M. Resch, R. Keller, V. Himmler, B. Krammer, and A. Schulz, Eds., Springer Verlag, pp. 139–155.

[18] LOFSTEAD, J. F., KLASKY, S., SCHWAN, K., PODHORSZKI, N., AND JIN, C. Flexible IO and integration for scientific codes through the adaptable IO system (ADIOS). In *Proceedings of the 6th International Workshop on Challenges of Large Applications in Distributed Environments (CLADE)* (2008), pp. 15–24.

[19] MPI FORUM. MPI-2: Extensions to the Message-Passing Interface. http://www.mpi-forum.org/docs/docs.html, 1997.

[20] MUELDER, C., GYGI, F., AND MA, K.-L. Visual analysis of inter-process communication for large-scale parallel computing. *IEEE Transactions on Visualization and Computer Graphics 15*, 6 (2009), 1129–1136.

[21] MUELDER, C., SIGOVAN, C., MA, K.-L., COPE, J., LANG, S., ISKRA, K., BECKMAN, P., AND ROSS, R. Visual analysis of I/O system behavior for high-end computing. In *Proceedings of the 3rd International Workshop on Large-Scale System and Application Performance (LSAP)* (2011).

[22] NISAR, A., LIAO, W., AND CHOUDHARY, A. Scaling parallel I/O performance through I/O delegate and caching system. In *Proceedings of 20th ACM/IEEE International Conference for High Performance Computing, Networking, Storage and Analysis (SC)* (2008).

[23] OHTA, K., KIMPE, D., COPE, J., ISKRA, K., ROSS, R., AND ISHIKAWA, Y. Optimization techniques at the I/O forwarding layer. In *Proceedings of the 12th IEEE International Conference on Cluster Computing (CLUSTER)* (2010).

[24] PEDRETTI, K., BRIGHTWELL, R., AND WILLIAMS, J. Cplant^{TM} runtime system support for multi-processor and heterogeneous compute nodes. In *Proceedings of the 4th IEEE International Conference on Cluster Computing (CLUSTER)* (2002), pp. 207–214.

[25] Petascale Data Storage Institute. http://www.pdsi-scidac.org/.

[26] PETERKA, T., GOODELL, D., ROSS, R., SHEN, H.-W., AND THAKUR, R. A configurable algorithm for parallel image-compositing applications. In *Proceedings of 21st ACM/IEEE International Conference for High Performance Computing, Networking, Storage and Analysis (SC)* (2009).

[27] ROMEIN, J. Fcnp: Fast I/O on the Blue Gene/P. In *Parallel and Distributed Processing Techniques and Applications (PDPTA'09)* (2009).

[28] SHIPMAN, G., DILLOW, D., ORAL, S., AND WANG, F. The Spider center wide file system; from concept to reality. In *Proceedings of the 51st Cray User Group Meeting (CUG)* (2009).

[29] VISHWANATH, V., HERELD, M., ISKRA, K., KIMPE, D., MOROZOV, V., PAPKA, M., ROSS, R., AND YOSHII, K. Accelerating I/O forwarding in IBM Blue Gene/P systems. In *Proceedings of 22nd ACM/IEEE International Conference for High Performance Computing, Networking, Storage and Analysis (SC)* (2010).

[30] WYLIE, B. J. N., GEIMER, M., MOHR, B., BÖHME, D., SZEBENYI, Z., AND WOLF, F. Large-scale performance analysis of Sweep3D with the Scalasca toolset. *Parallel Processing Letters 20*, 4 (2010), 397–414.

[31] YOSHII, K., ISKRA, K., NAIK, H., BECKMAN, P., AND BROEKEMA, P. C. Performance and scalability evaluation of 'Big Memory' on Blue Gene Linux. *International Journal of High Performance Computing Applications 25*, 2 (2011), 148–160.

[32] YU, H., SAHOO, R. K., HOWSON, C., ALMÁSI, G., CASTAÑOS, J. G., GUPTA, M., MOREIRA, J. E., PARKER, J. J., ENGELSIEPEN, T. E., ROSS, R. B., THAKUR, R., LATHAM, R., AND GROPP, W. D. High performance file I/O for the Blue Gene/L supercomputer. In *Proceedings of the 12th International Symposium on High-Performance Computer Architecture (HPCA)* (2006), pp. 187–196.

ISOBAR Hybrid Compression-I/O Interleaving for Large-scale Parallel I/O Optimization

Eric R. Schendel [1,2,+], Saurabh V. Pendse [1,2,+], John Jenkins [1,2], David A. Boyuka II [1,2], Zhenhuan Gong [1,2], Sriram Lakshminarasimhan [1,2], Qing Liu [2], Hemanth Kolla [3], Jackie Chen [3], Scott Klasky [2], Robert Ross [4], Nagiza F. Samatova [1,2,*]

[1] North Carolina State University, Raleigh, NC 27695, USA

[2] Oak Ridge National Laboratory, Oak Ridge, TN 37830, USA

[3] Sandia National Laboratory, Livermore, CA 94551, USA

[4] Argonne National Laboratory, Argonne, IL 60439, USA

* Corresponding author: samatova@csc.ncsu.edu
\+ Authors contributed equally

ABSTRACT

Current peta-scale data analytics frameworks suffer from a significant performance bottleneck due to an imbalance between their enormous computational power and limited I/O bandwidth. Using data compression schemes to reduce the amount of I/O activity is a promising approach to addressing this problem. In this paper, we propose a hybrid framework for interleaving I/O with data compression to achieve improved I/O throughput side-by-side with reduced dataset size. We evaluate several interleaving strategies, present theoretical models, and evaluate the efficiency and scalability of our approach through comparative analysis. With our theoretical model, considering 19 real-world scientific datasets both from the public domain and peta-scale simulations, we estimate that the hybrid method can result in a 12 to 46% increase in throughput on hard-to-compress scientific datasets. At the reported peak bandwidth of 60 GB/s of uncompressed data for a current, leadership-class parallel I/O system, this translates into an effective gain of 7 to 28 GB/s in aggregate throughput.

Categories and Subject Descriptors

D.4.2 [**Storage Management**]: Secondary storage—*parallel data compression, file storage*; D.2.8 [**Software Engineering**]: Metrics—*complexity measures, performance measures*

Keywords

ISOBAR; Hybrid Interleaving; Staging; High Performance Computing; Lossless Compression; I/O

1. INTRODUCTION

As exascale computing comes closer to becoming reality and more powerful High Performance Computing (HPC) systems become available, the complexity of scientific simulations and analyses has grown commensurately. Unfortunately, the level of disk I/O performance offered by these systems has not kept up, leading to a serious bottleneck in read and write performance in these applications. This problem is exacerbated by the increasing frequency of checkpoint operations performed by such computations due to their increasing vulnerability to node failures at this scale, which further adds to the I/O overload.

Ideally, the solution to the I/O bottleneck will involve both data reduction and parallel I/O access pattern optimization. Unfortunately, these two optimization methods have traditionally been in conflict. State-of-the-art I/O middleware solutions, such as ADIOS [22], HDF5 [37], and PnetCDF [20], have no native support for write compression in a parallel context, due to the complexity of handling the resultant non-uniform data, which requires synchronization between all nodes performing shared-file I/O. Further constraining the problem is the fact that scientists cannot sacrifice simulation fidelity, especially at checkpoints, which rules out lossy compression as a viable data reduction method. And yet, typical lossless compression techniques are ineffective on hard-to-compress floating-point data generally produced by such simulations.

However, we argue that these goals can in fact be complementary. Our key insight is that, by dynamically identifying a subset of highly-compressible data to process while asynchronously writing the remainder to storage, we can effectively hide the cost of compression and I/O synchronization behind this transfer, thus rendering parallel write compression viable. This interleaving method is a natural fit for data staging architectures, where various data transformations can occur while data is "in transit" or in-situ, from compute nodes to disk. Traditionally, staging has been used to compute statistical analyses or perform indexing operations [1, 2]. With interleaved compression and I/O, however, we can augment this functionality by performing compression as an in-situ transfer and storage optimization, as well.

The problem of identifying a highly-compressible subset of the original data is itself quite difficult, as scientific data is usually hard-to-compress with typical compression libraries. We argue that this is because I/O libraries optimized for scientific applications tend to view multi-byte data elements, such as floating-point values, as atomic units of data. Instead, by relaxing this notion and utilizing *byte-level analysis* of the scientific data, better results can be obtained. ISOBAR, or In-Situ Orthogonal Byte Aggregate Reduction, enables exactly this sort of analysis for lossless compression, and has been shown to be effective on such datasets [30]. By modifying ISOBAR's analysis methods to partition the data into compressible and incompressible byte streams, we form an effective basis for interleaving the usage of computing resources. By transmitting the incompressible data over the network immediately, we can hide the cost of compressing the remainder and synchronizing for non-uniform I/O to write it to disk.

Although we demonstrate performance gains when using our methodology in a leadership-class HPC system (the Cray XK6 Jaguar cluster), it is impossible to evaluate our system on every possible cluster configuration. For this reason, it is also desirable to have an analytical performance model, which would allow prediction of performance characteristics on new hardware and software, and would aid application developers in configuration choices.

Therefore, we present a *hybrid compression-I/O* methodology for data reduction and I/O optimization. By employing ISOBAR analysis within a data staging architecture and incorporating the popular ADIOS I/O framework as our I/O backend, we implement effective parallel compression with state-of-the-art I/O performance. Furthermore, we develop a resource interleaving strategy to process the compressible and incompressible components of the data simultaneously, as identified by ISOBAR-analysis. This enables immediate asynchronous transfer and writing of incompressible data while compression is applied concurrently to the remainder. Additionally, we develop a performance model for our methodology, which we demonstate to have a high degree of accuracy through validation against empirical data.

Our system exhibits read and write performance gains proportional to the degree of data reduction, which ranges as high as 46% on scientific datasets. This would translate into an effective increase of 28 GB/s bandwidth over the peak aggregate throughput of 60 GB/s of uncompressed data offered by the leadership-class Lustre parallel filesystem at Oak Ridge National Labs [24]. Even under worst-case conditions, where the dataset is highly entropic and difficult to compress, we show that our system still maintains a gain in throughput over the state-of-the-art.

2. BACKGROUND

2.1 ISOBAR

ISOBAR is a lossless compression method that we built specifically for data that varies in compressibility on a byte-by-byte basis [30]. A ubiquitous example of such data is scientific floating-point data, where the exponent bits can be highly similar while the significand bits are highly entropic. To this end, ISOBAR first performs a *preconditioner* on the linearized input data, selecting data to compress based on its expected degree of compressibility. This is performed by the ISOBAR-analyzer. The analyzer's objective is to identify high-entropic content within a dataset that negatively impacts the compression efficiency and reduces the burden on the compressor from processing the components with low compression potential. This enhances the compression algorithm in terms of the compression throughput as well as the compression ratio.

The input data is considered as a matrix of bytes, where each row is an input value (e.g., a double-precision floating-point) and each column is an individual byte of the input value. The preconditioner counts the frequency of each byte on a column basis and marks that column as compressible if the distribution appears to be non-random. Once these columns are identified, any general purpose compressor may be used, but ISOBAR automatically chooses the best one by user preference (compression ratio vs. speed).

2.2 ADIOS

High-performance computing applications leverage I/O libraries like HDF5 (Hierarchical Data Format), ADIOS (Adaptable I/O System), and PnetCDF (Parallel Network Common Data Form) that allow scientists to easily describe the data that needs to be written out and analyzed. These I/O libraries provide an enhanced I/O performance, by efficiently handling synchronization, and meta-data generation during shared-file writes. We choose to incorporate ADIOS for this paper, since it has been shown to deliver performance improvements of up to 300% at scale [24, 27] on the Cray Jaguar leadership-class computing facilities at ORNL.

ADIOS essentially provides an efficient componentization of the HPC I/O stack. Through an XML file, it provides the option to describe the data, and to choose the optimal transport methods like POSIX and MPI-IO without the need to recompile the application codes. The data written using ADIOS is in the form of a native BP (Binary Packed) file, comprising of "process groups," which are variables described in XML configuration, usually tagged according to their functionality. For example, checkpoint and restart data is written under a single process group, as is analysis data.

3. HYBRID COMPRESSION-I/O FOR DATA STAGING ARCHITECTURES

The prevailing I/O strategy in current peta-scale systems is to offload the burden of I/O to dedicated *staging nodes*, as shown in Figure 1. This allows minimal idle time on the compute nodes allocated for the simulation, as the I/O nodes handle the rate-limiting disk writes and reads collectively and network bandwidth is an order of magnitude faster than disk bandwidth. However, given the trend of ever-increasing simulation data sizes, combined with the need to checkpoint simulation state to minimize data loss in the face of node failure, the I/O offloading approach alone cannot keep up with the computational throughput available.

3.1 Method

A promising approach to aid in mitigating this problem is

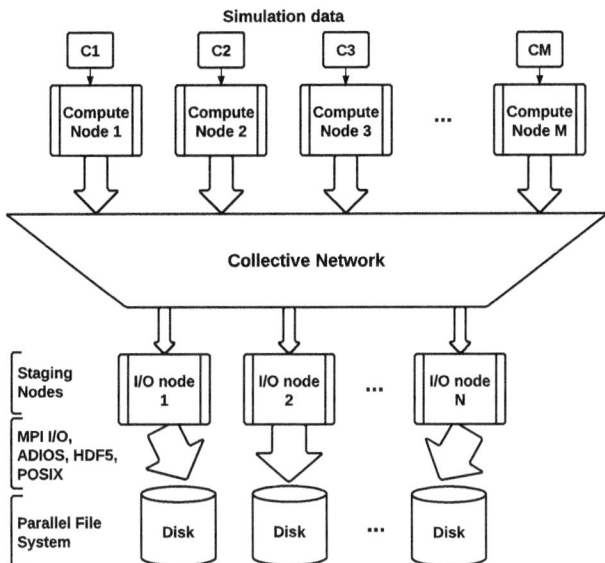

Figure 1: A peta-scale computing system with staging environment.

to write compressed data to the disk [36]. This reduces the aggregate amount of data to be written, which can alleviate the I/O bottleneck to some extent. However, there are a number of technical challenges in utilizing compression in the scientific computing environment. Most state-of-the-art compression algorithms do not provide enough compression throughput to justify the data reduction, and those that do sacrifice the compression ratio. Moreover, the target simulation data is notoriously "hard-to-compress;" traditional compression algorithms provide meager compression ratios [30]. In addition, compression brings up the non-trivial issue of managing the writes of variable sized chunks of data. This mandates a strategy to efficiently handle disk I/O, taking into account appropriate data organization and writer node synchronization while also keeping the overhead imposed by the associated metadata in check.

Current state-of-the art I/O frameworks such as ADIOS and HDF5 have no capability to compress and store simulation data when performing parallel writes to a parallel filesystem. In this work, we utilize the data staging model, based on the ISOBAR technology, to write and simultaneously compress simulation data. In addition to using the data staging paradigm, interleaving compression and I/O can also be directly integrated into I/O frameworks. ISOBAR was introduced as a high-throughput compressor built specifically for hard-to-compress datasets [30]. Especially important is the fact that we can use ISOBAR to produce multiple streams of data that, once defined by the analysis portion of ISOBAR, can be operated on independently. This presents the perfect opportunity to hide the compression costs by asynchronously writing streams (the incompressible byte streams) while operating on the remaining streams (compressing the compressible byte streams). We call this the *hybrid compression-I/O* approach. The interleaving of compression and I/O helps to hide the compression costs, while the reduction in data size reduces disk costs.

Figure 2 illustrates our generic hybrid approach. ISOBAR partitions the data into two streams: compressible and incompressible bytes, and incorporates a small, constant-sized

metadata block to each (containing the buffer size and the analysis array, a bitfield of marking which bytes are compressible). The compressible stream is compressed and then written to disk, while the incompressible stream can be immediately written to disk. There is no dependency between the two streams, so we may choose to order the operations how we wish. Thus, we issue an asynchronous write of the incompressible stream, then begin compressing the compressible stream. Finally, we write the compressible stream. This strategy has numerous benefits: we maximize resource utilization by performing network and I/O operations while compressing, and since compression throughput tends to be much higher than I/O bandwidth, it is possible to eliminate the compression costs entirely.

There are roughly two possible performance scenarios of interleaving, based on the individual performance of compression and file writing, shown in Figure 3. The worst case occurs when the uncompressed data is written before the remainder of the data is compressed. This is depicted in Figure 3a. In this scenario, the compression time is the bottleneck, and so is only partially hidden by the writing of the incompressible data to disk. However, this case generally occurs when most of the data is deemed compressible, in which case the increased compression cost directly translates into substantial data reduction; thus, overall time-to-disk is still reduced due to a higher compression ratio.

The second scenario shown in Figure 3b occurs if data compression finishes before the incompressible data has been fully written, and must wait to write the compressed data stream. In this scenario, compression time is completely hidden, and can be considered a "free" operation with respect to time. Also, the idle time can be used for other activities, such as running ISOBAR-analysis on another chunk if available. A related scenario to this is when data compression and incompressible data writing finish at approximately the same time resulting in full utilization of all resources. This case also completely hides the compression costs.

3.2 Data Layout in ADIOS

The layout of our compressed and uncompressed data on disk is managed by ADIOS's self-describing file format (.bp), which is specifically designed to attain scalable high performance I/O, to support delayed consistency and data characterization, and to maintain compatibility with standard file formats. Also, since this file format is log-based [27], new data can be appended without incurring any additional overhead, irrespective of the number of processes or timesteps. As a result, the performance improvements we report using our hybrid framework over a single timestep can be maintained over multiple timesteps.

For our system, we define two ADIOS groups (or "data containers"): one for the compressed data, and one for the uncompressed data. Every writing process submits data to each of the two groups. Depending on the transport method chosen in the configuration file, ADIOS can store data from all the writing processes into a single shared file using collective MPI-IO or multiple files using POSIX I/O with a separate file handle for each writing process. Fast access to data for a specific process or timestep is supported via footer indexes that avoid the known limitation of header-based formats [29], where any change to the length of the file data requires moving the index.

Figure 4 shows the ADIOS data layout specific to our ap-

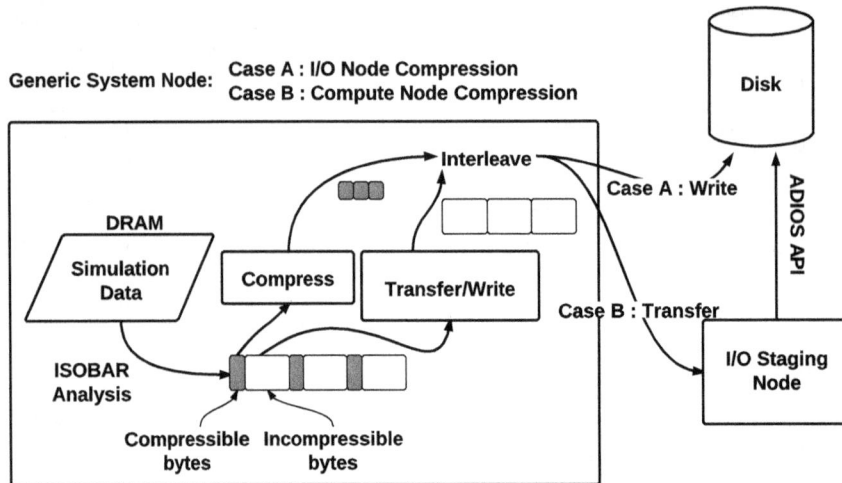

Figure 2: The hybrid compression-I/O method; interleaved compression may occur at the compute nodes or the I/O nodes.

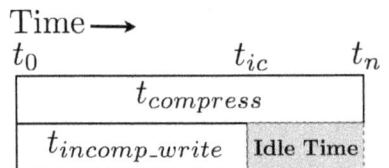

(a) Compression is the rate limiting factor.

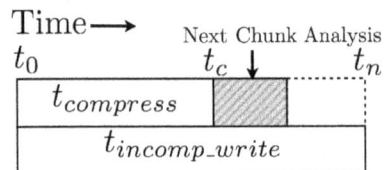

(b) Compression interleaving results in free time usable for the analysis of the next chunk.

Figure 3: Possible scenarios for compression and incompressible data write times.

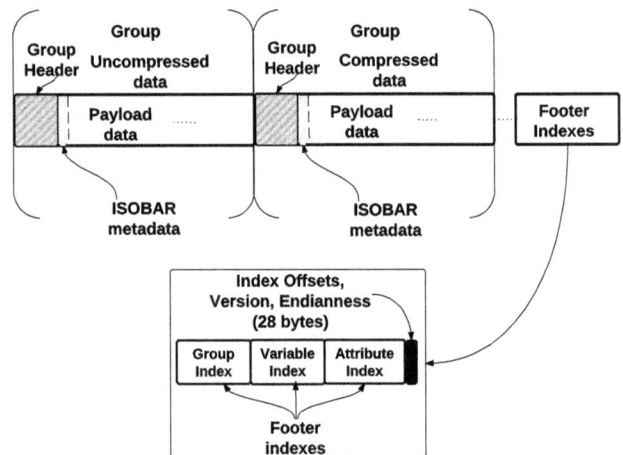

Figure 4: Data layout (with associated metadata) for a single timestep.

Table 1: Average metadata overhead for different interleaving strategies.

Test Case	Average Metadata Overhead (%)			
	ISOBAR		ADIOS	
	POSIX	MPI	POSIX	MPI
Base	0.00002	0.00002	0.00321	0.00148
ISOBAR at I/O nodes	0.00004	0.00004	0.00902	0.00417
ISOBAR at compute nodes	0.00007	0.00007	0.00978	0.00471
Serial ISOBAR	0.00004	0.00004	0.00806	0.00358

plication for a single timestep. ADIOS handles the data organization among groups via local group headers and indexes. The ISOBAR metadata is stored first within each group, followed by the payload data. The metadata size is dependent on the ADIOS system configuration, the chunk size, and the compute-I/O node ratio. The relative ordering of groups is arbitrary, dependent on the order in which the processes submit data and on synchronization among them (via a coordination token) [23]. The global footer indexes shown are used for query-driven data retrieval (accessing a specific timestep or process output). In this work, we confine our focus to data layout for the write-all/read-all paradigm, which is ubiquitous in HPC computing, especially in checkpoint and restart operations. From the standpoint of future work, however, our framework can be adapted for the WORM paradigm by leveraging previous work [13] to optimize the data layout on disk. In addition, support for compression schemes [19, 18, 17] which offer up to 7 times reduction in datasizes can be extended. Together, these possibilitie provide avenues for increasing throughput gains whilst maintaining read performance.

The metadata required to support this format is very small, requiring less than 0.01% overhead in the worst case, as summarized in Table 1. If applied to 1 GB of data, this translates into less than 100 KB of overhead. As shown in the table, the metadata can be split into two categories: that maintained specifically for ISOBAR, and that required by ADIOS. The exact amount of metadata is dependent on the transport method used (POSIX or MPI-IO) as well as the location of the compressor (compute node or I/O node). The overhead is minimal in the base case (no compression), as expected, and maximal when compressing at the compute nodes, which generates the most individual streams of data. The metadata cost is also higher for the POSIX transport method, since this allocates one file per writing process, as opposed to the single shared file maintained by MPI-IO.

4. PERFORMANCE MODELING

While we demonstrate that our hybrid compression-I/O methodology provides improved I/O performance in one testing environment, there are many supercomputing systems, each with widely-varying performance characteristics. Since our optimization algorithms exhibit a strong dependence on hardware parameters, it is important to devise an accurate performance model, so that we can generalize the results collected in Section 5 to other systems. This will enable application designers to estimate the benefit of compression given their particular hardware configuration, problem characteristics, etc. We therefore develop such a performance model, which we then validate against empirical data, as reported in Section 5.4.

4.1 Model Preliminaries

Given our target cluster architecture, we make some underlying assumptions in our model. We assume a fixed compute node to I/O node ratio, ρ, consistent with the majority of I/O staging frameworks currently in use. Furthermore, on each compute node, we assume fixed-size input *chunks* of size (C), which are all written following the bulk-synchronous parallel I/O model. This is a common mode of operation when writing checkpoint and restart data, which synchronously flushes the simulation state to file, then continues with the simulation. We also assume that the I/O staging framework (e.g., ADIOS) and the network architecture provide a relatively consistent I/O and transfer rate, respectively. As shown in numerous experiments with ADIOS [22, 23], this is a reasonable assumption to make. Finally, we require some *a priori* information about the compression performance in order to accurately predict overall system performance. Fortunately, this can be gathered easily by running the ISOBAR analysis stage on a small, representative set of data to predict overall performance [30].

To provide a complete model, there are three cases of writing from compute nodes to disk that we wish to consider for comparative purposes. The first is when no compression is performed, and data is written directly to disk (through the I/O nodes). This forms our base case to compare the other compression methods against, and allows us to check the sanity of our model before looking at the more complex compression models. The remaining cases use ISOBAR interleaved compression, but in different locations. The second case compresses at the compute-node level. If time-to-disk is our sole optimization metric, then we expect the second method of compute-node compression to perform best, exhibiting the greatest aggregate compression throughput due to the large number of compute cores utilized (by constrast, compressing at the I/O nodes yields less aggregate compression throughput by a factor of ρ, which is 8 in our experiments, but can be much higher). Our third and final case is compressing at the I/O-node level. This case is important as future staging architectures shift toward dedicating compute nodes strictly to simulation work [21], relying on

asynchronous RDMA to offload data to I/O nodes and prevent simulation stalls.

Table 2: Input symbols for the performance models.

Input Symbol	Description
C	The chunk size
ρ	Compute to I/O node ratio
θ	Throughput of the collective network between the compute and I/O nodes
δ	Size of the metadata
μ_r	Throughput of the disk reads
μ_w	Throughput of the disk writes
α	Fraction of the chunk that is compressible
σ	Compression ratio (compressed vs original)
T_{prec}	Throughput of the ISOBAR preconditioner
T_{comp}	Compression throughput
T_{decomp}	Decompression throughput

Table 3: Output symbols for the performance models.

Output Symbol	Description
t_{prec}	Time to run the ISOBAR preconditioner on the data
$t_{compress}$	Time to compress the data (algorithm dependent)
$t_{transfer}$	Total transfer time [1]
$t_{comp\_transfer}$	Transfer time for compressible data [1]
$t_{incomp\_transfer}$	Transfer time for incompressible data [1]
t_{write}	Time to write data to the disk
t_{comp_write}	Time to write compressible data to the disk
t_{incomp_write}	Time to write incompressible data to the disk
t_{write_depend}	Time for all the dependencies to complete before writing the compressible byte stream
$t_{decompress}$	Time to decompress the data (algorithm dependent)
t_{incomp_read}	Time to read the incompressible data from the disk
t_{comp_read}	Time to read the compressible data from the disk
$t_{combine}$	Time to reconstruct data from compressible and incompressible portions
$t_{combine\_depend}$	Time until all data is ready to be recombined into the original chunk
t_{comp_ion}	Intermediate processing time for handling compressible data at I/O nodes
t_{incomp_cn}	Itermediate processing time for handling incompressible data at compute nodes
t_{total}	Total end-to-end data transfer time
τ	Aggregate throughput

[1]Interpretation of transfer direction based on context of usage i.e., compute to I/O for writes and I/O to compute for reads.

In this work, we refer to the I/O node as a staging node on the system that receives the data from the compute nodes and sends it to the OSS (Object Storage Servers), which manage writing of the data to the Lustre File System. We do not operate at these file system nodes.

We will build the models in increasing order of complexity: the base case of no compression, compression at the I/O nodes, and compression at the compute nodes. Tables 2 and 3 summarize the symbols for parameters and output variables used in the model. In all scenarios, the aggregate throughput τ is given by

$$\tau = \frac{\rho \cdot C}{t_{total}}, \tag{1}$$

where ρ is the number of compute nodes and C is the chunk size.

4.2 Base Case: No Compression

In this scenario, we simply transfer the simulation data from the compute nodes to the I/O nodes ($t_{transfer}$), followed by writing the data to file (t_{write}), in a synchronous manner. The end-to-end transfer time for a chunk of data from the compute nodes to the disk ($t_{total} = t_{transfer} + t_{write}$) is similarly simple, given our assumptions on aggregate network and disk bandwidths:

$$t_{transfer} = \frac{C}{\theta} + \frac{C \cdot \rho}{\theta} \tag{2}$$

$$t_{write} = \frac{C \cdot \rho}{\mu_w} \tag{3}$$

$$t_{total} = \frac{C}{\theta}(1 + \rho) + \frac{C}{\mu_w}\rho \tag{4}$$

To reload the data from disk, the same operations occur in reverse, except with read throughputs instead of write throughputs.

4.3 I/O Node Compression Case

An overview of the compression-I/O workflow is shown in Figure 5. The I/O nodes implement the ISOBAR preconditioner and interleave the disk writes of the incompressible byte-columns with compression.

The compute nodes merely forward the raw data to the I/O nodes. In our design, we issue the I/O operation for the incompressible bytes asynchronously, allowing us to concurrently perform compression. Thus, the writing of the compressed data waits (if necessary) on the incompressible stream writing to complete. This can be captured more intuitively with the task dependency graph shown in Figure 6. Each vertex represents a task and directed edges represent task dependencies. If each edge is weighted to be the completion time of the originating task, then the longest path from the head vertex to the tail vertex, also known as the *critical path*, gives the overall run time of the interleaved process. Using this diagram, we can capture the overall runtime in a single equation. First, we define the cost of each individual task.

The total preconditioning time in this case is ρ times the preconditioning time of a single chunk. Moreover, the partitioning has to be handled by the I/O node. The partitioning throughput is approximately equal to the preconditioner throughput. Thus, the total preconditioning time is given

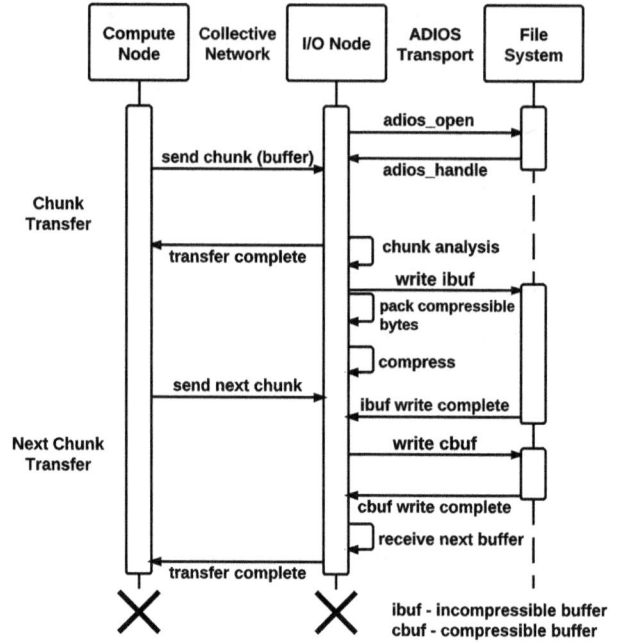

Figure 5: Compute-I/O interleaving strategy with compression at the I/O nodes.

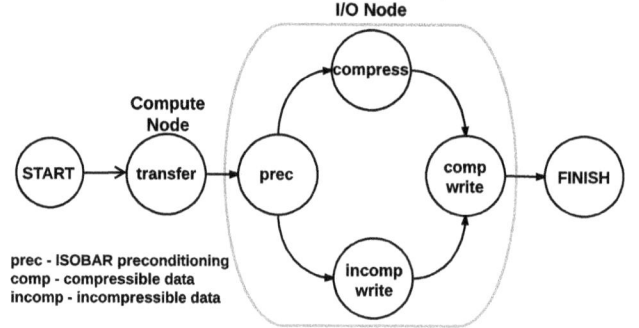

Figure 6: Task dependencies for the I/O node compression case.

by:

$$t_{prec} = 2\left(\frac{\rho C}{T_{prec}}\right) \tag{5}$$

$$t_{compress} = \frac{\rho \alpha C}{T_{comp}} \tag{6}$$

$$t_{incomp\_write} = \frac{\rho(1 - \alpha)C}{\mu_w} \tag{7}$$

$$t_{comp\_write} = \frac{(\alpha \sigma C + \delta)\rho}{\mu_w} \tag{8}$$

Looking at Figure 6, we see that incompressible write (t_{incomp_write}) and compression ($t_{compress}$) are interleaved. Thus, the length of the critical path, and therefore the overall writing time, can be calculated as

$$\begin{aligned} t_{total} &= t_{transfer} + t_{prec} \\ &+ \max(t_{compress}, t_{incomp\_write}) \\ &+ t_{comp\_write}. \end{aligned} \tag{9}$$

66

The reading stage of restoring the chunks into memory from disk requires the dependency graph to be inverted (that is, each directed edge reversed). This maintains the interleaving property of decompression and reading of incompressible byte-columns. The preconditioner task is replaced with reconstruction, which reorders the decompressed byte streams and the incompressible byte stream to their original locations in memory. The overall reading time can be calculated as

$$
\begin{aligned}
t_{total} = {} & t_{comp\_read} \\
& + \max(t_{decompress}, t_{incomp\_read}) \\
& + t_{combine} + t_{transfer}.
\end{aligned} \tag{10}
$$

4.4 Compute Node Compression Case

The integration of ISOBAR into the compute nodes is a more nuanced task. Figure 7 shows the general workflow of the interleaved compression and network-I/O, and Figure 8 shows the corresponding task-dependency graph for this scenario.

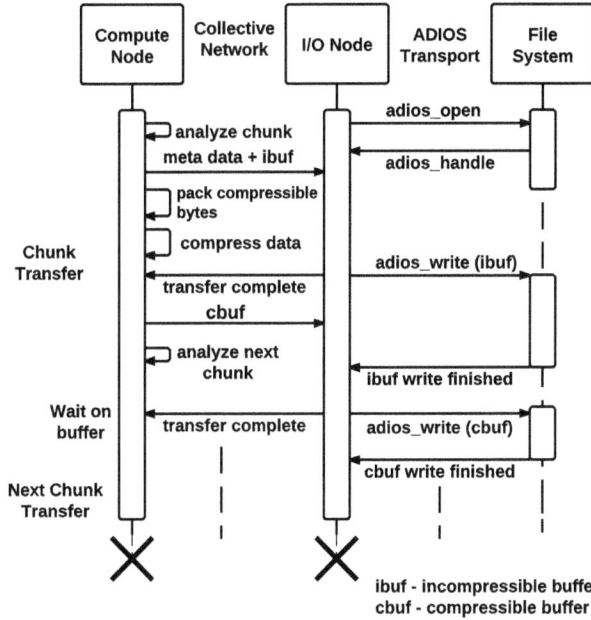

Figure 7: Compute-I/O interleaving strategy with compression at the compute nodes.

After the preconditioner is run, the incompressible byte-columns are sent asynchronously while the remaining byte-columns are compressed. Once the incompressible byte-columns are sent, the I/O nodes may immediately issue its asynchronous writing operation. Once the compression is complete, the compressed stream must wait for the incompressible network transfer to complete (if necessary) to transfer its results. Finally, once the incompressible bytes are written to disk, the compressed stream may be written.

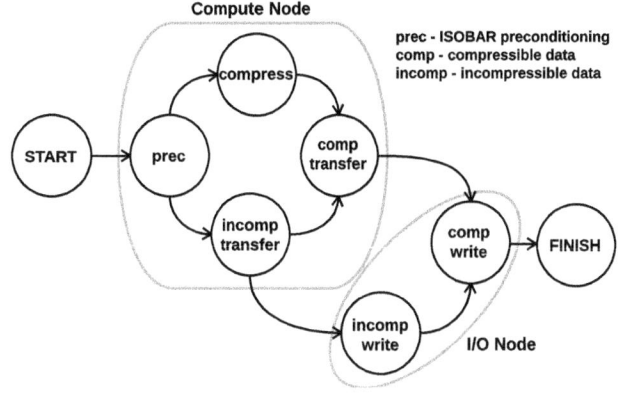

Figure 8: Task dependencies for the compute node compression case.

Individually, these operations are modeled as:

$$t_{prec} = \frac{C}{T_{prec}} \tag{11}$$

$$t_{incomp\_transfer} = \frac{(1-\alpha)C}{\theta}(1+\rho) \tag{12}$$

$$t_{incomp\_write} = \frac{(1-\alpha)C}{\mu_w}\rho \tag{13}$$

$$t_{compress} = \frac{\alpha C}{T_{comp}} \tag{14}$$

$$t_{comp\_transfer} = \frac{(\alpha\sigma C + \delta)}{\theta}(1+\rho) \tag{15}$$

$$t_{comp\_write} = \frac{(\alpha\sigma C + \delta)}{\mu_w}\rho \tag{16}$$

As discussed in Section 3 and seen in the dependency graph in Figure 8, interleaving is achieved through the compression and transfer/writing of network data. Additionally, there may be interleaving of the transfer of compressed byte-columns and the incompressible byte writing. Thankfully, given the structure of the graph and the residence of the tasks on different nodes, we may define the critical path using the following two quantities:

$$
\begin{aligned}
t_{comp\_ion} = {} & \max(t_{compress}, t_{incomp\_transfer}) \\
& + t_{comp\_transfer}
\end{aligned} \tag{17}
$$

$$
\begin{aligned}
t_{write\_depend} = {} & \max(t_{comp\_ion}, \\
& t_{incomp\_transfer} + t_{incomp\_write})
\end{aligned} \tag{18}
$$

t_{comp_ion} represents the time taken to compress and send the compressible byte-columns to the I/O nodes, accounting for stalls caused by a longer incompressible byte-column transfer. t_{write_depend} represents the time taken for all dependencies to clear before writing the compressible byte stream, including possible stalls at the second network-I/O interleaving level. Adding in the preconditioner and the compressible byte-column writing, the total time-to-disk can be defined as follows:

$$t_{total} = t_{prec} + t_{write\_depend} + t_{comp\_write} \tag{19}$$

Once again, the reading of hybrid-compressed data chunks causes an inversion of the dependency graph, except that write operations are replaced with read operations, the transfers are reversed, the compressed byte-columns are decompressed, and the preconditioner task is replaced with the reconstruction task. In fact, in this particular instance, the inverted task graph is isomorphic to the original task graph, thus simplifying building the read model. The compressible byte-columns are read and then asynchronously sent to the compute nodes while the incompressible byte-columns are read. Afterwards, the incompressible byte-columns are transferred asynchronously while the decompression process begins. Finally, the compressible and incompressible columns are recombined. This is captured in the following model:

$$t_{comp\_read} = \frac{(\alpha \sigma C + \delta)\rho}{\mu_r} \qquad (20)$$

$$t_{comp\_transfer} = \frac{\alpha \sigma C + \delta}{\theta} \qquad (21)$$

$$t_{decompress} = \frac{\alpha \sigma C}{T_{decomp}} \qquad (22)$$

$$t_{incomp\_read} = \frac{(1-\alpha)C\rho}{\mu_r} \qquad (23)$$

$$t_{incomp\_transfer} = \frac{(1-\alpha)C}{\theta} \qquad (24)$$

The reconstruction time is assumed to be constant for fixed sized data chunks. Similar to the write case, the critical paths are defined as follows:

$$t_{incomp\_cn} = \max(t_{incomp\_read}, t_{comp\_transfer})$$
$$+ \; t_{incomp\_transfer} \qquad (25)$$

$$t_{combine\_depend} = \max(t_{incomp\_cn},$$
$$t_{comp\_transfer} + t_{decompress}), \qquad (26)$$

where t_{incomp_cn} represents the time taken for the incompressible byte stream to reach the compute nodes, taking into account stalls as a result of the compressible byte stream being sent first, and $t_{combine\_depend}$ represents the time until all data is ready to be recombined into the original chunk of data. Thus, the total time to restore the data to its original state is

$$t_{total} = t_{comp\_read} + t_{combine\_depend} + t_{combine}. \qquad (27)$$

5. EXPERIMENTS AND RESULTS

In this section, we present the empirical evaluations of our framework via a set of microbenchmarks to evaluate the throughput performance for the writes as well as the reads. We report the percentage improvement in performance obtained using the hybrid compression-I/O framework (at the compute as well as the I/O nodes) over the base case without compression. We also report theoretical evaluations for the interleaving strategies discussed in Section 4 via performance model simulations. Lastly, we specify the parameters used for the simulations and present a comparison between the predicted and actual system performance.

5.1 Experimental Setup

Our experiments were conducted on the Cray XK6 Jaguar cluster at the Oak Ridge Leadership Computing Facility (OCLF). It consists of $18,688$ compute systems, each containing a 16-core 2.2 GHz AMD Opteron 6724 processor and 32 GB of RAM. It uses the Lustre [31] file system for parallel I/O and a high performance Gemini interconnect for communication. The compute-I/O node ratio for all experiments is kept fixed at $8 : 1$. The definitive choice of a single optimal ratio is non-trivial, since it depends on the size of

the data being moved, the degree of inter-node communication, as well as the memory requirement of the staging nodes. The study in this realm is the subject of future work.

We evaluated the system characteristics using a set of micro-benchmarks to measure the network and disk I/O throughputs. The aggregate network throughput for our experiment cases was measured to be 530 MB/s on an average, while the read and write throughputs were measured to be 62.6 MB/s and 15.6 MB/s per node, respectively. It should be noted that for all our experiments, we refer to the term "node" as a processing core on the Jaguar system.

We use the `gts_chkp_zion`, `flash_velx` and `s3d_temp` datasets discussed in [11, 9, 30, 33] for our analyses. The datasets are chosen so as to reflect the entire compressibility spectrum across a range of scientific datasets. The GTS dataset consists of about 2.4 million double precision values of the zion variable's checkpoint and restart data for each 10th timestep of the GTS simulation. It consists of entirely unique values. It has a high degree of apparent randomness and is one of the most "hard-to-compress" scientific dataset. Note that this is only *apparent* randomness; in reality, the dataset contains patterns that are non-trivial to isolate, preventing general-purpose compressors from leveraging them.

The FLASH dataset consists of about 68.1 million double precision values of the velocity variable with entirely unique values. It is also hard-to-compress and exhibits compressibility characteristics similar to most scientific datasets discussed in [30]. Therefore, it is a good representative for a large number of scientific datasets under consideration.

The S3D dataset, on the other hand, consists of about 20.2 million double precision values of the temperature variable with 46% unique values. It is relatively less hard-to-compress in comparision with the other two datasets.

The ISOBAR framework supports the use of any general purpose byte-level compression algorithm. However, for our evaluations, we use `zlib` [12], designed by Jean-loup Gailly and Mark Adler. It is a lossless compression /decompression algorithm that uses an LZ77 algorithm variant to compress the data in a block sequence. In addition to scoring high marks in general-purpose compression rate and compression throughput, the memory usage of `zlib` is independent of any input data.

In addition to the three interleaving strategies discussed in Section 4, we also include a serial compression case for completeness sake, wherein we apply ISOBAR compression serially, i.e., we do not interleave compressible and incompressible data processing. This is essentially an extension of the base case, allowing us to directly evaluate the impact of interleaving.

5.2 Write Performance

Figure 9 shows the results gathered from write micro-benchmarks. For each dataset, the results are reported in terms of the percent improvement in the write throughput relative to the base case, measured for each of the four scenarios (i.e. the base case, interleaving at compute nodes, and interleaving at I/O nodes, and the serial compression), versus the number of compute nodes.

We observe that both interleaved approaches (compute node and I/O node compression) yield an improvement in performance over state-of-the-art I/O middleware framework without compression (the base case). As expected, interleaving using compute node compression results in the highest

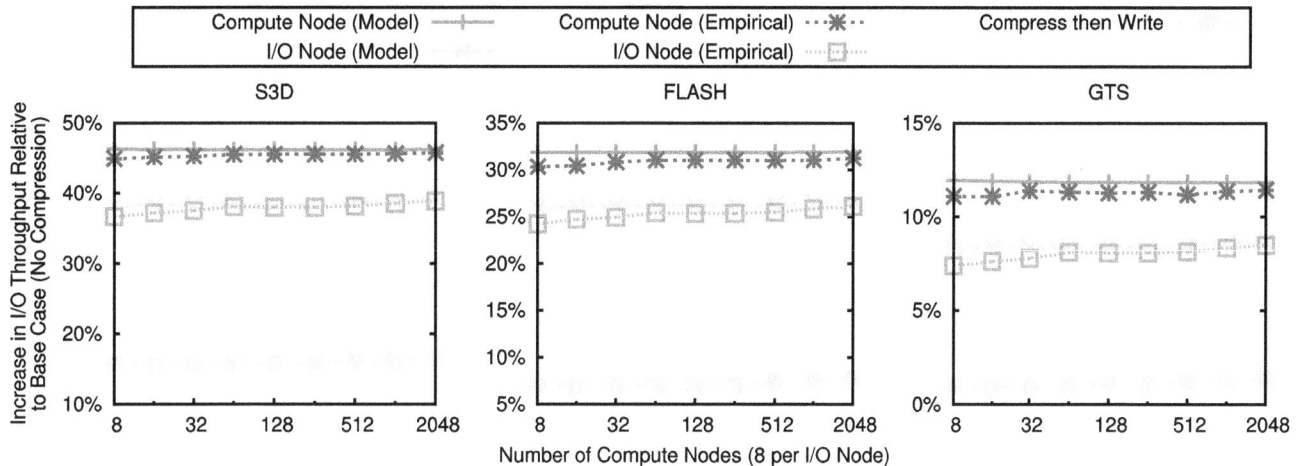

Figure 9: Model and empirical end-to-end write throughput versus number of compute nodes (weak scaling).

performance gain, from around 12% over the base case for the GTS dataset and to as high as 46% over the base case for the S3D dataset. Improvements for the FLASH dataset are 31% over the base case. On the other hand, interleaving using I/O node compression yields improvements in the range of about 8% for the GTS dataset, 37% for the S3D dataset, and 25% for the FLASH dataset. Using ISOBAR serially yields a modest 1% (GTS) to 16% (S3D) gain in throughput performance, suggesting that a significant portion of the performance boost comes from our compression-I/O interleaving strategy, affirming the efficacy of this approach.

The experiments are conducted with weak scaling up to 2048 nodes on the Jaguar system. The stability of the results over a varying number of cores suggests that the framework is, indeed, scalable.

5.3 Read Performance

We carried out equivalent read micro-benchmark tests on the disk data, evaluating the base case (without decompression) and each of the two interleaved decompression strategies (decompression at the compute nodes and at the I/O nodes).

The experimentation results of the read microbenchmarks are shown in Figure 10 in the form of percent improvements over the base case (i.e., direct reads without decompression). Both the interleaved approaches for the reads exhibit performance gains of the same order as reported for the writes for all the datasets. This suggests that the hybrid framework is symmetric with respect to reads as well as writes.

In order to support asynchronous processing of the compressible and incompressible portions of the data for the interleaved scenarios, we used a separate file per ADIOS group. The reason for this is that ADIOS currently reads data from all the groups upfront when using a single file and this operation is inherently blocking, i.e., a request for the read of only the compressed buffer requires the entire data to be read. The two-file-approach does not affect the write performance.

5.4 Performance Modeling

The performance models for evaluation were setup to use the following parameter values. The compute-I/O node ratio was chosen as $\rho = 8 : 1$. Compression efficiency is

sensitive to the chunk size for most lossless compression techniques that adapt based on calculated statistics of the subject data [35, 15]. We chose a chunk size $C = 3$ MB taking into account the sensitivity of most lossless compression techniques to the input chunk size [35]. The ISOBAR preconditioner operates at an approximate throughput of $T_{prec} = 500$ MB/s. Other ISOBAR specific parameters were chosen based on the statistical analyses of 24 different scientific datasets [30], 19 of which were "hard-to-compress." The average values of these parameters based on the application type (i.e., α, σ, T_{comp}, T_{decomp} from Table 2) are shown in Table 4.

The predicted performance for the data writes and reads for all the test scenarios and evaluation datasets are shown in Figure 9 and 10, respectively. It is evident that the theoretical performance improvements are generally consistent with the empirical results. Though some small overestimating bias is visible, it is itself relatively consistent, and can therefore be readily factored out (as has been done in Table 4). Additionally, the fact that the trends exhibited by the model predictions are equivalent to those of the measured results points to a mismeasured system parameter as the likely culprit for the minor discrepency that exists. Thus, the performance model can be used to closely approximate the true behavior of the system.

In addition, we also performed theoretical evaluations of our framework on other scientific datasets from various application domains. These include the MSG [7], OBS [7], and NUM [8, 28] datasets, all of which normally produce a reasonable amount of data per process. The results for the best strategy (interleaving at the compute nodes) for reads as well as writes are shown in the Table 4.

We observe that the expected theoretical performance gains for these more typical datasets are as high as 32%, even after accounting for the observed model bias. This shows that our framework improves significantly on less harder to compress datasets and that the performance gains are directly proportional to the compression ratio of datasets.

6. RELATED WORK

The ISOBAR hybrid compression framework utilizes the the I/O forwarding paradigm [3], which is a common tech-

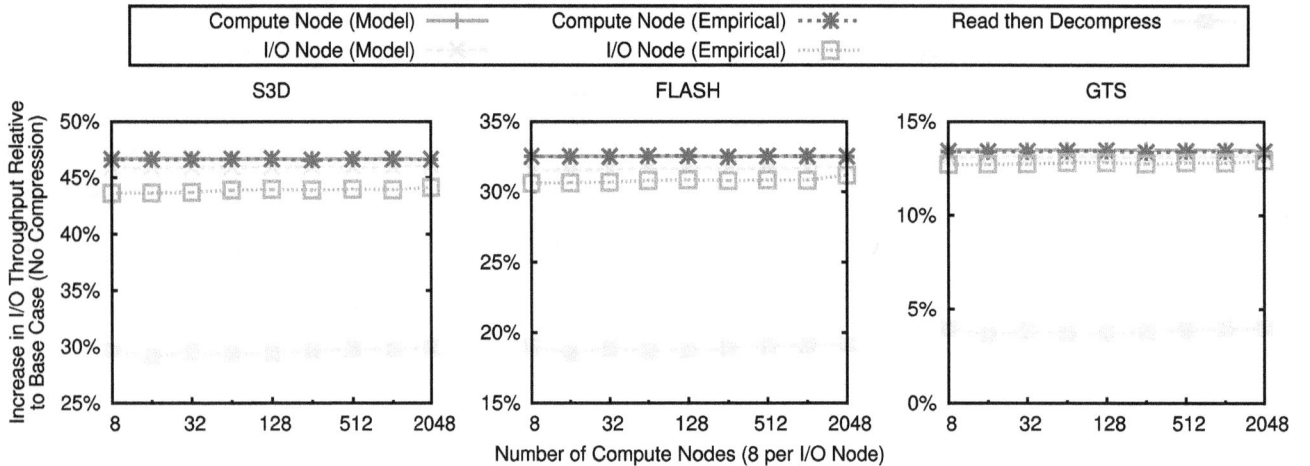

Figure 10: Model and empirical end-to-end read throughput versus number of compute nodes (weak scaling).

nique for alleviating the I/O bottleneck in super-computing environments, and is the subject of active research. The multithreaded ZOID architecture [16], developed under the ZeptoOS [4] project on the IBM BlueGene/P, is a state-of-the-art data staging system. LambdaRAM [32] is an asynchronous data staging system which mitigates WAN latency via dedicated staging nodes. IODC [26] is a portable MPI-IO layer implementing a caching framework wherein certain tasks, such as file caching, consistency control, and collective I/O optimization, are delegated to a small set of I/O Delegate nodes. Recent work in ADIOS includes the DataStager component [2], which focuses on I/O performance through data staging via network rate limiting and I/O phase prediction, and JITStaging [1], which provides a framework for placing data filter, analysis and organization code in the data pipeline to reduce overall time-to-data.

SCR [6] and PLFS [5] are well-known middleware approaches designed specifically for single (N-N) and shared (N-1) checkpointing, respectively. While SCR provides efficient checkpoints and improves system reliability by shifting checkpoint I/O workload to hardware better suited for the job, it is not suitable for applications that need process-global access to checkpoint files. Moreover, hardware and file system support is required to cache checkpoint files. PLFS, on the other hand, transparently rearranges shared checkpoint patterns into single patterns, thereby decreasing the checkpoint time by taking advantage of the increased bandwidth. However, this requires managing the overwhelming pressure resulting from the simultaneous creation of thousands of files within a single directory. Also, since PLFS is specifically a checkpoint file system and not a general purpose file system, certain usage patterns may suffer a significant performance hit [5].

Our approach differs in that we focus on optimizing data staging I/O throughput via compression and resource interleaving. Some recent work has examined compression in a data staging context [36]; however, only traditional compression algorithms are explored, which do not function well on the hard-to-compress scientific data we consider, and resource interleaving is not used to hide the compression and I/O synchronization costs.

Previous work on data deduplication can also be considered a form of compression, detecting and eliminating duplication in data with a goal to improving disk utilization. State-of-the-art deduplication systems include HYDRAstor [10], MAD2 [34], and others [14]. Deduplication can operate at either sub-file or whole-file scale; the relative merits of these aproaches have been explored [25]. Although these systems are scalable, provide a good deduplication efficiency, and attain near-optimal throughput for common filesystem data, they are unfortunately less effective when dealing with peta-scale scientific data. Unlike typical file system data, scientific data exhibits very few duplicate non-contiguous patterns, nullifying much of the effectiveness of the deduplication approach. Furthermore, the possibility of running compression *in-situ* remains desirable for performance reasons, which is not possible with filesystem-bound algorithms such as deduplication.

Table 4: Dataset evaluations for the best strategy of interleaving at the compute nodes.

Application	α	σ	T_{comp}	T_{decomp}	Avg. write gain (%)*	Avg. read gain (%)*
GTS [†]	0.25	0.527	90	414	11.26	13.40
FLASH [†]	0.25	0.019	149	127	30.87	32.53
S3D [†]	0.375	0.152	186	457	45.43	46.64
MSG	0.375	0.361	140	560	31.61	31.84
OBS	0.25	0.203	43	172	24.55	24.99
NUM	0.25	0.231	163	652	23.51	23.93

[†]Validated by experimental results.   *Adjusted for model bias.

7. CONCLUSION

The I/O staging paradigm has arisen to cope with the growing gap between computing power and I/O bandwidth in current peta-scale HPC environments. While providing increased and more consistent performance, the sheer scale of the data necessitates lossless compression as a data reduction methodology, leaving the technical challenge of absorbing the costs of compression and overhead in parallel I/O performance on nonuniform chunk sizes.

To meet these challenges, we presented the ISOBAR hybrid compression-I/O framework. The ISOBAR preconditioner allows us to separate the high-entropy components of the data from the low-entropy components, forming independent streams that may be interleaved. The high-entropy components are sent across the network and to disk asynchronously while the low-entropy data is compressed, hiding the compression costs and fully utilizing all compute, network, and I/O resources. Placement of the compression routine itself is an important issue, so we implement a hybrid approach where the compression phase may be placed either on the compute nodes or the I/O nodes, trading off between aggregate compression throughput and leaving the compute nodes free to run the application at hand. Finally, each of the implementations are accurately modeled by a set of performance metrics, allowing a generalization of our methodology's performance past the experimental environment.

We demonstrated the efficiency of compression-I/O interleaving, improving end-to-end I/O throughput by predicted values ranging from 12 to 46% on datasets that are considered particularly hard-to-compress. We therefore believe that data compression can be used effectively within an HPC environment to help bridge the computational and I/O performance gap.

8. ACKNOWLEDGEMENTS

We would like to thank ORNL's and ANL's leadership class computing facilities, OLCF and ALCF respectively, for the use of their resources. We would also like to acknowledge the use of those scientific data sets at Flash Center for Computational Science. This work was supported in part by the U.S. Department of Energy, Office of Science and the U.S. National Science Foundation (Expeditions in Computing). Oak Ridge National Laboratory is managed by UT-Battelle for the LLC U.S. D.O.E. under contract no. DEAC05-00OR22725

9. REFERENCES

[1] H. Abbasi, G. Eisenhauer, M. Wolf, K. Schwan, and S. Klasky. Just in time: Adding value to the IO pipelines of high performance applications with JITStaging. In *Proceedings of the 20th International Symposium on High Performance Distributed Computing*, HPDC '11, pages 27–36. ACM, 2011.

[2] H. Abbasi, M. Wolf, G. Eisenhauer, S. Klasky, K. Schwan, and F. Zheng. DataStager: Scalable data staging services for petascale applications. In *Proceedings of the 18th International Symposium on High Performance Distributed Computing*, HPDC '09, pages 39–48. ACM, 2009.

[3] N. Ali, P. Carns, K. Iskra, D. Kimpe, S. Lang, R. Latham, R. Ross, L. Ward, and P. Sadayappan. Scalable I/O forwarding framework for high-performance computing systems. In *International Conference on Cluster Computing and Workshops*, CLUSTER '09, pages 1–10. IEEE, 2009.

[4] P. Beckman, K. Iskra, K. Yoshii, and H. Naik. The ZeptoOS project. http://www.zeptoos.org/.

[5] J. Bent, G. Gibson, G. Grider, B. McClelland, P. Nowoczynski, J. Nunez, M. Polte, and M. Wingate. PLFS: a checkpoint filesystem for parallel applications. In *Proceedings of the Conference on High Performance Computing Networking, Storage and Analysis*, SC '09, pages 21:1–21:12. ACM, 2009.

[6] G. Bronevetsky and A. Moody. Scalable I/O systems via node-local storage: Approaching 1 TB/sec file I/O. Technical report, Lawrence Livermore National Laboratory, 2009.

[7] M. Burtscher and P. Ratanaworabhan. FPC: a high-speed compressor for double-precision floating-point data. *IEEE Transactions on Computers*, 58:18–31, 2009.

[8] M. Burtscher and I. Szczyrba. Numerical modeling of brain dynamics in traumatic situations - Impulsive Translations. In *Mathematics and Engineering Techniques in Medicine and Biological Scienes*, pages 205–211, 2005.

[9] J. H. Chen, A. Choudhary, B. Supinski, M. DeVries, E. Hawkes, S. Klasky, W. Liao, K. Ma, J. Mellor-Crummey, N. Podhorszki, R. Sankaran, S. Shende, and C. Yoo. Terascale direct numerical simulations of turbulent combustion using S3D. *Computational Science and Discovery*, 2(1):015001, 2009.

[10] C. Dubnicki, L. Gryz, L. Heldt, M. Kaczmarczyk, W. Kilian, P. Strzelczak, J. Szczepkowski, C. Ungureanu, and M. Welnicki. HYDRAstor: a scalable secondary storage. In *Proccedings of the 7th Conference on File and Storage Technologies*, pages 197–210. USENIX Association, 2009.

[11] B. Fryxell, K. Olson, P. Ricker, F. X. Timmes, M. Zingale, D. Q. Lamb, P. MacNeice, R. Rosner, J. W. Truran, and H. Tufo. FLASH: an adaptive mesh hydrodynamics code for modeling astrophysical thermonuclear flashes. *The Astrophysical Journal Supplement Series*, 131:273–334, Nov. 2000.

[12] J. Gailly and M. Adler. Zlib general purpose compression library. http://zlib.net/, Jan. 2012.

[13] Z. Gong, S. Lakshminarasimhan, J. Jenkins, H. Kolla, S. Ethier, J. Chen, R. Ross, S. Klasky, and N. F. Samatova. Multi-level layout optimization for efficient spatio-temporal queries on ISABELA-compressed data. In *Proceedings of the 26th IEEE International Parallel & Distributed Processing Symposium*, IPDPS '12, 2012.

[14] F. Guo and P. Efstathopoulos. Building a high-performance deduplication system. In *Proceedings of the 2011 USENIX Annual Technical Conference*, 2011.

[15] Y. He, R. Lee, Y. Huai, Z. Shao, N. Jain, X. Zhang, and Z. Xu. RCFile: a fast and space-efficient data placement structure in MapReduce-based warehouse systems. In *Proceedings of the 27th IEEE*

International Conference on Data Engineering, ICDE '11, pages 1199–1208, 2011.

[16] K. Iskra, J. M. Romein, K. Yoshii, and P. Beckman. ZOID: I/O-forwarding infrastructure for petascale architectures. In *Proceedings of the 13th ACM SIGPLAN Symposium on Principles and Practice of Parallel Programming*, pages 153–162, 2008.

[17] Y. Jin, S. Lakshminarasimhan, N. Shah, Z. Gong, C. Chang, J. Chen, S. Ethier, H. Kolla, S.-H. Ku, S. Klasky, R. Latham, R. Ross, K. Schuchardt, and N. F. Samatova. S-preconditioner for multi-fold data reduction with guaranteed user-controlled accuracy. In *Proceedings of the IEEE 11th International Conference on Data Mining*, ICDM '11, pages 290–299, 2011.

[18] S. Lakshminarasimhan, J. Jenkins, I. Arkatkar, Z. Gong, H. Kolla, S.-H. Ku, S. Ethier, J. Chen, C. Chang, S. Klasky, R. Latham, R. Ross, and N. F. Samatova. ISABELA-QA: Query-driven data analytics over ISABELA-compressed scientific data. In *Proceedings of the 2011 International Conference for High Performance Computing, Networking, Storage and Analysis*, SC '11, pages 31:1–31:11. ACM, 2011.

[19] S. Lakshminarasimhan, N. Shah, S. Ethier, S. Klasky, R. Latham, R. Ross, and N. Samatova. Compressing the incompressible with ISABELA: In-situ reduction of spatio-temporal data. In *Proceedings of the 17th International European Conference on Parallel and Distributed Computing*, Euro-Par '11, pages 366–379, 2011.

[20] J. Li, W.-K. Liao, A. Choudhary, R. Ross, R. Thakur, W. Gropp, R. Latham, A. Siegel, B. Gallagher, and M. Zingale. Parallel netCDF: a high-performance scientific I/O interface. In *Proceedings of the 2003 ACM/IEEE Conference on Supercomputing*, SC '03, page 39. ACM, 2003.

[21] J. Liu, J. Wu, and D. Panda. High performance RDMA-based MPI implementation over InfiniBand. *International Journal of Parallel Programming*, 32:167–198, 2004.

[22] J. Lofstead, S. Klasky, K. Schwan, N. Podhorszki, and C. Jin. Flexible IO and integration for scientific codes through the adaptable IO system (ADIOS). In *Proceedings of the 6th International Workshop on Challenges of Large Applications in Distributed Environments*, CLADE '08, pages 15–24. ACM, 2008.

[23] J. Lofstead, F. Zheng, S. Klasky, and K. Schwan. Adaptable, metadata rich IO methods for portable high performance IO. In *Proceedings of the 2009 IEEE International Symposium on Parallel & Distributed Processing*, IPDPS '09, pages 1–10, 2009.

[24] J. Lofstead, F. Zheng, Q. Liu, S. Klasky, R. Oldfield, T. Kordenbrock, K. Schwan, and M. Wolf. Managing variability in the IO performance of petascale storage systems. In *Proceedings of the 2010 ACM/IEEE International Conference for High Performance Computing, Networking, Storage and Analysis*, SC '10, pages 1–12, 2010.

[25] D. T. Meyer and W. J. Bolosky. A study of practical deduplication. *ACM Transactions on Storage*, 7(4):1–20, Feb. 2012.

[26] A. Nisar, W.-K. Liao, and A. Choudhary. Scaling parallel I/O performance through I/O delegate and caching system. In *Proceedings of the International Conference for High Performance Computing, Networking, Storage and Analysis*, SC '08, pages 1–12, 2008.

[27] M. Polte, J. Lofstead, J. Bent, G. Gibson, S. Klasky, Q. Liu, M. Parashar, N. Podhorszki, K. Schwan, M. Wingate, and M. Wolf. ...and eat it too: high read performance in write-optimized HPC I/O middleware file formats. In *Proceedings of the 4th Annual Workshop on Petascale Data Storage*, PDSW '09, pages 21–25. ACM, 2009.

[28] J. M. Prusa, P. K. Smolarkiewicz, and A. A. Wyszogrodzki. Simulations of gravity wave induced turbulence using 512 PE CRAY T3E. *International Journal of Applied Mathematics and Computational Science*, 11(4):883–898, 2001.

[29] R. Rew and G. Davis. NetCDF: an interface for scientific data access. *IEEE Computer Graphics and Applications*, 10(4):76–82, July 1990.

[30] E. R. Schendel, Y. Jin, N. Shah, J. Chen, C. Chang, S.-H. Ku, S. Ethier, S. Klasky, R. Latham, R. Ross, and N. F. Samatova. ISOBAR preconditioner for effective and high-throughput lossless data compression. In *Proceedings of the 28th International Conference on Data Engineering*, ICDE '12. IEEE, 2012.

[31] P. Schwan. Lustre: Building a file system for 1000-node clusters. In *Proceedings of the 2003 Linux Symposium*, pages 400–407, July 2003.

[32] V. Vishwanath, R. Burns, J. Leigh, and M. Seablom. Accelerating tropical cyclone analysis using LambdaRAM, a distributed data cache over wide-area ultra-fast networks. *Future Generation Computer Systems*, 25(2):184–191, 2009.

[33] W. X. Wang, Z. Lin, W. M. Tang, W. W. Lee, S. Ethier, J. L. V. Lewandowski, G. Rewoldt, T. S. Hahm, and J. Manickam. Gyro-kinetic simulation of global turbulent transport properties in tokamak experiments. *Physics of Plasmas*, 13:092505, 2006.

[34] J. Wei, H. Jiang, K. Zhou, and D. Feng. MAD2: a scalable high-throughput exact deduplication approach for network backup services. In *Proceedings of the IEEE 26th Symposium on Mass Storage Systems and Technologies*, MSST '10, pages 1–14, 2010.

[35] T. A. Welch. A technique for high-performance data compression. *Computer*, 17(6):8–19, June 1984.

[36] B. Welton, D. Kimpe, J. Cope, C. Patrick, K. Iskra, and R. Ross. Improving I/O forwarding throughput with data compression. In *International Conference on Cluster Computing*, CLUSTER '11, pages 438–445. IEEE, 2011.

[37] M. Yang, R. E. McGrath, and M. Folk. HDF5 - a high performance data format for earth science. In *21st International Conference on Interactive Information Processing Systems (IIPS) for Meteorology, Oceanography and Hydrology*, 2005.

QBox: Guaranteeing I/O Performance on Black Box Storage Systems

Dimitris Skourtis
skourtis@cs.ucsc.edu

Shinpei Kato
shinpei@cs.ucsc.edu

Scott Brandt
scott@cs.ucsc.edu

Department of Computer Science
University of California, Santa Cruz

ABSTRACT

Many storage systems are shared by multiple clients with different types of workloads and performance targets. To achieve performance targets without over-provisioning, a system must provide isolation between clients. Throughput-based reservations are challenging due to the mix of workloads and the stateful nature of disk drives, leading to low reservable throughput, while existing utilization-based solutions require specialized I/O scheduling for each device in the storage system.

Qbox is a new utilization-based approach for generic black box storage systems that enforces utilization (and, indirectly, throughput) requirements and provides isolation between clients, without specialized low-level I/O scheduling. Our experimental results show that Qbox provides good isolation and achieves the target utilizations of its clients.

Categories and Subject Descriptors

D.4.2 [**Operating Systems**]: Storage Management; D.4.8 [**Operating Systems**]: Performance

Keywords

Storage virtualization, quality of service, resource allocation, performance

1. INTRODUCTION

During the past decade there has been a significant growth of data with no signs of slowing. Due to that growth there is a real need for storage devices to be shared efficiently by different applications and avoid the extra costs of having more and more under-utilized devices dedicated to specific applications. In environments such as cloud systems, where multiple "clients", i.e., streams of requests, compete for the same storage device, it is especially important to manage the performance of each client. Failure to do so leads to low performance for some or all clients depending on complex factors such as the I/O schedulers used, the mix of client

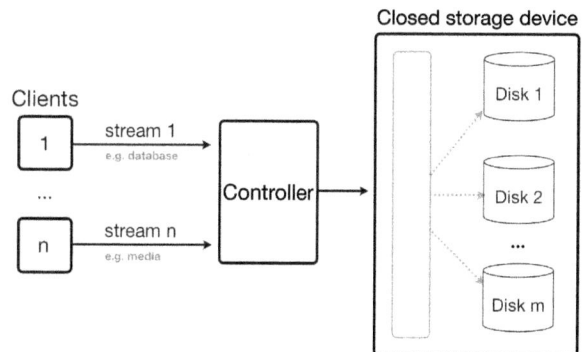

Figure 1: Given that we have no access to the storage device, we place a controller between the clients and the device to provide performance management to the clients, i.e., the request streams.

workloads, as well as storage-specific characteristics. Unfortunately, due to the nature of storage devices, managing the performance of each client and isolating them from each other is a non-trivial task. In a shared system, each client may have a different workload and each workload may affect the performance of the rest in undesirable and possibly unpredictable ways. A typical example would be a stream of random requests reducing the performance of a sequential or semi-sequential stream, mostly due to the storage device performing unnecessary seeks. The above is the result of storage devices trying to be equally fair to all requests by providing similar throughput to every stream. Of course, not all requests are equally costly, with sequential requests taking only a small fraction of a millisecond and random requests taking several milliseconds, 2-3 orders of magnitude longer. Note that a sequential stream does not have to be perfectly sequential–none ever truly are–and that real workloads often exhibit such behavior.

Providing a solution to the above problem may require using specific I/O schedulers for every disk-drive or node in a clustered storage system. Moreover, it could require changes to current infrastructure such as the replacement of the I/O scheduler of every client. Such changes may create compatibility issues preventing upgrades or other modifications to be applied to the storage system. Instead of making modifications to the infrastructure of an existing system it is often easier and in practice cheaper to deploy a solution between the clients and the storage. We call that the black box approach since it imposes minimal requirements on the clients and storage, and because it is agnostic to the specifications of either side. Our approach partly fits the grey-box framework for systems presented in [1], however, QBox requires fewer algorithmic assumptions about the underlying system. In this paper we take an almost agnostic approach and target the following problem: given a set of clients and a storage device, our goal is to manage the performance of each client's request stream in terms of disk-time utilization and provide each client with a pre-specified proportion of the device's time, while having no internal control of either the clients or the storage device, or requiring any modifications to the infrastructure of either side.

Clients want throughput reservations. However, except for highly regular workloads, throughput varies by orders of magnitude depending upon workload (Figure 2) and only a fixed fraction of the (highly variable) total may be guaranteed. By isolating each stream from the rest, utilization reservations allow a system to indirectly guarantee a specific throughput (not just a share of the total) based on direct or inferred knowledge about the workload of an individual stream, independent of any other workloads on the system and can allow much greater total throughput than throughput-based reservations [17]. Our utilization-based approach can work with Service Level Agreements (SLA); requirements can be converted to utilization as demonstrated in [18] and as long as we can guarantee utilization, we can guarantee throughput provided by an SLA.

To our knowledge there is no prior work on utilization-based performance guarantees for black box storage devices. Most work that is close to our scenario such as [15, 11] is based on throughput and latency requirements, which are hard to reserve directly without under-utilizing the storage for a number of reasons such the orders-of-magnitude cost differences between best- and worst-case requests. Moreover, throughput-based solutions create other challenges such as admission control. Without very specific knowledge about the workloads, the system must make worst-case assumptions, leading to extremely low reservable throughput. On the other hand, existing solutions based on disk utilization [18, 17, 10] only support single drives and if used in a clustered storage system they require their scheduler to be present on every node.

In this paper, we present a novel method for managing the performance of multiple clients on a storage device in terms of disk-time utilization. Unlike the management of a single drive, in the black box scenario it is hard to measure the service time of each request. Instead, our solution is based on the periodic estimation of the average cost of sequential and random requests as well as the observation that their costs have an orders-of-magnitude difference. We observe the throughput of each request type in consecutive time windows and maintain separate moving estimates for the cost of sequential and random requests. By taking into account the desired utilization of each client we schedule their requests by assigning them deadlines and dispatching them to the storage device according to the Earliest Deadline First (EDF) algorithm [13, 21]. Our results show that the desired utilization rates are achieved closely enough, achieving both good performance guarantees and isolation. Those results stand over any combination of random, sequential, and semi-sequential workloads. Moreover, due to our utilization-based approach, it is easy to decide whether a new client may be admitted to the storage system, possibly by modify-

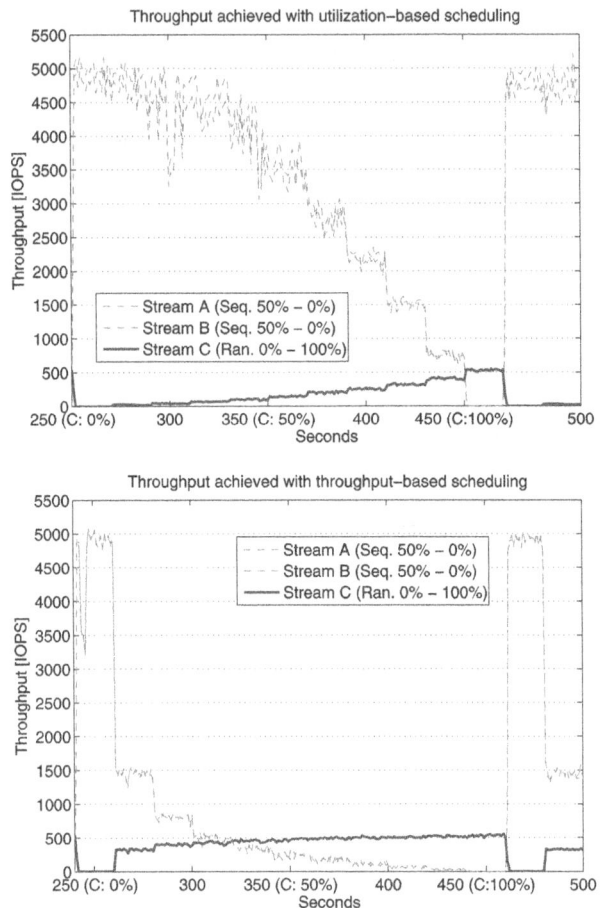

Figure 2: QBox (top) provides isolation, while the introduction of a random stream makes the throughput of sequential streams drop dramatically with throughput-based scheduling (bottom.)

ing the rates of other clients. Finally, all clients may access any file on the storage device and we make no assumptions about the location of the data on a per client basis.

2. SYSTEM MODEL

Our basic scenario consists of a set of clients each associated with a stream of requests and a single storage device containing multiple disks. Clients send requests to the storage device and each stream uses a proportion of the device's execution time. We call that proportion the utilization rate of a stream and it is either provided by the client or in practice, by a broker, which is part of our controller and translates SLAs into throughput and latency requirements as in [17, 18] or [10]. Briefly, to translate an SLA to utilization, we measure the aggregate throughput of the system for sequential and random requests separately over small amounts of requests (e.g., 20) and set a confidence level (e.g., 95%) to avoid treating all requests as outliers. Details about arrival patterns and issues such as head/track switches and bad layout are presented in [19].

The main characteristic of our scenario is that we treat the storage device as a black box. In other words, we only interact with the storage device by passing it client requests

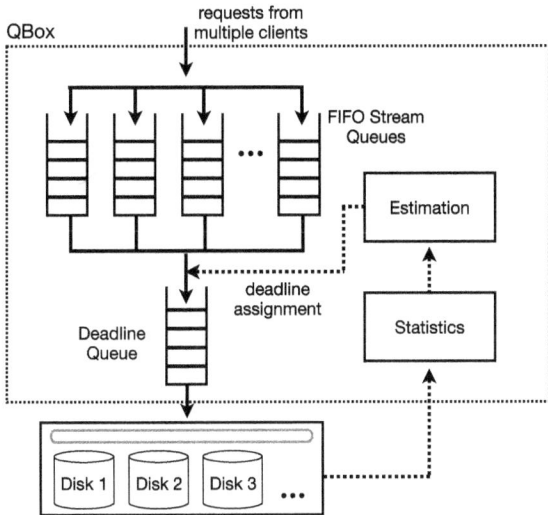

Figure 3: The controller architecture.

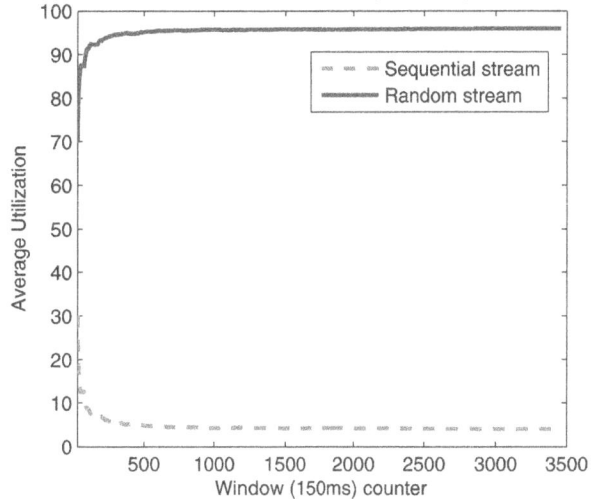

Figure 4: When our controller sends the requests in the order they are received from the clients, the system fails to provide the desired rates.

and receiving responses. For example, we cannot modify or replace the device's scheduler as is the case in [18] and do not assume it uses a particular scheduler. Moreover, we cannot control which disk(s) are going to execute each request and do not restrict clients to specific parts of the storage device. Due to those requirements the natural choice is to place a controller between the clients and the storage device. Hence, all client requests go through the controller, where they are scheduled and eventually dispatched to the device. As we will see, this setup allows us to gather little information regarding the disk execution times, which turns scheduling and therefore black box management into a challenge.

We manage the performance of the streams in a time-based manner. After a request reaches our controller, we assign it a deadline by keeping an estimate of the expected execution time e for each type of request (sequential or random) and by using the stream's rate r provided by the broker. Using e and r we compute the request's deadline by $d = e/r$. The absolute deadline of a request coming from stream s is set to $D_s = T_s + d$, where T_s is the sum of all the relative deadlines assigned so far to the requests of stream s. Although, we are using "deadlines" for scheduling, our goal is not to strictly satisfy deadlines. Instead, it is the relative values that matter with regards to the dispatching order. On the other hand, if we used a stricter dispatching approach e.g., [18], then the absolute times would be important for replacing the expected cost with the actual cost after the request was completed. In this paper we do not focus on urgent requests, however, it is possible to place such requests ahead of others in the corresponding stream queue by simply assigning them earlier deadlines.

Although we do not assume the storage device is using a specific disk scheduler, it is better to have a scheduler which tries to avoid starvation and orders the requests in a reasonable manner (as most do). A stricter dispatching policy such as [18] can be used on the controller side to avoid starvation by placing more emphasis on satisfying the assigned deadlines instead of overall performance. The next section presents our method for estimating execution times and managing the performance of each stream in terms of

time. We also discuss practical issues we faced while applying our method and discuss how we addressed them.

3. PERFORMANCE MANAGEMENT

In QBox we maintain a FIFO queue for each stream and a deadline queue, which may contain requests from any stream. The deadline queue is ordered according to the Earliest Deadline First (EDF) scheduler and the deadlines are computed as described in the previous section. Whenever we are ready to dispatch a request to the storage device the request with the smallest absolute deadline out of all the stream queues is moved to the deadline queue. To find the earliest-deadline request it suffices to look at the oldest request from each stream queue, since any other request before that has either arrived at a later time or is less urgent. Next, the request with the earliest deadline is removed from the deadline queue and dispatched to the device.

3.1 Estimating execution times

As mentioned earlier, we aim to provide performance management through a controller placed between the clients and the storage device. We wish to achieve this goal without knowledge of how the storage device schedules and distributes the requests among its disks and without access to the storage system internals. Most importantly, we are unaware of the time each request takes on a single disk, which we could otherwise measure by looking at the time difference between two consecutive responses, i.e., the inter-arrival time. In our case, the time between two consecutive responses does not necessarily reflect the time spent by the device executing the second request, because those two requests may have been satisfied by different disks.

On the other hand, we know the number of requests executed from each stream on the storage device. If all requests had the same cost, then we could take the average over a time window T, i.e., $e = T/n$, where n is the number of requests completed in T. Clearly, that would not solve

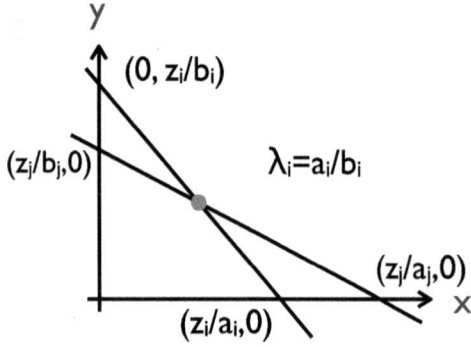

Figure 5: The intersection of the two lines from (3) gives us the average cost x of a sequential and y of a random request in the time windows z_i and z_j.

the problem since random requests are orders-of-magnitude more expensive than sequential requests, i.e., the disk has to spend significantly more time to complete a random request. Based on that observation, for each stream we classify its requests into sequential and random while keeping track of the number of requests completed by type per window. Assuming the clients saturate the device and the cost x of the average sequential request and the cost y of the average random request remain the same across two time windows z_i and z_j we are lead to the following system of linear equations:

$$\begin{cases} \alpha_i x + \beta_i y = z_i \\ \alpha_j x + \beta_j y = z_j, \end{cases} \quad (1)$$

where α_i is the number of sequential requests completed in window i, and similarly for the number of random requests denoted by β_i. Often, j will be equal to $i+1$. Solving the above system gives us the sequential and random average request costs for windows z_i and z_j:

$$x = \frac{z_j \beta_i - \beta_j z_i}{\alpha_j \beta_i - \alpha_i \beta_j}, \quad y = \frac{z_i}{\beta_i} - \frac{\alpha_i}{\beta_i} x. \quad (2)$$

The above equations may give us negative solutions due to system noise and other factors. Since execution costs may only be positive we restrict the solutions to positive (x,y) pairs (Figure 5), i.e., satisfying:

$$\begin{cases} z_i/\alpha_i < z_j/\alpha_j \\ z_i/\beta_i > z_j/\beta_j \\ \alpha_i/\beta_i > \alpha_j/\beta_j \end{cases} \text{ or } \begin{cases} z_i/\alpha_i > z_j/\alpha_j \\ z_i/\beta_i < z_j/\beta_j. \\ \alpha_i/\beta_i < \alpha_j/\beta_j \end{cases} \quad (3)$$

Intuitively, setting z_i equal to z_j in (3) would require that if the number of completed sequential requests goes down in window j, then the number of random requests has to go up (and vice-versa.) Otherwise, the intersection would contain a negative component. By focusing on the case where every time window has the same length we reduce the chances of getting highly volatile solutions and make the analytical solution simpler to intuitively understand. In that case the solution becomes

$$x = \frac{z}{\alpha_i + \beta_i \lambda}, \quad y = \lambda x, \quad (4)$$

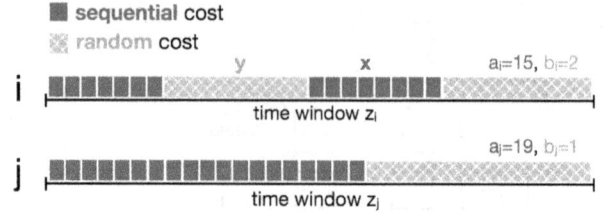

Figure 6: Counting sequential and random completions per window lets us estimate their average cost.

where

$$\lambda = \frac{\alpha_i - \alpha_j}{\beta_j - \beta_i}. \quad (5)$$

From (5) we see that the intersection solutions are expected to be volatile if the window size is small. On the other hand, if the window size is large and the throughput does not change, the intersection will often be negative, i.e., it will happen on a negative quadrant, since the two lines from Figure 5 will often have a similar slope. It would be easy to ignore negative solutions by skipping windows. However, depending on the window size and workload it is possible to get negative solutions more often than positive ones. That leads to fewer updates and therefore a slower convergence to a stable estimate. To face that issue we looked into two directions. One direction is to observe that if the window size is small enough, it is not important whether we take the intersection of the current window with the previous one or some other window not too far in the past. Based on that observation we consider the positive intersections of the current window with a number of the previous ones and take the average. That method increases the chance of getting a valid solution. In addition, updating more frequently allows the moving estimate to converge more quickly without giving a large weight on any of the individual estimates.

The other way we propose to face negative solutions is to compute the projection of the previous estimate on the current window assuming the x/y ratio remains the same along those two windows. In particular, we may assume that α_i/β_i is close to α_j/β_j. In that case, we can project the previous intersection point or estimate on the line describing the second window. The projection is given by

$$x = \frac{\alpha_j z_i}{\alpha_i (\mu \beta_j + \alpha_j)}, \quad y = \mu x, \quad (6)$$

where

$$\mu = \frac{1}{\beta_i} \left(\frac{z_i}{x} - \alpha_i \right). \quad (7)$$

The idea is that if both the number of completed sequential and random requests in a window drops (or increases) proportionally the cost must have shifted accordingly. Although we observed that the projection method works especially well, its correctness depends on the previous estimate. It could still be used when some intersection is invalid to keep updating the estimate but leave it as future work to determine whether it can enhance our estimates.

3.2 Estimation error and seek times

A key assumption is that the request costs are the same among windows. Assuming that at some point we have the true (x, y) cost and that the cost in the next window is not exactly the same due to system noise we expect to have error. To compute that error we replace z_j in the solution for x in (2) by its definition i.e., $\alpha_j x + \beta_j y$ and denote that expression by x'. Taking the difference between x and x' gives

$$\left| x - x' \right| = \frac{\beta_i}{\left| \alpha_j \beta_i - \alpha_i \beta_j \right|} \left| (\alpha_j x + \beta_j y) - z_j \right| \qquad (8)$$

and

$$\left| y - y' \right| = \frac{\alpha_i}{\beta_i} \left| x' - x \right| . \qquad (9)$$

So far we have not considered seek times between streams and how they might affect our estimates. In the typical case where m random requests are executed by a disk followed by n sequential requests, the first request out of the sequential ones will incur a seek. That seek is not fully charged to either type of request in our model, simply because it is either hard or impossible in our scenario. Intuitively, the total seek cost of a window is distributed across both request types. Firstly, because fewer requests of both types will end up being executed in that window and secondly due to the error formula (9) for y. In particular, assuming the delayed requests in some window i would also follow the α_i/β_i ratio we now show that seeks do not affect our scheduling.

Let $\alpha_i' = \alpha_i - \delta_i^{(\alpha)}$ and $\beta_i' = \beta_i - \delta_i^{(\beta)}$, where δ_i^{τ} is the number of requests of type τ that are not executed in window i due to seek events. From the above assumption, $\delta_i^{(\beta)} = \beta_i/\alpha_i \delta_i^{(\alpha)}$. Then $\alpha_i'/\beta_i' = (\alpha_i - \delta_i^{(\alpha)})/(\alpha_i - \delta_i^{(\beta)})$, which gives α_i/β_i and similarly, for window j. Using the original solution (2) for the sequential and random costs, consider the ratio of y/x as well as y'/x', which uses α' instead of α and similarly for β. By substituting, we get that $y/x = y'/x' = -\alpha_i'/\beta_i'$, which is independent of the number of seeks δ and by the above is equal to $-\alpha_i/\beta_i$.

From the above, we conclude that seeks do not affect the relative estimation costs and consequently our schedule. The reason the ratios are negative can be seen from Figure 5. Specifically, fixing every variable in (2), while increasing the x-cost, reduces the y-cost and vice versa. Therefore, the slope y/x is negative whether we have seeks or not.

3.3 Write support and estimating in practice

In this work, we only deal with read requests. Since writes typically respond immediately, it is harder to approximate the disk throughput over small time intervals. On the other hand, if a system is busy enough, the write throughput over large intervals (e.g., 5 seconds) is expected to have a smaller variance and be closer to the true throughput. Preliminary results suggest the above holds. There are still some challenges, such as the effect of writes on reads when there is significant write activity, which may be addressed by dispatching writes in groups. Adding support for writes is a priority for future work and is expected to lead into a more general solution supporting SSDs and hybrid systems.

In our implementation we took the approach of having small windows, e.g. 100ms, to increase the frequency of estimates and to give a small weight to each of them. As we compute intersections we keep a moving average and weight each estimate depending on its distance from the previous one. Due to the frequent updates, if there is a shift in the cost, the moving estimate will reach that value quickly. Moreover, to improve estimates, for each window we find its

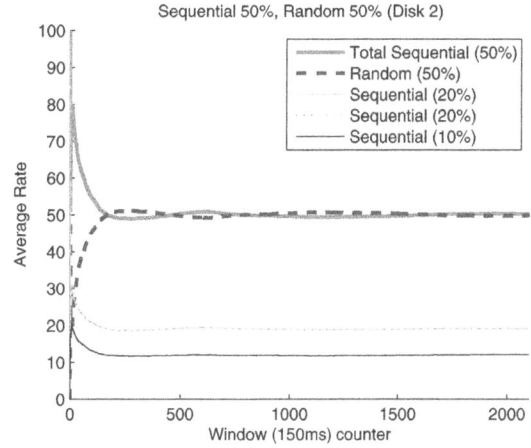

Figure 7: Using one disk and a mixture of sequential and random streams the rates are achieved and convergence happens quickly.

intersection with a number of the previous windows (e.g., 10.) Finally, if the λ cost ratio as defined in (5) is too small or too large we ignore that pair of costs. We set the bounds to what we consider safe values in that they will only take out clearly wrong intersections.

4. EXPERIMENTAL EVALUATION

In this section, we evaluate QBox in terms of utilization and throughput management. We first verify that the sequential and random request cost estimates are accurate enough and that the desired stream rates are satisfied in different scenarios. Next, we show that the throughput achieved is to a large degree in agreement with the target rates of each stream.

4.1 Prototype

In all our experiments we use up to four disks (different models) or a software RAID 0 over two disks. We forward stream requests to the disks asynchronously using Kernel AIO. We avoided using threads in order to keep a large number of requests queued up (e.g., 200) and to avoid race conditions leading to inaccurate inter-arrival time measurements. Up to subsection 4.4 we are interested in evaluating QBox in a time-based manner. For that purpose we avoid hitting the filesystem cache by enabling O_DIRECT and do not use Native Command Queuing (NCQ) in any of the disks. Moreover, we send requests in a RAID 0 fashion rather than using a true RAID. The above allows us to know the disk each request targets, which consequently lets us compute the service times by measuring the inter-arrival times and compare those with our estimates. The extra information is not used by our method since it is normally unavailable. It is used only for evaluation purposes. Starting from subsection 4.4 we gradually remove all the above restrictions and evaluate QBox implicitly in a throughput-based manner.

We evaluate QBox both with synthetic and real workloads depending on the goal of the experiment. All synthetic requests are reads of size 4KB unless we are using a RAID over two disks in which case they are 8KB. For the synthetic workload, each disk contains a hundred 1GB files. We use a subset of the Deasna2 [3] NFS trace with request sizes typ-

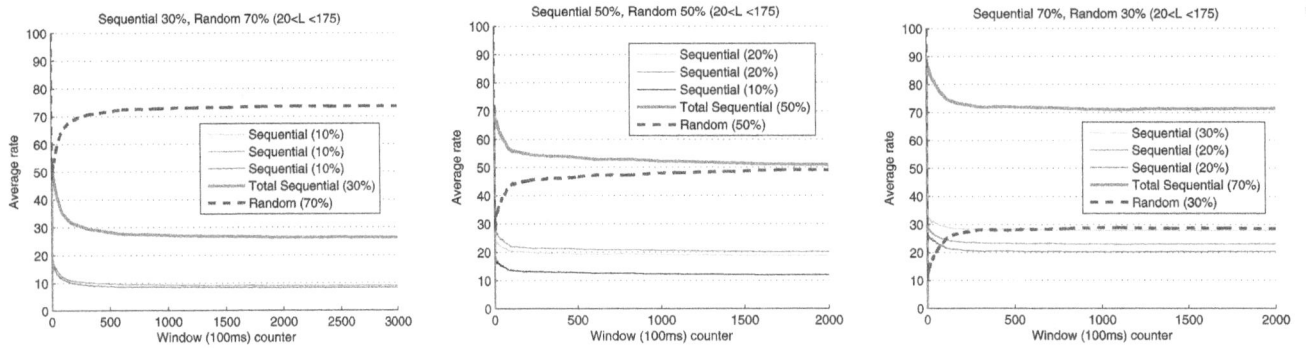

Figure 8: Using two disks and our scheduling and estimation method we achieve the desired rates most of the time relatively well. In the above we have three sequential streams and a random one.

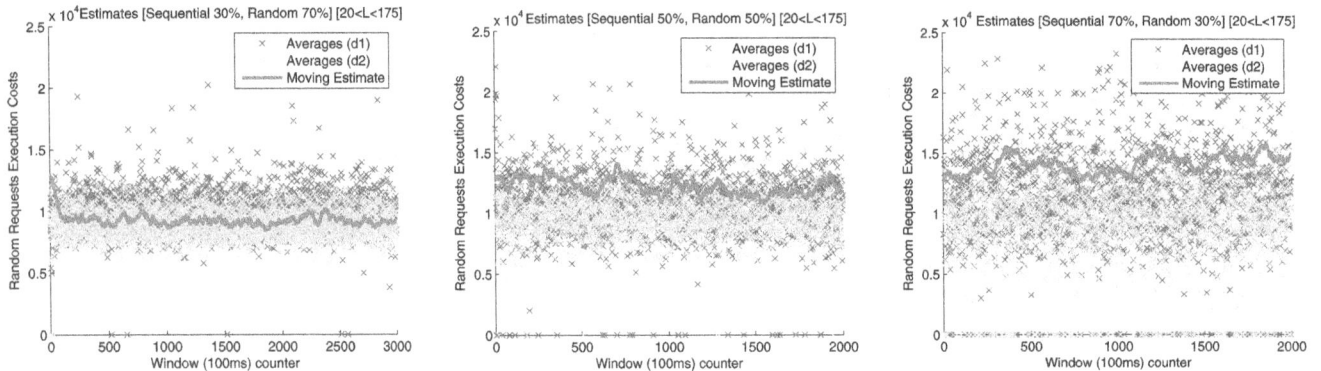

Figure 9: Using two disks (d1, d2) and our estimation method we maintain a moving estimate of the average random execution cost on the storage device.

ically being 32KB or 64KB. Finally, except for a workload containing idle time, we assume there are always requests queued up, since that is the most interesting scenario, and we bound the number of pending requests on the storage by a constant, e.g., 200. Finally, we do not assume a specific I/O scheduler is used by the storage device. In our experiments, the "Deadline Scheduler" was used, however, we have tried other schedulers and observed similar results.

4.2 Sequential and random streams

Our approach is based on the differentiation between sequential and random requests and so the first step in evaluating QBox is to consider a workload of fully sequential and random streams with the goal of providing isolation between them. Note that to provide isolation a prerequisite is that our cost estimates for the average sequential and random request are close enough to the true values, which are not known, and it is not possible to explicitly measure them in our black box scenario. In this set of experiments, the workload consists of three sequential streams and one random. Each sequential stream starts at a different file to ensure there are inter-stream seeks. Each request of the random stream targets a file and offset uniformly at random. For each stream we measure the average utilization provided by the storage device. We look into three sets of desired utilizations. Figure 8(a) shows a random stream with a utilization target of 70%, while each sequential stream has a target of 10% for a total of 30%. As the experiment runs, the cost

estimates take values within a small range and the average achieved utilization converges. In Figures 8(b) and (c) the sequential streams are given higher utilizations. In all three cases, the achieved utilizations are close to the desired ones. Again in Figures 8(b) and (c) the initial estimate was relatively close to the actual cost, so the moving rates approach the converging rates more quickly.

From Figure 9 we notice that estimates get above the average cost when there is many sequential requests even if the utilization targets are achieved (Figure 8). The main reason for that is that we keep track and store (in memory) large amounts of otherwise unnecessary statistics per request. Therefore, if in a window of e.g., 100ms there is a very large number of request completions, i.e., when the rate of sequential streams is high, 10ms ($10\mu s \cdot 1000$ requests) may be given to that processing and therefore the estimates are scaled up. Of course, those operations can be optimized or eliminated without affecting QBox. As expected, a similar effect happens with the estimated cost of sequential requests (not shown), therefore the ratio of the costs stays valid leading to proper scheduling as shown in Figure 8.

Besides the initial estimates, the convergence rate also depends on the window size, since a smaller size implies more frequent updates and faster convergence. However, if the window size becomes too small the number of completed requests become too few and the quality of the estimate may not be accurate enough due to the significant noise. Note that whether the window size is considered too small

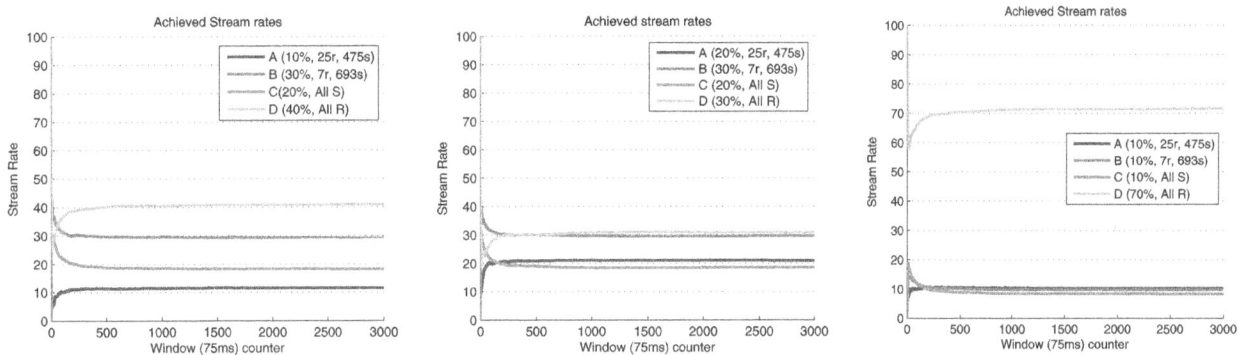

Figure 10: Using two disks and our scheduling and estimation method we achieve the desired rates most of the time relatively well. Stream A requires 20% of the disk time and sends 25 random requests every 475 sequential requests. Similarly for the rest of the streams.

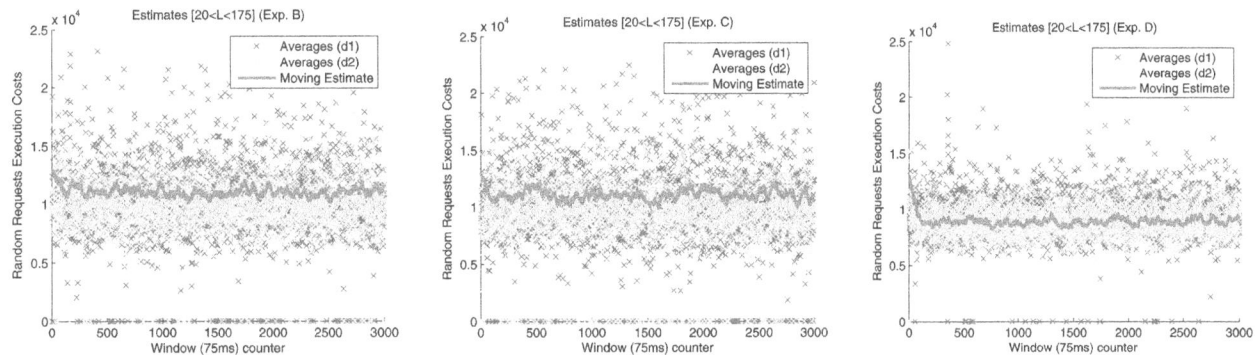

Figure 11: Using two disks (d1, d2) and our estimation method we maintain a moving estimate of the average random execution cost on the storage device.

depends on the number of disks in the storage system as having more disks implies that a greater number of requests complete per window. The window size we picked in the above experiment (Figure 8) is 100ms. Other values such as 150ms provide similar estimation quality and later we look at smaller windows of 75ms. Note that in Figure 9 there is a number of recorded averages that are 0 because random streams with low target rates are more likely to have no arrivals in a window. Not having any completed random requests in a window implies that we can estimate a new sequential estimate more easily.

Finally, in the above, we assume there is always enough queued requests from all streams. Without any modification to our method we see from Figure 12 that under idle time it is still possible to manage the rates. In particular, every 5000 requests (on average) dispatched to the storage device we delay dispatching the next request(s) for a (uniformly at) random amount of time between 0.5 to 1 second. From Figure 12 we see that the rates are still achieved, while there is slightly more noise in the estimates compared to Figure 9. We noted that if the idle times are larger than the window size, then our method is less affected. That was expected, since idling over a number of consecutive windows implies that new requests will be scheduled according to the previous estimates as the estimates will not be updated. Finally, although the start and end of the idle time window may affect the estimate, the effect is not significant since the

estimate moves only by a small amount on each update and most updates are not affected.

4.3 Mixed-workload streams

In practice, most streams are not perfectly sequential. For example, a stream of requests may consist of m random requests for every n sequential requests, where m is often significantly smaller than n. To face that issue, instead of characterizing each stream as either sequential or random we classify each request. Note that the first request of a sequential group of requests after m random ones is considered random if m is large enough. Although not all random requests cost exactly the same, we do not differentiate between them since we work on top of the filesystem and do not assume we have access to the logical block number of each file. Therefore, we do not have a real measure of sequentiality for any two I/O requests. However, as long as the cost of random requests does not vary significantly between streams we expect to achieve the desired utilization for each stream. Indeed, as it has been observed in [10], good utilization management can still be provided when random requests are assumed to cost the same. Moreover, from [3] we see that requests from common workloads are usually either almost sequential or fully random. Differentiating between cost estimates on a per stream basis is expected to improve the management quality and leave it as future work.

From Figure 10 we see that the targets are achieved in the

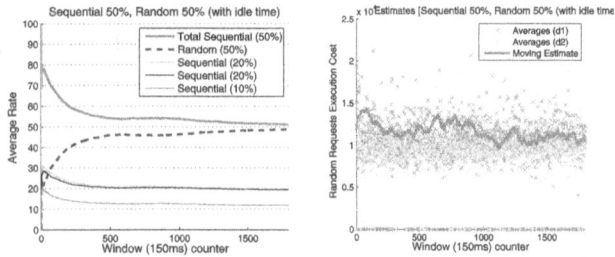

Figure 12: Using two disks (d1, d2), the desired rates are achieved well enough (reach 45% quickly) even when there is idle time in the workload.

presence of semi-sequential streams. In particular, in 10(a), stream A sends 25 random requests for every 475 sequential ones. Stream B sends 7 random requests for every 693 sequential ones, while streams C and D are purely sequential and random, respectively. Other target sets in Figure 10 are satisfied equally well. Note that each group of requests does not have to be completed before the next one is sent. Instead, requests are continuously dequeued and scheduled.

So far we have seen scenarios with fixed target rates. Our method supports changing the target rates online as long as the rate sum is up to 100%. Depending on the new target rates, the cost estimation updates can be crucial in achieving those rates. For example, increasing the rate of a random stream decreases the average cost of a random request and our estimates are adjusted automatically to reflect that. Figure 13(a) illustrates that the utilization rates are satisfied and Figure 13(b) shows how the random estimate changes as the clients adjust their desired utilization rates every thirty seconds. For this experiment we set the number of disks to four to illustrate our method works with a higher number of disks and to support our claim that it can work with any number of disks. The same experiment was run with two disks giving nearly identical results (figure omitted.)

As explained earlier, the disk queue depth is set to one for evaluation purposes. However, since a large queue depth can improve the disk throughput we implicitly evaluate QBox by comparing the throughput achieved when the depth is 1 and 31, while the target rates change. In particular, we look at semi-sequential and random streams. As expected and illustrated in Figure 15, having a depth of 31 achieves a higher throughput over a range of rates. Although, this does not verify our method works perfectly due to lack of information, it provides evidence that it works and, as we will see in the next subsection, that is indeed the case.

4.4 RAID utilization management

In our experiments so far, we have been sending requests to disks manually in a striping fashion instead of using an actual RAID device. That was done for evaluation purposes. Here, we use a (software) RAID 0 device and instead evaluate QBox indirectly. The RAID configuration consists of two disks with a chunk size of 4KB to match our previous experiments, while requests have a size of 8KB.

In the first experiment we focus on the throughput achieved by two (semi-)sequential streams as we vary their desired rates. Moreover, we add a random stream to make it more realistic and challenging. We fix the target rate of the random stream since otherwise it would have a variable effect on

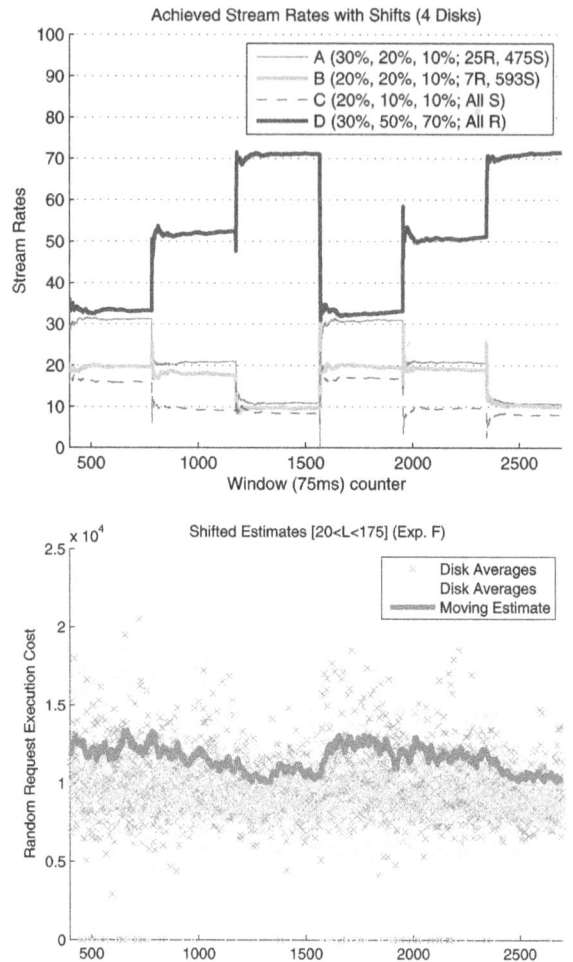

Figure 13: Using four disks and desired rates that shift over time, the rates are still achieved quickly under semi-sequential and random workloads.

the sequential streams throughput and make the evaluation uncertain. As long as the throughput achieved by each of the sequential streams varies in a linear fashion we are able to conclude that our method works. Indeed, from Figure 14 stream A starts with a target rate of 0.5 and goes down to 0, while stream B moves in the opposite direction. As the throughput of stream A goes down, the difference is provided to stream B. Moreover, in Figure 16 we see that having two random streams and a sequential one fixed at 50% (not plotted) has a similar behavior. The difference between those two cases is the drop in the total throughput of the first case with streams A and B having a lower throughput when their rates get closer to each other. That is due to the more balanced number of requests being executed from each sequential stream leading to a greater number of seeks between them. Since seeks are relatively expensive compared to the typical sequential request the overall throughput drops slightly. If that effect was not observed in Figure 14, then the random stream (C) would be getting a smaller amount of the storage time, which would go against its performance targets. Instead, the random stream throughput remains unchanged. On the other hand, in Figure 16 there

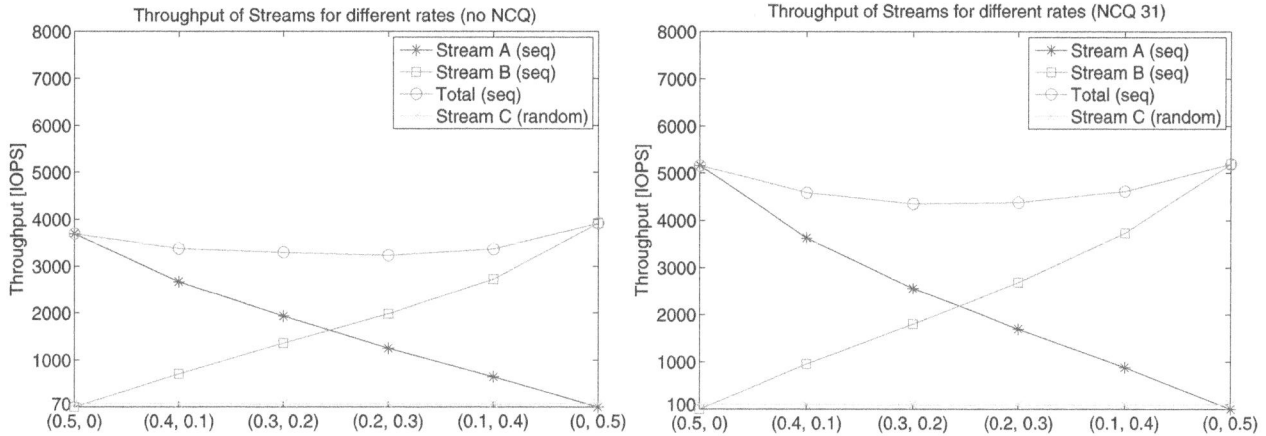

Figure 14: Using RAID 0 the throughput achieved by each sequential stream is in agreement with their target rates. Stream A has a varied target rate from 50% to 0 and the opposite for B. Random stream C requires a fixed rate of 50% of the storage time. Similarly for a large disk queue depth (NCQ.)

is no drop in the total throughput, which is expected since the cost of seeks between random requests are similar to the typical cost of a random request. Therefore, the total throughput remains constant. Moreover, the sequential stream (not plotted) reaches an average throughput of 3600 and 5060 IOPS with a depth of 1 and 31, respectively as in Figure 14. Finally, note that whether we use no NCQ or a depth of 31 the throughput behavior is similar in both Figures (14 and 16), which is desired since a large depth can provide a higher throughput in certain cases [26], along with other benefits such as reducing power consumption [24].

4.5 Evaluation using traces

To strengthen our evaluation, besides synthetic workloads we run QBox using two different days of the Deasna2 [3] trace as two of the three read streams, while the third stream sends random requests. Deasna2 contains semi-sequential traces of email and workloads from Harvard's division of engineering and applied sciences. As the requests wait to be dispatched, we classify them as either sequential or random depending on the other requests in their queue.

Unlike time, evaluating a method by comparing throughput values is hard because the achieved throughput depends on the stream workloads. However, by looking at the throughput achieved using QBox in Figure 17 and the results of throughput-based scheduling in Figure 18 it is easy to conclude that QBox provides a significantly higher degree of isolation and that the target rates of the streams are respected well enough. Moreover, looking more closely at Figure 17, we see that wherever the throughput is not in perfect accordance with the targets of streams A and B, there is an increase of random requests coming from the same streams. That effect is valid and due to the trace itself. On the other hand, Figure 18 demonstrates the destructive interference inherent in throughput-based reservation schemes with semi-sequential streams receiving a very low throughput.

4.6 Caches

So far our experiments have skipped the file system cache to more easily evaluate our method and to send requests asynchronously, since without O_DIRECT they become block-

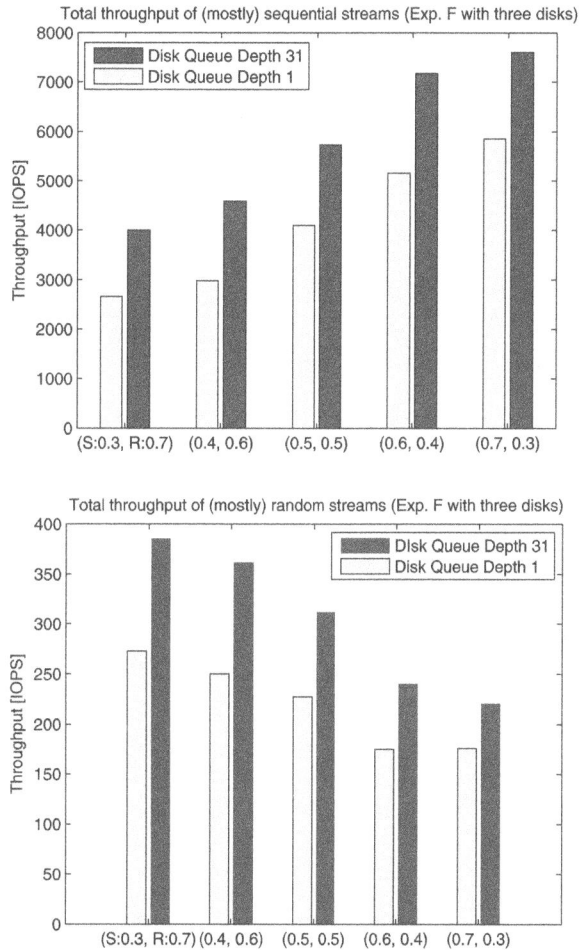

Figure 15: The throughput with an NCQ of 1 and 31 is maintained while the desired rates vary.

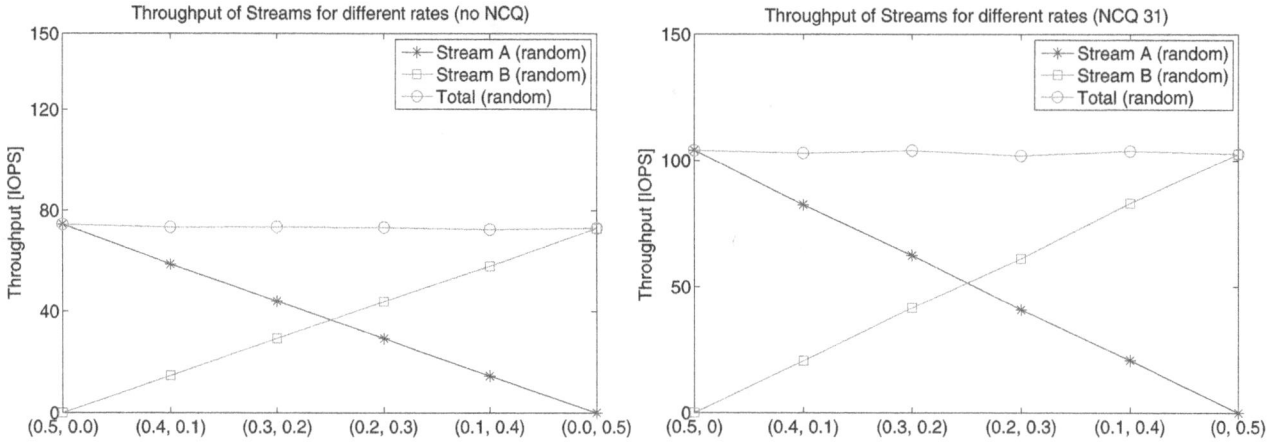

Figure 16: Using RAID 0 the throughput of each random stream is in agreement with its target. Stream A has a varied target rate from 50% to 0 and B from 0 to 50%. The sequential stream (not plotted) has a utilization of 50% leading to an average of 3600 and 5060 IOPS with no NCQ and a depth of 31, respectively.

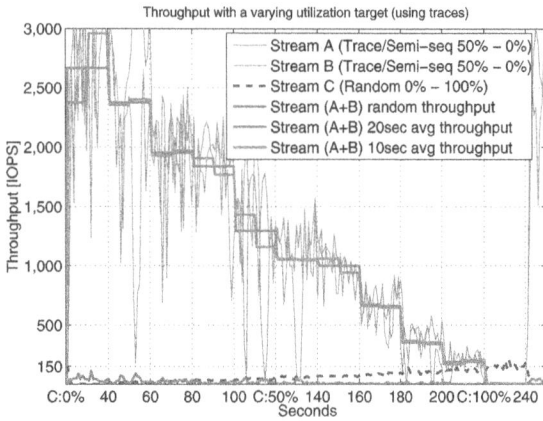

Figure 17: QBox provides streams of real traces the throughput corresponding to their rate close enough even in the presence of a random stream.

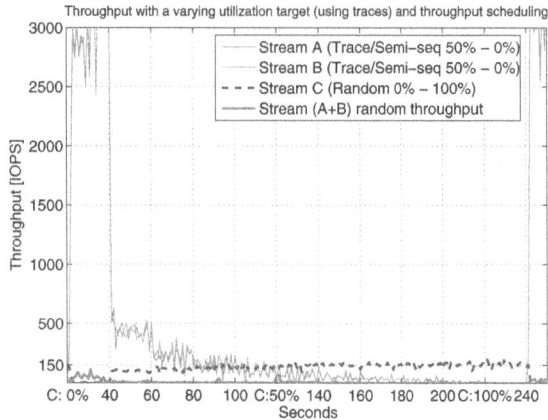

Figure 18: Random stream C affects throughput-scheduling leading to a low throughput for A and B.

ing requests. Although applications such as databases may avoid file system caches, we are interested in QBox being applicable in a general setting. For our purposes, request completions resulting from cache hits could be ignored or accounted differently. From our experiments, detection of random cache hits seems reliable and the well-known relation—as explained in [7]–between the queue size and the average latency may also be useful to improve accuracy as well as grey-box methods [1]. However, we cannot say the same for sequential requests due to prefetching. Moreover, since random workloads may cover a large segment of the storage, hits are not as likely. Hence, in this paper we treat hits as regular completions for simplicity.

Without modifying QBox we enable the file system cache and see from Figure 19 that although the throughput is noisier than in the previous experiments due to the nature of cache hits, we still manage to achieve throughput rates that are in accordance with the target rates. Scheduling based on throughput (Figure 20) gives similar results to Figure 18, supporting our position on throughput-based scheduling. Finally, using synthetic workloads we get an output of the same form as Figure 14 with a maximum sequential throughput of 1700 IOPS (figure omitted.)

4.7 Overhead

The computational overhead is trivial. We know the most urgent request in each stream queue and thus picking the next request to dispatch requires as many operations as the number of streams. Since the number of streams is expected to be low, that cost is trivial. In addition, on a request completion we increase a fixed number of counters and at the end of each window we compute a fixed, small number of intersections. The time it takes to compute each intersection is insignificant. Finally, updating the moving estimate only requires computing the new estimate weight. In total the procedure at the end of each window takes less than $10\mu s$.

5. RELATED WORK

A large body of literature exists related to providing guarantees over storage devices. Typically they either aim to

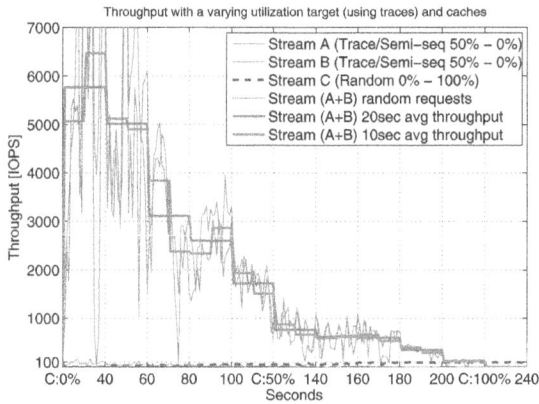

Figure 19: The throughput achieved by QBox in the presence of caches follows the target rates.

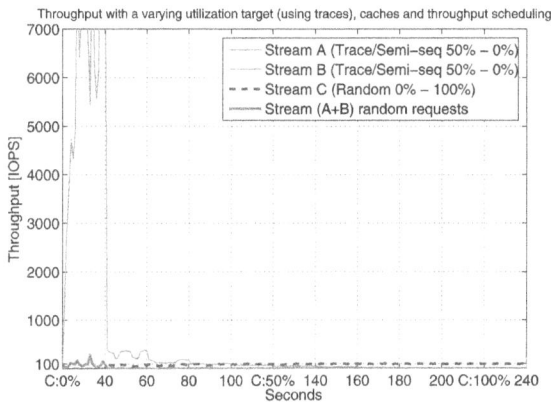

Figure 20: Throughput-based scheduling fails to isolate stream performance leading to a low throughput for semi-sequential streams.

satisfy throughput or latency requirements, or attempt to proportionally distribute throughput. Most solutions do not distinguish between sequential and random workloads, which leads to the storage being under-utilized. Avoiding that distinction leads to charging semi-sequential streams unfairly due to the significant cost difference between sequential and random requests. Instead, QBox uses disk service time rather than IOPS or Bytes/s to solve that problem.

Stonehenge [8] clusters storage systems in terms of bandwidth, capacity and latency, however, being based on bandwidth its reservations cover only a fraction of the disk performance. Other proposed solutions based on bandwidth, include [11, 15, 2] and take advantage of the relation - as was later explained in [7] - between the queue length and average latency to throttle requests. mClock [6] does not provide performance insulation, while both [6] and pClock [5] do not differentiate between sequential and random requests. Other solutions such as [9, 11, 15, 16] do not provide insulation either. On the other hand, Argon [22] provides insulation, however, workload changes may affect its provided soft bounds. In [14], distribution-based QoS is provided to a percentage of the workload to avoid over-provisioning. [12] attempts to predict response times rather than service times

through statistical models. PARDA [4] provides guarantees by assuming a specific scheduler resides on each host, unlike QBox, which does not assume access to the hosts/clients.

Facade [15] aims to provide performance guarantees described by an SLA for each virtual storage device. It places a virtual store controller between a set of hosts and storage devices in a network and throttles client requests so that the devices do not saturate. In particular, it adjusts the queue size dynamically, which affects the latency of each workload. However, a single set of low latency requests may decrease the queue size of the system and it is hard to determine whether a new workload may be admitted.

YouChoose [27] tries to provide the performance of reference storage systems by measuring their performance off-line and mimicking it online. It is based on an off-line machine learning process, similar to [23], which can be hard to prepare due to the challenging task of selecting a representative set of training data. Moreover, the safe admission of new virtual storage devices can be challenging.

Solutions based on execution time estimates such as [18, 17, 10] assume we have low-level control over each hard-drive. Moreover, in Horizon [18] it was shown that such a solution can be used in distributed storage systems with single-disk nodes using the Horizon scheduler. Our work is also based on disk-time utilization and deadline assignment, however, we treat the storage device as a black box and therefore do not assume our own scheduler is in front of every hard-drive. Finally, [25, 20] reserve I/O rates using worst-case execution times, therefore, they can only reserve a fraction of the storage device time.

6. CONCLUSIONS

In this paper, we targeted the problem of providing isolation and performance guarantees in terms of storage device utilization to multiple clients with different types of workloads. We proposed a "plug-n-play" method for isolating the performance of clients accessing a single file-level storage device treated as a black box. Our solution is based on a novel method for estimating the expected execution times of sequential and random requests as well as on assigning deadlines and scheduling requests using the Earliest Deadline First (EDF) scheduling algorithm. Our experiments show that QBox provides isolation between streams having different characteristics with changing needs and on storage systems with a variable number of disks.

There are multiple directions for future work. Extensions include support for SSDs based on the cost difference of reads and writes as well as hybrid systems. Adding support for writes and RAID 4, 5 is another direction. Technical improvements include a better use of the history of requests in computing estimates and sophisticated methods to detect sudden and stable changes. Finally, we would like to verify QBox works on Network Attached Storage, test it at the hypervisor level in a virtualized environment and explore the case where there is multiple controllers and storage devices.

7. REFERENCES

[1] A. C. Arpaci-Dusseau and R. H. Arpaci-Dusseau. Information and control in gray-box systems. In *Proceedings of the eighteenth ACM symposium on Operating systems principles*, SOSP '01, pages 43–56, New York, NY, USA, 2001. ACM.

[2] D. D. Chambliss, G. A. Alvarez, P. Pandey, D. Jadav, J. Xu, R. Menon, and T. P. Lee. Performance virtualization for large-scale storage systems. In *In Proceedings of the 22th International Symposium on Reliable Distributed Systems (SRDSÕ03*, pages 109–118, 2003.

[3] D. Ellard, J. Ledlie, P. Malkani, and M. Seltzer. Passive nfs tracing of email and research workloads. In *Proceedings of the 2nd USENIX Conference on File and Storage Technologies*, FAST '03, pages 203–216, Berkeley, CA, USA, 2003. USENIX Association.

[4] A. Gulati, I. Ahmad, and C. A. Waldspurger. Parda: proportional allocation of resources for distributed storage access. In *Proccedings of the 7th conference on File and storage technologies*, pages 85–98, Berkeley, CA, USA, 2009. USENIX Association.

[5] A. Gulati, A. Merchant, and P. J. Varman. pclock: an arrival curve based approach for qos guarantees in shared storage systems. In *Proceedings of the 2007 ACM SIGMETRICS international conference on Measurement and modeling of computer systems*, SIGMETRICS '07, pages 13–24, New York, NY, USA, 2007. ACM.

[6] A. Gulati, A. Merchant, and P. J. Varman. mclock: handling throughput variability for hypervisor io scheduling. In *Proceedings of the 9th USENIX conference on Operating systems design and implementation*, OSDI'10, pages 1–7, Berkeley, CA, USA, 2010. USENIX Association.

[7] A. Gulati, G. Shanmuganathan, I. Ahmad, C. Waldspurger, and M. Uysal. Pesto: online storage performance management in virtualized datacenters. In *Proceedings of the 2nd ACM Symposium on Cloud Computing*, SOCC '11, pages 19:1–19:14, New York, NY, USA, 2011. ACM.

[8] L. Huang, G. Peng, and T.-c. Chiueh. Multi-dimensional storage virtualization. In *Proceedings of the joint international conference on Measurement and modeling of computer systems*, SIGMETRICS '04/Performance '04, pages 14–24, New York, NY, USA, 2004. ACM.

[9] W. Jin, J. S. Chase, and J. Kaur. Interposed proportional sharing for a storage service utility. *SIGMETRICS Perform. Eval. Rev.*, 32:37–48, June 2004.

[10] T. Kaldewey, T. Wong, R. Golding, A. Povzner, S. Brand, and C. Maltzahn. Virtualizing disk performance. In *Real-Time and Embedded Technology and Applications Symposium, 2008. RTAS '08. IEEE*, pages 319–330, April 2008.

[11] M. Karlsson, C. Karamanolis, and X. Zhu. Triage: Performance differentiation for storage systems using adaptive control. *Trans. Storage*, 1:457–480, November 2005.

[12] T. Kelly, I. Cohen, M. Goldszmidt, and K. Keeton. Inducing models of black-box storage arrays. *In Technical Report HPL-SSP-2004-108*, 2004.

[13] C. L. Liu and J. W. Layland. Scheduling algorithms for multiprogramming in a hard-real-time environment. *J. ACM*, 20:46–61, January 1973.

[14] L. Lu, P. Varman, and K. Doshi. Graduated qos by decomposing bursts: Don't let the tail wag your server. In *Distributed Computing Systems, 2009. ICDCS '09. 29th IEEE International Conference on*, pages 12–21, June 2009.

[15] C. R. Lumb, A. Merchant, and G. A. Alvarez. Facade: Virtual storage devices with performance guarantees. In *Proceedings of the 2nd USENIX Conference on File and Storage Technologies*, pages 131–144, Berkeley, CA, USA, 2003. USENIX Association.

[16] A. Merchant, M. Uysal, P. Padala, X. Zhu, S. Singhal, and K. Shin. Maestro: quality-of-service in large disk arrays. In *Proceedings of the 8th ACM international conference on Autonomic computing*, ICAC '11, pages 245–254, New York, NY, USA, 2011. ACM.

[17] A. Povzner, T. Kaldewey, S. Brandt, R. Golding, T. M. Wong, and C. Maltzahn. Efficient guaranteed disk request scheduling with fahrrad. In *Proceedings of the 3rd ACM SIGOPS/EuroSys European Conference on Computer Systems 2008*, Eurosys '08, pages 13–25, New York, NY, USA, 2008. ACM.

[18] A. Povzner, D. Sawyer, and S. Brandt. Horizon: efficient deadline-driven disk i/o management for distributed storage systems. In *Proceedings of the 19th ACM International Symposium on High Performance Distributed Computing*, HPDC '10, pages 1–12, New York, NY, USA, 2010. ACM.

[19] A. S. Povzner. *Efficient guaranteed disk i/o performance management*. PhD thesis, University of California at Santa Cruz, Santa Cruz, CA, USA, 2010. AAI3429522.

[20] L. Reuther and M. Pohlack. Rotational-position-aware real-time disk scheduling using a dynamic active subset (das). In *In Proceedings of the 24th IEEE Real-Time Systems Symposium (RTSS 2003). IEEE*, page 374. IEEE Computer Society, 2003.

[21] M. Spuri, G. Buttazzo, and S. S. S. Anna. Scheduling aperiodic tasks in dynamic priority systems. *Real-Time Systems*, 10:179–210, 1996.

[22] M. Wachs, M. Abd-El-Malek, E. Thereska, and G. R. Ganger. Argon: performance insulation for shared storage servers. In *Proceedings of the 5th USENIX conference on File and Storage Technologies*, pages 5–5, Berkeley, CA, USA, 2007. USENIX Association.

[23] M. Wang, K. Au, A. Ailamaki, A. Brockwell, C. Faloutsos, and G. R. Ganger. Storage device performance prediction with cart models. *SIGMETRICS Perform. Eval. Rev.*, 32:412–413, June 2004.

[24] Y. Wang. Ncq for power efficiency. *White paper*, February 2006.

[25] T. M. Wong, R. A. Golding, C. Lin, and R. A. Becker-szendy. Zygaria: storage performance as a managed resource. In *In IEEE Real Time and Embedded Technology and Applications Symposium (RTAS 06*, pages 125–134, 2006.

[26] Y. J. Yu, D. I. Shin, H. Eom, and H. Y. Yeom. Ncq vs. i/o scheduler: Preventing unexpected misbehaviors. *Trans. Storage*, 6:2:1–2:37, April 2010.

[27] X. Zhang, Y. Xu, and S. Jiang. Youchoose: Choosing your storage device as a performance interface to consolidated i/o service. *Trans. Storage*, 7:9:1–9:18, October 2011.

A Hybrid Local Storage Transfer Scheme for Live Migration of I/O Intensive Workloads

Bogdan Nicolae
Joint Laboratory for Petascale Computing
INRIA, France
bogdan.nicolae@inria.fr

Franck Cappello
Joint Laboratory for Petascale Computing
INRIA, France
University of Illinois at Urbana-Champaign, USA
fci@lri.fr

ABSTRACT

Live migration of virtual machines (VMs) is key feature of virtualization that is extensively leveraged in IaaS cloud environments: it is the basic building block of several important features, such as load balancing, pro-active fault tolerance, power management, online maintenance, etc. While most live migration efforts concentrate on how to transfer the memory from source to destination during the migration process, comparatively little attention has been devoted to the transfer of storage. This problem is gaining increasing importance: due to performance reasons, virtual machines that run large-scale, data-intensive applications tend to rely on local storage, which poses a difficult challenge on live migration: it needs to handle storage transfer in addition to memory transfer. This paper proposes a memory-migration independent approach that addresses this challenge. It relies on a hybrid active push / prioritized prefetch strategy, which makes it highly resilient to rapid changes of disk state exhibited by I/O intensive workloads. At the same time, it is minimally intrusive in order to ensure a maximum of portability with a wide range of hypervisors. Large scale experiments that involve multiple simultaneous migrations of both synthetic benchmarks and a real scientific application show improvements of up to 10x faster migration time, 10x less bandwidth consumption and 8x less performance degradation over state-of-art.

Categories and Subject Descriptors

D.4.2 [**OPERATING SYSTEMS**]: Storage Management

General Terms

Design, Performance, Experimentation

Keywords

live migration; block migration; local storage transfer; I/O intensive workloads; IaaS cloud computing; data-intensive applications

1. INTRODUCTION

Over the last few years, a large shift was recorded from privately own and managed hardware to Infrastructure-as-a-Service (IaaS) cloud computing [7]. Using IaaS, users can lease storage space and computation time from large datacenters in order to run their applications, paying only for the consumed resources.

Virtualization is the core technology behind IaaS clouds. Computational resources are presented to the user in form of virtual machines (VMs), which are fully customizable by the user. This equivalent to owning dedicated hardware, but without any long term cost and commitment. Thanks to virtualization, IaaS cloud providers can isolate and consolidate the workloads across their datacenter, thus being able to serve multiple users simultaneously in a secure way.

Live migration [11] is a key feature of virtualization. It gives the cloud provider the flexibility to freely move the VMs of the clients around the datacenter in a completely transparent fashion, which for the VMs is almost unnoticeable (i.e. they typically experience an interruption in the order of dozens of milliseconds or less). This ability can be leveraged for a variety of management tasks, such as:

Load balancing. the VMs can be rearranged across the physical machines of the datacenter in order to evenly distribute the workload and avoid imbalances caused by frequent deployment and termination of VMs.

Online maintenance. when physical machines need to be serviced (e.g. upgraded, repaired or replaced), VMs can be moved to other physical machines while the maintenance is in progress, without the need to shutdown or terminate any VM.

Power management. if the overall workload can be served by less physical machines, VMs can be consolidated from the hosts that are lightly loaded to hosts that are more heavily loaded [21]. Once the migration is complete, the hosts initially running the VMs can be shutdown, enabling the cloud provider to save on energy spending.

Proactive fault tolerance. if a physical machine is suspected of failing in the near future, its VMs can be pro-actively moved to safer locations [20]. This has the potential to reduce the failure rate experienced by the user, thus enabling the provider to improve the conditions stipulated in the service level agreement. Even if the machine will not completely fail, migration may still prevent VMs from running with degraded performance.

A particularly difficult challenge arises in the context of live migration when the VMs make use of local storage. This scenario is frequently encountered in practice [5]: VMs need a "scratch space", i.e. a place where to store temporary data generated during their runtime. Such a feature can significantly speed up large-scale data-intensive applications, as it eliminates the need to rely on a much slower parallel file system or cloud repository. To this end, cloud providers typically install local disks on the physical machines that are running the user workloads and enable the VMs to access it. Since one of the goals of live migration is to relinquish the source as fast as possible, no residual dependencies on the source host should remain after migration. Thus, the complete disk state needs to be transferred to destination while it is actively changed by the VM.

In this paper we propose a live storage transfer mechanism that complements existing live migration approaches in order to address the challenge mentioned above. Our approach is specifically optimized to withstand rapid changes to the disk state during live migration, a scenario that is frequently caused by VMs executing I/O intensive workloads. We aim to minimize the migration time and network traffic overhead that live migrations generate under these circumstances, while at the same time minimizing the I/O performance degradation perceived by the VMs. This is an important issue: as noted in [31], the impact of live migration on a heavy loaded VM cannot be neglected, especially when service level agreements need to be met.

Our contributions can be summarized as follows:

- We present a series of design principles that facilitate efficient transfer of local storage during live migration. Unlike conventional approaches, our proposal is designed to efficiently tolerate I/O intensive workloads inside the VM while the live migration is in progress. (Section 4.1)

- We show how to materialize these design principles in practice through a series of algorithmic descriptions, that are applied to build a completely transparent implementation with respect to the hypervisor. (Sections 4.2, 4.3 and 4.4)

- We evaluate our approach in a series of experiments, each conducted on hundreds of nodes provisioned on the Grid'5000 testbed, using both synthetic benchmarks and real-life applications. These experiments demonstrate significant improvement in migration time and network traffic over state-of-art approaches, while reducing at the same time the negative impacts of live migration on performance inside the VMs. (Section 5)

2. THE PROBLEM OF STORAGE TRANSFER DURING LIVE MIGRATION

In order to migrate a VM, its state must be transferred from the host node to the destination node where it will continue running. This state consists of three main components: *memory*, *state of devices* (e.g. CPU, network interface) and *storage*. The state of devices typically comprises a minimal amount of information (hardware buffers, processor execution state, etc.) and is usually considered negligible.

However, the size of memory and storage however can explode to huge sizes and can take extended periods of time to transfer.

One solution to this problem is to simply pay for the cost of interrupting the application while transferring the memory and storage, which is known as *offline migration*. However, distributed data-intensive applications do not work in isolation: there are dependencies between distributed processes running in different VM instances. Thus, offline migration causes an unacceptably long downtime during which the VM is not not able to communicate with the outside, which leads to accumulation of jitter that degrades the performance of the whole application.

To alleviate this issue, *live migration* [11] is a potential solution: it enables a VM to continue almost uninterrupted (i.e. with a downtime in the order of dozens of milliseconds) while experiencing minimal negative effects due to migration. In order to be possible, live migration needs to solve a difficult problem: keeping a *consistent view* of memory and storage at all times for the VM, while performing background transfers that converge to a state where the memory and storage is fully available on the destination and the source is not needed anymore. Techniques to do so efficiently in the context of HPC applications have been studied before for memory [16], but how to achieve this for storage remains an open issue.

Initially, the problem of keeping a consistent view of storage between the source and destination was simply avoided by using a parallel file system rather than local disks. Thus, the source and destination are always fully synchronized and no transfer of storage is necessary. However, under normal operation, this approach can have several disadvantages: (1) it consumes system bandwidth and storage space on shared disks for temporary I/O that is not intended to be shared; (2) it limits the sustained throughput that the VM can achieve for I/O; (3) it raises scalability issues, especially considering the growing sizes of datacenters.

Given these disadvantages, such a solution is not feasible to adopt just for the purpose of supporting live migrations. It is important to enable VMs to use local storage as scratch space, while still providing efficient support for live migration. As a consequence, in order to obtain a consistent view of storage that does not indefinitely depend on the source, storage must be transferred from the source to the destination.

Apparently, transferring local storage is highly similar to the problem of transferring memory: one potential solution is simply to consider local storage as an extension of memory. However, such an approach does not take into account the differences between the I/O workload and memory workload, potentially performing sub-optimally. Furthermore, unlike memory, VM storage does not always need to be fully transferred to the destination, as a large part of it is never touched during the lifetime of the VM and can obtained in a different fashion, for example directly from the cloud repository.

In this context, the storage transfer strategy plays a key role. To quantify the efficiency of such a strategy, we rely on a series of performance metrics. Our goal is to optimize the storage transfer according to these metrics:

Migration time.

is the total time elapsed between the moment when the live migration was initiated on the source and the moment when all resources needed by the VM instance are fully available at the destination. This parameter is important because it indicates the total amount of time during which the source is busy and cannot be reallocated to a different task or shut down. Even if migration time for a single VM instance is typically in the order of seconds and minutes, when considering the economy of scale, multiple migrations add up to huge amounts of time during which resources are wasted. Thus, a low migration time is highly desirable.

Network traffic.

is the amount of network traffic that can be traced back to live migration. This includes memory (whose transfer cannot be avoided), any direct transfer of storage from source to destination, as well as any traffic generated as a result of synchronizing the source with the destination through shared storage. Network traffic is expensive: it steals away bandwidth from VM instances, effectively diminishing the overall potential of the datacenter. Thus, it must be lowered as much as possible.

Impact on application performance.

is the extent to which live migrations cause a performance degradation in the application that runs inside the VM instances. This is the effect of consuming resources (bandwidth, CPU time, etc.) during live migrations that could otherwise be leveraged by the VM instances themselves to finish faster. Obviously, it is desirable to limit the overhead of migration as much as possible, in order to minimize any potential negative effects on the application.

3. RELATED WORK

If downtime is not an issue, *offline migration* is a solution that potentially consumes the least amount of resources. This is a three-stage procedure: freeze the VM instance at the source, take a snapshot of its memory and storage, then restore the VM state at the destination based on the snapshot. Several techniques to take a snapshot of VM instances have been proposed, such as: dedicated copy-on-write image formats [12, 30], dedicated virtual disk storage services based on shadowing and cloning [26], fork-consistent replication systems based on log-structuring [13], de-duplication of memory pages [28]. Many times, for HPC applications it is cheaper to save the state of the application inside the virtual disk of the VM instance and then reboot the VM instance on the destination, rather than save the memory inside the snapshot [27]. Approaches such as *VMFlock* [4] are specifically optimized to migrate a whole set of VMs simultaneously in an offline fashion between clouds, by taking advantage of similarities between their corresponding images and de-duplicating them in a distributed fashion.

Extensive live migration research was done for memory-to-memory transfer. The *pre-copy* strategy [11, 22] is by far the most widely adopted approach implemented in production hypervisors. It works by copying the bulk of memory to the destination in background, while the VM instance in running on the source. If any transmitted memory pages are modified in the mean time, they are re-sent to the target subsequently, based on the assumption that eventually the memory on the source and destination converge up to a point when it is cheap to synchronize them and transfer control to the destination. Several techniques can be used to reduce

the overhead incurred by the background transfers, such as online compression [29, 24].

However, pre-copy has its limitations: if memory is modified faster than it is copied in the background to the destination, this solution never converges. To address this limitation, Ibrahim et al. [16] propose an optimized pre-copy strategy that dynamically adapts to the memory change rate in order to guarantee convergence. Other approaches, such as Checkpoint/Restart and Log/Replay were successfully adopted by Liu et al. [18] to significantly reduce downtime and network bandwidth consumption over pre-copy. A *post-copy* strategy was proposed by Hines et al. [15]. Unlike pre-copy, control is transferred to the destination from the beginning, while relying on the source to fetch the needed content in the background up to the point when the source is not needed anymore. This approach copies each memory page only once, thus guaranteeing convergence regardless of how often the memory is modified.

Although not directly related to live migration, live memory transfer techniques were also proposed by Lagar-Cavilla et al. [17] in from of *VM cloning*, an abstraction for VM replication that works similar to the fork system call. This is similar to live migration in that the destination must receive a consistent view of the source's memory, however, the goal is to enable the source to continue execution on a different path rather than shut it down as quickly as possible.

The problem of storage transfer was traditionally avoided in favor of shared storage that is fully synchronized both at source and destination. However, several attempts break from this tradition.

A widely used approach in production is incremental block migration, as available in QEMU/KVM [3]. In this case, copy-on-write snapshots of a base disk image, shared using a parallel system, are created on the local disks of the nodes that run the VMs. Live migration is then performed by transferring the memory together with the copy-on-write snapshots, both using pre-copy. Thus, this approach inherits the drawbacks of pre-copy for I/O: under heavy I/O pressure the disk content may be changed faster than it can be copied to the destination, which introduces an infinite dependence on the source.

Bradford et al. [8] propose a two-phase transfer: in the first phase, the whole disk image is transferred in the background to the destination. Then, in the second phase the live migration of memory is started, while all new I/O operations performed by the source are also sent in parallel to the destination as incremental differences. Once control is transferred to the destination, first the hypervisor waits for all incremental differences to be successfully applied, then resumes the VM instance. However, waiting for the I/O to finish can increase downtime and reduce application performance. Furthermore, since a full disk image can grow in the order of many GB, the first phase can take a very long time to complete, negatively impacting the total migration time.

A similar approach, called *mirroring*, is proposed by Haselhorst et al. [14]: the first phase transfers the disk content in the background to the destination, while in the second phase all writes are trapped and issued in parallel to the destination. However, unlike Bradford et al., writes complete on the source only after they also complete on the destination. Under I/O intensive workloads, this can lead to increased latency and decreased throughput for writes that happen before control is transferred to the destination. Furthermore, it can happen that some workloads repeatedly overwrite the same location. In this case, mirroring unnecessarily slows down migration and consumes bandwidth. To alleviate this, Mashtizadeh et al. [19] complemented mirroring with hot block avoidance. However, according to the authors, this introduced a high complexity and did not work for certain workloads.

Our own effort tries to overcome these limitations while achieving the goals presented in Section 2.

4. OUR APPROACH

To address the issues mentioned in Section 2, in this section we propose a completely transparent live storage transfer scheme that complements the live migration of memory. We introduce a series of design principles that are at the foundation of our approach (Section 4.1), then show how to integrate them in an IaaS cloud architecture (Section 4.2) and finally introduce a series of algorithmic descriptions (Section 4.3) that we detail how to implement in practice (Section 4.4).

4.1 Design principles

Transfer only the modified contents of the VM disk image to the destination. Conceptually, the disk space of the VMs is divided into two parts: (1) a basic part that holds the operating system files together with user applications and data; (2) a writable part that holds all temporary data written during the lifetime of the VM. The basic part is called the base disk image. It is configured by the user, stored persistently on the cloud's repository and then used as a template to deploy multiple VM instances.

As this part is never altered, it must not necessarily be transferred from the source to the destination: it can be obtained directly from the cloud repository. Thus, we propose to transfer only the actually written data from the source to the destination, while any data that is required from the basic part is directly accessed from the cloud repository where the base disk image is stored.

To reduce latency and improve read throughput on the destination, we transparently prefetch the hot contents of the base disk image according to hints obtained from the source. Note that under concurrency, this can incur a heavy load on the repository. To avoid any potential bottleneck introduced by read contention, we assume a distributed repository is present that can evenly distribute a read workload under concurrency. Under these circumstances, we can store the disk image in a striped fashion: it is split into small chunks that are distributed among the storage elements of the repository.

Transparency with respect to the hypervisor. The I/O workload of the VM can be very different from its memory workload. At one extreme, the application running inside the VM can change the memory pages very frequently but rarely generate I/O to local storage. At the other extreme, the application may generate heavy I/O to local storage but barely touch memory (e.g. it may need to flush in-memory data to disk). For this reason, the best way to transfer memory can be different from the best way to transfer storage.

To deal with this issue, we propose to separate the storage transfer from memory transfer and handle it independently from the hypervisor. Doing so has two important advantages. First, it enables a high flexibility in choosing what strategy to apply for the memory transfer and how to fine tune it depending on the memory workload. Second, it offers high portability, as the storage transfer can be used in tandem with a wide selection of hypervisors without any modification.

Note that this separation implies that our approach is not directly involved in the process of transferring control from source to destination. This is the responsibility of the hypervisor. How to detect this moment and best leverage it to our advantage is detailed in Section 4.4.

Hybrid active push-prioritized prefetch strategy. Under an I/O intensive workload, the VM rapidly changes the disk state, which under live migration becomes a difficult challenge for the storage transfer strategy. Under such circumstances, attempting to synchronize the storage on the source and destination before transferring control to the destination introduces two issues:

- The same disk content may change repeatedly. In this case, content is unnecessarily copied at the destination, eventually being overwritten before the destination receives control. Thus, migration time is increased and network traffic is generated unnecessarily.

- Disk content may change faster than it can be copied to the destination. This has devastating consequences, as live migration will never finish and control will never be transferred to the destination. Thus all network traffic and negative impact on the application is in vain, not to mention keeping the destination busy.

To avoid these issues, we propose a hybrid strategy described below.

As long as the hypervisor did not transfer control to the destination, the source actively pushes all local disk content to the destination, While the VM is still running at the source, we monitor how many times each chunk was written. If a chunk was written more times than a predefined *Threshold*, we mark this chunk as *dirty* and avoid pushing it to the destination. Doing so enables us deal with the first issue: each chunk is transferred no more than *Threshold* times to the destination.

Once the hypervisor transfers control to the destination, we send the destination the list of remaining chunks that it needs from the source in order to achieve a consistent view of local storage. At this point, our main concern is to eliminate the dependency on the source as fast as possible. In order to do so, we prefetch the chunks in decreasing order of access frequency. This ensures that *dirty* chunks, which are likely to be accessed in the future, arrive first on the destination. If the destination needs a chunk from the source before it was prefetched, we suspend the prefetching and serve the read request with priority.

Doing so enables us to deal with the second issue, since storage does not delay in any way the transfer of control to the destination. No matter how fast disk changes, once control arrives at the destination, the source is playing a passive role and does not generate any new disk content, thus leaving only a finite amount of data to be pulled from the source.

4.2 Architecture

The simplified architecture of an IaaS cloud that integrates our approach is depicted in Figure 1. The typical elements found in the cloud are illustrated with a light background, while the elements introduced by our approach are illustrated by a darker background.

The *shared repository* is a service that survives failures and is responsible to store the base disk images that are used as a template by the compute nodes. It can either use a dedicated set of resources or simply aggregate a part of each of the local disks of the compute nodes into a common pool. For example, *Amazon S3* [6] or a parallel file system can serve this role. The cloud client has direct access to the repository and is allowed to upload and download the base disk images.

Using the *cloud middleware*, which is the frontend of the user to the cloud, an arbitrary number of VM instances can be deployed starting from the same base disk image. Typically these VM instances form a virtual distributed environment where they communicate among each other. The cloud middleware is also responsible to coordinate all VM instances of all users in order to meet its service level agreements, while minimizing operational costs. In particular, it implements the VM scheduling strategies that leverage live migration in order to perform load-balancing, power saving, pro-active fault tolerance, etc.

Each compute node runs a *hypervisor* that is responsible for running the VM instances. All reads and writes issued by the hypervisor to the underlying virtual disk are trapped by the *migration manager*, which is the central actor of our approach and is responsible to implement our live storage migration strategy.

Under normal operation, the migration manager presents the disk image to the hypervisor as a regular file that is accessible from the local disk. Whenever the hypervisor writes to the image file, the migration manager generates new chunks that are stored locally. Whenever the hypervisor reads a region of the image that has never been touched before, the chunks that cover that region are fetched from the repository and copied locally. Thus, future accesses to a region that has been either read or written before are served from the local disk directly. Using this strategy, the I/O pressure put on the repository is minimal, as contents is fetched on-demand only. At the same time, the migration manager is listening for migration requests and implements the design principles presented in Section 4.1. The next section is dedicated to detail this aspect.

4.3 Zoom on the migration manager

The migration manager is designed to listen for two types of events: *migration requests* and *migration notifications*.

The cloud middleware can send migration requests to the migration manager using the MIGRATION_REQUEST primitive (Algorithm 1). Upon receipt of this event, the migration manager assumes the role of *migration source* (by setting the *isSource* flag). At this point, all chunks that were locally modified (part of *ModifiedSet*) are queued up into the *RemainingSet* for active pushing to the destination in the background. Furthermore, it starts keeping track of how many times each chunk is modified during the migration process. This information is stored in *WriteCount*, initially 0 for all chunks. Once this initialization step completed, it sends a migration notification to the migration

---

Algorithm 1 Migration request on the source

1: **procedure** MIGRATION_REQUEST(*Destination*)
2:     $RemainingSet \leftarrow ModifiedSet$
3:     **for all** $c \in VirtualDisk$ **do**
4:         $WriteCount[c] \leftarrow 0$
5:     **end for**
6:     start BACKGROUND_PUSH
7:     $isSource \leftarrow$ **true**
8:     invoke MIGRATION_NOTIFICATION on *Destination*
9:     forward migration request to the hypervisor
10:     notify BACKGROUND_PUSH
11: **end procedure**
12: **procedure** BACKGROUND_PUSH
13:     **while true do**
14:         wait for notification
15:         **while** $\exists c \in RemainingSet : WriteCount[c] < Threshold$ **do**
16:             $buf \leftarrow$ contents of c
17:             push (c, buf) to *Destination*
18:             $RemainingSet \leftarrow RemainingSet \setminus \{c\}$
19:         **end while**
20:     **end while**
21: **end procedure**

---

manager running on *Destination*, which assumes the role of *migration destination* and starts accepting chunks that are pushed from the source. At the same time, the source forwards the migration request to the hypervisor, which independently starts the migration of memory from the source to the destination. As soon as the migration has started, the BACKGROUND_PUSH task is launched, which starts pushing all chunks whose access count is less than *Threshold* to the source.

If a chunk c is modified before control is transferred to the destination, its write count is increased. This results in the BACKGROUND_PUSH task being notified (which potentially wakes up if not already busy with pushing other chunks). A simplified WRITE primitive that achieves this (but does not handle writes to partial chunks or writes spanning multiple chunks) is listed in Algorithm 2.

Algorithm 2 Simplified writes of single full chunks

1: **function** WRITE(c, *buffer*)
2:     **if** *isDestination* **then**
3:         cancel any pull(c) in progress
4:         $RemainingSet \leftarrow RemainingSet \setminus \{c\}$
5:     **end if**
6:     contents of $c \leftarrow buffer$
7:     $ModifiedSet \leftarrow ModifiedSet \cup \{c\}$
8:     **if** *isSource* **then**
9:         $WriteCount[c] \leftarrow WriteCount[c] + 1$
10:         $RemainingSet \leftarrow RemainingSet \cup \{c\}$
11:         notify BACKGROUND_PUSH
12:     **end if**
13:     **return** success
14: **end function**

Once the hypervisor is ready to transfer control to the destination and invokes SYNC on the disk image exposed by the migration manager, the BACKGROUND_PUSH task is stopped and the source enters in a passive phase where it

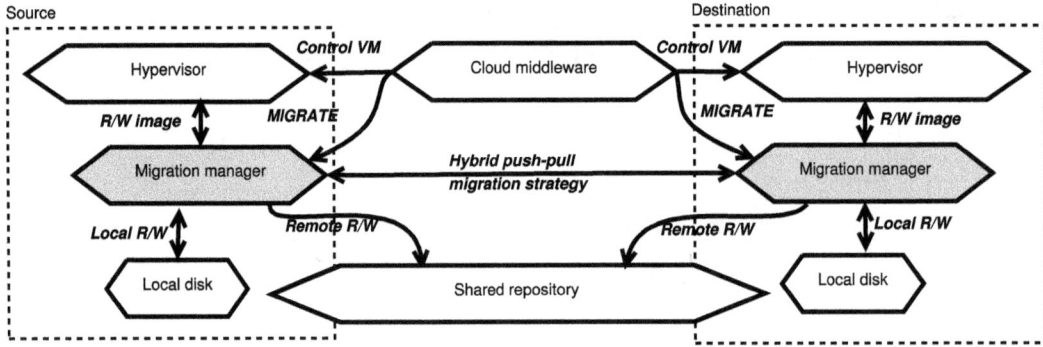

Figure 1: Cloud architecture that integrates our approach via the migration manager (dark background).

listens for pull requests coming from the destination. In order to signal that it is ready for this, the source invokes TRANSFER_IO_CONTROL on the destination, as shown in Algorithm 3. The TRANSFER_IO_CONTROL primitive receives as parameters the remaining set of chunks that need to be pulled from the source, together with their write counts. It then starts the BACKGROUND_PULL task, whose role is to prefetch all remaining chunks from the source. Priority is given to the chunks with the highest write count, under the assumption that frequently modified chunks will also be modified in the future.

Algorithm 3 Migration notification and transfer of control on destination
---
1: **procedure** MIGRATION_NOTIFICATION
2:    $isDestination \leftarrow$ **true**
3:    accept chunks from $Source$
4: **end procedure**
5: **procedure** TRANSFER_IO_CONTROL(RS, WC)
6:    $RemainingSet \leftarrow RS$
7:    $WriteCount \leftarrow AC$
8:    start BACKGROUND_PULL
9: **end procedure**
10: **procedure** BACKGROUND_PULL
11:    **while** $RemainingSet \neq \emptyset$ **do**
12:       $c \leftarrow c' \in RemainingSet : WriteCount[c'] = max(WriteCount[RemainingSet])$
13:       $RemainingSet \leftarrow RemainingSet \setminus \{c\}$
14:       pull(c) from $Source$
15:    **end while**
16: **end procedure**

Note that chunks may be needed earlier than they are scheduled to be pulled by BACKGROUND_PULL. To accommodate this case, the READ primitive needs to be adjusted accordingly. A simplified form that handles only reads of single full chunks is listed in Algorithm 4. There are two possible scenarios: (1) the chunk c that is needed is already being pulled - in this case it is enough to wait for completion; (2) c is scheduled for prefetching but the pull has not started yet - in this case BACKGROUND_PULL is suspended and resumed at a later time in order to allow READ to pull c. On the other hand, if a chunk c that is part of the $RemainingSet$ is modified by WRITE, the old content must not be pulled from the source anymore and any pending pull of chunk c must be aborted.

Once all remaining chunks have been pulled at the destina-

Algorithm 4 Simplified reads of single full chunks

1: **function** READ(c)
2:    **if** $isDestination$ **and** $c \in RemainingSet$ **then**
3:       **if** c is being pulled by BACKGROUND_PULL **then**
4:          wait until c is available
5:       **else**
6:          suspend BACKGROUND_PULL
7:          pull(c) from $Source$
8:          $RemainingSet \leftarrow RemainingSet \setminus \{c\}$
9:          resume BACKGROUND_PULL
10:       **end if**
11:    **end if**
12:    fetch c from repository if c not available locally
13:    **return** contents of c
14: **end function**
---

tion, the source is not needed anymore. Both the hypervisor and the migration manager can be stopped and the source can be shut down (or its resources used for other purposes). At this point, the live migration is complete.

A graphical illustration of the interactions performed in parallel by the algorithms presented above, from the initial migration request on the source to the moment when the live migration is complete, is depicted in Figure 2. Solid arrows are used to represent interactions between the migration managers. A dotted pattern is used to represent interactions between the migration manager and the hypervisor, as well as the interactions between the hypervisors themselves. Note that the transfer of memory is not explicitly represented, as our approach is completely transparent with respect to the hypervisor and its migration strategy.

4.4 Implementation

We implemented the *migration manager* on top of *FUSE* (File System in UserspacE) [1]. Its basic functionality (i.e. to intercept the reads and writes of the hypervisor with the purpose of caching the hot contents of the base disk image locally, while storing all modifications locally as well) is based on our previous work presented in [26]. The migration manager exposes the local view of the base disk image as file inside the mount point, accessible to the hypervisor through the standard POSIX access interface.

To keep a maximum of portability with respect to the hypervisor, we exploit the fact that the hypervisor calls the sync system call right before transferring control to the destination. Thus, our implementation of the sync system

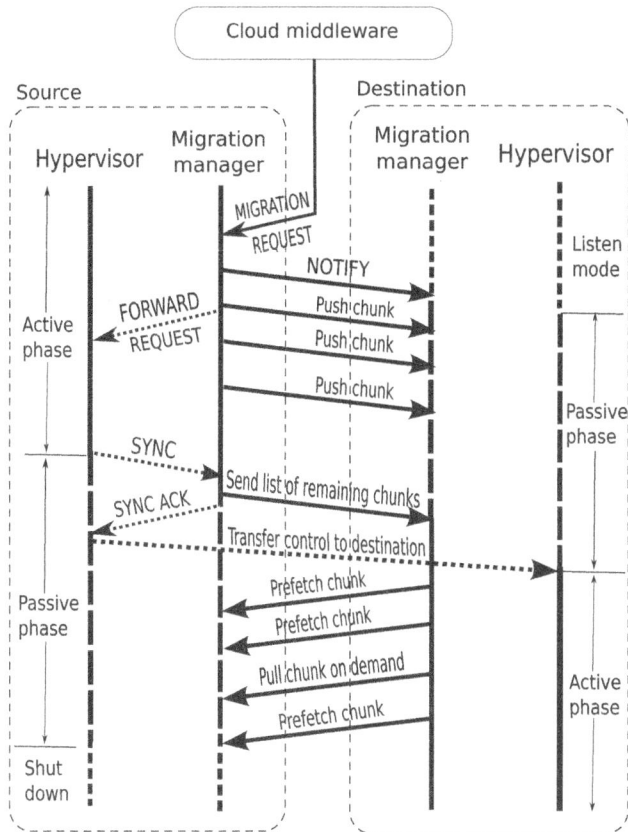

Figure 2: Overview of the live storage transfer as it progresses in time.

call invokes TRANSFER_IO_CONTROL on the destination, ensuring that the destination is ready to intercept reads and writes before the hypervisor transfers control to the VM instance itself. Furthermore, we strive to remain fully POSIX-compliant despite the need to support migration requests. For this reason, we implemented the MIGRATION_REQUEST primitive as an *ioctl*.

Finally, the migration manager is designed to integrate with *BlobSeer* [23, 25], which acts as the repository that holds the base VM disk images. BlobSeer enables *scalable aggregation of storage space* from a large number of participating nodes, while featuring transparent data striping and replication. This enables it to reach high aggregated throughputs under concurrency while remaining highly resilient under faults.

5. EVALUATION

5.1 Experimental setup

The experiments were performed on Grid'5000, an experimental testbed for distributed computing that federates nine sites in France. We used 100 nodes of the graphene cluster from the Nancy site, each of which is equipped with a quad-core Intel Xeon X3440 x86_64 CPU with hardware support for virtualization, local disk storage of 278 GB (access speed $\simeq$55 MB/s using SATA II ahci driver) and 16 GB of RAM. The nodes are interconnected with Gigabit Ethernet (mea-

sured 117.5 MB/s for TCP sockets with MTU = 1500 B with a latency of $\simeq$0.1 ms).

We use QEMU/KVM [3] 1.0 as the hypervisor. It is running on all compute nodes is , while the operating system is a recent Debian Sid Linux distribution. For all experiments, a 4 GB raw disk image file based on the same Debian Sid distribution was used as the guest environment. We rely on the standard live migration implemented in QEMU (pre-copy) in order to transfer the memory. In order to minimize the overhead of migration, we set the maximum migration speed to match the maximum bandwidth of the network interface (i.e. 1G).

5.2 Methodology

The experiments we perform involve a set of VM instances, each of which is running on a different compute node. We refer to the nodes where the VM instances are initially running as *sources*. The rest of the nodes act as *destinations* and are prepared to receive live migrations at any time.

We compare five approaches throughout our evaluation:

5.2.1 Live storage transfer using our approach

In this setting we rely on BlobSeer to store base disk image and on the FUSE-based migration manager (described in Section 4.4) to expose a locally modifiable view of the disk image to the hypervisor. BlobSeer is deployed on all compute nodes and stores the initial base disk image (4 GB) in a distributed fashion, using a stripe size of 256 KB (which from our previous experience is large enough to avoid excessive fragmentation overhead, yet small enough to avoid contention under concurrent read accesses). Any live migration request is treated according to the strategy described in Section 4.3. Both the transfer of storage and memory proceed concurrently and independently. For the rest of this paper, we refer to this setting as our−approach.

5.2.2 Live storage transfer using other techniques

We compare our approach to three other techniques: (1) a pure pre-copy approach (denoted precopy), in which case we assume the local modifications are stored in a qcow2 [12] disk snapshot and the storage transfer is performed using QEMU/KVM's standard incremental block migration; (2) an improved precopy approach (denoted mirror), based on our FUSE implementation, that performs all writes synchronously both at the source and destination with the intent to reproduce the approach presented in [14]; and finally (3) a pure post-copy approach (denoted postcopy), that is a based on our approach and simply remains passive during the push phase, deferring any transfer until after the moment when control is transferred to the destination.

5.2.3 Synchronization through a parallel file system

We include in our evaluation a third setting where the modifications to the base disk image are not stored locally but are synchronized on the source and destination through a parallel file system (denoted pvfs−shared). This corresponds to the traditional solution that avoids storage transfer during live migration altogether. For the purpose of this work, we have chosen PVFS [10] as the parallel file system, as it is a popular POSIX-compliant high performance storage solution that hypervisors can use for storage synchronization. In this setting, the base disk image is stored in a PVFS deployment that spans all compute nodes, while the local modifications are shared between the source and the destination through a qcow2 disk snapshot that is stored in the same PVFS deployment.

Table 1: Summary of compared approaches

Approach	Local storage transfer strategy
our−approach	As presented in Section 4.3
mirror	Sync writes both at src and dest
postcopy	Pull from src after transfer of control
precopy	Push to dest before transfer of control
pvfs−shared	Does not apply (All writes go to PVFS)

These approaches are summarized in Table 1 and are compared based on the performance metrics defined in Section 2:

- *Migration time*: is the time elapsed between the moment when the migration has been initiated and the source has been relinquished. For precopy, mirror and pvfs−shared, the live migration ends as soon as the control is transferred to the destination. For our−approach and postcopy, migration time also includes the time spent by the destination to pull all remaining local modifications from the source.

- *Network traffic*: is the total network traffic generated during the experiments by the VM instances due to I/O to their virtual disks and live migration. Except pvfs−shared, this traffic includes all memory and storage transfers. In the case of pvfs−shared, it includes the memory transfers and all I/O generated during the lifetime of the VMs (which is redirected to PVFS), regardless whether inside or outside of migration.

- *Impact on application performance*: is the performance degradation perceived by the application during live migration when compared to the case when no migration is performed. For the purpose of this work, we are interested in the impact on the sustained I/O throughput in various benchmarking scenarios, as well as the impact on total runtime for data-intensive HPC applications.

5.3 Live migration performance of I/O intensive benchmarks

Our first series of experiments evaluates the performance of live migration for two I/O intensive benchmarks: *IOR* [2] and *AsyncWR*.

IOR is a popular HPC I/O benchmarking tool. It measures read and write throughput using various access interfaces (POSIX, HDF5, MPI-IO). For the purpose of this work, we focus on the POSIX access interface, as it is the choice of many HPC applications that typically write output data and checkpointing data through it. Our benchmark consists in performing 10 iterations of IOR using a single process running inside the VM that writes and then reads a 1 GB large file in blocks of 256 KB. Under no live migration, the maximal achieved read and write performance is 1 GB/s and 266 MB/s respectively.

AsyncWR is a benchmarking tool that we developed to simulate the behavior of data-intensive applications that mix computations with intensive I/O. It runs a fixed number of iterations, each of which performs a computational task that keeps the CPU busy (increments a counter) while generating random data into a memory buffer. This memory buffer

is copied at the beginning of next iteration into an alternate memory buffer and written asynchronously to the file system. Using this workload, we aim to study the impact of storage migration in a scenario where a moderate constant I/O pressure is generated inside the VM instances while the CPU is busy. We fixed the number of iterations to 180 using a data size of 1 MB/iteration, which corresponds to a constant I/O pressure of about 6 MB/s when no live migration occurs.

The experiment consists in launching each of the benchmarks inside a VM instance and then performing a live migration after a delay of 100 seconds. This gives the VM instance a warm-up period that avoids instant migrations due to lack of accumulated changes, while at the same time forcing the live migration to withstand the full I/O pressure from the beginning. The amount of RAM available to the VM instance is fixed at 4 GB.

The total migration time is depicted in Figure 3(a). As can be noticed, for the highly I/O intensive *IOR* workload there is a large difference between the five approaches. Since the pvfs−shared approach needs to transfer memory only, it is the fastest of all three. Comparatively, our−approach manages to perform a complete storage transfer during live migration in about 4x more time, which itself is more than 3x faster than postcopy. This underlines the importance of the push phase in overlapping the memory transfer with the storage transfer, which ultimately reduces overall migration time. Pure precopy seems to transfer a lot of storage more than once, which explains its more than 10x slower migration time when compared to our−approach. Although this problem is alleviated by mirror, it slows down writes, making it about 2.8x slower than our−approach. However, for *AsyncWR* (i.e. when the I/O workload is moderate), mirroring can lead to a faster migration than our−approach. Still, our approach is faster than pure postcopy and precopy. As expected, pvfs−shared is the fastest in the *AsyncWR* case as well.

When comparing network traffic (Figure 3(b)), a clear trend is visible: our−approach and postcopy have a clear advantage over the other approaches, with postcopy slightly better due to the fact that it needs to transfer only a minimal amount of data. Pure precopy generates a lot of network traffic due to accumulation of writes on the source, which can be alleviated by mirroring. Finally, the worst of all approaches is as expected pvfs−shared: it generates network traffic for every I/O request, regardless whether it is during live migration or not. Compared to pvfs−shared, our approach conserves bandwidth by more than an order of magnitude in the *IOR* case.

Finally, the impact of live migration on the performance results of *IOR* and *AsyncWR* is illustrated in Figure 3(c). We focus on the achieved throughputs for the IOR benchmark, both for reading (*IOR-Read*) and writing (*IOR-Write*), as well as the write throughput achieved for *AsyncWR*. Due to large differences between the absolute values of the three throughput types, we have chosen to normalize the average values obtained during the experiment with respect to the maximal achieved values when no live migration is performed. These maximal values are: 1 GB/s for *IOR-Read*, 266 MB/s for *IOR-Write* and 6 MB/s for *AsyncWR*.

For the IOR benchmark, a large gap can be observed between pvfs−shared and the other approaches. Here it becomes clearly visible that under I/O intensive scenarios, synchro-

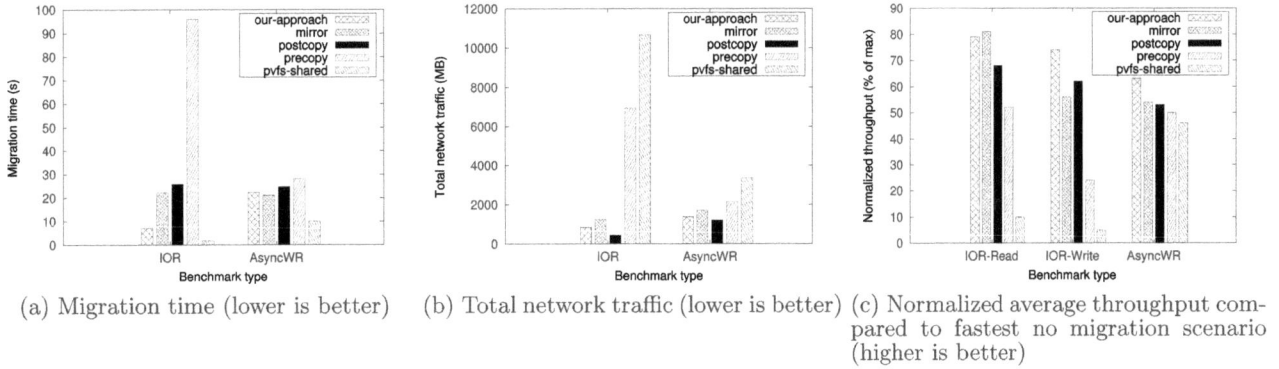

(a) Migration time (lower is better) (b) Total network traffic (lower is better) (c) Normalized average throughput compared to fastest no migration scenario (higher is better)

Figure 3: Migration performance of a VM instance (4 GB of RAM) that performs I/O intensive workloads

nizing through the parallel file system in order to avoid storage transfer during live migration has a high price: the total read throughput is less than 10% of the maximum achievable throughput, while the write throughput is less than 5%. Our approach achieves 80% of maximal read throughput, which is marginally surpassed only by mirror, due to the fact that no data resides on the source anymore and thus it does not trigger on-demand pulls after the control was transferred to the destination. This effect is also visible when comparing our approach to postcopy: in this case, our approach achieves 10% more read bandwidth due to the fact that the push phase diminishes the amount of data that needs to be pulled on-demand after the transfer of control. The repeated transfers of the same data triggered by precopy are also visible in the sustained throughput: it reaches only 50% of the maximal read throughput and 25% of the maximal write throughput. Our approach is the clear winner when comparing the sustained write throughputs: it performs by almost 15% better than postcopy. This also demonstrates the trade-off necessary to achieve a slightly higher read throughput using mirror: the achieved write throughput is by 20% smaller than our approach.

In the case of *AsyncWR*, an overall drop in sustained write throughput can be observed when comparing to the *IOR* case. The only exception to this is pvfs–shared, which significantly catches up with the other approaches, but still offers the lowest throughput. This is explained by the fact that unlike *IOR*, which is a purely I/O oriented workload, *AsyncWR* performs memory-intensive operations on the data before it is written, which increases the overhead of the memory transfer, ultimately leading to contention for bandwidth between memory and storage transfer, thus the observed effect. Nevertheless, our approach achieves at least 10% more bandwidth when compared to the other approaches, whose performance is quite close one to another.

5.4 Performance of concurrent live migrations

Our next series of experiments aims to evaluate the performance of all five approaches in a highly concurrent scenario where multiple live migrations are initiated simultaneously. To this end, we use the *AsyncWR* benchmark presented in Section 5.3.

The experimental setup is as follows: we fix the number of sources to 30 and gradually increase the number of destinations from 1 to 30, in steps of 10. On all sources we launch

the *AsyncWR* benchmark, wait until a warm-up period of 100 seconds has elapsed, and then simultaneously initiate the live migrations to the destinations. We keep the same configuration as in the previous section: the total amount of data is fixed at 1800 MB, while the amount of RAM available to the VM instance is fixed at 4 GB.

As can be observed in Figure 4(a), with increasing number of live migrations, all approaches except precopy keep an almost constant average migration time. On the other hand, precopy experiences a steady increase in average migration time, which reaches over 50% for 30 migrations when compared to 1 migration.

In order to explain this finding, it needs to be correlated to the total network traffic, depicted in Figure 4(b). As can be noticed, precopy experiences a sharp increase in network traffic, whereas the rest of approaches experience a much milder trend. Except for pvfs–shared, all approaches generate network traffic exclusively because of the live migrations. Thus, the depicted network traffic is concentrated over very short periods of time. Since the total system bandwidth (approx. 8 GB/s provided by a Cisco Catalyst switch) is insufficient to accommodate the instantaneous needs of precopy, a slowdown in transfer speed occurs when increasing the number of live migrations, which ultimately reflects into increased average migration time.

Thanks to earlier transfer of control to the destination, our approach and postcopy enables new data to be generated directly at the destination, greatly reducing the network traffic induced by the storage migration, which enables it to avoid reaching the system bandwidth limit. Although counter-intuitive, reaching this limit is also avoided by mirror. This happens because mirroring actually slows down writes, which in itself slows down the application and thus reduces the rate at which memory is changed. Nevertheless, the benefits of mirroring are smaller when compared to our approach and postcopy. Note that although very high, the network traffic generated by pvfs–shared is not generated over short periods of time, which enables it to remain scalable with respect to average migration time.

The impact on the computation is depicted in Figure 4(c). We measure the overall amount of computation lost due to live migrations as a percent of the maximum computational potential achieved in a migration-free scenario. Since the *AsyncWR* computation is simply meant to keep the CPU busy (i.e. increment a counter) we define the computational

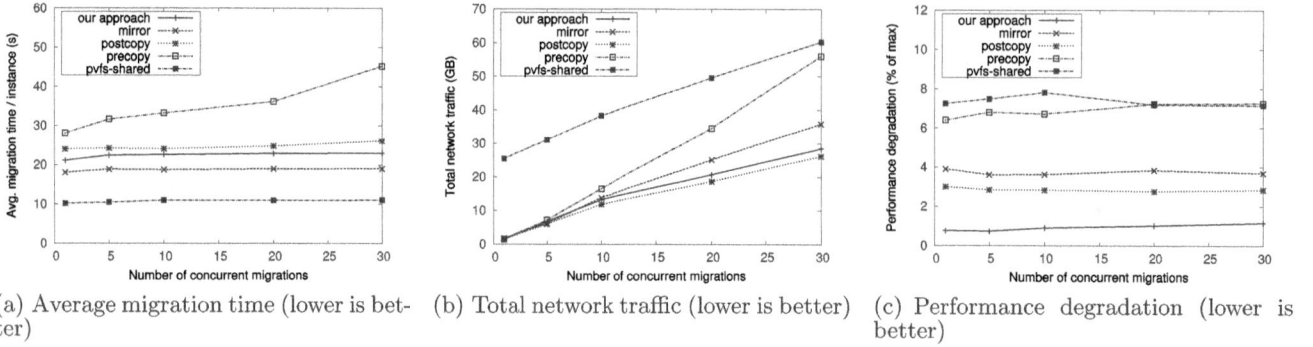

(a) Average migration time (lower is better) (b) Total network traffic (lower is better) (c) Performance degradation (lower is better)

Figure 4: AsyncWR when increasing the number of concurrent live migrations from 1 to 30

potential as simply the aggregate end-value of the counters from all processes of all VM instances. As can be observed, our approach manages to reach a degradation of slightly more than %1. This is up to 8x better than pvfs−shared and precopy and 3x-4x better than postcopy and mirror.

Overall, we conclude that under a concurrent migration scenario, our approach remains highly scalable both with respect to migration time and network traffic, while having a minimal on performance.

5.5 Impact on real life applications

Our next series of experiments illustrates the behavior of our proposal in real life. For this purpose we have chosen *CM1*, a three-dimensional, non-hydrostatic, non-linear, time-dependent numerical model suitable for idealized studies of atmospheric phenomena. This application is used to study small-scale processes that occur in the atmosphere of the Earth, such as hurricanes.

CM1 is representative of a large class of HPC stencil applications that model a phenomenon in time which can be described by a spatial domain that holds a fixed set of parameters in each point. The problem is solved iteratively in a distributed fashion by splitting the spatial domain into subdomains, each of which is managed by a dedicated MPI process. At each iteration, the MPI processes calculate the values for all points of their subdomain, then exchange the values at the border of their subdomains with each other, which is a highly network intensive process. After a certain number of iterations was successfully completed, each MPI process dumps the values of the subdomain it is responsible for into a file on the local storage, which generates a moderately intensive I/O write pressure. These files are then asynchronously collected and processed in order to visualize the evolution of the phenomenon in time. For the purpose of this work, we omitted the visualization part.

The experiment consists in deploying a fixed number of 64 sources, each of which hosts a VM instance that runs a process of CM1. The memory size of each instance is 4 GB, while the number of allocated cores is 2. As input data for CM1, we have chosen a 3D hurricane that is a version of the Bryan and Rotunno simulations [9]. We split the spatial domain into 8x8 subdomains, each of which has a size of 200x200. The output frequency is set at 30 seconds of simulated time, which for this configuration roughly translates to 40 seconds of computation time, during which

approx. 200 MB of data per process are generated. While CM1 is running, we perform an increasing number of live migrations, starting from 1 to 7. The migrations are initiated successively at an interval of 60 seconds in the following pattern: source 1 is migrated to a target node after 60 seconds, source 2 is migrated to a target node after 120 seconds, etc. This simulates a highly dynamic datacenter where live migrations happen frequently.

The *cumulated* migration time, i.e. the sum of the migration time from all sources is depicted in Figure 5(a). As expected, all five approaches exhibit a linear trend in growth as the number of successive migrations increases. Interestingly enough, our approach outperforms pvfs−shared by a small margin, despite transferring local storage in addition to memory. This effect can be traced back to the lower I/O throughput sustained by pvfs−shared, which ultimately impacts the memory access pattern in a way that generates more memory transfer overhead than our own approach. Compared to precopy, we observe a steady decrease in cumulated migration time of about 2x. The same trend is visible when comparing to mirror: we observe a decrease of up to 33%. This indicates that mirroring significantly improves precopy in practice, but is still far from postcopy, which is close to our own approach.

The network traffic incurred by live migrations is shown in Figure 5(b). Since CM1 generates network traffic during normal operation, we subtracted this amount from the total observed network traffic in order to obtain the network traffic that can be traced back to live migration. As can be noticed, a huge gap exists between pvfs−shared and the rest of approaches. Thanks to local storage, this translates to more than 90% less network traffic. Since CM1 does not overlap computation with I/O, precopy performs much closer to the other approaches than in our AsyncWR benchmark. Still, our approach outperforms precopy and mirror by an overall 10-15% less network traffic overhead. However, it is outperformed by postcopy in its turn by 12%.

Finally, the impact on application performance is shown in Figure 5(c). As can be observed, live migration introduces a considerable increase in execution time that even surpasses the cumulated migration time, despite the fact that the application was not interrupted. This shows how sensitive HPC workloads are to performance degradation (one single slow VM can drag all other VMs down), underling the importance of minimizing the negative impact of

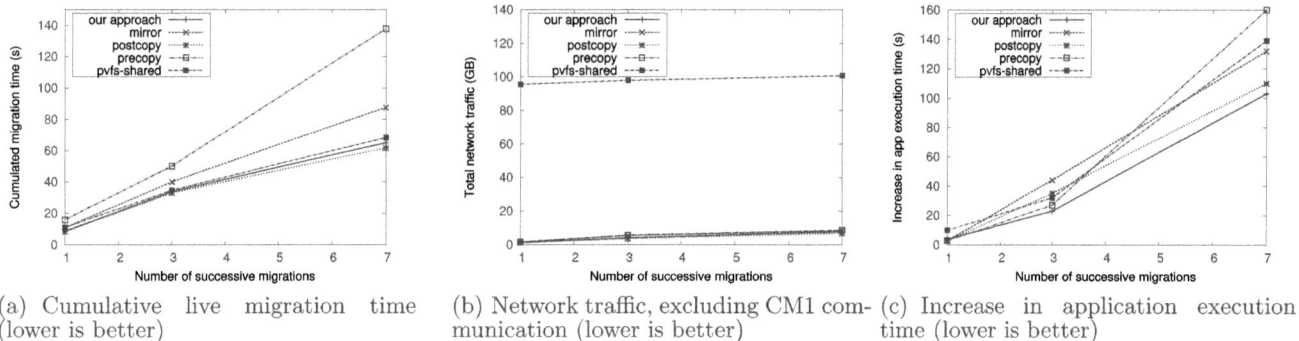

(a) Cumulative live migration time (lower is better)

(b) Network traffic, excluding CM1 communication (lower is better)

(c) Increase in application execution time (lower is better)

Figure 5: Performance of CM1 when performing an increasing number of live migrations separated by a one minute interval

live migration. In this context, our approach generates up to 10% less increase in total execution time when compared to postcopy. This number grows as high as 40% when compared to pvfs−shared and mirror, which is further augmented up to 62% when compared to precopy.

When further increasing the number of live migrations, an even higher gap can be expected.

6. CONCLUSIONS

Live migration is a key feature of virtualization. It enables a large variety of management tasks (such as load balancing, offline maintenance, power management and pro-active fault tolerance) that are critical in the maintenance of large IaaS cloud datacenters that run scientific data-intensive applications. In such datacenters, virtual machines often take advantage of locally available storage space in order to efficiently handle I/O intensive workloads. However, this poses a difficult challenge for live migration.

In this paper, we have presented a storage transfer proposal for live migration that is highly efficient under such circumstances. Unlike other state-of-art live migration approaches, we propose a memory-independent approach that relies on a hybrid active push-prioritized prefetch strategy. This enables us to separate the memory transfer strategy from the storage transfer strategy, enabling high migration flexibility for I/O intensive workloads regardless of memory access pattern.

We demonstrated the benefits of our approach through experiments that involve hundreds of nodes, using both benchmarks and real applications. When pushed to the extreme, such as the live migration of I/O benchmarks, our approach finished the migration up to 10x faster, consumed up to 10x less bandwidth and sustained the highest I/O write throughput inside the VM instance when compared to other state-of-art approaches, while showing up to 8x less negative impact on application performance.

Overall, we argue that synchronization through a parallel file system as an alternative to local storage is not scalable and expensive both in terms of performance and resources. Furthermore, we believe that the wide adoption of I/O pre-copy in practice as a consequence of its perceived higher safety (i.e. tolerates the failure of the destination during migration) does not justify the performance penalty and extra consumed resources in the context of large-scale sci-

entific applications (which already implement fault-tolerant protocols). Finally, we argue that pure I/O post-copy is not enough on its own and can be further augmented to better adapt to the migration process, as illustrated by our approach.

Based on these results, we plan to explore the problem of storage transfer for live migration more extensively. In particular, we did not find acceptable implementations of alternate memory transfer techniques in practice (e.g. post-copy), but plan to experiment how our approach behaves in such a context on the first occasion. This might reveal interesting directions with respect to optimizing the storage transfer. Furthermore, we plan to study techniques such as de-duplication to further reduce the migration cost and potentially improve performance despite extra computational overhead. Finally, we plan to monitor I/O patterns with the purpose of predicting the best moment to initiate a live migration. Such information could be leveraged by the cloud middleware to better orchestrate live migrations within the datacenter.

Acknowledgments

We thank Eugen Feller for his remarks on the usefulness of live migration in the context of power management. This work was supported in part by the ANR MAPREDUCE, ANR-JST FP3C, ANR RESCUE projects and the Joint Laboratory for Petascale Computing (INRIA, UIUC, NCSA). The experiments presented in this paper were carried out using the Grid'5000/ALADDIN-G5K experimental testbed, an initiative of the French Ministry of Research through the ACI GRID incentive action, INRIA, CNRS, RENATER and other contributing partners (see http://www.grid5000.fr/).

7. REFERENCES

[1] File System in UserspacE (FUSE). http://fuse.sourceforge.net.

[2] IOR. http://sourceforge.net/projects/ior-sio/.

[3] QEMU/KVM. http://www.linux-kvm.org.

[4] S. Al-Kiswany, D. Subhraveti, P. Sarkar, and M. Ripeanu. Vmflock: virtual machine co-migration for the cloud. In *HPDC '11: Proceedings of the 20th International Symposium on High Performance Distributed Computing*, pages 159–170, San Jose, USA, 2011.

[5] Amazon Elastic Compute Cloud (EC2). http://aws.amazon.com/ec2/.

[6] Amazon Simple Storage Service (S3). http://aws.amazon.com/s3/.

[7] M. Armbrust, A. Fox, R. Griffith, A. D. Joseph, R. Katz, A. Konwinski, G. Lee, D. Patterson, A. Rabkin, I. Stoica, and M. Zaharia. A view of cloud computing. *Commun. ACM*, 53:50–58, April 2010.

[8] R. Bradford, E. Kotsovinos, A. Feldmann, and H. Schiöberg. Live wide-area migration of virtual machines including local persistent state. In *VEE '07: Proceedings of the 3rd International Conference on Virtual Execution Environments*, pages 169–179, San Diego, USA, 2007.

[9] G. H. Bryan and R. Rotunno. The maximum intensity of tropical cyclones in axisymmetric numerical model simulations. *Journal of the American Meteorological Society*, 137:1770–1789, 2009.

[10] P. H. Carns, W. B. Ligon, R. B. Ross, and R. Thakur. PVFS: A parallel file system for Linux clusters. In *Proceedings of the 4th Annual Linux Showcase and Conference*, pages 317–327, Atlanta, USA, 2000.

[11] C. Clark, K. Fraser, S. Hand, J. G. Hansen, E. Jul, C. Limpach, I. Pratt, and A. Warfield. Live migration of virtual machines. In *NSDI'05: Proceedings of the 2nd Symposium on Networked Systems Design & Implementation*, pages 273–286, Boston, USA, 2005.

[12] M. Gagné. Cooking with Linux—still searching for the ultimate Linux distro? *Linux J.*, 2007(161):9, 2007.

[13] J. G. Hansen and E. Jul. Scalable virtual machine storage using local disks. *SIGOPS Oper. Syst. Rev.*, 44:71–79, December 2010.

[14] K. Haselhorst, M. Schmidt, R. Schwarzkopf, N. Fallenbeck, and B. Freisleben. Efficient storage synchronization for live migration in cloud infrastructures. In *PDP '11: Proceedings of the 19th Euromicro International Conference on Parallel, Distributed and Network-based Processing*, pages 511–518, Ayia Napa, Cyprus, 2011.

[15] M. R. Hines, U. Deshpande, and K. Gopalan. Post-copy live migration of virtual machines. *SIGOPS Oper. Syst. Rev.*, 43:14–26, July 2009.

[16] K. Z. Ibrahim, S. Hofmeyr, C. Iancu, and E. Roman. Optimized pre-copy live migration for memory intensive applications. In *SC '11: 24th International Conference for High Performance Computing, Networking, Storage and Analysis*, pages 40:1–40:11, Seattle, USA, 2011.

[17] H. A. Lagar-Cavilla, J. A. Whitney, R. Bryant, P. Patchin, M. Brudno, E. de Lara, S. M. Rumble, M. Satyanarayanan, and A. Scannell. Snowflock: Virtual machine cloning as a first-class cloud primitive. *ACM Trans. Comput. Syst.*, 29:2:1–2:45, February 2011.

[18] H. Liu, H. Jin, X. Liao, L. Hu, and C. Yu. Live migration of virtual machine based on full system trace and replay. In *HPDC '09: Proceedings the 18th ACM international symposium on High Performance Distributed Computing*, pages 101–110, Garching, Germany, 2009.

[19] A. Mashtizadeh, E. Celebi, T. Garfinkel, and M. Cai. The design and evolution of live storage migration in VMware ESX. In *USENIX ATC '11: Proceedings of the 2011 USENIX Annual Technical Conference*, pages 1–14, Portland, USA, 2011.

[20] A. B. Nagarajan, F. Mueller, C. Engelmann, and S. L. Scott. Proactive fault tolerance for hpc with xen virtualization. In *ICS '07: Proceedings of the 21st Annual International Conference on Supercomputing*, pages 23–32, Seattle, USA, 2007.

[21] R. Nathuji and K. Schwan. Virtualpower: Coordinated power management in virtualized enterprise systems. In *SOSP '07: Proceedings of 21st ACM SIGOPS Symposium on Operating Systems Principles*, pages 265–278, Stevenson, USA, 2007.

[22] M. Nelson, B.-H. Lim, and G. Hutchins. Fast transparent migration for virtual machines. In *ATEC '05: Proceedings of the 2005 USENIX Annual Technical Conference*, pages 1–25, Anaheim, USA, 2005.

[23] B. Nicolae. *BlobSeer: Towards Efficient Data Storage Management for Large-Scale, Distributed Systems*. PhD thesis, University of Rennes 1, November 2010.

[24] B. Nicolae. On the benefits of transparent compression for cost-effective cloud data storage. *Transactions on Large-Scale Data- and Knowledge-Centered Systems*, 3:167–184, 2011.

[25] B. Nicolae, G. Antoniu, L. Bougé, D. Moise, and A. Carpen-Amarie. Blobseer: Next-generation data management for large scale infrastructures. *J. Parallel Distrib. Comput.*, 71:169–184, 2011.

[26] B. Nicolae, J. Bresnahan, K. Keahey, and G. Antoniu. Going back and forth: Efficient multideployment and multisnapshotting on clouds. In *HPDC '11: 20th International ACM Symposium on High-Performance Parallel and Distributed Computing*, pages 147–158, San José, USA, 2011.

[27] B. Nicolae and F. Cappello. BlobCR: Efficient checkpoint-restart for HPC applications on IaaS clouds using virtual disk image snapshots. In *SC '11: 24th International Conference for High Performance Computing, Networking, Storage and Analysis*, pages 34:1–34:12, Seattle, USA, 2011.

[28] E. Park, B. Egger, and J. Lee. Fast and space-efficient virtual machine checkpointing. In *VEE '11: Proceedings of the 7th International Conference on Virtual Execution Environments*, pages 75–86, Newport Beach, USA, 2011.

[29] P. Svärd, B. Hudzia, J. Tordsson, and E. Elmroth. Evaluation of delta compression techniques for efficient live migration of large virtual machines. In *VEE '11: Proceedings of the 7th International Conference on Virtual Execution Environments*, pages 111–120, Newport Beach, USA, 2011.

[30] C. Tang. Fvd: a high-performance virtual machine image format for cloud. In *ATEC '11: Proc. of the 2011 USENIX Annual Technical Conference*, pages 1–18, Portland, USA, 2011.

[31] W. Voorsluys, J. Broberg, S. Venugopal, and R. Buyya. Cost of virtual machine live migration in clouds: A performance evaluation. In *CloudCom '09: Proceedings of the 1st International Conference on Cloud Computing*, pages 254–265, Beijing, China, 2009.

A Virtual Memory Based Runtime to Support Multi-tenancy in Clusters with GPUs

Michela Becchi[1], Kittisak Sajjapongse[1], Ian Graves[1], Adam Procter[1],
Vignesh Ravi[2], Srimat Chakradhar[3]

[1]University of Missouri, [2]Ohio State University, [3]NEC Laboratories America

becchim@missouri.edu, ks5z9@mail.mizzou.edu, ilggdd@mail.mizzou.edu,
proctera@missouri.edu, raviv@cse.ohio-state.edu, chak@nec-labs.com

ABSTRACT

Graphics Processing Units (GPUs) are increasingly becoming part of HPC clusters. Nevertheless, cloud computing services and resource management frameworks targeting heterogeneous clusters including GPUs are still in their infancy. Further, GPU software stacks (e.g., CUDA driver and runtime) currently provide very limited support to concurrency.

In this paper, we propose a runtime system that provides abstraction and sharing of GPUs, while allowing isolation of concurrent applications. A central component of our runtime is a memory manager that provides a virtual memory abstraction to the applications. Our runtime is flexible in terms of scheduling policies, and allows dynamic (as opposed to programmer-defined) binding of applications to GPUs. In addition, our framework supports dynamic load balancing, dynamic upgrade and downgrade of GPUs, and is resilient to their failures. Our runtime can be deployed in combination with VM-based cloud computing services to allow virtualization of heterogeneous clusters, or in combination with HPC cluster resource managers to form an integrated resource management infrastructure for heterogeneous clusters. Experiments conducted on a three-node cluster show that our GPU sharing scheme allows up to a 28% and a 50% performance improvement over serialized execution on short- and long-running jobs, respectively. Further, dynamic inter-node load balancing leads to an additional 18-20% performance benefit.

Categories and Subject Descriptors

C.1.4.1 [**Computer Systems Organization**]: Processor Architectures - Parallel Architectures, Distributed Architectures.

General Terms

Performance, Design, Experimentation.

Keywords

Cluster computing, runtime systems, virtualization, GPU, CUDA.

1. INTRODUCTION

Many-core processors are increasingly becoming part of high performance computing (HPC) clusters. Within the last two to three years GPUs have emerged as a means to achieve extreme-scale, cost-effective, and power-efficient high performance computing. The peak single-precision performance of the latest

GPU from NVIDIA – the Tesla C2050/C2070/C2075 card - is more than 1 Teraflop, resulting in a price to performance ratio of $2-3 per Gigaflop. Meanwhile, Intel has announced the upcoming release of the Many Integrated Core processor (Intel MIC), with peak performance of 1.2 Teraflops. Early benchmarking results on molecular dynamics and linear algebra applications have been demonstrated at the International Supercomputing Conference, Hamburg, Germany, in June 2011.

Today some of the fastest supercomputers are based on NVIDIA GPUs, including three of the top five fastest supercomputers in the world. For example, Tianhe-1A, the second fastest system, is equipped with 7,168 NVIDIA Fermi GPUs and 14,336 CPUs. Almost 80% of the HPC clusters in the top-500 list are currently powered with Intel multi-core processors. The next challenge for Intel will be to successfully position its MIC processor in the many-core market.

Given the availability of these heterogeneous computing infrastructures, it is essential to make efficient use of them. One classical way to schedule batch jobs on HPC clusters is via PBS cluster resource managers such as TORQUE [25]. Another practical way to manage large clusters intended for multi-user environments involves using virtualization, treating clusters as private clouds (e.g. Eucalyptus [24]). This model [18][19] has several benefits. First, end-users do not need to be aware of the characteristics of the underlying hardware: they see a service-oriented infrastructure. Second, resource management and load balancing can be performed in a centralized way by the private cloud administrator. Finally, when the overall resource requirements exceed the cluster's availability, more hardware resources can be externally rented using a hybrid cloud model, in a way that is dynamic and fully transparent to the user [19]. The convergence of heterogeneous HPC and the cloud computing model is confirmed by Amazon EC2 Cluster GPU instances [26]. Other vendors, such as Nimbix [27] and Hoopoe [28], are also offering cloud services for GPU computing.

The use of GPUs in cluster and cloud environments, however, is still at an initial stage. Recent projects - GViM [1], vCUDA [2], rCUDA [3] and gVirtuS [4] - have addressed the issue of allowing applications running within virtual machines (VMs) to access GPUs by intercepting and redirecting library calls from the guest to the CUDA runtime on the host. These frameworks either rely on the scheduling mechanisms provided by the CUDA runtime, or allow applications to execute on GPU in sequence, possibly leading to low resource utilization and consequent suboptimal performance. Ravi et al [6] have considered GPU sharing by allowing concurrent execution of kernel functions invoked by different applications. All these proposals have the following limitations. First, they assume that the overall memory requirements of the applications mapped onto the same GPU fit the device memory capacity. As data sets become larger and

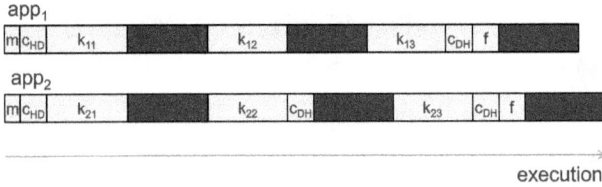

Figure 1: Example of two applications that can effectively time-share a GPU. Light-grey blocks represent GPU phases (m = device memory allocations, c_{HD} = host-to-device data transfers, k_{ij} = kernel executions, c_{DH} = device-to-host data transfers, and f = device memory de-allocations). Black blocks represent CPU phases.

resource sharing increases, this assumption may not hold true. Second, the proposed frameworks *statically* bind applications to GPUs (that is, they do not allow runtime application-to-GPU re-mapping). Not only can this lead to suboptimal scheduling, but it also forces a complete application restart in case of GPU failure, and prevents efficient load balancing if GPU devices are added to or removed from the system.

One important problem to address when designing runtime support for GPUs within cluster and cloud environments is the following. In cluster settings, resource sharing and dynamic load balancing are typical techniques aimed to increase the resource utilization and optimize the aggregate performance of concurrent applications. However, GPUs have been conceived to accelerate single applications; as a consequence, *software stacks for GPUs currently include only very limited support for concurrency*. As an example, if multiple CUDA applications use the same GPU, the CUDA driver and runtime will serve their requests in a first-come-first-served fashion. *In the presence of concurrency, the CUDA runtime will fail in two scenarios: first, if the aggregate memory requirements of the applications exceed the GPU capacity; second, in case of too many concurrent applications.* In fact, the CUDA runtime associates a CUDA context on GPU to each application thread, and reserves an initial memory allocation to each CUDA context. Therefore, the creation of too many contexts will lead to exceeding the GPU memory capacity. On a NVIDIA Tesla C2050 device, for example, we experimentally observed that the maximum number of application threads supported by the CUDA runtime in the absence of conflicting memory requirements is eight. This fact has the following implication: *existing GPU virtualization frameworks and resource managers for heterogeneous clusters that rely on the CUDA runtime serialize the execution of concurrent applications, leading to GPU underutilization*. Further, *existing runtime systems statically bind applications to GPU devices, preventing dynamic scheduling and limiting the opportunities for load balancing*. We aim to overcome these limitations.

Current high-end GPUs have two important characteristics: first, they have a device memory that is physically separated from the host memory; second, they can be programmed using library APIs. For example, NVIDIA GPUs can be programmed using CUDA [22] or OpenCL. GPU library calls, which originate on the CPU, come in at least three kinds: device memory allocations, data transfers, and kernel launches (whereby kernels are GPU implementations of user-defined functions). Since efficient GPU memory accesses require regular access patterns, the use of nested pointers is discouraged in GPU programming. As a consequence, most GPU applications do not use pointer nesting. Moreover, even if NVIDIA has recently introduced the possibility to dynamically allocate memory within CUDA kernels, this feature

is not found in publicly available GPU benchmarks. *In this work, we focus on optimizing the handling of traditional GPU applications.* However, we also support pointer nesting by requiring the programmer to register nested data structures using our runtime API. Finally, we allow applications that perform dynamic memory allocation within kernels to use our runtime system, but we exclude them from our sharing and dynamic scheduling mechanisms. Both pointer nesting and dynamic device memory allocation can be detected by intercepting and parsing the pseudo-assembly (PTX) representation of CUDA kernels sent to the GPU devices.

Applications that use GPUs alternate CPU and GPU phases. Because of this alternation, *statically* binding applications to GPUs (that is, using the *programmer-defined* mapping of GPU phases to GPU devices) may lead to inefficiencies. This holds particularly for applications having multiple GPU phases (e.g.: iterative solvers) and in the presence of multi-tenancy. We observe that the application programmer optimizes its application assuming dedicated and well-known resources; our runtime aims at providing dynamic load balancing in multi-tenant clusters, where the availability and utilization of the underlying resources is hidden from the users and not known *a-priori*.

As an example, suppose we wish to schedule the two applications app_1 and app_2 illustrated in Figure 1 on a single GPU. Moreover, let us assume that the memory footprint of each application in isolation fits within the device memory, but their aggregate memory requirements exceed the GPU memory capacity. In this situation, if the two applications are run on the bare CUDA runtime, they must be serialized (otherwise the execution will fail with an out-of-memory error). However, serializing the two applications will lead to resource underutilization, in that the GPU will be idle during the CPU phases of both app_1 and app_2. A better scheduling consists of time-sharing the GPU between app_1 and app_2, so that one application uses the GPU while the other is running a CPU phase. Such scheduling requires periodically unbinding and binding each application from/to the GPU. In turn, *dynamic binding* involves data transfers between CPU and GPU in order to restore the state of the application. Note that the runtime must determine: (i) when unbinding is advisable, and (ii) which data transfers must be performed. For example, app_1 has no explicit data transfers between the kernel calls k_{11}, k_{12} and k_{13}: all necessary data transfers must be added by the runtime. On the other hand, a data transfer between k_{22} and k_{23} is already part of app_2. In summary, providing dynamic binding implies designing a *virtual memory* capability for GPUs. In Section 2, we discuss other scenarios where dynamic binding of applications to GPUs is desirable.

1.1 Our Contributions

In this work, we propose a runtime component that provides *abstraction* and *sharing* of GPUs, while allowing *isolation* of concurrent applications. Our contributions can be summarized as follows.

- We propose *dynamic (or runtime) application-to-GPU binding* as a mechanism to maximize device utilization and thereby improve performance in the presence of multi-tenancy. In particular, dynamic binding is suitable for applications with multiple GPU phases, and in the presence of GPUs with different capabilities.

- We identify *virtual memory for GPUs* as an essential mechanism to provide dynamic binding. Specifically, we propose a virtual memory based runtime. As added value, our design enables: (i) detecting badly written applications in the runtime and therefore avoiding overloading the GPU with erroneous calls, and (ii) optimizing memory transfers between the multi-core host and the GPU device.

- We introduce two forms of memory swapping in our runtime: *intra-application* and *inter-application*. The former enables applications whose kernels fit the device memory to run on the GPU, even if their overall memory requirements exceed the device memory capacity. The latter allows concurrent applications whose aggregate memory requirements exceed the device memory capacity to time-share the GPU.

- We provide a generic runtime component that easily supports different scheduling mechanisms.

- We include in our runtime support for *load balancing in case of GPU addition and removal, resilience to GPU failures*, and *checkpoint-restart capabilities*.

The remainder of this paper is organized as follows. In Section 2, we discuss in more detail the objectives of our design. In Section 3, we describe our reference hardware and software architecture. In Section 4, we present our design and prototype implementation. In Section 5, we report results from our experimental evaluation. In Section 6, we relate our work to the state of the art. We conclude our discussion in Section 7.

2. OBJECTIVES

The overall goal of this work is to provide a runtime component that allows multiple applications to run concurrently on a heterogeneous cluster whose nodes comprise CPUs and GPUs. We foresee the use of our runtime system in two scenarios (Figure 2): (i) in combination with VM-based cloud computing services (e.g.: Eucalyptus [24]), and (ii) in combination with HPC cluster resource managers (e.g.: TORQUE [25]). In both cases a cluster-level scheduler assigns VMs or jobs to heterogeneous compute nodes. Our runtime component is replicated on each node and schedules library calls originated by applications on the available GPUs so as to optimize the overall performance. Our framework must allow integration with cluster-level schedulers intended for both homogeneous and heterogeneous clusters (the former oblivious of the presence of GPUs).

Note that heterogeneous clusters that include GPUs require scheduling at two granularities: on one hand, jobs must be mapped onto compute nodes (*coarse-grained scheduling*); on the other, specific library calls must be mapped onto GPUs (*fine-grained scheduling*). Existing cluster-level schedulers perform coarse-grained scheduling, whereas our runtime performs fine-grained scheduling. The two schedulers may interact in two ways. First, the cluster-level scheduler may be completely oblivious of the GPUs installed on each node. In case of overloaded GPUs, the node-level runtime may offload the computation to other nodes. To this end, the runtime system must include a node-to-node communication mechanism enabling inter-node code and data transfer. Alternatively the node-level runtime may expose some information to the cluster-level scheduler (e.g.: number of GPUs, load level, etc.), so as to guide the cluster-level scheduling decisions. While the first form of interaction may lead to suboptimal scheduling decisions, it allows a straightforward integration with existing cluster resource managers and VM-based cloud computing services targeting homogeneous clusters.

Until recently, GPUs could not be accessed from applications executing within VMs. Several projects – GViM [1], vCUDA [2], rCUDA [3] and gVirtuS [4] - have addressed this issue for

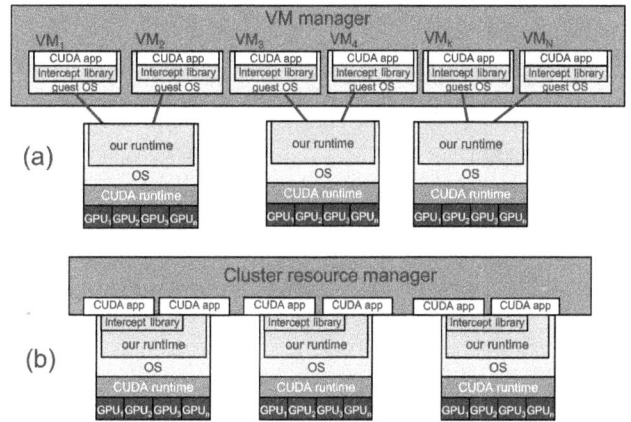

(a)

(b)

Figure 2: Two deployment scenarios for our runtime: (a) VM-based cloud computing service and (b) HPC cluster resource manager.

applications using the CUDA Runtime API to access GPUs. The general approach is to use *API remoting* to bridge two different OS spaces: the guest-OS where the applications run and the host-OS where the GPUs reside. In particular, API remoting is implemented by introducing an interposed *front-end* library in the guest-OS space and a *back-end* daemon in the host-OS. The front-end library, which overrides the CUDA Runtime API, intercepts CUDA calls and redirects them to the back-end through a socket interface. In turn, the back-end issues those calls to the CUDA runtime. Note that this mechanism provides GPU *visibility* from within VMs, but does not add any form of *abstraction*. In fact, applications still use CUDA Runtime primitives to direct their calls to specific GPUs residing on the host where the VMs are deployed. Moreover, the bare use of the scheduling mechanisms offered by the CUDA Runtime may not be optimal when multiple or multi-threaded applications are mapped onto a single GPU.

In this work, we aim to design a runtime that provides *abstraction* and *sharing* of GPUs, while allowing *isolation* of concurrent applications. In addition, the runtime must be *flexible* in terms of *scheduling policies*, and allow *dynamic binding* of applications to GPUs. Finally, the runtime must support *dynamic upgrade* and *downgrade* of GPUs, and be *resilient to GPU failures*. More detail on these objectives is provided below.

- *Abstraction* - GPUs installed in the cluster need to be abstracted (or hidden) from the user's direct access. GPU programming APIs generally require the application programmer to explicitly select the target GPU (for example, using the CUDA runtime `cudaSetDevice` primitive). This gives the application control of the number of GPU devices to use. Our design masks the explicit procurement of GPUs, thus allowing a transparent mapping of applications onto GPUs. As a side effect, applications can be efficiently mapped onto a number of devices different from that for which they have been originally programmed. Note that this abstraction is coherent with the traditional parallel programming model for general purpose processors. When a user writes a multithreaded program, for example, he targets a generic multi-core processor. At runtime, the operating system distributes processing threads onto the available cores.

- *GPU Sharing* – As mentioned above, applications targeting heterogeneous nodes alternate general-purpose CPU code with library calls redirected and executed on GPUs. In the presence of multi-tenancy, assigning each application a dedicated GPU device for the entire lifetime of the application may not be

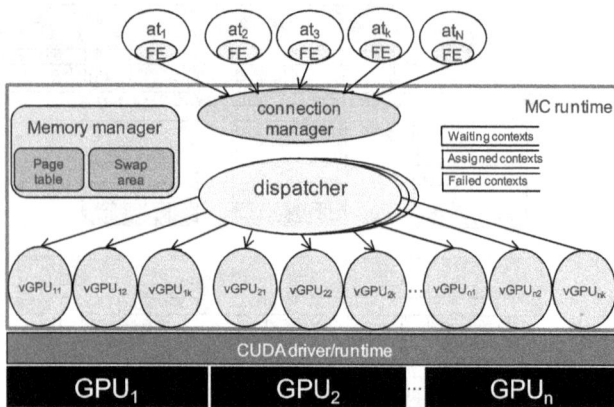

Figure 3: Overall design of runtime.

optimal, in that it may lead to resource underutilization. GPU sharing is an obvious way to improve resource utilization. However, sharing must be done judiciously: excessive sharing may lead to high overhead and be counterproductive.

- *Isolation* – In the presence of resource sharing, concurrent applications must run in complete isolation from one another. In other words, each application must have the illusion of running on a dedicated device. State-of-the-art runtime support for GPUs provides partial isolation of different process contexts. In particular, each process is assigned its own process space on the GPU; however, GPU sharing is possible only as long as the cumulative memory requirements of different applications do not exceed the physical capacity of the GPU. Our work aims to handle such memory issues seamlessly, allowing GPU sharing irrespective of the overall memory requirements of the applications. In other words, we want to extend the concept of *virtual memory* to GPUs.

- *Configurable Scheduling* – The quality of a scheduling policy depends on the objective function and assumptions about the workload. A simple first-come-first-served scheduling algorithm can be adequate in the absence of profiling information. A credit-based scheduling algorithm may be more suitable to settings that include fairness in the objective function. Further, a scheduling algorithm that prioritizes short running applications can be preferable if profiling information is available. Yet another scheduling policy may be adopted in the presence of expected quality of service requirements (e.g.: execution deadlines). Our goal is to provide a runtime system that can easily accommodate different scheduling algorithms.

- *Dynamic Binding* – In existing runtime systems (including the CUDA runtime) the mapping of GPU kernels to GPU devices is static, or programmer-defined. A dynamic application-to-GPU binding may be preferable in several scenarios. First, let us consider the situation of a node having GPU devices with different compute capabilities. Existing work in the context of heterogeneous multi-core systems [21] has shown that performance can be optimized by maximizing the overall processor utilization while favoring the use of more powerful cores. The application of this concept to nodes equipped with different GPUs suggests that the system throughput can be maximized by dynamically migrating application threads from less to more powerful GPUs as they become idle. Second, dynamic binding can help when GPUs are shared by applications cumulatively exceeding the memory capacity. In fact, dynamically migrating application threads to different devices may minimize waiting times. Finally, resuming application threads on different devices allows load balancing

when GPUs are added or removed from the system (*dynamic upgrade and downgrade*), and is beneficial in case of *GPU failures* (by preventing a whole application restart).

- *Checkpoint-Restart Capability* – Along with dynamic binding, our runtime provides a checkpoint-restart mechanism that allows efficiently redirecting an application thread to a different GPU. A checkpoint can be explicitly specified by the user, or automatically triggered by the runtime. For example, the runtime may monitor the execution time of particular library calls (e.g. kernel functions) on a GPU. An automatic checkpoint may be advisable after long-running kernel calls to decrease the restart penalty in case of GPU failures. Note that this kind of checkpoint is inserted dynamically at runtime.

3. REFERENCE ARCHITECTURE

The overall reference architecture is represented in Figure 2. The underlying hardware platform consists of a cluster of heterogeneous nodes. Each node has one or more multi-core processors and a number of GPUs. The operating system performs scheduling and resource management on the general-purpose processors. Access to the GPUs is mediated by the CUDA driver and runtime library API. Our runtime performs scheduling and resource management on the available GPUs.

Each GPU has a device memory. Among others, the CUDA runtime library contains functions to: (i) target a specific device (cudaSetDevice), (ii) allocate and de-allocate device memory (e.g., cudaMalloc/Free), (iii) perform data transfers between the general purpose processor and the GPU devices (e.g., cudaMemcpy), (iv) transfer code onto the GPUs (the internal functions __cudaRegisterFunction/FatBinary), and (v) trigger the execution of user-written kernels (cudaConfigureCall and cudaLaunch).

In addition, the CUDA runtime offers some CPU multi-threading support. For example, CUDA 3.2 associates a CUDA context to each application thread. Several contexts can coexist on the GPU. Each of them has a dedicated virtual address space; contains references to textures, modules and other entities; and is used for error handling. CUDA contexts allow different application threads to time-share the GPU processing cores, and space-share the GPU memory. In CUDA 4.0, the use of CUDA contexts is slightly modified to allow data sharing and concurrent kernel execution across threads belonging to the same application. As mentioned in Section 1, with both versions of the CUDA runtime, the number of parallel CUDA contexts that can be supported at runtime is limited by the device memory capacity.

As shown in Figure 2, our runtime component interacts with a cluster-level scheduler, operates at the node level and must be installed on all the nodes of the cluster. The cluster-level scheduler maps jobs onto compute nodes. During execution, the GPU library calls issued by applications are intercepted by our frontend library and redirected to our runtime daemon on the node where the job has been scheduled. Since our runtime is a stand-alone process, a mechanism for inter-process communication between the job and our runtime demon is needed. In our prototype, we use the socket-based communication framework provided as part of the open-source project gVirtuS [4][5]. This framework relies on *afunix* sockets in a non-virtualized environment and on proprietary *VM-sockets* in a virtualized one.

Although the design of an optimal cluster-level scheduler for heterogeneous clusters is beyond the scope of this work, we want to be able to integrate our runtime with existing cloud computing services and cluster resource management frameworks that target homogeneous clusters. In this situation, the cluster-level scheduler in use is unaware of both the GPU devices installed on the compute nodes, and the fraction of execution time that each job will spend on GPUs. Therefore, in the presence of nodes with different hardware setups, simple cluster-level scheduling policies may lead to queuing on nodes containing a lower number of GPUs (or assigned a higher number of jobs targeting GPU). To tackle this problem, we allow nodes to offload GPU library calls to other nodes in the cluster. For this purpose, we introduce inter-node communication between our runtime components. Note that this mechanism operates at the granularity of GPU library calls, and does not affect the portion of the job running on CPU.

4. DESIGN AND METHODOLOGY

In this section, we describe the design of our proposed runtime. Our prototype implementation targets NVIDIA GPUs programmed through the CUDA 3.2 runtime API. In Section 4.8, we summarize the changes required to support CUDA 4.0.

4.1 Overall Design

The overall design of our runtime is illustrated in Figure 3. The basic components are: *connection manager*, *dispatcher*, *virtual-GPUs (vGPUs)*, and *memory manager*. As mentioned before, when applications execute on the CPU, library calls directed to the CUDA runtime are intercepted by a frontend library and redirected to our runtime. We say that each application establishes a *connection* with the runtime, and uses the connection to issue a sequence of CUDA calls and receive their return code. Multiple applications establish concurrent connections. The connection manager accepts and enqueues incoming connections. The dispatcher dequeues pending connections and schedules their calls on the available GPUs. If the devices on the node are overloaded, the dispatcher may offload some connections to other nodes using an inter-node communication mechanism. To allow controlled GPU sharing, each GPU has an associated set of virtual-GPUs. The dispatcher schedules applications onto GPUs by *binding* their connections to the corresponding virtual-GPUs. Applications bound to virtual-GPU $vGPU_{ik}$ share GPU_i. Finally, the memory manager provides a virtual memory abstraction to applications. Dispatcher and virtual-GPUs interact with the memory manager to enable: (i) GPU sharing in the presence of concurrent applications with conflicting memory requirements, (ii) load balancing in case of GPU with different capabilities, GPU addition and removal, (iii) GPU fault tolerance, and (iv) checkpoint-restart capabilities.

4.2 Connection Manager

When used natively, the CUDA 3.2 runtime spawns a CUDA context on the GPU for each application thread. Different application threads can be directed to different GPUs by using the cudaSetDevice primitive. One of the goals of our runtime is to preserve the CUDA semantics. To this end, our frontend library opens a separate connection for each application thread. CUDA calls belonging to different connections can therefore be served independently either on the same or on distinct GPUs. The connection manager enqueues connections generated by concurrent application threads in a *pending connections* list.

4.3 Dispatcher

The primary function of the dispatcher is to schedule CUDA calls issued by application threads onto GPUs. The dispatcher can be configured to use different scheduling algorithms: first-come-first-served, shortest-job-first, credit-based scheduling, etc. Some scheduling algorithms (e.g. shortest-job-first) require the dispatcher to make scheduling decisions based on the kernels executed by the applications, their parameters, and their execution configuration. Higher resource utilization and better performance can be achieved by supporting dynamic binding of applications to GPUs: the dispatcher must be able to modify the application-to-GPU mapping between kernel calls, and to unbind applications from GPUs during their CPU-phases. These scheduling actions must be hidden from the users.

To enable informed scheduling decisions, the dispatcher must be able to delay application-to-GPU binding until the first kernel launch is invoked. Unfortunately, the very first CUDA calls issued by a CUDA application are not kernel launches, but synchronous internal routines used to register the GPU machine code (_cudaRegisterFatBinary), kernel functions (_cudaRegisterFunction), variables and textures (_cudaRegisterVar, _cudaRegisterSharedVar, _cudaRegisterShared and _cudaRegisterTexture) to the CUDA runtime. Moreover, kernel launches are never the first non-internal CUDA calls issued by application threads: at the very least, they must be preceded by memory allocations and data transfers. Before kernel launches can be invoked by the client, all of these previous calls must be serviced.

Two observations help us overcome this problem. First, registration functions are always issued to the runtime prior to CUDA contexts' creation on the GPU. Therefore, these internal calls can be safely issued by the dispatcher well before the corresponding applications are bound to virtual-GPUs. The same holds for device management functions, some of which are ignored by our runtime (e.g. cudaSetDevice) or overridden (e.g. cudaGetDeviceCount will return the number of virtual, not physical, GPUs). Second, it is possible to delay GPU memory operations until the related data are accessed within kernel calls: the runtime responds to memory allocation requests by returning *virtual addresses*, and these virtual pointers are mapped to real device pointers at a later stage.

In summary, the dispatcher dequeues application threads from the list of *pending connections*, and handles them as follows. First, it issues registration functions to the CUDA runtime. Second, it services device management functions (and typically overrides them so as to hide the hardware setup of the node from the users). Third, it handles memory operations with the aid of the memory manager. In particular, the dispatcher does not issue memory operations directly to the CUDA runtime, but instead operates entirely in terms of virtual addresses generated by the memory manager. Fourth, if there are any free virtual-GPUs, the dispatcher schedules application threads to virtual-GPUs (and enqueues them in the list of *assigned contexts*). If all virtual-GPUs are busy, application threads are enqueued in the list of *waiting contexts* for later scheduling. In addition, any failure during the execution of an application thread will cause it to be enqueued in a list of *failed contexts*, which is used by the dispatcher for recovery.

To prevent the dispatcher from being a bottleneck, its implementation is multithreaded: each dispatcher thread processes a different connection. All queues used within the runtime (*pending connections*; *waiting, assigned and failed contexts*) are accessed using mutexes.

4.4 Virtual GPUs

In order to allow time-sharing of GPUs, we spawn a configurable number of virtual-GPUs for each GPU installed on the system. A virtual-GPU is essentially a worker thread that issues calls originated from within application threads to the CUDA runtime.

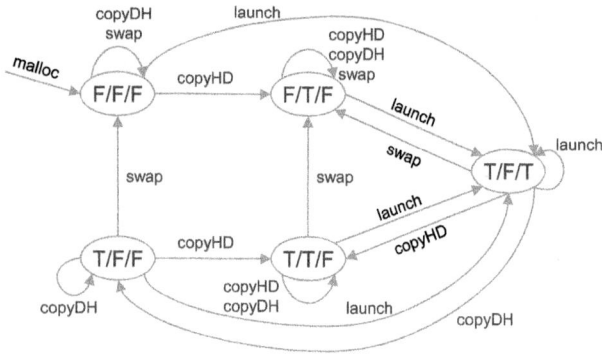

Figure 4: State diagram showing the transitions of `isAllocated/toCopy2Dev/toCopy2Swap` flags.

Virtual-GPUs are statically bound to physical GPUs through a `cudaSetDevice` invoked at system startup. Each virtual-GPU can service one application thread at a time. A virtual-GPU is idle when no application thread is bound to it, and is active otherwise. Note that, since our runtime maps application threads onto virtual-GPUs and the CUDA runtime spawns a CUDA context for each virtual-GPU, this infrastructure preserves the semantics of the CUDA runtime. We experimentally observed (see Section 5) that the CUDA runtime cannot handle an arbitrary number of concurrent threads. Therefore, limiting the number of virtual-GPUs prevents our framework from overloading the CUDA runtime, and allows proper operation even in the presence of a large number of CUDA applications.

4.5 Memory Manager

The goal of the memory manager is to provide a virtual memory abstraction for GPUs. Two ideas are at the basis of the design. First, applications will not see device addresses returned by the CUDA runtime, but they will see virtual addresses generated by the runtime. Second, data resides in the host memory, and is moved to the device only on demand. In this way, *the host memory represents a lower level in the memory hierarchy*: when some data must be moved to the device memory but the device memory capacity is exceeded, the memory manager *swaps* data from the device memory to the host memory. We allow memory swapping in two situations: (i) within a single application, and (ii) in the presence of multi-tenancy. The latter scenario is characterized by the presence of concurrent applications, each of whose memory footprints in isolation would fit within the device memory, but whose aggregate memory requirements exceed the GPU memory capacity. In addition, the swap functionality allows an application to migrate from a less capable to a more capable GPU when the latter becomes available.

Host-to-device data transfers deferral must be done judiciously. Data transfers *preceding* the first kernel call cannot overlap with GPU computation, and can thus be deferred without incurring performance losses. After the first kernel call, application-to-GPU binding is known and our runtime can be configured to either defer or not defer data transfers. Not deferring allows computation-communication overlapping at the expenses of an increased swap overhead; deferring has the opposite effect.

The memory manager has two components: a *page table[1]*, and a

swap area. The page table stores the address translation, and the swap area contains not yet allocated or swapped-out GPU data. The main data structures used in the memory manager are the following.

```
/* PAGE TABLE */
typedef struct {
    void      *virtual_ptr;
    void      *swap_ptr;
    void      *device_ptr;
    size_t    size;
    bool      isAllocated;
    bool      toCopy2Dev;
    bool      toCopy2Swap;
    entry_t   type;
    void      *params;
    nesting_t nested;
} PageTableEntry;

map<Context*, list<PageTableEntry*> *> PageTable;

/* CAPACITY AND UTILIZATION of AVAILABLE GPUs */
int numGPUs;
uint64_t *CapacityList;
uint64_t *MemAvailList;
map<Context *, size_t> MemUsage;
```

Each page table entry (PTE), which is created upon a memory allocation operation, contains three pointers: the virtual pointer which is returned to the application (`virtual_ptr`), the pointer of the data in the swap area (`swap_ptr`), and, if the data are resident on the device, the device pointer (`device_ptr`). In addition, each entry has a `size`, a `type`, and possible additional parameters (`params` and `nested`). Finally, the flags `isAllocated`, `toCopy2Dev`, and `toCopy2Host` are used to guide device memory allocations, de-allocations and data transfers, and indicate whether the PTE has been allocated on device, whether the actual data reside only on the host, and whether the actual data reside only on device, respectively. The state transitions of the three flags depending on the call invoked by the application are illustrated in Figure 4. In particular, `malloc` represents any allocation operation (`cudaMalloc`, `cudaMallocArray`, etc.), whereas copy$_{DH}$ and copy$_{HD}$ represent any device-host and host-device data transfer function (`cudaMemcpy`, `cudaMemcpy2D`, etc.), respectively. Figure 4 assumes data transfer deferral and that all data referenced in a kernel launch can be modified by the kernel execution: a more fine-grained handling is possible if the information about read-only and read-write parameters is available. The attributes `type` and `params` allow distinguishing different kinds of memory allocations and data transfers associated with the entry. The `nested` attribute indicates whether the virtual address points to a nested data structure, or whether it is a member of it. Nested data structures must be declared to the runtime using a specific runtime API call, and are associated additional attributes describing their structure. These attributes are used by the memory manager in order to ensure consistency between virtual and device pointers within nested structures.

Each application thread (or *context*) has an associated list of PTEs: the page table contains all the PTEs for all the active and pending contexts in the node. In addition, the memory manager keeps track of the capacity and the memory availability of each GPU (`CapacityList` and `MemAvailList`) and of the

---

[1] Strictly speaking this is a misnomer, since allocation need not occur in multiples of any fixed "page size", but we retain the term to make the analogy with conventional virtual memory systems clear.

memory usage of each context (`MemUsage`). This information is used to determine whether binding an application thread to a GPU can potentially lead to exceeding its memory capacity.

Table 1 shows the actions performed by the runtime for each memory-related call invoked by the application. For simplicity, we show the data transfer deferral configuration. Note that, in this case, *malloc* and *copy$_{HD}$* (data copy from host to device) do not trigger any CUDA runtime actions. *Swap* is an internal function which is triggered by the runtime when some data must be swapped from device to host memory to make room for data on the GPU. Like *malloc*, *swap* operates on a single page table entry. Two scenarios are possible: *intra-application swap* and *inter-application swap*. Independent of the kind, the swap operation can be triggered by the runtime while trying to allocate device memory to execute a kernel launch. Memory operations on nested structures will be extended also to their PTE members.

Intra-application swap – Consider the following sequence of calls coming from the same application *app*, where *matmul* is a matrix multiplication kernel for square matrices.

```
1.  malloc(&A_d, size);
2.  malloc(&B_d, size);
3.  malloc(&C_d, size);
4.  copyHD(A_d, A_h, size);
5.  matmul(A_d, A_d, B_d);    //B_d = A_d * A_d
6.  matmul(B_d, B_d, C_d);    //C_d = B_d * B_d
7.  copyDH(B_h, B_d, size);
8.  copyDH(C_h, C_d, size);
```

If the above application is run on the bare CUDA runtime and the data sizes are such that only two matrices fit the device memory, the execution will fail on the third instruction (that is, when trying to allocate the third matrix). On the other hand, when our runtime is used, no memory allocation is performed until the first kernel launch (instruction 5). Previous instructions update only page table and swap memory. Instruction 5 will cause the allocation of matrices A_d and B_d and the data transfer of A_h to A_d, and will execute properly. During execution of instruction 6, the runtime will detect the need for freeing device memory. Before trying to swap and unbind other applications from the GPU, the runtime will analyze the page table of *app* and detect that data A_d, not required by instruction 6, can be swapped to host. This will allow the application to complete with no error. In summary, *intra-application swap enables the execution of applications that would fail on the CUDA runtime even if run in isolation*. In other words, the maximum memory footprint of the "larger" kernel (rather than the overall memory footprint of the application) will determine whether the application can correctly run on the device.

Inter-application swap – This kind of swap may take place when concurrent applications mapped onto the same device have conflicting memory requirements. In particular, if device memory cannot be allocated and intra-application swap is not possible, the memory manager will be queried for applications running on the same GPU and using the amount of memory required. If such an application exists, it will be asked to swap. The application may or may not accept the request: for instance, an application running in a CPU phase with no pending requests may swap, but an application in the middle of a kernel call may not. If no application honors the swap request, the calling application will unbind from the virtual-GPU and retry later. Otherwise, all the page table entries belonging to the application that accepts the request will be swapped, and such application will be temporarily unbound from the GPU. There may be situations where multiple applications must swap for the required memory to be freed. To reduce complexity and avoid inefficiencies, we do

Table 1: For each application call, actions performed by our runtime and possible errors returned. A blank in the third column indicates any error generated by the CUDA runtime (i.e., result codes ≠ `cudaSuccess`). PTE = page table entry.

Application call	Actions performed by runtime	Errors returned by the runtime
Malloc	Create PTE	A virtual address cannot be assigned
	Allocate swap	Swap memory cannot be allocated
Copy$_{HD}$	Check valid PTE	No valid PTE
	Move data to swap	Swap-data size mismatch
Copy$_{DH}$	Check valid PTE	No valid PTE
	If (PTE.toCopy2Swap) cudaMemcpy$_{DH}$	-
Free	Check valid PTE	No valid PTE
	De-allocate swap	Cannot de-allocate swap
	If (PTE.isAllocated) cudaFree	-
Launch	Check valid PTE	No valid PTE
	If (^PTE.isAllocated) cudaMalloc	-
	If (PTE.toCopy2Dev) cudaMemcpy$_{HD}$	-
	cudaLaunch	-
Swap	Check valid PTE	No valid PTE
	If (PTE.toCopy2Swap) cudaMemcpy$_{DH}$	-
	If (PTE.isAllocated) cudaFree	-

not trigger the swap in these situations. Note that inter-application swap implies coordination among virtual-GPUs and, as a consequence, has a higher overhead than intra-application swap. To avoid dead-locks, synchronization is required while accessing the page table. Finally, note that enabling swaps only during CPU phases allows GPU intensive applications to make full use of the GPU.

To determine whether a memory allocation can be serviced, the runtime will first use the memory utilization data in the memory manager (`CapacityList`, `MemAvailList`, and `MemUsage`). However, because of possible memory fragmentation on GPU, the runtime may need to use the return code of the GPU memory allocation function to ensure that the request can be honored. Moreover, there may be cases where only some GPUs have the required memory capacity.

Finally, we point out two additional benefits of our design. First, bad memory operations (for instance, data transfers beyond the boundary of an allocated area) can be detected by the memory manager without overloading the CUDA runtime with calls that would fail. Second, multiple data copy operations within the same allocated area (i.e., the same page table entry) will trigger a single, bulk memory transfer to the device memory.

4.6 Fault Tolerance & Checkpoint-Restart

The memory manager provides an implicit checkpoint capability that allows load balancing if more powerful GPU become idle, if

GPUs are dynamically added and removed from the system, and recovery in case of GPU failures. For each application thread, the page table and the swap memory contain the state of the device memory. In addition, an internal data structure (called *Context*) contains other state information, such as: a link to the *connection* object, the information about the last device call performed, and, if the application thread fails, the error code. With this state information, dynamic binding allows redirecting contexts to different GPUs and resuming their operation. The dispatcher will monitor the availability of the devices and schedule contexts from the *failed contexts* list (in case of GPU failure or removal) and unbind and reschedule applications from the *assigned contexts* list in case of GPU addition. Our mechanism can be combined with BLCR [29] in order to enable these mechanisms also after a full restart of a node. Finally, our runtime has an internal check-pointing primitive that can be dynamically triggered after long running kernels, to allow fast recovery in case of failures.

4.7 Inter-node Offloading

If the GPUs installed on a node are overloaded, our runtime can offload some application threads to other nodes. Note that this mechanism allows transferring only the CUDA calls originating within an application, and not its CPU phases. In particular, the runtime redirects application threads in the list of *pending connections* to other nodes using a TCP socket interface. A measure of the load on the system is provided by the size of the list of *pending connections*. We allow the dispatcher to process *pending connections* only if the number of *pending contexts* is below a given threshold.

4.8 CUDA 4 Support

We briefly discuss the modifications required by our runtime in order to support CUDA 4.0. The most significant changes in CUDA 4.0 are the following: (i) all threads belonging to the same application are mapped onto the same CUDA context, and (ii) each application thread can use multiple devices by issuing multiple `cudaSetDevice` calls. The first change has been introduced to enable application threads to share data on GPU.

Our current implementation does not differentiate threads belonging to the same application from threads belonging to different ones. Moreover, to avoid explicit procurement of threads to GPUs, our runtime ignores all `cudaSetDevice` calls issued by applications. Compatibility with CUDA 4.0 requires the following changes. First, each thread connection should carry the information about the corresponding application identifier. This information will be used to ensure that application threads sharing data are mapped onto the same device. Second, `cudaSetDevice` calls can be used to identify groups of CUDA calls that can potentially be assigned to different GPUs. Note that, because of the dynamic binding capability of our runtime, the latter modification is not strictly required. However, its introduction can help making efficient scheduling decisions with minimal overhead. Finally, CUDA 4.0 allows a more efficient and direct GPU-to-GPU data transfer. Our runtime can take advantage of this mechanism to provide faster thread-to-GPU remapping.

5. EXPERIMENTAL RESULTS

The experiments were conducted in two environments: on a single node and on a three-node cluster. Unless otherwise indicated, the metric reported in all experiments is the overall execution time for a batch of concurrent jobs (that is, the time elapsed between the

Table 2: Benchmark programs.

Program	Description	Kernel calls #
Short-running applications		
Back Propagation (*BP*)	Training of 20 neural networks with 64K nodes per input layer	40
Breadth-First Search (*BFS*)	Traversal of graph with 1M nodes	24
HotSpot (*HS*)	Thermal simulation of 1M grids	1
Needleman-Wunsch (*NW*)	DNA sequence alignment of 2K potential pairs of sequences	256
Scalar Product (*SP*)	Scalar product of vector pair (512 vector pairs of 1M elements)	1
Matrix Transpose (*MT*)	Transpose (384x384) matrix	816
Parallel Reduction (*PR*)	Parallel reduction of 4M elements	801
Scan (*SC*)	Parallel prefix sum of 260K elements	3,300
Black Scholes - small (*BS-S*)	Processing of 4M financial options	256
Vector Addition (*VA*)	100M-element vector addition	1
Long-running applications		
Small Matrix Multiplication (*MM-S*)	200 matrix multiplications of 2Kx2K square matrices and variable CPU phases	200
Large Matrix Multiplication (*MM-L*)	10 matrix multiplications of 10Kx10K square matrices and variable CPU phases	10
Black Scholes - large (*BS-L*)	Processing of 40M financial options	256

first job starts and the last job finishes processing). We observed analogous trends when considering the average execution time across the jobs in the batch.

In all experiments, we adopted a *first-come-first-served scheduling policy* that assigns jobs to physical GPUs in a round-robin fashion and attempts to perform load balancing (by keeping the number of active *vGPUs* uniform across all available GPUs). The runtime is configured to defer all data transfers. *All data reported in experiments using our runtime include all the overheads introduced by our framework*: call interception, queuing delays, scheduling, memory management, and, whenever performed, swap operations and relating synchronizations. Given the parallel nature of the system, such overheads are not additive.

5.1 Hardware Setup

The system used in our node-level experiments includes eight Intel Xeon E5620 processors running at 2.40 GHz and is equipped with 48 GB of main memory and three NVIDIA Fermi GPUs (two Tesla C2050s and one Tesla C1060). Each Tesla C2050 has 14 streaming multiprocessors (SMs) with 32 cores per SM, each running at 1.15 GHz, and 3 GB of device memory. The Tesla C1060 has 30 SMs with 8 cores per SM, and 4 GB of device memory. In one experiment, we replaced the Tesla C1060 with the less powerful NVIDIA Quadro 2000 GPU, equipped with four 48-core SMs and 1 GB device memory. In our cluster-level experiments we used an additional node with the same CPU configuration but equipped with a single Tesla C1060 GPU card.

5.2 Benchmarks

The benchmark applications used in our experiments are listed in Table 2. These applications, obtained from Rodinia Benchmark Suite [30] and NVIDIA's CUDA SDK, cover several application

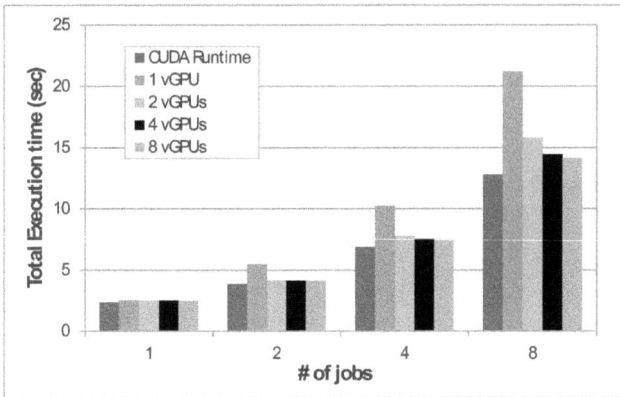

Figure 5: Execution time reported with a variable number of short-running jobs on a node with 1 GPU. The bare CUDA runtime is compared with our runtime.

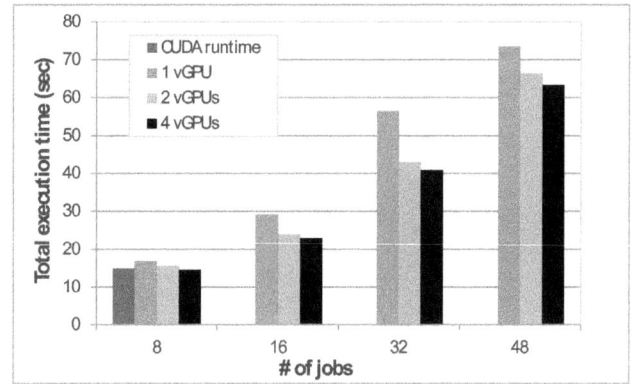

Figure 6: Execution time reported with a variable number of short-running jobs on a node with 3 GPUs. The bare CUDA runtime cannot handle more than 8 concurrent jobs.

domains, and differ in their memory occupancy, their GPU intensity and their interleaving of computation between CPU and GPU. We divide the workload into two categories: *short-running* and *long-running* applications. When using a Tesla C2050 GPU, the former report a running time between 3 and 5 seconds each, and the latter between 30 and 90 seconds (depending on the CPU phase injected – see Section 5.3.3). In the third column of Table 2, we report the number of kernel calls performed by each application. All short-running applications and *BS-L* are GPU intensive and have memory requirements well below the capacity of the GPUs in use. *MM-S* and *MM-L* are injected CPU phases of different length; *MM-L* has high memory requirements.

5.3 Node-level Experiments

5.3.1 Overhead Evaluation

First, we measured the overhead of our framework with respect to the CUDA runtime. We allowed our runtime to use only one physical GPU, and varied the number of virtual GPUs (*vGPUs*). The execution time of the bare CUDA runtime gives a lower bound that allows us to quantify the overhead associated with our framework. The data in Figure 5 were obtained by randomly drawing jobs from the pool of short-running applications in Table 2, and averaging the results over ten runs. To ensure apple-to-apple comparison, we run each of the randomly drawn combination of jobs on all 5 reported configurations (bare CUDA runtime and our runtime using 1, 2, 4 and 8 *vGPUs*).

Since our experiments showed that the CUDA runtime cannot handle more than eight concurrent CUDA contexts, we limited the number of jobs to eight. As can be seen in Figure 5, the total execution time of our runtime approaches the lower limit (CUDA runtime) as we increase the number of *vGPUs*. Increasing the number of *vGPUs* means increasing the sharing of the physical GPU, thus amortizing the overhead of the framework (which, in the worst case, accounts for about 10% of the execution time). Note that the percentage overhead would decrease on long-running applications.

5.3.2. Benefits of GPU Sharing

In our second set of experiments we evaluated the effect of GPU sharing in the presence of more (three) physical GPUs. We used the same workload as in Section 5.3.1, and again varied the number of *vGPUs* per device. We recall that the number of *vGPUs* represents the number of jobs that can time-share a GPU.

As mentioned in the previous section, we found that the CUDA

runtime does not currently support more than eight concurrent jobs stably. Therefore, we do not report results using the bare CUDA runtime beyond eight jobs. Figure 6 shows that, when using four *vGPUs* per device, our runtime reports some performance gain compared to the bare CUDA runtime. In fact, the overhead of our framework is compensated by its ability to load balance jobs on different physical GPUs. When running higher number of concurrent jobs, our results confirm our previous finding that increasing the amount of GPU sharing positively impacts the performances. However, we do not observe significant performance improvements when more than four *vGPUs* are employed. We believe that four *vGPUs* per device provide a good compromise between resource sharing and runtime overhead, and we use this setting in the rest of our experiments.

5.3.3. Conflicting Memory Needs: Effect of Swapping

The effect of swapping can be evaluated by using memory-hungry applications. To this end, we considered large matrix multiplication (*MM-L*). This benchmark program performs ten square matrix multiplications on randomly generated matrices. We set the data set size so to have conflicting memory requirements when more than two jobs are mapped onto the same GPU. In addition, we injected in the matrix multiplication benchmark CPU phases of various size. CPU phases are interleaved with kernel calls, and simulate different level of post-processing on the product of the matrix multiplication.

The effect of swapping is evaluated by running 36 *MM-L* jobs concurrently. In order to compare the swapping and no-swapping cases, we conducted experiments with one *vGPU* (no swapping required) and four *vGPUs* (swapping required). We recall that, in the one *vGPU* case, jobs run sequentially on a physical GPU, and therefore there is no memory contention. In the experiment, the fraction of CPU work is varied while maintaining the level of GPU work. Figure 7 shows that the total execution time grows linearly with the fraction of CPU work in the case of serialized execution (1 *vGPU*). In the case of GPU sharing (4 *vGPUs*), the overall execution time is kept constant even if the amount of work in each job increases. In fact, swapping can effectively reduce the total execution time by hiding the CPU-driven latency. In the chart, the number on the top of each bar indicates the swap operations occurred during execution. This experiment demonstrates that our swapping mechanism can effectively resolve resource conflicts among the concurrently running applications. In addition, despite its overhead, this mechanism provides performance improvement to applications with a considerable fraction of CPU work.

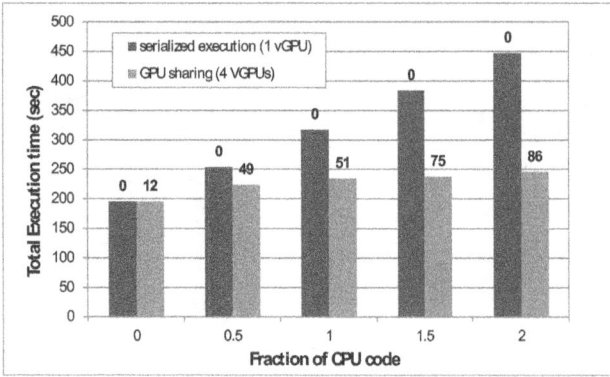

Figure 7: 36 *MM-L* jobs (with conflicting memory requirements) are run on a node with 3 GPUs. The fraction of CPU code in the workload is varied. We indicate the number of *swap* operations occurred on top of each bar.

We next investigated the performance of our runtime when combining applications with different amount of CPU work. In particular, we mixed *BS-L* with *MM-L* at different ratio (Figure 8). *BS-L* is a GPU-intensive application with very short CPU phases, whereas *MM-L* was set to have a fraction of CPU work equal to 1. The memory requirements of *BS-L* are below those of *MM-L*. Again, we run 36 jobs concurrently. The results of these experiments are shown in Figure 8. Again, the number on the top of each bar indicates the number of swap operations occurred during execution. As one might expect, the performance gain from GPU sharing increases as *MM-L* becomes dominant. Because *BS-L* is a GPU intensive application and swapping adds additional overhead, this results in a longer execution time for four *vGPUs* at a 75/25 mix of *BS-L* and *MM-L*.

5.3.4 Benefits of Dynamic Load Balancing

In Figure 9, we show the results of experiments performed on an unbalanced node that contains two *fast* and one *slow* GPUs: two Tesla C2050s and one Quadro 2000, respectively. In one setting, our runtime performs load balancing as follows. The dispatcher keeps track of fast GPUs becoming idle, and, in the absence of pending jobs, it migrates running jobs from slow to fast GPUs.

The experiments are conducted on *MM-S* jobs with varying CPU fraction, and using 4 *vGPUs* per device. The number of jobs migrated is reported on top of each bar. As can be seen, despite

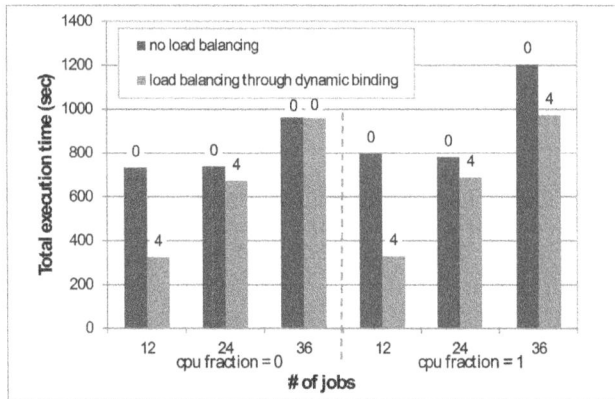

Figure 9: Unbalanced node with 2 Tesla C2050s and 1 Quadro 2000: effect of load balancing through dynamic binding. The number of *MM-S* jobs migrated to *fast* GPUs is reported on top of each bar.

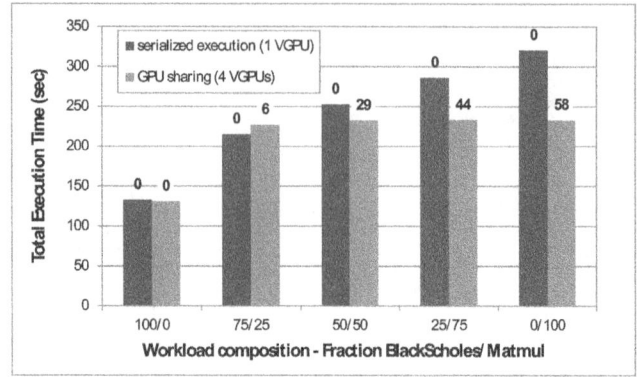

Figure 8: 36 jobs (*BS-L* and *MM-L*) are run on a node with 3 GPUs. The workload composition is varied. We indicate the number of *swap* operations occurred on top of each bar.

the overhead due to job migration, load balancing through dynamic binding of jobs to GPUs is an effective way to improve the performances of an unbalanced system. This holds especially in the presence of small batches of jobs and of applications alternating CPU and GPU phases. As the number of concurrent jobs increases, the system performs load balancing by scheduling on fast GPUs pending jobs, rather than by migrating jobs already running on slow devices.

5.4 Cluster-level Experiments

We have integrated our runtime with TORQUE, a cluster-level scheduler that can be used to run GPU jobs on heterogeneous clusters. In this section, we show experiments performed on a cluster of three nodes. The jobs are submitted at a head node and executed on two compute nodes. The hardware configuration of the compute nodes is described in Section 5.1. Having a three- and a single-GPU compute node, our cluster is unbalanced.

When TORQUE is used on a cluster equipped with GPUs, it relies on the CUDA runtime to execute GPU calls. Since the CUDA runtime does not provide adequate support to concurrency, TORQUE does not allow any form of GPU sharing across jobs. Therefore, when configured to use compute nodes equipped with GPUs, TORQUE serializes the execution of concurrent jobs by enqueuing them on the head node and submitting them to the compute nodes only when a GPU becomes available. *By coupling TORQUE with our runtime system, we are able to provide GPU sharing to concurrent jobs.*

When coupling TORQUE with our runtime, we conducted experiments with three settings. In all cases, to force TORQUE to submit to the compute nodes more jobs than available GPUs, we hid from TORQUE the presence of GPUs, and handled it only within our runtime. In the first setting, our runtime was configured to use only one *vGPU* per device, and therefore to serialize the execution of concurrent jobs. In the second setting, we allowed GPU sharing by using four *vGPUs* per device. In the third setting, we additionally enabled load balancing across compute nodes by allowing inter-node communication and offloading. We also performed experiments using TORQUE natively on the bare CUDA runtime. However, the results reported using this configuration are far worse than those reported using TORQUE in combination with our runtime. Therefore, we show the use of our runtime with one *vGPU* per device as example of no GPU sharing.

In Figure 10, we show experiments conducted using a variable number of short-running jobs drawn from the applications in

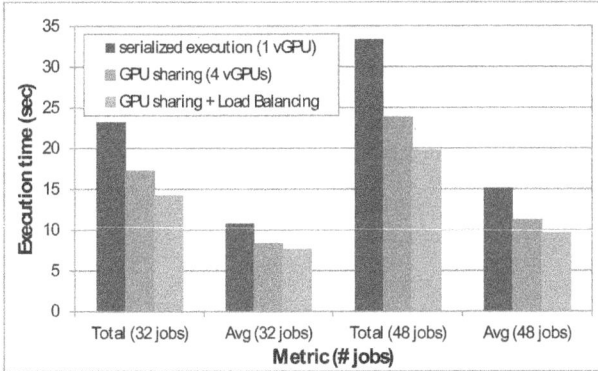

Figure 10: Two-node cluster using TORQUE: effect of GPU sharing and load balancing via inter-node offloading in the presence of short-running jobs and in the absence of conflicting memory requirements.

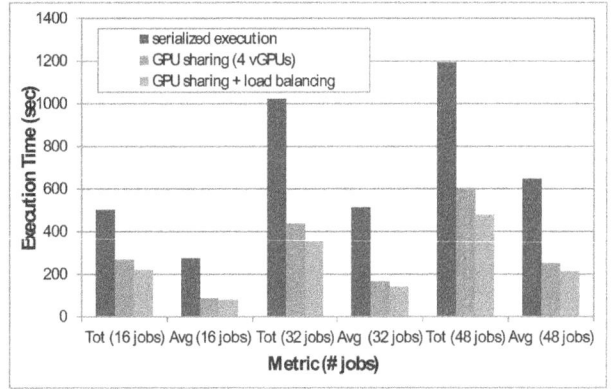

Figure 11: Two-node cluster using TORQUE: effect of GPU sharing and load balancing via inter-node offloading in the presence of long-running jobs and conflicting memory requirements.

Table 2. In this set of experiments, jobs do not exhibit conflicting memory requirements. Again, we average the results reported over ten runs. As can be seen, GPU sharing allows up to a 28% performance improvement over serialized execution. However TORQUE, which relies on our runtime and is unaware of the number and location of the GPUs in the cluster, divides the workload equally between the two nodes. Thus, the node with only one GPU is overloaded compared to the other node with three GPUs. When, in addition to GPU sharing, we allow load balancing through our inter-node offloading technique, the overall throughput is further improved by up to 18%.

Finally, we want to show the benefits of our runtime system in a cluster in the presence of jobs with conflicting memory requirements. To this end, we run 16, 32 and 48 *BS-L* and MM-L jobs (25/75 distribution). We recall that these two applications have long runtimes. The results of this experiment are shown in Figure 11. Again, serialized execution allows avoiding memory conflicts. From the figure, it is clear that allowing jobs to share GPUs increases the throughput significantly (up to 50%), despite the overhead due to the need for swap operations. Moreover, in the presence of load imbalances, the execution is further accelerated by allowing the overloaded node to offload the excess jobs remotely.

6. RELATED WORK

Our proposal is closely related to two categories of work: runtime systems to enable GPU virtualization [1][2][3][4][6], and memory-aware runtimes for heterogeneous nodes including CPUs and GPUs [8][9]. As mentioned previously, GViM [1], vCUDA [2], rCUDA [3] and gVirtuS [4] use API *remoting* to provide GPU visibility from within virtual machines. GViM and vCUDA leverage the multiplexing mechanism provided by the CUDA runtime in order to allow GPU sharing among different applications. In addition, GViM uses a Working Queue per GPU to evenly distribute the load across different GPUs. However, as discussed, the CUDA runtime cannot properly handle a large number of concurrent applications, nor concurrent applications whose aggregate memory requirements exceed the memory capacity of the underlying GPU device. Our work addresses both these issues, and allows dynamic scheduling of jobs on GPUs.

As additional feature, GViM provides a mechanism to minimize the overhead of memory transfers when GPUs are used within virtualized environments. In particular, its authors propose using the `mmap` Unix system call to avoid the data copy between the

guest OS and the host OS. Whenever possible, they also propose using page locked memory (along with the `cudaMallocHost` primitive) in order to avoid the additional data copy between host OS and GPU memory. Memory transfer optimization is orthogonal to the objectives of this work. In the future, we plan to include these optimizations in our runtime.

Guevara et al [7] propose kernel consolidation as a way to share GPUs. They show that this mechanism is particularly effective in the presence of kernels with complementary resource requirements (e.g.: compute intensive and memory intensive kernels). The concept of kernel consolidation has been reconsidered and explored in the context of GPU virtualization by Ravi et al [6]. Differently from us, Ravi et al assume that the overall memory footprint of the consolidated applications fits the device memory, and statically bind applications to GPUs. Our proposal is in a way orthogonal to [6]. In fact, the delayed application-to-GPU binding and the deferral of memory operations offered by our runtime should allow easy and efficient integration of kernel consolidation.

Gelado et al [8] and Becchi et al [9] propose two similar memory-management frameworks for nodes including CPUs and GPUs. The primary goal of these proposals is to hide the underlying distributed memory system from the programmer, and automatically move data between CPU and GPU as they are needed. By doing so, these frameworks eliminate some unrequired memory transfers between CPU and GPU. These proposals, however, do not target multi-tenancy and conflicting memory requirements among concurrent applications, which are the main focus of our work. On one hand, the memory module we design has some similarities with these two proposals (tracking of mapping between CPU and GPU address spaces, memory transfer deferral and optimization); on the other hand, it extends these frameworks and focuses on the multi-tenancy scenario.

NVCR [15] provides a checkpoint-restart mechanism for CUDA applications written using the CUDA driver and runtime APIs. The framework is intended to be integrated with BLCR [29] Checkpoints are inserted at each memory and kernel operation using an intercept library. To ensure memory consistency and reconstruct the device pointer information, NVCR requires replaying all memory allocations performed by the application after every restart, leading to a potentially high overhead. Our virtual memory abstraction allows us to replay only memory operations required by not-yet-executed kernel calls.

Our runtime assumes that the memory footprint of each application fits the most capable GPU in the system. Under this assumption, we allow concurrency among applications with conflicting memory requirements. *In addition, our intra-application swap capability allows relaxing the memory requirements for applications to run on GPU.* Related work [16][17] has considered the problem of limiting the memory requirements of single applications by reorganizing their memory access patterns and splitting operators.

Finally, the interest in using GPUs for general purpose computing is confirmed by recent work on automatic generation of CUDA code [13][14], and on programming models and runtime systems for heterogeneous nodes [10][11][12]. These proposals are orthogonal to the work presented in this paper.

7. CONCLUSIONS AND FUTURE WORK

In conclusion, we have proposed a runtime system that provides abstraction and sharing of GPUs, while allowing isolation of concurrent applications. Two fundamental features of our runtime are: (i) *dynamic application-to-GPU binding* and (ii) *virtual memory for GPUs*. In particular, dynamic binding maximizes device utilization and improves performances in the presence of concurrent applications with multiple GPU phases and of GPUs with different compute capabilities. Besides dynamic binding, the virtual memory abstraction enables the following features: (i) load balancing in case of GPU addition and removal, (ii) resilience to GPU failures, and (iii) checkpoint-restart capabilities.

Our prototype implementation targets NVIDIA GPUs. In the future, we intend to extend our runtime to support other many-core devices, such as the Intel MIC. In addition, we intend to evaluate our runtime on larger clusters and on multi-node applications. Finally, we plan to explore alternative mapping and scheduling algorithms, as well as security concerns related to heterogeneous cluster and cloud computing infrastructures.

8. ACKNOWLEDGEMENTS

The authors thank the anonymous reviewers for the feedback that helped improve the paper. This work has been supported by NEC Research Laboratories. Adam Procter has been supported by U.S. Department of Education GAANN grant no. P200A100053.

9. REFERENCES

[1] V. Gupta et al. 2009. GViM: GPU-accelerated virtual machines. In *Proc. of HPCVirt '09*. ACM, New York, NY, USA, pp. 17-24.

[2] L. Shi, H. Chen, and J. Sun. 2009. vCUDA: GPU accelerated high performance computing in virtual machines. In *Proc. of IPDPS '09*, Washington, DC, USA, pp. 1-11.

[3] J. Duato et al. 2010. rCUDA: Reducing the number of GPU-based accelerators in high performance clusters. In *Proc. of HPCS '10*, pp. 224–231.

[4] G. Giunta, R. Montella, G. Agrillo, and G. Coviello. 2010. A GPGPU transparent virtualization component for high performance computing clouds. In *Proc. of Euro-Par 2010*, Heidelberg, 2010.

[5] gVirtuS: http://osl.uniparthenope.it/projects/gvirtus

[6] V. Ravi, M. Becchi, G. Agrawal, and S. Chakradhar. 2011. Supporting GPU sharing in cloud environments with a transparent runtime consolidation framework. In *Proc. of HPDC '11*. ACM, New York, NY, USA, pp. 217-228.

[7] M. Guevara, C. Gregg, K. Hazelwood, and K. Skadron. 2009. Enabling Task Parallelism in the CUDA Scheduler. In *Workshop on Programming Models for Emerging Architectures*, Sep. 2009.

[8] I. Gelado et al. 2010. An asymmetric distributed shared memory model for heterogeneous parallel systems. In *Proc. of ASPLOS '10*. ACM, New York, NY, USA, pp. 347-358.

[9] M. Becchi, S. Byna, S. Cadambi, and S. Chakradhar. 2010. Data-aware scheduling of legacy kernels on heterogeneous platforms with distributed memory. In *Proc. of SPAA '10*. ACM, New York, NY, USA, pp. 82-91.

[10] M. D. Linderman, J. D. Collins, H. Wang, and T. H. Meng. 2008. Merge: a programming model for heterogeneous multi-core systems. In *Proc. of ASPLOS '08*. ACM, New York, NY, USA, pp. 287-296.

[11] B. Saha et al. 2009. Programming model for a heterogeneous x86 platform. In *Proc. of PLDI '09*. New York, NY, USA, pp. 431-440.

[12] C.-K. Luk, S. Hong, and H. Kim. 2009. Qilin: exploiting parallelism on heterogeneous multiprocessors with adaptive mapping. In *Proc. of MICRO '09*. ACM, New York, NY, USA, pp. 45-55.

[13] S.-Z. Ueng, M. Lathara, S. Baghsorkhi, and W.-M. Hwu. 2008. CUDA-Lite: Reducing GPU Programming Complexity. In *Languages and Compilers for Parallel Computing*, Lecture Notes in Comp. Sc., Vol. 5335. Springer-Verlag, Berlin, Heidelberg pp. 1-15.

[14] S. Lee and R. Eigenmann. 2010. OpenMPC: Extended OpenMP Programming and Tuning for GPUs. In *Proc. of SC '10*. Washington, DC, USA, pp. 1-11. Nov 2010.

[15] A. Nukada, H. Takizawa, and S. Matsuoka, 2011. NVCR: A Transparent Checkpoint-Restart Library for NVIDIA CUDA. In *Proc. of IPDPDW '11*, Shanghai, China, pp. 104-113, Sep 2011.

[16] N. Sundaram, A. Raghunathan, and S. Chakradhar. 2009. A framework for efficient and scalable execution of domain-specific templates on GPUs. In *Proc. of IPDPS '09*. IEEE Computer Society, Washington, DC, USA, pp. 1-12.

[17] J. Kim, H. Kim, J. Hwan Lee, and J. Lee. 2011. Achieving a single compute device image in OpenCL for multiple GPUs. In *Proc. of PPoPP '11*. ACM, New York, NY, USA, pp. 277-288.

[18] H. Lim, S. Babu, J. Chase, and S. Parekh. 2009. Automated control in cloud computing: challenges and opportunities. In *Proc. of ACDC '09*. ACM, New York, NY, USA, pp. 13-18.

[19] P. Marshall, K. Keahey, and T. Freeman. 2010. Elastic Site: Using Clouds to Elastically Extend Site Resources. In *Proc. of CCGrid 2010*, pp. 43-52, May 2010.

[20] P. Padala et al. 2009. Automated control of multiple virtualized resources. In *Proc. of EuroSys '09*. New York, NY, USA, pp. 13-26.

[21] M. Becchi and P. Crowley. 2006. Dynamic thread assignment on heterogeneous multiprocessor architectures. In *Proc. of CF '06*. ACM, New York, NY, USA, pp. 29-40.

[22] J. Nickolls, I. Buck, M. Garland, K. Skadron. 2008. Scalable Parallel Programming with CUDA. In *ACM Queue*. April 2008.

[23] G. Teodoro et al. 2009. Coordinating the use of GPU and CPU for improving performance of compute intensive applications. In *Proc. of CLUSTER*, pp. 1–10, 2009.

[24] Eucalyptus: http://www.eucalyptus.com

[25] TORQUE Resource Manager: http://www.clusterresources.com/products/TORQUE-resource-manager.php

[26] Amazon EC2 Instances: http://aws.amazon.com/ec2/

[27] Nimbix Informatics Xcelerated: http://www.nimbix.net

[28] Hoopoe: http://www.hoopoe-cloud.com

[29] BLCR: https://ftg.lbl.gov/projects/CheckpointRestart

[30] Rodinia : https://www.cs.virginia.edu/~skadron/wiki/rodinia/index.php/Main_Page

Interference-driven Resource Management for GPU-based Heterogeneous Clusters

Rajat Phull, Cheng-Hong Li, Kunal Rao, Srihari Cadambi, and Srimat Chakradhar

NEC Laboratories America, Inc.
Suite 200, 4 Independence Way, Princeton, NJ 08540, USA
{rphull, chenghong, kunal, cadambi, chak}@nec-labs.com

ABSTRACT

GPU-based clusters are increasingly being deployed in HPC environments to accelerate a variety of scientific applications. Despite their growing popularity, the GPU devices themselves are under-utilized even for many computationally-intensive jobs. This stems from the fact that the typical GPU usage model is one in which a host processor periodically offloads computationally intensive portions of an application to the coprocessor. Since some portions of code cannot be offloaded to the GPU (for example, code performing network communication in MPI applications), this usage model results in periods of time when the GPU is idle. GPUs could be time-shared across jobs to "fill" these idle periods, but unlike CPU resources such as the cache, the effects of sharing the GPU are not well understood. Specifically, two jobs that time-share a single GPU will experience resource contention and *interfere* with each other. The resulting slow-down could lead to missed job deadlines. Current cluster managers do not support GPU-sharing, but instead dedicate GPUs to a job for the job's lifetime.

In this paper, we present a framework to predict and handle interference when two or more jobs time-share GPUs in HPC clusters. Our framework consists of an analysis model, and a dynamic interference detection and response mechanism to detect excessive interference and restart the interfering jobs on different nodes. We implement our framework in Torque, an open-source cluster manager, and using real workloads on an HPC cluster, show that interference-aware two-job colocation (although our method is applicable to colocating more than two jobs) improves GPU utilization by 25%, reduces a job's waiting time in the queue by 39% and improves job latencies by around 20%.

Categories and Subject Descriptors

C.4 [**PERFORMANCE OF SYSTEMS**]: Modeling techniques, measuring techniques

General Terms

Measurement, Performance, Design

Keywords

GPU, Co-processor, Interference, Cluster, Scheduling, Iterative applications

1. INTRODUCTION

GPUs have been shown to provide a $10 - 100\times$ performance boost for computationally-intensive kernels such as linear system solvers, physical simulations, partial differential equations solvers and flow visualizations [25, 28, 31]. Many of these kernels are integral components of HPC applications, for which GPUs can provide significant end-to-end speedups. As a result, they are being increasingly deployed in HPC clusters and supercomputers, such as [4], as well as cloud infrastructures such as Amazon's EC2 [8]. Three of the top five supercomputers in the Top500 List use GPUs [3].

However, GPUs are usually under-utilized when viewed from an overall application perspective. Good coprocessor utilization, which is the fraction of time the coprocessor is busy, is an important consideration because coprocessors are expensive and power-hungry [17]. We argue that the current GPU usage model does not facilitate achieving high utilization. Specifically, a host processor manages the overall application and periodically offloads computationally intensive kernels over the PCI bus to the GPU coprocessor. However there are some blocks of code that cannot or should not be offloaded to the GPU. These could be code blocks (i) that are not parallelizable and therefore do not run faster on the many-core GPU or (ii) whose performance benefits are over-shadowed by data movement across the PCI bus or (iii) that perform I/O operations such as accessing network or disk. This creates "gaps" in a job's GPU access pattern, or periods where the GPU is idle because the CPU is busy executing tasks that are ill-suited for the GPU such as when multi-node MPI jobs perform inter-process communication.

Such idle periods lower coprocessor utilization. Note that this is different from the actual core utilization on the GPU: GPU-optimized kernels often fully utilize the cores on the GPU to achieve as much speedup as possible. But these GPU kernels comprise intermittent portions of the entire job, with execution periodically reverting to the host. This is true even for an application like Himeno [6] that overlaps computation and MPI communications. In general we observe this low utilization in many real, GPU-accelerated HPC applications. For instance, when we examined the

WRF application that uses the GPU to accelerate numerical weather prediction [15], we found that on a 4-node cluster with each node containing one NVIDIA Tesla C2050 GPU, the devices were busy less than 10% of the time![1] Similarly, other MPI-based multi-node GPU applications such as Amber [1], the molecular simulation tool, use the GPU under 30% of the time on average.

In this paper, we propose improving GPU utilization by *time-sharing* GPU devices across multiple jobs; in other words, we schedule multiple jobs to run on the same compute nodes to GPUs. We leverage each job process's intermittent GPU usage such that when one process's computation reverts to the host CPU, another process of a different job uses the GPU. Colocated jobs must be dispatched by the cluster manager to the same nodes. Since multiple jobs now access the same GPU devices, the GPUs would be better utilized, especially if one job's GPU access patterns could potentially fill in the idle periods of another job's access patterns.

However, most current cluster managers supporting GPUs do not offer this sharing feature; rather, they dedicate entire GPU devices to each job for as long as the job runs. One reason for this is that when jobs time-share GPUs, they contend for common resources, and will consequently *interfere* with each other. This interference degrades performance and may result in missed deadlines. The open-source cluster manager Torque [5] does allow users to specify that their jobs can share GPUs, but then the responsibility for any performance degradation or missed deadlines rests with the user. As far as we know, existing cluster managers do not automatically analyze how jobs that time-share GPUs might slow down due to interference. Thus, they cannot make "compatible" jobs share GPUs, and ensure "incompatible" jobs are kept apart. Unlike in the CPU domain, where cache and memory interference are better understood, *there is no prior work that looks into predicting as well as handling the effects of inter-job interference when jobs contend for a common GPU device.* While our proposed framework can be extended to more than two colocated jobs, we believe an investigation of the effects of two jobs contending for a common GPU is a reasonable starting point, and we attempt to do that thoroughly in this paper. In addition, colocating too many jobs will likely increase memory pressure on the relatively scarce GPU memory resources. Technologies to manage GPU memory during multi-tenancy have recently been proposed [9], and complement the ideas in this paper.

The ability to schedule jobs to share GPUs and offer performance guarantees is useful for an HPC cluster manager, and critical if coprocessor utilization must be increased. To this end, we propose a three-pronged approach to *predict* and *dynamically handle* interference between colocated jobs on GPUs. First, we statically profile an instance of each job offline, and extract GPU usage patterns for the job. Second, we build an interference analysis model that uses the patterns to predict the performance degradation of two jobs when they are colocated and time-share GPUs. Third, we monitor the performance of colocated jobs, and dynamically relocate jobs that cause excessive or unacceptable performance loss due to interference.

The interference analysis model allows a cluster manager

to employ heuristics on top of our scheme and decide if two jobs could time-share GPUs or not. We implement our prediction scheme as well as our dynamic interference handling mechanisms in Torque, an open-source cluster manager [5]. We test our framework on an HPC cluster with NVIDIA C2050 GPUs, and experimentally measure the benefits of GPU sharing for a number of real workloads.

To summarize, the contributions of this work are:

- We present performance and utilization trade-offs when real HPC workloads time-share GPU coprocessors, thereby motivating "coprocessor interference-driven" cluster management.

- We propose a three-pronged approach for HPC cluster managers to utilize GPUs more efficiently: offline GPU usage pattern extraction, an interference analysis model and online monitoring/response to interference-related performance degradation.

- We implement coprocessor interference-awareness in PBS Torque, the well-known cluster-level resource management framework, and experimentally show improved utilization as well as overall performance gains on several real HPC workloads.

The rest of the document is organized as follows. In Section 2, we illustrate the magnitude of GPU interference, and explain the causes using examples. In Section 3, we describe coprocessor interference modeling and slowdown prediction. We present the interference analysis framework in Section 4. Section 5 presents experimental results. We discuss related work in Section 6 and conclude in Section 7.

2. COPROCESSOR INTERFERENCE

In this section, we illustrate interference due to contention for the GPU coprocessor by way of example, and explain the reasons for the observed variations in performance degradation. Our hardware infrastructure for this experiment is a small 2-node cluster, with each node consisting of dual quad core 2.4GHz Xeon E5620 processors, and one NVIDIA C2050 GPU. We use the following three applications, all of which are MPI-based 2-node jobs using 1 GPU per node (but configurable to use the CPU instead of the GPU): WRF, Openfoam, and K-means.[2]

Magnitude of GPU interference. Our first goal is to quantify the effect of GPU contention on application performance. To do this, we run different combinations of MPI jobs (with two MPI processes each) simultaneously on the 2 nodes, and measure performance degradation both with and without GPU usage.

Table 1 quantifies the results of GPU interference. The left column shows all pairwise combinations of our 3 HPC jobs. For each combination, we run the two jobs concurrently on the 2-node cluster, and measure the performance slowdown relative to when the jobs run exclusively, i.e., with no contention for any resource. Each job uses both nodes in the cluster and runs one MPI process on each node. In the case when a job runs exclusively on the two nodes, each node has only one MPI process. If two jobs run concurrently on the cluster, each node is shared by two different MPI processes.

---

[1]We do not take into account how many cores of the GPU were actually busy. A busy GPU is one in which some or all cores are busy, while an idle GPU is one in which no core is busy.

---

[2]Section 5 provides detailed descriptions of these applications.

Colocated Jobs	Slowdown of Host-Only Versions	Slowdown of Host+GPU Versions
(WRF, Openfoam)	(2.8%, 11%)	(5.0%, 8.3%)
(K-means, Openfoam)	(0.8%, 0.2%)	(0.8%, 51.5%)
(K-means, WRF)	(0.4%, 0.8%)	(0.7%, 24.4%)

Table 1: Performance loss of colocated jobs with and without GPU contention.

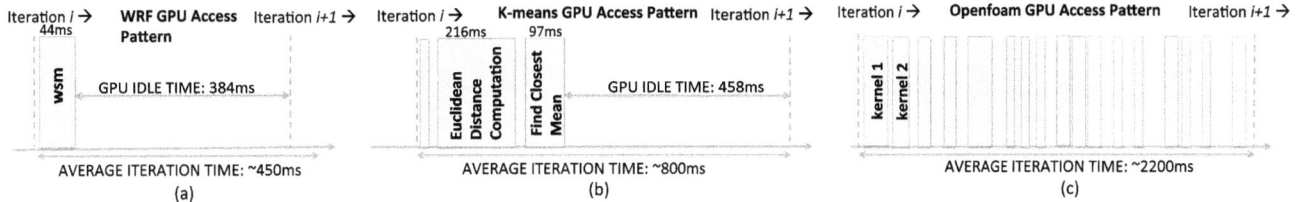

Figure 1: GPU usage patterns of (a) WRF, (b) K-means, and (c) Openfoam.

The second and third column of the table show individual slowdown experienced by the 2 jobs respectively. Thus, (0.8%, 0.2%) for (K-means, Openfoam) indicates that when the host-only versions of these jobs are run together, K-means and Openfoam are 0.8% and 0.2% slower than when they run by themselves with exclusive access to all resources, respectively. This column quantifies the performance loss due to contention for non-GPU resources, such as the cache, memory system, network and so on. We ensure the total number of threads of any pair of the jobs is less then the number of cores, so contention for the CPU cores is not a factor. We notice that K-means together with Openfoam, as well as K-means together with WRF experience little slowdown (under 1%) when they run concurrently on the same nodes without using GPU.

The fourth and fifth column of Table 1 report individual slowdown experienced by two host+GPU jobs respectively when the jobs are concurrently run, thus time-sharing the GPUs of both nodes. For the same pair of K-means and Openfoam, the slowdown of Openfoam now is 51.5%, *a major increase due to sharing of the GPU with another job.*

There are two important take-aways:

- Compared to the performance loss when the host-only versions compete for CPU and other resources, performance loss when competing for the GPU is larger. The effects of contention for non-GPU resources such as the cache are better understood [18]. However GPU contention has not yet been studied, and is the focus of this paper.

- The extent of performance loss arising due to GPU contention ranges from 0.7% to 51.5%. In many cases, a 0.7% slowdown is negligible, but a 51.5% slowdown may not be. Therefore, a cluster manager must be able to predict and handle interference if it schedules jobs to share GPUs.

GPU interference: looking deeper. When GPUs are time-shared between two jobs, the key factor that determines each job's performance degradation is the manner in which its processes access the GPU devices, i.e., their GPU access patterns. All our applications, and in general HPC applications, are iterative in nature, and each iteration of a process accesses the GPU device in a very similar manner.

Any variations in the GPU access pattern, say due to actual data values, are very small.

Qualitatively two aspects relating to the GPU access patterns of an application's process affect the performance degradation experienced by the process and its co-running processes, and the application as a whole. First we assume that the CUDA runtime executes kernels from different processes in a FIFO order, allowing only one kernel access to the GPU at any given time. (Later in Section 3 we will present evidences suggesting the CUDA runtime indeed serializes kernels for GPU access and grants access in FIFO order.) Based on this, the performance degradation due to GPU interference depends on the length of each kernel and the frequency of kernel launches by a process. Particularly, we found that a process using short kernels has less impact on its co-running process's performance because the waiting time of queued kernels from the co-running process is short. Also the performance of a process that launches kernels less frequently is less susceptible to interference due to GPU sharing. In the following we will use three real applications to further explain these effects.

Figure 1(a) shows how a WRF's process accesses a GPU device over time when running by itself with exclusive GPU access. The figure shows the access pattern for one iteration of the WRF's process. During each iteration, the GPU is accessed by 1 main CUDA kernel. Between kernel invocations, the GPU is idle when the CPU performs other tasks (for e.g., network I/O or MPI barrier synchronization). Similarly, Figure 1(b) and Figure 1(c) show the GPU access patterns for one iteration of K-means's and Openfoam's processes, respectively.

Looking at the GPU usage patterns for WRF and Openfoam, we can see that WRF's pattern of one iteration has considerable periods during which the GPU is idle. That is, WRF launches kernels relatively less frequently. These idle periods offer an opportunity for time-sharing the GPU. When run concurrently, both jobs will attempt to launch their GPU kernels, but the CUDA runtime will serialize access to the GPU. For example, the CUDA runtime may receive kernel launches in this order: wsm kernel from WRF, kernel 1 and 2 (and the rest of kernels) from Openfoam. In that case, the wsm kernel is launched first, while the kernels 1 and 2 from Openfoam are queued by the CUDA runtime. When wsm is done, instead of idling for 384ms, the

CUDA runtime launches Openfoam kernels. Since WRF only launches a relatively short kernel (44ms) in comparison with the length of its iteration (450ms), and Openfoam's kernels are also very short (less than 1ms), whenever a kernel is queued by the CUDA runtime, its wait time will not be long. In addition, the large gaps between successive kernel calls of WRF means Openfoam's kernels seldom gets delayed. Both of these factors explain the low interference overhead for these two applications. In other words, these applications are "compatible".

When K-means is run together with either Openfoam or WRF, both Openform and WRF experience a much higher slowdown (24.4% and 51.5%) while the performance degradation of K-means is negligible. Because K-means's kernels are long, Openfoam's (and WRF's) kernels may need to wait longer if they are queued by the CUDA runtime. The fact that Openfoam launches kernels more frequently than WRF does means that Openfoam's kernels may get delayed more often by the CUDA runtime, and thus Openfoam suffers more performance degradation than WRF when either one of them shares GPUs with K-means.

One of the key contributions in this paper is to predict the effect of interference given the exclusive GPU access patterns. In the next section, we describe our coprocessor interference analysis model that algorithmically predicts the performance slowdown.

3. INTERFERENCE ANALYSIS

This section introduces the proposed interference analysis framework. The goal of the interference analysis is to predict the slowdown of co-running jobs due to contention of the shared resources, like GPU devices and the PCIe buses.

Our interference analysis is modeling-based. It only relies on the profiling of a job when the job runs with dedicated resources without GPU sharing. Given the profiling information of a number of jobs, our interference analysis predicts the performance slowdown for all combinations of the co-running jobs.

Several assumptions and observations of GPU-accelerated MPI applications underlies our interference analysis. First we assume that the slowdown of a GPU-accelerated MPI job due to GPU contention is determined by the maximum slowdown across all MPI processes of the job. Therefore, we focus on the analysis of interference between individual MPI processes on the same compute node.

Second we assume that a process of a multi-node HPC job using GPUs for acceleration has a repetitive GPU usage pattern. Such a pattern consists of a series of kernel launches separated by CPU processing (called a "gap") between them, as explained in Section 2. In this paper we target NVIDIA's GPUs and its CUDA programming framework. In CUDA, when two processes issue GPU kernels, their kernel executions will be interleaved by the CUDA runtime (time sharing). Further such time sharing of GPU device is multi-programmed, i.e., each kernel runs to its completion without preemption. Figure 2(a) illustrates a possible time-multiplexed execution sequence of GPU kernels issued from two different application processes. In addition, we focus on iterative-convergence, multi-node HPC applications using MPI for communications. As shown in Figure 2(b), such applications spend most of its computation in a main loop; each iteration of the loop invokes one or more

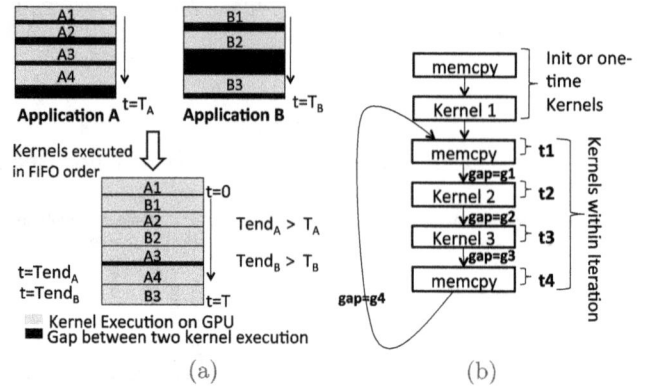

Figure 2: GPU usage: (a) interleaved execution on GPU; (b) Repetitive GPU usage patterns.

GPU kernels, and all the iterations have the same GPU kernels.

Based on these observations and assumptions our interference analysis framework extracts the repetitive GPU usage patterns of an application process without GPU contention and then uses such patterns to predict the performance slowdown of two or more co-running processes sharing the same GPU. In the following we first discuss how to obtain the GPU usage pattern of a MPI process using GPU, and then how the patterns can be used to construct an interference analysis model predicting the performance slowdown.

GPU usage patterns. In order to obtain the GPU usage pattern of a process our interference analysis framework uses a profiling tool called The CUDA Performance Tool Interface (CUPTI). CUPTI allows users to register callback functions which are invoked upon specific CUDA runtime events. In particular, we use the callback functions to intercept events of GPU kernel launches, completions, and data transfer operations. Such callback notifications enable our framework to maintain a history table of GPU kernel usage across multiple iterations of an application. The history table is further used to identify the repetitive GPU usage pattern in the application. For the identified GPU usage pattern, the framework measures average execution time and gaps between CUDA runtime API calls.

Our implementation of the GPU usage profiling does not require any code changes or recompilations of applications. To achieve this goal, we use mpiP [30], a lightweight, link-time profiling library for MPI applications. The mpiP library intercepts each MPI call (for profiling) and forwards the call to the native MPI library. As the first MPI call for each MPI application is `MPI_Init()`, we registered our CUPTI callbacks behind intercepted `MPI_Init()` call, while forwarding other intercepted MPI calls immediately.

Interference analysis model. The interference analysis model takes as inputs the repetitive GPU usage patterns of multiple processes obtained by the aforementioned method and predicts the performance slowdown of each process when the processes share one GPU device. Two prediction methods have been developed. One is based on simulation, while the other is based on timed Petri nets (TPN). The simulation model mimics the FIFO ordering scheduling policy and produces the interleaved execution pattern of multiple processes by using their GPU usage patterns. The individual execution time is compared with the interleaved execution time to predict the slowdown for each process. The TPN method algorithmically computes the slowdown of co-running processes based on cyclic structures in the TPN's state space. Although both methods can handle two or more processes sharing the same GPU device, due to limited space we will focus on the TPN method for two processes sharing one GPU device in the following.

A Petri net is a formal model very suitable for modeling concurrent systems. Usually it is presented as a directed and bipartite graph. It consists of two disjoint sets of vertices: *transitions* $T = \{t_1, \ldots, t_m\}$ and *places* $P = \{p_1, \ldots, p_n\}$, and edges $E \subseteq (P \times T) \cup (T \times P)$. Figure 3(a) shows a PN, where transitions are solid bars and places are circles. A *marking* $m : P \to \{0, 1, 2, \ldots\}$ is an assignment of *tokens* to places. For example, p_1 in Figure 3(a) has one token, represented as a small solid circle. A transition is *enabled* if each of its input places has at least one token. An enabled transition *fires* immediately. A fired transition removes one token from each of its input places and deposits one token to each of its output places. We use $t^-(p)$ and $t^+(p)$ to denote the changes of the number of tokens at place p due to the firing of transition t: $t^-(p)$ is 1 if $(p, t) \in E$, otherwise $t^-(p)$ is 0. Similarly, $t^+(p)$ is 1 if $(t, p) \in E$, otherwise $t^+(p)$ is 0.

For the purpose of performance modeling the notion of time is introduced into original Petri nets and such Petri nets are called timed Petri nets (TPNs). Our interference model uses the variant TPN in which time is associated with transitions [22, 26]. In such TPNs the firing of a transition t takes some non-negative delay $d(t)$, specified by function $d : T \to R^+ \cup \{0\}$. For example, in Figure 3(a) $d(t_1) = 5$ and $d(t_2) = 7$. During the time interval of the firing $[0, d(t))$, one token at each of the input places of t is *reserved*. A token reserved by transition t cannot enable any other transition except t. After $d(t)$ time units elapses, transition t completes its firing and removes the reserved tokens from its input places and adds new, unreserved tokens to its output places. Incorporating the above definitions, the basic structure (the bipartite graph) (P, T, E), the initial marking m_0, and the firing delay function D together fully specify a TPN N as a tuple $N = (P, T, E, m_0, d)$.

The behavior of a TPN can be characterized by its reachable *states*. A state of a TPN has two components: a marking m and a remaining-firing-time (RFT) function $k : T \to \mathbb{R}^+ \cup \{0\}$ assigning to each transition a non-negative number as the amount of firing time remained on the transition [34]. If a transition t is not enabled, $k(t) = 0$. The marking of the initial state of a TPN is the initial marking m_0. The RFT function of the initial state assigns each enabled transition t at m_0 its firing delay $d(t)$ and the disabled transitions 0. Given a TPN $N = (P, T, E, m_0, d)$ at state $s_i = (m_i, r_i)$, a transition t_s enabled at s_i is the *first-to-complete* transition if t_s's RFT is the smallest among all of the enabled transition at state s_i. When t_s completes its firing, the TPN enters a new state $s_j = (m_j, k_j)$. We say state s_j is directly reachable from state s_i, denoted as $s_i \xrightarrow{t_s} s_j$. The new state s_j can be computed from s_i as follows:

$$\forall p \in P, \; m_j(p) = m_i(p) - t_s^-(p) + t_s^+(p),$$

$$\forall t \in T, \; k_j(t) = \begin{cases} d(t), & t \text{ is disabled at } m_i \\ & \text{but enabled at } m_j; \\ \max\{k_i(t) - k_i(t_s), 0\} & \text{otherwise} \end{cases}$$

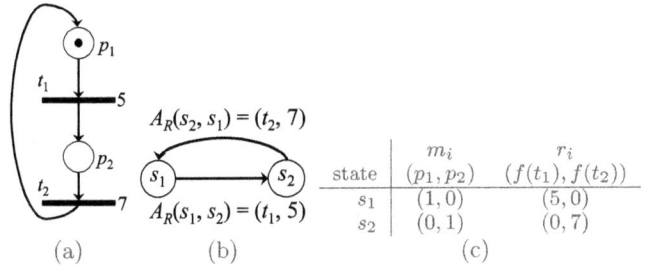

Figure 3: (a) A simple TPN, (b) its state graph, and (b) the states s_1 and s_2.

More generally, state s_{i_k} is reachable from s_{i_0} if there exists a sequence of states $s_{i_1}, s_{i_2}, \ldots$ and transitions $t_{i_0}, t_{i_1}, t_{i_2}, \ldots$ such that t_{i_j} is the first-to-complete transition enabled at state s_{i_j}. That is, $s_{i_0} \xrightarrow{t_{i_0}} s_{i_1} \xrightarrow{t_{i_1}} s_{i_2} \xrightarrow{t_{i_2}} \cdots \xrightarrow{t_{i_{k-1}}} s_{i_k}$. We use $R(s)$ to represent the set of all of the reachable states from state s, including state s.

From the reachability relation between states a directed *state graph* $G = \{V_R, E_R, A_R\}$ annotated with timing information can be constructed for a TPN N [34]. Given N's initial state s_0 and s_0's reachable states $R(s_0)$, each vertex $u \in V_R$ corresponds to a state $s_u \in R(s_0)$. There is an edge connecting from vertex u to v, or $(u, v) \in E_R$, if and only if s_v is immediately reachable from state s_u. The function A_R annotates each edge $(u, v) \in E$ with two information: the transition t_u that brings state s_u to s_v, and the RFT of t_u at s_u, which is the elapsed time of the state transition from s_u to s_v.

Our TPN interference model is derived "compositionally" from the GPU usage patterns of the individual processes. We assume at most two processes share the same GPU-equipped compute node. Further we assume that the CUDA's runtime schedules kernels from different processes in FIFO order. Figure 4 shows the complete TPN model for two GPU-sharing processes. The TPN modeling the interference between two processes has two groups of transitions and places, each of which corresponds to the GPU usage pattern of one of the two processes. Each activity a in the usage pattern of a process is modeled by a TPN fragment, which is a place p_a and its output transition t_a. The transition's firing time equals the activity's duration. If an activity a is followed by activity b in the usage pattern, transition t_a is connected to activity b's place p_b. The place of the first activity in the usage pattern of a process has one initial token, representing the process's control flow.

The GPU as a shared resource is modeled in the TPN as a place p_{GPU} connecting to transitions corresponding to activities accessing the GPU. Both kernel executions and data transfers between the host and the GPU (cudaMemcpy) are such activities. In the case that a kernel execution and a memory transfer are overlapped, both the execution and the memory transfer will be treated as one GPU-accessing activity. Place p_{GPU} has an equal number of initial tokens as the number of GPUs of the compute node, and is assumed to be one in our discussion. If activity a uses GPU, transition t_a is both an input and output transition of p_{GPU}, meaning t_a is enabled only if there is a token in place p_a (the program control flow reaches the point to start activity a) and p_{GPU}

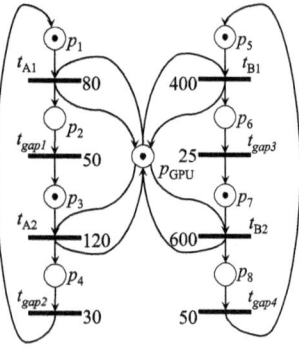

Figure 4: A complete TPN interference model of two processes.

(the GPU is idle). Once t_a's firing completes, it deposits the GPU token back to place p_{GPU}.

The runtime slowdown experienced by two processes sharing the GPU on a compute node can be estimated from the state graph of their TPN interference model. Because our TPN model is structurally bounded and has a finite number of reachable states because of its rational firing delay, any instance of our TPN model has a bounded state space and its state graph is cyclic. Based on these observations, the following simple algorithm computes the elapsed runtime of one iteration of the repeatable pattern of a process:

1. Select an activity a in the repeatable pattern of the process.

2. For each edge (i, j) (annotated with a transition t_{ij} and the transition's RFT $k(t_{ij})$) on the state graph, assign a weight $\tau_{ij} = 1$ to edge labeled with transition $t_{ij} = t_a$ and 0 for any other transition.

3. For a cycle W in the state graph, define a ratio $c(W) = \sum_{(i,j) \in W} k(t_{ij}) / \sum_{(i,j) \in W} \tau_{ij}$. Compute the maximum ratio $\mu = \max_W \{c(W)\}$ across all cycles in the state graph using the *minimum cost-to-time ratio cycle algorithm* [7]. Return μ.

The computed maximum ratio μ in the last step is an predicted upper bound of the elapsed runtime of one iteration of the process's repeatable pattern. Notice that the TPN model is not completely accurate, so the predicted upper bound of the runtime may be smaller than the actual.

Validation. We implemented our analysis model and algorithm in an open source TPN analysis tool called Roméo [13]. We then used six real-world, GPU-accelerated MPI applications to validate our interference analysis method. Each application is configured to run with two MPI processes, each of which offloads certain amount of computation to a GPU. In each experimental run, two jobs were run on the two nodes. Each job used both compute nodes and thus shared the GPUs with another job. Figure 5 shows the actual slowdown and the predicted slowdown experienced by the six MPI applications running simultaneously with another MPI application on the two compute nodes. The top chart (a) shows the full length of each bar, while the bottom chart (b) highlights the majority of the cases where the slowdown is below 3. (Here the slowdown is the ratio between the runtime with sharing and the runtime without sharing.) The results indicates that in most of the cases

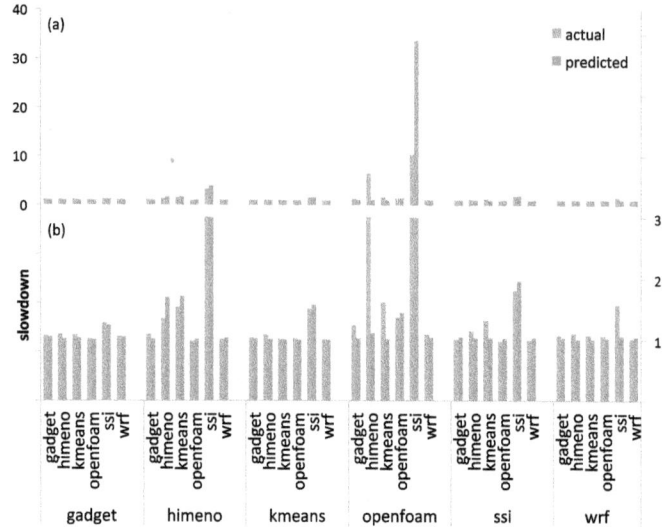

Figure 5: The actual and the TPN-predicted slowdown of pairs of two-node, colocated MPI applications.

(48 in total) our model's predictions are very close to the actual slowdown. The results also confirm our hypothesis that the CUDA runtime orders kernel execution of different applications in FIFO order.

4. INTERFERENCE-AWARE CLUSTER RESOURCE MANAGER

This section describes the architecture of an interference-aware cluster resource manager. We first provide a high-level overview and then explain each component in detail.

Overview. Figure 6 describes the architecture of our interference-aware scheduler and resource manager (the framework). It consists of several components running on a management server and one or more user-level monitoring agents running on each compute node. In particular, on the server side the scheduler maintains one or more job queues, selects a job from the queue (JOB SELECTION), assigns the processes of the selected job to compute nodes (NODE SELECTION), while continuously responding to monitoring agents running on each compute node. A monitoring agent is a light-weight, user-level runtime that observes the performance of a process and reports its findings to the server-side scheduler. It also receives instructions from the server-side scheduler to perform corrections if excessive interference is detected.

To make our interference-aware framework as general as possible we designed it as an enhancement to a conventional job scheduler like Torque [5]. Our interference-aware framework starts to schedule jobs to share compute nodes and their co-processors only after the conventional job scheduler cannot find enough idle nodes to be dedicated to the next job waiting in the queue. Therefore to simplify our discussions we will assume the situation that there are not enough idle compute nodes and our framework is triggered to schedule jobs to share resources.

Although our framework can handle all types of jobs, it only allows jobs satisfying certain requirements to share

114

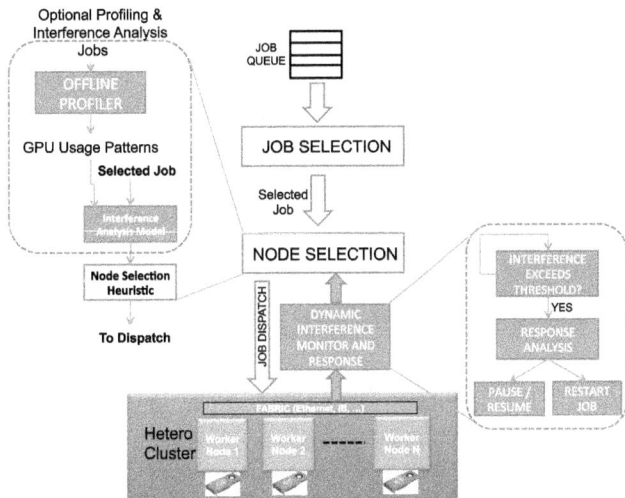

Figure 6: Architecture of the cluster manager showing interference awareness.

compute nodes and co-processors with other jobs. The first requirement is that a job's peak GPU device memory footprint must be known to the framework. Using the information of the peak GPU memory footprint, our framework avoids scheduling two job processes whose total GPU memory footprint exceeds the amount of memory on the GPU device on the same compute node. The peak GPU memory footprint can be obtained through profiling or runtime monitoring tools like `nvidia-smi`. We assume that users provide the peak GPU memory footprints of their applications to the framework.

The second requirement is that the processes of a job must have repetitive GPU usage patterns. This is because our interference-aware framework relies on repetitive kernel calls to perform an on-line monitoring and response mechanism (explained shortly) to mitigate or eliminate excessive interference between multiple job processes running on the same node. Notice that our framework does *not* need to know the patterns in advance, as long as the patterns are detectable at runtime. If a job does not meet either of the two requirements, our framework will schedule it to only run on dedicated compute nodes without any sharing.

GPU usage pattern profiling (optional). GPU usage profiling extracts the GPU usage patterns of a job required for interference analysis as described in Section 3. We assume that either the user uses the GPU usage characterization method discussed in Section 3 to extract the GPU usage pattern for each process of the job, or other approaches that can obtain GPU usage patterns without user involvement are adopted. For the latter, one possibility is to use an infrastructure like the Google-Wide profiling [24] to continuously profile running jobs and store the collected patterns in a database for later use. The scheduler can also perform a pilot run with dedicated compute nodes of a submitted job to get the usage patterns. In our prototype we assume that the GPU usage patterns of a job is user-provided.

Since job profiling may not always be possible, our scheduler does not require such information to be provided. If a job's GPU usage patterns are not available, our framework will skip the interference analysis and schedule the job to

share randomly selected compute nodes with other active jobs. Although a random scheduling decision may lead to excessive interference between multiple job processes running on the same node, our framework employs a novel on-line monitoring and response mechanism to handle such a situation (explained shortly).

Job selection. Different selection policies can be used to select a job from the job queue. Examples include FCFS, shortest-job-first (SJF), or other priority-based policies adopted by system administrators. The job queue can thus be viewed as a priority queue, where the priority function can be the job submission time in FCFS policy, the estimated job runtime in SJF, or some customized assignments based on local administrative policies.

Node selection. Our framework uses two node selection heuristics to dispatch the processes of the selected job to compute nodes. The choice between the two heuristics depends on whether the GPU usage patterns of the job processes are available. The first heuristic schedules the selected job to run on randomly selected compute nodes. It is used if the GPU usage patterns of the selected job are not available.

The second node selection heuristic dispatches the processes of the selected job to compute nodes in a way that the performance degradation due to runtime interference is minimized. The framework uses this heuristic if the GPU usage patterns of the selected job for interference analysis (see Section 3) is available. To predict potential interference, the framework also stores copies of the GPU usage patterns of all of the running jobs. Based on these stored patterns, the framework applies the interference analysis to estimate the runtime slowdown of different node selections. Using the slowdown estimation as the cost function, the scheduler then uses a dynamic programming algorithm to select one node for each process of the selected job such that the cost of interference is minimized.

The dynamic programming (DP) algorithm finds the optimal node assignment for each of the m processes of a job to n compute nodes. We assume that all of the m processes have identical GPU usage patterns[3] and all of the n compute nodes have the same computing capability. Let $c(p, k)$ be the minimum cost of scheduling p processes of the selected job to the first k compute nodes of the cluster. We have

$$c(p, k) = \min \left\{ c(p, k-1), c(f(p-1, k-1) \| (p \to k)) \right\}, \quad (1)$$

where $f(p-1, k-1)$ is the optimal node assignment for the $(p-1)$ processes to the first $(k-1)$ compute nodes, and $c(f(p-1, k-1) \| (p \to k))$ is the cost of combining the solution $f(p-1, k-1)$ and assigning the p-th process to the k-th compute node. The base cases of the dynamic programming procedure are the respective cost of assigning one process to different compute nodes, which can be predicted by the interference analysis model. Using (1) the node selection algorithm iterates over a m-by-n table to compute $c(m, n)$. With some additional bookkeeping the optimal node selection $f(m, n)$ can be easily constructed.

The DP algorithm can also handle a job that needs to run on dedicated compute nodes. Such scenarios can arise if the peak GPU memory footprint of any of the job's processes does not leave room for any other job process to run on the

---

[3]If a job has different GPU usage patterns, the most "interfering" one, the one caused most slowdown based on the interference analysis model is used.

same compute node, or the service agreement of a job mandates dedicated resources. To make sure a compute node k is never selected by the algorithm, we can simply set the cost of scheduling any process to k to a very large value.

Several different cost functions can be used. We use the maximum predicted slowdown experienced across all job processes, including the ones already running and the ones to be scheduled. Another option is to take the sum of the slowdown of each job (the slowdown of a job is the maximum slowdown across all of the job's processes).

Monitoring and response. Our framework employs an on-line monitoring mechanism to detect excessive interference. If a job is scheduled to run on compute nodes with active jobs, the interference between the co-running jobs is monitored. If a newly scheduled job causes too much interference and therefore results in excessive performance loss, the new job is terminated. The terminated job is immediately re-submitted (retaining its original position in the queue) for scheduling. The terminated job will only be rescheduled on idle nodes and will therefore have dedicated resources. Although the rescheduled job runs on dedicated nodes initially, later on our framework may schedule other jobs to be colocated with it. Overall our monitoring and response mechanism is coordinated between the server-side scheduler and local monitoring agents.

The server-side scheduler coordinates with local monitoring agents to monitor the behavior and measure the performance of each active job in two phases for a limited period of time. The first monitoring phase identifies whether a job has repetitive kernel calls and measures the performance of a job *without* any interference, while the second one measures the performance of a job *with* interference due to contentions to *all* resources, not just the GPU devices.

The first monitoring phase takes place right after a job is started to run on compute nodes. During this phase the local monitoring agents ensure that the processes of the job run in exclusive mode without any interference by temporarily stopping processes of any other job running on the same nodes. A local monitoring agents identifies any repetitive CUDA kernel call and computes the average frequency of the identified repetitive kernel call (the identification and measuring mechanism will be detailed shortly). The monitoring agents then report their findings back to the server-side scheduler. The lowest kernel-call frequency among all processes of the job is used as the job's performance *under no interference* and cached by the server-side scheduler.

If two or more processes of different jobs share the same compute node, our framework triggers the second monitoring phase following the first monitoring phase. In the second monitoring phase all processes are run simultaneously free from any throttling. The local monitoring agent measures the kernel frequency of each process and sends the measured values back the server-side scheduler. For each monitored job, the server-side scheduler uses the lowest kernel frequency across all of the job's processes as its performance *under interference*.

Notice that using the kernel frequency captured in the second monitoring phase as the performance measure reflects all possible interferences not limited to the GPU contention. Such a performance measure is also independent from various optimization techniques, like running multiple kernels issued by different processes simultaneously [23] and overlapping communication and computation [6]. This is because factors like optimizations or other interferences due to memory system and network contentions essentially affect not just the elapsed run time but also the intervals between repetitive kernel calls.

Each local monitoring agent uses a function-intercepting technique to carry out process monitoring and throttling. The monitor agent intercepts both CUDA and MPI function calls initiated by processes. For performance monitoring, the monitoring agent measures how frequently a process launches a specific CUDA kernel. More specifically, once a kernel function is initiated, the monitoring agent intercepts the call, records the wall time of the call, and then immediately forwards the call to the real CUDA runtime library. For a process to be identified as having repetitive kernel calls, at least the same kernel call must be initiated N times within T seconds. In our prototype N is set to 25 and T is 30 seconds. If this condition is not satisfied, the process is treated as not having repetitive kernel calls. Otherwise the local monitoring agent computes the kernel frequency using the elapsed time of the N successive calls as the performance metric. The measured performance is returned to the server-side scheduler by a dedicated communication thread to minimize the disruption of normal execution. The thread also handles throttling instructions from the scheduler. Once the throttling message is received, the thread sets a flag which causes either the next CUDA or MPI call to be blocked. On the other hand, when the scheduler sends a message to resume the execution, the thread clears the flag to re-activate the blocked call. For the CUDA and MPI function calls to be intercepted, the execution binary of a job is dynamically linked to customized proxy libraries of CUDA and MPI, which are based on NVIDIA's CUPTI and mpiP [30].

After receiving performance measurements with and without interference, the framework decides whether the performance degradation is acceptable. Let P_i and P_i' be the lowest kernel frequency of job J_i without and with interference, respectively, two possible interference criteria are considered. The first criterion caps the slowdown to a predetermined threshold T, that is, $\max P_i/P_i' \leq T$. The second criterion allows job J_N to continue if and only if for each job $J_i \in \{J_1, \ldots, J_k\}$ that compute nodes with J_N,

$$\max\{\frac{1}{P_i'}, \frac{1}{P_N'}\} \leq K(\frac{1}{P_i} + \frac{1}{P_N}), \qquad (2)$$

where K is a number between 0 and 1, referred to as the *interference threshold*.

Our prototype implementation uses (2) to decide if the interference caused by new job J_N is excessive. If the interference is excessive, two response mechanisms are possible: (a) the scheduler terminates J_N's execution and reschedules it by inserting J_N back to its original position in the job queue. J_N will then be rescheduled to idle compute nodes, or (b) the scheduler allows J_N to continue its execution in a restrained fashion by periodically throttling J_N's execution using the on-line throttling mechanism described earlier. The length of the throttling period is dynamically adjusted based on whether the interference criterion (like (2)) is satisfied. Currently our prototype uses method (a).

If the local monitoring agent cannot detect any repetitive kernel calls of a process, our framework will schedule the job to run exclusively on the dedicated compute nodes. If a job without detectable repetitive kernel calls is launched on compute nodes where no other jobs are running, our framework will run the job exclusively and avoid to schedule any new job to be colocated with it. On the other hand, if a job without detectable repetitive kernel calls is run on compute nodes with other existing active jobs, the job will be terminated and rescheduled as if it causes excessive interference.

5. EXPERIMENTAL RESULTS

In this section, we quantify the benefits of our interference-aware scheduling and resource management framework for a co-processor-based heterogeneous cluster. Our goal is to identify how much improvement the interference-awareness provides when added to an existing state-of-the-art cluster manager. We use PBS Torque [5], an open-source cluster manager, as our baseline. Along with its derivatives such as PBS Professional [21], Torque is used in several existing HPC installations such as [4].

We augment Torque with our interference-aware scheduling and resource management framework as described in the previous sections. We refer to the augmented version of Torque as **I-Torque**. We quantify the benefits of co-processor interference-awareness along three dimensions: (i) individual job latencies, (ii) coprocessor utilization and (iii) the *makespan* or the total latency for a set of jobs.

Our HPC cluster consists of 12 nodes, each with dual 2.4GHz quad-core Intel Xeon E5620 processors and 48GB of RAM, running Ubuntu 10.04 Linux. Each node has one 1 NVIDIA C2050 Fermi GPU coprocessor with 3GB of memory connected via a 16x PCIe bus. The nodes are interconnected using gigabit ethernet. We use Supermico 7046-GT TRF servers with the X8DTG-QF motherboard.

Table 2 lists job instances of six real MPI-based HPC applications used in our experiments. Each application has kernels programmed in CUDA to use GPUs. Scaling these applications to different numbers of nodes, and using them with different parameters (such as data size) enables us to generate larger sets of jobs.

As mentioned in Section 4, we link the applications with NVIDIA's CUPTI and mpiP [30] to enable dynamic monitoring and response. For our experiments, we construct a job set consisting of 31 jobs, each of which is an instance of the above applications. A job is a randomly selected application with a different set of parameters, scaled to run on 2-nodes or 4-nodes.

To quantify the benefits of interference-awareness, we set up our controlled experiments as follows. Both Torque and I-Torque use the same job selection algorithm (for e.g., FIFO). Their node selection algorithm however is different only in that I-Torque allows jobs to share the same nodes while Torque does not. Thus with Torque, each GPU is exclusively allocated to a job process until the job process completes. I-Torque on the other hand allows jobs to be colocated with other jobs if the performance degradation due to interference is below certain threshold.

For the first set of experiments, we use FIFO as the common job selection heuristic for both Torque and I-Torque. The node assignment in I-Torque is as described in Section 4. **Makespan.** For the above job set, we first report the makespan or the total latency for the entire job set. This is the time from when the entire job set is issued, to when the *last* job completes. The makespan cannot be larger than the sum of individual job latencies, which are presented next. We use the makespan to evaluate the effect of the inter-

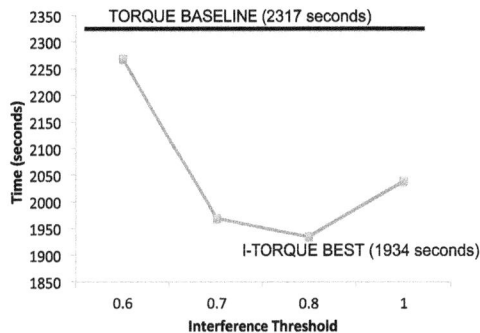

Figure 7: The effect of interference threshold on the total latency of the job set (makespan).

ference threshold, from Equation 2. Figure 7 shows the makespan as we vary the interference threshold from 0.6 to 1.0. A threshold of 0.8 provides the lowest makespan: the entire job set finishes in 1934 seconds, about 17% faster than the makespan of the baseline Torque which takes 2317 seconds for the job set.

Individual job latencies. When a job is submitted to a cluster manager, it's overall latency is comprised of its (i) wait time in the queue and (ii) actual execution time. In general, when a job is colocated with another job sharing GPUs, *its wait time in the queue decreases while actual execution time increases.* Figure 8 shows the queue wait times and execution times of all 31 jobs with and without using our interference-aware framework, i.e., for Torque and I-Torque. Table 2 summarizes the input dataset, GPU memory used per node, the number of the job instances for each job in the job set, and the number of MPI ranks. For each job in the above job set, on average, I-Torque reduces the queue wait time by 39%, but increases the execution time 12.9%. Overall a job's total latency is decreased by 23% in average. In addition, in the baseline Torque, each of the 31 jobs spends an average of 68% of its total latency waiting in the queue, while in I-Torque, the average queue wait time is reduced to 53% of the job's total latency.

Coprocessor utilization. We expect I-Torque to improve coprocessor utilization since colocated jobs will reduce GPU idle times. Figure 9 shows how average GPU utilization across the cluster changes with time. It is clear that I-Torque has better coprocessor utilization besides completing all jobs earlier. Compared to Torque, I-Torque increases the average cluster-wide coprocessor utilization from 32% to 40%, a 25% improvement (or an increase of 8 percentage points).

Summary. Table 3 summarizes the benefits of interference-awareness for different job scheduling heuristics: FIFO, Shortest-Job-First (SJF) and Backfill [16]. We note that significant improvements on all metrics can be achieved when I-Torque uses FIFO job selection. However with SJF job selection, the benefits of I-Torque appear low. This is because the longest job is started at the end, and runs by itself for most of the time without overlapping with other, shorter jobs (which have all completed).

We also augment Torque's Backfill scheduling [16] with interference awareness. In this case, we also see an improvement in all metrics: average coprocessor utilization increases from 31% to 42% while the makespan decreases by 20%.

We also note that under FIFO, SJF and Backfill, I-Torque attempted to schedule 19, 16 and 16 jobs to be colocated re-

Job	Description	GPU memory usage (MB/node)	Dataset	No. of instances	No. of MPI ranks
wrf1	weather	285	Run days=10, Run hours=12	5	2
wrf2	simulation [15]	285	Run days=25, Run hours=24	1	2
kmeans1		251	No. of points=2500000	3	2
kmeans2	clustering algorithm	119	No. of points=1250000	1	4
kmeans3		163	No. of points=2500000	1	4
kmeans4		162	No. of points=1250000	1	2
himeno1	fluid analysis solving	84	Grid Size=64X64X128	3	2
himeno2	Poisson's equation	200	Grid Size=128X128X256	1	2
himeno3	using Jacobi iteration [6]	78	Grid Size=64X64X128	1	4
openfoam	fluid dynamics [2]	132	No. of Cells=955000	2	2
ssi	supervised semantic indexing [11]	890	No. of documents=1863573	5	2
gadget	cosmological simulations [27]	73	No.of particles = 110592	7	2

Table 2: Summary of the job set.

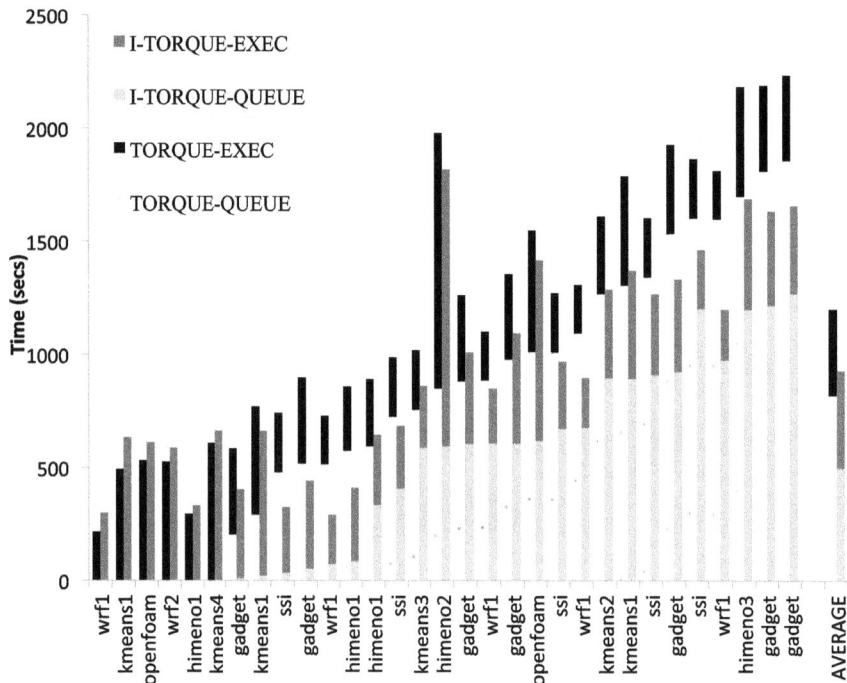

Figure 8: Job latencies with Torque and Torque with interference analysis (I-Torque). Each bar shows a job's wait time in the queue and actual execution time.

spectively out of the total 31 jobs. Out of these attempts for jobs to be colocated, 4, 5 and 7 jobs respectively were killed and relocated when excessive dynamic interference was detected (for an interference threshold of 0.8).

6. RELATED WORK

Job scheduling and effects of interference due to shared resource contention have been studied intensively in the literature. This section summarizes the previous work popular job scheduling approaches and existing methods of predicting performance degradation due to interference.

For most HPC computing platforms like clusters or supercomputers the resources are shared among users. Users submit their jobs to a scheduler (like PBS Pro [21] or Load-Leveler [14]), and the scheduler selects and schedules a number of jobs to execute concurrently, sharing the compute and network resources. One common form of sharing is *space* sharing, where the compute nodes are divided up into

groups, each of which is dedicated to a scheduled job. Jobs can be ordered by certain priority function and selected accordingly. However, selecting jobs following a strict order (e.g., FCFS) can result in resource underutilization, that is, there are jobs waiting in the queue while some compute nodes are idle. To solve this problem, backfilling is proposed where small jobs can be selected out-of-order to keep idle nodes busy, as long as they do not delay the execution of jobs queued in front of them [16].

Another sharing strategy is *time* sharing [10,12,20,32,33]. Both coscheduling [20] and gang scheduling [20,32,33] time multiplex multiple jobs in a way that processes of the same job are synchronized to execute at the same time to ensure progress. In both schemes each job is given a time slice in which the job runs on dedicated compute nodes. Once the time slice expires the job is preempted. While coscheduling and gang scheduling try to maximize resource utilization, Benoit et al. proposed scheduling algorithms that adjust the execution speed of jobs consisting of independent tasks

Scheduling Heuristic	Makespan (sec)		Cumulative Job Latencies (sec)		Coprocessor Utilization	
	Torque	I-Torque	Torque	I-Torque	Torque	I-Torque
FIFO	2317	1934	37180	28783	32%	40%
SJF	2599	2502	35033	32877	29%	28.5%
Backfill	2390	1915	35932	27956	31%	42%

Table 3: Summary of I-Torque benefits for different job scheduling mechanisms.

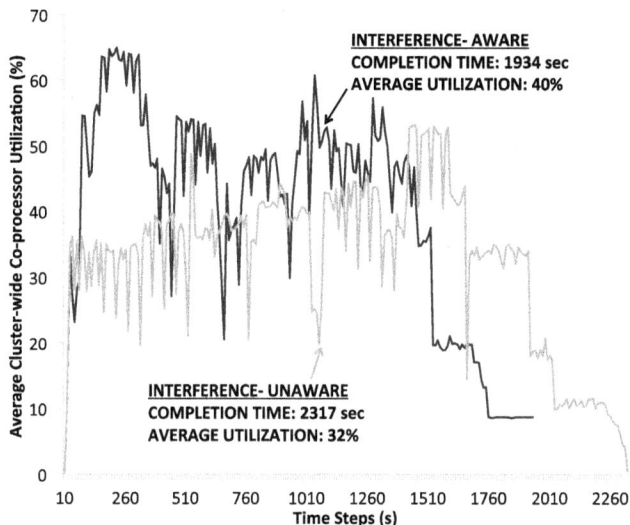

Figure 9: Average cluster-wide coprocessor utilization.

("bags-of-tasks") to minimize performance degradations due to resource sharing [10]. Comparing to classic coscheduling or gang scheduling, our scheduling framework differs in the way of context switching (our scheduler does not preempts jobs but relies on CUDA runtime for local scheduling) and main compute resources to be shared (CPU vs GPU). On the other hand, our scheduler targets multi-node jobs consisting of communicating processes, different from the bags-of-task model in [10]. Further our scheduling framework uses a novel interference analysis model and monitoring and response mechanism to guarantee that the performance of individual jobs are not penalized due to resource sharing.

Wiseman and Feitelson proposed "paired" gang scheduling where a CPU-bound and an I/O-bound jobs share the same time slice in gang scheduling [32]. When two jobs are paired to share the same time slice, their executions are scheduled by the local OS. Although our scheduler also pairs jobs based on their GPU usage patterns, the pairing decision in our scheduler is based on a novel interference analysis model instead of a simple GPU utilization rate.

Performance profiling of different combinations of processes sharing the same resource have been suggested in [18, 23, 29], which are then used to make scheduling decisions. If there are N jobs, the methods suggested in [23, 29] require $O(N^2)$ profiling runs, i.e., these methods essentially try out all combinations of job coscheduling. In contrast, our interference prediction is modeling-based and requires only $O(N)$ profiling runs, each of which is applied to one job running with dedicated resources. The method suggested by Mars et al. in [18] also adopts a modeling-based approach to study

cache contention and takes $O(N)$ profiling runs, while we address the problem of GPU sharing.

The on-line monitoring and response mechanism have been proposed by Mars et al. in [19]. Our monitoring mechanism differs from the one in [19] in terms of the performance measurement, the targeted applications, and the throttling mechanism. In [19] the performance is indirectly inferred from the miss rate of the last-level shared cache, while in our monitoring it is measured as the "throughput" or frequency of off-loaded kernels. In [19] the mechanism is applied to multi-threaded applications running on a single compute node, while our targets are multi-node applications using GPUs. Finally, since our framework targets multi-node applications, the monitoring and response mechanism needs to be exercised across all of the processes running on different compute nodes.

7. CONCLUSION

In this paper we address the issue of low coprocessor utilization in HPC clusters. Although GPUs are well utilized (in terms of cores) by compute-intensive kernels, an entire end-to-end application only intermittently offloads computations to GPUs, often causing them to stay idle and thus reducing its utilization.

Current cluster managers do not time-share GPUs across jobs to improve coprocessor utilization. An important reason for this is jobs that share GPUs interfere with each other. To the best of our knowledge, the effects of interference due to coprocessor contention has not been studied before. We address this by proposing an interference-driven cluster management framework for GPU-based heterogeneous clusters. The framework consists of a novel interference analysis model to predict the performance slowdown of co-running jobs sharing GPU coprocessors, and an on-line dynamic interference monitoring and response mechanism that automatically restarts jobs if the measured interference exceeds a threshold. In principle our framework allows multiple jobs to share the same set of GPUs under the GPU memory constraint; for practical reasons we implement our framework for two-job colocation in Torque, an open-source cluster manager. Using real-world, multi-node, GPU-accelerated HPC applications, our framework improves GPU utilization by 25%, reduces a job's waiting time in the queue by 39% and improves job latencies by 20%.

Acknowledgments

The authors would like to thank Dr. Yeh-Ching Chung and Meng-Kai Liao at National Tsing Hua University, Hsinchu, Taiwan for their help of setting up the Gadget benchmark.

8. REFERENCES

[1] Amber 11 NVIDIA GPU Acceleration Support. http://ambermd.org/gpus/.

[2] OpenFoam: The Open Source CFD Toolbox. http://www.openfoam.com.

[3] Top 500 list (November 2011).

[4] Tsubame2 system architecture.

[5] Adaptive Computing. Torque Resource Manager. http://www.adaptivecomputing.com.

[6] Advanced Center for Computing and Communication, RIKEN. Himeno Benchmark. http://accc.riken.jp/HPC_e/himenobmt_e.html.

[7] R. K. Ahuja, T. L. Magnanti, and J. B. Orlin. *Network Flows: Theory, Algorithms, and Applications.* Prentice Hall, 1993.

[8] Amazon Elastic Compute Cloud (Amazon EC2). http://www.amazon.com/b?ie=UTF8&node=201590011.

[9] M. Becchi, K. Sajjapongse, I. Graves, A. Procter, V. Ravi, and S. Chakradhar. A virtual memory based runtime to support multi-tenancy in clusters with GPUs. In *Proc. of the Intl. Symposium on High Perf. Distributed Computing,* 2012.

[10] A. Benoit, L. Marchal, J.-F. Pineau, Y. Robert, and F. Vivien. Scheduling concurrent bag-of-tasks applications on heterogeneous platforms. *IEEE Computer,* 59(2):202–217, Feb. 2010.

[11] S. Byna, J. Meng, S. T. Chakradhar, A. Raghunathan, and S. Cadambi. Best Effort Semantic Document Search on GPUs. In *Proc. of the Workshop on GPUGPU,* Mar. 2010.

[12] D. G. Feitelson and M. A. Jette. Improved utilization and responsiveness with gang scheduling. In *Job Scheduling Strategies for Parallel Processing,* Lecture Notes in Computer Science, pages 238–261. Springer Berlin/Heidelberg, 1997.

[13] G. Gardey, D. Lime, M. Magnin, and O. Roux. Roméo: A tool for analyzing time Petri nets. In K. Etessami and S. Rajamani, editors, *Computer Aided Verification,* volume 3576 of *Lecture Notes in Computer Science,* pages 261–272. Springer Berlin/Heidelberg, 2005.

[14] IBM. Tivoli workload scheduler LoadLeveler. http://www-03.ibm.com/systems/software/loadleveler.

[15] John Michalakes and Manish Vachharajani. GPU Acceleration of Numerical Weather Prediction. http://www.mmm.ucar.edu/wrf/WG2/GPU/WSM5.htm.

[16] D. Lifka. The ANL/IBM SP scheduling system. In *Job Scheduling Strategies for Parallel Processing,* volume 949 of *Lecture Notes in Computer Science,* pages 295–303. Springer Berlin/Heidelberg, 1995.

[17] A. Majumdar, S. Cadambi, and S. Chakradhar. An energy-efficient heterogeneous system for embedded learning and classification. volume 3, pages 42 –45, march 2011.

[18] J. Mars, L. Tang, R. Hundt, K. Skadron, and M. L. Soffa. Bubble-up: Increasing utilization in modern warehouse scale computers via sensible co-locations. In *Proc. of the Annual IEEE/ACM Intl. Symposium on Microarchitecture,* Dec. 2011.

[19] J. Mars, N. Vachharajani, R. Hundt, and M. L. Soffa. Contention aware execution: online contention detection and response. In *Proc. of the IEEE/ACM Intl. Symposium on Code Generation and Optimization,* pages 257–265, Apr. 2010.

[20] J. Ousterhout. Scheduling techniques for concurrent systems. In *Proceedings of the International Conference on Distributed Computing Systems,* pages 22–30, Oct. 1982.

[21] PBS Works. GPU Scheduling with PBS Professional. http://www.pbsworks.com.

[22] C. Ramchandani. *Analysis of Asynchronous Concurrent Systems by Timed Petri Nets.* PhD thesis, Massachusetts Institute of Technology, Cambridge, MA, USA, 1974.

[23] V. T. Ravi, M. Becchi, G. Agrawal, and S. Chakradhar. Supporting GPU sharing in cloud environments with a transparent runtime consolidation framework. In *Proc. of the Intl. Symposium on High Perf. Distributed Computing,* pages 217–228, 2011.

[24] G. Ren, E. Tune, T. Moseley, Y. Shi, S. Rus, and R. Hundt. Google-wide profiling: A continuous profiling infrastructure for data centers. *IEEE Micro,* 30(4):65–79, Jul.–Aug. 2010.

[25] J. Schneider, M. Kraus, and R. Westermann. GPU-based euclidean distance transforms and their application to volume rendering. In *Computer Vision, Imaging and Computer Graphics. Theory and Applications,* volume 68 of *Communications in Computer and Information Science,* pages 215–228. Springer Berlin Heidelberg, 2010.

[26] J. Sifakis. Performance evaluation of systems using nets. In *Net Theory and Applications,* volume 84 of *Lecture Notes in Computer Science,* pages 307–319. Springer Berlin/Heidelberg, 1980.

[27] V. Springel. The cosmological simulation code gadget-2. *Monthly Notices of the Royal Astronomical Society,* 364(4):1105–1134, 2005.

[28] J. A. Stuart, C.-K. Chen, K.-L. Ma, and J. D. Owens. Multi-GPU volume rendering using MapReduce. In *Proc. of the Intl. Symposium on High Perf. Distributed Computing,* pages 841–848, June 2010.

[29] L. Tang, J. Mars, N. Vachharajani, R. Hundt, and M. L. Soffa. The impact of memory subsystem resource sharing on datacenter applications. In *Proc. of the Annual Symposium on Computer Architecture,* pages 283–294, June 2011.

[30] J. Vetter and C. Chambreau. mpiP: Lightweight, scalable MPI profiling. http://mpip.sourceforge.net.

[31] V. Volkov and J. W. Demmel. Benchmarking GPUs to tune dense linear algebra. In *Proc. of the ACM/IEEE Conf. on Supercomputing,* pages 1–11, Nov. 2008.

[32] Y. Wiseman and D. G. Feitelson. Paired gang scheduling. *IEEE Tran. on Parallel and Distributed Syst.,* 14(6):581–592, June 2003.

[33] Y. Zhang, H. Franke, J. Moreira, and A. Sivasubramaniam. An integrated approach to parallel scheduling using gang-scheduling, backfilling, and migration. *IEEE Tran. on Parallel and Distributed Syst.,* 14(3):236–247, Mar. 2003.

[34] W. M. Zuberek. Timed Petri nets and preliminary performance evaluation. In *Proc. of the Annual Symposium on Computer Architecture,* pages 88–96, 1980.

Exploring the Performance and Mapping of HPC Applications to Platforms in the Cloud

Abhishek Gupta,
Laxmikant V. Kalé
University of Illinois at
Urbana-Champaign, Urbana,
IL, USA
(gupta59,kale)@illinois.edu

Filippo Gioachin,
Verdi March,
Chun Hui Suen,
Bu-Sung Lee
HP Labs, Singapore
(gioachin, verdi.march,
chun-hui.suen,
francis.lee)@hp.com

Paolo Faraboschi,
Richard Kaufmann,
Dejan Milojicic
HP Labs, Palo Alto, CA, USA
(paolo.faraboschi,
richard.kaufmann,
dejan.milojicic)@hp.com

ABSTRACT

This paper presents a scheme to optimize the mapping of HPC applications to a set of *hybrid* dedicated and cloud resources. First, we characterize application performance on dedicated clusters and cloud to obtain application signatures. Then, we propose an algorithm to match these signatures to resources such that performance is maximized and cost is minimized. Finally, we show simulation results revealing that in a concrete scenario our proposed scheme reduces the cost by 60% at only 10-15% performance penalty vs. a non optimized configuration. We also find that the execution overhead in cloud can be minimized to a negligible level using thin hypervisors or OS-level containers.

Categories and Subject Descriptors

D.1.3 [**Concurrent Programming**]: Parallel Programming; K.6.4 [**System Management**]: Centralization/decentralization

Keywords

High Performance Computing, Clouds, Resource Scheduling

1. INTRODUCTION

A recent study reaffirmed that dedicated supercomputers are still more cost-effective than cloud for large-scale HPC applications [2]. This is largely due to the high overhead of virtualization on I/O latency which hinders the adoption of cloud for large-scale HPC applications [2, 6]. However, our preliminary study indicated that cloud resources could be cost-effective for small and medium-scale HPC applications [5]. As such, resource allocation should be aware of application and resource characteristics to maximize application performance yet minimizing cost.

This paper describes a proposed scheme to intelligently map an HPC application to a set of *hybrid* resources consisting of a mix of dedicated and cloud resources. Section 2 begins with our in-depth performance characterization for HPC applications on various dedicated clusters and cloud. We discover that the cloud overhead can be minimized to a negligible level using thin hypervisors or OS-level contain-

Table 1: Experimental Test-bed

Platform	Ranger	Taub	Open Cirrus	Euca-cloud	HPLS
Cores/ node	16 @2.3GHz	12 @2.67GHz	4 @3.00GHz	2 @2.67GHz	12 @2.67GHz
Network	Infiniband	Infiniband	10 GigaE	1 GigaE	1 GigaE

ers. Then, we propose an algorithm that leverages the performance characteristics to map an application to resources. In Section 3 we present our simulation results showing that our scheme reduces the cost by 60% compared to a non-optimized configuration, while the performance penalty is kept at 10-15%. Finally, Section 4 discusses the lessons learned and potential implications of our study.

2. APPROACH

We benchmarked a variety of platforms spanning different architecture (see Table 1). Ranger and Taub are supercomputers, while Open Cirrus is a dedicated cluster with slower interconnect. HPLS and Eucalyptus are typical cloud environment. We also compare lightweight virtualization using dedicated network (VM-thin) and Linux containers (LXC) using NAMD [4], a highly scalable molecular dynamics application with the ApoA1 input (92k atoms).

Figure 1 shows the scaling behavior of our testbeds for (a) different platforms and (b) for different virtualization techniques applied to a typical cloud node. Due to superior network performance on the supercomputers (Taub, Ranger), NAMD scales well over the test range, while we observe scaling problems on Open cirrus and even more on cloud (Eucalyptus, HPLS) due to inferior network performance, which we verified by measuring the time spent in communication. Networking on cloud is further impacted by the I/O virtualization overhead, although through a more in-depth study we show alternative techniques (b) that can partially mitigate the overhead. VM-thin assigns a dedicated network interface to each VM via an IOMMU pass-through, and achieves near native performance ('bare'). We also show that the slowdown incurred by CPU virtualization is minimal, compared to conventional network virtualization ('VM-plain'). Interference from the OS and hypervisor causes additional slowdown on VMs. Figure 1(c) shows the distribution of execution slowdown from the ideal $1000\mu s$ execution step measured on a virtualized node.

Based on these findings and our previous work [5], we developed a mapper tool shown in Figure 2. Starting from an HPC application, through characterization we extract a

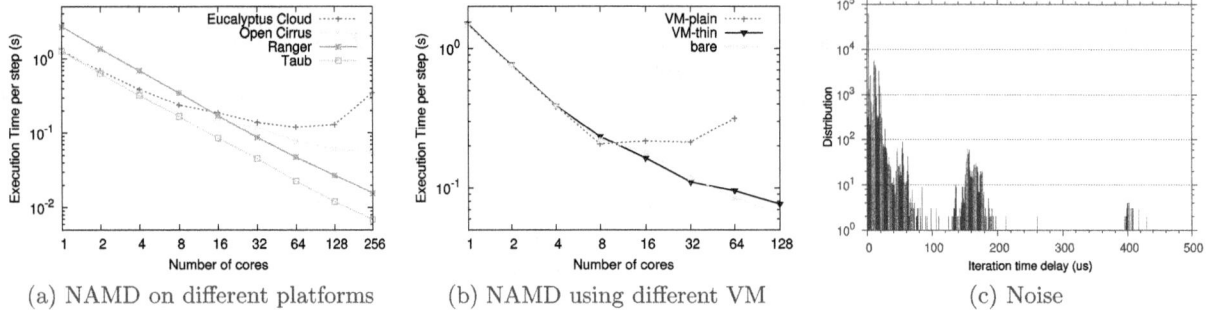

(a) NAMD on different platforms   (b) NAMD using different VM   (c) Noise

Figure 1: (a,b) Execution time vs. Number of cores for NAMD (c) Noise Benchmark on a VM

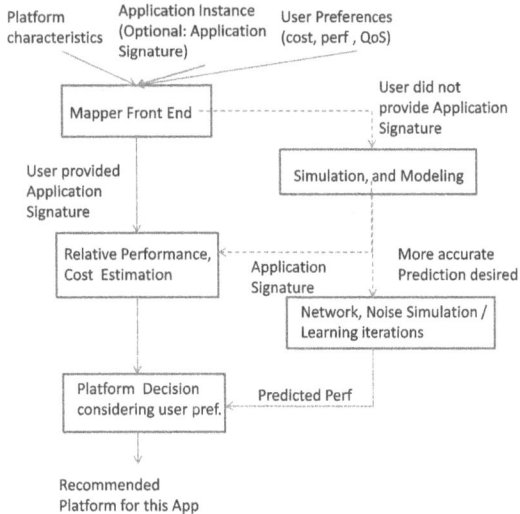

Figure 2: Mapper Approach

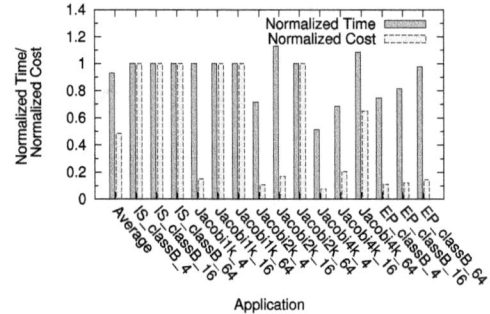

Figure 3: Normalized Performance and Cost (intelligent mapping vs execution on supercomputer)

lem sizes, that is input matrix dimensions (e.g. size 1k ×
1k). For this application set, our scheme reduces the cost on
average by 60% compared to a non-optimized configuration,
while the performance penalty is kept at 10-15%. Further
details can be found in the technical report on this work [3].

4. LESSONS LEARNED, CONCLUSIONS

We have shown that the adoption of intelligent mapping
techniques is pivotal to the success of hybrid platform environments that combine supercomputer and typical hypervisor-based clouds. In some cases, a hybrid cloud-supercomputer
platform environment can outperform its individual constituents. We learned that application characterization in
HPC-Cloud space is a challenging problem, but the benefits
are substantial. Finally, we demonstrated that lightweight
virtualization is important to remove "friction" from HPC in
cloud.

We described the concept and initial implementation of a
static tool to automate the mapping, using a combination
of application characteristics, platform parameters, and user
preferences. In the future, we plan to extend the mapping
tool to also perform a dynamic adjustment of the static mapping through run-time monitoring.

signature capturing the most important dimensions: number and size of messages, computational grain size (FLOPS),
overlap percentage of computation and communication, presence of synchronization barriers and load balancing. Subsequently, given a set of applications to execute and a set
of target platforms, we define heuristics to map the applications to the platforms that optimize *parallel efficiency*.
In doing so, we consider several target platforms spanning
a variety of processor configurations, interconnection networks, and virtualization environments. Platform characteristics, such as CPU frequency, interconnect latency and
bandwidth, platform costs (using a pay-per-use charging
rate based model) and user preferences are considered. The
output of the tool are platform recommendations to optimize practical scenarios such as best performance within a
constrained budget, or cost minimization with performance
guarantees.

3. RESULTS

We evaluated the results obtained by our mapper and
studied the benefits using it to map a set of application
to supercomputer (Ranger) and Eucalyptus cloud. Figure 3
shows the significant cost savings achieved while meeting
performance guarantees using our intelligent mapper. Embarrassingly parallel (EP) and Integer sort (IS) benchmarks
are part of NPB Class B benchmark suite [1] and Jacobi2D
is a kernel which performs 5-point stencil computation to
average values in a 2-D grid. The application suffix is the
number of processors; for Jacobi, we consider multiple prob-

5. REFERENCES

[1] NPB. http://www.nas.nasa.gov/Resources/Software/npb.html.
[2] Magellan Final Report. Technical report, U.S. Department of
    Energy (DOE), 2011.
[3] Exploring the Performance and Mapping of HPC Applications
    to Platforms in the Cloud. Technical report, HP Labs, 2012.
[4] A. Bhatele et al. Overcoming scaling challenges in biomolecular
    simulations across multiple platforms. In *IPDPS 2008*.
[5] A. Gupta and D. Milojicic. Evaluation of HPC Applications on
    Cloud. In *Best Student Paper, Open Cirrus Summit*, 2011.
[6] E. Walker. Benchmarking Amazon EC2 for high-performance
    scientific computing. *LOGIN*, 2008.

Towards a Common Model for Pilot-Jobs

Andre Luckow, Ole Weidner,
Andre Merzky, Sharath Maddineni
Center for Computation and Technology
Louisiana State University
Baton Rouge, LA
{aluckow, oweidern, amerzky,
smaddini}@cct.lsu.edu

Mark Santcroos
Bioinformatics Laboratory
Academic Medical Center
University of Amsterdam
Amsterdam, The Netherlands
m.a.santcroos@amc.uva.nl

Shantenu Jha[*]
CAC/ECE
Rutgers University
Piscataway, NJ
shantenu.jha@rutgers.edu

ABSTRACT

Pilot-Jobs (PJ) have become one of the most successful abstractions in distributed computing. In spite of extensive uptake, there does not exist a well defined, unifying conceptual model of Pilot-Jobs, which can be used to define, compare and contrast PJ implementations. This presents a barrier to extensibility and interoperability. This paper is an attempt to, (i) provide a minimal but complete model (P*) of Pilot-Jobs, (ii) establish the generality of the P* Model by mapping various well-known Pilot-Job frameworks such as Condor and DIANE to P*, (iii) demonstrate the interoperable and concurrent usage of *distinct* pilot-job frameworks on different production distributed cyberinfrastructures via the use of an extensible API for the P* Model (Pilot-API).

Categories and Subject Descriptors

D.2.10 [**Software Design**]: Methodologies

Keywords

Distributed Systems, Interoperability, Abstractions

1. INTRODUCTION AND OVERVIEW

Distributed cyber/e-infrastructure is by definition comprised of a set of resources that is fluctuating – growing, shrinking, changing in load and capability (in contrast to a static resource utilization model of traditional cluster computing systems). The ability to utilize a dynamic resource pool is thus an important attribute of any application that needs to utilize distributed cyberinfrastructure (DCI) efficiently. Pilot-Jobs (PJ) provide an effective abstraction for dynamic execution and resource utilization in a distributed context. As a consequence of providing a simple approach for decoupling workload management and resource assignment/scheduling, Pilot-Jobs have been one of the most successful abstractions in distributed computing. Not surprisingly, there are multiple, distinct and incompatible imple-

---

[*]contact author

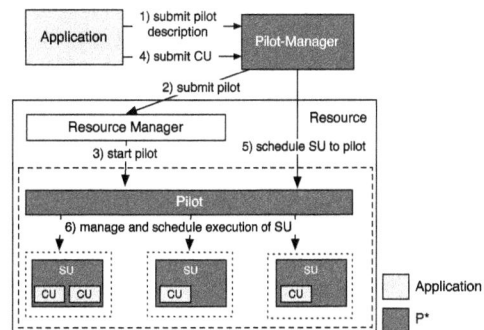

Figure 1: **P* Model: Elements and Interactions:** The manager has two functions: it manages 1) Pilots (step 1-3) and 2) the execution of CUs. After a CU is submitted to the manager, it transitions to an SU, which is scheduled to a Pilot by the PM.

mentations of Pilot-Jobs. Often, these implementations are coupled to the infrastructure they were designed for.

Our objective is to provide a minimal, but complete model of Pilot-Jobs: The P* Model provides a conceptual basis to compare and contrast different PJ frameworks. We perform experiments demonstrating interoperability across middleware, platform and different PJ frameworks, and to establish the effectiveness of the Pilot-API.

2. THE P* MODEL OF PILOT-ABSTRACTIONS

The P* model is derived from an analysis of many PJ implementations; based upon this analysis, we present the common *elements* of the P* Model, followed by a description of the overall functioning of a PJ framework. The P* Model defines the following elements:

- **Pilot (Pilot-Compute):** The Pilot is the entity that actually gets submitted and scheduled on a resource. The PJ provides application (user) level control and management of the set of allocated resources.
- **Compute Unit (CU):** A CU encapsulates a self-contained piece of work (a task) specified by the application that is submitted to the Pilot-Job framework. There is no intrinsic notion of resource associated with a CU.
- **Scheduling Unit (SU):** SUs are the units of scheduling,

P* Element	BigJob	DIANE	Condor-G/Glide-in
Pilot-Manager	BigJob Manager	RunMaster	condor_master condor_collector condor_negotiator condor_schedd
Pilot	BigJob Agent	Worker Agent	condor_master condor_startd
CU	Task	Task	Job
SU	Sub-Job	Task	Job

Table 1: Mapping P* elements and PJ Frameworks: While each PJ framework maintains its own vocabulary, each of the P* elements can be mapped to one (or more) components of the different frameworks.

internal to the P* Model, i.e., it is not known by or visible to an application. Once a CU is under the control of the Pilot-Job framework, it is assigned to an SU.

• **Pilot-Manager (PM):** The PM is responsible for (i) orchestrating the interaction between the Pilots as well as the different components of the P* Model (CUs, SUs) and (ii) decisions related to internal resource assignment (once resources have been acquired by the Pilot-Job). For example, an SU can consists of one or more CUs. The PM determines how to group them and when SUs are scheduled and executed on a resource via the Pilot.

Figure 1 illustrates the interactions between the elements of the P* Model. First, the application specifies the capabilities of the resources required using a Pilot-Job description (step 1). The PM then submits the necessary number of Pilots to fulfill the resource requirements of the application (step 2). Each Pilot is queued at the resource manager, which is responsible for starting it (step 3). The application can submit CUs to the PM at any time (step 4). A submitted CU becomes an SU, i.e. the PM is now in control of it. In the simplest case one CU corresponds to one SU.

As shown in table 1, the above elements can be mapped to specific entities in different Pilot-Jobs framework, e.g. BigJob [1], Condor [2] and DIANE [3]. While most of these frameworks share many properties, they often differ in their implementation (e.g. of the communication mechanism) and usage modalities. The aim of the Pilot-API [4] is to provide an abstract, unified interface to PJ frameworks that adhere to the P* Model. Figure 2 shows how the Pilot-API enables the user to run applications interoperably on different production and research infrastructures. For this purpose we investigate the performance of BFAST, a genome sequencing application. BFAST is very I/O sensitive – we observed for example, an I/O bottleneck if many BFAST CUs are run on the same shared file system. The Pilot-API enables applications to scale to different infrastructures in such cases.

3. DISCUSSION AND FUTURE WORK

Although a variety of PJ frameworks have emerged, which are, for the most parts, functionally equivalent, it is often impossible to use them interoperably or even just to compare them. The primary contribution of this work is the development of the P* Model, the usage of the P* elements to describe and characterize PJ frameworks such as DIANE and Condor-G/Glide-in. We demonstrated the practical relevance of this work by using different PJ frameworks via a unified API, and enabling applications to scale across different infrastructures and utilize performance advantages.

Pilot-abstractions provide significant future research &

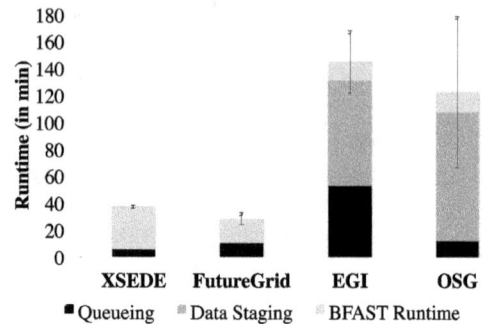

Figure 2: PJ Framework Performance on XSEDE, FutureGrid, EGI and OSG: Running 128 BFAST match tasks on 128 cores. The longer runtimes on EGI and OSG are mainly caused by longer queuing times and the necessity to stage all input files.

development opportunities, especially in their use for data-intensive applications. The management, placement and scheduling of data in distributed systems remains a challenge due to various reasons: (i) the placement of data is often decoupled from the placement of Compute Units and Pilots, i.e. the application must often manually stage in and out its data using simple scripts; (ii) heterogeneity, e.g. with respect to storage, filesystem types and paths, often prohibits late binding decisions; (iii) absence of capabilities that allow applications to specify their data dependencies on an abstract, logical level (rather than on file basis) are not available; (iv) due to lack of a common treatment for compute and data, optimizations of data/compute placements are often not possible. In addition, applications must cope with various other challenging, data-related issues, e.g. varying data sources (such as sensors and/or other application components), fluctuating data rates, transfer failures, optimizations for different queries, data-/compute co-location etc. While these issues can be handled in an application-specific manner, the use of general-purpose, infrastructure independent capabilities, such as a common Pilot-based abstraction for compute and data presents several advantages. This motivates an abstraction for data, that is analogous to Pilot-Jobs, that we refer to as *Pilot-Data (PD)*.

4. REFERENCES

[1] A. Luckow, L. Lacinski, and S. Jha, "SAGA BigJob: An Extensible and Interoperable Pilot-Job Abstraction for Distributed Applications and Systems," in *IEEE/ACM CCGrid*, 2010, pp. 135–144.

[2] J. Frey, T. Tannenbaum, M. Livny, I. Foster, and S. Tuecke, "Condor-G: A Computation Management Agent for Multi-Institutional Grids," *Cluster Computing*, vol. 5, no. 3, pp. 237–246, July 2002.

[3] J. Moscicki, "Diane - distributed analysis environment for grid-enabled simulation and analysis of physics data," in *Nuclear Science Symposium Conference Record, 2003 IEEE*, vol. 3, 2003, pp. 1617 – 1620.

[4] Pilot API, https://github.com/saga-project/BigJob/blob/master/pilot/api/, 2012.

A System-Aware Optimized Data Organization for Efficient Scientific Analytics

Yuan Tian
Dept. of Computer Science
Auburn University
tianyua@auburn.edu

Scott Klasky
Oak Ridge National Lab
Oak Ridge, 37831
klasky@ornl.gov

Weikuan Yu
Dept. of Computer Science
Auburn University
wkyu@auburn.edu

Hasan Abbasi
Oak Ridge National Lab
Oak Ridge, 37831
habbasi@ornl.gov

Bin Wang
Dept. of Computer Science
Auburn University
bzw0012@auburn.edu

Norbert Podhorszki
Oak Ridge National Lab
Oak Ridge, 37831
pnorbert@ornl.gov

ABSTRACT

Large-scale scientific applications on High End Computing systems produce a large volume of highly complex datasets. Such data imposes a grand challenge to conventional storage systems for the need of efficient I/O solutions during both the simulation runtime and data post-processing phases. With the mounting needs of scientific discovery, the read performance of large-scale simulations has becomes a critical issue for the HPC community. In this study, we propose a system-aware optimized data organization strategy that can organize data blocks of multidimensional scientific data efficiently based on simulation output and the underlying storage systems, thereby enabling efficient scientific analytics. Our experimental results demonstrate a performance speedup up to 72 times for the combustion simulation S3D, compared to the logically contiguous data layout.

Categories and Subject Descriptors

D 4.3 [**Operating System**]: File Systems Management—*Access Method, File organization*

General Terms

Design, Experimentation, Performance

Keywords

I/O, Data Layout

1. INTRODUCTION

The increasing growth of leadership computing capabilities, in terms of both system complexity and computational power, has enabled scientific applications to solve complex scientific problems at large scale. Such phenomenon is accompanied by a gigantic volume of complex scientific data produced, driving the impetus for

data intensive computing as a very significant factor in scientific computing.

Many efforts, both past and present, have focused on examining and improving the I/O performance by studying the output side of the problem [7, 8], despite the importance of read performance in driving the scientific insight through scientific simulation, analysis workflows and visualization. Worse yet, current I/O technique often overlook the need of good read performance and, as a result, have a substantial negative impact on the read performance. The main reason is the discrepancy between the physical limitations of linearly ordered magnetic storage and the common access patterns [5] of the multidimensional scientific data. Significant "dimension dependency" [4] has been observed for range queries, due to the expense of coping with noncontiguity of data points with extra disk seeks or retrieving extra data between needed segments.

We propose a System-aware Optimized Data Organization strategy which uses 1) an Optimized Chunking model to produces the *ideal* sized data chunks based on the simulation output and system parameters; and 2) a Space Filling Curve reordering to ensure the close-to-optimal data concurrency. The initial experimental result on the Jaguar Cray XT5 [3] supercomputer at Oak Ridge National Laboratories (ORNL) demonstrated that our strategy is able to provide both good balance and high performance for challenging access patterns in scientific applications. Up to 72x speedup to the planar read is achieved for S3D [2] compared to the logically contiguous data layout.

2. OUR APPROACH

Chunking has been commonly recognized as an efficient data layout for multidimensional arrays [4]. For a chunk based data organization, the size of chunks plays a critical role in determining the read performance for query on a data subset.

Intuitively there is a *sweet spot* for the chunk size where the overhead on the seek operation (to traverse through the data chunks) and redundant data retrieval (to read extra data to avoid seeks) achieves the best balance for the slow dimension. Such a sweet spot is where the optimal read performance can be expected. We develop the Optimized Chunking model to pinpoint an *ideal* chunk size for a multidimensional data on a HPC system. We show that significantly varying the chunk size towards either direction results in performance degradation as the I/O becomes burdened by overhead or dominated by disk seeks. Given a 3-D variable, the relationship between the performance for planar read and the chunk size is shown in Figure 1, where N_{ocs} is the sweet spot.

Because dividing large data chunk breaks the contiguity on the

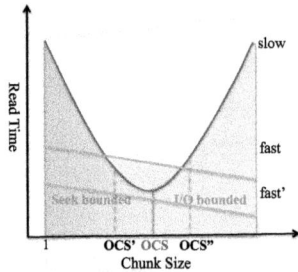

Figure 1: The Read Time vs. the Chunk Size

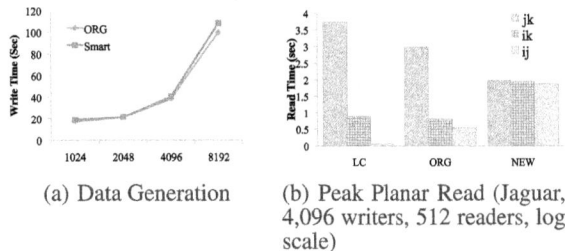

(a) Data Generation

(b) Peak Planar Read (Jaguar, 4,096 writers, 512 readers, log scale)

Figure 2: I/O Performance

fast dimension, the read performance degrades proportionally with the decreasing chunk size, where the data was originally contiguous. This results in two scenarios as shown in Figure 1, represented by two orange lines. In view of the general performance on all the dimensions, the fastest total read time may not incur at the point *OCS* but still within the *Optimized Region* of *OCS'* and *OCS''*. The performance difference inside such region is within a small margin. As this study is aimed at finding an *optimized* chunk size, we use our solution of *OCS* as the guidance for data organization. Our experimental results in Section 3 demonstrate that this value provides satisfactory performance. After a series mathematical derivation (the detail of the derivation can be found in [6], we can then determine the Optimized Chunk Size: $OCS = BW_{io} \times (CC + T_s)$, where $BW_{i/o}$ is the I/O bandwidth, T_s is the time unit for each seek operation, and CC is the communication cost unit. For a simplified analytical model, the external and internal interferences to the storage system are ignored. Such modeling can help pinpoint a solution that enables near-optimal I/O performance tuning in a timely fashion.

After the *correct* sized data chunks are produced, a Hilbert Space Filling Curve reordering is applied to shuffle the placement of the data chunks on storage targets. This approach is to achieve a close-to-optimal data concurrency for reading based on our earlier study [5].

3. EXPERIMENTAL EVALUATION

We have implemented our new approach within ADaptive I/O System (ADIOS) [1], and evaluated it on the *Jaguar* supercomputer at ORNL. A 3-D variable with a process local dimension of $256 \times 256 \times 256$ is generated by S3D [2]. Based on our equation for optimized chunk size and system parameters, each data chunk is divided into 49 subchunks. Figure 2(a) shows such strategy only introduces a negligible write overhead.

A planar read is then performed on each of three dimensions k, j and i, where k is the fastest dimension. The number of readers varies from 32 to 512. We compare the performance between three different data organizations, namely Logically Contiguous (LC), the original ADIOS (ORG) and our Optimized Data Organization (NEW). The peak performance is shown in Figure 2(b). Our Optimized Data Organization achieves a maximum improvement of 12x

compared to ORG and 72x compared to LC, respectively. Moreover, the dimension dependency is significantly alleviated.

4. CONCLUSION

We propose a system-aware optimized data organization to enable the efficient scientific data analytics. Under the governance of Optimized Chunking model and SFC-based chunk reordering, we demonstrate that a balanced and high performance reading for challenging access patterns of scientific data is achieved.

5. ACKNOWLEDGEMENT

This work is funded in part by a UT-Battelle grant to Auburn University, and in part by National Science Foundation award CNS-1059376. This research is also supported by an UT-Battelle grant (UT-B-4000103043) to Auburn University. It used resources of the NCCS at ORNL, which is supported by the Office of Science of the U.S. Department of Energy under Contract No. DE-AC05-00OR22725.

6. ADDITIONAL AUTHORS

Additional authors: Ray Grout(National Renewable Energy Laboratories, email: Ray.Grout@nrel.gov) and Matt Wolf (Georgia Institute of Technology, email: mwolf@cc.gatech.edu).

7. REFERENCES

[1] Adaptable I/O System. http://www.nccs.gov/user-support/center-projects/adios.

[2] J. H. Chen et al. Terascale direct numerical simulations of turbulent combustion using S3D. *Comp. Sci. & Disc.*, 2(1):015001 (31pp), 2009.

[3] NCCS. http://www.nccs.gov/computing-resources/.

[4] T. Shimada, T. Tsuji, and K. Higuchi. A storage scheme for multidimensional data alleviating dimension dependency. In *Digital Information Management, 2008. ICDIM 2008. Third International Conference on*, pages 662 –668, nov. 2008.

[5] Y. Tian, S. Klasky, H. Abbasi, J. Lofstead, N. P. R. Grout, Q. Liu, Y. Wang, and W. Yu. Edo: Improving read performance for scientific applications through elastic data organization. In *CLUSTER '11: Proceedings of the 2011 IEEE International Conference on Cluster Computing*, Washington, DC, USA, 2011. IEEE Computer Society.

[6] Y. Tian and W. Yu. Finding the optimized chunking for multidimensional array on large-scale systems. Technical Report AU-CSSE-PASL/12-TR01, Auburn University, 2012.

[7] W. Yu and J. Vetter. ParColl: Partitioned Collective I/O on the Cray XT. In *International Conference on Parallel Processing (ICPP'08)*, Portland, OR, 2008.

[8] W. Yu, J. Vetter, and H. Oral. Performance characterization and optimization of parallel I/O on the cray XT. *IPDPS*, pages 1–11, April 2008.

Dynamic Binary Rewriting and Migration for Shared-ISA Asymmetric, Multicore Processors

Summary

Giorgis Georgakoudis
University of Thessaly
ggeorgakoudis@gmail.com

Spyros Lalis
University of Thessaly
lalis@inf.uth.gr

Dimitrios S. Nikolopoulos
Queen's University of Belfast
d.nikolopoulos@qub.ac.uk

Categories and Subject Descriptors: D.3.4 [Programming Languages]: Processors–*Code generation*; C.1.3 [Processor Architectures]: Other Architecture Styles–*Heterogeneous systems*; D.4.1 [Operating systems]: Process Management

General Terms: Experimentation, Performance

Keywords: Heterogeneous multicore, Shared asymmetric ISA, Binary Rewriting, Code optimization

1. INTRODUCTION

Asymmetric multicore processors have demonstrated strong potential for improving performance, power efficiency and area efficiency of computing systems [1, 2, 5, 6]. Disjoint ISA systems, such as AMD Fusion, ARM Tegra and the Cell broadband engine, are becoming widespread. Although disjoint-ISA systems have exhibited high performance, they are hard to program [6]. Single-ISA, performance heterogeneous systems [7, 10] are simpler to program, as the same code can run on any core in the system. However, that implies that certain threads will be unable to exploit performance enhancing features which are available on selected cores and exposed to the ISA, through specialized instructions.

Shared-ISA asymmetric multicore architectures [9] provide programmability and code customization simultaneously. Shared-ISA architectures use a *baseline ISA*, which some performance enhanced (PE) cores extend with additional, PE instructions. Existing solutions for code portability–such as using only baseline code, fat binaries, programmer's effort for different versions of code, or fault-and-migrate [8]–suffer in efficiency, adaptivity or programmability. Hardware asymmetry should be transparently handled, enabling applications to utilize available cores efficiently.

We propose a new dynamic binary rewriting and migration method for shared-ISA asymmetric multicore processors which has the following strengths: (i) it enables code portability while making use of performance enhancements when possible, (ii) rewriting occurs at the binary level, thus there is no need for special tools or effort from the programmer, (iii) it is applied dynamically, on demand, invoked by the operating system when a thread is scheduled to a core with different performance capabilities, (iv) it enables scheduling/migrations to happen between cores, thus permitting schedulers to meet high-level optimization objectives seamlessly.

We implement and evaluate our binary rewriting scheme on real hardware, specifically an FPGA prototype of a shared-ISA Microblaze multicore processor architecture where PE cores have additional hardware FP and integer arithmetic functional units. These hardware units reflect to the processor's ISA in the form of extra instructions available on top of a baseline ISA. This paper makes the following contributions:

- We introduce a new binary rewriting method for shared-ISA asymmetric multicore processors, enabling code portability with performance enhancement and allowing seamless migration between cores.
- We present an evaluation on real hardware, an FPGA prototype platform, using benchmarks from the SPEC CPU2006 and Rodinia [3] benchmark suites.
- We present a case study of multiprogram workloads consisting of applications that exhibit heterogeneous performance enhancement capabilities. We propose a scheduling policy, minimizing workload's average turnaround time, which relies on thread migrations.

2. DYNAMIC BINARY REWRITING AND MIGRATION

Our binary rewriting is triggered by scheduling decisions, adapting a binary at runtime according to the scheduled core's performance capabilities. The application along with its libraries is compiled without any PE instructions, so that code generated is compatible with any available core type. Disassembling the stripped binary code provides enough information for rewriting.

Binary rewriting takes place in three phases. The first phase builds a static call graph and determines the code boundaries of discovered functions. To accomplish that, we employ control flow analysis and function prologue/epilogue matching techniques [4]. The second phase identifies patching/de-patching targets within each function depending on the scheduled core capabilities. Specifically we find calls to libgcc SW emulation routines and instruction patterns that are equivalent to a hardware, PE instruction. Conversely for de-patching, we identify hardware instructions that need reverting back to baseline code. The third phase examines those targets and rewrites the binary. Intra-procedural code is relocated to remove superfluous instructions due to patching. However, we preserve the procedure's code memory footprint to maintain inter-procedural control flow, thus relinking only intra-procedural branches, and to use as a placeholder for reinstating baseline instructions. Rewriting updates the runtime machine state of a running thread, such as the call stack, to account for relocations.

We present a scheduling policy which aims at minimizing average turnaround time in a multiprogram workload based on the observation that applications with higher speedup potential benefit more when scheduled to PE cores. We implement an online, software profiler to identify hotspots in code. A thread's speedup potential is estimated based on possible patching targets in those hotspots. After a sampling period, we migrate higher speedup

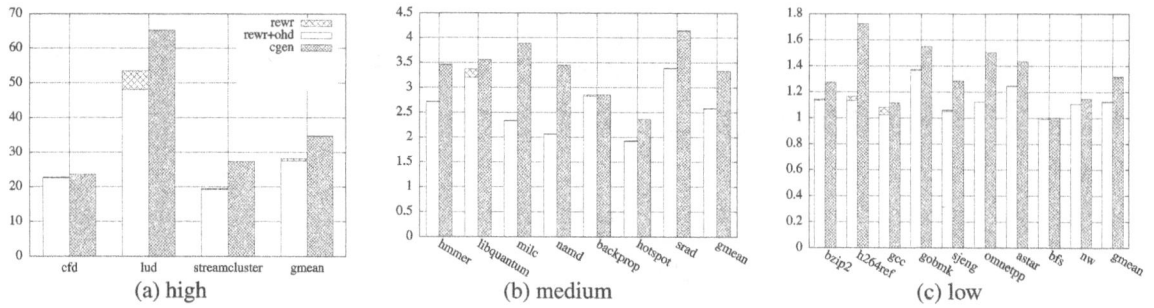

| (a) high | (b) medium | (c) low |

Figure 1: Speedup vs baseline

threads to PE cores, while swapping lower speedup ones to baseline cores.

3. EVALUATION

We evaluate our dynamic binary rewriting efficiency by comparing it against portable, but performance handicapped code consisting only of baseline instructions and performance enhanced, nonportable code generated by the compiler for a PE core. We perform single-program measurements, calculating the speedup obtained by binary rewriting and statically targeted code against baseline code. Results are shown in Figure 1, categorizing benchmarks based on speedup achieved as *high*, *medium* and *low*; "rewr" shows speedup accounting only for pure benchmark execution time, while "rewr+ohd" shows lower speedup achieved by including the rewriting overhead delay. Compiler generated, statically targeted code speedup –an ideal case– is denoted as "cgen" and the geometric mean is denoted by "gmean". Rewriting improves significantly baseline code and in several cases performs on par to statically targeted code, being at worse 30% slower, while the overhead accounts for less that 2%.

We also evaluate our scheduling policy, enabled by binary rewriting, in multiprogram workloads. Our octo-core HW platform configuration has the following modes: (i) *BASE* is the lower bound and baseline for performance: all cores are baseline ones, (ii) *UNF*, *MIG* and *ORAC* have a heterogeneous configuration of four PE and four baseline cores. In *UNF*, initial assignment of threads to cores is inverse to speedup potential, rewriting is enabled and migrations are not enabled. In *MIG*, we keep the handicapped initial assignment but we enable both rewriting and migrations to enable better thread-to-core mapping. In *ORAC*, initial thread-to-core assignment matches speedup potential; both rewriting and migrations are enabled. (iii) *PE-REWR* and *PE-STATIC* have all PE cores. *PE-REWR* involves rewriting benchmarks for PE instructions, while for *PE-STATIC* code is statically targeted. The "high-low" workload has four high speedup and four low speedup benchmarks, "high-med" has the same high speedup applications and four medium speedup ones, while "med-low" uses the medium and low speedup benchmarks of previous setups. We calculate the average turnaround time (*ANTT*) and results are shown in Figure 2. *MIG* and *ORAC* reduce *ANTT* significantly, while performing close to *PE-REWR* and *PE-STATIC*.

4. CONCLUSIONS

We presented a dynamic binary rewriting method which enables dynamic performance optimization at the instruction level and code portability in asymmetric, shared-ISA multiprocessor systems. Binary rewriting is invoked dynamically by the operating system when a thread is scheduled/migrated to a core. It performs closely

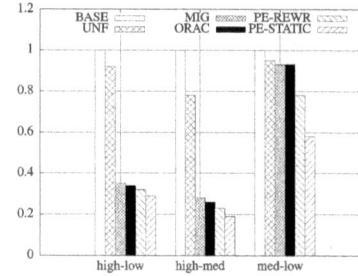

Figure 2: *ANTT* of multiprogram workloads

to slightly worse compared with non-portable, statically targeted code for PE instructions. Moreover, migrations, enabled by binary rewriting, reduce significantly the *ANTT* in multiprogram workloads where applications exhibit varying speedup potential from PE instructions.

5. ACKNOWLEDGEMENTS

This work has been partially supported by the European Commission under the I-CORES project (FP7 MCF-IRG Contract #224759)

6. REFERENCES

[1] T. Agerwala and S. Chatterjee. Computer architecture: Challenges and opportunities for the next decade. *IEEE Micro*, 25(3):58–69, 2005.
[2] M. Annavaram, E. Grochowski, and J. P. Shen. Mitigating amdahl's law through epi throttling. In *ISCA*, pages 298–309, 2005.
[3] S. Che, M. Boyer, J. Meng, D. Tarjan, J. W. Sheaffer, S.-H. Lee, and K. Skadron. Rodinia: A benchmark suite for heterogeneous computing. In *IISWC*, pages 44–54, 2009.
[4] L. C. Harris and B. P. Miller. Practical analysis of stripped binary code. *SIGARCH Comput. Archit. News*, 33:63–68, December 2005.
[5] M. D. Hill. Amdahl's law in the multicore era. In *HPCA*, page 187, 2008.
[6] R. Kumar, D. M. Tullsen, N. P. Jouppi, and P. Ranganathan. Heterogeneous chip multiprocessors. *IEEE Computer*, 38(11):32–38, 2005.
[7] R. Kumar, D. M. Tullsen, P. Ranganathan, N. P. Jouppi, and K. I. Farkas. Single-isa heterogeneous multi-core architectures for multithreaded workload performance. In *ISCA*, pages 64–75, 2004.
[8] T. Li, P. Brett, R. C. Knauerhase, D. A. Koufaty, D. Reddy, and S. Hahn. Operating system support for overlapping-isa heterogeneous multi-core architectures. In *HPCA*, pages 1–12, 2010.
[9] D. Reddy, D. A. Koufaty, P. Brett, and S. Hahn. Bridging functional heterogeneity in multicore architectures. *Operating Systems Review*, 45(1):21–33, 2011.
[10] J. C. Saez, D. Shelepov, A. Fedorova, and M. Prieto. Leveraging workload diversity through os scheduling to maximize performance on single-isa heterogeneous multicore systems. *J. Parallel Distrib. Comput.*, 71(1):114–131, 2011.

Coupling Scheduler for MapReduce/Hadoop

Jian Tan, Xiaoqiao Meng, Li Zhang
IBM T. J. Watson Research Center
Hawthorne, NY 10562
{tanji,xmeng,zhangli}@us.ibm.com

ABSTRACT

Current schedulers of MapReduce/Hadoop are quite successful in providing good performance. However improving spaces still exist: map and reduce tasks are not jointly optimized for scheduling, albeit there is a strong dependence between them. This can cause job starvation and bad data locality. We design a resource-aware scheduler for Hadoop, which couples the progresses of mappers and reducers, and jointly optimize the placements for both of them. This mitigates the starvation problem and improves the overall data locality. Our experiments demonstrate improvements to job response times by up to an order of magnitude.

Categories and Subject Descriptors

H.4 [**Information Systems Applications**]: Miscellaneous; D.2.10 [**Software Engineering**]: Design—*Methodologies*

Keywords

MapReduce/Hadoop, Coupling Scheduler, Fair Scheduler, Implementation, Experimentation

1. INTRODUCTION

MapReduce [2], as well as its open source implementation Hadoop [3], has emerged as a dominant paradigm for processing large datasets in parallel on compute clusters. Schedulers are critical in enhancing the performance of Hadoop, among which Fair Scheduler is the de facto industry standard. Though quite successful, it still has improving spaces.

1. Map and reduce tasks are scheduled separately without joint optimization. First, Fair Scheduler only guarantees the fairness of the map phase, and is not really fair for reducers, since it launches reducers greedily to a maximum. We argue that allocating excess computing resources without balancing with the map progress will lead to underutilization, which is evidenced by the starvation problem [4]. Second, most of the existing data locality algorithms only consider local inputs for map tasks and ignore that the intermediate data generated from maps also need to be fetched by reducers, through either networks or local disks. The placements of map and reduce tasks have impacts on each other.

2. Hadoop relies on Delay Scheduling to improve the data locality for map tasks. We observe that the introduced delays can degrade the performance in heterogeneous environments, e.g., when the input data are not distributed evenly on a large fraction of nodes.

In view of these observations, we propose a resource-aware scheduler, termed Coupling Scheduler. It couples the progresses of map and reduce tasks to mitigate starvation, jointly optimizes the placements for both to improve data locality of reducers using Wait Scheduling, and utilizes Random Peeking Scheduling to enhance the data locality of mappers.

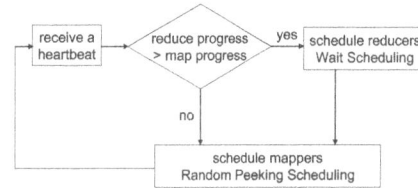

Figure 1: Schematic diagram of Coupling Scheduler

2. SCHEDULING REDUCERS

Map tasks are small and independent, which can run in parallel. Differently, reducers are long-run tasks that contain copy/merge and reduce phases. In most of the current implementations a job that has launched a reducer will not release the slot until finished, which may starve other jobs that arrive later. This problem is even more pronounced for typical work flows that contain small jobs after large ones. A real experiment illustrates this problem in Fig. 2, showing the number of running map and reduce tasks of two jobs at every time point. Job 2 can not launch its re-

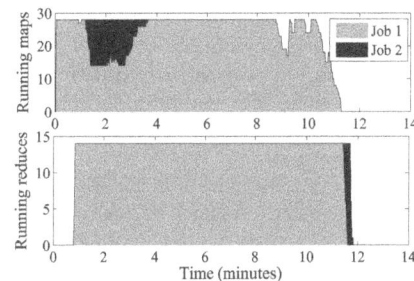

Figure 2: Starvation problem with Fair Scheduler

ducers until job 1 releases some slots at time 11.3 minutes. Ideally, a stop-and-resume control for job 1 may solve this problem, which can incur large overhead [4]. Killing running tasks to free resources for other jobs is also an option, but it wastes the partially accomplished work. A better approach is to avoid or alleviate this problem, if possible, from the beginning. To this end, we introduce a simple but effective approach: launch reducers gradually (e.g., the percentage y of started reducers) according to the progress of the mappers (e.g., the percentage x of finished map tasks) through a function $f : [0, 1] \rightarrow [0, 1]$. If reduce progress lags behind map progress $f(x) > y$, then this job should have a better chance to launch reducers; otherwise it should not acquire more slots that can be used by others. Repeating the same

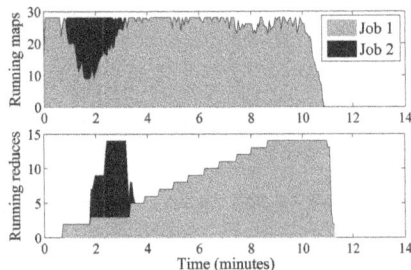

Figure 3: Repeat with Coupling Scheduler

experiment, Fig. 3 demonstrates that the starvation problem can be mitigated with the new approach. Note that reducers are not work-conserving: the gray area for the number of running reducers in Fig. 3 is almost half of that in Fig. 2.

More importantly, this way of gradually launching reducers depending on the map progress enables new ways to consider the data locality jointly for both mappers and reducers, which is absent in all existing approaches. Mappers take the input data and reducers fetch the intermediate data through either network or local disk. It is a joint control that places 1) map tasks closer to the input data as well as the running reducers and 2) reducers closer to a "centrality" of generated intermediate data. The placements of mappers determine where the intermediate data are stored. In turn, the placements of reducers impact how map outputs are fetched. However, it is difficult to predict the future run-time information, e.g., map output bytes, interactions among multiple jobs, etc. The greedy approach to launching reducers taken by existing schedulers can make wrong decisions at the beginning since it is unaware of the evolving job dynamics. For long-run reducers, an early mistake takes much more effort to correct. Existing approaches rely on recomputations and speculative executions. Our unique way of gradually launching reducers opens up new possibilities: initially both mappers and reducers may not know their optimal placements with the common goal for better data locality; as the job evolves, new run-time information becomes available such that mappers and reducers can alternatively optimize step by step depending on the decisions taken by the other phase.

The heartbeats sent by slave nodes arrive at the master node in a random order. When it is ready to launch a reducer ($f(x) > y$), the slave node that just sent the heartbeat is not necessarily an optimal place. We propose Wait Scheduling, which allows a reducer to check up to a certain number of heartbeats before making a decision. The decision is based on computing a good placement for the new reducer. It is similar to Delay Scheduling [4], but used for reducers instead of mappers, different in the sense that it

needs to find a data "centrality" for the already generated intermediate data on the assumed tree network for Hadoop.

3. SCHEDULING MAPPERS

Fair Scheduler utilizes Delay Scheduling to improve data locality for mappers [4] by allowing them to wait for a period of time T to check whether local data are available or not. Interestingly, we find that the mappers are sensitive to the introduced delay T. The waiting time T effectively specifies the rate of launching map tasks. Suppose that on average the map tasks of the considered job last for K seconds. Then, when the number S of nodes that are running local map tasks exceeds a certain number such that $S/K > 1/T$, the map assign rate of a job becomes less than the rate at which the mappers complete on the cluster. This can cause an underutilization problem: the number of mappers running simultaneously will not reach the desired number, and change with large variations over time. We illustrate this problem using an experiment (WordCount with 427 mappers on 15 nodes with 4 map slots per node) in Fig. 4.

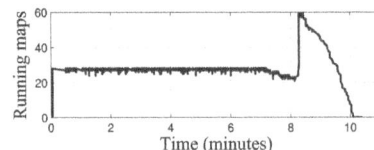

Figure 4: Only 7 nodes have local data and 8 nodes do not store any input data. In most time Delay Scheduling only launches 4×7 mappers concurrently.

Since mappers are sensitive to delays, we propose Random Peeking Scheduling. When receiving a heartbeat, the master node randomly selects K out of the N total nodes and checks how many (say, K_1) has local map inputs and how many (say, K_2) has available map slots for a given job. Then it estimates the percentage of nodes that have local map inputs $\hat{p}_m = K_1/K$ and the total number $\hat{N}_m$ of nodes that have available map slots $\hat{N}_m = N \times K_2/K$. The random sampling technique is only for the purpose of reducing the time complexity for a large cluster. A medium/small size cluster can set $K = N$. Now, when the master node finds that a slave node does not have local data, it launches a remote map task with probability p, which is a function of $\hat{p}_m, \hat{N}_m$ and the number of pending mappers. Choosing a good p is based on the intuition that 1) if many other nodes have local data and available slots, then the schedule should skip the current heartbeat with high probability; 2) if a job has a large number of pending map tasks compared with $\hat{N}_m$, it is beneficial to launch remote mappers immediately with a certain probability.

4. REFERENCES

[1] Fair Scheduler, http://hadoop.apache.org/mapreduce/docs/r0.21.0/fair_scheduler.html.

[2] J. Dean and S. Ghemawat. Mapreduce: simplified data processing on large clusters. *Commun. ACM*, 51:107–113, January 2008.

[3] Hadoop. http://hadoop.apache.org.

[4] M. Zaharia, D. Borthakur, J. S. Sarma, K. Elmeleegy, S. Shenker, and I. Stoica. Job scheduling for multi-user mapreduce clusters. Technical Report, University of California, Berkeley, April 2009.

Performance Evaluation of Interthread Communication Mechanisms on Multicore/Multithreaded Architectures

Massimiliano Meneghin
IBM Research Lab
Dublin, Ireland
massimin@ie.ibm.com

Davide Pasetto
IBM Research Lab
Dublin, Ireland
pasetto_davide@ie.ibm.com

Hubertus Franke
IBM TJ Watson
Yorktown Heights, NY
frankeh@us.ibm.com

Fabrizio Petrini
IBM TJ Watson
Yorktown Heights, NY
fpetrin@us.ibm.com

Jimi Xenidis
IBM Research Lab
Austin, TX
jimix@us.ibm.com

ABSTRACT

The three major solutions for increasing the nominal performance of a CPU are: multiplying the number of cores per socket, expanding the embedded cache memories and use multi-threading to reduce the impact of the deep memory hierarchy. Systems with tens or hundreds of hardware threads, all sharing a cache coherent UMA or NUMA memory space, are today the de-facto standard. While these solutions can easily provide benefits in a multi-program environment, they require recoding of applications to leverage the available parallelism. Threads must synchronize and exchange data, and the overall performance is heavily influenced by the overhead added by these mechanisms, especially as developers try to exploit finer grain parallelism to be able to use all available resources.

Categories and Subject Descriptors

C.4 [**Performance of Systems**]: Performance attributes;
D.1 [**Concurrent Programming**]: Parallel Programming

General Terms

Performance,Experimentation

1. CONTRIBUTION

This work (full version is available online [1]) examines two synchronization mechanisms - locks and queues - in the context of multi and many cores systems with tens of hardware threads. Locks are typically used in non streaming environments to synchronize access to shared data structures, while queues are mainly used as a support for stream computing. Several mechanisms are available today, and they can broadly be classified into: (1) lock-based schemes and (2) non-blocking schemes including wait-free protocols [4] and lock-free protocols [3]. As the number of cores increases, the *desired grain of parallelism becomes smaller* and understanding the overhead and tradeoff of the core-to-core communication mechanism is becoming increasingly important. The analysis examines how the algorithmic aspect of the implementation, the interaction with the operating system and

the availability of supporting machine language mechanisms contribute to the overall performance.

While an extensive amount of work has been performed on locks and queues, a comprehensive comparison of their runtime performance characteristics and scalability on modern architectures is still missing. This work wants to address the following open questions:

- Can modern CPU architectures effectively execute *fine grain* parallel programs that utilize all available hardware resources in a coordinated way?

- What is the overhead and the scalability of the supporting synchronization mechanisms?

Experiments run on Intel $X86^{TM}$ and IBM $PowerEN^{TM}$ [2] and focus on fine grain parallelism - where the task performed on each data item requires only a handful of microseconds. The two systems use completely different solutions to implement atomic operations: a lock instruction prefix is used on X86, while PowerPC architectures utilize the load reservation / store conditional. The PowerEN architecture also introduces a userspace `wrlos` instruction that allows for the thread to wait, i.e. not being dispatched, until a reservation is lost.

2. REFERENCES

[1] D.Pasetto and M.Meneghin and F.Petrini and H.Franke and J.Xenidis. Performance Evaluation of Interthread Communication Mechanisms on Multicore Multithreaded Architectures - full paper.

[2] H.Franke, J.Xenidis, B.Bass, C.Basso, S.Woodward, J.D.Brown, and C.L.Johnson. Introduction to the Wirespeed Architecture and Processor. *IBM Journal of Research and Development*, 2010.

[3] A. LaMarca. A performance evaluation of lock-free synchronization protocols. In *Proceedings of the thirteenth annual ACM symposium on Principles of distributed computing*, PODC '94, pages 130–140, New York, NY, USA, 1994. ACM.

[4] R. Newman-Wolfe. A protocol for wait-free, atomic, multi-reader shared variables. In *Proceedings of the sixth annual ACM Symposium on Principles of distributed computing*, PODC '87, pages 232–248, New York, NY, USA, 1987. ACM.

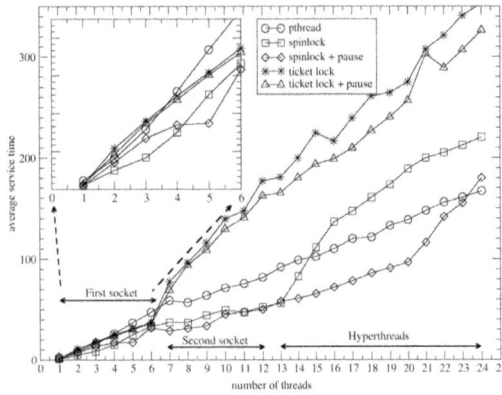

(a) Normalized X86 lock time

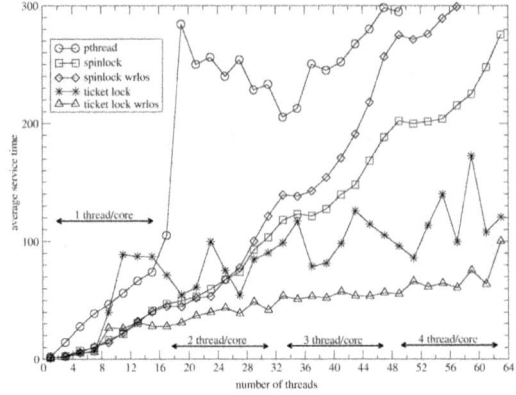

(b) Normalized PowerEN lock time

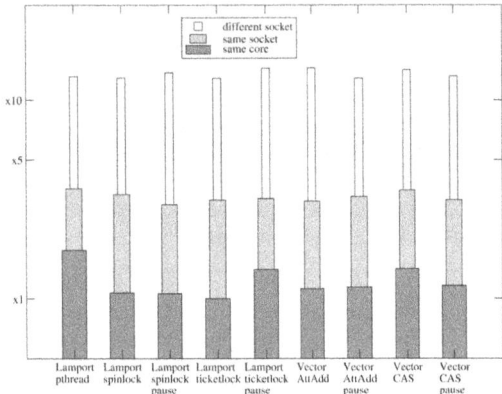

(c) Normalized queue latency on X86

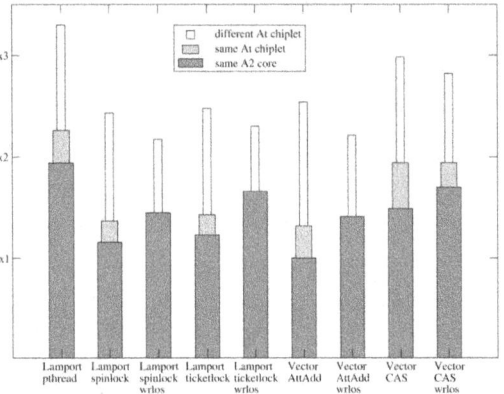

(d) Normalized queue latency on PowerEN

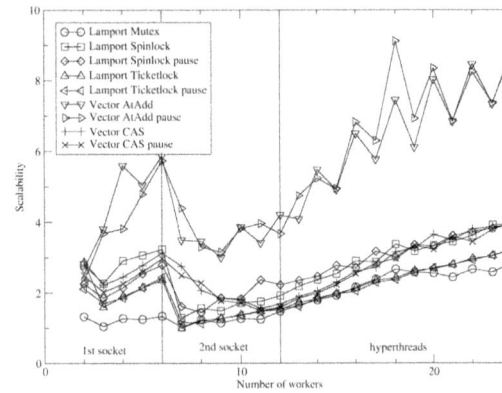

(e) Fan-out BW on X86

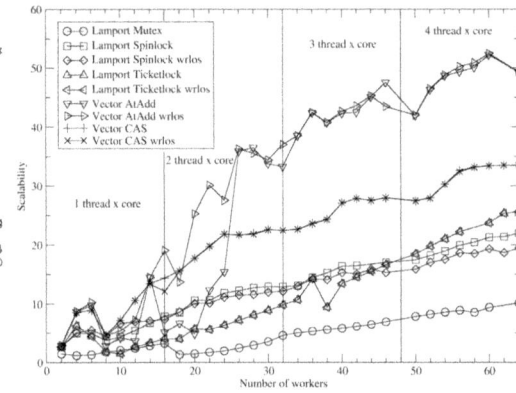

(f) Fan-out BW on PowerEN

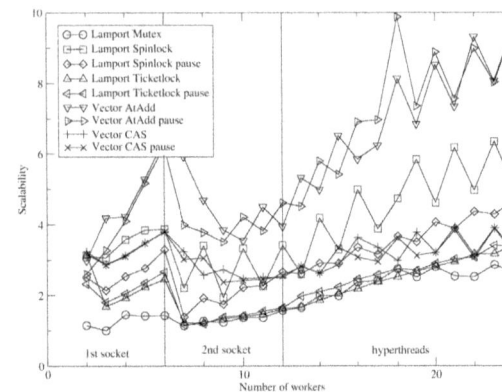

(g) Normalized Fin BW on X86

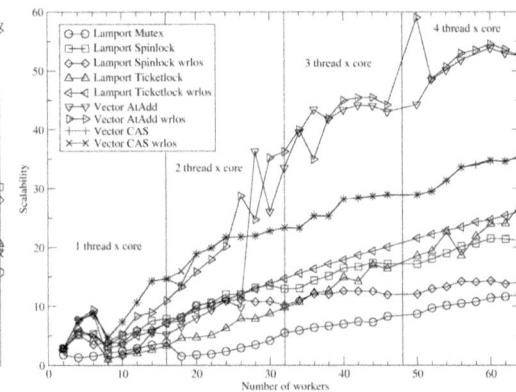

(h) Normalized Fin BW on PowerEN

132

Fault Tolerant Parallel Data-Intensive Algorithms

Mucahid Kutlu
Department of Computer
Science and Engineering
Ohio State University
Columbus, OH, 43210
kutlu@cse.ohio-state.edu

Gagan Agrawal
Department of Computer
Science and Engineering
Ohio State University
Columbus, OH, 43210
agrawal@cse.ohio-state.edu

Oguz Kurt
Department of Mathematics
Ohio State University
Columbus, OH, 43210
oguz@math.ohio-state.edu

ABSTRACT

Fault-tolerance is rapidly becoming a crucial issue in high-end and distributed computing, as increasing number of cores are decreasing the mean-time to failure of the systems. In this work, we present an algorithm-based fault tolerance solution that handles fail-stop failures for a class of iterative data intensive algorithms. We intelligently replicate the data to minimize data loss in multiple failures and decrease re-execution in recovery by little modifications in the algorithms. We evaluate our approach by using two data mining algorithms, kmeans and Apriori. We show that our approach has negligible overhead and allows us to gracefully handle different number of failures. In addition, our approach outperforms Hadoop both in absence and presence of failures.

Categories and Subject Descriptors

D.1.3 [**Programming Techniques**]: Concurrent Programming—*Parallel programming*

Keywords

Fault Tolerance, Data-Intensive Computing

1. INTRODUCTION

Growing computational and data processing needs are currently being met with increasing number of cores, as there is almost no improvement in single core's performance. However, with growing number of cores, the Mean-Time-To-Failure (MTTF) of the systems is decreasing. As a result, fault-tolerance is rapidly becoming a major topic in high-end computing.

Several different approaches to fault-tolerance have been taken, depending upon the nature of the parallel application and programming model used. There is a large number of efforts on MPI fault-tolerance, which focus on checkpointing (e.g. [4]). However, the main issue with checkpointing is the high overhead, especially, as systems are becoming larger, and disk bandwidths are not improving. For the future exascale systems, it is being argued that checkpointing and recovery time (with current methods) will even exceed the MTTF, leading to the need for alternative methods [2].

A promising alternative is *algorithm-based fault-tolerance* which uses specific properties of the algorithms to reduce the amount of information that needs to be cached. Although these methods are less general than checkpointing, they have lower overheads. In developing fault-tolerant algorithms, we have two main goals. First, we want to minimize the data loss, since the lost data needs to be

HPDC'12, June 18–22, 2012, Delft, The Netherlands.
ACM 978-1-4503-0805-2/12/06.

reread from the storage cluster, resulting in slowdown. Second, we want to minimize re-processing of the lost data. In this work, we examine algorithm-level fault-tolerance for data-intensive algorithms. In our approach, we divide the dataset into smaller parts before replication and distribute the replicated data parts with the aim of keeping the maximum data intersection between any two processors minimum. This allows us to have minimum data loss when multiple failures occur and to have better load balance after failure. In addition, the results of the small data parts are also replicated to decrease the amount of re-processing of the lost data.

2. OUR APPROACH

We focus on only the *fail-stop* failures. In addition, we do not use any additional node for the failed one to recover or be replaced, and instead, continue the execution with the remaining nodes. We use master and slave approach for parallelization. We first divide the data into smaller parts. Then we replicate these data parts and distribute them among processors such that the maximum intersection between any two processors is minimum. Each processor has two types of data, *primary data* and the *replicas*. Each processor normally processes only its own primary data and replicas can be processed only in case of failures. After processing each data part, the result(or summary) is sent to the master node and slaves that also store that data part as replica.

Having smaller parts as a unit of processing and replication allows us to have better load balance after failure, and to decrease the amount of data loss when we have multiple failures. Exchanging the summaries reduces the amount of work that has to be redone after a failure.

Now let's see how we recover the system when multiple slave nodes fail. This case is shown in the Figure 1. In this example, the replication factor, R, and number of data parts per processor (for primary data), S, are both 2 and the number of slave nodes is 4. The boxes below processors represent the data blocks where the dark ones are the data blocks that will be impacted by the failures. The data blocks in the first row are the primary ones whereas those in the second row are the replicas.

Let's assume that P1 and P2 fail at the beginning of an iteration. D2-D4 are available on slave nodes that are still operational. So, the master node notifies P3 to process D2 and D3 and, similarly, asks P4 to process D4. However, D1 is not available on any of the slave nodes, and therefore, it needs to be read from the storage cluster. The master node reads D1 and sends it to the P4 to process it. Here, P4 is chosen for processing D1 to get a better load balance.

In this study, we focused on only k-means and apriori algorithms. But, in our previous work [5], we made the observation that parallel versions of several well-known data mining techniques share a relatively similar reduction structure. Therefore, besides k-means

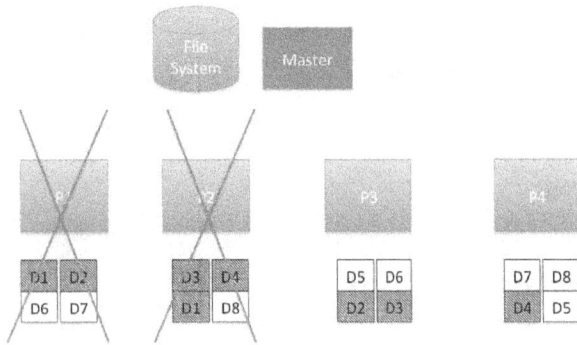

Figure 1: Multiple Slave Nodes Failure

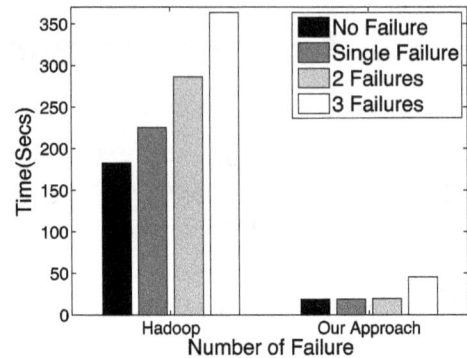

Figure 3: Total Execution Time that Changes with the Number of Failures

clustering and apriori association mining, our approach can be applied to several data mining algorithms.

3. EXPERIMENTS

In our experiments, we used single node with 8 cores 2.5 GHz Opterons processor and 24 GB memory. We implemented apriori algorithm in C programming language with MPI library. We run each test 5 times and calculated the average of three after eliminating the maximum and the minimum. The size of the dataset is 0.96 GB.

In the first experiment, we tested the impact of frequency of summary exchange with different number of failures. Particularly, all failures occur at the beginning of the iteration and there is no replication. Thus, any failure requires that certain portion of the data be read from the storage cluster.

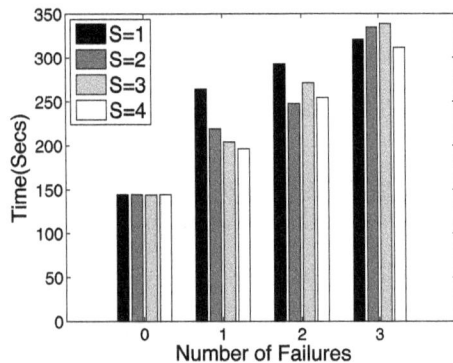

Figure 2: Impact of Frequency of Summary Exchange: Varying Number of Failures

The results are shown in Figure 2. When there is no failure, the execution time is nearly same for all S values for both algorithms. It shows that the overhead of summary exchange is negligible. When there is only one failure, we get the best results in the $S = 4$ case and the worst results with the $S = 1$ case. In other words, increasing value of S helps to improve the performance because as we divide the data into more parts, we are able to get better load balance in case of failures. When we have 2-3 failures, the results of $S = 3$ case is worse than $S = 2$ case since the performance depends on the node with the maximum data and after 2-3 failures, the maximum data in $S = 2$ case is larger than the one in $S = 3$ case. However, this will not be the case when we have more nodes.

Map-reduce [3] is a popular solution for developing data-intensive applications, which also supports fault-tolerance. Thus, in the sec-

ond experiment, we compared our approach with Hadoop[1], the open-source implementation of map-reduce. We used Hadoop implementations of apriori algorithm of [1]. The configurations and parameters were as follows. Because we cannot control failure of individual processes in Hadoop, 8 nodes, with 1 core per node, were used for Hadoop and our approach. We did not use any backup nodes for either of the implementations, i.e. failure recovery occurs with fewer nodes. Replication factor is set to 3 in both implementations. Default chunk sizes are used in Hadoop and the frequency of summary exchange, S, is 4 in our implementation.

There is a large performance difference between Hadoop and our approach. Therefore, we compared relative slowdowns of the systems in case of failures. The results are shown in Figure 3. When there were three failures, Hadoop could recover in only 2 of the 10 executions we tried. In other runs, the program failed completely. The results shown in Figure 3 are for the average of the two successful executions. In all cases, there is also a significant difference in the performance. Our approach's execution time increases 1%, 4% and 139% while Hadoop's execution time increases 23%, 57% and 99% for 1, 2 and 3 failures, respectively. When there are 3 failures, the relative slowdown in our approach is higher than Hadoop's. But, as we stated above, Hadoop could not recover in 80% of the cases.

4. REFERENCES

[1] T. Bicer, Wei Jiang, and G. Agrawal. Supporting fault tolerance in a data-intensive computing middleware. In *Parallel Distributed Processing (IPDPS), 2010 IEEE International Symposium on*, pages 1 –12, april 2010.

[2] Franck Cappello, Al Geist, Bill Gropp, Laxmikant V. Kalé, Bill Kramer, and Marc Snir. Toward exascale resilience. *IJHPCA*, 23(4):374–388, 2009.

[3] Jeffrey Dean and Sanjay Ghemawat. MapReduce: Simplified Data Processing on Large Clusters. In *OSDI*, pages 137–150, 2004.

[4] J. Hursey, J.M. Squyres, T.I. Mattox, and A. Lumsdaine. The design and implementation of checkpoint/restart process fault tolerance for open mpi. In *Parallel and Distributed Processing Symposium, 2007. IPDPS 2007. IEEE International*, pages 1 –8, march 2007.

[5] Ruoming Jin and Gagan Agrawal. Shared Memory Paralellization of Data Mining Algorithms: Techniques, Programming Interface, and Performance. In *Proceedings of the second SIAM conference on Data Mining*, 2002.

---

[1]http://hadoop.apache.org/

Leveraging Renewable Energy in Data Centers: Present and Future

Keynote Summary

Ricardo Bianchini
Department of Computer Science
Rutgers University
ricardob@cs.rutgers.edu

ABSTRACT

Interest has been growing in powering data centers (at least partially) with renewable or "green" sources of energy, such as solar or wind. However, it is challenging to use these sources because, unlike the "brown" (carbon-intensive) energy drawn from the electrical grid, they are not always available. In this keynote talk, I will first discuss the tradeoffs involved in leveraging green energy today and the prospects for the future. I will then discuss the main research challenges and questions involved in managing the use of green energy in data centers. Next, I will describe some of the software and hardware that researchers are building to explore these challenges and questions. Specifically, I will overview systems that match a data center's computational workload to the green energy supply. I will also describe Parasol, the solar-powered micro-data center we have just built at Rutgers University. Finally, I will discuss some potential avenues for future research on this topic.

Categories and Subject Descriptors

A.1 [**Introductory and Survey**]; C.5.5 [**Computer System Implementation**]: Servers; D.4.1 [**Operating Systems**]: Process Management

Keywords

Renewable energy, energy-aware scheduling, data centers.

1. INTRODUCTION

Data centers consume an enormous amount of energy [13]. In recent years, large data center operators, like Google and Microsoft, have significantly improved the energy efficiency of their multi-megawatt data centers. However, the majority of the energy consumed by data centers is actually due to small and medium-sized data centers [13], which are much more numerous and much less efficient. These facilities may range from a few dozen servers housed in a machine room to several hundreds of servers housed in a larger enterprise installation. Many of these facilities run high-performance computing workloads, such as data analytics and scientific simulations.

The energy consumed by data centers represents a financial burden on the organizations that operate them, and an infrastructure burden on power utilities. In addition, data centers contribute to climate change, since most of the electricity produced in the US and around the world derives from carbon-intensive fuels, such as coal and natural gas.

HPDC'12, June 18–22, 2012, Delft, The Netherlands.
ACM 978-1-4503-0805-2/12/06.

Due to these concerns and societal pressure, we are starting to see many "green" data centers powered (at least partially) by renewable sources of energy [2, 4]. These green data centers either generate their own electricity or draw directly from a nearby renewable power plant. Among other advantages, these types of renewable plant/data center co-location reduce the energy losses involved in power conversion and transmission over long distances.

Solar and wind are two of the most promising sources of green energy for data centers, as they are clean and broadly available. However, solar and wind do have two main limitations today: the space they require and their capital costs.

Fortunately, predicted improvements in efficiency and reductions in cost/Watt will alleviate these problems significantly in the future. For example, improvements in photovoltaic (PV) solar panels and new PV technologies are expected to triple today's efficiencies until 2030 [12]. Over the same period, the cost/Watt of PV panels is expected to become less than half of what it is today. In addition, governments currently provide incentives for green energy generation. For example, federal and state incentives in New Jersey can reduce the capital cost of solar installations by 60% [3]. If these incentives continue, cost may not be a significant factor in the future.

These trends suggest that solar and/or wind power will become increasingly attractive, especially for small and medium data centers as they require smaller and cheaper installations. Moreover, solar panels and/or wind turbines can be deployed in small increments for these data centers.

2. RESEARCH CHALLENGES

The main challenge with solar and wind energy is that, unlike brown energy drawn from the grid, it is variable. To mitigate this variability, data centers could "bank" green energy in batteries or on the grid itself. However, these approaches incur energy losses and high additional costs in the case of batteries. Instead, data centers can maximize the use of the available green energy by matching the energy demand (computational work) to the supply.

The need to match energy demand and supply prompts many interesting research questions. For example, what kinds of data center workloads are amenable to green data centers? What kinds of techniques can we apply to better match the demand for energy to the variable energy supply? Should we allow programmers to specify what types of techniques can be used? How well can we predict solar and wind availability? If batteries are available, how should we manage them? Can we leverage geographical distribution to maximize our use of green energy? If we have a choice, where should be place green data centers to strike a good compromise between high energy generation and data center costs?

Researchers have started building software and hardware to address these questions, e.g. [5, 6, 7, 8, 9, 10, 11]. The next section describes some software efforts, whereas Section 4 describes Parasol, a solar-powered μdata center we just built at Rutgers.

3. SOFTWARE FOR GREEN DATA CENTERS

We have recently built two load-scheduling systems for green data centers: GreenSlot [5] and GreenHadoop [6]. Both systems assume that (1) the data center is connected to a solar array and the electrical grid, and (2) there are no batteries. Their goal is to maximize the use of solar energy; brown energy should only be consumed when solar energy is not available.

GreenSlot extends the SLURM scheduler for batch jobs. Green-Slot maximizes the solar energy consumption while meeting the jobs' deadlines. If brown energy must be used to avoid deadline violations, GreenSlot schedules jobs for times when brown energy is cheap. In more detail, it first predicts the amount of solar energy that will likely be available in the future, using historical data and weather forecasts. Based on its predictions and the information provided by users, it schedules the workload by creating resource reservations into the future. Whenever servers are not needed, GreenSlot transitions them to a sleep (ACPI S3) state.

Along similar lines, GreenHadoop extends the Hadoop data-processing framework. Scheduling the energy consumption of Hadoop jobs is challenging, because they do not specify the number of servers to use, their run times, or their energy needs. Moreover, power-managing servers here requires guaranteeing that the data to be accessed by the active jobs remains available. Besides managing energy consumption and brown energy costs, GreenHadoop manages the cost of peak brown power consumption.

Instead of adapting to the availability of green energy through job scheduling, researchers from UMass Amherst have proposed to modulate the servers' duty cycle using fast sleep states [10]. In contrast, researchers from UC Berkeley have proposed to adjust the quality of the replies provided to users in interactive workloads [7]. For mixed interactive and batch workloads, researchers from UC San Diego have proposed to adapt the amount of batch processing dynamically [1]. Finally, several groups have considered load distribution across green data centers to "follow the renewables", e.g. [8, 9, 11].

4. PARASOL: OUR GREEN DATA CENTER

Parasol is our research platform for studying the use of renewable energy in data centers. It comprises a small container, a set of solar panels, and batteries. The container lies on a steel structure placed on the roof of our building. The 16 solar panels are mounted on top of the steel structure and shade the container from the sun most of the time. We expect that the panels will produce up to 3KW of AC power (after derating). Figure 1 shows the steel structure, the container, and the solar panels.

The container hosts two racks of energy-efficient IT equipment. The racks currently host 64 Atom-based half-U servers equipped with solid-state drives, but we will install many more of these servers soon (the maximum capacity of Parasol is roughly 150 of these servers). The container uses free cooling whenever possible, and direct-exchange air conditioning (HVAC) otherwise. Our desire to study free cooling is the main reason we place the servers on the roof, rather than inside our building. Besides the solar panels, Parasol can draw energy from its batteries and/or the electrical grid. Three manual switches enable different configurations for the supply of energy. For example, we can configure Parasol to operate completely off the electrical grid.

Parasol includes an extensive monitoring infrastructure to quantify resource utilization, power generation and consumption, server

Figure 1: Final stage of the construction of Parasol.

and data center temperatures, and air flow and quality. A powerful server located in one of the racks collects all the monitoring information and backs it up to our main laboratory.

Acknowledgements

I am very grateful to my collaborators in this area: Josep L. Berral, Íñigo Goiri, Jordi Guitart, Md E. Haque, William Katsak, Kien Le, Margaret Martonosi, Thu D. Nguyen, and Jordi Torres. My group's research has been partially funded by NSF grants CSR-0916518 and CSR-1117368, and the Rutgers Green Computing Initiative.

5. REFERENCES

[1] B. Aksanli et al. Utilizing Green Energy Prediction to Schedule Mixed Batch and Service Jobs in Data Centers. In *HotPower*, 2011.

[2] Data Center Knowledge. Apple Plans 20MW of Solar Power for iDataCenter, 2012. http://www.datacenterknowledge.com/archives/2012/02/20/-apple-plans-20mw-of-solar-power-for-idatacenter/.

[3] DSIRE. Database of State Incentives for Renewables and Efficiency. http://www.dsireusa.org/.

[4] EcobusinessLinks. Green Hosting - Sustainable Solar & Wind Energy Web Hosting, 2012. http://www.ecobusinesslinks.com/green_web_hosting.htm.

[5] I. Goiri et al. GreenSlot: Scheduling Energy Consumption in Green Datacenters. In *Supercomputing*, 2011.

[6] I. Goiri et al. GreenHadoop: Leveraging Green Energy in Data-Processing Frameworks. In *EuroSys*, 2012.

[7] A. Krioukov et al. Design and Evaluation of an Energy Agile Computing Cluster. Technical Report EECS-2012-13, UC Berkeley, 2012.

[8] K. Le et al. Cost- And Energy-Aware Load Distribution Across Data Centers. In *HotPower*, 2009.

[9] Z. Liu et al. Greening Geographical Load Balancing. In *SIGMETRICS*, 2011.

[10] N. Sharma et al. Blink: Managing Server Clusters on Intermittent Power. In *ASPLOS*, 2011.

[11] C. Stewart and K. Shen. Some Joules Are More Precious Than Others: Managing Renewable Energy in the Datacenter. In *HotPower*, 2009.

[12] Technology Roadmap – Solar Photovoltaic Energy. International Energy Agency, 2010. http://www.iea.org.

[13] US Environmental Protection Agency. Report to Congress on Server and Data Center Energy Efficiency, 2007.

Work Stealing and Persistence-based Load Balancers for Iterative Overdecomposed Applications

Jonathan Lifflander
University of Illinois
Urbana-Champaign
jliffl2@illinois.edu

Sriram Krishnamoorthy
Pacific Northwest National Lab
sriram@pnnl.gov

Laxmikant V. Kale
University of Illinois
Urbana-Champaign
kale@illinois.edu

ABSTRACT

Applications often involve iterative execution of identical or slowly evolving calculations. Such applications require incremental rebalancing to improve load balance across iterations. In this paper, we consider the design and evaluation of two distinct approaches to addressing this challenge: persistence-based load balancing and work stealing. The work to be performed is overdecomposed into *tasks*, enabling automatic rebalancing by the middleware. We present a hierarchical persistence-based rebalancing algorithm that performs localized incremental rebalancing. We also present an active-message-based *retentive* work stealing algorithm optimized for iterative applications on distributed memory machines. We demonstrate low overheads and high efficiencies on the full NERSC Hopper (146,400 cores) and ALCF Intrepid systems (163,840 cores), and on up to 128,000 cores on OLCF Titan.

Categories and Subject Descriptors

D.1.3 [**Programming Techniques**]: Concurrent Programming—*Parallel programming*; J.2 [**Physical Sciences and Engineering**]: Chemistry

Keywords

dynamic load balancing, work stealing, persistence, iterative applications, task scheduling, hierarchical load balancer

1. INTRODUCTION

Applications often involve iterative execution of identical or slowly evolving calculations. Many such applications exhibit significant complexity and runtime variation to preclude effective static load balancing, requiring incremental rebalancing to improve load balance over successive iterations.

A popular approach to addressing the load balancing challenge is *overdecomposition*. Rather than parallelize to a specific processor core count, the application-writer exposes parallelism by decomposing work into medium-grained tasks.

Each task is coarse enough to enable efficient execution (tiling, vectorization, etc.) and potential migration, while being fine enough to expose significantly higher application-level parallelism than is required by the hardware. This allows the middleware to manage the mapping of the tasks to processor cores, and rebalance them as needed.

This paper focuses on balancing the computational load across processor cores for overdecomposed applications, where static or start-time approaches are insufficient in achieving effective load balance. Such applications require periodic rebalancing of the load to ensure continued efficiency.

Applications that retain the computation balance over iterations, with gradual change, are said to adhere to the *principle of persistence*. Persistence-based load balancers redistribute the work to be performed in a given iteration based on measured performance profiles from previous iterations. We present a hierarchical persistence-based load balancing algorithm that attempts to localize the rebalance operations and migration of tasks. The algorithm greedily rebalances "excess" load rather than attempting a globally optimal partition, which could potentially incur high space overheads.

Work stealing is an attractive alternative for applications with significant load imbalance within a phase, or applications with workloads that cannot be easily profiled. Work stealing ameliorates these problems by actively attempting to find work until termination of the phase is detected. This approach has been successfully employed in domains where the load imbalance cannot be computed a priori or varies significantly across consecutive invocations [19]. We present an active-message-based work stealing algorithm optimized for iterative applications on distributed memory machines. The algorithm minimizes the number of remote roundtrip latencies incurred, reduces the duration of locked operations, and takes into account data transfer time when stealing tasks across the communication network. *Retentive* work stealing augments this algorithm with knowledge of execution profiles from the previous iteration to enable incremental rebalancing.

The scalability and overheads incurred by these algorithms are evaluated using candidate benchmarks. We observe that the persistence-based load balancer produces effective load distributions with low overheads. We demonstrate work stealing at over an order of magnitude higher scale than prior published results. While more scalable than widely believed, work stealing does not perform as well as persistence-based load balancing. Retentive stealing, which borrows from the persistence-based load balancer to retain information from the previous iteration, is shown to adapt better to iterative applications, achieving higher efficiencies and lower stealing overheads.

The primary contributions of this paper are:

- A hierarchical persistence-based load balancing algorithm that performs greedy localized rebalancing
- An active-message-based retentive work stealing algorithm optimized for distributed memory machines
- First comparative evaluation of persistence-based load balancing and work stealing
- Most scalable demonstration of work stealing — on up to 163,840 cores
- Demonstration of the benefits of retentive stealing in incrementally rebalancing iterative applications

2. CHALLENGES

An effective load balancer should achieve good load balance at scale while incurring low overheads. In particular, the cost of rebalancing should be related to the degree of imbalance incurred and not the total work. In an iterative application, the load balancing overhead should decrease as the calculation evolves towards a stable state, increasing only when the application induces additional load imbalance.

Persistence-based load balancers cannot adapt to immediate load imbalance and incur periodic rebalancing overheads. If a processor runs out of work too early in a phase, it needs to wait until the end of the phase for the imbalance to be identified and corrected. Minimizing task migration for such load balancers can be beneficial by retaining data locality and topology-awareness that guided the initial distribution.

Work stealing algorithms typically employ random stealing to quickly propagate available work. This interferes with locality optimizations and topology-aware distributions. Termination detection is a challenge at scale on distributed-memory machines. While hierarchical termination detectors approximate the cost of tree-based reduce operations in principle, they incur higher costs in practice. Termination detectors run concurrent with the application, introducing additional overheads throughout the application's execution.

The cost of stealing itself is significant on a distributed-memory machine due to the associated communication latency and time to migrate the stolen work. Work stealing also ignores prior rebalancing, incurring repeated stealing costs across iterations. Due to these reasons, work stealing has traditionally been confined to shared-memory systems. In addition, given all the "noise" introduced by work stealing, it is typically employed in applications that incur significant load imbalance and are not amenable to an initial distribution. Typical approaches to distributed-memory load balancing consider hierarchical schemes due to the perceived limitations associated with work stealing.

3. RELATED WORK

Load imbalance is a well-known problem and has been widely studied in the literature. Applications involving regular data structures, such as dense matrices, achieve load balance by choosing a data distribution (e.g., multipartitioning [12]) and carefully orchestrating communication. These approaches are specialized for regular computations and do not directly extend to other classes.

Iterative calculations on less regular structures (e.g., sparse matrices [7] or meshes [28]) employ an inspector-executor approach to load balancing where the data and associated computation balance is analyzed at runtime before the start of the first iteration to rebalance the work (e.g., CHAOS [13]) Typical approaches to such start-time load balancing employ a partitioning scheme [18]. Scalable parallelization of such partitioners [8, 21] is non-trivial.

Overdecomposition is instantiated in a variety of forms by different compilers and runtimes, including Cilk [5], Intel Thread Building Blocks [24], OpenMP [16], Charm++ [20], Concurrent Collections [9], and ParalleX [17]. Many application frameworks that understand domain-specific data structures implicitly employ this approach [11].

Charm++ [20] supports a variety of persistence-based load balancing algorithms. The typical approach involves gathering statistics for objects, measuring the amount of imbalance, and executing the corresponding rebalancing algorithms in either a centralized or hierarchical [29] fashion. Such hierarchical persistence-based load balancers are employed in several scalable applications [23]. Unlike the hierarchical schemes considered by Zheng et al. [29], we focus on the development of a localized rebalancing algorithm that also incurs lower space overheads due to greedy rebalancing.

Irregular algorithms whose workload cannot be predicted at start-time, or work partitioned into sub-units, pose a significant challenge to the above load balancing approaches. Applications in this class include state-space search, combinatorial optimization, and recursive parallel codes. Work stealing is a popular approach to load balancing such applications. Cilk [5] is a widely-studied depth-first scheduling algorithm for fully-strict computations with optimal space and time bounds. It has been shown to scale well on shared memory machines and implementations are available for networks of workstations [6] and wide-area networks [27]. Prior work on extending work stealing to distributed-memory adapted the algorithm to employ remote memory access (RMA) operations using ARMCI [22], demonstrating scaling to 8192 cores [14]. An implementation in X10 extended this algorithm to reduce the interference caused by steal operations [25]. These approaches employed work stealing in a memoryless fashion. We present work stealing for distributed-memory machines using a threaded active message library developed on MPI, demonstrating scaling to significantly higher core counts.

Work stealing has not been evaluated at this scale (100,000+ cores on multiple platforms) for any application on any hardware platform using any prior algorithm. The largest prior demonstration was on up to 8192 cores [14]. The domains employing work stealing and persistence-based load balancing have traditionally been disjoint. We are not aware of any prior work comparing the effectiveness of these two schemes for iterative applications, or any other application domain.

4. PROGRAMMING MODEL

The algorithms presented in this paper are implemented in the context of a MPI-based runtime library. The runtime acts both as a user-level library for distributed memory task-based execution and as the runtime target for language constructs such as X10 async [10] that support non-SPMD execution modes. All processes in a group or an MPI communicator collectively switch between SPMD and task processing phases. The code snippet below illustrates the repeated execution of a task processing phase as part of an iterative application. Throughout the paper, we employ

C++ style notation except for a few shorthands in place of detailed implementation-specific API.

```
TslFuncRegTbl *frt = new TslFuncRegTbl();
TslFunc tf = frt->add(taskFunc);
TaskCollProps props;
props.functions(tf,frt)
    .taskSize(sizeof(Task))
    .localData(&procLocalObj,sizeof(procLocalObj))
    .maxTasks(localQueueSize);
UniformTaskCollSplit utc(props); //collective
for (..) {
  Task task(..); //setup task
  utc.addTask(&task, sizeof(Task)); //local operation
}
while(..) {
  utc.process(); //collective
  utc.restore(); //implicit collective
}
```

The fundamental construct in the computation is a task collection seeded with one or more tasks. The library supports several task collection variants, each specialized to exploit specific properties of the task collection known at runtime. The above example shows a task collection, called UniformTaskCollectionSplit, which optimizes for a collection of tasks of identical size, with a known upper bound on the number of tasks on any individual processor core, and additional information common across all tasks (provided as the opaque struct procLocalObj). Function pointers associated with a task execution are translated into portable handles using the function registration table, TslFuncRegTbl. These properties are used to construct a task collection object that implements the split queue work stealing algorithm, explained in Section 6. The choice of task collection can be explicitly specified by the programmer or chosen by the runtime depending on the task collection properties specified. The task collection objects are collectively created on a per-process or a per-thread basis.

The task collection objects are then seeded with tasks to begin execution. This allows for distributed locality-aware initialization. The copy overhead of task insertion in the above illustration can be avoided through in-place task initialization. The task collection, once seeded, is processed in a collective fashion using the process() method. Tasks, during their execution, can create additional tasks to be executed as part of the same or another task collection. The process() method returns when all tasks, seeded and subsequently created, have been executed and the task collection is empty, determined through a distributed termination detection algorithm. The process() method is the runtime equivalent of an X10 finish statement and corresponds to a *terminally-strict* sub-computation.

In an iterative computation, the task queue can be restored to its state prior to invocation of process() using the restore() method. This resets the termination detector and the task distribution enabling re-execution of the task collection. Execution profiles from the previous execution of the task collection can be used to adapt the seeding of tasks and scheduling algorithms employed for subsequent iterations.

5. PERSISTENCE-BASED LOAD BALANCER

On each processor core, the persistence-based load balancer collects statistical data on the durations of each task executed in the current iteration. This load database is then

---

Algorithm 1 Centralized load balancer

$peLoad \Leftarrow \{ \text{ this processor's load } \}$
$lbD \Leftarrow \{ \text{ database of tasks } \}$
$localTaskPool \Leftarrow \{ \text{ empty task pool } \}$
$sumLoad \Leftarrow \{ \text{ distributed reduction } \}$
$avgLoad \Leftarrow \dfrac{sumLoad}{number\ of\ cores}$
while $peLoad > C \cdot avgLoad$ **do**
   $task \Leftarrow removeSmallestTask(lbD)$
   $addTask(localTaskPool, task)$
   $peLoad\ \text{-=}\ getDuration(task)$
end while
$sendTo0(localTaskPool, peLoad)$
if $processor = 0$ **then**
   $taskPool \Leftarrow \{ \text{ received tasks } \}$
   $peLoads \Leftarrow \{ \text{ load for each PE } \}$
   $makeMaxHeap(taskPool)$
   $makeMinHeap(peLoads)$
   while $t \Leftarrow removeMaxTask(taskPool)$ **do**
     $assign(t, getMinPE(peLoads))$
   end while
   $\{ \text{ send out new tasks to each PE } \}$
else
   $\{ \text{ receive new load from PE 0 } \}$
end if

---

used to rebalance the load for the next iteration after the current iteration has terminated.

The first step in utilizing the persistence properties that an application might exhibit is collecting data. Each task that is executed by a core is timed and stored in a local database. Storing the exact duration of each task (assuming a double-precision timer), requires $\Theta(n)$ doubles and $\Theta(n)$ task descriptors, where n is the number of tasks that each core executes. To reduce the amount of storage required, the scheduler times each task, truncates the duration, and bins it with other tasks that are of approximately the same duration. This reduces the storage to $\Theta(n) + b$, where n is the number of task descriptors and b is the number of bins. These bins are kept in a sorted structure, allowing the load balancer to access the database in roughly duration order.

5.1 Centralized Load Balancing

The baseline strategy, referred to as the centralized scheme, performs load balancing on one core, much like RefineLB as described by Zheng et al. [29]. Algorithm 1 details this strategy. First, the average load is calculated in parallel using a sum-reduction. If a core's load is sufficiently above the average load, the core removes the shortest duration task from its load database and moves it into a local task pool, until its load is below a constant, referred to as C, times the average load. These tasks (descriptors that compactly represent the task) in the local task pool, along with the core's new load, are sent to core 0, which attempts to redistribute the load.

Core 0 receives the donated tasks from overloaded cores, storing them into a task pool. It also receives each core's total load. From this data it creates a min-heap of the loads of each core and a max-heap of the durations in the task pool. It then assigns the longest task to the most underloaded core until the task pool is empty. These assignments are then sent to the cores.

To maximize the scalability of this approach, the local task pool from each core is collected on core 0 using MPI_Gatherv, and new assignments are redistributed using MPI_Scatterv.

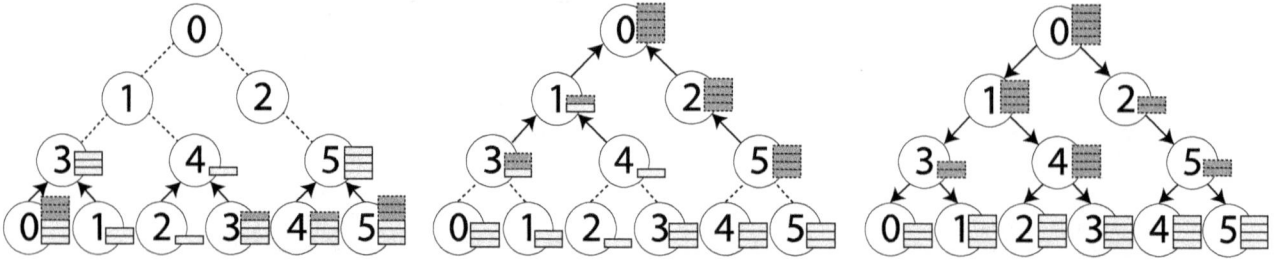

(a) All the leaves of the tree send their excess load (any load above a constant, referred to as C, times the average load) to their parent, selecting the work units from shortest duration to longest.

(b) Each core receives excess load from its children and saves work for underloaded children until their load is above a constant D times the average load. Remaining tasks are sent to the parent.

(c) Starting at the root, the excess load is distributed to each child applying the centralized greedy algorithm: maximum-duration task is assigned to minimum-loaded child.

Figure 1: The hierarchical persistence-based load balancing algorithm for 6 cores. The rectangles represent work units; a shaded rectangle with a dotted border indicates the work unit moves during that step.

5.2 Hierarchical Load Balancing

Algorithm 2 details the procedure and Figure 1 illustrates the structure of the load-balancing tree. The cores are organized as an n-ary tree where every core is a leaf. First, the average load across all cores is determined. Each core locally chooses its shortest tasks to donate while reducing its anticipated load to be below the average times a threshold.

An underloaded core contains an empty set of tasks to be donated. Each core then sends its load information together with the set of donated tasks to its parent. Each core above the first level in the tree then receives the tasks and load from each child. These cores redistribute the donated tasks to balance the lightly loaded cores using the same procedure as the centralized algorithm. Each core then sends the total surplus or deficit in its sub-tree, together with donated tasks left over from the distribution, to its parent. This algorithm is repeated recursively up the tree to the root. The root redistributes leftover tasks down the tree to further improve load balance. Any tasks provided by a core's parent are redistributed down the tree to the leaf nodes, where they are enqueued for the next iteration.

This algorithm is greedy since it locally optimizes for the children of a node as work moves up the tree, assigning tasks to underloaded children, and down the tree to distribute the work. The average child load (total load of that subtree divided by the subtree size) at each node is used to make a local decision about which child to assign work. Such a greedy approach reduces communication and the amount of storage required at each level by considering only the immediate children and assigning them work immediately. This also reduces the amount of time to rebalance at each level because fewer tasks must be considered. In addition, tasks are assigned to locally deficit cores, better preserving data and topology locality than the centralized rebalancing scheme.

On the other hand, the quality of the load balance may diminish when the tree is extremely unbalanced because local decisions based on averages do not cause work to be migrated aggressively. Also, when there is a great disparity in the work unit size, large work units may be assigned to a locally deficit core rather than the most underloaded core, not effectively addressing the load imbalance problem.

Note that tasks themselves can be distributed directly from the donating core to the designated core, rather than through the tree. The greedy algorithm can also be applied to other organizations of the cores (e.g., torus) to better match the underlying communication network's topology.

Algorithm 2 Hierarchical greedy load balancer

$peLoad \Leftarrow \{$ this processor's load $\}$
$lbD \Leftarrow \{$ database of tasks $\}$
$localTaskPool \Leftarrow \{$ empty task pool $\}$
$sumLoad \Leftarrow \{$ distributed reduction $\}$
$avgLoad \Leftarrow \dfrac{sumLoad}{number\ of\ cores}$
while $peLoad > C \cdot avgLoad$ **do**
  $task \Leftarrow removeSmallestTask(lbD)$
  $addTask(localTaskPool, task)$
  $peLoad\ \text{-=}\ getDuration(task)$
end while
$sendToParent(localTaskPool, peLoad)$
$\{$ wait for children $\}$
if processor is not root **then**
  $\{$ wait for children $\}$
  $taskPool \Leftarrow \{$ received tasks $\}$
  $peLoads \Leftarrow \{$ load for each child PE $\}$
  $makeMaxHeap(taskPool)$
  $makeMinHeap(peLoads)$
  while $t \Leftarrow removeMaxTask(taskPool)\ \wedge$
      $getMinPELoad(peLoads) < D \cdot avgLoad$ **do**
    $assign(t, getMinPE(peLoads))$
  end while
else
  $\{$ wait for children $\}$
end if
if processor is not leaf **then**
  $taskPool \Leftarrow \{$ received tasks $\}$
  $peLoads \Leftarrow \{$ load for each child PE $\}$
  $makeMaxHeap(taskPool)$
  $makeMinHeap(peLoads)$
  while $t \Leftarrow removeMaxTask(taskPool)$ **do**
    $assign(t, getMinPE(peLoads))$
  end while
  for all p in children **do**
    $sendTasks(p)$
  end for
else
  $\{$ wait to receive tasks $\}$
  $\{$ add tasks to pool $\}$
end if

---

6. RETENTIVE WORK STEALING

In this section, we present our implementation of distributed memory work stealing. Work stealing begins with all participating cores seeded with zero or more tasks. A core with local work takes the role of a worker, processing local tasks, as long as they are available. Once local work is exhausted, a worker becomes a thief, searching for other available work. A thief randomly chooses a victim and attempts to steal work from the victim's collection of tasks. On a successful steal, a thief returns to the worker state, continuing to process its local tasks. This procedure repeats until all workers have exhausted their tasks and termination is detected.

The randomness in the choice of the victim ensures quick distribution of work even in highly imbalanced cases (e.g., only one worker starts with all the work). If sufficient parallel slack is present, generally more cores will be in worker state rather than searching for work as a thief. Therefore, work stealing implementations, as pioneered by Cilk, attempt to avoid the overheads of synchronization or atomic operations on the executing worker, forcing much of the synchronization overhead on the thieves.

Shared memory implementations employ a deque in which the worker inserts the tasks on one end (referred to as the *head*), while thieves steal from the other end (the *tail*). Fence instructions are employed by the worker to ensure that its insertions at the head are visible to potential thieves in the correct order. A thief obtains a lock on the deque to preclude other concurrent steals. More details of the algorithm can be found in Blumofe et al. [5]

We employ a distributed-memory work stealing algorithm that considers the differing costs involved in distributed-memory machines.

```
Task taskBuf[BSIZE];//array holding tasks on the deque
Lock lock; //lock to arbitrate access to the deque
int head; //head: accessed only by worker
volatile int split; //split: worker reads/writes; thief reads
volatile int stail; //position of next steal; thief reads/writes;
        worker reads
volatile int itail; //intermediate tail: worker reads, thief writes
int ctail; //completed tail: accessed only by worker
Initial values:
    lock.unlock();
    head = split = stail = itail = ctail = 0;
```

A distributed-memory implementation of work stealing requires tasks to be copied to local memory, rather than just obtaining a pointer. On many architectures, such data transfer is more efficient from a contiguous memory rather than an arbitrary data structure (such as a linked list of tasks). We therefore employ a bounded-buffer circular deque implementation on a fixed-sized array.

The operations on the deque are depicted in Figures 2, 3, and 4. The dotted arrows correspond to locked or atomic operations, while the vertical dotted lines depict updated values for the variables being modified.

Each worker (a processor core in our case) allocates such a deque and associated state variables. The reuse of taskBuf allows it to reside in "registered" memory, enabling efficient data transfer. Rather than allowing all tasks in the deque to be stolen by a thief, we employ a split deque. All tasks between head and split are local to the worker owning the deque and cannot be stolen by a thief. This enables a worker to add and remove tasks at the head, without the potential need for fence instructions. The tasks past the split are in the shared portion of the deque and are available for stealing by thieves.

Individual remote memory operations (obtaining a lock, adjusting indices, releasing a lock, etc.) incur significant latencies. This not only increases the cost of a steal but slows down work propagation by precluding other steals. In order to enable contesting thieves to make quick progress, a split-phase stealing protocol is employed so that stolen tasks can be concurrently transferred while other thieves make progress. The shared portion between split and stail represents tasks that are available to be stolen. The shared portion between stail and ctail corresponds to stolen tasks that are being copied into the thieves' local memories.

The state of the deque can be identified by the following:

```
bool full() {
    return head==ctail && (split!=head || split!=ctail);
}
bool sharedEmpty() { return split==stail; }
bool localEmpty() { return head==split; }
int sharedSize() { return (split−stail+BSIZE)%BSIZE;}
int localSize() { return (head−split+BSIZE)%BSIZE;}
```

Note that the state of the deque queried without holding a lock is speculative if any of the variables associated with computing the state is marked as volatile. The only exception is split, which can only be modified by the worker and therefore can be read by it without holding the lock.

Adding a task into the deque by a worker (addTask()) involves inserting the task at the head. The method also resets the space available for insertion by adjusting ctail. This employs the invariant:

$$(\text{itail}==\text{stail}) \equiv \text{no pending steals on taskBuf[stail..ctail]} \quad (1)$$

```
void releaseToShared(int sz) {
    memfence();
    split = (split+sz)%BSIZE;
}
void addTask(Task task) {
    do {
        if(itail==stail) ctail = stail;
    } while(full());
    taskBuf[head] = task;
    head = (head+1)%BSIZE;
    if (sharedEmpty())
        releaseToShared(localSize() / 2);
}
```

When a worker observes the shared portion of its deque to be empty, it releases tasks from its local portion, shown by the routine releaseToShared(). Note that a memory fence operation is required while adding or getting tasks only when releasing work to the shared portion of the deque.

```
bool acquireFromShared() {
    lock();
    if(sharedEmpty()) return false;
    int nacquire = min(sharedSize()/2,1);
    split = (split − nacquire + BSIZE) % BSIZE;
    unlock();
    return true;
}
bool getTask(Task *task) {
    if(localEmpty())
        if(!acquireFromShared()) return false;
    *task = taskBuf[head];
    head = (head − 1 + BSIZE) % BSIZE;
    if (sharedEmpty())
        releaseToShared(localSize() / 2);
    return true;
}
```

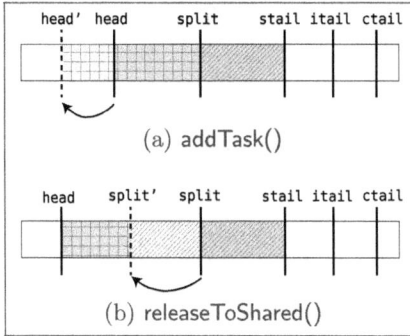

(a) addTask()

(b) releaseToShared()

Figure 2: Routines related to adding tasks into the deque

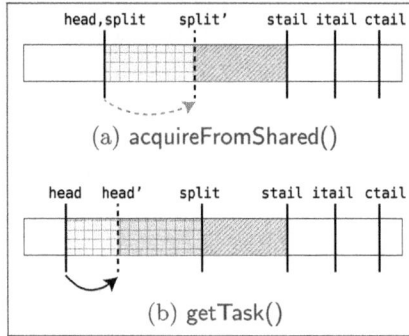

(a) acquireFromShared()

(b) getTask()

Figure 3: Routines for a worker getting tasks from its deque

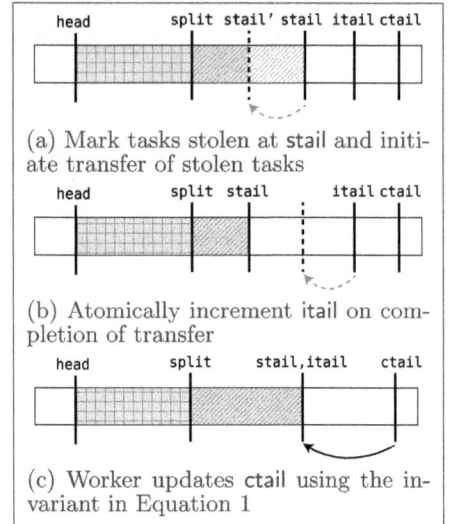

(a) Mark tasks stolen at stail and initiate transfer of stolen tasks

(b) Atomically increment itail on completion of transfer

(c) Worker updates ctail using the invariant in Equation 1

Figure 4: Steps in a steal operation

	HF-Be256	HF-Be512 (20/40)	TCE
Total tasks	84.9M	21.7B / 1.36B	470K
Non-null tasks	213K	9.10M / 862K	470K

Table 1: Number of tasks in first (all tasks) and subsequent iterations (non-null tasks). The chunk size for HF-Be512 is shown in parentheses.

Extracting a task from the deque first involves transferring tasks from the shared to the local portion, if the local portion is empty. The task at the head is then returned.

When a worker runs out of local work (getTask() returns false), it attempts to steal work from a random worker proc. This is implemented as an active message executed on the victim. The block of code executed as an active message is annotated by @proc in the code snippet. The victim's deque is locked and any tasks to be stolen are marked (using stail) before unlocking the deque. The stolen tasks are then transferred to the thief through an asynchronous operation (sendResponse()). When that operation is complete (detected by other runtime system components), the completion is noted in the deque by atomically updating itail. Note that multiple thieves could initiate the transfer of stolen tasks and complete the transfers out-of-order. Hence, ctail, which denotes completed steals, cannot be updated by a thief upon completion of its transfer, but needs to be updated by the worker using the invariant shown in Equation 1.

```
bool steal(int proc) {
  if(hasTerminated()) return false;
  //post a recv for incoming response
  @proc { //active message executed on proc
    lock();
    if(sharedEmpty()) { sendResponse(NULL); }
    int nsteal = min((sharedSize()+1)/2, BSIZE-stail);
    int oldtail = stail;
    int newtail = (stail + nsteal) % BSIZE;
    int nshift = newtail - oldtail;
    stail = newtail;
    unlock();
    sreq = sendResponse(taskBuf[oldtail..(oldtail+nsteal)]);
    when sreq.localComplete() {
      atomic itail += nshift;
    }
  }
  //wait on recv
  if(recvSize()>0) {
    lock();
    // adjust head, split, ...
    unlock();
    return true;
  }
  return false;
}
```

The stolen tasks are directly transferred from the victim's deque to the thief's deque, without additional copy operations. In the meanwhile, any attempts to steal from the thief would fail since the state variables denote the deque to be empty. On completion of a successful data transfer, and receipt of non-zero number of tasks, the state variables are updated under a lock to denote the availability of tasks.

```
void process() {
  while (!hasTerminated()) {
    Task task;
    while (getTask(&task)) {
      executeTask(&task);
    }
    bool got_work = false;
    while(got_work == false && !hasTerminated()) {
      do {
        p = rand() % nproc();
      } while (p == me());
      got_work = steal(p);
    }
  }
}
```

The overall execution procedure is shown above. All participating processor cores execute this routine. Each core executes all local tasks in the worker role, then turns into a thief searching for work. On finding work, the thief turns back into a worker. This cycle is repeated until termination is detected.

The tasks executed by each core are logged throughout the execution. In the next iteration, the processing begins with each core's local queue seeded with tasks executed by it in the previous iteration. Given that work stealing attempts to dynamically balance the load each time it runs, this retained task distribution is anticipated to be more balanced than the initial seeding.

Essentially by retaining the previous execution profile, the advantages of persistence-based load balancing are applied to work stealing, and depending on the degree to which the persistence principle applies, the number of attempted and successful steals diminish in subsequent iterations with this optimization (shown in Figures 8 and 9). This strategy also maintains the primary advantage of work stealing: the ability of the runtime to adapt to major dynamic imbalances during an iteration.

```
set<Task> executedTasks;
void executeTask(Task task) {
  executedTasks.insert(task);
  // execute task
}
void restore() {
  foreach task in executedTasks {
    addTask(task);
  }
  executedTasks.clear();
}
while(..) {
  process();
  restore();
}
```

Note that the balance determined by the work stealing algorithm includes associated overheads. Therefore significant imbalance, together with work stealing, can still be expected in subsequent iterations. In Section 7, we show that this approach incrementally improves the load balance while also reducing the work stealing overheads.

Termination detection is done using Francez's termination detection algorithm [15], involving a tree in which thieves propagate termination messages in the form of rounds up and down the tree. Any round is invalidated by a thief that was a victim of a steal since the last round. Termination is detected when all workers have turned thieves, participated in the termination detection procedure, and none of them have been stolen from since the last round. The organization of the workers/thieves into a tree results in a theoretical logarithmic overhead of termination detection after all tasks have been executed.

7. EXPERIMENTAL EVALUATION

The experiments were performed on three systems: Cray XE6 NERSC Hopper [2], IBM BG/P Intrepid [1], and Cray XK6 Titan [3]. Hopper is a 6384-node system, each node consisting of two twelve-core 2.1GHz AMD 'MagnyCours' processors and 32GB DDR3 memory. Titan is a 18688-node system, each node consisting of one sixteen-core 2.2GHz AMD 'Bulldozer' processor and 32GB DDR3 memory. Hopper and Titan employ the Gemini interconnection network with a peak of 9.8GB/s bandwidth per Gemini chip. The Intrepid system consists of 40960 nodes, each with one quad-core 850MHz PowerPC 450 processor and 2GB DDR2 memory.

Our codes were compiled using the Intel compiler suite versions 12.0.4.191 and 12.1.1.256 on Hopper and Titan, respectively. Cray MPICH2 XT versions 5.3.3 and 5.4.1 were used on Hopper and Titan, respectively. On Intrepid, our codes were compiled with IBM XL C/C++ version 9.0. All communication was performed using two-sided MPI operations (MPI_Isend(), MPI_Irecv(), and MPI_Wait()), except the collectives employed in the persistence-based load balancing, as specified in Section 5. We developed a thread-based implementation with one thread pinned to each core throughout the execution, all of them sharing data, with MPI initialized in MPI_THREAD_MULTIPLE mode. We evaluated various configurations by varying the number of worker threads and "server" threads, and found that the best performance (in all the configurations we evaluated) was achieved with 23 worker threads and 1 server thread on Hopper, 15 worker

threads and 1 server thread on Titan, and 3 worker threads and 1 server thread on Intrepid. We report all our results for these configurations. Given the server thread is still employed in communication progress for the application, we report all results as if the application is utilizing all the cores.

We evaluated the following schemes:

- **StealAll:** Work stealing of all tasks in the calculation
- **Steal:** Work stealing non-null tasks (same as StealAll for TCE)
- **StealRet:** Retentive work stealing on non-null tasks
- **PLB:** Persistence-based load balancing
- **Ideal:** Ideal scaling expected, for comparison

7.1 Benchmarks

The algorithms presented were evaluated using the following two benchmarks:

Tensor Contraction Expressions: Tensor Contraction Expressions (TCE) [4] comprise the entirety of Coupled Cluster methods, employed in accurate descriptions of manybody systems in diverse domains. Tensors are generalized multi-dimensional matrices organized into dense rectangular tiles. A tensor contraction can be viewed as a collection of tile-tile products. The sparsity in the tensors, which can be algebraically determined through inexpensive local integer operations, induces inhomonegenity in the computation of dense tile-tile contractions, which vary widely in their computational requirements, spanning in structure from inner products to outer products.

Hartree-Fock: The Hartree-Fock (HF) method is a single-determinant theory [26] that forms the basis for higher-level electronic structure theories such as Møller-Plesset perturbation theory and Coupled Cluster theory. The benchmark consists of the two-electron contribution component of Hartree-Fock, the computationally dominant part of the method. The work to be performed is divided into smaller units based on the user-specific tile size. The work to be performed is determined by the schwarz screening matrix. Unlike the TCE benchmark, the sparsity induced by the schwarz matrix depends on the specific input and cannot be determined at compile-time. The screening produces variability in the execution time of individual tasks and potentially results in *null* tasks, i.e., tasks that do not perform any work. These null tasks are pruned in subsequent iterations.

For the Hartree-Fock benchmark, we considered two different molecular systems for evaluation, one consisting of 256 beryllium atoms (HF-Be256) and the other 512 atoms (HF-Be512). The matrices involved in the Hartree-Fock calculation (schwarz, fock, and dens matrices) were block-cyclically distributed amongst the cores with a tile size of 40 for evaluation on Hopper. A tile size of 20 was used on Titan and Intrepid to expose additional parallelism and enable evaluation on larger core counts. The number of total and non-null tasks is shown in Table 1. Note that the number of non-null tasks quadruples when the number of atoms is doubled. The tasks themselves do not necessarily incur the same execution time due to the sparsity induced by the schwarz matrix.

For TCE, we evaluate the following expression:
$$C[i,j,k,l] += A[i,j,a,b] * B[a,b,k,l]$$

Each dimension is split into four spatial blocks. Indices $i, j, k,$ and l are organized into spatial blocks $240, 180, 100,$ and 210; indices a and b are of size 84 and are organized into spatial blocks $20, 24, 20,$ and 20. The tensors are partitioned into dense blocks with a tile size 20 and distributed in the global address space. Detailed explanation of the benchmark can be found in Baumgartner et al. [4]

We observed that applications converged faster to the best achievable efficiency on Hopper and present five iterations for each application. Both schemes required many more iterations to converge to the best possible efficiency on Titan and Intrepid. We present results for the first fourteen iterations on these systems. Complete results for all configurations considered are not presented due to space limitations.

Persistence-based load balancing is typically performed only when significant load imbalance is detected to amortize the cost of load balancing. We load balance every iteration to quickly evaluate the effectiveness of load balancing. For the experiments, the load balancer constants C (Algorithm 1) and D (Algorithm 2) were set to 1.003; the branching factor used in the hierarchical version was 3. The results presented do not include the load balancing cost, which is evaluated separately in section 7.3.

7.2 Scalability and Efficiency

The execution times of the various schemes for both applications are shown in Figure 5. For the HF benchmark, the execution time for stealing all tasks corresponds to the zero-th iteration of all runs, before pruning the null tasks, while other times presented correspond to the last iteration for the respective runs. Lines marking ideal speedup (with respect to the smallest core count shown in the corresponding graph as the baseline) are shown for comparison. For the HF benchmark, executing all tasks is significantly more expensive than executing only the non-null tasks. This is primarily due to the communication and computation associated with identifying the null tasks (checking the schwarz matrix). The schemes also scale well with increase in core count. Traditional work stealing scales better when executing all tasks, given the increased degree of available parallelism. This demonstrates that random work stealing can scale to large core counts provided sufficient parallelism.

When executing only the non-null tasks, work stealing is less scalable than the other approaches evaluated. Persistence-based load balancing and retentive stealing achieve the best performance. The TCE benchmark exhibits super-linear scaling due to the working set fitting in the cache. This effect is countered by load imbalance at higher scales. Retentive work stealing appears to address the problems associated with work stealing.

In order to better evaluate the observed performance and evolution of the schemes with iterations, we plotted their efficiency for each of the iterations on the non-null tasks. For each problem size, the efficiency is measured with respect to the best performance achieved by any of the schemes at any core count considered for that problem size.

The efficiency of retentive work stealing is shown in Figure 7. The efficiency of traditional work stealing is that achieved by the first iteration. Retentive work stealing steadily improves its efficiency with subsequent iterations; for HF-Be512 the best points achieve over 90% efficiency on 76,800 cores of Hopper, over 91% efficiency on 163,940 cores of Intrepid, and over 81% efficiency on 128,000 cores of Titan. Given that the effectiveness of work stealing is influenced by the parallel slack, we plot the average number of tasks, with error bars showing the standard deviation across different processor cores, for each core count. This plot shows the similarity of task distributions across the problem sizes. For

each problem size, the efficiency begins to deteriorate when less than 10 tasks per processor core are available on average. For a given number of tasks per processor core, the efficiency decreases with core count.

7.3 Cost and Effectiveness of Persistence-Based Load Balancers

In this section, we evaluate the effectiveness of the centralized and hierarchical persistence-based load balancers using micro-benchmarks constructed from the execution times for each task in the HF-Be256 run on Hopper. In order to simulate various degrees of load imbalance and stress the load balancers, the tasks are sorted by duration and distributed to the cores in a round-robin fashion, favoring every n-th core by giving it m tasks. For example, when $n = 2$ and $m = 4$ every other core receives 4 tasks, instead of 1 task.

By varying m and n, the performance of both schemes is evaluated under severe amounts of load imbalance. As the problem is scaled on more cores, due to the number of tasks remaining constant, much more load imbalance arises because there is more variance in duration between the tasks that each core selects. For example, when $n = 4$ and $m = 4$, on 2400 cores, the core with the highest load has 252% the average amount of work; on 38400 cores, the highest loaded core has 691% the average. As illustrated by these data points, the imbalance increases with the number of cores, necessitating that substantially more tasks be migrated.

Table 3 shows execution times and quality of the load balance achieved by both schemes on Hopper. The quality of load balance is measured as percentage deterioration in the execution time over the ideal load balance. The execution time for a given distribution of tasks is defined by the load on the core with the maximum load, while the ideal is the average of the load across all cores. Since the ideal load balance is not always achievable, we compare the hierarchical algorithm with the centralized algorithm.

The centralized load balancer achieves a consistently good load balance, given its global view of the computation at all scales. The variations in the load balance quality are due to the differences in tasks assigned to different cores. The hierarchical algorithm suffers from worse load balance quality due to the greedy rebalancing employed. At scale, the few tasks available per core exacerbates the challenges encountered by greedy rebalancing. However, it is still competitive given sufficient number of tasks to rebalance. The execution times of the load balancers clearly demonstrate the benefits of the hierarchical approach.

7.4 Quantifying Work Stealing Overheads

In order to study the improvements in performance obtained by retentive stealing, we measured the number of attempted and successful steals for the various problems. Figure 8 and Table 2 show the number of attempted steal operations for the first, second, and fifth iterations. We observe that the number of steals, of any form, does not increase dramatically with an increased process count. For example, on iteration 1 of HF-Be512 on Hopper, the average number of attempted steals decreases from 5661 on 9600 cores to 5471 on 38400 cores.

If sufficient parallelism is present, the number of steals is influenced more by the problem size and initial task distribution than the number of concurrent executing cores. When the degree of application parallelism dries out, as happens in

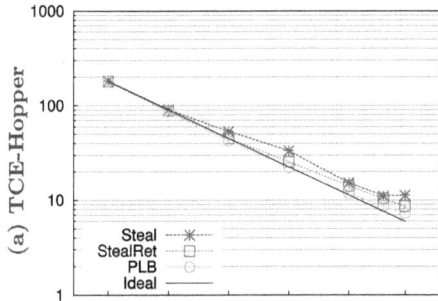

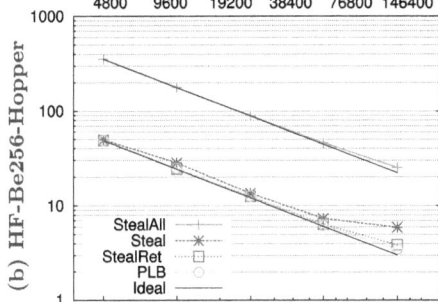

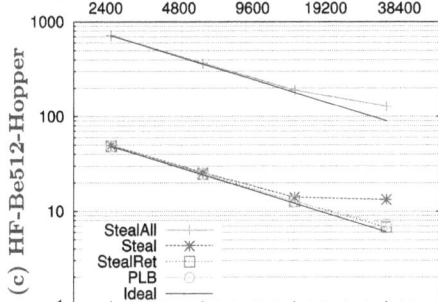

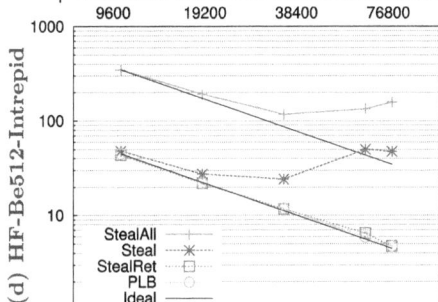

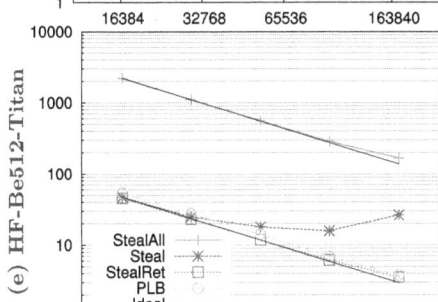

Figure 5: Execution times for first and last iteration. x-axis — number of cores; y-axis — execution time in seconds

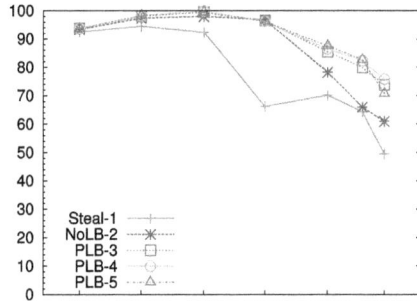

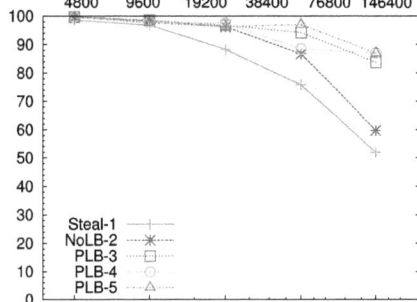

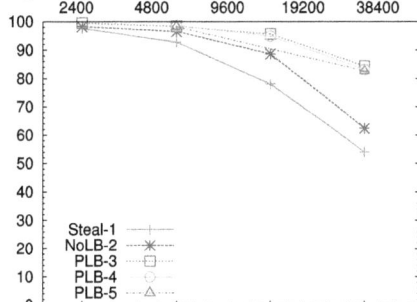

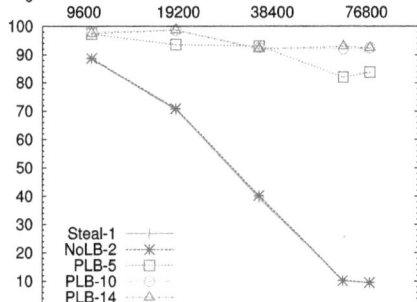

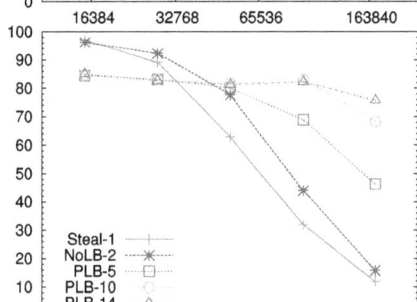

Figure 6: Efficiency of persistence-based load-balancing across iterations for the three system sizes, relative to the ideal anticipated speedup. x-axis — number of cores; y-axis — efficiency

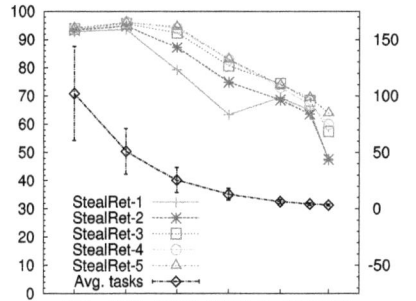

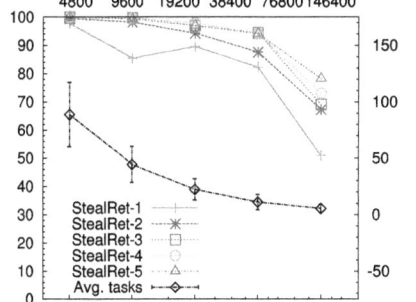

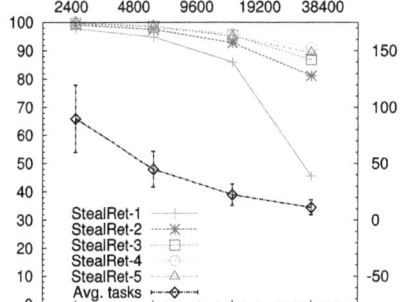

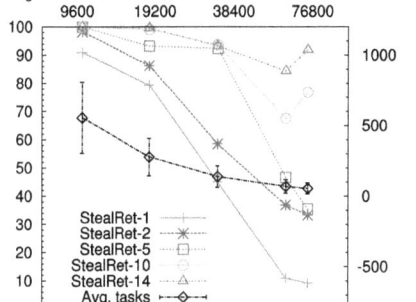

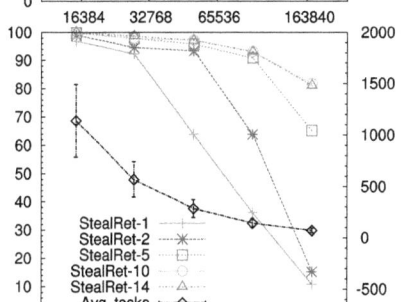

Figure 7: Efficiency of retentive work stealing across iterations relative to ideal anticipated speedup and tasks per core. x-axis — core count; left y-axis — efficiency; right y-axis — tasks per core (error bar: std. dev.)

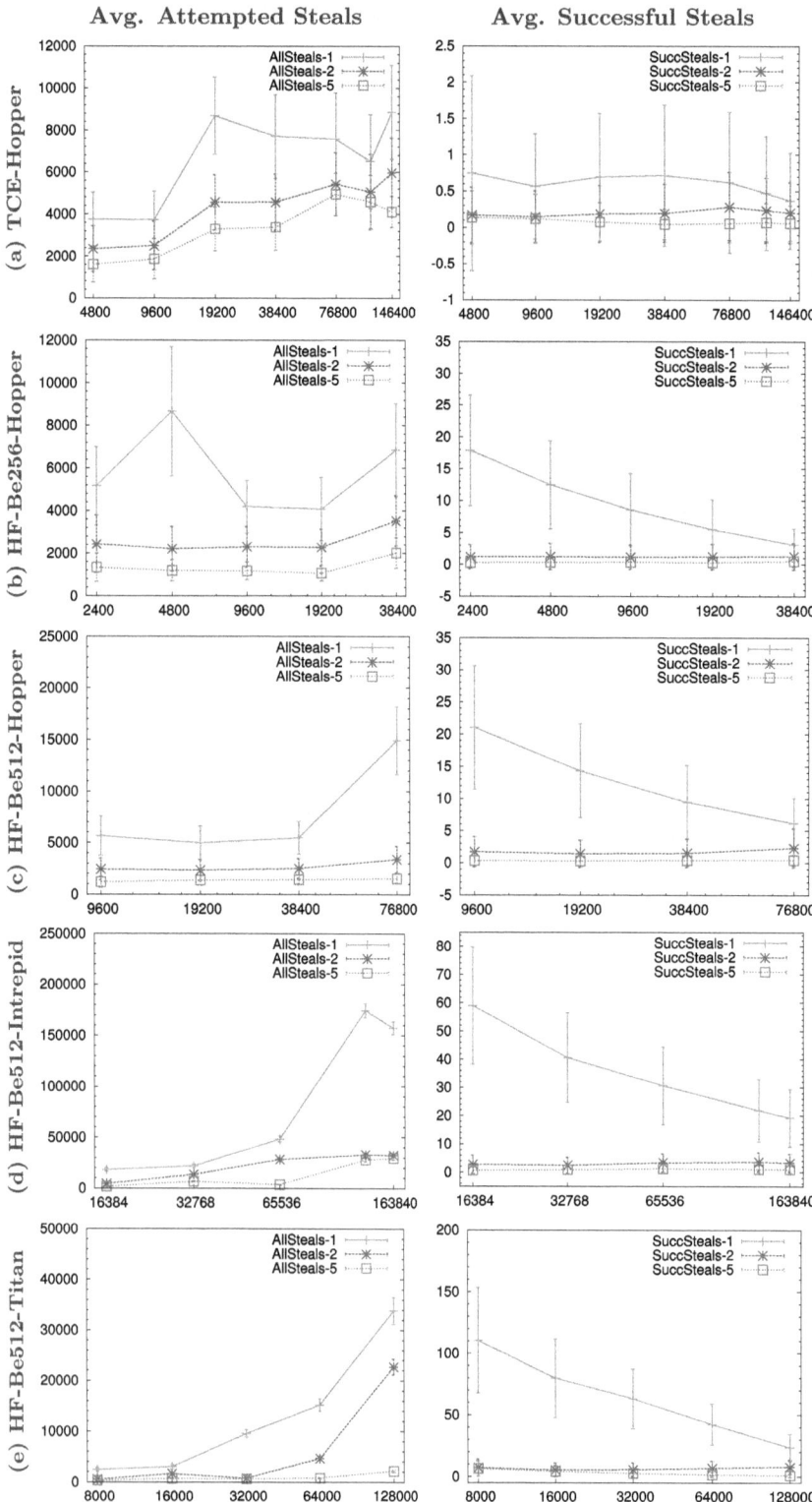

Avg. Attempted Steals

(a) TCE-Hopper · (b) HF-Be256-Hopper · (c) HF-Be512-Hopper · (d) HF-Be512-Intrepid · (e) HF-Be512-Titan

(Legends: AllSteals-1, AllSteals-2, AllSteals-5)

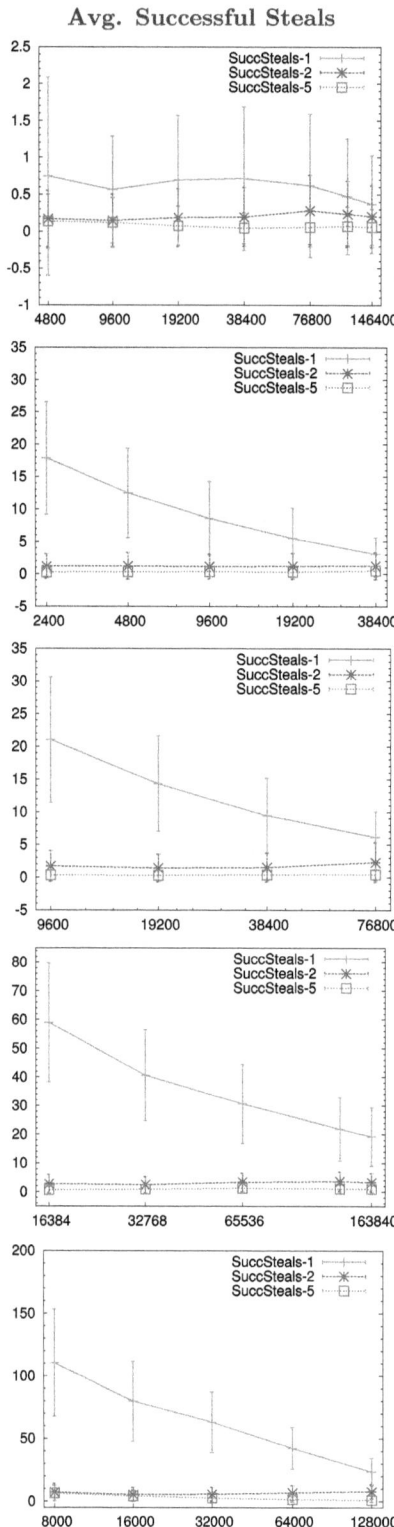

Avg. Successful Steals

(Legends: SuccSteals-1, SuccSteals-2, SuccSteals-5)

Iter	Avg / Std Attempted Successful		Avg / Std Attempted Successful	
	4800 Cores		9600 Cores	
1	3745/1294	0.7/1.3	3735/1350	0.6/0.7
2	2347/1086	0.2/0.4	2507/1155	0.1/0.4
5	1610/868	0.1/0.4	1864/964	0.1/0.3
	19200 Cores		38400 Cores	
1	8691/1840	0.7/0.9	7694/1987	0.7/1.0
2	4563/1306	0.2/0.4	4570/1325	0.2/0.4
5	3291/1049	0.1/0.3	3381/1095	0.04/0.2
	78600 Cores		146000 Cores	
1	7573/2196	0.6/1.0	8859/2238	0.4/0.7
2	5426/1496	0.3/0.5	5967/1663	0.2/0.4
5	4944/1019	0.1/0.2	4109/739	0.1/0.2
	2400 Cores		4800 Cores	
1	5168/1831	18/8.7	8662/3034	12/6.9
2	2436/1356	1.2/1.9	2209/1056	1.2/2.1
5	1333/667	0.3/0.7	1192/498	0.3/0.7
	9600 Cores		19200 Cores	
1	4190/1221	8.6/5.7	4073/1476	5.5/4.7
2	2298/966	1.1/1.9	2275/873	1.2/2
5	1171/412	0.3/0.8	1066/360	0.3/0.7
	38400 Cores			
1	6837 / 2178	3.1 / 2.6		
2	3528 / 1186	1.2 / 2.1		
5	2015 / 715	0.5 / 0.9		
	9600 Cores		19200 Cores	
1	5661/1897	21/9.6	4975/1602	14/7.3
2	2428/1047	1.7/2.4	2336/1020	1.4/2.1
5	1202/549	0.3/0.8	1375/457	0.3/0.7
	38400 Cores		76800 Cores	
1	5471/1571	9,4/5.7	14899/3267	6.1/4
2	2512/965	1.5/2.2	3382/1278	2.3/3.1
5	1430/412	0.4/0.8	1537/439	0.4/0.9
	16384 Cores		32768 Cores	
1	18220/1569	59.0/20.6	21736/1615	40/15
2	4386/633	2.8/3.1	13522/844	2.5/2.8
5	1697/231	0.7/1.1	6548/373	0.9/1.3
	65536 Cores		131072 Cores	
1	48315/3026	30/14	174496/6860	21/11
2	28249/1583	3.4/3.2	32904/1793	3.7/3.4
5	3694/318	1.2/1.6	27914/1620	1.1/1.5
	163840 Cores			
1	157353/6307	19/10		
2	32368/1813	3.3/3.2		
5	29479/1516	1/1.4		
	8000 Cores		16000 Cores	
1	2461/356	110/42	2994/410	79/31
2	538/113	7.3/6.9	1652/142	5.4/5.5
5	320/87	6.5/6.1	714/84	4.2/4.5
	32000 Cores		64000 Cores	
1	9592/713	63/24	15180/1225	42/17
2	770/118	5.6/5.3	4680/412	6.8/5.7
5	631/76	2.6/3.1	814/86	1.6/2.1
	128000 Cores			
1	33844/2634	24/11		
2	22725/1571	8.0/5.8		
5	2155/217	1.0/1.4		

Figure 8: Average (error bar: standard deviation) number of attempted steals for the first, second, and fifth iteration of retentive stealing. x-axis — number of cores; y-axis — average number of steals.

Figure 9: Average (error bar: standard deviation) number of successful steals for the first, second, and fifth iteration of retentive stealing. x-axis — number of cores; y-axis — average number of steals.

Table 2: Average (Avg) number and standard deviation (Std) of attempted and successful steals for retentive work stealing for TCE, HF-Be256, and HF-Be512 benchmarks on Hopper Cray XE6, Intrepid IBM BG/P, and Titan Cray XK6.

146

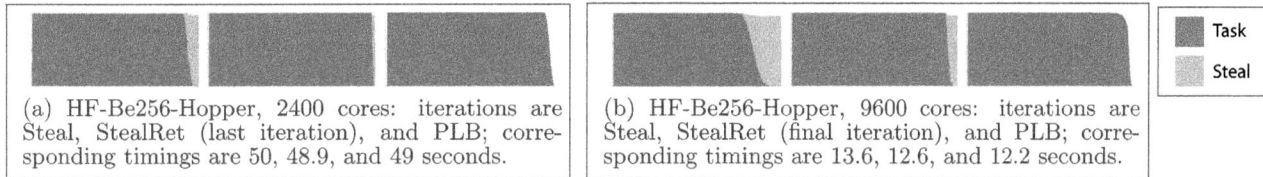

(a) HF-Be256-Hopper, 2400 cores: iterations are Steal, StealRet (last iteration), and PLB; corresponding timings are 50, 48.9, and 49 seconds.

(b) HF-Be256-Hopper, 9600 cores: iterations are Steal, StealRet (final iteration), and PLB; corresponding timings are 13.6, 12.6, and 12.2 seconds.

Task
Steal

Figure 10: Utilization for all worker threads over time. x-axis — time; y-axis — percent utilization.

	Load Balancer Execution Time (seconds)					Load Balancer Quality (percent over ideal)				
	2400	4800	9600	19200	38400	2400	4800	9600	19200	38400
$n\ m$	C / H	C / H	C / H	C / H	C / H	C / H	C / H	C / H	C / H	C / H
1 1	1.57 / 1.42	1.98 / 1.12	5.76 / 1.08	14.8 / 1.92	35.6 / 1.04	0.03 / 0.06	0.03 / 0.18	0.03 / 0.4	0.03 / 2.0	5.8 / 12
2 2	4.83 / 0.07	6.33 / 0.16	8.42 / 0.81	13.0 / 0.77	43.8 / 1.00	0.03 / 0.14	0.03 / 0.54	0.03 / 1.1	1.7 / 6.6	5.8 / 12
2 4	7.40 / 0.35	10.0 / 0.66	13.0 / 0.33	18.3 / 0.31	37.7 / 1.14	0.03 / 0.26	0.03 / 0.68	0.03 / 4.0	0.03 / 7.1	5.8 / 12
2 8	9.24 / 0.34	11.4 / 0.30	13.0 / 0.33	18.4 / 1.62	45.2 / 4.40	0.03 / 0.28	0.03 / 2.2	0.03 / 3.7	0.1 / 7.3	5.8 / 18
4 2	1.40 / 0.08	2.00 / 0.30	3.82 / 0.48	16.9 / 0.82	39.5 / 0.75	0.03 / 0.17	0.03 / 0.53	0.03 / 1.3	2.8 / 5.7	5.8 / 11
4 4	2.84 / 0.09	4.13 / 0.20	6.65 / 0.56	13.4 / 0.36	37.0 / 0.65	0.03 / 0.29	0.03 / 0.60	0.03 / 2.4	1.3 / 7.4	5.8 / 15
4 8	4.34 / 0.28	6.27 / 0.97	9.07 / 0.58	15.1 / 0.26	43.0 / 0.85	0.03 / 0.29	0.03 / 0.58	0.03 / 3.9	0.03 / 6.9	5.8 / 13
8 2	0.45 / 0.04	0.75 / 0.11	2.73 / 0.25	15.0 / 0.79	36.2 / 0.36	0.03 / 0.30	0.03 / 0.73	0.03 / 1.2	2.9 / 5.4	6.6 / 13
8 4	0.98 / 0.06	1.52 / 0.07	3.03 / 0.19	11.9 / 0.65	38.1 / 0.55	0.03 / 0.50	0.03 / 1.0	0.03 / 3.1	2.3 / 7.6	5.8 / 12
8 8	1.88 / 0.06	2.70 / 0.10	5.01 / 0.49	11.4 / 0.38	36.7 / 0.63	0.03 / 0.49	0.03 / 1.0	0.03 / 4.6	0.9 / 7.9	5.8 / 15

Table 3: LHS — execution time (seconds) on Hopper for rebalancing 12 initial distributions of tasks of the HF-Be256 system, comparing centralized (C) and hierarchical (H) persistence-based schemes. RHS — load balance quality, computed as the maximum percentage over the ideal execution time (perfectly balanced load). The ideal execution times are 48, 24, 12, 6, and 3 seconds, respectively.

our application in the highest scale considered for each problem, steal attempts significantly increase. For iteration 1 of HF-Be512 on Hopper, increasing the number of cores from 38400 to 76800 increases the average number of attempted steals from 5471 to 14898. This trend is due to a lack of parallel slack, not just the increasing core counts. The high standard deviation shows that different cores are provided with different initial loads and attempt a varying number of steals to find work.

The number of attempted steals provides insight into the improvements in the performance achieved by retentive stealing. As the load balancing becomes iteratively refined with retentive stealing, the number of attempted steals decreases and stabilizes across process counts. In addition, the gradual balancing of the load is accompanied by a lower standard deviation. Intuitively, when each processor core finishes the work initially assigned to it, all cores reach a similar state and the entire application is close to completion. For iteration 5 of HF-Be512 on Hopper, increasing the number of cores from 38400 to 76800 after retentive stealing has been applied for several iterations, only increases the average number of attempted steals from 1430 to 1537.

The number of successful steals, shown in Figure 9 and Table 2, confirms our intuition from the number of attempted steals. A successful steal depends on the availability of pending work, which decreases with increase in core count. More importantly, retentive stealing balances the load well enough that for the last iteration the number of successful steals is very small. For iteration 5 of HF-Be512 on Hopper, for core counts 9600, 19200, 38400, and 76800, the average number of successful steals are 0.3, 0.3, 0.4, and 0.4, respectively.

The efficiency of persistence-based load balancing, using the hierarchical load balancer, is shown in Figure 6. The first iteration plotted on the graph is the efficiency of work stealing after the null tasks have been pruned. The significant change in the work distribution from iteration 0 to 1 renders persistence-based load balancing ineffective, result-ing in large observed execution times. Instead, we resorted to work stealing in the first iteration, in this evaluation.

For the second iteration, to show the overhead of work stealing, tasks are seeded based on the previous iteration, but work stealing is disabled and no load balancer is used. Efficiency improves slightly in this case because the overheads associated with stealing and termination detection are removed. In subsequent iterations, the hierarchical load balancer is executed before the start of the iteration, using the data collected from the previous iteration. The first time the hierarchical load balancer is run, load balance improves significantly; for example, on Hopper efficiency increases by 7% on 76800 cores for the TCE calculation, 24% on 38400 cores for the HF-Be256 system, and 22% on 76800 cores for the HF-Be512 system. The second application of the load balancer improves the performance slightly in the HF-Be256 case on Hopper. The third application does not seem to have much impact on Hopper, but Titan and Intrepid require more applications of the load balancer before HF-Be512 converges.

Figure 10 shows the processor utilization over time for two HF-Be256 runs on 2400 and 9600 cores of Hopper. The graph demonstrates that for the first iteration of the computation, before retentive stealing is applied, performance is low due to many cores spending time trying to steal tasks. As the problem is strong scaled, the amount of time spent stealing increases dramatically. Retentive work stealing reduces this time in both cases, increasing the amount of time spent executing tasks. With retention, work stealing performs almost as well as persistence-based load balancing.

8. CONCLUSION

We presented scalable algorithms for persistence-based load balancing and work stealing. The hierarchical persistence-based load balancing algorithm presented locally rebalances the load in a greedy fashion. The work stealing algorithm is optimized for distributed memory machines, by coalescing remote operations, reducing the duration of locked operations, and enabling concurrent steal operations that allow overlapped task migration. We presented retentive stealing to further adapt work stealing for iterative applications.

Work stealing is traditionally considered not to scale beyond small core counts, due to its perceived limitations: randomization, the need to repeatedly rebalance, the cost of termination detection, and the potential interference with application execution. While not universally applicable, we demonstrate that work stealing scales better than commonly believed. Retentive stealing is also shown to improve execution efficiency by incrementally improving the load balance and reducing the overheads associated with stealing.

ACKNOWLEDGEMENTS

This work was supported in part by the DOE Office of Science, Advanced Scientific Computing Research, under award number 59193, and by the U.S. Department of Energy's Pacific Northwest National Laboratory under the Extreme Scale Computing Initiative. This research used resources of the Argonne Leadership Computing Facility at Argonne National Laboratory, the National Energy Research Scientific Computing Center and the Oak Ridge Leadership Computing Facility at the Oak Ridge National Laboratory, which are supported by the Office of Science of the U.S. Department of Energy under contracts DE-AC02-06CH11357, DE-AC02-05CH11231, and DE-AC05-00OR22725, respectively.

9. REFERENCES

[1] ALCF Intrepid. http://www.alcf.anl.gov/intrepid.
[2] NERSC Hopper. http://www.nersc.gov/users/computational-systems/hopper.
[3] OLCF Titan. http://www.olcf.ornl.gov/computing-resources/titan.
[4] G. Baumgartner et al. Synthesis of high-performance parallel programs for a class of ab initio quantum chemistry models. *Proc. of IEEE*, 93(2):276–292, 2005.
[5] R. D. Blumofe, C. F. Joerg, B. C. Kuszmaul, C. E. Leiserson, K. H. Randall, and Y. Zhou. Cilk: An Efficient Multithreaded Runtime System. In *PPoPP*, pages 207–216, July 1995.
[6] R. D. Blumofe and P. A. Lisiecki. Adaptive and reliable parallel computing on networks of workstations. In *USENIX*, pages 10–10, 1997.
[7] Ü. V. Çatalyürek and C. Aykanat. Hypergraph-partitioning-based decomposition for parallel sparse-matrix vector multiplication. *IEEE Trans. Parallel Distrib. Syst.*, 10(7):673–693, 1999.
[8] Ü. V. Çatalyürek, E. G. Boman, K. D. Devine, D. Bozdag, R. T. Heaphy, and L. A. Riesen. A repartitioning hypergraph model for dynamic load balancing. *JPDC*, 69(8):711–724, 2009.
[9] A. Chandramowlishwaran, K. Knobe, and R. Vuduc. Performance evaluation of concurrent collections on high-performance multicore computing systems. In *IPDPS*, 2010.
[10] P. Charles, C. Grothoff, V. Saraswat, et al. X10: an object-oriented approach to non-uniform cluster computing. In *OOPSLA*, pages 519–538, 2005.
[11] N. H. Darach Golden and S. McGrath. Parallel adaptive mesh refinement for large eddy simulation using the finite element methods. In *PARA*, pages 172–181, 1998.
[12] A. Darte, J. Mellor-Crummey, R. Fowler, and D. C. Miranda. Generalized multipartitioning of multi-dimensional arrays for parallelizing line-sweep computations. *JPDC*, 63(9):887–911, 2003.
[13] R. Das, Y.-S. Hwang, M. Uysal, J. Saltz, and A. Sussman. Applying the CHAOS/PARTI library to irregular problems in computational chemistry and computational aerodynamics. In *Scalable Parallel Libraries Conference*, pages 45 –56, oct 1993.
[14] J. Dinan, D. B. Larkins, P. Sadayappan, S. Krishnamoorthy, and J. Nieplocha. Scalable work stealing. In *SC*, 2009.
[15] N. Francez. Distributed termination. *ACM Trans. Program. Lang. Syst.*, 2:42–55, January 1980.
[16] E. Gabriel et al. Open MPI: Goals, concept, and design of a next generation MPI implementation. In *European PVM/MPI*, September 2004.
[17] G. R. Gao, T. L. Sterling, R. Stevens, M. Hereld, and W. Zhu. Parallex: A study of a new parallel computation model. In *IPDPS*, pages 1–6, 2007.
[18] B. Hendrickson and R. Leland. An improved spectral graph partitioning algorithm for mapping parallel computations. *SIAM J. Sci. Comput.*, 16:452–469, March 1995.
[19] C. Joerg and B. C. Kuszmaul. Massively parallel chess. In *Proceedings of the Third DIMACS Parallel Implementation Challenge, Rutgers*, 1994.
[20] L. Kalé and S. Krishnan. CHARM++: A Portable Concurrent Object Oriented System Based on C++. In *OOPSLA '93*, pages 91–108, September 1993.
[21] G. Karypis, K. Schloegel, and V. Kumar. Parmetis: Parallel graph partitioning and sparse matrix ordering library. *Version 1.0, Dept. of Computer Science, University of Minnesota*, 1997.
[22] J. Nieplocha, V. Tipparaju, M. Krishnan, and D. K. Panda. High performance remote memory access communication: The ARMCI approach. *Int. J. High Perform. Comput. Appl.*, 20(2):233–253, 2006.
[23] J. C. Phillips et al. Scalable molecular dynamics with namd. *Journal of Computational Chemistry*, 26(16):1781–1802, 2005.
[24] J. Reinders. *Intel Threading Building Blocks: Outfitting C++ for Multi-Core Processor Parallelism*. O'Reilly Media, 2007.
[25] V. A. Saraswat, P. Kambadur, S. B. Kodali, D. Grove, and S. Krishnamoorthy. Lifeline-based global load balancing. In *PPoPP*, pages 201–212, 2011.
[26] A. Szabo and N. S. Ostlund. *Modern Quantum Chemistry*. McGraw-Hill Inc., New York, 1996.
[27] R. V. van Nieuwpoort, T. Kielmann, and H. E. Bal. Efficient load balancing for wide-area divide-and-conquer applications. In *PPoPP*, pages 34–43, 2001.
[28] R. D. Williams. Performance of dynamic load balancing algorithms for unstructured mesh calculations. *Concurrency: Pract. Exper.*, 3:457–481, October 1991.
[29] G. Zheng, A. Bhatele, E. Meneses, and L. V. Kale. Periodic Hierarchical Load Balancing for Large Supercomputers. *IJHPCA*, 2010.

Highly Scalable Graph Search
for the Graph500 Benchmark

Koji Ueno
Tokyo Institute of Technology / JST CREST

ueno.k.ac@m.titech.ac.jp

Toyotaro Suzumura
Tokyo Institute of Technology
IBM Research – Tokyo / JST CREST

suzumura@cs.titech.ac.jp

ABSTRACT

Graph500 is a new benchmark to rank supercomputers with a large-scale graph search problem. We found that the provided reference implementations are not scalable in a large distributed environment. We devised an optimized method based on 2D partitioning and other methods such as communication compression and vertex sorting. Our optimized implementation can handle BFS (Breadth First Search) of a large graph with 2^{36} (68.7 billion vertices) and 2^{40} (1.1 trillion) edges in 10.58 seconds while using 1366 nodes and 16,392 CPU cores. This performance corresponds to 103.9 GE/s. We also studied the performance characteristics of our optimized implementation and reference implementations on a large distributed memory supercomputer with a Fat-Tree-based Infiniband network.

Categories and Subject Descriptors

G.2.2 [**Discrete Mathematics**]: Graph Theory – *Graph algorithms*; D.1.3 [**Programming Techniques**]: Concurrent Programming – *Distributed programming*

General Terms

Algorithms, Performance.

Keywords

Graph500, BFS, Supercomputer

1. INTRODUCTION

Large-scale graph analysis is a hot topic for various fields of study, such as social networks, micro-blogs, protein-protein interactions, and the connectivity of the Web. The numbers of vertices in the analyzed graph networks have grown from billions to tens of billions and the edges have grown from tens of billions to hundreds of billions. Since 1994, the best known de facto ranking of the world's fastest computers is TOP500, which is based on a high performance Linpack benchmark for linear equations. As an alternative to Linpack, Graph500 [1] was recently developed. We conducted a thorough study of the algorithms of the reference implementations and their performance in an earlier paper [19]. Based on that work, we now propose a scalable and high-performance implementation of an optimized Graph500 benchmark for large distributed environments.

Here are the main contributions of our new work:

1. Optimization of the parallel level-synchronized BFS (Breadth-First Search) method to improve the cache-hit ratio through various optimizations in the 2D partitioning, graph structure and vertex sorting.

2. Optimization of the complete flow of the Graph500 as a lighter-weight benchmark with better graph construction and validation.

3. A new traversal record of 103.9 giga-edges/second with our optimized method on the currently 5th-ranked Tsubame 2.0 supercomputer.

4. A thorough study of the performance characteristics of our optimized method and those of the reference implementations.

Here is the organization of our paper. In Section 2, we give an overview of Graph500 and parallel BFS algorithms. In Section 3, we describe the scalability problems of the reference implementations. We explain the proposed optimized BFS method in Section 4, and the optimized graph construction and validation in Section 5. In Section 6, we describe our performance evaluation and give detailed profiles from our optimized method running on the Tsubame 2.0 supercomputer. We discuss our findings in Section 7, review related work in Section 8, and conclude and consider future work in Section 9.

2. GRAPH500 AND PARALLEL BFS ALGORITHMS

In this section, we give an overview of the Graph500 benchmark [1], the parallel level-synchronized BFS method, and then the mapping of this method for the sparse-matrix vector multiplication.

2.1 Graph500 Benchmark

In contrast to the computation-intensive benchmark used by TOP500, Graph500 is a data-intensive benchmark. It does breadth-first searches in undirected large graphs generated by a scalable data generator based on a Kronecker graph [16]. The benchmark has two kernels: Kernel 1 constructs an undirected graph from the graph generator in a format usable by Kernel 2. The first kernel transforms the edge tuples (pairs of start and end vertices) to efficient data structures with sparse formats, such as CSR (Compressed Sparse Row) or CSC (Compressed Sparse Column). Then Kernel 2 does a breadth-first search of the graph from a randomly chosen source vertex in the graph.

The benchmark uses the elapsed times for both kernels, but the rankings for Graph500 are determined by how large the problem is and by the throughput in TEPS (Traversed Edges Per Second).

This means that the ranking results basically depend on the time consumed by the second kernel.

After both kernels have finished, there is a validation phase to check if the result is correct. When the amount of data is extremely large, it becomes difficult to show that the resulting breadth-first tree matches the reference result. Therefore the validation phase uses 5 validation rules. For example, the first rule is that the BFS graph is a tree and does not contain any cycles.

There are six problem sizes: toy, mini, small, medium, large, and huge. Each problem solves a different size graph defined by a Scale parameter, which is the base 2 logarithm of the number of vertices. For example, the level Scale 26 for *toy* means 2^{26} and corresponds to 10^{10} bytes occupying 17 GB of memory. The six Scale values are 26, 29, 32, 36, 39, and 42 for the six classes. The largest problem, huge (Scale 42), needs to handle around 1.1 PB of memory. As of this writing, Scale 38 is the largest that has been solved by a top-ranked supercomputer.

2.2 Level-synchronized BFS

All of the MPI reference implementation algorithms of the Graph500 benchmark use a "level-synchronized breadth-first search", which means that all of the vertices at a given level of the BFS tree will be processed (potentially in parallel) before any vertices from a lower level in the tree are processed. The details of the level-synchronized BFS are explained in [2][3].

Algorithm I: Level-synchronized BFS

1 for all vertices v parallel do
2 | **PRED**[v]← -1;
3 | **VISITED** [v] ← 0;
4 **PRED** [r] ← 0
5 **VISITED**[r] ← 1
6 Enqueue(CQ, r)
7 While **CQ** != Empty do
8 | **NQ** ← empty
9 | for all **u** in **CQ** in parallel do
10 | | u ← Dequeue(**CQ**)
11 | | for each **v** adjacent to **u** in parallel do
12 | | | if **VISITED** [v] = 0 then
13 | | | | **VISITED** [v] ← 1;
14 | | | | **PRED** [v] ← u;
15 | | | | Enqueue(**NQ**, v)
16 | swap(**CQ, NQ**);

Algorithm I is the abstract pseudocode for the algorithm that implements level-synchronized BFS. Each processor has two queues, *CQ* and *NQ*, and two arrays, PRED for a predecessor array and *VISITED* to track whether or not each vertex has been visited.

At any given time, CQ (Current Queue) is the set of vertices that must be visited at the current level. At level 1, CQ will contain the neighbors of *r*, so at level 2, it will contain their pending neighbors (the neighboring vertices that have not been visited at levels 0 or 1). The algorithm also maintains NQ (Next Queue), containing the vertices that should be visited at the next level. After visiting all of the nodes at each level, the queues CQ and NQ are swapped at line 16.

VISITED is a bitmap that represents each vertex with one bit. Each bit of VISITED is 1 if the corresponding vertex has been

already visited and 0 if not. PRED has predecessor vertices for each vertex. If an unvisited vertex *v* is found at line 12, the vertex u is the predecessor vertex of the vertex v at line 14. When we complete BFS, PRED forms a BFS tree, the output of kernel2 in the Graph500 benchmark.

The Graph500 benchmark provides 4 different reference implementations based on this level-synchronized BFS method. Their details and algorithms appear in an earlier paper [19]. However we found out that the fundamental concept of the level synchronized BFS can be viewed as a sparse-matrix vector multiplication. With reference to the detailed algorithmic explanations in [19], we only explain the basic BFS method here.

2.3 Representing Level-Synchronized BFS as Sparse-Matrix Vector Multiplication

The level-synchronized BFS in II-B is analogous to a Sparse-Matrix Vector multiplication (SpMV) [20] which is computed as $y = Ax$ where x and y are vectors and A is a sparse matrix.

A is an adjacency matrix for a graph. Each element of this matrix is 1 if the corresponding edge exists and 0 if not. The vector x corresponds to CQ (Current Queue) where $x(v) = 1$ if the vertex v is contained in CQ and $x(v) = 0$ if not. $x(v)$ means the v-th element of vector x. Then the neighboring vertices of CQ can be represented as the vertex v where $y(v) \geq 1$. We get the neighboring vertices from SpMV. Then we can compute the lines 12 to 15 in the Algorithm I.

2.4 Mapping Reference Implementations to SpMV

In a distributed memory environment, the graph data and vertex data must be distributed. There are four MPI-based reference implementation of Graph500: replicated-csr (R-CSR), replicated-csc (R-CSC), simple (SIM), and one_sided (ONE-SIDED).

All four of the reference implementations use 1D partitioning method. The method of vertex distribution is the same in these four implementations. Assume that we have a total of P processors. VISITED, PRED and NQ are simply divided into P blocks and each processor handles one block. There are two partitioning methods for the sparse matrix shown in Figure 1. For the Figure 1, we assume that the edge list of the given vertex is a column of the matrix. With the vertical partitioning (left), each processor has the edges incident to the vertices the processor owns. With the horizontal partitioning (right), each processor has the edges emanating from the vertices the processor owns. Figure 1 also shows how SpMV can be computed in parallel with P processors. The computation of the reference implementations can be abstracted as the computation of SpMV. R-CSR and R-CSC use vertical partitioning for SpMV while SIM and ONE-SIDED use horizontal partitioning for SpMV.

$$\begin{bmatrix} A_1 \\ \hline A_2 \\ \hline \vdots \\ \hline A_P \end{bmatrix} \times x \qquad \begin{bmatrix} A_1 & A_2 & \cdots & A_P \end{bmatrix} \times x$$

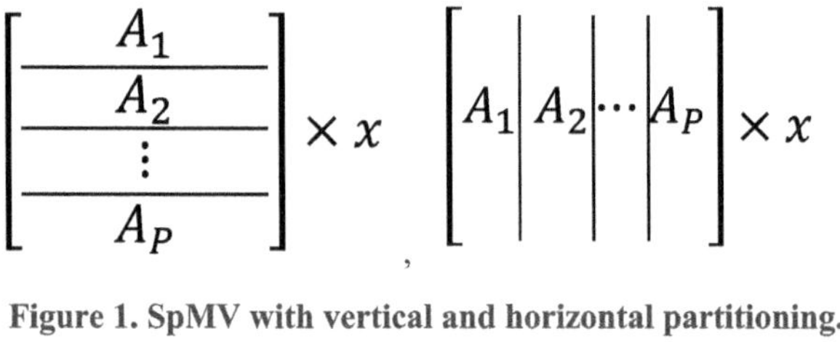

Figure 1. SpMV with vertical and horizontal partitioning.

3. SCALABILITY ISSUES OF REFERENCE IMPLEMENTATIONS

In this section we give overviews of three reference implementations of Graph500, R-CSR (*replicatedc-csr*), R-CSC (replicated-csc), and SIM (*simple*) and we use experiments and quantitative data to show why none of these algorithms can scale well in large systems.

Before moving to the detailed descriptions of each implementation, we need to cover how CQ (Current Queue) is implemented in the reference implementations. The reference implementations also use bitmaps with one bit for each vertex in CQ and NQ. In these bitmaps, if a certain vertex v is in a queue (CQ or NQ), then the bit that corresponds to that vertex v is 1 and if not, then the bit is 0.

We categorize the reference implementations into replication-based and non-replicated methods, which are described in Sections 3.1 and 3.2. Then in Section 3.3 we present a scalable BFS approach with 2D partitioning.

3.1 Replication-based method

3.1.1 Algorithm Description
For the R-CSR and R-CSC methods that divide an adjacency matrix vertically, CQ is duplicated to all of the processes. Then each processor independently computes NQ for its own portion.

Copying CQ to all of the processors means each processor sends its own portion of NQ to all of the other processors. CQ (and NQ) is represented as a relatively small bitmap. For relatively small problems with limited amounts of distribution, the amounts of communication data are reasonable and this method is effective.

However, since the size of CQ is proportional to the number of vertices in the entire graph, this copying operation leads to a large amount of communication for large problems with large distribution.

3.1.2 Quantitative Evaluation for Scalability
Figure 2 shows the communication data volume for each node with the replication-based implementation and SCALE of 26 for each node as the problem size. This is a weak-scaling version, and computes the theoretical results when using 2 MPI processes per node. In such a weak-scaling setting, the number of vertices increases in proportion to the increasing number of nodes. This result clearly shows that the Replication-based method is not scalable for a large distributed environment.

3.2 Non-replicated Method

3.2.1 Algorithm Description
The simple reference implementation or SIM that divides an adjacent matrix in a horizontal fashion, locates the portion of the CQ by dividing it into P. The NQ queue is already divided into P blocks, and so each processor can use the NQ queue from the previous level as the CQ of the current level.

Edge lists of the vertices in CQ are merged to form a set N of edges. The edges of a set N are the edges emanating from the vertices in CQ and incident to the neighboring vertices. These N include both the edges to be handled by the local processor and by other processors. The edges incident to the vertex owned by remote processors are transmitted to those processors.

The number of edges to be transmitted to remote processors can be up to the number of edges of the adjacency matrix owned by the sender-side processor. Thus the communication data volume is constant without regard to the number of nodes.

However, the Replication-based method with vertical partitioning transmits CQ as a bitmap. On the other hand in the *simple* implementation, SIM needs to send edges, pairs of a CQ vertex and neighboring vertex because the predecessor vertex is needed to update PRED, the predecessor array. Therefore, the Replication-based approach with vertical partitioning is better than the *simple* approach in a small-scale environment with fewer nodes.

3.2.2 Quantitative Evaluation for Scalability
The other two reference implementations with horizontal partitioning are called "*simple*" and "*one_sided*". In these implementations all-to-all communication that sends a different data set to each of the other processors is needed when sending the set of N edges. This all-to-all communication is not scalable for large distributed environments.

Figure 3 shows the communication speed of the all-to-all communication on Tsubame 2.0 when using 4 MPI processes per node. We used MVAPICH2 1.6 as the MPI implementation. The communication was implemented with the *MPI_Alltoall* function, and we used three different transmission buffer sizes, 64 MB, 256 MB, and 1,024 MB.

The amount of data that each node transmits to other nodes is 4 MB when using the 1,024 MB buffer size, 64 nodes, and 256 MPI processes. The results shown in Figure 3 show that the all-to-all communication is not scalable.

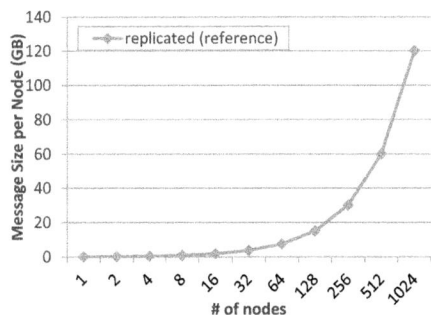

Figure 2. Theoretical message size per node (GB)

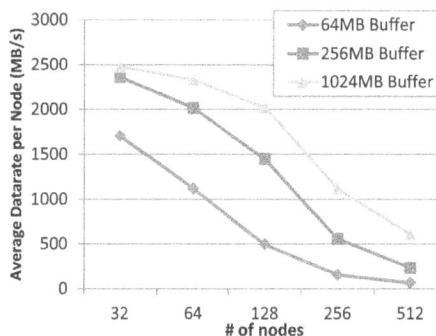

Figure 3. Average data rate per node with all-to-all communication

With 512 nodes, the performance is quite slow even with a small buffer size such as 64 MB. Also, even if we use 1,024 MB as the buffer size, the performance is 1/4 of 32 nodes.

Our experimental testbed, Tsubame 2.0, uses a Fat-Tree structure with its Infiniband network. If the theoretical peak performance were achieved, there would be no performance degradation even for all-to-all communication is among all of the nodes. However, the communication latency cannot be ignored in a large system. The actual performance is always less than the theoretical maximum.

3.3 Scalable Approach: 2D Partitioning-Based BFS

To solve the scalability problems described in Section 3.1 and Section 3.2, a scalable distributed parallel breadth-first search algorithm was proposed in [4]. Their scalable approach uses a level-synchronized BFS and 2D partitioning technique to reduces the communication costs since it can handle both vertical and horizontal partitioning, unlike 1D partitioning. Our proposed method optimizes this 2D partitioning technique and also uses some other optimization techniques. Here is a brief overview of the 2D partitioning technique.

Assume that we have a total of P processors, where the $P = R \cdot C$ processors are logically deployed in a two dimensional mesh which has R rows and C columns. We use the terms processor-row and processor-column with respect to this processor mesh. Adjacency matrix is divided as shown in Figure 4 and the processor (i, j) is responsible for handling the C blocks from $A_{i,j}^{(1)}$ to $A_{i,j}^{(C)}$. The vertices are divided into $R \cdot C$ blocks and the processor (i, j) handles the k-th block, where k is computed as $(j-1) \cdot R + i$.

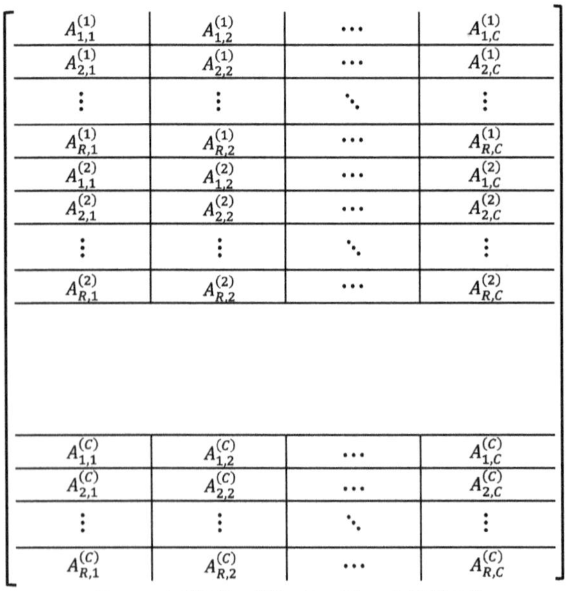

$$
\begin{bmatrix}
A_{1,1}^{(1)} & A_{1,2}^{(1)} & \cdots & A_{1,C}^{(1)} \\
A_{2,1}^{(1)} & A_{2,2}^{(1)} & \cdots & A_{2,C}^{(1)} \\
\vdots & \vdots & \ddots & \vdots \\
A_{R,1}^{(1)} & A_{R,2}^{(1)} & \cdots & A_{R,C}^{(1)} \\
A_{1,1}^{(2)} & A_{1,2}^{(2)} & \cdots & A_{1,C}^{(2)} \\
A_{2,1}^{(2)} & A_{2,2}^{(2)} & \cdots & A_{2,C}^{(2)} \\
\vdots & \vdots & \ddots & \vdots \\
A_{R,1}^{(2)} & A_{R,2}^{(2)} & \cdots & A_{R,C}^{(2)} \\
& & & \\
A_{1,1}^{(C)} & A_{1,2}^{(C)} & \cdots & A_{1,C}^{(C)} \\
A_{2,1}^{(C)} & A_{2,2}^{(C)} & \cdots & A_{2,C}^{(C)} \\
\vdots & \vdots & \ddots & \vdots \\
A_{R,1}^{(C)} & A_{R,2}^{(C)} & \cdots & A_{R,C}^{(C)}
\end{bmatrix}
$$

Figure 4. 2D Partitioning Based BFS [4]

Each level of the level-synchronized BFS method with 2D partitioning is done in 2 communication phases called "*expand*" and "*fold*". In the *expand* phase, every processor copies its CQ to all of the other processors in the same processor-column, similar to vertical 1D partitioning. Then the edge lists of the vertices in CQ are merged to form a set N. In the *fold* phase, each processor sends the edges of N to the owner of their incident vertices, similar to horizontal 1D partitioning. With the 2D partitioning, these owners are in the same processor-row. 2D partitioning method is equivalent to a method of combining the two types of 1D partitioning. If C is 1, this corresponds to the vertical 1D partitioning and if R is 1, it corresponds to the horizontal 1D partitioning.

The advantage of 2D partitioning is to reduce the number of processors that need to communicate. Both types of 1D partitioning require all-to-all communication. However, with the 2D partitioning, each processor only communicates with the processors in the processor-row and the processor-column.

4. U-BFS: SCALABLE BFS METHOD

Our BFS implementation is based on a 2D partitioning method and is highly optimized for a large-scale distributed computing environment by using various optimization techniques. In this section we present these techniques. As described in Section 3.3, in the 2D partitioning, the $P = R \cdot C$ processors are deployed in a $R \cdot C$ mesh.

4.1 Overview of Oprimized 2D Partioning-based BFS (U-BFS)

Our U-BFS optimization also uses the 2D partitioning technique. The communication method of the *expand* phase is the same approach as R-CSC, one of the reference implementations. Each set of vertices in CQ is represented as a bitmap and each processor gathers CQ at each level by using the *MPI_AllGather* function.

The communication of the *fold* phase is optimized in our implementation by compression of the data described in Section 4.2. Because the amount of data communicated in each *fold* phase is much larger than that of the *expand* phase when we use a naïve method, compression of the data is important.

We divide the processing of the *fold* phase into senders and receivers. The senders send the edges emanating from the vertices in CQ as compressed data. The receivers receive data from the senders, decompress the data to edges, and process edges. Both senders and receivers are handled by multiple parallel threads and the communication can be done asynchronously. Our proposed method has highly efficient processing with this parallel and asynchronous communication.

In addition, our method can efficiently utilize the CPU caches by vertex sorting (Section 4.4), binding the threads to CPU cores (Section 4.3), and then giving higher priority to the receiver threads (Section 4.3) to reduce the cache replacements from thread switching.

The algorithm appears as Algorithm II. CQ and NQ are bitmaps. In Lines 1-2, NQ is initialized and the BFS root is inserted into NQ in line 3. Lines 5-10 are done by all of the processors. Line 6 is the *expand* communication. In Line 7, Task A and Task B run in parallel. Task A is the receiver processing and Task B is the sender processing.

Algorithm II: Optimized 2D partitioning algorithm
Variables: MAP which is described in the Section 4.4 is for conversion from the sorted number to the original number.

Main
```
1    for all vertexes lu in NQ do
2    |  NQ[lu] ← 0
3    NQ [root] ← 1
4    fork;
5    for level = 1 to ∞
6    |  CQ ← all gather NQ in this processor-column;
7    |  parallel Task A and Task B
8    |  Synchronize;
9    |  if NQ = φ for all processors then
10   |  |  terminate loop;
11   join;
```

Task A (sender)
```
1    for all vertexes u in CQ parallel do (contiguous access)
2    |  if CQ [u] = 1 then
3    |     for each vertex v' adjacent to u do
4    |     |  compress the edge (u, v') and send it to the owner of vertex v'
```

Task B (receiver)
```
1    for each received data parallel do
2    |  decompress the data and get the edge (u, v')
3    |  if visited[v'] = 0 then
4    |  |  VISITED[v'] ← 1;
5    |  |  v ← MAP[v'];
6    |  |  PRED[v] ←u;
7    |  |  NQ [v] ← 1;
```

4.2 Optimized Communication with Data Compression

The compression of communication data is greatly important because the bottleneck of the distributed BFS is often the communication. We optimized the communication of the *fold* phase because the amount of data communicated in the *fold* phase is much larger than that of the *expand* phase when we use a naïve method. In the *fold* phase, sender side sends the edges emanating from the vertices in CQ. The edges are represented as a list of a tuple (u, v) where u is the vertex of CQ and v is the neighboring vertex of CQ. We compress vertex u and v with different compression techniques.

Here is our compression method for vertex u. Since CQ is a bitmap, by checking CQ in order of bitmap array, the vertices in u will be sorted in ascending-order. Thus the average difference between two vertex u in successive edges will be small. The vertex u is represented by simply encoding the difference from the prior tuple with variable-length quantity which is used by the standard MIDI file format and Google's protocol buffers etc. We use general variable-length quantity (VLQ) for unsigned integer. An integer

value will be one or more bytes. Smaller numbers will be smaller number of bytes. The most significant bit (MSB) of each byte indicates whether another VLQ byte follows. If the MSB is 1, another VLQ byte follows and if 0, this is the last byte of the integer. The rest 7 bits of each byte form an integer. The least significant will be first in a stream.

For example, we assume that the CQ bitmap is '01100001' which means three vertices 1, 2 and 7 are in the CQ and we also assume that the numbers of edges emanating from the vertices 1, 2 and 7 are 2, 1 and 3 respectively. The series of vertices u will be '1, 1, 2, 7, 7, 7' because we check the CQ in order. Then we will get the difference from the prior vertex, '-, 0, 1, 5, 0, 0'. With VLQ, a smaller number will be encoded into smaller number of bytes. Therefore, we can compress the vertices u.

For the compression of vertex v, each edge (u, v) will be sent to the owner of vertex v. We distribute these vertices with a round robin method. The owner of vertex v' is computed by dividing v by P. For example, the owner of vertex v ($= v_{local} \cdot P + v_{proc}$) is v_{proc}. Thus by sending $v_{local} = v/P$ instead of v, we can reduce the size of the data for vertex v.

The data representation of vertex u is compressed by using the differences from the preceding data. However to support multi-threaded processing, we need to introduce a packet, a unit which can be decoded independently. If we send a series of edges in one packet containing (300, 533), (301, 12), (301, 63), (303, 1222) as (u, v), then the data representation of the vertex u without VLQ encoding, but with the difference technique is "300, 1, 0, 2". With the VLQ encoding, it becomes "0xAC, 0x01, 0x01, 0x00, 0x02".

When there are P processors, the data representation of the vertex v is "8, 0, 0, 19". Without this optimization, the size of each data tuple (v, u) would be 16 bytes, since each vertex is represented as 8 bytes, but with this optimization, the data size is about 5 bytes on average, since the vertex v consumes 4 bytes and the vertex u consumes about 1 byte as long as the difference between the contiguous values is less than 128 with the VLQ encoding.

4.3 Parallelizing the Sender and Receiver Processing

Our optimized implementation uses hybrid parallelism of MPI and OpenMP for communication and computational efficiency. As our multi-threading strategy to use **N** CPU cores for MPI processes, we run (N-1) threads for the sender-side processing (Task A) and (N-1) threads for the receiver side (Task B), and only 1 thread for communication. In total, (2N-1) threads run in parallel. The communication dataflow in the *fold* phase appears in Figure 5. Each thread at the sender side reads the graph data and CQ,

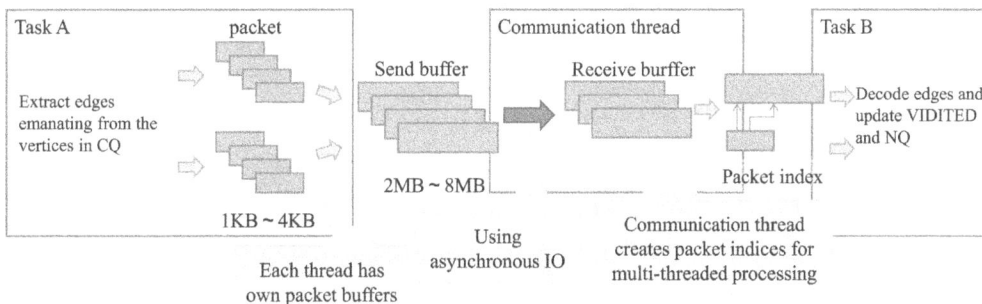

Figure 5. A dataflow diagram of the *fold* communication.

compress edges and then store compressed edge data into the packet buffer prepared for each sender thread.

Once the packet buffer is full, the data is passed to the communication thread and emitted with the asynchronous MPI sender function *MPI_Isend*. When a communication thread receives the data, it creates a packet index for multi-threaded processing and passes it to the receiver thread. Once the receiver thread receives the packet index and the data, the thread decodes it, updates the VISITED bitmap, and creates NQ.

The receiver thread decodes the incoming edge (v, u) where u is the vertex of CQ and v is the neighboring vertex of CQ, determines whether vertex v was already visited by checking the VISITED bitmap, and if not, updates the VISITED bitmap and NQ. However since the incoming vertices v are received at random, the random access to the VISITED bitmap can degrade the performance. We optimize updating VISITED bitmap in the next section.

We also optimize for the NUMA architecture. If we have N CPU cores for MPI processes, then *(2N – 1)* threads are created. Unless these threads are bound to a CPU, the OS scheduler will allocate more than N CPU cores. For a multi-socket CPU like that of Tsubame 2.0, if a thread is moved to another CPU core at a different CPU socket, then the cache hit ratio is reduced. Also, for a NUMA architecture, the memory and the CPU where the data processing thread is running should be kept close together.

To reduce cache misses due to thread switches, the threads for the receiver side have higher priority to the threads for the sender side. This thread priority also reduces the amount of buffers required for receiver processing.

4.4 Improving Cache Hit Ratio with Vertex Sorting

We explained in the previous section that each receiver thread (Task B) generates random memory access to the VISITED bitmap, which lowers the cache hit ratio. The distribution of the degrees follows Zipf's law as observed in our earlier work [19], since Graph500 uses a Kronecker graph [16]. The frequency of access to VISITED is determined by the vertex degree (the number of edges of each vertex). If the degree of vertex v is high, then v-th element of VISITED will be accessed more frequently. The high cost of random memory access can be reduced by sorting the vertices in decreasing order of degrees. We call this optimization *Vertex Sorting*.

To optimize accessing the VISITED bitmap, we use the sorted order in the row index of the adjacent matrix. We do not use the sorted order in the column index. If we use the sorted order in both row and column index, the conversion of PRED from the sorted order to original order is necessary. This conversion needs all-to-all collective communication which we need to pay expensive cost. Therefore, in the adjacent matrix, the row index and the column index for the same vertex are different.

In Algorithm II, v' is the sorted number and v is the original number. The number we get from the adjacent matrix is the sorted one. We change the sorted number to the original one in line 5 of Task B (receiver-side processing) by using MAP.

In the 2D partitioning, vertices are divided into $R \cdot C$ blocks and each block is allocated to a processor. We sort the vertices only in a local block. Therefore, *Vertex Sorting* does not affect the vertex partitioning and the graph partitioning. The adjacent matrix and the

MAP in Algorithm II are created in the construction phase (kernel 1). The method of sorting the vertices in the construction phase is described in Section 5.1.

5. GRAPH CONSTRUCTION FOR U-BFS AND OPTIMIZING VALIDATION

In this section we present the method of the construction phase for optimized BFS described in the previous section and the method of optimizing validation.

The current Graph500 benchmark must conduct 64 iterations of the BFS executions and validations. The validation phase dominates the overall time of the Graph500 benchmark, and so it is critically important to accelerate this phase to speed up the entire experiment.

5.1 Graph Construction

In the construction phase, we construct a sparse matrix representation of the graph from the edge list generated in the generation phase. Our optimized algorithm of the construction phase is shown in Algorithm III.

Algorithm III: Graph Construction
Input: L is a generated edge list.
Output: Two arrays of a sparse matrix representation for the graph, P and V. P is a pointer array and V is an index array. MAP for conversion from the sorted number to the original number.
C and I are arrays that have the same length of P. S is an array whose length is the number of local vertices.
1   for each column **v** of local adjacency matrix
2 | P[v] ← 0
3 | C[v] ← 0
4 | I[v] ← 0
5   for each local vertex **v**
6 | S[v] ← 0
7   for each edge (v0, v1) in L
8 | send edge (v0, v1) to its owner
9 | send edge (v1, v0) to its owner
10 for each received edge (**u**, **v**)
11 | C[v] ← C[v] + 1
12 | send vertex **v** to its owner
13 for each received vertex **v**
14 | S[v] ← S[v] + 1
15 sort S and create MAP for conversion from sorted number to original number and MAP' for inverse conversion
16 for **v** is 1 to the number of columns of local adjacency matrix
17 | P[v] ← P[v-1] + C[v]
18 for each edge (v0, v1) in L
19 | send edge (v0, v1) to its owner
20 | send edge (v1, v0) to its owner
21 for each received edge (**u**, **v**)
22 | send vertex **u** to its owner
23 | receive vertex **u** and send MAP'[**u**] to sender processor
24 | receive MAP'[**u**] as **u'**
25 | V[P[**v**] + I[**v**]] ← **u'**
26 | I[v] ← I[v] + 1

In our implementation, the matrix is 2D partitioned. Both edges and vertices have their owner processor. In Algorithm III, *local adjacency matrix* is a portion of the adjacency matrix allocated to the processor and *local vertices* are the vertices the processor owns.

154

5.2 Validation

The validation determines the correctness of the BFS result based on the edge tuples generated in the graph generation phase. By profiling the validation phase of the reference implementation, we found two validation rules in the Graph500 specification dominating the all-to-all communications.

1) Each edge in the input list has vertices with levels that differ by at most one or neither is in the BFS tree

2) Each node and its parent are joined by an edge in the original graph.

A processor that owns an edge tuple (v0, v1) needs to communicate with the owner processor of v0 and the owner processor of v1. Implemented in a naïve fashion, this requires all-to-all communication involving all of the processors, which is not scalable. We devised an approach that divides the edge tuples with 2D partitioning and allocates them to each processor before the first BFS execution. The number of processors involved in communication is fewer than the original version, making the work scalable.

6. PERFORMANCE EVALUATION

We used Tsubame 2.0, the fifth fastest supercomputer in the TOP500 list of June 2011, to evaluate the scalability of our optimized implementation.

6.1 Overview of the Tsubame 2.0 supercomputer

Tsubame 2.0 is a production supercomputer operated by the Global Scientific Information and Computing Center (GSIC) at the Tokyo Institute of Technology. Tsubame 2.0 has more than 1,400 compute nodes interconnected by high-bandwidth full-bisection-wide Infiniband fat nodes.

Each Tsubame 2.0 node has two Intel Westmere EP 2.93 GHz processors (Xeon X5670, 256-KB L2 cache, 12-MB L3), three NVIDIA Fermi M2050 GPUs, and 50 GB of local memory. The operating system is SUSE Linux Enterprise 11. Each node has a theoretical peak of 1.7 teraflops (TFLOPS). The main system consists of 1,408 computing nodes, and the total peak performance can reach 2.4 PFLOPS. Each of the CPUs in Tsubame 2.0 has six physical cores and supports up to 12 hardware threads with Intel's hyper-threading technology, thus achieving up to 76 gigaflops (GFLOPS).

The interconnect that links the 1,400 computing nodes with storage is the latest QDR Infiniband (IB) network, which has 40 Gbps of bandwidth per link. Each computing node is connected to two IB links, so the communication bandwidth for the node is about 80 times larger than a fast LAN (1 Gbps). Not only the link speed at the endpoint nodes, but the network topology of the entire system heavily affects the performance for large computations. Tsubame 2.0 uses a full-bisection fat-tree topology, which handles applications that need more bandwidth than provided by such topologies as a torus or mesh.

6.2 Evaluation Method

In the software environment we used gcc 4.3.4 (OpenMP 2.5) and MVAPICH2 version 1.6 with a maximum 512 nodes. Tsubame 2.0 is also characterized as a supercomputer with heterogeneous

processors and a large number of GPUs, but we did not use those parts of the system. Each node of Tsubame 2.0 has 12 physical CPU cores and 24 virtual cores with SMT (Simultaneous Multithreading). Our implementation treats 24 cores as a single node and the same number of processors is allocated to each MPI process.

In our experiments, the 2D-partitioning-based processor allocation $R \cdot C$ was per Table 1. R and C were determined with the policy of allocating division numbers as similarly as possible. The number of MPI processes should be a power of two and the value of R and C was determined by the MPI processes irrespective of the number of nodes.

The result in this paper is the maximum performance of 16 iteration BFS runs. But the result of the Graph500 list is the median of 64 BFS runs. Therefore, there is a little difference between the performance result in this paper and our official score of the Graph500 list.

Table 1. The values of R and C with the # of MPI processes

# of MPI processes	1	2	4	8	16	32
R	1	1	2	2	4	4
C	1	2	2	4	4	8
# of MPI processes	64	128	256	512	1024	2048
R	8	8	16	16	32	32
C	8	16	16	32	32	64

6.3 Performance of U-BFS

Figure 6 shows the performance of U-BFS in a weak-scaling fashion with SCALE 26 per node. We use 2 MPI processes for each node. We get the performance of 99.0 GE/s (TEPS) with 1024 nodes and SCALE 36. We also conducted the experiment with 1366 nodes and our optimized implementation achieved 103.9 GE/s (TEPS) with 1366 nodes (16,392 CPU cores) and SCALE 36.

6.4 Comparison with Reference Implementations

We compared U-BFS with the latest version (2.1.4) of the reference implementations in Figure 7 and Figure 8. This experiment was done in a weak-scaling fashion, so the problem size for each node was held constant, SCALE 24 in Figure 7 and SCALE 26 in Figure 8. The horizontal axis is the number of nodes and the vertical axis is the performance in GE/s.

U-BFS and the two reference implementations, R-CSR and R-CSC use 2 MPI processes for each node. The reference implementation, *simple*, uses 16 MPI processes for each node, since the implementation does not use multithreading parallelism. As shown in the graph, there were some results that could not be measured due to problems in the reference implementations. When the number of nodes is increased for SIM, the system ran out of memory. With R-CSR and SCALE 32, a validation error occurred and there was a segmentation fault at higher SCALE values. With R-CSC, the construction phase crashes above SCALE 34. Figure 7 and Figure 8 show that U-BFS outperformed R-CSC and SIM for all of the nodes. With numbers of nodes fewer than 32, the R-CSR implementation is best, but our method shows performance advantages with more than 32 nodes. For example, our optimized method is 2.8 times faster than R-CSR with 128 nodes and SCALE 26 for each node. (All of the final problem sizes were SCALE 33.)

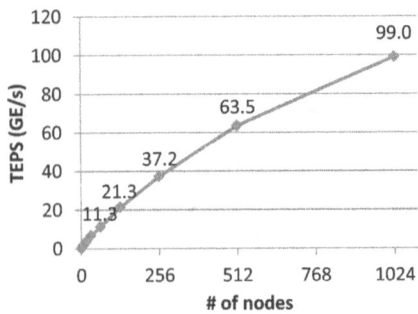

Figure 6. Performance of optimized BFS (U-BFS) (Scale 26 per node)

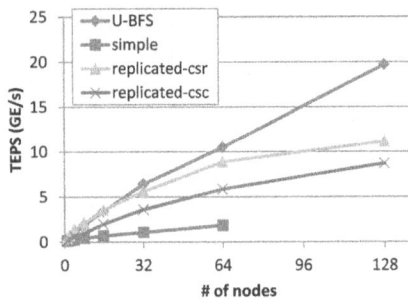

Figure 7. Comparison with Reference implementations (Scale 24 per node)

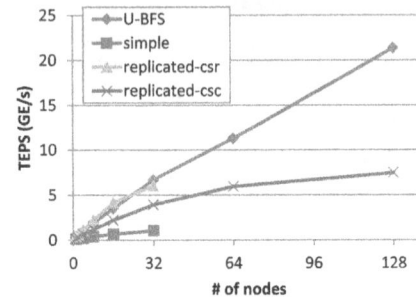

Figure 8. Comparison with Reference implementations (Scale 26 per node)

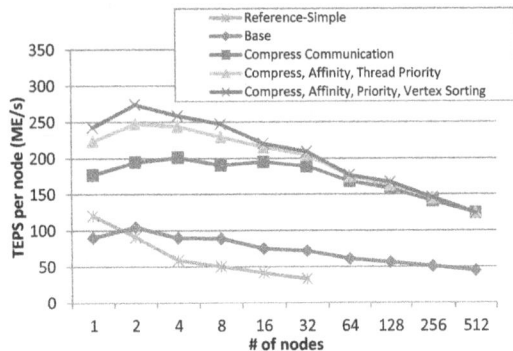

Figure 9. Effect of each optimization

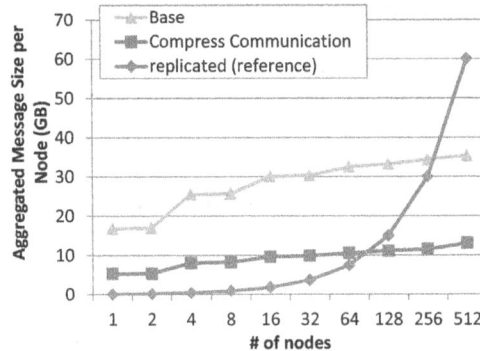

Figure 10. Comparing Communication Data Volume

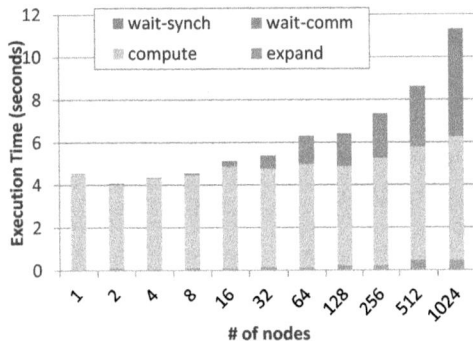

Figure 11. Performance breakdown of the overall execution times

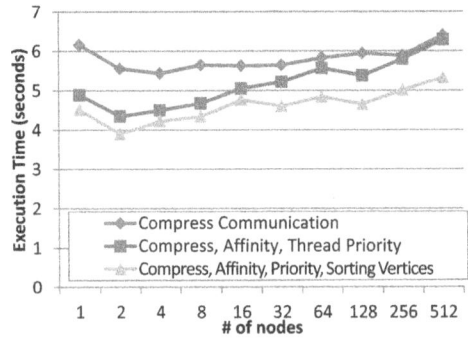

Figure 12. Execution times without communication wait times

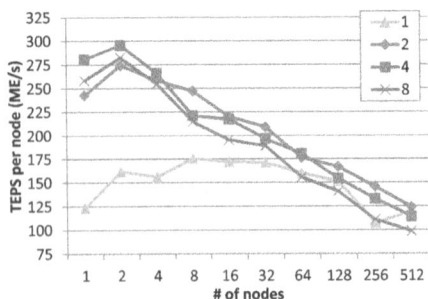

Figure 13. Performance comparison with varying number of MPI processes (1, 2, 4, and 8) per node

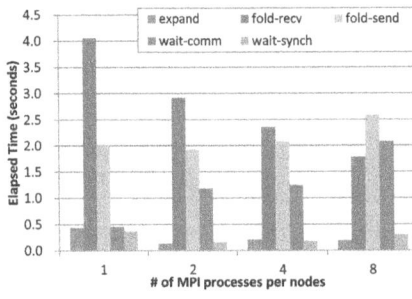

Figure 14. Performance breakdown with 64 nodes and varying number of MPI processes per node

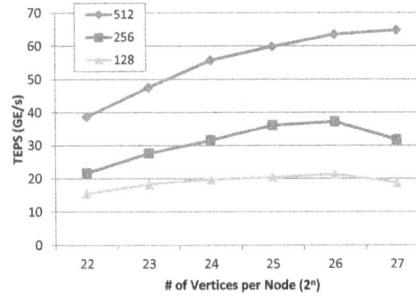

Figure 15. Performance with varying problem size per node

6.5 Effect of Each Optimization

Figure 9 shows the performance effects of each of our proposed optimization techniques. For the reference data, we also show the performance of *SIM*. The Fold phase, which is the main computation part of 2D partitioning-based algorithm, uses the same approach as the *simple* reference implementation. Therefore, our optimization should show similar performance characteristics.

We also prepared a "base" version as a multi-threaded implementation with 2D partitioning. This version parallelizes the senders and receivers, and also uses asynchronous communication. Even without any optimizations, this almost doubles the performance over the *simple* reference implementation.

Compared with the *base* version, the communication compression technique (Section 4.2) boosts the performance by 2 to 3 times. We also had a maximum of a 27% performance improvement due to the CPU affinity and the technique (Section 4.3) of giving higher priority to the receiver processing. Another 10% came from the technique of vertex sorting (Section 4.4). However, these optimizations except for the communication compression were not effective with larger numbers of nodes because the network communications became the major bottleneck.

Figure 10 compares the communication data volume of our optimized method and the reference implementation in a weak-scaling setting. The vertical axis is the transmitted data volume (GB) per node involved in one traversal of BFS with the SCALE 26 problem size. This profiling used 2 MPI processes per node.

The data volume of the Replication-based reference implementations including R-CSC and R-CSR is a theoretical value since we could not measure the data with more than 256 nodes because of the limitations of the reference implementations. This graph shows the measured data for the 2D-partitioning-based optimization methods comparing communication compression and no compression.

The communication data volume increases in proportion to the number of nodes for the weak-scaling setting since the Replication-based implementation needs to send CQ to all of the other processes. Meanwhile, the 2D-based partitioning method is scalable since the communication data volume becomes relatively smaller. With the data compression technique used by U-BFS, the communication data volume can be reduced to around one third of the *base* version. For example, the data volume was reduced from 32.3 GB to 13.1 GB with 512 nodes.

Figure 11 shows the breakdown of the execution time with U-BFS in a weak-scaling setting. The vertical axis is the execution time of BFS with SCALE 26 for a single node that runs 2 MPI processes. Since the communication at the *fold* phase is asynchronous, the communication waits only occur when the communication cannot keep up with the computation. The synchronization wait is the waiting time when synchronizing with all of the other nodes just before the level-synchronized BFS moves to the next step.

In our profiling results, the communication costs for the Expand phase is relatively small. A large part of the execution time is spent in the computations. However with more than 16 nodes, the communication wait time is increasing, which increases the overall execution time. This means the bottleneck of U-BFS with more than 16 nodes is the communication. More analysis appears in the Discussion section.

With the profiling result, the overall execution time, which excludes the communication wait time of each optimization, is shown in Figure 12. This result shows that the execution time without the communication wait time decreases as expected with our optimization techniques. This is also observed even with relatively large numbers of nodes where communications becomes the bottleneck.

6.6 Performance comparison with varying number of MPI processes

Figure 13 shows the performance characteristics when varying the number of MPI processes per node in a weak-scaling setting. The result does not show great differences between 2 or 4 MPI processes, but the performance is degraded with 1 and 8 MPI processes.

Figure 14 shows that the processing time at the receiver side decreases with larger numbers of nodes. The processing time at the receiver side (which requires the random access to the *visited* bitmap) can be reduced by increasing the cache hit ratio, since the number of vertices allocated for each MPI process decreases with more MPI processes.

Meanwhile the processing time at the sender side is increasing with larger numbers of MPI processes. This is because the number of CPU cores allocated for each MPI process, N, is decreased since $(N-1)$ threads are running as senders. The communication time is also increased for 1 and 8 MPI processes. For these reasons, performance degradation is seen with 1 and 8 MPI processes per node.

6.7 Performance with varying problem size per node

Figure 15 shows the performance characteristics as the problem size changes. U-BFS executes 2 MPI processes per node. The maximum problem size U-BFS can compute on the Tsubame 2.0 environment is SCALE 27. The experimental results shown in Figure 15 show the best performance is obtained with SCALE 26 per node when using 128 and 256 nodes. With 512 nodes, the SCALE 27 problem size shows the best performance. Also, we ran the same experiments with less than 64 nodes for reference, although our proposed optimization targets large environments. SCALE 26 per node shows the best performance with 1, 2, 4, 8, 16, 32, and 64 nodes.

6.8 Profiling Execution Time and Communication Data Size at Each Level

Figure 16 compares the reference implementations, R-CSR and R-CSC, with U-BFS in terms of the execution time at each level of the level-synchronized BFS method. Note that the reference implementations only use 32 nodes and our optimized method uses 128 nodes, but the problem size per node is the same, so this is a fair comparison.

The Kronecker graph adopted by the Graph500 benchmark is a scale-free graph. With such a graph, the search range becomes greatly expanded once it reaches vertexes with high degrees that have large numbers of edges. Since R-CSR computes the CSR-based algorithm, the execution time at each level depends on the number of unvisited vertices.

Therefore this method consumes more time in the shallow portions. In contrast, R-CSC and U-BFS use the CSC-based method. Unlike the CSR-based method, the execution time at

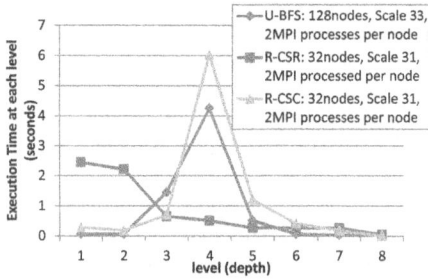

Figure 16. Execution time at each level (Scale 26 per node)

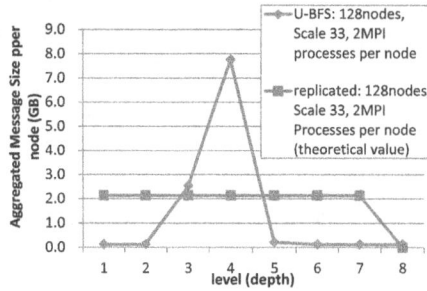

Figure 17. Aggregated message size per node at each level

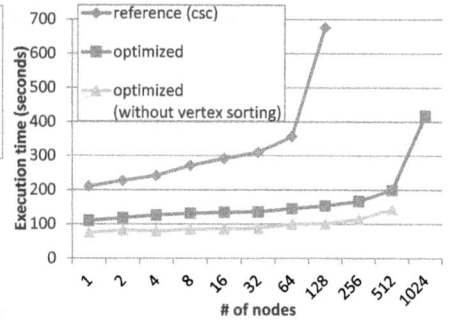

Figure 18. Performance comparison of the construction phase

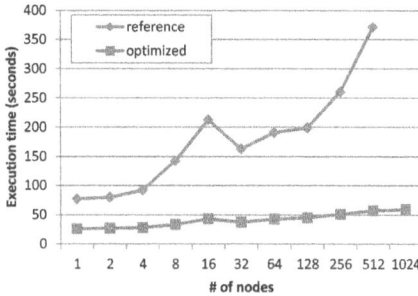

Figure 19. Performance comparison of the validation phase

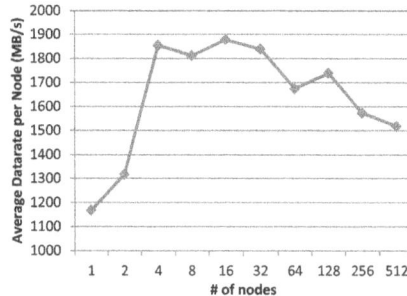

Figure 20. Average data rate per node with varying numbers of nodes

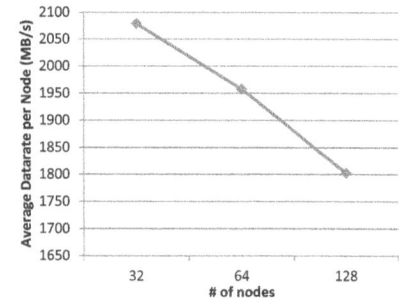

Figure 21. Effect of all-to-all collective communication of 32 nodes against other groups

each level is almost proportional to the number of adjacent vertices of CQ.

Figure 17 compares the reference implementations and U-BFS for the communication data volume per node at each level of the level-synchronized BFS. The reference implementations show the theoretical values of R-CSR and R-CSC since both implementations use the same approach and their data volumes are similar.

The Replication-based implementation needs to copy the CQ bitmap to all of the MPI processes, so the communication data volume is similar at each level. However, the communication data volume of U-BFS is almost proportional to the number of adjacent vertices, so the execution time at each level shown in Figure 16 reflects this characteristic.

Our optimized method has high performance processing even for smaller numbers of vertices, and thus the random graph and a real road network with a large graph diameter can be efficiently processed with our method.

6.9 Performance of Construction and Validation

Figure 18 compares the construction phases of the optimized version and the reference implementations in a weak-scaling setting. U-BFS with sorting functionality is 1.5 times slower than without sorting. However, it finishes the construction phase twice as quickly compared to the reference implementation.

Figure 19 compares our method of validation with the reference implementation, where our method finishes the validation phase with less than one-third of the time of the original implementations.

7. DISCUSSION

7.1 Performance with Fat-Tree Network Topology

The performance evaluation of our method in a weak scaling setting reveals that the performance per node is degraded by increasing numbers of nodes. According to the profiling result, we also found that the bottleneck is the communication and this performance result came from the increased communication waits.

The network topology of Tsubame 2.0 is a Fat-Tree. Therefore if the theoretical peak performance is achieved, even all-to-all collective communication with all of the nodes should have the same performance as two arbitrary nodes communicating with each other, since the communication path between arbitrary pairs of nodes will not overlap. However in reality, the communication paths interfere when the communication between nodes is simultaneous, which leads to performance degradation. This interfere is described in [22] as a hotspot.

Figure 20 is the average transmission rate per node with U-BFS. This value is measured by simply dividing the entire data transmission rate by the BFS execution time. The result shows that the transmission rate is decreasing with increasing numbers of nodes.

We also measured the effect on other group communication when the groups, each consisting of 32 nodes, did all-to-all collective communication to all of the involved nodes transmitting different data to the other nodes). The result is shown in Figure 21. In the figure, 2 and 4 groups of 32 nodes simultaneously did all-to-all collective communication with 64 nodes and 128 nodes, respectively. No communication is done between any arbitrary nodes. This experimental result reveals and verifies that communication by other groups influences the transmission data rate due to the hotspot.

Therefore the performance degradation of our optimized method with increased numbers of nodes is caused by the limitations of the Fat-Tree-based network topology. The overlap problem of this Fat-Tree communication routing has been investigated by various methods, and the unexpected communication degradation shown in Figure 9 might possibly solved by applying some of these approaches.

7.2 Comparing with 3D-torus based systems

Our optimized approach achieves 103.9 GE/s as TEPS with SCALE 36 and 1366 nodes of Tsubame 2.0. When comparing this value with other systems based on the Graph500 benchmark results announced in November 2011, the top-ranked system achieves 254.3 GE/s as TEPS with SCALE 32 and 4,096 nodes of BlueGene/Q. Another leading TEPS score was the system called Hopper that achieves 113.4 GE/s with SCALE 37 and 1,800 nodes.

8. RELATED WORK

Yoo [4] presents a distributed BFS scheme with 2D graph partitioning that scales on the IBM BlueGene/L with 32,768 nodes. Our implementation is based on their distributed BFS method but we optimized the method further. Bader [3] describes the performance of optimized parallel BFS algorithms on multithreaded architectures such as the Cray MTA-2.

Aydin[21] conduct the performance evaluation of a distributed BFS with 1D partitioning and 2D partitioning on the Cray XE6 and the Cray XT4. His work is similar to our work but his method of 2D partitioning is different from Yoo[4]'s method and his method needs additional communication that degrade the performance of BFS. Their achieved score in [21] was only 17.8 GE/s on Hopper with 40,000-cores.

Agarwal [2] proposes an efficient and scalable BFS algorithm for commodity multicore processors such as the 8-core Intel Nehalem EX processor. With the 4-socket Nehalem EX (Xeon 7560, 2.26 GHz, 32 cores, 64 threads with HyperThreading), they ran 2.4 times faster than a Cray XMT with 128 processors when exploring a random graph with 64 million vertices and 512 million edges, and 5 times faster than 256 BlueGene/L processors on a graph with an average degree of 50. The performance impact of their proposed optimization algorithm was tested only on a single node, but it would be worthwhile to extend their proposed algorithm to larger machines with commodity multicore processors, which includes Tsubame 2.0.

Harish [10] devised a method of accelerating single-source shortest path problems with GPGPUs. Their GPGPU-based method solves the breadth-first search problem in approximately 1 second for 10 million vertices of a randomized graph where each vertex has 6 edges on average. However, the paper concluded that the GPGPU-method does not match the CPU-based implementation for scale-free graphs such as the road network of the 9th DIMACS implementation challenge, since the distribution of degrees follows a power law in which some vertices have much higher degrees than others. However since the top-ranked supercomputers in TOP500 have GPGPUs for compute-intensive applications, it would be worthwhile to pursue the optimization of Graph500 by exploiting GPGPUs.

9. CONCLUDING REMARKS AND FUTURE WORK

In this paper we proposed an optimized implementation of the Graph500 benchmark in a large-scale distributed memory environment. The reference code samples provided by the Graph500 site were neither scalable nor optimized for such a large environment. Our optimized implementation is based on the level-synchronized BFS with 2D partitioning and we propose some optimization methods such as communication compression and vertex sorting. Our implementation does 103.9 GE/s as TEPS (Traversal Edges Per Second) with SCALE 36 and 1366 nodes of Tsubame 2.0. This score is 3rd score in the ranking list announced in November 2011. We found the performance of our optimized BFS is limited by the network bandwidth. We also propose approaches for optimizing the validation phase, which can accelerate the overall benchmark. Many of our proposed approaches in this paper can also be effective for other supercomputers such as Cray and BlueGene. For future work we will show the effectiveness of our implementation in other large systems.

10. REFERENCES

[1]   Graph500 : http://www.graph500.org/

[2]   Virat Agarwal, Fabrizio Petrini, Davide Pasetto, and David A. Bader. 2010. Scalable Graph Exploration on Multicore Processors. In Proceedings of the 2010 ACM/IEEE International Conference for High Performance Computing, Networking, Storage and Analysis (SC '10). IEEE Computer Society, Washington, DC, USA, 1-11

[3]   David A. Bader and Kamesh Madduri. 2006. Designing Multithreaded Algorithms for Breadth-First Search and st-connectivity on the Cray MTA-2. In Proceedings of the 2006 International Conference on Parallel Processing (ICPP '06). IEEE Computer Society, Washington, DC, USA, 523-530

[4]   Andy Yoo, Edmond Chow, Keith Henderson, William McLendon, Bruce Hendrickson, and Umit Catalyurek. 2005. A Scalable Distributed Parallel Breadth-First Search Algorithm on BlueGene/L. In Proceedings of the 2005 ACM/IEEE conference on Supercomputing (SC '05). IEEE Computer Society, Washington, DC, USA, 25-.

[5]   D.A. Bader, J. Feo, J. Gilbert, J. Kepner, D. Koester, E. Loh, K. Madduri, W. Mann, and Theresa Meuse, HPCS Scalable Synthetic Compact Applications #2 Graph Analysis (SSCA#2 v2.2 Specification), 5 September 2007.

[6]   D. Chakrabarti, Y. Zhan, and C. Faloutsos, R-MAT: A recursive model for graph mining, SIAM Data Mining 2004.

[7]   Bader, D., Cong, G., and Feo, J. 2005. On the architectural requirements for efficient execution of graph algorithms. In Proc. 34th Int'l Conf. on Parallel Processing (ICPP). IEEE Computer Society, Oslo, Norway.

[8]   K. Madduri, D.A. Bader, J.W. Berry, and J.R. Crobak, ``Parallel Shortest Path Algorithms for Solving Large-Scale Instances,'' 9th DIMACS Implementation Challenge -- The Shortest Path Problem, DIMACS Center, Rutgers University, Piscataway, NJ, November 13-14, 2006.

[9]   Richard C. Murphy, Jonathan Berry, William McLendon, Bruce Hendrickson, Douglas Gregor, and Andrew Lumsdaine, "DFS: A Simple to Write Yet Difficult to

Execute Benchmark,", IEEE International Symposium on Workload Characterizations 2006 (IISWC06), San Jose, CA, 25-27 October 2006.

[10] Pawan Harish and P. J. Narayanan. 2007. Accelerating large graph algorithms on the GPU using CUDA. In Proceedings of the 14th international conference on High performance computing (HiPC'07), Srinivas Aluru, Manish Parashar, Ramamurthy Badrinath, and Viktor K. Prasanna (Eds.). Springer-Verlag, Berlin, Heidelberg, 197-208.

[11] Daniele Paolo Scarpazza, Oreste Villa, and Fabrizio Petrini. 2008. Efficient Breadth-First Search on the Cell/BE Processor. IEEE Trans. Parallel Distrib. Syst. 19, 10 (October 2008), 1381-1395.

[12] Douglas Gregor and Andrew Lumsdaine. 2005. Lifting sequential graph algorithms for distributed-memory parallel computation. SIGPLAN Not. 40, 10 (October 2005), 423-437.

[13] Grzegorz Malewicz, Matthew H. Austern, Aart J.C Bik, James C. Dehnert, Ilan Horn, Naty Leiser, and Grzegorz Czajkowski. 2010. Pregel: a system for large-scale graph processing. In Proceedings of the 2010 international conference on Management of data (SIGMOD '10). ACM, New York, NY, USA, 135-146.

[14] U. Kang, Charalampos E. Tsourakakis, and Christos Faloutsos. 2009. PEGASUS: A Peta-Scale Graph Mining System Implementation and Observations. In Proceedings of the 2009 Ninth IEEE International Conference on Data Mining (ICDM '09). IEEE Computer Society, Washington, DC, USA, 229-238.

[15] Toshio Endo, Akira Nukada, Satoshi Matsuoka, and Naoya Maruyama. Linpack Evaluation on a Supercomputer with Heterogeneous Accelerators. In IEEE International Parallel & Distributed Processing Symposium (IPDPS 2010).

[16] J. Leskovec, D. Chakrabarti, J. Kleinberg, and C. Faloutsos, "Realistic, mathematically tractable graph generation and evolution, using kronecker multiplication," in Conf. on Principles and Practice of Knowledge Discovery in Databases, 2005.

[17] MVAPICH2: http://mvapich.cse.ohio-state.edu/

[18] OpenMPI : http://www.open-mpi.org/

[19] Toyotaro Suzumura, Koji Ueno, Hitoshi Sato, Katsuki Fujisawa and Satoshi Matsuoka. Performance characteristics of Graph500 on large-scale distributed environment, IEEE IISWC 2011 (IEEE International Symposium on Workload Characterization) , November 2011, Austin, TX, US.

[20] Umit Catalyurek and Cevdet Aykanat. 2001. A hypergraph-partitioning approach for coarse-grain decomposition. In Proceedings of the 2001 ACM/IEEE conference on Supercomputing (SC '01). ACM, New York, NY, USA.

[21] Aydin Buluç and Kamesh Madduri. 2011. Parallel breadth-first search on distributed memory systems. In Proceedings of 2011 International Conference for High Performance Computing, Networking, Storage and Analysis (SC '11). ACM, New York, NY, USA, Article 65 , 12 pages.

[22] Torsten Hoefler, Timo Schneider, Andrew Lumsdaine. Multistage switches are not crossbars: Effects of static routing in high-performance networks. 2008 IEEE International Conference on Cluster Computing, Tsukuba, Japan. pp.116-125.

PonD: Dynamic Creation of HTC Pool on Demand Using a Decentralized Resource Discovery System

Kyungyong Lee
University of Florida
ACIS Lab. Dept of ECE.
klee@acis.ufl.edu

David Wolinsky
Yale University
Computer Science Dept.
david.wolinsky@yale.edu

Renato Figueiredo
University of Florida
ACIS Lab. Dept of ECE.
renato@acis.ufl.edu

ABSTRACT

High Throughput Computing (HTC) platforms aggregate heterogeneous resources to provide vast amounts of computing power over a long period of time. Typical HTC systems, such as Condor and BOINC, rely on central managers for resource discovery and scheduling. While this approach simplifies deployment, it requires careful system configuration and management to ensure high availability and scalability. In this paper, we present a novel approach that integrates a self-organizing P2P overlay for scalable and timely discovery of resources with unmodified client/server job scheduling middleware in order to create HTC virtual resource Pools on Demand (PonD). This approach decouples resource discovery and scheduling from job execution/monitoring — a job submission dynamically generates an HTC platform based upon resources discovered through match-making from a large "sea" of resources in the P2P overlay and forms a "PonD" capable of leveraging unmodified HTC middleware for job execution and monitoring. We show that job scheduling time of our approach scales with $O(\log N)$, where N is the number of resources in a pool, through first-order analytical models and large-scale simulation results. To verify the practicality of PonD, we have implemented a prototype using Condor (called C-PonD), a structured P2P overlay, and a PonD creation module. Experimental results with the prototype in two WAN environments (PlanetLab and the FutureGrid cloud computing testbed) demonstrates the utility of C-PonD as a HTC approach without relying on a central repository for maintaining all resource information. Though the prototype is based on Condor, the decoupled nature of the system components - decentralized resource discovery, PonD creation, job execution/monitoring - is generally applicable to other grid computing middleware systems.

Keywords

Resource discovery; self-configuration; P2P; virtual resources; high-throughput computing

Categories and Subject Descriptors

C.2.4 [**COMPUTER-COMMUNICATION NETWORKS**]: Distributed Systems

1. INTRODUCTION

High Throughput Computing (HTC) refers to computing environments that deliver vast amounts of processing capacities over a non-negligible period of time (e.g., days, months, years). This continuous computing throughput is a vital factor in solving advanced computational problems for scientists and researchers. Widely-used HTC middleware such as Condor [1] and BOINC [2] enable sharing of commodity resources connected over a local or wide-area network. Commonly, these systems use central managers to aggregate resource information and to schedule tasks. While this approach provides a straightforward means to discover available resources and schedule jobs, it can impose administrative overheads and scalability constraints. Namely, the central manager needs to be closely administered, and the failure of the manager node can render its managed resources unavailable for scheduling new tasks.

The growing adoption of on-demand computing-as-a-service cloud provisioning models and a large number of resources in data centers motivate the need for solutions that scale gracefully and tolerate failures, while limiting management overheads. These traits are commonly found in peer-to-peer (P2P) systems; nevertheless, the current prevailing approaches for job scheduling rely on specialized configuration of responsibilities for resources, e.g. for information collection and job match-making. With proper configuration, such approaches have been demonstrated to scale to several thousands of resources.

Scalability limitations of HTC middleware beyond current targets have been addressed in the literature. Raicu et. al. [3] addressed the inherent scalability constraint in existing HTC schedulers by proposing a fast and lightweight task execution framework which demonstrated improved scalability in a pool of tens of thousands resources processing millions of tasks. Sonmez et. al [4] measured the workflow scheduling performance in multi-cluster grids in simulated and real environments. The real-environment experiment was executed on the DAS-3 (a multi-cluster grid system in the Netherlands) revealing that limited capabilities of head-nodes result in overall system performance degradation as workflow size increases.

In this paper, we propose a novel HTC middleware approach, PonD, which leverages a scalable and flexible P2P decentralized resource discovery system to form a job execution Pool-on-Demand (PonD) dynamically from a large-scale resource pool. Within a PonD, unmodified client/server HTC middleware modules are self-configured on-demand, and take over the responsibility for job execution and monitoring. A key contribution of this paper, which differentiates PonD from related work, is the integration of decentralized resource discovery with a traditional centralized job-scheduling approach supporting existing job schedulers. By leveraging decentralized resource discovery during scheduling, we avoid the need for a central aggregator of information, and by using a centralized scheduler we can reuse existing HTC middleware. In addition to the enhancement on the scheduling scalability, this approach is able to provide improvements on the fault-tolerance, and combined with virtualization and infrastructure-as-a-service (IaaS) technologies, the PonD approach allows increased flexibility of scaling up/down virtual resource pools.

Our approach supports a large scale P2P overlay consisting of various candidate resources capable of joining a PonD. As typical in P2P systems, each resource, by default, can take the role of both job submitter and worker. Thus all members in a PonD, or connected resources, have the ability to dynamically create, join, and leave a PonD based on their queued-job demands. When creating a PonD, the requirements for the job are passed to the decentralized resource discovery module. This module forms a query and distributes it through a self-organizing, distributed query tree, which in turn aggregates the results in order to find resources which satisfy the job's requirements. The resource discovery module invites a portion of the usable resources to join a PonD owned by the job's submitter. Each resource handles the request by automatically configuring the HTC middleware to treat the job owner as the centralized manager, after which jobs are immediately scheduled and run.

Figure 1 illustrates the overall operation of PonD. Node A has a list of jobs in its job queue, and it sends a resource discovery query with job requirements. Using the query result, node A sends an invitation to nodes that satisfy ClassAd requirements to join its PonD — node A becomes the central manager node for its own PonD. Then, job scheduling and execution are processed by underlying HTC middleware. After job completion, Node A releases workers back into the larger resource pool, and returns to its initial status. In an abstract view, participating nodes exist in a large-scale, loosely-coupled resource "sea" — for instance, a wide-area opportunistic computing Desktop Grid, or a system that federates across multiple public/private clouds. When a node needs to run a job, it discovers and invites worker nodes to join a "pond" that is much smaller — for instance, a virtual cluster with hundreds of nodes aggregated into a single virtual resource pool. Upon job completion, nodes return to the "sea" and await other invitations or initiate their own PonDs. The discovery process is non-binding, and nodes are able to decide to accept or decline membership on a PonD according to local policies; once bound to a PonD, scheduling policies of the HTC middleware deployed apply.

The practicality in our work derives largely from our experiences with a Condor-based PonD implementation, C-PonD. We present both the construction of C-PonD as well as experimental results from analysis, simulation, and deployment on PlanetLab [5] and the FutureGrid distributed cloud computing infrastructure [6]. The simulation results verify the scalability of PonDs — specifically, pool creation

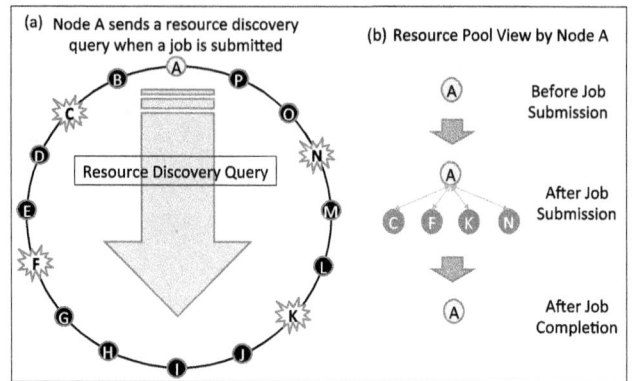

Figure 1: On-Demand pool creation when a job is submitted: (a)Node A sends a resource discovery query when it has a idle job in its job queue. (b)Based on the query result, Node A forms a condor pool with job requirement satisfying nodes (Node C, F, K, and N). After a job completion, worker nodes are released.

time grows as a function of $O(\log N)$, where N is the number of resources. The simulation results also evaluate the scheduling result correctness in case dynamically changing attributes are queried or participating nodes have unstable uptime. Experiments using FutureGrid resources capture a cluster/cloud scenario, and an experimental deployment on PlanetLab highlights a Desktop Grid scenario to demonstrate the feasibility of C-PonD on environments where resources are shared and widely distributed.

In summary, the main contributions of this work are:

- We propose a novel HTC system which integrates resource discovery with flexible query/resource representation in a decentralized query processing fashion based on P2P multicast trees, and dynamic middleware configuration to create resource pools on demand.

- We demonstrate this system by reusing existing, *unmodified* HTC middleware through a prototype implementation. It supports rich query processing and on-demand creation/tear-down of Condor pools.

- We evaluate the system from the perspectives of asymptotic scalability and its ability to provide timely resource discovery results through simulation-based analyses at large scales, and of its practical feasibility through experiments with smaller scale deployments of the prototype in WAN testbeds (FutureGrid and PlanetLab).

2. BACKGROUND

Focusing on Condor PonDs, in this section we give a brief description of its building blocks: Condor [1], a structured P2P network overlay, and a self-organizing multicast-tree build on a P2P network.

2.1 Condor

Condor [1] is a high-throughput computing framework that harnesses both dedicated and non-dedicated computing resources to create a resource pool. After gathering submitted jobs and available resource information from participating nodes, Condor negotiates and schedules inactive jobs to idle machines. Condor also provides Classified Advertisements (ClassAds) [7] that support a flexible and expressive way to describe job characteristics and requirements as well as resource information in order to determine matches.

In Condor, nodes can play the role of central managers, worker nodes, or job submitters. Roles are determined by running the appropriate daemons (i.e., *condor_startd*, *condor_schedd*, *condor_collector*, and *condor_negotiator*), and a single node may assume multiple roles.

condor_startd: This daemon is responsible for advertising resource capabilities and policies expressed using ClassAds to the *condor_collector* daemon of central manager as well as receiving and executing tasks delegated by the central manager. A node that runs this daemon is regarded as a worker node.

condor_schedd: A node which wants to submit a job runs this daemon. *condor_schedd* is in charge of storing user-submitted jobs at a local queue and sending resource requests to a *condor_collector* at a central manager node.

condor_collector: The role of this daemon is collecting resource information expressed using ClassAds and a list of *condor_schedd* with inactive jobs in their queue. A *condor_startd* periodically updates resource information ClassAds to their *condor_collector*. *condor_collector* also retrieves a list of inactive jobs from *condor_schedd* daemons at the time of negotiation.

condor_negotiator: This daemon is responsible for matchmaking between inactive jobs and idle resources. At each negotiation cycle, this daemon retrieves a list of inactive jobs and resource ClassAds from *condor_collector* daemon.

Usually, a condor pool consists of a single central manager that runs both an instance of the *condor_collector* and *condor_negotiator* daemons along with many worker nodes and submitters which run *condor_startd* and *condor_schedd* daemons, respectively. In order to provide reliable services in case of central manager node failure, fail-over central managers can be deployed using the high availability daemon.

In order to enable cross-domain resource sharing, Condor has two extensions, Condor-Flock [8] and Condor-G [9]. With these approaches, each node maintains a pre-configured list of other pools' central managers. Each central manager node also has to keep a list of allowed remote submitters. To overcome the pre-configuration requirements of condor flocking, Butt et al. [10] presented a self-organizing Condor flock that was built upon a structured P2P network. A locality-aware P2P pool is formed with central managers of each condor pool. When a central manager has available resources, it announces to other managers via the P2P overlay. When a central manager requires additional resources, it checks announcement messages from other central managers to determine where available resources are located. While our approach shares similar features to self-organizing Condor-flock [10] (self-configuration, and dynamic resource instantiation in response to jobs in the queue), the core mechanism for discovering nodes and self-organizing pools based on unstructured P2P queries with a logarithmically increasing overhead is a key differentiating factor.

Condor Glide-in [11] also provides a way to share idle resources across different administrative domains without a pre-configured list of other pools' central managers. When jobs are waiting in a queue of the *condor_schedd* daemon, *pilots* are created to find available resources for execution. In order to find available resources, a Glidein Factory manages a list of available resources across multiple Condor pools.

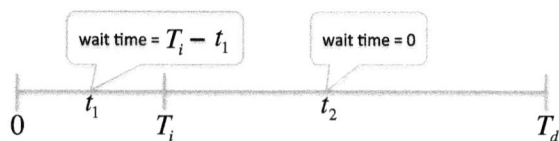

Figure 2: Condor negotiation procedure. T_d means the default scheduling period, and T_i means the minimum inter-scheduling time. A job submitted at t_1, where $t_1 < T_i$, has to wait $T_i - t_1$ for matchmaking.

Though the approach of flocking provides opportunities to share resources across different domains with bounded management overheads at a central manager, the cost of sequentially traversing pools in a flock list introduces non-negligible additional scheduling latencies at scale. Condor maintains a default negotiation period, T_d, and a minimum inter-negotiation time, T_i where $T_d \geq T_i$, as system configurations. Upon job submission, the negotiator checks if T_i has elapsed since the last negotiation cycle. If so, it starts a new negotiation cycle immediately. Otherwise, it waits until T_i elapses. The procedure is explained in Figure 2. In order to analyze the effect of the minimum inter-negotiation time to the overall waiting time in a queue until a matchmaking, the expected waiting time can be computed as follows.

$$
\begin{aligned}
E(T_{wait}) &= \frac{1}{T_d} \int_0^{T_d} (T_{wait} \text{ at time } t) \, dt \\
&= \frac{1}{T_d} \times \left(\int_0^{T_i} (T_i - t) \, dt + \int_{T_i}^{T_d} 0 \, dt \right) \quad (1) \\
&= \frac{T_i^2}{2 \times T_d} \quad (2)
\end{aligned}
$$

Equation 1 describes the waiting time of a job upon arrival at time t that can be explained with Figure 2. In the default Condor setup, T_d is 60 seconds and T_i is 20 seconds. Thus, the expected waiting time at each central manager during a flocking procedure is 3.3 seconds. Considering the sequential traversal of central managers during flocking, the waiting time increases linearly.

2.2 P2P system

P2P systems can provide a scalable, self-organizing, and fault-tolerant service by eliminating the distinction between service provider and consumer. C-PonD uses a structured P2P network, Brunet [12], which implements the Kleinberg small-world network [13]. Each Brunet node maintains two types of connections: (1) a constant number of near connections to its nearest left and right neighbors on a ring using the Euclidian distance in a 160-bit node ID space, and (2) approximately $log(N)$ (where N is the number of nodes) far connections to random nodes on a ring, such that the routing cost is $O(log(N))$. The overlay uses recursive greedy routing in order to deliver messages.

2.3 Tree-based Multicast on P2P

By leveraging existing connections in a structured P2P system, Vishnevsky et. al [14] presented a means to create an efficient distribution of messages in Chord and Pastry using a self-organizing tree. Each node recursively partitions responsible multicast regions by using the routing information at each node. DeeToo [15] presents a similar tree creation method on a small-world style P2P network, which is leveraged in PonD for decentralized resource discovery.

In a recursive-partitioning tree, each node is allocated a sub-region of the P2P ring over which to disseminate a message. A node then redistributes the message to neighboring nodes inside this region allocating new sub-regions to them. This process continues until the message is disseminated over the entire sub-region. For example, if a node, n_0, is assigned $[begin, end]$ region for message distribution, the node checks its routing table to get a list of neighboring nodes that exist in $[begin, end]$. Assuming that node n_0 has neighboring nodes n_1, n_2, ..., n_{i-1}, n_i within $[begin, end]$, n_0 assigns sub-region $[begin, n_2)$, $[n_2, n_3)$, ..., $[n_{i-1}, n_i)$, $[n_i, end]$ to nodes n_1, n_2, ..., n_{i-1}, n_i, respectively. These steps continue recursively until reaching leaf nodes that have no neighbors in the allocated sub-region.

In comparison to statically-built trees [16–18], the dynamic and self-organizing tree provides prompt responsiveness to node failures without the additional cost of maintaining pointers for children and parent nodes. Furthermore, a message does not have to be delivered to the static root node in order to be propagated to the entire set of resources.

3. ARCHITECTURE AND DESIGN

This section details the system design and the techniques used in resource discovery and self-organization of PonDs.

3.1 Decentralized resource discovery

Decentralized resource discovery in PonD shares similar motivations from related works of resource discovery in P2P [10, 19–23] but follows a fundamentally different approach. In a practical HTC system, the number of resource attributes can be large; for instance, default Condor installations have several dozens of attributes, and furthermore, users can provide their own attributes. Queries can be complex and include combinations of exact, ranges, and regular-expression matching, thus making resource discovery based on DHT key/value lookups or range-based queries insufficient.

Modifying the middleware or imposing limits to its utility is not a viable approach either. The approach taken by PonD ensures that unmodified HTC middleware can be used seamlessly. We leverage Condor ClassAds [7] and its matchmaking library for distributed query processing during discovery. By doing so, our decentralized resource discovery module inherits most of ClassAd characteristics, e.g. supporting range queries and regular expressions. For query dissemination and result aggregation, we use a self-organizing multicast tree. This approach can be applied to other structured P2P methods (e.g., Chord and Pastry) that support scalable multicasting with different resource representations and match-making engines (e.g., RDF and semantic queries).

3.1.1 Matchmaking module

The matchmaking module is responsible for matching requirements of jobs and resources by ranking nodes based upon their ability to satisfy a query. In order to obtain and distribute resource information, each resource uses *condor_startd* daemon which produces ClassAds. For matchmaking, requirements for desired resources and rank criteria are delivered as arguments. The following example illus-

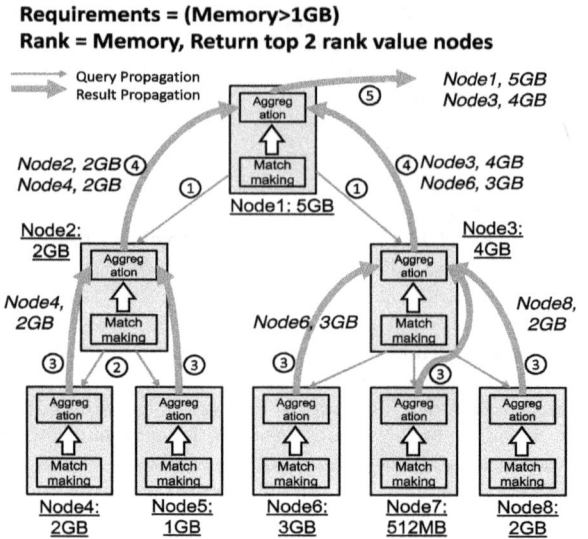

Figure 3: Resource discovery example. *Node1* wants to find the top two available Memory machines whose memory is greater than 1GB. *NodeID:Memory Size* value means matchmaking result, and NodeID:Memory Size value means available resource status.

trates arguments based on ClassAd syntax.[1]

Requirement=Memory>1GB && SWInstalled.Has ("Matlab") && regexp("*.edu",Hostname)

Rank = (Memory) + (KeyboardIdle*10)

The **Requirement** says the target resource's memory has to be greater than 1GB. The target machine also has to have *Matlab* installed, and the hostname of target machine has to end with ".edu". If a node satisfies the *Requirement*, it calculates a rank value. **Rank** is used to determine optimal candidates. This approach allows users to have the flexibility to specify their own job requirements and rank values.

3.1.2 Aggregation module

Upon completing the processing of a match-making task, a node returns the result to its aggregation module. The local aggregator waits for results from child nodes to aggregate its own and children nodes' matchmaking results. The aggregation is executed by sorting the rank value of query satisfying nodes and extracting the top ranked value nodes. After completing aggregation, the node returns the result to the parent node's aggregation function.

As with matchmaking, aggregation is processed independently at each node in a self-organizing multicast tree, and results are propagated back through the tree. This hierarchical information aggregation method provides scalability in a distributed information management system. The parallel processing of match-making and aggregation module is comparable to MapReduce [24] distributed computing: the match-making process is akin to a Map task, and result aggregation is akin to a Reduce task [25].

Figure 3 shows an example of the decentralized resource

---

[1]In the example, we modified ClassAd syntax for readability.

discovery. NodeID:Memory Size (underline) is the current resource status of each node, and *NodeID:Memory Size* (italic) is an aggregation result. Node1 (the root node) initiates a resource discovery query by specifying a requirement: e.g. a node's memory should be larger than 1GB. Nodes satisfying the requirement are ordered based on Memory size, and the two with the largest sizes are returned. The narrow line shows query propagation using a self-organizing multicast tree. The Aggregation module orders child nodes' result and returns a list of required number of nodes (thick line).

3.1.3 First-Fit Mode

In order to maximize the efficiency of aggregation and to discover the list of nodes that maximize rank, a parent node in a recursive-partitioning tree waits until all child nodes' aggregated results are returned. However, if it is acceptable to execute tasks on resources that satisfy the requirement but might not be the best-ranked ones, the query response time can be improved by executing a resource discovery query in *First-Fit* mode. With First-Fit, an intermediate node in a tree can return an aggregated result to its parent node as soon as the number of discovered nodes are larger than the number of requested nodes.

3.1.4 Redundant Topology to Improve Fault-Tolerance

While a tree architecture provides a dynamic and scalable basis for a parallel query distribution and result aggregation, it might suffer from result incompleteness due to internal node failures during an aggregation task. For instance, in Figure 3, the failure of *Node 3* in the middle of query processing would result in the loss of the query results for nodes *6, 7*, and *8*. In order to reduce the effect of internal node failure to completeness of the query result, we propagate a query concurrently through a redundant tree topology.

One such method is to execute parallel requests in opposite directions in the overlay. In a recursive-partitioning tree discussed in Section 2.3, a node is responsible for a region in its clockwise-direction; node $n2$ is assigned a region $[n2, n3)$, note that $n2 < n3$. In a counter-clockwise direction tree, a node $n2$ is allocated a region $(n1, n2]$. This approach can compensate missing results in one tree from another if the missing region is not assigned to failed nodes in both trees.

3.2 PonD self-configuration

After acquiring a list of available resources from a resource discovery module, invitations are sent to those nodes to join a PonD of a job submitter. As invited nodes join a PonD, deployed HTC middleware takes roles of task execution and monitoring. In C-PonD, which is an implementation of PonD with Condor, we leverage system configuration "CONDOR_HOST" to create/join a PonD dynamically.

Condor job scheduling is performed at *condor_negotiator* daemon with available resource information and inactive job lists that are fetched at the time of negotiation from the *condor_collector* daemon. Generally, the two daemons run at the central manager node, while worker nodes (*condor_startd* daemon) and job submit nodes (*condor_schedd* daemon) identify the central manager using a condor configuration value "CONDOR_HOST", which can be set independently for daemons on the same resource. The "CONDOR_HOST" configuration can be changed at run-time by using Condor commands (e.g., *condor_config_val* and *condor_reconfig*).

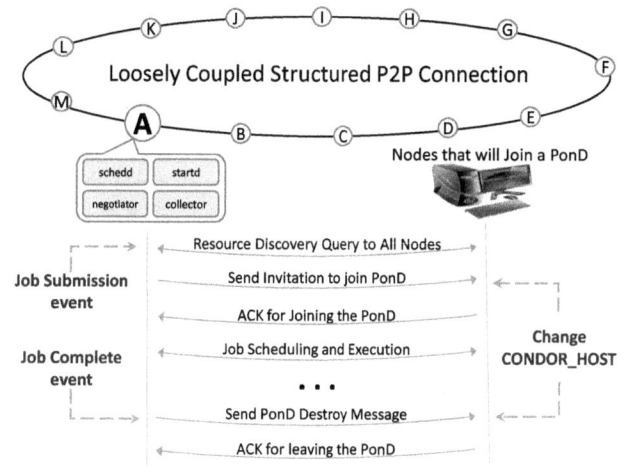

Figure 4: Steps to create a C-PonD through dynamic condor re-configuration.

Figure 4 shows an overall procedure of creating a PonD with Condor for job execution. In the figure, all resources are connected through a structured P2P network, and every node runs *condor_negotiator, condor_collector, condor_startd*, and *condor_schedd* daemon locally. We will show how Node A creates a PonD for a job execution.

○ Upon detecting a job submission, Node A sends a resource discovery query with a job requirement, rank criteria, and the number of required nodes, which are derived from the ClassAds of the local submission queue in the *condor_schedd*.

○ Upon the query completion, Node A sends a PonD join invitation to nodes that are discovered from the query. When receiving the invitation, nodes that accept it set "CONDOR_HOST" value of *condor_startd* daemon to the address of Node A.

○ Nodes send ACK message to confirm joining the PonD.

○ When a PonD is created, Node A becomes the central manager of the PonD, and *condor_negotiator* daemon of Node A schedules inactive jobs to available resources. The scheduled jobs are executed using *condor_starter* of worker nodes and *condor_shadow* daemon of Node A.

○ Upon job completion, Node A sends a PonD destroy message to nodes in the PonD. When receiving the message, nodes set "CONDOR_HOST" value to the address of itself.

○ Each node sends an ACK message to Node A when leaving the PonD.

Note that every node in the resource pool can create a PonD. It is also possible for a node to discover available resources for other PonDs in case a central manager of a PonD is not capable of executing resource discovery query.

3.2.1 Leveraging virtual networking

C-PonD is designed to provide an infrastructure that supports scaling to a large number of geographically distributed resources in a wide area network — a common environment in Desktop Grids. Due to the constraints of Network Address Translation (NAT)/firewalls, however, supporting direct communication between peers for PonD invitation/join, job execution/monitoring using Condor daemons is one of essential features for a successful deployment in the real-world. In order to address this requirement, we adopt IP-over-P2P (IPOP) [26, 27] to build a virtual networking overlay that enables routing IP messages atop a structured P2P network. This approach has benefits with respect to self-management, resilience to failures, and ease-of-use from the user's perspective. The practicality of this approach is well presented by GridAppliance [28] as the authors demonstrated over several years of operation in a WAN environment.

These network challenges present a problem for systems deriving from Condor GlideIn or Flocking, which need publicly available IP addresses on a pilot node, worker/submitter, or central manager node. C-PonD's use of virtual networking allows direct messaging between peers after an IP-layer virtual overlay network has been established.

3.2.2 Multiple Distinct Jobs Submission

In the case that multiple jobs with distinct requirements are submitted concurrently by a $condor\_schedd$, discovered resources need to be distinguishable by the initiating query. Let us assume that two distinct jobs, $\mathcal{J}_i$ and $\mathcal{J}_k$, are submitted with requirements $\mathcal{R}_i$ and $\mathcal{R}_k$, and a list of discovered resources is $\mathbb{N}_i$ and $\mathbb{N}_k$, respectively. If $\mathcal{R}_i \subset \mathcal{R}_k$ satisfies, jobs in $\mathcal{J}_i$ might suffer from the dearth of resources when jobs in $\mathcal{J}_k$ are scheduled to resources in $\mathbb{N}_i$; $\mathcal{R}_i \subset \mathcal{R}_k$ means that jobs in $\mathcal{J}_k$ can be executed in resources of $\mathbb{N}_i$, but there is no guarantee that jobs in $\mathcal{J}_i$ can be executed in nodes of $\mathbb{N}_k$. In order to deal with this issue, we add a ClassAds attribute dynamically to the $condor\_startd$ about the ID of a job that matched during resource discovery. Jobs matching the ID will be prioritized to run on that resource.

3.2.3 Minimum Inter-Scheduling Time

Equation 2 describes the effect of the minimum inter-scheduling to the expected queueing time of a job before scheduling. Unlike in a typical Condor environment, where one negotiator may deal with multiple job submitters, a negotiator in a C-PonD will handle a single job submitter so that we can decrease the minimum inter-scheduling time significantly without posing large processing overheads to a $condor\_negotiator$ daemon.

3.3 Discussion

Overheads : While Condor provides a scalable service by deploying multiple managers and fault-tolerant capability with duplicated fail-over servers, the administrative overhead to configure and manage these servers is non-negligible and can incur significant communication costs at scale. In contrast, C-PonD self-configures manager nodes on demand, and because of its ability to reuse unmodified middleware, it can be extended to discover and self-configure nodes for high-availability fail-over services. Though a PonD is still a centralized architecture with a central manager node (a PonD creator) and multiple worker nodes, failures are isolated. A crash of a central manager node does not keep other nodes from creating other PonDs. Worker nodes that are registered at a PonD periodically check the status of the central manager of the PonD. If the central manager is detected to be offline or inactive, it withdraws from the PonD.

Middleware reuse : C-PonD uses unmodified Condor binary files. This is made possible by the use of a decentralized resource discovery module and run-time configuration

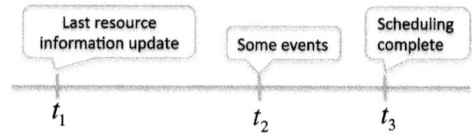

Figure 5: Based on the event at $t2$ (e.g., attribute value change, node crash), scheduling result at $t3$ might be stale.

scripts. By using Condor intact, we reduce the possibility of bugs in scheduling and job execution/monitoring due in large part to the over 20 years use and development of Condor. This feature differentiates C-PonD from many other decentralized HTC middleware which try to build a system from scratch. Reusing the ClassAds module for matchmaking allows us to inherit most of characteristics of ClassAds, such as regular expression matching and dynamic resource ranking mechanisms. No source code modification also implies that our approach can be applied to other HTC schedulers (e.g., XtremWeb [29], Globus toolkit, and PBS).

Resource fair sharing : In order to guarantee fair resource sharing amongst nodes, a manager node in Condor records job priority and user priority. Based on the priority, different users can get different levels of services when there is a resource contention. While there is no central point that keeps global information across all nodes in C-PonD, we can leverage DHT, a distributed shared storage in a P2P, by mapping a job submitter ID to a DHT key.

4. EVALUATION

In this section, we evaluate PonD from different perspectives. We use first-order analytical models to determine resource discovery latency and bandwidth costs. From there, we perform a simulation-based quantitative analysis of C-PonD in terms of scalability of scheduling throughput with respect to the number of resources and the matchmaking result staleness under various attribute dynamics and node uptime. By *staleness*, we check if scheduled resources still satisfy query requirements after matchmaking. Due to discrepancy between the timestamp of resource information and matchmaking, scheduled nodes might no longer satisfy requirements after matchmaking. For instance, in Figure 5, a scheduling is completed at t_3 with resource information that was updated at t_1, where $t_1 < t_3$. If an event happens at t_2 that changes status of the scheduled nodes, such as attribute value change or crash, the scheduling result that was conducted with resource information at $t1$ might not satisfy job requirements at t_3, and we define this result discrepancy as *stale*. We complete the evaluation by examining the performance of C-PonD prototype deployed on actual wide-area network testbeds.

4.1 System analysis

Scheduling Latency : The scheduling time of C-PonD with respect to the number of resources (N) is primarily determined by the latency of a resource discovery query. A recursive partitioning tree is known to have $O(\log N)$ tree depth [15], which determines the query latency, as the number of nodes increases. Note that the query latency can be decreased using the *First-Fit* mode described in Section 3.1.3. After discovering available resources, pool invitations are sent in parallel (with $O(\log N)$ routing cost) and a PonD is created as worker nodes join with a cost of $O(1)$. Thus, the asymptotic complexity of the time to create a C-PonD is $O(\log N)$.

Condor performs matchmaking sequentially node by node, which results in linearly increasing pattern with respect to the number of resources. Though the scheduling latency might not be a dominant factor in a pool with modest number of resources considering the overall job execution time (such as within a C-PonD), the linearly increasing pattern can become a non-negligible overhead as the pool size increases.

If we consider Condor-flocking in a large scale environment, the matchmaking time at each central manager might not be a prevailing factor for a scheduling latency, because we can assume that the number of resources will be evenly distributed amongst flocking servers. However, as Equation 2 implies, the scheduling time can be affected by the minimum inter-scheduling time while traversing different central managers sequentially. Thus, we can expect that the scheduling time increases with $O(S_f)$, where S_f means the number of flocking servers to traverse.

Other than the number of resources, the scheduling latency is dependent on the number of jobs for matchmaking. Condor has *auto-clustering* feature to improve job scheduling throughput. At the time of scheduling, *condor_schedd* daemon checks *SIGNIFICANT_ATTRIBUTES* (SA), which is a subset of attributes of *condor_startd* and *condor_schedd*. Job ClassAds whose values of SA are same are grouped in a cluster, and they are scheduled at once, which improves the scheduling throughput [30]. The auto-clustering can be also applied to C-PonD to decrease the number of resource discovery queries.

Network Bandwidth Overheads : C-PonD incurs bandwidth consumption during resource discovery query processing, PonD join invitation messages, and *condor_startd* ClassAds updates while a PonD is active. In order to understand query overheads, we assume that the number of resources is N, the size of default arguments (e.g., task name, query range) is S_D, a size of query requirement is S_Q, a P2P address size is S_A, and the number of required resources is k. The bandwidth consumption between a child and parent node is $(S_D + S_Q + S_A \times k)$ for a query distribution and a result aggregation. Using a recursive-partitioning tree, a message is routed only to 1-hop neighbors, so the total query bandwidth usage is $(N-1) \times (S_D + S_Q + S_A \times k)$. In order to analyze per edge bandwidth consumption, dividing total bandwidth consumption by the number of edges gives constant factors $(S_D + S_Q + S_A * k)$. In other words, (N-1) edges are traversed in a query, and each edge corresponds to two messages (send/receive), thus the average per-edge bandwidth consumption follows $O(S_D + S_Q + S_A \times k)$. In the typical case where k is a constant, the average per-edge bandwidth consumption is $O(1)$. In a tree, nodes located closer to the root node are likely to have more child nodes. Based on the underlying P2P-topology of C-PonD, the number of neighboring connections of a node is bounded by the log of total number of nodes. Accordingly, in the worst case, a node is responsible for $O(\log N)$ edges.

Unlike C-PonD, Condor incurs inactive job fetching overheads during the negotiation phase and periodic *condor_startd* ClassAds update regardless of job submission status. Assuming that a pool size is N, S_c is the size of *condor_startd* ClassAds (usually several KBytes in a typical Condor set-

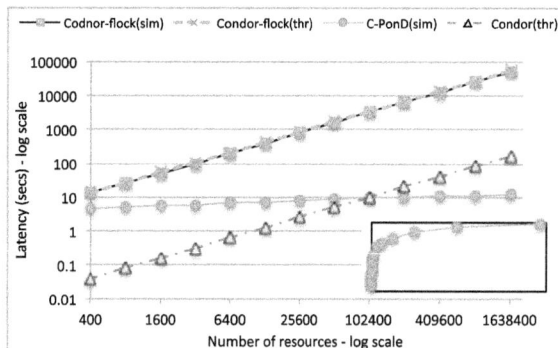

Figure 6: Scheduling latency increasing pattern of Condor-flock, C-PonD, and Condor in various pool sizes. *sim* shows a simulation result, and *thr* shows a theoretical analysis. A bottom-right inner-graph shows a logarithmic pattern of C-PonD resource discovery time.

ting), and T_u is the update period (300 seconds in default setting), the update bandwidth is $N \times S_c \times \frac{1}{T_u}$ per second at the central manager node. As T_u gets longer, the overhead of the central manager decreases, but the longer update period can result in a stale scheduling result in case dynamic attributes are specified as requirements.

Matchmaking Result Staleness : Condor relies on periodically updated resource information for matchmaking, therefore the scheduling result correctness depends on the dynamics of attributes and the information update period. In addition, the varying uptime of worker nodes can also influence the result correctness. Condor adopts soft-state to keep *condor_startd* ClassAds of available resources, and a resource that has not updated its ClassAds during the past 15 minutes (default configuration) are removed from the worker node list, which can also result in stale matchmaking results during the soft-state time span.

In C-PonD, the matchmaking is performed using local ClassAds, so the only component that influences result staleness is the query result transmission time. We compare the matchmaking result staleness of Condor and C-PonD through simulations under a controlled environment with synthetic attribute dynamics and resource uptime.

4.2 Simulations

In order to evaluate C-PonD on a large scale simulated environment, we implemented an event-driven simulation framework using C++ language and Standard Template Library (STL) aimed at minimizing the memory footprint in order to perform a simulation of millions of nodes[2]. We used Archer [31] in order to run simulations on distributed computing resources efficiently. After a resource pool is formed with a given number of resources, nodes remain in the pool until a simulation finishes.

4.2.1 Evaluation on Scheduling Scalability

Figure 6 presents the scheduling latency of Condor and Condor with flocking, and resource discovery time of C-PonD in the Y axis and the number of resources in a pool in the X axis (both represented in log-scale). The dotted lines show expected latency based on the analysis, and the solid lines show the response time from simulations. Because

---

[2]https://github.com/kyungyonglee/PondSim

there currently is no enviromnent capable of precise simulation of Condor at the scale of millions of nodes, and because the latency of each method is dependent on constants associated with system environments (e.g., network latency, computing capacity of scheduler, number of resources in each pool for flocking, available bandwidth), the focus of this analysis is to highlight trends of increasing scheduling latency as the number of resources increases and gauge the expected magnitude of a system where the latency of decentralized discovery becomes apparent.

In the simulation, the expected scheduling time of Condor is derived from experiment results from Bradley et. al [32] — the latency of one round of matchmaking, which schedules a single job (or multiple jobs clustered by *auto-clustering*) to top-ranked resources, being one second in a pool of 10,000 worker nodes. Based on the fact that Condor performs sequential traversing of all worker nodes, we apply a linear model to predict the scheduling time for different numbers of worker nodes. For C-PonD, we assume a widely distributed WAN resource pool and set the transmission delay of an edge between 50 ms and 300 ms following a uniform distribution [33]. In Condor-flocking, we set an average number of resources in a pool as 100 with default negotiation cycle of 60 seconds and the minimum inter-negotiation cycle of 20 seconds, which is the default Condor configuration value. In addition to the simulation, we also present a analytical result based on Equation 2.

As shown in the figure, Condor and Condor-flock have a linearly increasing pattern, and C-PonD shows a logarithmic pattern as the number of resources increases; this can be clearly observed in the bottom-right inner graph, where the horizontal and vertical axis values are represented in the absolute value scale. The figure also shows that results from Equation 2 the almost identical values of Condor-flock simulation and theory. Though the magnitude of latency can vary according to system configurations, we can observe that the latency of C-PonD outperforms Condor when the number of resources is larger than 100,000, which asserts the necessity of careful system design with respect to the target number of resources. From this simulation, in summary, we would like to address that the possibility of scheduling throughput limitations of centralized HTC middleware in a large scale can be relieved by leveraging a decentralized resource discovery mechanism, while supporting existing HTC middleware for job scheduling.

4.2.2 Matchmaking Result Staleness

In this section, we discuss the staleness of a scheduling result of C-PonD and compare it to Condor to illustrate the ability of C-PonD to cope with the dynamics of resource uptime and attributes. Condor relies on soft-state to determine if a worker node is alive or not; at a default system configuration, a worker node that does not update ClassAds for the last 15 minutes is deemed to be non-accessible. Thus, scheduling to a non-accessible worker node can be made within the time-span of soft-state period. In contrast, in C-PonD, heart-beat messages are exchanged between resources every few seconds, allowing the underlying P2P network to deal with node failures in a decentralized fashion. In order to address the staleness of a scheduling result quantitatively in a controlled environment, we perform a simulation by making worker nodes join and leave a pool dynamically with different mean session times following exponential dis-

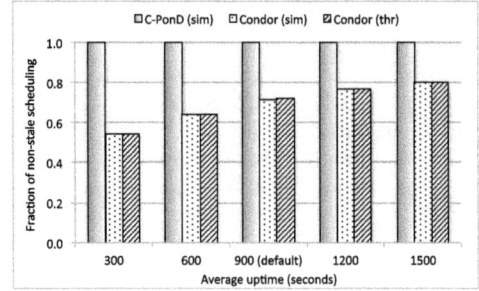

(a) Scheduling based on non-stale information for simulated Condor and C-PonD, and based on Equation 4 (Condor-thr)

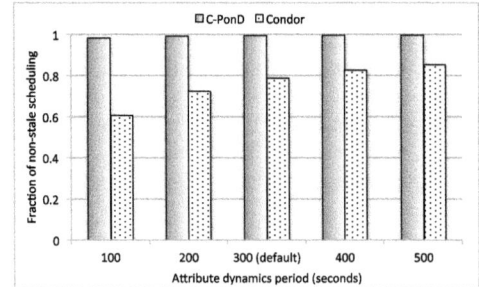

(b) The scheduling result of Condor varies according to the dynamics of attributes

Figure 7: Scheduling result staleness of C-PonD and Condor

tribution. Upon joining a pool, a node updates its ClassAds to the central manager every 300 seconds until it leaves the pool. The central manager keeps the ClassAds until the soft-state period expires.

Let us assume that the default ClassAds update period of Condor as T_d, a soft-state expiration time as T_s. Given an exponentially distributed join/leave event of worker nodes with a mean event rate of λ and assuming that a worker node is alive at time t_0, the probability of the node being inactive - the next event happens - after t elapses is defined as $\lambda e^{-\lambda t}$. If $0 < t \leq T_s - T_d$, given that $T_s > T_d$, the inactive node is deemed as alive to the central manager. If $T_s - T_d < t < T_s$, the node is deemed to be down or up according to the last ClassAds update time. Given the memoryless property of exponential distribution, we can calculate the probability of a ClassAds of inactive node still exist at a central manager as $\frac{T_s - t}{T_d}$. Finally, given that a node is alive at t_0, we can calculate the probability of a scheduling result being stale after t elapses, $P(Stl_t)$, as

$$P(Stl_t) = \int_0^{T_s - T_d} \lambda e^{-\lambda t}\, dt + \int_{T_s - T_d}^{T_s} \lambda e^{-\lambda t} \times \frac{T_s - t}{T_d}\, dt \tag{3}$$

Due to the alternating event of join/leave, the probability of a node being active at arbitrary time t_0 is $\frac{1}{2}$. Thus we can calculate the probability of scheduling result being non-stale after t elapses from t_0 as

$$P(non - stl_t) = 1 - \frac{1}{2} \times P(Stl_t) \tag{4}$$

In order to validate Equation 4 and to present a quantitative comparison between C-PonD and Condor, we per-

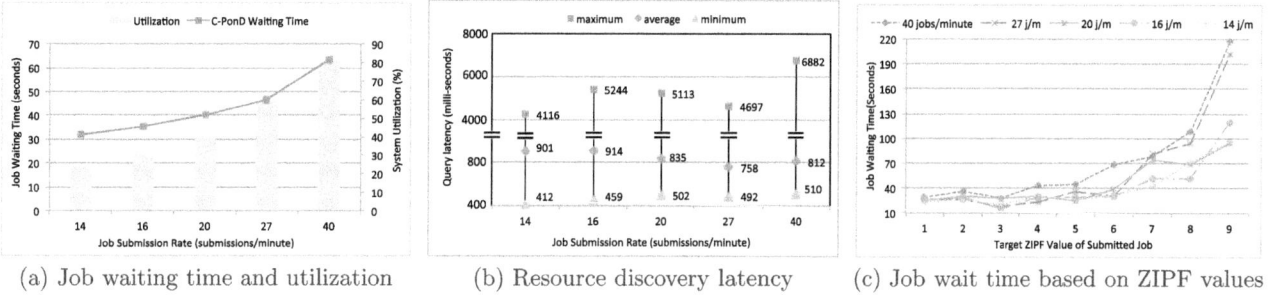

| (a) Job waiting time and utilization | (b) Resource discovery latency | (c) Job wait time based on ZIPF values |

Figure 8: The performance metrics measured from a deployment of C-PonD on FutureGrid

formed a simulation in a pool of 10^6 worker nodes setting edge latencies between 50 and 300 msec uniformly with the different value of worker node's join/leave event rate $\lambda - \frac{1}{300}, \frac{1}{600}, \frac{1}{900}, \frac{1}{1200}, \frac{1}{1500}$ per second. For a Condor pool, we adopted the default system configuration value. For C-PonD, we assume the node join and departure are handled via the underlying P2P network topology. Figure 7a shows the fraction of non-stale scheduling results according to the different average uptime. The left-most solid-bar shows the simulated value of C-PonD, the dotted grid bar shows the simulation result of Condor, and the diagonal bar shows an expected value calculated based on Equation 4 for Condor. We can observe that C-PonD has almost no impact for the given worker nodes uptime, because the only factor that can influence the result staleness is the aggregated result propagation time that is of the order of tens of seconds in a 10^6 pool. In case of Condor, the staleness of the scheduling result has a non-negligible impact based on the dynamics of worker nodes. For instance, 20% of scheduling results are stale when the average uptime of a node is 25 minutes. The results also claim the correctness of the analytical model of the scheduling result non-staleness in Equation 4 - the similar value of Condor(sim) and Condor(thr).

Next, we present the effect of attribute value dynamics to the scheduling result. In C-PonD, the matchmaking is performed with resource information that is available from the local *condor_startd* daemon. Otherwise, in Condor, the matchmaking result might be as stale as the information update period (300 seconds in the default Condor configuration). In order to model scheduling with a requirement of non-uniform likelihoods of resource matching, we add a synthetic ClassAd attribute, *ZipfAttribute* whose value follows Zipf-distribution. A worker node selects an integer value from one to ten with skew value of 1.0 and heavy portion of the distribution at one (35% of nodes). At the simulation, a node changes the *ZipfAttribute* value at a rate of λ following the exponential distribution. The scheduling staleness is measured as the fraction of nodes that still satisfies the requirement after the matchmaking. We do not show detailed analysis for this model due to the similarity with Equation 3.

The vertical axis of Figure 7b shows the fraction of non-stale scheduling result, and the horizontal axis shows the mean time of attribute change event. As shown in the figure, Condor has a higher impact than C-PonD as an attribute value changes more dynamically. In case of Condor, about 20% of scheduling results are stale when the average

attribute value change rate is the same as Condor ClassAds update period (300 seconds).

4.3 Deployment on FutureGrid

In order to demonstrate the correctness of the implementation and the feasibility of C-PonD approach as a real-world HTC middleware in a wide area network environment, we conducted experiments on a cloud computing infrastructure, FutureGrid [6]. A total of 260 Virtual Machine (VM) instances were deployed across USA using a VM image that has C-PonD modules installed. Specifically, we setup 80 VMs at the University of Chicago, 80 VMs at Texas Advanced Computing Center (TACC), 70 VMs at San Diego Supercomputer Center (SDSC), and 10 VMs at the University of Florida. Each VM instance was assigned a single-core CPU and 1 GB of RAM.

In order to evaluate the system in a realistic setup created a synthetic job submission scenario by referencing DAS-2 trace from the grid workload archive [34]. From the trace, we extracted memory usage information, the number of independent concurrent execution for each job, and the running time of each job. An extra resource attribute named *ZipfAttribute* was added to resource ClassAds to allow the experiments to vary the likelihood of resource discovery queries to find available resources. During the experiment, each submitted job selects an integer target value from one to ten following a Zipf-distribution as a requirement. Each worker node also selects *ZipfAttribute* value at the C-PonD initialization time.

During the match-making process, nodes that satisfy requirements extracted from the DAS-2 trace file and whose *ZipfAttribute* is same as the selected Zipf value are returned. In a real grid computing scenario, finding nodes with high ZipfAttribute value can be thought of as searching for best machines with higher capabilities than other machines in a resource pool. We differentiated average job inter-arrival time that follows the exponential distribution to observe the system performance under different system utilizations. The experiment is conducted for two hours per each job submission rate. A job that is composed of multiple independent concurrent tasks is submitted at an arbitrary node while keeping the overall job submission rate of the system.

Figure 8a shows the average job waiting time of C-PonD at the primary vertical axis under different job submission rates shown in the horizontal axis. The job waiting time is the elapsed time since the job submission until the job execution begin time. The secondary vertical axis shows system utilization that is calculated as

$$\frac{\sum JobRunningTime}{ExperimentTime * NumberofResources}$$

As the job submission rate increases, the system utilization and job waiting time also increase due to resource contention. In order to clarify the reason for longer waiting time as the job submission rate increases, we present the average, minimum, and maximum query latency for different job submission rates in Figure 8b. In Figure 8b, we can observe that the resource discovery query latency does not have a strong correlation with the job submission rate; regardless of the contention, it took less than a second to traverse 260 resources distributed in a WAN network. We can also observe the occasional longer query latency that might be caused by internal lagging nodes in a tree during the aggregation task, which can be improved by heuristics dealing with abnormalities in a tree, such as First-Fit and redundant topology in Section 3.1.3 and 3.1.4 (which were not applied in this experiment).

Figure 8c shows an average job waiting time of C-PonD based on the different target *ZipfAttribute* value under different job submission rates. The horizontal axis shows the target Zipf value at a submission, and the vertical axis shows the corresponding wait time. As we can see, the waiting time gets longer when the number of requirement satisfying resources is reduced (e.g., higher *ZipfAttribute* value). It can be explained as follow: a job is composed of a large number of independent concurrent tasks that can run on different machines. Thus, when a job with requirements of high *ZipfAttribute* is submitted, a resource contention is likely to happen among multiple independent tasks in a job.

These experiments validates the functionality of C-PonD in a real-world WAN environment while showing a good query response time regardless of the job submission rate and resource utilization.

4.4 C-PonD running on PlanetLab

In this experiment, we observe the dynamic behavior of C-PonD creation through resource status snapshots over a 65 hour period while running C-PonD on 440 PlanetLab nodes. After installing C-PonD module on each PlanetLab node, we add the geographic coordinate information that is extracted from the IP address of each node as *condor_startd* ClassAds attributes. We leverage this attribute to build a query requirement. In a HTC pool that is deployed on a widely distributed environment, we can explicitly specify a region of job execution using a geospatial-aware query based on latitude/longitude range. This is a useful scenario in case a communication cost is a substantial factor determining job performance. The flexibility of adding new attributes addresses an advantage of C-PonD over other decentralized resource discovery systems.

In Figure 9, *Req.1* region in the horizontal axis, jobs are submitted with a requirement that says *ZipfAttribute* is one of the values from one to ten. In the *Req.2* region, jobs are submitted with a requirement of worker nodes being in America. In *Req.3* region, jobs are submitted with a requirement of worker nodes being in Europe, and *Req.4* requires worker nodes being in Asia. The vertical axis shows the number of available resources in America (top horizontal line), Europe (middle line), and Asia (bottom line) continent. The number of running jobs at the time is shown at

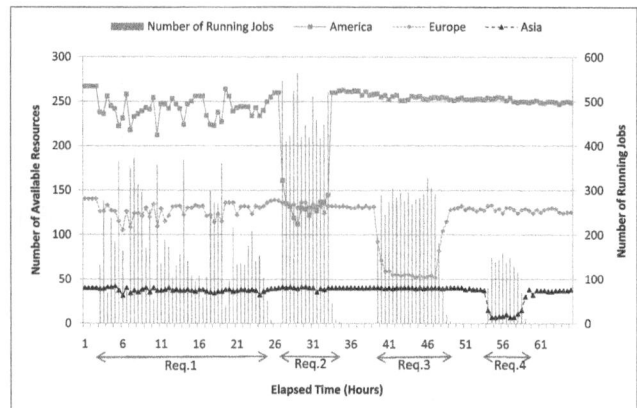

Figure 9: The number of available resources and running jobs status snapshots of C-PonD execution on 440 PlanetLab nodes during 65 hours of experiment. In Req. 2, 3, and 4 region, jobs runs on America, Europe, and Asia nodes, respectively.

the vertical bar whose value can be referenced at the secondary vertical axis.

We controlled the job submission rate not to overwhelm PlanetLab nodes, as they are shared resources not dedicated to a single user. Based on observation with varying requirements, C-PonD showed a flawless operation for a PonD creation and job execution.

From the figure, we can observe that the number of running jobs at a time is more than the number of claimed machines (equal to total number of nodes minus the number of available nodes). The reason is as follows: if a worker node has multi-core CPU, the *condor_startd* daemon recognizes each core as a distinct worker node, and those distinct worker nodes execute jobs independently. Thus, a node with multiple cores can run multiple jobs at a time.

5. RELATED WORK

Decentralized resource discovery methods are proposed from various aspects. In a structured P2P network, Sword [19] and Mercury [21] enhance DHTs to support range queries by mapping attribute names and values to the DHT key. Kim et. al [20], Squid [22], and Artur et. al [35] discuss resource locating methods on a multi-dimensional P2P network. Kim et. al [20] maps a resource attribute to one dimension in CAN [36], and a requirement confirming zone is created from a query requirement. Squid [22] leverages Space Filling Curve (SFC) to convert a multi-dimensional space to a one-dimensional ring space, where the locality preserving feature of SFC allows a range query. However, the limitation of locality-preservation for dimensions over five limits scalability of Squid. Artur et. al [35] converts multi-dimensional spaces into one dimension ring space. The correlation between multiple dimensions and attribute values are leveraged for match-making. This algorithm has a scalability limitation for a large number of attributes. Similar to our work, Armada [18] use a tree-structure for match-making by assigning an Object ID based on an attribute value, where a partition tree is constructed based on the proximity of the object ID. The resource discovery module of PonD has advantages in the aspects of rich query processing capacity and appropriateness for dynamic attributes over these works.

In an unstructured network, Iamnitchi et. al [37] proposes a flooding-based query distribution for match-making on a P2P network with query forwarding optimization method leveraging previous query result and similarity of queries. Due to the characteristics of flooding, duplicated messages hurt the query efficiency. Shun et. al [38] uses super-peers which keep the resource status of worker nodes. In order to minimize information update overhead, they use threshold to decide whether to distribute updated resource information. Thomas et. al [39] uses hybrid approach of flooding-based approach and structured id based propagation method. Different from the resource discovery module of PonD, these methods do not guarantee that a resource discovery query can be resolved even there is a node that satisfies job requirements. Periodic resource information update can also result in result-staleness.

MyGrid [40] provides a software abstraction to allow a user to run tasks on resources that are available to the user regardless of scheduler middleware. Based on MyGrid work, OurGrid [41] toolkit provides a mechanism to allow users to gain access to computing resources on other administrative domains while guaranteeing a fair resource sharing among resources that are connected through P2P network.

BonjourGrid [42] and PastryGrid [23] are decentralized grid computing middlewares. For resource discovery, BonjourGrid [42] uses publish/subscribe multicast mechanism. Without structured multicast mechanism, resource discovery results can flood the query initiating node. Due to reliance on IP-layer multicast, it has no guarantee to work on WAN environment. We solved this issue by leveraging P2P-based virtual overlay network. PastryGrid [23] is built on a structured P2P network, Pastry [43], and the resource discovery is performed by sequentially traversing nodes until a required number of nodes is discovered. Though they did not measure efficiency of resource discovery method, the cost of sequential traversing (e.g., $O(N)$, where N is the number of query satisfying nodes) is much more expensive than our parallel resource discovery mechanism, which is $O(logN)$.

MyCluster [44] presents a method to submit and run jobs across different administrative cluster domains. In their approach, a proxy is used to reserve a specific amount of CPUs in other clusters for some periods of time. The proxy is also responsible for setting task execution environment across different clusters in a user-transparent way. Due to the resource reservation mechanism for a specific amount of time, resource underutilization can happen after job completion.

Celaya et. al. [33] proposes a decentralized scheduler for HTC using a statically built tree for resource information aggregation and resource discovery. A parent node keeps aggregated resource information of a sub-tree rooted at itself, and the information is leveraged for scheduling. Due to the periodic resource information update, the scheduling result might be misleading, and it supports a limited number of attributes for resource discovery (e.g., memory, disk space). Without a solid mechanism to handle internal node failures in a statically built tree, the system can not guarantee a reliable service.

6. CONCLUSIONS

This paper presents and evaluates PonD, a novel approach for scalable, self-organizing and fault-tolerant HTC service.

The system combines a P2P overlay for resource discovery across a loosely-coupled resource "sea" in order to create a small "pond" of resources using unmodified HTC middleware for job execution and monitoring. Our approach removes the need for a central server or set of servers which monitor the state of all resources in an entire pool. A decentralized resource discovery module provides a mechanism to discover a list of nodes in the pool which satisfy job requirements by leveraging a self-organizing tree for a query distribution and result aggregation. Through the first-order performance analysis and simulations, we compared our approach with an existing HTC approach, Condor. In terms of scalability, a job execution pool creation time of PonD grew logarithmically as the number of resources increases. The evaluation on scheduling result correctness under a dynamic environment presents the robustness of our approach to dynamic attribute value changes and worker node churn. In order to demonstrate the validity of our proposed approach, we deployed and experimented a prototype implementation of C-PonD using unmodified Condor binary files leveraging run-time configurations setup in the real-world - PlanetLab and FutureGrid. Although C-PonD implementation is centered on a Condor, the clean separation of decentralized resource discovery and PonD creation module from the HTC middleware makes this approach generalizable and applicable to other HTC middleware, and a further differentiation from other decentralized HTC platforms that try to cover all phases of operation (e.g., resource discovery, scheduling, job execution and monitoring).

7. ACKNOWLEDGMENTS

We would like to thank our shepherds Douglas Thain and Thilo Kielmann, anonymous reviewers, and Alain Roy for their insightful comments and feedback. This work is sponsored by the National Science Foundation (NSF) awards 0751112 and 0910812.

8. REFERENCES

[1] Jim Basney and Miron Livny. *Deploying a High Throughput Computing Cluster.* Prentice Hall, 1999.

[2] David P. Anderson. Boinc: A system for public-resource computing and storage. In *Fifth IEEE/ACM Inter. Workshop on GRID*, 2004.

[3] I. Raicu, Y. Zhao, C. Dumitrescu, I. Foster, and M. Wilde. Falkon: a fast and light-weight task execution framework. In *Proceedings of the 2007 ACM/IEEE conference on Supercomputing*, 2007.

[4] O. Sonmez, N. Yigitbasi, S. Abrishami, A. Iosup, and D. Epema. Performance analysis of dynamic workflow scheduling in multicluster grids. HPDC '10, 2010.

[5] B. Chun, D. Culler, T. Roscoe, A. Bavier, L. Peterson, M. Wawrzoniak, and M. Bowman. Planetlab: an overlay testbed for broad-coverage services. *SIGCOMM Comput. Commun. Rev.*, 2003.

[6] Gregor von Laszewski and et. al. Design of the futuregrid experiment management framework. In *GCE2010 at SC10*, New Orleans, 11/2011 In Press.

[7] Solomon. M. Ruman. R, Livny. M. Matchmaking: distributed resource management for high throughputcomputing. In *7th HPDC*, 1998.

[8] D.H.J. Epema, M. Livny, R. van Dantzig, X. Evers, and J. Pruyne. A worldwide flock of Condors: Load

sharing among workstation clusters. *Future Generation Computer Systems*, 12:53–65, 1996.

[9] J. Frey, T. Tannenbaum, M. Livny, I. Foster, and S. Tuecke. Condor-g: a computation management agent for multi-institutional grids. In *HDPC*, 2001.

[10] Ali R. Butt, Rongmei Zhang, and Y. Charlie Hu. A self-organizing flock of condors. *J. Parallel Distrib. Comput.*, 66:145–161, January 2006.

[11] I. Sfiligoi. glideinWMS a generic pilot-based workload management system. *Journal of Physics Conference Series*, 119(6):062044–+, July 2008.

[12] P.Oscar Boykin and et al. A symphony conducted by brunet, 2007.

[13] J. M. Kleinberg. Navigation in a small world. *Nature*, 406, August 2000.

[14] V. Vishnevsky, A. Safonov, M. Yakimov, E. Shim, and A. D. Gelman. Scalable blind search and broadcasting over distributed hash tables. *Comput. Commun.*, 2008.

[15] T. Choi and P. O. Boykin. Deetoo: Scalable unstructured search built on a structured overlay. In *7th Workshop on Hot Topics in P2P Systems*, 2010.

[16] A. I. T. Rowstron, A. Kermarrec, M. Castro, and P. Druschel. Scribe: The design of a large-scale event notification infrastructure. In *Proceedings of the Third International COST264 Workshop on Networked Group Communication*, 2001.

[17] J. Kim, B. Bhattacharjee, P. J. Keleher, and A. Sussman. Matching jobs to resources in distributed desktop grid environments. 2006.

[18] D. Li, J. Cao, X. Lu, and K. C. C. Chen. Efficient range query processing in peer-to-peer systems. *IEEE Trans. on Knowl. and Data Eng.*, 2009.

[19] J. Albrecht, D. Oppenheimer, A. Vahdat, and D. A. Patterson. Design and implementation trade-offs for wide-area resource discovery. *ACM Trans. Internet Technol.*, 2008.

[20] Jik-Soo Kim, Peter Keleher, Michael Marsh, Bobby Bhattacharjee, and Alan Sussman. Using content-addressable networks for load balancing in desktop grids. In *HPDC*, 2007.

[21] A. R. Bharambe, M. Agrawal, and S. Seshan. Mercury: supporting scalable multi-attribute range queries. *SIGCOMM Comput. Commun. Rev.*, 2004.

[22] C. Schmidt and M. Parashar. Squid: Enabling search in dht-based systems. *J. Par. Distrib. Comput.*, 2008.

[23] Heithem A., Christophe C., and Mohamed J. A decentralized and fault-tolerant desktop grid system for distributed applications. In *Concurrency and Computation: Practice and Experience*, 2010.

[24] J. Dean and S. Ghemawat. Mapreduce: simplified data processing on large clusters. *Commun. ACM*, 2008.

[25] K. Lee and et. al. Parallel processing framework on a p2p system using map and reduce primitives. In *8th Workshop on Hot Topics in P2P Systems*, 2011.

[26] A. Ganguly, A. Agrawal, P. Boykin, and R. Figueiredo. Ip over p2p: enabling self-configuring virtual ip networks for grid computing. In *IPDPS*, 2006.

[27] David Isaac Wolinsky and et. al. On the design of scalable, self-configuring virtual networks. In *Proceed. of Super Computing*, SC '09, 2009.

[28] David Isaac Wolinsky and Renato Figueiredo.

Experiences with self-organizing, decentralized grids using the grid appliance. HPDC '11. ACM, 2011.

[29] G. Fedak, C. Germain, V. Neri, and F. Cappello. Xtremweb: A generic global computing system. CCGRID '01, 2001.

[30] condor auto clustering. `https://condor-wiki.cs.wisc.edu/index.cgi/wiki?p=AutoclustingAndSignificantAttributes`.

[31] Renato J. Figueiredo and et al. Archer: A community distributed computing infrastructure for computer architecture research and education. In *Collaborative Computing*, 2009.

[32] D Bradley, T St Clair, M Farrellee, Z Guo, M Livny, I Sfiligoi, and T Tannenbaum. An update on the scalability limits of the condor batch system. *Journal of Physics: Conference Series*, 331(6):062002, 2011.

[33] J. Celaya and U. Arronategui. A highly scalable decentralized scheduler of tasks with deadlines. In *Grid Computing (GRID), 2011*, 2011.

[34] A. Iosup, H. Li, M. Jan, S. Anoep, C. Dumitrescu, L. Wolters, and D. H. J. Epema. The grid workloads archive. *Future Gener. Comput. Syst.*, 2008.

[35] A. Andrzejak and Z. Xu. Scalable, efficient range queries for grid information services. In *P2P '02*, 2002.

[36] S. Ratnasamy, P. Francis, M. Handley, R. Karp, and S. Schenker. A scalable content-addressable network. In *SIGCOMM*, 2001.

[37] A. Iamnitchi and I. T. Foster. On fully decentralized resource discovery in grid environments. GRID, 2001.

[38] Shun K. K. and Jogesh K. M. Resource discovery and scheduling in unstructured peer-to-peer desktop grids. *Parallel Processing Workshops*, 2010.

[39] T. Fischer, S. Fudeus, and P. Merz. A middleware for job distribution in peer-to-peer networks. In *Applied Parallel Computing. State of the Art in Scientific Computing*. 2007.

[40] Lauro B. C., Loreno F., Eliane A., Gustavo M., Roberta C., Walfredo C., and Daniel F. Mygrid: A complete solution for running bag-of-tasks applications. In *In Proc. of the SBRC*, 2004.

[41] N. Andrade, W. Cirne, F. Brasileiro, and P. Roisenberg. Ourgrid: An approach to easily assemble grids with equitable resource sharing. In *Proceedings of the 9th Workshop on Job Scheduling Strategies for Parallel Processing*, 2003.

[42] Heithem A., Christophe C., and Mohamed J. Bonjourgrid: Orchestration of multi-instances of grid middlewares on institutional desktop grids. *Parallel and Distributed Processing Symposium*, 2009.

[43] Antony Rowstron and Peter Druschel. Pastry: Scalable, distributed object location and routing for large-scale peer-to-peer systems, 2001.

[44] E. Walker, J.P. Gardner, V. Litvin, and E.L. Turner. Creating personal adaptive clusters for managing scientific jobs in a distributed computing environment. In *Challenges of Large Applications in Distributed Environments*, 2006.

SpeQuloS: A QoS Service for BoT Applications Using Best Effort Distributed Computing Infrastructures

Simon Delamare
INRIA/LIP, Univ. Lyon, France
Simon.Delamare@inria.fr

Gilles Fedak
INRIA/LIP, Univ. Lyon, France
Gilles.Fedak@inria.fr

Derrick Kondo
INRIA, Univ. Grenoble, France
Derrick.Kondo@inria.fr

Oleg Lodygensky
IN2P3, Univ. Paris XI, France
Oleg.Lodygensky@lal.in2p3.fr

ABSTRACT

Exploitation of Best Effort Distributed Computing Infrastructures (BE-DCIs) allow operators to maximize the utilization of the infrastructures, and users to access the unused resources at relatively low cost. Because providers do not guarantee that the computing resources remain available to the user during the entire execution of their applications, they offer a diminished Quality of Service (QoS) compared to traditional infrastructures. Profiling the execution of Bag-of-Tasks (BoT) applications on several kinds of BE-DCIs demonstrates that their task completion rate drops near the end of the execution.

In this paper, we present the SpeQuloS service which enhances the QoS of BoT applications executed on BE-DCIs by reducing the execution time, improving its stability, and reporting to users a predicted completion time. SpeQuloS monitors the execution of the BoT on the BE-DCIs, and dynamically supplies fast and reliable Cloud resources when the critical part of the BoT is executed. We present the design and development of the framework and several strategies to decide when and how Cloud resources should be provisioned. Performance evaluation using simulations shows that SpeQuloS fulfill its objectives. It speeds-up the execution of BoTs, in the best cases by a factor greater than 2, while offloading less than 2.5% of the workload to the Cloud. We report on preliminary results after a complex deployment as part of the European Desktop Grid Infrastructure.

Categories and Subject Descriptors

C.2.4 [**Distributed Systems**]: Distributed applications

Keywords

Distributed Computing Infrastructures, QoS, Grids, Cloud

1. INTRODUCTION

There is a growing demand for computing power from scientific communities to run large applications and process huge volumes of scientific data. Meanwhile, Distributed Computing Infrastructures (DCIs) for scientific computing continue to diversify. Users can not only select their preferred architectures amongst Clusters, Grids, Clouds, Desktop Grids and more, based on parameters such as performance, reliability, cost or quality of service, but can also combine transparently several of these infrastructures together. The quest for more computing power also depends on the emergence of infrastructures that would both offer lower operating costs and larger computing power.

Amongst the existing DCIs, *Best Effort* DCIs are able to meet these two criteria. We call Best Effort DCIs (BE-DCIs) an infrastructure or a particular usage of an existing infrastructure that provides unused computing resources without any guarantees that the computing resources remain available to the user during the complete application execution. Desktop Grids (Condor[25], OurGrid[6], XtremWeb[15]) and Volunteer Computing Systems (BOINC[4]), which rely on idle desktop PCs are typical examples of Best Effort DCIs. But, one can think of other examples: Grid resource managers such as OAR[11] manage a best effort queue to harvest idle nodes of the cluster. Tasks submitted in the best effort queue have the lowest priority; at any moment, a regular task can steal the node and abort the on-going best effort task. In Cloud computing, Amazon has recently introduced EC2 Spot instances[2] where users can bid for unused Amazon EC2 instances. If the market Spot price goes under the user's bid, a user gains access to available instances. Conversely when the Spot price exceeds his bid, the instance is terminated without notice. Similar features exist in other Cloud services[29].

Although BE-DCIs are prone to node failures and host churn, they are still very attractive because of the vast computing power provided at an unmatched low cost. Unsurprisingly, several projects such as EDGeS [36] or SuperLink [16] propose technologies to make BE-DCIs, in particular Desktop Grids, available to Grid users as regular computing element such as clusters.

However, because BE-DCIs trade reliability against lower prices, they offer poor Quality of Service (QoS) with respect to traditional DCIs. This study presents how the execution of BoTs, which are the most common source of parallelism in the Grid [30], is affected by the unreliable nature of BE-DCIs: the main source of QoS degradation in BE-DCIs is due to the *tail effect* in BoT execution. That is, the last fraction of the BoT causes a drop in the task completion throughput.

To enhance QoS of BoT execution in BE-DCIs, we propose a complete service called SpeQuloS which abbreviates "Speculative execution and Quality of Service". SpeQuloS improves the QoS in three ways: *i*) by reducing time to complete BoT execution, *ii*) by improving BoT execution stability and *iii*) by informing user about a statistical prediction of BoT completion.

To achieve this objective, SpeQuloS dynamically deploys fast and trustable workers from Clouds that are available to support the BE-DCIs. The issue of outliers tasks slowing down the executions has been addressed by the Mantri system for MapReduce applications [3]. We propose a different approach which does not require knowledge of the resources that make up the infrastructure. By monitoring the BoT execution progress, very few information are needed to detect the tail effect. This allows to deliver SpeQuloS as an online multi-BoT, multi-users service and able to serve several BE-DCI simultaneously. In this paper, we describe strategies based on BoT completion thresholds and task execution variance for deciding when to assign tasks to Cloud workers. We also investigate two approaches for Cloud resource provisioning and different methods for workload assignment on Cloud resources. We evaluate these strategies using trace-driven simulations based from actual Grid, Cloud, and Desktop Grid infrastructures. Our simulator models two middleware which represents two different approaches for handling hosts volatility. One middleware, called XtremWeb-HEP (XWHEP), uses host failure detection based on heartbeats. The second middleware, called BOINC, uses task deadlines and task replication.

Our simulation results show that SpeQuloS correctly addresses the tail effect: In half of the cases the tail has totally disappeared, in the other half it has been significantly reduced. As a consequence, both for XtremWeb-HEP and BOINC the execution of BoT applications is greatly improved on every BE-DCIs investigated and for various kind of BoT workloads. Nevertheless, the strategies implemented are shown to make a minimal use of the Cloud resources: In the best cases where a speed-up greater than 2 is achieved, we observe that less 2.5% of the BoT has been offloaded to the Cloud. Finally, our evaluation shows that users experience can be greatly improved as success rate on the prediction of the BoT completion time is 90% on average.

We also describe the implementation and deployment of SpeQuloS in the scope of the European Desktop Grid Initiative FP7 project[13] (EDGI). Dealing with the deployment of a such a complex infrastructure had strong a consequence on the design of the service. Its architecture is modular and distributed through several independent components. It supports several Desktop Grid middleware (XtremWeb-HEP, BOINC) and Cloud technologies (Amazon EC2, Open-Nebula, Nimbus, Rackspace) In this paper, we present the development of the prototype and some preliminary results after being deployed on part of the production European Desktop Grid Infrastructure (EDGI).

The rest of the paper is organized as follow. In Section 2, we introduce our analysis of running BoT applications on best effort infrastructures. The SpeQuloS framework is presented in Section 3. Section 4 presents performance evaluation. Section 5 reports on real-world deployment. Related works are presented in Section 6 and finally we conclude in Section 7.

2. BEST EFFORT DISTRIBUTED COMPUTING INFRASTRUCTURES

In this section, we define Best Effort Distributed Computing Infrastructures (BE-DCIs). The key principle of BE-DCIs is that participating nodes can leave the computation at any moment. We investigate how this characteristic impacts on BoT execution performance.

2.1 BE-DCI Types

The different types of BE-DCIs that we study are as follows:

Desktop Grids (DGs) are grids composed of regular desktop computers typically used for computation when no user activity is detected. A node becomes unavailable when the user resumes his activity or when the computer is turned off. DGs can be supported by volunteer computing projects, such as SETI@home, where individuals offer their computing resources. DGs can also be internal to an institution which uses its collection of desktop computers to build a computational Grid.

Best Effort Grids are regular Grids used in Best Effort mode. Grid resource management systems, such as OAR[11], allow submission in a Best Effort queue. Tasks submitted to that queue have a lower priority and can be preempted by any other task. Therefore, if available grid resources are exhausted when a regular task is submitted, the resource manager kills as many best effort tasks as needed to allow its execution.

Cloud Spot Instances are variable-priced instances provided by Amazon EC2 Cloud service. Contrary to regular EC2 instances, which have a fixed price per hour of utilization, Spot instance prices vary according to a *market* price. An user can *bid* for a Spot instance by declaring how much he is willing to pay for one hour of utilization. If the market price goes lower than the user's bid, the instance is started. The user will only be charged at the price of the market, not at its bid price. If the market price goes higher than the bid, the instance is stopped. The Nimbus Cloud system has recently added support for Cloud Spot instances, as well as "Backfill" instances[29], which are low priority instances started when host resources are unused.

2.2 BoT Execution on BE-DCIs

Bag of Tasks (BoT) are set of tasks that can be executed individually. Although there are many solutions for BoT execution on cross-infrastructure deployments, we assume that a Desktop Grid middleware is used to schedule tasks on the computing resources. We adopt the following terminology to describe the main components of Desktop Grid middleware: the server which schedules tasks, the user who submits tasks to the server, and workers which fetch and execute tasks on the computing resources.

Desktop Grid middleware have several desired features to manage BE-DCI resources: resilience to node failures, no reconfiguration when new nodes are added, task replication or task rescheduling in case of node failures and push/pull protocols that help with firewall issues. We consider two well-established Desktop Grid middleware: BOINC which runs many large popular volunteer computing projects such

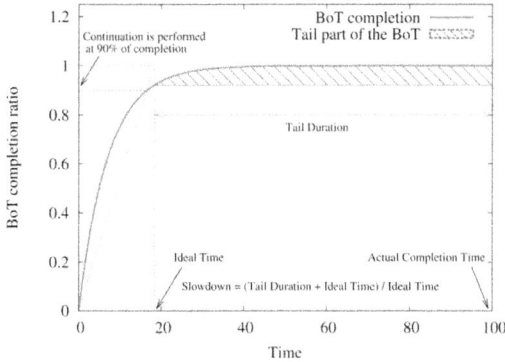

Figure 1: Example of BoT execution with noteworthy values

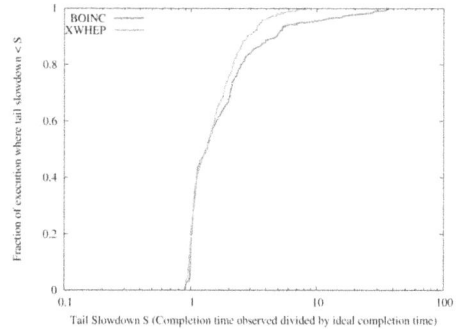

Figure 2: Profiling execution of BoTs in BE-DCIs: Tail Slowdown is the BoT completion time divided by the ideal completion time (i.e. determined by assuming a constant completion rate). The cumulative distribution function of observed slowdowns is represented.

Table 1: Average fraction of Bag of Tasks in the tail, i.e. the ratio between the number of tasks in the tail versus the total number of tasks in the BoT and average percentage of execution time in tail, i.e. the percentage of BoT execution time (makespan) spent in the tail.

	Avg. % of BoT in tail		Avg. % of time in tail	
BE-DCI Trace	**BOINC**	**XWHEP**	**BOINC**	**XWHEP**
Desktop Grids	4.65	5.11	51.8	45.2
Best Effort Grids	3.74	6.40	27.4	16.5
Spot Instances	2.94	5.19	22.7	21.6

as SETI@Home, and XtremWeb-HEP, which is an evolution of XtremWeb for the EGI Grid which implements several security improvements such as handling of Grid certificates. Condor and OurGrid would have also been excellent candidates, but we focus on middleware already deployed in EDGI infrastructure.

User tasks are submitted to the BOINC or XtremWeb-HEP server. Then, depending on the BE-DCIs targeted, the BoT is executed in the following way; on Desktop Grids, a desktop node runs the worker software. On the Grid , the worker software is submitted as a PilotJob, i.e. when the Grid task is executed, it starts the worker which connects to the DG server and can start executing tasks from this server. When using Cloud resources, we follow a similar procedure by creating an instance which contains the worker software and runs it at start-up. Several projects [35, 16, 27] follow a similar approach, and find it to be efficient and scalable.

We captured several BoT executions, using the experimental environment described in Section 4.1. BoT execution profiles denote a slowdown in BoT completion rate during the last part of its execution. Indeed, examination of individual BoT execution traces showed that most of time, BoTs execution progression follows a pattern illustrated by Figure 1: The last fraction of the BoT takes a large part of the total execution time. We called this phenomenon the **tail effect**.

To characterize this tail effect, we investigate the difference between the BoT actual completion time and an ideal completion time. The ideal completion time is the BoT completion time that would be achieved if the completion rate, calculated at 90% of the BoT completion, was constant. Therefore, the ideal completion time is $\frac{t_c(0.9)}{0.9}$, where $t_c(0.9)$ is the elapsed time when 90% of the BoT is completed. Figure 1 illustrates this definition. The ideal completion time is computed at 90% of completion because we observed that except during start-up, the BoT completion rate remains approximately constant up to this stage of execution. Therefore, the ideal completion would have been equivalent if it had been calculated at 50% or 75% of BoT completion.

Intuitively, the ideal completion time could be obtained in an infrastructure which would offer constant computing capabilities.

We define the *tail slowdown* metric as the ratio between ideal completion time and actual BoT completion time. The tail slowdown reflects the BoT completion time increase factor resulting from the tail effect. Figure 2 presents the cumulative distribution functions of tail slowdowns observed during BoT executions in various BE-DCI environments.

One can observe that the distribution is largely skewed and in some cases, the slowdown seriously impacts BoT completion time. About one half of BoT executions are not extremely affected by the tail effect. In those cases, the tail slowdown does not exceed 1.33, meaning that tail effect slows the execution by no more than 33%. Other cases are less favorable; the tail effect doubles the completion time from 25% of executions with XWHEP middleware to 33% with BOINC. In the worst 5% of execution, the tail slowdown is to 400% with XWHEP and 1000% for BOINC. These results are mostly due to host volatility and the fact that Desktop Grid middleware have to wait for failure detection before reassigning tasks.

The tail part of a BoT execution is the set of tasks executed during the tail effect, i.e. later than the ideal completion time. These tasks create the tail effect by taking unusually long to complete. Table 1 shows characteristics of BoT tails, according to middleware and types of BE-DCIs considered.

In the table, we see that a few percent of BoTs' tasks belong to the tail, whereas an significant part of the execution takes place during the tail. Therefore, the completion time of a small fraction of a BoT is many times longer than completion time of most of the BoT. This also explains why the ideal time remains approximately the same when it is calculated up to 90% of BoT completion; the tail effect never appears before that stage.

Results of this section show that the tail effect can affect all kind of BE-DCIs, whatever is its volatility, or amount of resources, for both BOINC and XW-HEP middleware.

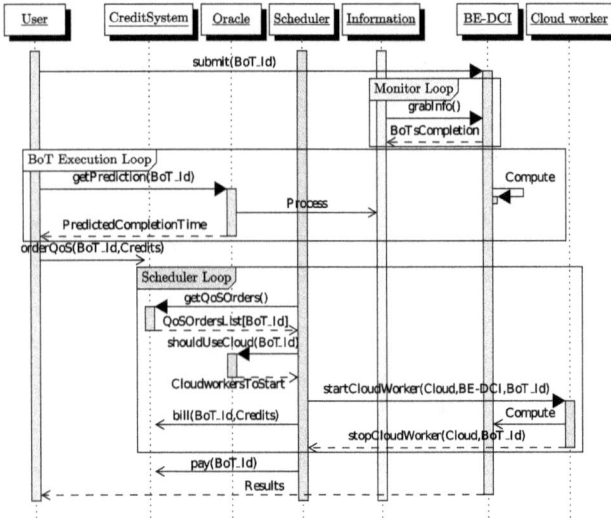

Figure 3: Sequence diagram of SpeQuloS interactions in a typical use-case scenario

It may strongly slow down the completion time of BoTs executed on BE-DCIs and cause high execution variance, precluding any performance prediction.

3. SPEQULOS

In this section, we are describing SpeQuloS service and implementation, which aims at providing QoS to BoT execution on BE-DCIs.

3.1 Overview of the SpeQuloS Service

SpeQuloS is a service which provide QoS to users of Best Effort DCIs managed by Desktop Grids (DG) middleware, by provisioning stable resources from Cloud services.

To supply resources to a BE-DCI, SpeQuloS uses Infrastructure as a Service (IaaS) Cloud to instantiate a virtual instance, called a Cloud worker. To be able to process tasks from the BE-DCI, a Cloud worker typically runs the DG middleware worker software that is used in the BE-DCI.

SpeQuloS implements various strategies to ensure efficient usage of Cloud resources and provides QoS features to BE-DCI users. As access to Cloud resources is costly, SpeQuloS provides a framework to regulate access to those resources among users and account for their utilization.

SpeQuloS is composed of several modules as shown in Figure 3. The Information module gathers and stores information from BE-DCIs (see Section 3.2). The Credit System module is in charge of the billing and accounting of Cloud-related operations (Section 3.3). The Oracle module helps SpeQuloS determine how to efficiently deploy the Cloud resources, and gives QoS information to users (Section 3.4 and 3.5). The Scheduler module manages the BoT and the Cloud workers during its execution (Section 3.6).

Figure 3 presents a simplified sequence diagram of a typical usage of SpeQuloS and the different interactions between the components of the system.

The progression of the scenario is represented vertically, and the various function calls between SpeQuloS modules are represented by arrows. A description of the various steps of this scenario is as follows:

- The first step of the scenario is a user submitting a BoT tagged with the *BoT_Id* to a BE-DCI. The BoT execution is then monitored by the Information module.

- At any moment, the user can request the Oracle to predict the BoT completion time to estimate QoS benefits of using Cloud resources. Then, the user may order to the Credit System QoS support for his BoT by allocating an amount of credits. The Credit System verifies that there are enough credits on the user's account to allow the order, and then it provisions credits to the BoT.

- The Scheduler periodically asks the Credit System if there are credits allocated for some BoTs. If credits are provisioned for a BoT, it asks the Oracle if it should start Cloud workers to accelerate the BoT execution.

- Cloud workers are started by the Scheduler to take part in the BoT execution. The Scheduler has to ensure that appropriate BE-DCI tasks are assigned to Cloud workers.

- At each fixed period of time, the Cloud resource usage must be billed. For each Cloud worker started, the Scheduler reports to the Credit System the corresponding credits used. If all the credits allocated to the BoT have been spent, or if the BoT execution is completed, Cloud workers are stopped.

- The Scheduler finally asks to the Credit System to pay for the Cloud resources usage. The Credit System closes the order relative to the BoT. If the BoT execution was completed before all the credits have been spent, the Credit System transfers back the remaining credits to the user's account.

3.2 Monitoring BoT Executions

SpeQuloS collects information on BoT executions which are relevant to implement QoS strategies with two objectives: 1) provide real-time information on BoT execution and BE-DCI computational activities and 2) archive BoT execution traces from which a statistical model can be extracted in order to compute a prediction of BoT execution time. To do so, the Information module stores in a database the BoT completion history as a time series of the number of completed tasks, the number of tasks assigned to workers and the number of tasks waiting in the scheduler queue. The amount of information transmitted per BoT is less than few hundreds bytes per minute, which allows the system to handle many BoTs and infrastructures simultaneously.

One key point is to hide infrastructure idiosyncrasies, i.e., different Desktop Grid middleware that have specific ways of managing queues should appear in an unified format. Because we monitor the BoT execution progress, a single QoS mechanism can be applied to a variety of different infrastructures.

3.3 Cloud Usage Accounting and Arbitration

Because Cloud resources are costly and shared among users, a mechanism is required to account for Cloud resource usage and to enable Cloud usage arbitration. The Credit System module provides a simple credit system whose interface is similar to banking. It allows depositing, billing and paying via virtual credits.

176

BE-DCI users spend their credits to support a BoT execution. Credits denote an amount of Cloud worker usage. At the moment, the Credit Systems uses a fixed exchange rate; 1 *CPU.hour* of Cloud worker usage costs 15 credits. At the end of the BoT execution, the amount of credits corresponding to the actual usage of Cloud resources is withdrawn from the user's credit account.

SpeQuloS manages users' accounts. A deposit policy is used by administrators for the provisioning of these accounts. Although simple, the system is flexible enough to give administrators control over Cloud usage. For instance, a simple policy that limits SpeQuloS usage of a Cloud to 200 nodes per day would be to write a deposit function, run once every 24 hours, which deposits $d = max(6000, 6000 - user\_credit\_spent)$ credits into an account. Furthermore, the mechanism allows one to easily implement more complex policies, such as the "network of favors"[5], which would allow cooperation among multiple BE-DCIs and multiple Clouds providers.

3.4 Providing QoS Estimation to BE-DCI users

Providing QoS features to BE-DCI users requires one to appropriately inform these users on the QoS level they can expect. These objectives are the responsibility of the Oracle module and are allowed by a careful exploitation of history of BoT execution traces collected by the Information module as well as real-time information about the progress of BoT execution. With this information, the Oracle module is able to compute a predicted completion time for the BoT. This prediction helps users to decide if it worth spending credits for BoT QoS.

The following prediction methods are currently used in SpeQuloS: when a user asks for a prediction, SpeQuloS retrieves the current user BoT completion ratio (r) and the elapsed time since BoT submission $(t_c(r))$, using the BoTs execution history stored in the Information module. It computes the predicted completion time t_p as: $t_p = \alpha \cdot \frac{t_c(r)}{r}$. SpeQuloS then returns this predicted time and its associated statistical uncertainty.

The α factor allows one to adjust the prediction based on the history of previous BoT executions in a given BE-DCI. At initialization, α factor is set to 1. Then, after some BoTs executions, the value of α is adjusted to minimize the average difference between the predicted time and the completion times actually observed. The statistical uncertainty returned to the user is the success rate (with a $\pm$ 20% tolerance) of predictions performed on previous BoT executions, observed from the historical data.

3.5 Cloud Resources Provisioning Strategies

We design and evaluate several different strategies for the Oracle module to decide when and how many Cloud workers should be started. We introduce three strategies to decide when to launch Cloud workers:

- Completion Threshold (9C): Cloud workers are started as soon as the number of completed tasks reaches 90% of the total BoT size.

- Assignment Threshold (9A): Cloud workers are started as soon as the number of tasks assigned to workers reaches 90% of total BoT size.

- Execution Variance (V): Let $t_c(x)$ be the time at which x percent of BoT tasks are completed and $t_a(x)$ be

the time at which x percent of BoT tasks were assigned to workers. We call the execution variance $var(x) = t_c(x) - t_a(x)$. Intuitively, the sudden change in the execution variance indicates that the system in no longer in steady state. Cloud workers are launched when the execution variance doubles compared to the maximum one measured during the first half of the BoT execution. More precisely, if c is the fraction of the BoT completed, Cloud workers are started as soon as $var(c) \geq 2.max_{x \in [0,50\%]}(var(x))$.

Assuming that users spend an amount of credits corresponding to S cpu.hours of Cloud usage, we propose two approaches to decide how many Cloud workers to start:

- Greedy (G): S workers are immediately started. Cloud workers that do not have tasks assigned stop immediately to release the credits. Doing so, other workers which have obtained tasks can complete their task.

- Conservative (C): Let $t_c(x)$ be the elapsed time at which x percent of BoT tasks are completed. Then $\frac{t_c(x)}{x}$ is the BoT completion rate. At time t_e, x_e and $t_c(x_e)$ are known from the SpeQuloS Information module monitoring. We can give an estimation of the remaining time t_r by assuming a constant completion rate:

$$t_r = t_c(1) - t_e = t_c(1) - t_c(x_e) = \frac{t_c(x_t)}{x_t} - t_c(x_t)$$

Then, $max(\frac{S}{t_r}, S)$ Cloud workers are launched, ensuring that there will be enough credits for them to run during the estimated time needed for the BoT to be completed.

We present three methods in the way of using these Cloud resources :

- Flat (F): Cloud workers are not differentiated from any regular workers by the DG server. Thus, in this strategy, all workers compete to get the remaining tasks of the tail.

- Reschedule (R): In contrast with Flat, the DG server differentiates Cloud workers from the regular workers. Cloud workers are served first with pending tasks if there are some, and if not with a duplicate of the tasks which are being executed on regular workers. This strategy ensures that tasks executed on regular workers and which may cause the tail are scheduled in the Cloud. However, the strategy is optimistic in the sense that it allows a regular worker which has computed a result to send the result and finish the task.

- Cloud Duplication (D): Cloud workers do not connect to DG server, but connect to a dedicated server hosted in the Cloud. All uncompleted tasks (even those under execution) are duplicated from the DG server to this Cloud server and are processed by Cloud workers. This strategy allows one to execute all the tasks of the tail on the stable Cloud resources, while keeping Cloud workers separated from regular Cloud workers.

Note that these strategies have different implementation complexities. Flat is the simplest one which does not need modification of the DG scheduler. Reschedule requires one to modify the DG scheduler in order to differentiate Cloud workers from regular one, which is not always possible in a production infrastructure where system administrators are reluctant to patch their DG servers. Cloud Duplication allows one to keep the DG scheduler unchanged but requires that SpeQuloS implement the task duplication from DG to Cloud server and the merging of results coming from Cloud workers and the regular BE-DCI.

3.6 Starting Workers on the Cloud

The Scheduler module manages the Cloud resources provisioned to support execution of the BoT for which users have required QoS. If credits have been allocated, and the Oracle decides that Cloud workers are needed, the Scheduler starts Cloud workers to support a BoT execution. As soon as Cloud resources are not needed anymore, or allocated credits are exhausted, the Cloud workers are shutdown remotely.

Technically, this feature is achieved by building Cloud instances which embed the DG worker middleware. We use the *libcloud* library, which allows unifying access to various IaaS Cloud technologies in a single API. Once the Cloud worker is executed on a Cloud resource, the Scheduler connects through SSH to the instance and configures the worker to connect to the BE-DCI for processing tasks from the appropriate BoT. Indeed, it is important to ensure that a Cloud worker on which a user is spending credits is not computing tasks belonging to other users.

Algorithms 1 and 2 present the various operations performed by the Scheduler module to monitor BoT execution and to manage Cloud workers.

Algorithm 1 MONITORING BOT

---

for all B in BoTs **do**
  if Oracle.shouldUseCloud(B) **then**
    if CreditSystem.hasCredits(B) **then**
      for all CW in Oracle.cloudWorkersToStart(B) **do**
        CW.start()
        configure(B.getDCI(),CW)
      end for
    end if
  end if
end for

Algorithm 2 MONITORING CLOUD WORKERS

---

for all CW in startedCloudWorkers **do**
  B ← CW.getSupportedBoT()
  if (Info.isCompleted(B)) **or** (not CreditSystem.hasCredits(B)) **then**
    CW.stop()
  else
    CreditSystem.bill(B,CW)
  end if
end for

3.7 Implementation

SpeQuloS has been developed as a set of independent modules, using the Python programming language and MySQL databases. Communication between modules use web services, therefore modules can be deployed on different networks. Several BE-DCIs and Cloud services can be connected at the same time to a single SpeQuloS server.

The SpeQuloS implementation targets a production level of quality. Testing and deployment are performed by differ-

ent teams of the EDGI consortium. The SpeQuloS source code is publicly available[1].

Desktop Grids Middleware and Grids Integration

SpeQuloS supports both BOINC and XWHEP middleware which are used in BE-DCIs. To distinguish QoS-enabled BoT from others, tasks belonging to these BoT are tagged by the users using a special field in the middleware task description (`batchid` in BOINC and `xwgroup` in XWHEP).

One issue is to ensure that Cloud workers only compute tasks belonging to the BoT for which credits has been provisioned. We solve this situation in BOINC by adding a new policy to the matchmaking mechanism. Note that BOINC requires that scheduling policies be coded and specified by compile time, which requires patching the BOINC server. For XWHEP, developers agreed to include a new configuration option in version 7.4.0 that met our needs.

Another challenge is to enable SpeQuloS support in hybrid infrastructures, where regular Grids are used. The 3G-Bridge[36] developed by SZTAKI is used in the EDGI infrastructure to provide Grid and Desktop Grid interoperability. Tasks submitted to a regular Grid's computing element connected to the 3G-Bridge may be transparently redirected to a Desktop Grid. To enable SpeQuloS's support of BoTs submitted using the 3G-Bridge, it has been adapted to store the identifier used by SpeQuloS to recognize a QoS-enabled BoT.

Cloud Services Support

Thanks to the versatility of the libcloud library, SpeQuloS supports the following IaaS Cloud technologies: Amazon EC2 and Eucalyptus (which are two compliant technologies deployed either on commercial or private Clouds), Rackspace (which is a commercial Cloud), OpenNebula and StratusLab (which implement the Open Cloud Computing Interface specification, delivered through the Open Grid Forum), and Nimbus (a Cloud system targeting scientists). In addition, we have developed a new driver for libcloud so that SpeQuloS can use Grid5000[8] as an IaaS cloud.

4. EVALUATION

In this section we report on the performance evaluation of SpeQuloS using simulations.

We have developed simulator of BOINC and XWHEP, which uses node availability traces from real infrastructure and generates traces of BoT execution. It also optionally simulates SpeQuloS utilization.

4.1 Simulations Setup

4.1.1 BE-DCIs Availability Traces

There have been many studies around nodes volatility for BE-DCIs. In particular several data-sets are provided by the Failure Trace Archive [23]. However, to our knowledge, there was no availability measurement for Cloud Spot instances or Grid systems used in best effort mode. As summarized in Table 2, we collected following traces:

- *Desktop Grid:* For this study we consider the public volunteer computing project SETI@Home (`seti`) ran

---

[1]`http://graal.ens-lyon.fr/~sdelamar/spequlos/`

by BOINC[21], and the private Desktop Grid deployments at University Notre Dame, ran by Condor[34] (nd). All these traces are provided by the Failure Trace Archive[23].

- *Best Effort Grid:* We consider using best effort queues of Grid5000[8] (G5K) infrastructure. We generated traces from the Gantt utilization charts for both Lyon (g5klyo) and Grenoble (g5kgre) G5K clusters for December 2010 period. The unused resources reported in charts are considered as resources available in best effort. In other words, a node is available in Best Effort Grid traces when it does not compute regular tasks, and vice-versa.

- *Cloud Spot Instances:* Cloud Spot instances such as Amazon EC2 Spot instances are variable-priced instances. These instances are only started if an user bid is higher than their current price. Thus, with Spot instances, the host availability depends both on the user's bids and the instance price market variation.

We consider the following usage of Spot instance: a total renting cost per hour (S) is set by the user to use several instances. As this cost is constant while the market price varies, the number of provisioned instances will vary. To implement this scenario, we use the following strategy: We place a sequence of n bids at price $\frac{S}{i}$, where $i \in 1..n$. n should be chosen high enough so that $\frac{S}{n}$ is lower than the lowest possible Spot Instance price. Hence, we ensure that the maximum number of Spot Instances are started for total renting cost of S.

Bids are placed using the *persistent* feature, which ensures that the requests will remain in consideration after each instance termination. Using price market history provided by Amazon from January to March 2011, we have generated the instances availability traces of the *c1.large* instance for a renting cost of 10 dollars (spot10) and 100 dollars (spot100) per hour.

Computing power of BE-DCI nodes depends on its nature. As DG workers use regular desktop computers, their computing power is much lower than Grid or Cloud ones. In addition, whereas Grid computing resources are usually homogeneous, DG and even Cloud resources show heterogeneity. Previous works[17, 24] allow us to model nodes power. Table 2 shows BE-DCIs workers computing power drawn from that studies: Cloud and Grid nodes are three times faster than DG nodes average and DG and Cloud computing power is heterogeneous and follows a normal distribution.

4.1.2 BoT Workloads

BoT applications are a major source of DCIs workload. We follow the definition of BoT given in [30, 19] where a BoT is an ordered set of n independent tasks: $\beta = \{T_1, ..., T_n\}$. All tasks in β have the same owner and the same group name or group identifier. In addition, Desktop Grid systems impose users to register applications in the server, thus we also have the requirement that tasks refer to the same application. Tasks may not be submitted at the same time. We define $AT(T_i)$, the arrival time of the task T_i and we have $AT(T_i) <$

$AT(T_j)$ id $i < j$. More, we define ϵ, the maximal time between two tasks arrivals, thus we have $\forall i$ in$(1, n)$, $AT(T_{i+1}) - AT(T_i) < \epsilon$. A typical ϵ value is 60 seconds, as used [30].

BoTs are also defined by their *size* i.e. the number of tasks. Each task also has a number *nops* of instructions to be processed. In homogeneous BoT, all the tasks have the same number of instructions. Conversely, in heterogeneous BoTs, the number of operations per tasks follows a probabilistic distribution.

The BoT workloads that we selected in our experimentation come from our experience in distributed computing infrastructures, such as the ones used in the EDGI project. The BIG workload is representative of BoT observed in public volunteer computing projects, and SMALL workload is representative of BoT observed in Grids such as Grid5000[18]. The RANDOM workload is statistically generated based on scientific studies conducted by Minh and Al, cited in [30]. Those BoTs vary in terms of size, number of instructions per task and task arrival times. Table 3 summarizes the BoT attributes. As shown in the table, SMALL and LARGE BoTs are homogeneous BoT, whereas RANDOM is heterogeneous.

4.1.3 Simulations parameters

Simulators are configured with DG middleware standard parameters. For the BOINC simulator, each task is replicated 3 times (*target_nresult=3*), and 2 replicas results are needed to consider a task completed (*min_quorum=2*). Two task replicas cannot be executed on the same worker (*one_result_per_user_per_wu=1*). After it is assigned to a worker, the maximum time to receive a replica result before reassigning it is set to 1 day (*delay_bound=86400*). For XW simulator, workers send a *keep alive* message every minute (*keep_alive_period=60*). When the server does not receive any *keep alive* message from a worker for 15 minutes (*worker_timeout=900*), it reassigns task executed on this worker to another one.

Pseudorandom number generator used in simulators can be initialized by a seed value to reproduce exactly the same simulation executions. Therefore, using the same seed value allows a fair comparison between a BoT execution where SpeQuloS is used and the same execution without SpeQuloS.

SpeQuloS users can choose the amount of credits they allocate to support BoT executions. In simulations, the amount of credits is set to be equivalent, in terms of *CPU.hour*, to 10% of total BoT workload. Therefore, depending on the BoT category considered, the number of provisioned credits varies. The BoT workload is computed as its size multiplied by tasks' wall clock time. Task wall clock time is an estimated upper bound for individual task execution time and is set to 11000 seconds for SMALL BoTs, 180 seconds for BIG BoTs and 2200 seconds for RANDOM BoTs.

The simulator executes the various BoTs described in table 3 on selected BE-DCIs representative of Desktop Grids (seti, nd), Best Effort Grids (g5klyo, g5kgre) and Clouds (spot10, spot100), using BOINC and XWHEP. Different BoT submission times are used in order to simulate execution in different time period of the BE-DCI traces. Results of this section are produced thanks to simulations of more than 25000 BoT executions.

4.2 Evaluation of Cloud Resources Provisioning Strategies

In this section, we report on the performance evaluation

Table 2: Summary of the Best Effort DCI traces. The trace length, number of nodes average (*mean*), standard deviation (*std. dev.*), minimum (*min*) and maximum (*max*) are presented. *av. quartiles* and *unav. quartiles* are the nodes availability and unavailability duration quartiles, in seconds. *avg. power* and *power std. dev.* are the average node power (in instructions per second) and node power standard deviation.

trace	length (days)	mean	deviation	min	max	av. quartiles (s)	unav. quartiles (s)	avg. power (nops/s)	power std. dev.
seti	120	24391	6793	15868	31092	61,531,5407	174,501,3078	1000	250
nd	413.87	180	4.129	77	501	952,3840,26562	640,960,1920	1000	250
g5klyo	31	90.573	105.4	6	226	21,51,63	191,236,480	3000	0
g5kgre	31	474.69	178.7	184	591	5,182,11268	23,547,6891	3000	0
spot10	90	82.186	3.814	29	87	4415,5432,17109	4162,5034,9976	3000	300
spot100	90	823.95	4.945	196	877	1063,5566,22490	383,1906,10274	3000	300

Table 3: Characteristic of BoT workload: *size* is the number of tasks in the BoT, *nops/task* is the number of instructions per tasks and *arrival* the repartition function of tasks arrival time. *weib* is the Weibull distribution and *norm*, the Normal distribution.

	Size	nops / task	Arrival time
SMALL	1000	3600000	0
BIG	10000	60000	0
RANDOM	$norm(\mu = 1000, \sigma^2 = 200)$	$norm(\mu = 60000, \sigma^2 = 10000)$	$weib(\lambda = 91.98, k = 0.57)$

of SpeQuloS strategies for Cloud provisioning presented in Section 3.5. We evaluate every combination of the strategies to find which one gives the best performance. We evaluate these combined strategies via trace-driven simulation for different middleware (BOINC or XWHEP), different BE-DCI availability traces, and different classes of BoTs. We look for the best strategy over all scenarios. The naming of the strategy combinations follows this scheme: 9A-G-D means that Cloud workers will start when 90% of the tasks have been assigned (Assignment Threshold), all the Cloud workers are started at once (Greedy) and all uncompleted tasks are duplicated to the Cloud (Cloud Duplication).

4.2.1 Tail Removal Efficiency

The first experiment aims at comparing the efficiency of the Cloud provisioning strategies to alleviate the tail effect. We define the *Tail Removal Efficiency (TRE)* as the percentage reduction of the tail duration with SpeQuloS compared to without SpeQuloS. We calculate TRE as $TRE = 1 - \frac{t_{speq} - t_{ideal}}{t_{nospeq} - t_{ideal}}$, where $t_{nospeqs}$ is the completion time measured without SpeQuloS (which is likely to be affected by tail), t_{speq} is the completion time measured for the same BoT execution when SpeQuloS is used. t_{ideal} is the ideal completion time for that execution without the tail.

Figures 4a, 4b and 4c present the complementary cumulative distribution function of TRE for several combinations of Cloud resource provisioning strategies. For a given efficiency, the figures show the fraction of BoT executions which obtained a greater efficiency.

We first observe that all the strategies are able to significantly address the tail effect. In the best cases (Fig. 4c, 9A-G-D, 9A-C-D), the tail has disappeared in one half of the BoT executions (TRE=100%) and for 80% of the BoT executions the tail has been at least halved (TRE>50%), which is satisfactory.

A comparison of the strategies shows that for the Flat deployment strategy (Fig. 4a) has the worst performances regardless of the combination used : in half of the BoT executions the tail has not been significantly reduced (TRE<30%). Reschedule (Fig. 4b) and Cloud Duplication strategies (Fig. 4c) both performs better than Flat if the Execution Variance is excluded : 80% of the BoT executions have addressed

the tail effect (TRE>30%). Clearly, the Execution Variance causes a severe drop of performance of any combinations which include this strategy. The Assignment threshold strategy has slightly better results than the Completion threshold strategy, and Reschedule is slightly better than Cloud duplication, especially when the Completion threshold strategy is used.

The Flat strategy cannot reach the same level of performance as the others because Cloud resources are in competition with BE-DCIs resources. In this strategy, tasks are assigned without distinction between Cloud workers and normal workers, which leads to Cloud workers not receiving tasks from DG server even during the tail part of the BoT execution. The Execution Variance strategy which tries to dynamically detect the tail effect by monitoring the variation of tasks' execution time, is shown to be less efficient than the others. We observed that unfortunately this strategy starts Cloud workers too late for a significant number of executions.

4.2.2 Cloud Resource Consumption

The second criteria for the performance comparison of the strategies is the Cloud resource consumption. Lower is the resource consumption, better is the strategy. In our system, 1 CPU.hour of Cloud workers usage is billed as 15 credits. The metric used to measure the Cloud utilization is the number of credits spent during the execution.

Figure 5 shows the average percentage of credits spent against the credits provisioned. In most cases, less than 25% of provisioned credits are spent. In our evaluation, provisioned credits are equivalent to 10% of the total BoT workload in terms of Cloud worker *CPU.hours*. Our results mean that actually, less than 2.5% of the BoT workload is executed in the Cloud, and so is the equivalent consumption of credits.

Figure 5 shows that credit consumption of the Cloud duplication strategy is lower than Flat which is lower than Reschedule. Indeed, in this last strategy, Cloud workers are continuously busy because they receive uncompleted task duplicates until the BoT execution is finished. Results also show that Assignment threshold consumes more than the others because it starts Cloud workers earlier, and that Conservative method saves a little more credits than Greedy.

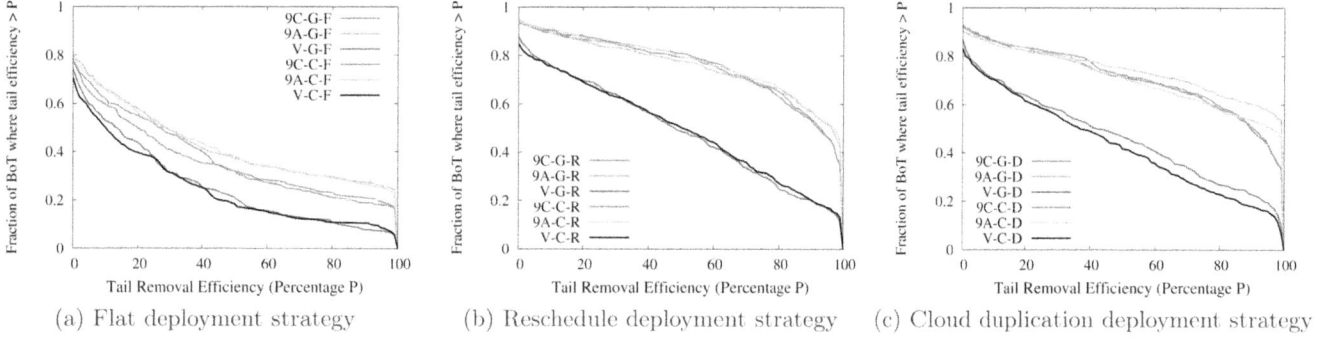

| (a) Flat deployment strategy | (b) Reschedule deployment strategy | (c) Cloud duplication deployment strategy |

Figure 4: Complementary cumulative distribution functions of Tail Removal Efficiency for several combinations of Cloud resources provisioning strategies. Tail removal efficiency denotes the reduction percentage of the tail duration using SpeQuloS compared to without SpeQuloS.

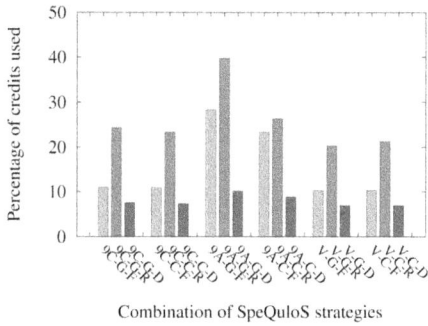

Figure 5: Credits consumption of various SpeQuloS strategies combinations. Lower is better.

Overall, our strategies have a low credit consumption. It ensures that enough credits are supplied to support the BoT execution until it ends and leaves more credits to users to support other BoT executions.

4.3 SpeQuloS Performance

In this section, we evaluate SpeQuloS performance to effectively enhance QoS of BoT executed on BE-DCIs. The results of this section use the Completion threshold, Conservative and Reschedule (9C-C-R) strategy combination, which is a good compromise between Tail Removal Efficiency performance, credits consumption and ease of implementation.

4.3.1 Completion Speedup

Figures 6a, 6b, 6c, 6d, 6e and 6f show the average BoT completion time measured with and without SpeQuloS. Each figure presents results from one DG middleware and BoT. Each figure's pair of columns show results for each BE-DCI trace.

The results show that in all cases, SpeQuloS decreases the completion time. Performance enhancement depends on the BE-DCI, BoT and middleware considered. More important gains are observed with BOINC, seti, and the RANDOM BoT, for which average completion time is reduced from 28818 seconds to 3195 seconds. In contrast, with XWHEP, spot10 and BIG BoT, the average completion is not much improved (from 2524 to 2521 seconds).

More important benefits are observed with highly volatile

BE-DCIs (seti, nd, g5k1yo). As the tail effect is more important in these BE-DCIs, using SpeQuloS can significantly increase the performance.

Benefits are also more important for SMALL BoTs, which are made of long tasks, and RANDOM BoTs, which are heterogeneous, in particular with Desktop Grid DCIs (seti & nd), for which node characteristics (low power and high volatility) make it difficult to execute such BoTs without SpeQuloS.

Even if BOINC and XWHEP completion times cannot be compared, as these middleware differ in the way they detect and handle task execution failures, one can note that XWHEP is slightly less improved than BOINC when SpeQuloS is used.

4.3.2 Execution Stability

One additional QoS enhancement that SpeQuloS aims to provide to BE-DCI users is execution stability. The execution stability is the ability to observe similar BoT completion times on the same execution environment (i.e., the BE-DCI considered, BoT workload, and DG middleware used). Providing a stable execution allows users to deduce from previous executions the QoS level they can expect from a BE-DCI. Figures 7a and 7b show the repartition functions of normalized BoT completion times around the average. Each execution's completion time is divided by the average completion time measured under the same execution environment in terms of BE-DCI availability traces, DG middleware used, and BoT category. Figures report on results obtained with every BE-DCI traces and BoT categories mixed.

For the XWHEP middleware, the execution stability is not much improved by SpeQuloS, as it was already good without it. However, the execution stability of BoTs using BOINC middleware is significantly improved by SpeQuloS. Without SpeQuloS, Figure 7a shows that a high number of executions have a normalized completion time lower than 1. This means that the average completion time is increased by a few, lengthy executions. As SpeQuloS is able to avoid such problematic cases, the average completion time becomes much more representative. This leads to a very satisfactory execution stability, actually better than for XWHEP.

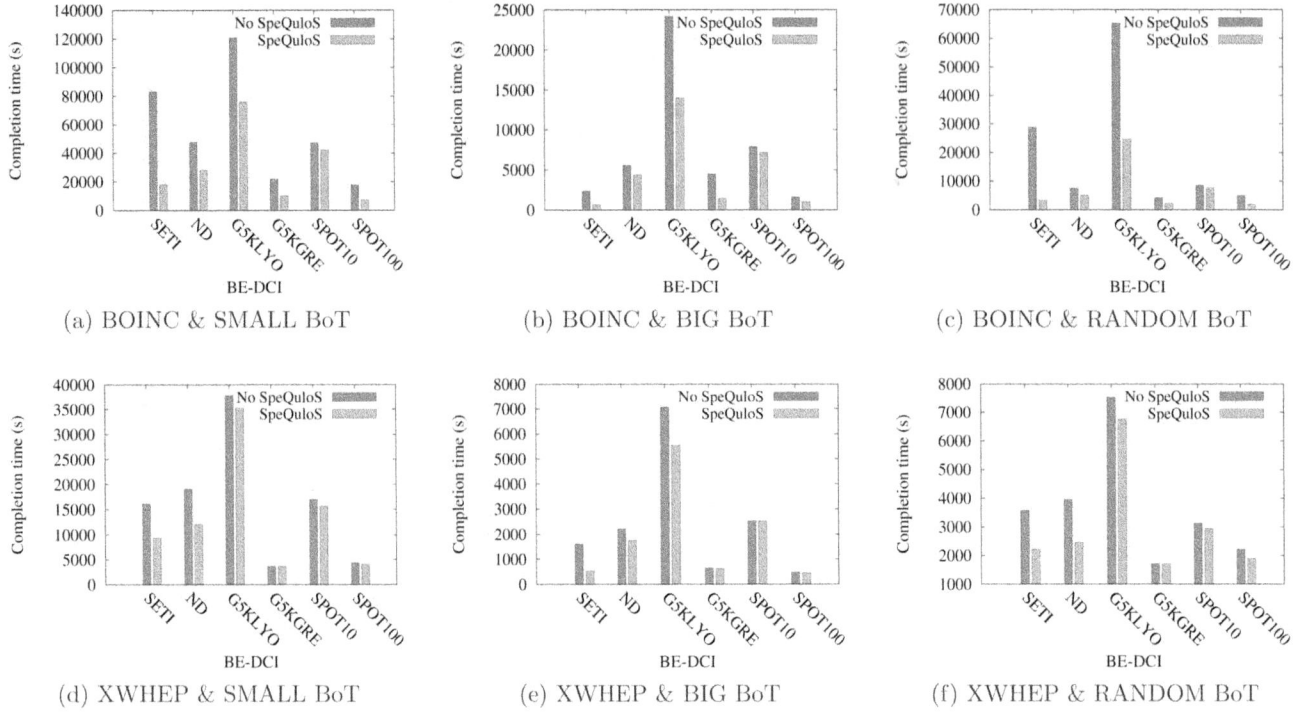

| (a) BOINC & SMALL BoT | (b) BOINC & BIG BoT | (c) BOINC & RANDOM BoT |
| (d) XWHEP & SMALL BoT | (e) XWHEP & BIG BoT | (f) XWHEP & RANDOM BoT |

Figure 6: Average completion time measured with and without SpeQuloS under various execution environments.

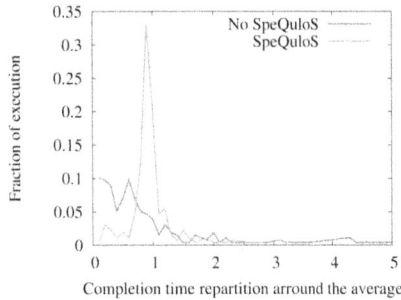

(a) BOINC

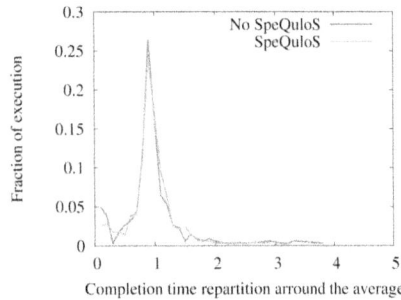

(b) XWHEP

Figure 7: Repartition functions of execution completion time normalized with the average completion time observed under same environment (BE-DCI traces, DG middleware, BoT). Curves centered around *1* denote stable executions.

Table 4: Percentage of success for SpeQuloS completion time prediction, according to BoT execution environment. A successful prediction is reported when the actual BoT completion time is comprised between ± 20% of the predicted completion time.

| | BoT category & Middleware | | | | | | |
| | SMALL | | BIG | | RANDOM | | |
BE-DCI	BOINC	XWHEP	BOINC	XWHEP	BOINC	XWHEP	Mixed
seti	100	100	100	82.8	100	87.0	94.1
nd	100	100	100	100	100	96.0	99.4
g5klyo	88.0	89.3	96.0	87.5	75	75	85.6
g5kgre	96.3	88.5	100	92.9	83.3	34.8	83.3
spot10	100	100	100	100	100	100	100
spot100	100	100	100	100	76	3.6	78.3
Mixed	97.6	96.1	99.2	93.5	89.6	65.3	**90.2**

4.3.3 Completion Time Prediction

Table 4 shows the percentage of successful SpeQuloS predictions, described in Section 3.4, made when the BoT completion is 50%. A successful prediction is reported when the actual completion time fits the SpeQuloS predicted time associated with an uncertainty of ± 20% (meaning that the actual completion time is comprised between 80% and 120% of the predicted time). For each BoT execution profiled, the α factor is computed using all available BoT executions with same BE-DCI trace, middleware, and BoT category. In other words, the "learning phase" (during which α is adjusted), is discarded and we assume perfect knowledge of the history of previous BoT executions.

Results show that the success rate of SpeQuloS prediction is high, except for some execution environments for which prediction is an issue. Still, the overall success rate is higher than 90%, meaning than the predicted completion time given by SpeQuloS is correct within ± 20% in 9 cases out of 10, which is remarkable given the unpredictable nature of BE-DCIs. Results also show that predictions are slightly better with BOINC middleware than with XtremWeb-HEP, which can be explained by the more stable execution of this middleware, as reported in previous section. Another observation is that the RANDOM BoTs gives inferior prediction quality. Indeed, as this BoT is highly heterogeneous, predicting completion time is harder as task execution times vary greatly amongst BoT executions.

Results of this section have shown that SpeQuloS is able to effectively enhance the QoS of BoTs executed on BE-DCIs. Indeed, using SpeQuloS, BoT completion time is accelerated by a factor of as much as 5, while assigning to Cloud resources less than 2.5% of the total workload. Additionally, SpeQuloS increases the execution stability, meaning that BoTs executed in similar environments will present similar performance. Finally, SpeQuloS can accurately predict the BoT completion time and provide this information to BE-DCI users.

5. SPEQULOS DEPLOYMENT IN EDGI

In this section, we present the deployment of SpeQuloS as a part of the European Desktop Grid Infrastructure[13] (EDGI). EDGI connects several private and public Desktop Grids (IberCivis, University of Westminster, SZTAKI, CNRS/University of Paris XI LAL and LRI DGs) to several Grids (European Grid Infrastructure (EGI), Unicore, ARC) and private Clouds (StratusLab and local OpenStack, OpenNebula).

The main objective of EDGI is to transparently provide the vast amount of computing power of DGs to EGI users. Ultimately, these users would submit their applications to regular Computing Elements and thanks to EDGI, these tasks can be executed on DGs without any difference noticed by the user. SpeQuloS is one element amongst a full software stack, featuring a bridge from Grids to Desktop Grids, a data distribution network, monitoring, eScience portal and more.

We present the current preliminary deployment of SpeQuloS, on part of the EDGI production infrastructure, which is illustrated in Figure 8. The current deployment includes a production infrastructure, composed of two DGs, XW@LRI and XW@LAL, both ran by XWHEP and managed by the University of Paris-XI. For testing purposes, XW@LRI is connected to Grid'5000 and gathers resources in best effort mode from 6 of its clusters with a bound on 200 nodes at a time. SpeQuloS uses Amazon EC2 as a supporting Cloud for XW@LRI. The XW@LAL server is connected to the local Desktop Grid of the laboratory. XW@LAL can also harvest computing resources from the EGI Grids through the EDGI's 3G Bridge[36]. A local OpenNebula part of the StratusLab infrastructure is used as a supporting Cloud for the LAL Desktop Grid. An interesting side-effect of this setup is that BoTs submitted through XtremWeb-HEP to EGI can eventually benefit from the QoS support provided by SpeQuloS using resources from StratusLab. In the context of the EDGI project, another SpeQuloS deployment is in progress, to provide QoS support to other EDGI's DGs, such SZTAKI's one, through a fully-dedicated OpenNebula Cloud service.

Several EDGI applications are installed and used regularly, such as DART (a Framework for Distributed Audio

Table 5: The University Paris-XI part of the European Desktop Grid Infrastructure. The table reports on the number of tasks executed on XW@LAL and XW@LRI Desktop Grids, as well as the number of EGI tasks executed on those DGs and the number of tasks assigned by SpeQuloS to StratusLab and Amazon EC2 Cloud services.

	XW@LAL	XW@LRI	EGI	StratusLab	EC2
#tasks	557002	129630	10371	3974	119

Analysis and Music Information Retrieval by Cardiff University), BNB-Grid (which is aimed at solving hard combinatorial, discrete and global optimization problems) and IS-DEP (which is a fusion plasma application which simulates the Tokamak of ITER). Table 5 summarizes the usage of the infrastructure during the first half of 2011 where SpeQuloS has been gradually deployed.

6. RELATED WORK

Many scenarios motivate the assemblage of Grids or Clouds with Best Effort infrastructures, and in particular Desktop Grids. GridBot [35] puts together Superlink@Technion, Condor pools and Grid resources to execute both throughput and fast-turnaround oriented BoTs. The European FP7 projects EDGeS[36] and EDGI[13] have developed bridge technologies to make Desktop Grid infrastructure transparently available to any EGI Grid users as a regular Computing Element. Similarly, the Latin America EELA-2 Grid has been bridged with the OurGrid infrastructures [9].

In [33], authors investigate the cost and performance of running a Grid workload on Amazon EC2 Cloud. Similarly, in [24], the authors introduce a cost-benefit analysis to compare Desktop Grids and Amazon EC2. ElasticSite[28] offloads a part of the Grid workload to the Cloud when there is peak user demand. In [1], authors propose a Pareto efficient strategy to offload Grid BoTs whith deadlines on the Cloud.

Providing QoS features in Grids is hard and not solved yet satisfactorily [12, 20, 38]. It is even more difficult in an environment where there are no guaranteed resources [7]. Unlike aforementioned work, we do not modify the resource manager scheduling policies to incorporate QoS features. Instead, we use an extrinsic approach by providing additional resources. However, the two approaches could coexist by classifying the DG workers according to their historical behavior and allocating applications with QoS needs to the more trustable and faster workers. In [37], a framework is presented to extend Grid resources using Cloud computing. Similarly, Aneka [10] supports the integration between Desktop Grids and Clouds. These works would be the closest to ours although we went further in term of implementation and evaluation.

There exists a large literature about predicting tasks completion time. For instance QBETS [31] uses time series to model and forecast task queues. Closer to our context [14], proposes a framework to model and predicts the various steps (submission, validation, waiting in the scheduler queue) that a work unit spend in a volunteer computing project. Our work differs by the fact that we address heterogeneous environments. As a result, we adopted an unique representation based on BoT progression to hide idiosyncrasies of BE-DCIs. Thus, the Oracle never accesses directly

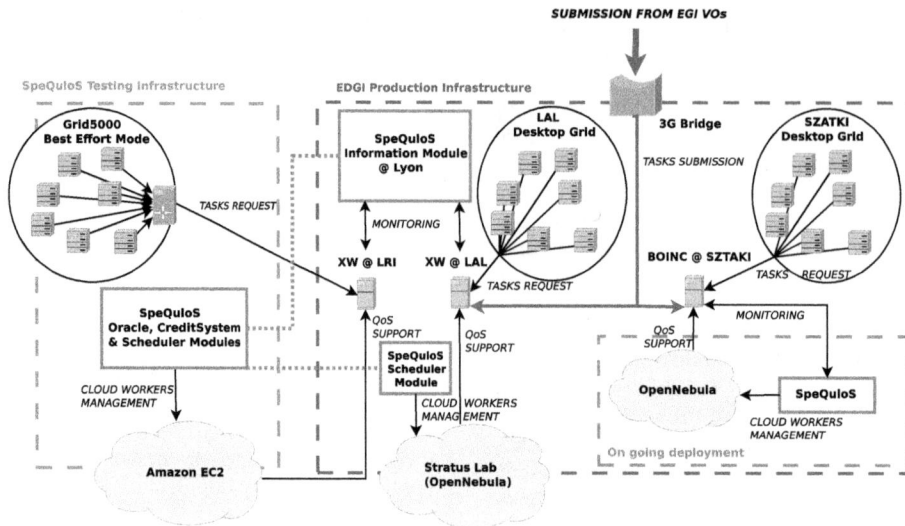

Figure 8: SpeQuloS' current deployment as a part of the EDGI infrastructure. SpeQuloS' modules are split and duplicated across the deployment.

the BoT Queue, but rather a history of past BoTs and online monitoring information.

Mitigation of the tail in Desktop Grid computing has been addressed in the past [22]. The difference between that prior work and ours is that we provide prediction and stability estimates for QoS, we devise new algorithms for using dedicated cloud resources, and we evaluate these algorithms more completely in a wide range of scenarios (in terms of different BoT classes, desktop grid middleware, and platforms with different degrees of volatility and heterogeneity).

In [39], authors propose the LATE (Longest Approximate Time to End) scheduling to alleviate outliers in MapReduce computation. The LATE scheduler monitors tasks execution and speculatively executes those of the tasks which are anticipated to have the latest finished time on the fastest hosts. Recently, the Mantri system[3] have been proposed, where the authors identifies several causes of dramatic slowdown of computation, including workload imbalance due to data skew, network contention due to disadvantageous communication patterns and overloaded machine. Because these MapReduce systems run within a cluster, they assume a finer grain of information: individual task monitoring versus global BoT progress rate monitoring in the case of SpeQuloS. SpeQuloS deals with considerably large infrastructures, potentially hundreds of thousands hosts with very different characteristics in the case of Desktop Grids. As infrastructures are treated as black box, SpeQuloS cannot implement MapReduce speculative execution heuristics which relies on a per-hosts information or network topologies information in the case of Mantri.

Providing cost-effective usage of Cloud resources is a topic of growing interest. Authors of [26] propose a mechanism to minimize the cost of scheduling an entire workflow on Cloud resources, while trying to satisfy a user-supplied deadline. Conversely, [32] presents a scheduler that minimizes completion time of BoT executed on multiple Clouds under a constrained budget. In our work, most of workload is processed by BE-DCIs and we only use Cloud resources to process its most critical part. However, these works could be consisered to optimize Cloud resources usage by SpeQuloS.

7. CONCLUSION AND FUTURE WORKS

Although Best Effort Distributed Computing Infrastructures (BE-DCIs) such as Desktop Grids, Best Effort Grids or Cloud Spot instances are the "low cost" solution available to high-throughput computing users, they are now getting more widely accessible. We have introduced SpeQuloS, a framework to enhance QoS for BoT applications when executed in BE-DCIs. We hope that this effort will help to make BE-DCIs "first class citizens" in the computing landscape.

The main principle of SpeQuloS is to monitor the execution of BoTs and dynamically provision external stable and powerful Cloud resources to help BE-DCIs to execute the most critical part of the BoT. We proposed several strategies and evaluated them using trace-driven simulations. Providing QoS to grid computing is considered a difficult issue, however our approach is able to substantially improve QoS with respect to several criteria, namely completion time, completion time stability and prediction, and just as important, feedback to the user on the predicted QoS benefits.

Development and deployment of SpeQuloS have shown the potential but also the difficulties of mixing hybrid infrastructures. Our framework is composed of several small independent and distributed modules which accomplish several key tasks: information retrieval and archiving, accounting and arbitration, prediction and forecasting, scheduling and resource provisioning. We have demonstrated its applicability to the European Desktop Grid Infrastructure, where the service provides QoS support for two Desktop Grids and one Best-effort Grid connected to three different Clouds. We are now working to integrate the system into the project's Grid portal so that end-users can benefit from the service, and we hope to significantly improve their experience of using the infrastructure.

Our future work will focus on improving the performance of tail detection and mitigation. In particular, we would like to anticipate when a BoT is likely to produce a tail by correlating the execution with the state of the infrastructure: resource heterogeneity, variation in the number of computing resources and rare events such as massive failures or network partitioning.

Acknowledgment

Authors would like to thank Peter Kacsuk, Jozsef Kovacs, Michela Taufer, Trilce Estrada and Kate Keahey for their insightful comments and suggestions throughout our research and development of SpeQuloS.

Some of the experiments presented in this paper were carried out using the Grid'5000 experimental testbed, being developed under the INRIA ALADDIN development action with support from CNRS, RENATER and several Universities as well as other funding bodies.

This work was funded by EDGI project, supported by the European Commission FP7 Capacities Programme under grant agreement RI-261556.

8. REFERENCES

[1] O. Agmon Ben-Yehuda, A. Schuster, A. Sharov, M. Silberstein, and A. Iosup. ExPERT: Pareto-efficient task replication on grids and clouds. Technical Report CS-2011-03, Technion, 2011.

[2] Amazon Web Services. An introduction to spot instances. Technical report, Amazon Elastic Compute Cloud, 2009.

[3] G. Ananthanarayanan, S. Kandula, A. Greenberg, I. Stoica, Y. Lu, B. Saha, and E. Harris. Reining in the outliers in map-reduce clusters using mantri. In *Proceedings of the 9th USENIX conference on Operating systems design and implementation*, OSDI'10, 2010.

[4] D. Anderson. BOINC: A system for public-resource computing and storage. In *proceedings of the 5th IEEE/ACM International GRID Workshop*, Pittsburgh, USA, 2004.

[5] N. Andrade, F. Brasileiro, W. Cirne, and M. Mowbray. Automatic grid assembly by promoting collaboration in peer-to-peer grids. *Journal of Parallel and Distributed Computing*, 67(8), 2007.

[6] N. Andrade, W. Cirne, F. Brasileiro, and P. Roisenberg. OurGrid: An approach to easily assemble grids with equitable resource sharing. In *Proceedings of the 9th Workshop on Job Scheduling Strategies for Parallel Processing*, 2003.

[7] C. Anglano, J. Brevik, M. Canonico, D. Nurmi, and R. Wolski. Fault-aware scheduling for bag-of-tasks applications on desktop grids. In *Proceedings of the 7th IEEE/ACM International Conference on Grid Computing*, GRID '06, 2006.

[8] R. Bolze and all. Grid5000: A large scale highly reconfigurable experimental grid testbed. *International Journal on High Peerformance Computing and Applications*, 2006.

[9] F. Brasileiro, A. Duarte, D. Carvalho, R. Barber, and D. Scardaci. An approach for the co-existence of service and opportunistic grids: The EELA-2 case. In *Latin-American Grid Workshop*, 2008.

[10] R. N. Calheiros, C. Vecchiola, D. Karunamoorthy, and R. Buyya. The Aneka platform and QoS-driven resource provisioning for elastic applications on hybrid clouds. *Future Generation Computer Systems*, 2011.

[11] N. Capit, G. Da Costa, Y. Georgiou, G. Huard, C. Martin, G. Mounie, P. Neyron, and O. Richard. A batch scheduler with high level components. In *Proceedings of the Fifth IEEE International Symposium on Cluster Computing and the Grid (CCGrid'05)*, Washington, DC, USA, 2005.

[12] F. Dong and S. G. Akl. Scheduling algorithms for grid computing: State of the art and open problems. Technical report, Queen's University Kingston, 2006.

[13] European desktop grid infrastructure. http://edgi-project.eu/, 2010.

[14] T. Estrada, K. Reed, and M. Taufer. Modeling job lifespan delays in volunteer computing projects. In *9th IEEE International Symposium on Cluster Computing and Grid (CCGrid)*, 2009.

[15] G. Fedak, C. Germain, V. Neri, and F. Cappello. XtremWeb: A Generic Global Computing Platform. In *CCGRID'2001 Special Session Global Computing on Personal Devices*, 2001.

[16] M. Fishelson and D. Geiger. Exact genetic linkage computations for general pedigrees. *Bioinformatics. 2002;18 Suppl 1:S189-98.*, 2002.

[17] E. Heien, D. Kondo, and A. David. Correlated resource models of internet end hosts. *31st International Conference on Distributed Computing Systems (ICDCS), Minneapolis, Minnesota, USA*, 2011.

[18] A. Iosup, H. Li, M. Jan, S. Anoep, C. Dumitrescu, L. Wolters, and D. H. Epema. The grid workloads archive. *Future Generation Computer Systems*, 24(7), 2008.

[19] A. Iosup, O. Sonmez, S. Anoep, and D. Epema. The performance of bags-of-tasks in large-scale distributed systems. In *Proceedings of the 17th international symposium on High performance distributed computing*, HPDC '08, 2008.

[20] M. Islam, P. Balaji, P. Sadayappan, and D. Panda. QoPS: A QoS based scheme for parallel job scheduling. In *Job Scheduling Strategies for Parallel Processing*, Lecture Notes in Computer Science. Springer, 2003.

[21] B. Javadi, D. Kondo, J. Vincent, and D. Anderson. Mining for statistical availability models in large-scale distributed systems: An empirical study of SETI@home. In *17th IEEE/ACM International Symposium on Modelling, Analysis and Simulation of Computer and Telecommunication Systems (MASCOTS)*, 2009.

[22] D. Kondo, A. Chien, and H. Casanova. Resource management for rapid application turnaround on enterprise desktop grids. In *ACM Conference on High Performance Computing and Networking, SC 2004, USA*, 2004.

[23] D. Kondo, B. Javadi, A. Iosup, and D. Epema. The Failure Trace Archive: Enabling comparative analysis of failures in diverse distributed systems. In *10th IEEE/ACM International Symposium on Cluster, Cloud and Grid Computing (CCGrid)*, 2010.

[24] D. Kondo, B. Javadi, P. Malecot, F. Cappello, and D. Anderson. Cost-benefit analysis of cloud computing versus desktop grids. In *18th International Heterogeneity in Computing Workshop*, 2009.

[25] M. Litzkow, M. Livny, and M. Mutka. Condor - a hunter of idle workstations. In *Proceedings of the 8th International Conference of Distributed Computing Systems (ICDCS)*, 1988.

[26] M. Mao and M. Humphrey. Auto-scaling to minimize cost and meet application deadlines in cloud workflows. In *International Conference for High Performance Computing, Networking, Storage and Analysis*, SC '11. ACM, 2011.

[27] A. C. Marosi and P. Kacsuk. Workers in the clouds. *Parallel, Distributed, and Network-Based Processing, Euromicro Conference on*, 2011.

[28] P. Marshall, K. Keahey, and T. Freeman. Elastic site: Using clouds to elastically extend site resources. In *Proceedings of CCGrid'2010, Melbourne, Australia*, 2010.

[29] P. Marshall, K. Keahey, and T. Freeman. Improving utilization of infrastructure clouds. In *IEEE/ACM International Symposium on Cluster, Cloud and Grid Computing (CCGrid 2011)*, 2011.

[30] T. N. Minh and L. Wolters. Towards a profound analysis of bags-of-tasks in parallel systems and their performance impact. In *High-Performance Parallel and Distributed Computing*, 2011.

[31] D. C. Nurmi, J. Brevik, and R. Wolski. QBETS: queue bounds estimation from time series. In *Proceedings of the 2007 ACM SIGMETRICS international conference on Measurement and modeling of computer systems*, SIGMETRICS '07, 2007.

[32] A.-M. Oprescu and T. Kielmann. Bag-of-tasks scheduling under budget constraints. In *CloudCom*, 2010.

[33] M. R. Palankar, A. Iamnitchi, M. Ripeanu, and S. Garfinkel. Amazon S3 for science grids: a viable solution? In *Proceedings of the 2008 international workshop on Data-aware distributed computing*, DADC '08, 2008.

[34] B. Rood and M. J. Lewis. Multi-state grid resource availability characterization. In *8th Grid Computing Conference*, 2007.

[35] M. Silberstein, A. Sharov, D. Geiger, and A. Schuster. GridBot: execution of bags of tasks in multiple grids. In *Proceedings of the Conference on High Performance Computing Networking, Storage and Analysis*, SC '09, 2009.

[36] E. Urbah, P. Kacsuk, Z. Farkas, G. Fedak, G. Kecskemeti, O. Lodygensky, A. Marosi, Z. Balaton, G. Caillat, G. Gombas, A. Kornafeld, J. Kovacs, H. He, and R. Lovas. EDGeS: Bridging egee to boinc and xtremweb. *Journal of Grid Computing*, 2009.

[37] C. Vázquez, E. Huedo, R. S. Montero, and I. M. Llorente. On the use of clouds for grid resource provisioning. *Future Gener. Comput. Syst.*, 2011.

[38] C. Weng and X. Lu. Heuristic scheduling for bag-of-tasks applications in combination with qos in the computational grid. *Future Generation Computer Systems*, 21(2), 2005.

[39] M. Zaharia, A. Konwinski, A. Joseph, R. Katz, and I. Stoica. Improving mapreduce performance in heterogeneous environments. In *OSDI'08*, 2008.

Understanding the Effects and Implications of Compute Node Related Failures in Hadoop

Florin Dinu and T. S. Eugene Ng
Dept. of Computer Science, Rice University
Houston, TX, USA

ABSTRACT

Hadoop has become a critical component in today's cloud environment. Ensuring good performance for Hadoop is paramount for the wide-range of applications built on top of it. In this paper we analyze Hadoop's behavior under failures involving compute nodes. We find that even a single failure can result in inflated, variable and unpredictable job running times, all undesirable properties in a distributed system. We systematically track the causes underlying this distressing behavior. First, we find that Hadoop makes unrealistic assumptions about task progress rates. These assumptions can be easily invalidated by the cloud environment and, more surprisingly, by Hadoop's own design decisions. The result are significant inefficiencies in Hadoop's speculative execution algorithm. Second, failures are re-discovered individually by each task at the cost of great degradation in job running time. The reason is that Hadoop focuses on extreme scalability and thus trades off possible improvements resulting from sharing failure information between tasks. Third, Hadoop does not consider the causes of connection failures between its tasks. We show that the resulting overloading of connection failure semantics unnecessarily causes an otherwise localized failure to propagate to healthy tasks. We also discuss the implications of our findings and draw attention to new ways of improving Hadoop-like frameworks.

Categories and Subject Descriptors

C.4 [**Computer Systems Organization**]: Performance of Systems-Fault Tolerance

General Terms

Measurement, Performance, Reliability

Keywords

Failures, Hadoop, Speculative Execution

1. INTRODUCTION

Hadoop has become a cloud workhorse [7]. Major Internet companies rely on Hadoop for their everyday needs involving extremely

large data sets [43, 44, 9]: management tasks involving log processing [16, 8], business intelligence applications or the deployment of new products and platforms [18, 44]. Cloud service providers have added Hadoop to their list of offerings [10, 3]. Scientists use Hadoop for a wide range of purposes. To name only a few examples, Hadoop facilitated the implementation of scalable solutions and algorithms for data-intensive text processing [2], assembly of large genomes [4], graph mining [12], machine learning and data mining [1] and large scale social network analysis [13]. Hadoop has also received much attention from the research community. Several studies propose performance improvements [28, 34] or extensions to Hadoop: running Hadoop on a wider range of job types [19, 21], in more challenging environments [50], as a back-end in other large scale systems [44, 38] or as part of a hybrid architecture [14]. As a result of its widespread use and of the critical nature of the applications running on top of it, ensuring good performance for Hadoop jobs is essential.

In this paper, we focus on Hadoop's behavior under compute node failures. The same cloud environments that host Hadoop applications are typically prone to compute node failures failures. Studies show [22, 45, 5] tens of compute node related failures per day and multiple failures per average compute job. Moreover, various environmental conditions such as network components failing or bandwidth quotas being exceeded can be indistinguishable at application level from compute node failures. Rightfully so, compute node failures are becoming a driving force behind the design of large-scale cloud applications [24]. Despite the pervasiveness of failures in the cloud, little research work has been done on analyzing Hadoop's performance under failures and understanding the efficiency of its design decisions in the context of failures.

Given Hadoop's popularity and the fact that failures are the norm rather than the exception in the cloud environment this research direction has immediate practical relevance. Our paper is the first to provide a thorough analysis of Hadoop under failures. The problem of dealing with failures is complex and our goal is to provide deep and insightful technical analysis. We view our paper as a necessary first step for solving what has become a chronically over-looked aspect: designing and building more robust failure detection and recovery algorithms for Hadoop. To this end, a collaborative effort from the community is needed: failure characteristics, job characteristics and cloud resource occupancy in real deployments need to be analyzed. Thus, in addition to the practical relevance this research direction is rich in avenues for impactful future work.

Specifically, in this paper we analyze Hadoop's behavior under fail-stop failures of entire compute nodes and under fail-stop failures of the Hadoop components running on compute nodes (Task-Tracker and DataNode). DataNode failures are important because they affect the availability of job input and output data and also delay read and write data operations which are central to Hadoop's performance. TaskTracker failures are equally important because they affect running tasks as well as the availability of intermediate data (i.e. map outputs). Unlike failures affecting logically centralized Hadoop components (JobTracker and NameNode) which can be addressed by distributed coordination mechanisms [39], compute node failures require Hadoop to take explicit measures for detection and recovery and are more likely to cause subtle interactions with the environment or between Hadoop's components.

Our measurements point to a real need for improvement. Surprisingly, we discover that a single failure can lead to large, variable and unpredictable job running times. For example, the running time of a job that takes 220s without failures can vary from 220s to as much as 1000s under TaskTracker failures and to 700s under DataNode failures. This is especially important for short jobs which are frequently encountered in the cloud and have been shown to be a major use case for Hadoop [50, 23, 20]. Such large performance variations are detrimental. They cause unpredictable user costs and prolonged waiting for results, decrease overall cloud utilization and complicate scheduling. In our experiments on a predictable cloud environment, the primary causes for the performance variations are internal to Hadoop's design, namely the inefficiencies in Hadoop's failure detection and recovery algorithms.

We expose three important inefficiencies in Hadoop's design which manifest themselves under compute node failures. First, Hadoop makes unrealistic assumptions about task progress rates. Hadoop seems to think that, with the exception of a few underperforming outliers, tasks progress at comparable rates. For Hadoop this warrants the use of a statistical speculative aggregation algorithm centered around average progress rates. Unfortunately, Hadoop's assumption can be easily invalidated in practice. Both the cloud environment as well as other Hadoop design decisions can result in very fast progressing tasks. For example, a number of recent proposals for improved cloud network design [35, 46] advocate accelerating specific network paths. Alternatively, imbalanced computations can lead to reducer tasks which are very fast because they process little data. Also, in a Hadoop job with multiple reducer waves, reducer tasks not belonging to the first wave can progress at very high rates because they do not have to wait for their input. We show that when Hadoop's assumption is invalidated, a negative effect which we call *delayed speculative execution* can appear. This consists in one speculative execution decision severely delaying or even precluding subsequent speculative executions at great overall costs for the job running time.

Second, Hadoop trades off possible improvements resulting from communication between tasks for extreme scalability. Therefore, each compute task performs failure detection and recovery on its own. The unfortunate effect of this lack of sharing failure information is that multiple tasks could be left wasting time re-discovering a failure that has already been identified by another task. Moreover, a speculated task may have to re-discover the same failure that hindered the progress of the original task in the first place. We find that both Hadoop's speculative execution algorithm as well as the LATE algorithm [50] can be significantly impacted by failures. Importantly, these findings suggest that even state-of-the-art approaches to cause-aware speculative execution [15] may be insufficient. This is because a good speculative execution decisions can be invalidated at runtime when the speculated task is affected by a failure. To ensure that speculated tasks help improve job running time, failure information needs to be effectively shared between tasks at job runtime.

Third, Hadoop uses connection failures between its tasks as a heuristic for detecting node failures. In part, this is warranted by the limited visibility a cloud application can obtain about the cloud environment. Unfortunately, several factors can cause connection failures without implying node failures. Temporary overload conditions such as network congestion or excessive end-host load can cause connection failures. All these conditions are common in data centers [17, 22]. As a result, from only the news of a connection failure Hadoop cannot reliably distinguish an underlying cause. We show that this limitation unnecessarily introduces additional failures into the system. Specifically, otherwise localized failures involving a compute node can propagate to tasks running on healthy nodes. We call this the *induced reducer death* problem.

Our findings are not obvious. The points we highlight about real-life system building decisions and real-life subtle interactions are crucial. In practice, these decisions and interactions often invalidate benefits obtainable through smart solutions built on top. See for example the unexpected but serious ways in which failures affect the LATE and Hadoop speculative execution algorithms.

The paper is organized as follows. In §2 we review relevant Hadoop material. In §3 we present how Hadoop deals with failures today. In §4 we give detailed experimental evidence of Hadoop's design inefficiencies. We discuss implications, lessons learned and new ways of improving Hadoop-like frameworks in §5. Finally, we review related work in §6 and conclude in §7.

2. BACKGROUND AND NOTATION

2.1 Notation

For brevity we use the term speculation to refer to *speculative execution*. We say that a task was *speculated* when a new instance of the task was speculatively executed. We distinguish between the *initial* instance of a task and subsequent speculative instances of the same task. We use WTO, RTO and CTO to signify write, read and connect timeouts.

2.2 Hadoop Background

Hadoop [6, 49] separates a job computation into two types of tasks: mappers and reducers. First, mappers read the job input data from Hadoop's distributed file system (HDFS) and produce as their output key-value pairs. These map outputs are stored locally on compute nodes, they are not written to HDFS. The map outputs comprise the input for the reducer tasks. Each reducer processes a separate key range. For this, reducers copy the part of the map outputs which contains values within that key range. This copy phase is called shuffling. Oftentimes, reducers needs to copy part of the output of every single map. Finally, a reducer writes the job output data to HDFS.

Each task has a progress score which attempts to capture how close the task is to completion. The score is 0 at the task's start and 1 at completion. For a reducer, a score of 0.33 signifies the end of the copy (shuffle) phase. At 0.33 all map outputs have been read. A score of 0.66 signifies the end of the sort phase. Between 0.66 and 1 a reduce function is applied and the output data is written to HDFS. The progress rate of a task is the ratio of the progress score over the current task running time. For example, it can take a task 15s to reach a score of 0.45, for a progress rate of 0.03/s.

HDFS is composed of a centralized NameNode and of distributed DataNodes running on compute nodes. DataNodes handle the read and write operations to the HDFS. The NameNode manages the file system metadata and decides which DataNodes data should be read from or written to. HDFS write operations are pipelined. In a pipelined write an HDFS block is replicated at the same time on a number of nodes dictated by a configured replication factor. For example, if data is stored on node A and needs to be replicated on B and C, then, in a pipelined write, data flows from node A to B and from B to C. A WTO/RTO occurs when a HDFS write/read operation is interrupted by a DataNode failure. WTOs occur for reducers while RTOs occur for mappers. CTOs can occur for both mappers and reducers, when they cannot connect to a DataNode.

A TaskTracker is a distributed Hadoop component running on compute nodes which is responsible for starting and managing tasks locally. TaskTrackers are configured with a number of mapper and reducer slots, the same number for every TaskTracker. If a TaskTracker has two reduce slots then a maximum of two reducers can concurrently run on it. If a job requires more reducers (or mappers) than the number of reducer (mapper) slots in the system then the reducers (mapper) are said to run in multiple waves. A Task-Tracker communicates regularly with a Job Tracker, a centralized Hadoop component that manages jobs and decides when and where to start new tasks.

2.3 Speculative Execution Background

The JobTracker runs a speculative execution algorithm which attempts to improve job running time by duplicating under-performing tasks. The algorithm in Hadoop 0.21.0 (the version we use in this paper) is a variant of the LATE algorithm [50]. Both algorithms rely on progress rates. Both select a set of candidate tasks for speculation and then execute the candidate task that is estimated to finish farthest in the future. The difference lies in the method used to select the candidates. Hadoop takes a statistical approach. A candidate for speculation is a task whose progress rate is slower by at least one standard deviation than the average progress rate of all started tasks of the same kind (i.e. map or reduce) that belong to one job. Let $Z(T_i)$ be the progress rate of a task T_i and T_{set} the set of all running or completed tasks of the same kind. A task T_{cur} can be speculatively executed if:

$$avg(Z(T_i)_{T_i \in T_{set}}) - std(Z(T_i)_{T_i \in T_{set}}) > Z(T_{cur}) \quad (1)$$

Intuitively Hadoop speculates an under-performing task only when large variations in progress rates occur. In contrast, LATE attempts to speculate tasks as early as possible. For LATE, the candidates are the tasks with the progress rate below a SlowTaskThreshold, which is a percentile of the progress rates for a specific task type. Both algorithms speculate a task only after it has ran for at least 60s. To minimize the impact on available resources both algorithms cap the number of active speculative task instances at 1.

3. FAILURES IN HADOOP

In this section we describe the mechanisms that Hadoop uses to guard against failures. Alongside the speculative execution algorithm described in (§2.3) these mechanisms cause the serious inefficiencies that we uncover in this paper.

We identified these mechanisms by performing source code analysis on Hadoop version 0.21.0. The experiments in the rest of the paper are also based on 0.21.0. At the beginning of November 2011 version 0.21.0 was still the highest Hadoop version available. Recently, Hadoop has moved from the 0.2x versions to the 1.0.x versions. While we have not tested these latest version we have performed a code-level comparison between versions 0.21.0 and 1.0.0. We find that the mechanisms described in this section have remained the same, thus showing that the mechanisms are not short-lived but rather are deeply rooted in Hadoop's design philosophy. The one change we have found concerns the speculative execution algorithm. In 1.0.0, Hadoop has reverted to an older algorithm found in versions 0.20.x. Unfortunately, that particular algorithm has already been shown to have serious inefficiencies [50],

a conclusion which lead to the development of the improved algorithm that we analyze in this paper.

3.1 How Hadoop Deals with TaskTracker Failures

Hadoop infers TaskTracker failures by comparing task state variables against tunable threshold values. Table 1 lists the variables used by Hadoop. These variables are constantly updated by Hadoop during the course of a job. For clarity, we omit the names of the thresholds and instead use their default numerical values.

As we examine in detail the decisions related to TaskTracker failures, it shall become apparent that tolerating network congestion and compute node overload is a key driver of many aspects of Hadoop's design. It also seems that Hadoop attributes non-responsiveness primarily to congestion or overload rather than to failure, and has no effective way of differentiating the two cases. To highlight some findings:

- Hadoop is willing to wait for non-responsive nodes for a long time (on the order of 10 minutes). This conservative design allows Hadoop to tolerate non-responsiveness caused by network congestion or compute node overload.

- A *completed* map task whose output data is inaccessible is re-executed very conservatively. This makes sense if the inaccessibility of the data is rooted in congestion or overload. This design decision is in stark contrast to the much more aggressive speculative re-execution of straggler tasks that are *still running* [50].

- The health of a reducer is a function of the progress of the shuffle phase (i.e. the number of successfully copied map outputs). However, Hadoop ignores the underlying cause of unsuccessful shuffles.

3.1.1 Declaring a TaskTracker Dead

TaskTrackers send heartbeats to the JobTracker every 3s. The JobTracker detects TaskTracker failures by checking every 200s if any TaskTrackers have not sent heartbeats for at least 600s. If a TaskTracker is declared dead, the tasks running on it at failure time are restarted on other nodes. Map tasks that completed on the dead TaskTracker are also restarted if the job is still in progress and contains any reducers.

3.1.2 Declaring Map Outputs Lost

The loss of a TaskTracker makes all map outputs it stores inaccessible to reducers. Hadoop recomputes a map output early (i.e. does not wait for the TaskTracker to be declared dead) if the JobTracker receives enough notifications that reducers are unable to obtain the map output. The output of map M is recomputed if:

$$N_j(M) > 0.5 * R_j \quad \text{and} \quad N_j(M) \geq 3.$$

Let L be the list of map outputs that a reducer R wants to copy from TaskTracker H. A notification is sent immediately if a read error occurs while R is copying the output of some map M1 in L. $F_j^R(M)$ is incremented only for M1 in this case. If on the other hand R cannot connect to H, $F_j^R(M)$ is increased by 1 for every map M in L. If, after several unsuccessful connection attempts $F_j^R(M) \bmod 10 = 0$ for some M, then the TaskTracker responsible for R sends a notification to the JobTracker that R cannot copy M's output. A back-off mechanism is used to dictate how soon after a connection error a node can be contacted again for map outputs. After every failure, for every map M for which $F_j^R(M)$ is incremented, a penalty is computed for the node running M:

Var.	Description	Var.	Description	Var.	Description
P_j^R	Time from reducer R's start until it last made progress	R_j	Nr. of reducers currently running	T_j^R	Time since reducer R last made progress
M_j	Nr. of maps (input splits) for a job	D_j^R	Nr. of map outputs copied by reducer R	S_j^R	Nr. of maps reducer R failed to shuffle from
$F_j^R(M)$	Nr. of times reducer R failed to copy map M's output	A_j^R	Total nr. of shuffles attempted by reducer R	Q_j	Maximum running time among completed maps
$N_j(M)$	Nr. of notifications that map's output is unavailable.			K_j^R	Nr. of failed shuffle attempts by reducer R

Table 1: Variables for failure handling in Hadoop. The format is $X_j^R(M)$. A subscript denotes the variable is per job. A superscript denotes the variable is per reducer. The parenthesis denotes that the variable applies to a map.

$$penalty = 10 * (1.3)^{F_j^R(M)}.$$

A new timer is set to *penalty* seconds in the future. Whenever a timer fires another connection is attempted.

3.1.3 Declaring a Reducer Faulty

A TaskTracker considers a reducer running on it to be faulty if the reducer failed too many times to copy map outputs. Three conditions need to be simultaneously true for a reducer to be considered faulty. First,

$$K_j^R \geq 0.5 * A_j^R.$$

In other words at least 50% of all shuffles attempted by reducer R need to fail. Second, either

$$S_j^R \geq 5 \quad \text{or} \quad S_j^R = M_j - D_j^R.$$

Third, either the reducer has not progressed enough or it has been stalled for much of its expected lifetime.

$$D_j^R < 0.5 * M_j \quad \text{or} \quad T_j^R \geq 0.5 * max(P_j^R, Q_j).$$

Note that for Hadoop only the existence of a connection failure is important but not the cause of the failure.

3.2 How Hadoop Deals with DataNode Failures

Hadoop detects DataNode failures using connection errors and timeouts. If a timeout expires or an existing connection is broken, the read or write operation is restarted with new source or destination nodes obtained from the NameNode.

The timeouts used by HDFS requests to recover from DataNode failures are conservatively chosen, likely in order to accommodate transient congestion episodes which are known to be common to data centers [17]. Both an initial task and a speculative task can suffer from these timeouts. RTOs and CTOs are on the order of 60s while the WTOs are on the order of 480s. Differences of 5s-15s in absolute timeout values exist and depend on the position of a DataNode in the HDFS write pipeline. For this paper's argument these minute differences are inconsequential.

4. EXPERIMENTS EXPOSING THE INEF-FICIENCIES OF FAILURE DETECTION AND RECOVERY IN HADOOP

4.1 Methodology

For our experiments we used 15 machines from 4 racks in the OpenCirrus testbed [11]. One node is reserved for the JobTracker and NameNode, the rest of the nodes run DataNode and TaskTracker processes. Each node has 2 quad-core Intel Xeon E5420 2.50 Ghz CPUs. The network is 10 to 1 oversubscribed. We run Hadoop 0.21.0 with the default configuration. Importantly, the compute nodes as well as the network were not shared with other users. The resources were solely used by our Hadoop jobs. Even more, the compute nodes were not virtualized. As a result the performance of our testbed was predictable. This allows us to clearly identify the performance variations caused by Hadoop's design.

We independently study DataNode and TaskTracker failures because in many Hadoop deployments DataNodes and TaskTrackers are collocated and therefore, under compute node failures it would be hard to single-out the underlying cause. We first analyze Task-Tracker failures. After the TaskTracker failure experiments one of the compute nodes became permanently disabled because of a hardware issue and this left us with one less compute node for the DataNode failure analysis. Fortunately, the two sets of results are independent, therefore this failure does not affect out findings.

The job we use for this paper sorts 10GB of random data using 2 map slots per node and 2 reduce slots per node. In the experiments we vary the number of reducers and the number of reducer waves. 200 runs are performed for each experiment. Without failures the job takes on average 220s to complete. We chose this relatively short job because current studies show the significant popularity of short jobs in cloud workloads [50, 23, 20]. Our goal is not to exhaustively and quantitatively analyze Hadoop performance over many job and failure types. Instead, our aim is to expose the inefficiencies, the subtle interactions and the underlying design decisions in Hadoop. Nevertheless, we argue that the thorough understanding obtained from our paper is also insightful for longer jobs and for jobs running on larger deployments. Hadoop's failure detection and recovery algorithms (§3) remain the same regardless of scale because they use non-adaptive timeouts and the proportion of TCP connection failures. Even for multiple failures (which are more probable in larger deployments or longer jobs), the same algorithms apply. Also, oftentimes the multiple failures are independent and they have a cumulative effect. This effect can be estimated as the sum of the effect of single failures.

We consider TaskTracker and DataNode processes failures as well as the failure of the entire compute node running these processes. The difference between the two failure types lies in the existence of TCP reset (RST) packets that are sent by the host OS when a process is killed. RST packets may serve as an early failure signal. We induce the single DataNode (or TaskTracker) fail-stop failures by randomly killing one of the DataNodes (or TaskTrackers) at a random time after the job is started and before the 220s mark. At the end of each run we restart Hadoop. We simulate a fail-stop failure of the compute node running a DataNode (or Task-Tracker) by filtering all RST packets sent after the failure if the

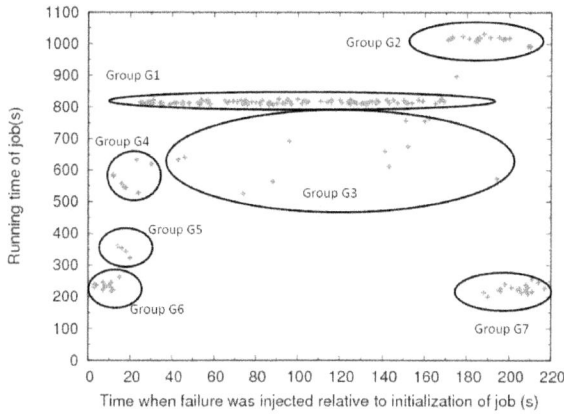

Figure 1: Clusters of job running times under TaskTracker failure. Without any failures the average job running time is 220s

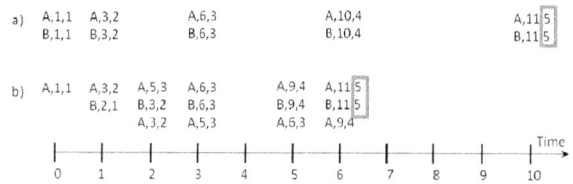

Figure 2: Illustration of early notifications. The tuple format is (map name, time the penalty expires, $F_j^R(M)$). For example, (A,3,2) means at time 3 a new connection should be attempted to get map output A, and there have been 2 failed attempts so far. The tuple values are taken immediately after the corresponding timestamp. This example considers that notifications are sent when $F_j^R(M) = 5$. Note that this occurs at different moments, shown by rectangles.

source port of the RST packet corresponds to the ports used by the failed DataNode (or TaskTracker). In our experiments we look at how failures impact the job running time and the job startup time. We consider the job startup time to be the time between the job submission and the job start assuming no waiting for task slots and no job queueing delays. We consider the job running time to be the time between the job start and job end.

Here is a quick roadmap of the experiments that follow. Details and arguments for our experiment choices can be found alongside the experiments. In the first experiment we analyze in great detail TaskTracker process failures and find significant performance variations. The subsequent three experiments confirm and expand on our findings for an increased number of reducers, for running a second concurrent job and for simulating TaskTracker node failures. For DataNode failure we start by explaining delayed speculative execution - an important inefficiency - using one sample run. We then analyze this inefficiency over three experiments each with a different number of reducers and reducer waves. We then change the speculative execution algorithm. We use LATE [50] and show the downside of Hadoop's philosophy to not share failure information. Our last experiment shows that DataNode failure can even significantly affect the job preparation stage.

4.2 TaskTracker Failure Analysis

Our first experiment details Hadoop's behavior under Task-Tracker process failures. For this first experiment we chose process failures because the presence of RST packets enabled us to perform a more thorough analysis. In the absence of RST packets, CTOs would slow down Hadoop's reaction considerably and would mask the effect of important subtle interactions.

4.2.1 Detailed Analysis

Figure 1 plots job running time against TaskTracker failure injection time. 14 reducers in 1 wave are used in this experiment. Out of 200 runs, 193 are plotted and 7 failed. Note the large variation in job running time. This is due to a large variation in the efficiency of Hadoop's failure detection and recovery mechanisms. To explain, we cluster the results into 8 groups based on the underlying causes. The first 7 groups are depicted in the figure. The 7 failed runs form group G8. The highlights that the reader may want to keep in mind are:

- When the failure affects few reducers, failure detection and recovery is exacerbated.

- Detection and recovery time in Hadoop is unpredictable – an undesirable property in a distributed system. The time it takes reducers to send notifications is variable and so is the time necessary to detect TaskTracker failures.

- The mechanisms used to detect lost map outputs and faulty reducers interact badly. As a result otherwise localized failure propagate in the system. Many reducers die unnecessarily as a result of attempting connections to a failed Task-Tracker. This leads to unnecessary re-executions of reducers, thus exacerbating recovery.

Group G1. In G1, at least one map output on the failed Task-Tracker was copied by all reducers before the failure. After the failure, the reducer on the failed TaskTracker is speculated on another node and it will be unable to obtain the map outputs located on the failed TaskTracker. According to the penalty computation (§3.1.2) the speculative reducer needs 10 failed connections attempts to the failed TaskTracker (416s in total) before a notification about the lost map outputs can be sent. For this one reducer to send 3 notifications and trigger the re-computation of a map, more than 1200s (i.e. 3 notifications each necessitating 416s) would typically be necessary. The other reducers, even though still running, do not help send notifications because they already copied the lost map outputs. Thus, the TaskTracker timeout (§3.1.1) expires first. Only then are the maps on the failed TaskTracker restarted. This explains the large job running times in G1 and their constancy. G1 shows that the efficiency of failure detection and recovery in Hadoop is impacted when few reducers are affected and map outputs are lost.

Group G2. This group differs from G1 only in that the job running time is further increased by roughly 200s. This is caused by the mechanism Hadoop uses to check for failed TaskTrackers (§3.1.1). To explain, let D be the interval between checks, T_f the time of the failure, T_d the time the failure is detected, T_c the time the last check would be performed if no failures occurred. Also let $n * D$ be the time after which a TaskTracker is declared dead for not sending any heartbeats. For G1, $T_f < T_c$ and therefore $T_d = T_c + n * D$. However, for G2, $T_f > T_c$ and as a result $T_d = T_c + D + n * D$. In Hadoop, by default, $D = 200s$ and $n = 3$. The difference between T_d for the two groups is exactly the 200s that distinguish G2 from G1. In conclusion, the timing of the TaskTracker failure with respect to the JobTracker checks can further increase job running time.

Group G3. In G3, the reducer on the failed TaskTracker is also speculated but sends notifications considerably earlier than the usual 416s. We call these *early notifications*. 3 early notifications are sent and this causes the map outputs to be recomputed before the TaskTracker timeout expires (3.1.2). To explain early notifications consider the simplified example in Figure 2 where the penalty (3.1.2) is linear ($penalty = F_j^R(M)$) and the threshold for sending notifications is 5. A more detailed example is available in [25]. Reducer R needs to copy the output of two maps A and B located on the same node. Case a) shows regular notifications and occurs when connections to the node cannot be established.

Case b) shows early notifications and can be caused by a read error during the copy of A's output. Due to the read error, only $F_j^R(A)$ is initially incremented. This de-synchronization between $F_j^R(A)$ and $F_j^R(B)$ causes the connections to the node to be attempted more frequently. As a result, failure counts increase faster and notifications are sent earlier.

Because the real function for calculating penalties in Hadoop is exponential (§3.1.2), a faster increase in the failure counts translates into large savings in time. As a result of early notifications, runs in G3 finish by as much as 300s faster than the runs in group G1.

Group G4. For G4, the failure occurs after the first map wave but before any of the map outputs from the first map wave is copied by all reducers. With multiple reducers still requiring the lost outputs, the JobTracker receives enough notifications to start the map output re-computation §(3.1.2) before the TaskTracker timeout expires. The trait of the runs in G4 is that not enough early notifications are sent to trigger the re-computation of map outputs early.

Group G5. As opposed to G4, in G5 enough early notifications are sent to trigger map output re-computation earlier.

Group G6. The failure occurs during the first map wave, so no map outputs are lost. The maps on the failed TaskTracker are speculated and this overlaps with subsequent maps waves. As a result, there is no noticeable impact on the job running time.

Group G7. This group contains runs where the TaskTracker was failed after all its tasks finished running correctly. As a result, the job running time is not affected.

Group G8. This group contains the failed jobs. The failed jobs are caused by Hadoop's default behavior to abort a job if one of the job's tasks fails 4 times. A reduce task can fail 4 times because of the induced death problem described next.

4.2.2 Induced Reducer Death

In several groups we encounter the problem of induced reducer death. Otherwise localized failures propagate to healthy tasks in the system. This is the case for the reducers which although run on healthy nodes, their death is caused by the repeated failure to connect to the failed TaskTracker. Such a reducer dies (possibly after sending notifications) because a large percent of its shuffles failed, it is stalled for too long and it copied all map output but the failed ones §(3.1.3). We also see reducers die within seconds of their start (without having sent notifications) because the conditions in §(3.1.3) become temporarily true when the failed node is chosen among the first nodes to connect to. In this case most of the shuffles fail and there is little progress made. Induced reducer death wastes time by causing task re-execution and wastes resources since shuffles need to be repeated.

4.2.3 Effect of Alternative Configurations

Subsection (§3.1) suggests failure detection is sensitive to the number of reducers. We increase the number of reducers to 56 and the number of reduce slots to 6 per node. Figure 3 shows the results. Considerably fewer runs rely on the expiration of the Task-Tracker timeout compared to the 14 reducer case because more reducers means more chances to send enough notifications to trigger map output re-computation before the TaskTracker timeout expires.

However, Hadoop still behaves unpredictably. The variation in job running time is more pronounced for 56 reducers because each reducer can behave differently: it can suffer from induced death or send notifications early. With a larger number of reducers these different behaviors yield many different outcomes.

Next, we run two concurrent instances of the 14 reducer job and analyze the effect the second scheduled job has on the running time of the first. Figure 4 shows the results for the first scheduled job compared to the case when it runs alone. Without failures, the first scheduled job finishes after a baseline time of roughly 400s. The increase from 220s to 400s is caused by the contention with the second job. The large variation in running times is still present. The second job does not directly help detect the failure faster because the counters in (§3.1) are defined per job. However, the presence of the second job indirectly influences the first job. Contention causes longer running time and in Hadoop this leads to increased speculation of reducers. A larger percentage of jobs finish around the baseline time because sometimes the reducer on the failed Task-Tracker is speculated before the failure and copies the map outputs that will become lost. This increased speculation also leads to more notifications so fewer jobs rely on the TaskTracker timeout expiration. Note also the running times around 850s. These jobs rely on the TaskTracker timeout expiration but suffer from the contention with the second job.

The next experiment mimics the failure of an entire node running a TaskTracker. Results are shown in Figure 5 for the 56 reducer job. The lack of RST packets means every connection attempt is subject to a 180s timeout. There is not enough time for reducers to send notifications so all jobs impacted by failure rely on the TaskTracker timeout expiration in order to continue. Moreover, reducers finish only after all their pending connections finish. If a pending connection is stuck waiting for the 180s timeout to expire, this stalls the whole reducer. This delay can also cause speculation and therefore increased network contention. These factors are responsible for the variation in running time starting with 850s.

4.3 DataNode Failure Analysis - Delayed Speculative Execution

The DataNode experiments simulate the failure of entire compute nodes running DataNodes. Thus, RST packets do not appear. We do not present the effect of DataNode process failures since their impact is low. While a DataNode failure is expected to cause some job running time variation and performance degradation, the speculative execution algorithm should eliminate significant negative effects. Our results show the opposite. As a quick example consider Figure 8. In this experiment, the speculative execution algorithm is largely ineffective after the map phase finishes (80s). The complete results for different number of reducers and reducer waves are plotted in Figures 8, 9, 10 and 11.

4.3.1 Understanding Delayed Speculative Execution

To understand the DataNode failure results, we first take a deeper look at the interactions between DataNode failures and the speculative execution algorithm. We show that these interactions can cause a detrimental effect which we deem delayed speculative execution. This consists in one speculation substantially delaying future speculations, or in the extreme case precluding any future speculations. The reason lies with the statistical nature of Hadoop's speculative execution algorithm (§2.3).

To explain delayed speculative execution, consider the sample run in Figure 6 which plots the progress rates of two reducers alongside the value of the left side of equation (1) from (§2.3). We call this left side the *limit*. For this run, 13 reducers are started in total,

192

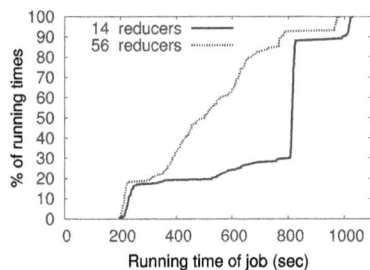

Figure 3: Increased nr of reducers

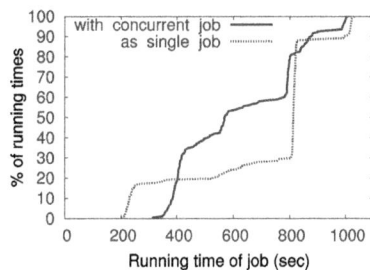

Figure 4: Single vs two concurrent jobs

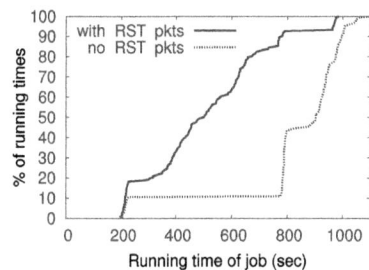

Figure 5: Effect of RST packets

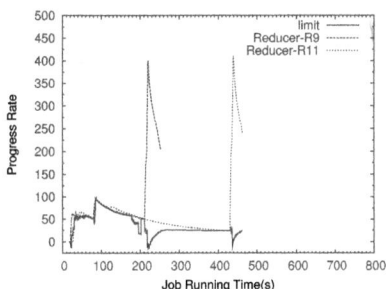

Figure 6: Delayed speculative exec.

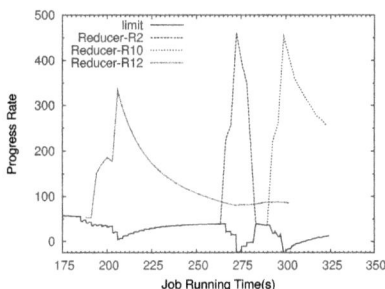

Figure 7: Types of progress rate spikes

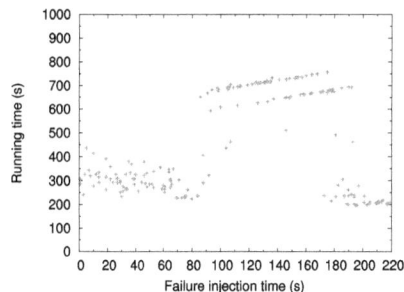

Figure 8: 52 reducers - 1 wave

all in 1 wave. In Hadoop, the progress rate for one task is the maximum rate over the progress rates of the initial task instance and the speculative instance. When an instance of the task completes, the final progress rate for the task is that of the completed instance. Initially, the reducers need to wait for the map phase to end. Their progress rates are close to the average rate and the standard deviation is small. Hence, the limit is relatively high and close to the average rate. A DataNode failure occurs at time 176s and affects reducers R9 and R11. The failure interrupted the write phase of these reducers and therefore R9 and R11 are stuck in a WTO. At time 200s, R9 is speculated. The progress rate for the speculative R9 is very high because it does not need to wait for map outputs to be computed. The outputs are readily available for copying. The sort phase is also fast and this helps further increase the progress rate of speculative R9. In Figure 6 this high rate is visible as a sudden large spike. As a result of the first spike, the average rate increases but the standard deviation increases more. Consequently, the limit decreases. Around 200s, the progress rate for R9 decreases because the speculative R9 needs time to finish the write phase. Because of this progress rate decrease the limit increases but not to the point where it would allow R11 to be speculated. R11 is speculated only around 450s when its progress rate becomes lower than the limit due to the prolong stall in the WTO. In the extreme case, if the limit is lowered too much (can even become negative) then no further speculation may be possible. To continue, all reducers stuck in an WTO would need to wait for the WTO to expire, because they cannot be speculated. In the general case, spikes need not be isolated as in our example. Several reducers can have progress rate spikes at the same time.

The influence that a speculation has on the limit and consequently on the start of subsequent speculations depends on the shape of the spike it creates. We plot these shapes in Figure 7. The ascending part of the spike decreases the limit. The severity of this ascending part depends on the amount of data the reducer needs to shuffle and on the speed of the network transfers. If little data is necessary or network transfers are very fast, then the reducer quickly finishes the shuffle and sort phases with a very

high progress rate. The decreasing part of the spike influences how much the limit increases. In our runs we see three distinct decreasing shapes each of which influences the limit differently. A short decrease signals that the write phase proceeded normally (reducer R10). A longer decrease signals that the speculative task also encountered a CTO because of the DataNode failure (reducer R12). A sharp decrease signals that the initial reducer finished shortly after the speculative reducer finished the shuffle and sort phases (reducer R2).

4.3.2 Effects of Delayed Speculative Execution on the Reduce Phase

Next, we explain in detail the results for DataNode failures injected during the reduce phase but after the map phase ends at roughly 80s.

For the 52-reducer, 1-wave case in Figure 8 the Hadoop speculative execution algorithm is ineffective after the map phase ends (∼80s). Notice the two parallel clusters of increasing job running time greater than 600s. The high job running times are caused by delayed speculative execution. Due to delayed speculative execution there is usually at least one reducer that cannot be speculated and therefore has to wait for the WTO to expire before continuing. The reason why two clusters exist lies in a Hadoop code-level design choice where a reducer does not remember a failed DataNode if it caused a WTO. Thus, the same failed DataNode can cause the reducer to get stuck in a CTO after the WTO. On the other hand, after a CTO, the reducer remembers the failed DataNode and no further CTOs are caused by that failure. If the WTO occurs at the last block that the reducer needs to write, no CTOs can follow. Therefore, one cluster is formed by reducers suffering only from a WTO while the other cluster is comprised of reducers suffering from both a WTO and a CTO. The steady increase in job running time for each of the clusters is a function of how close to the end of the job the failure was injected.

For the 13-reducer, 1-wave case in Figure 9 the speculative execution algorithm is more effective after the map phase end (∼80s). Large job running times caused by delayed speculative execution

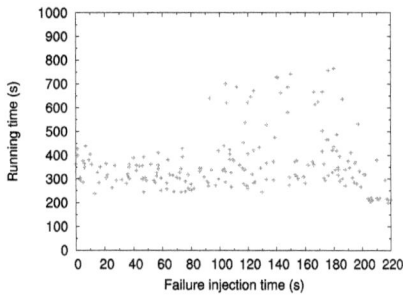

Figure 9: 13 reducers - 1 wave

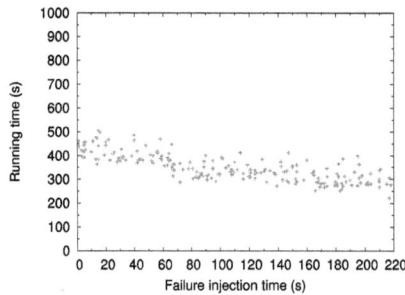

Figure 10: 52 reducers - 4 waves

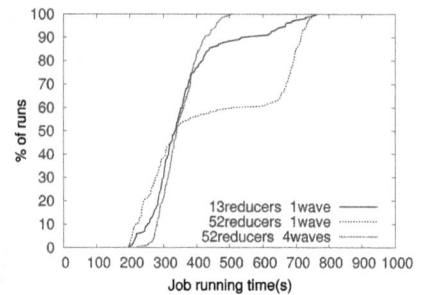

Figure 11: CDF for Figures 8, 9, 10

are still common but faster running times also exist. Compared to the 52-reducer case, each of the 13 reducers is responsible for writing 4 times more blocks and this considerably increases the chance that a CTO affects the write phase of a speculative reducer. As a result of these CTOs the limit is increased more and speculation becomes possible again thus resulting in some faster running times. Moreover, with only 13 reducers, less speculations are necessary overall since fewer reducers are impacted by the failure. Sometimes only 1 or 2 speculations are necessary overall and if both are started at the same time (in the first spike) there is no other speculation to be delayed.

For the 52-reducer, 4-wave case presented in Figure 10 the speculative execution algorithm performs well. The reason is that the reducers in the last 3 waves all have very high progress rates initially since the map outputs are already available and the sort phase is fast. As a result, the limit becomes high and less influenced by subsequent spikes. Consequently, further speculation is not impaired.

4.3.3 Effects of Speculative Execution on the Map Phase

We next explain the results for the experiments in Figures 8, 9, 10, and 11 when the failure is injected before 80s. During the first 80s, failures overlap with the map phase and reducers are not yet in the write phase. We did not see cases of delayed speculative execution for the map phase because mappers, unlike reducers, did not have to wait for their input data to be available and the map progress rates were similar. In theory, delayed speculative execution is also possible for the map phase when there is a large variation in progress rates among maps. This can happen in a topology with variable bandwidth. In these cases fast maps could skew the statistics.

Nevertheless, for the map phase we also identified speculative execution inefficiencies under DataNode failures. We encounter needless speculative execution caused by not including in the decision process information about why a task is slow . For example, a map task can stall on a 60s CTO but the speculative execution algorithm speculates a task only after the task has run for at least 60s. The speculation can be needless here because it oftentimes occurs exactly when the CTO expires and the initial map task can continue and quickly finish.

When the failure occurs during the map phase, the job running times are smaller than when reducers are affected. However, job running time variation still exists and is caused by several factors most of which are common to all 3 experiments from Figures 8, 9, 10, and 11. For example, sometimes the NameNode encounters a CTO at the end of a job, when it writes to HDFS a file with details about the run. This delays the delivery of the job results to the user even though all tasks, and therefore the computation are finished.

Also, if one of the maps from the last map waves suffers from a CTO this impacts job running time more since the CTO cannot be overlapped with other map waves. The reducers are delayed until the map stuck in the CTO finishes. Specific to the 52-reducer, 4-wave case is the fact that timeouts are possibly encountered by reducers in every of the 4 waves. As a result, job running times are slightly larger for this scenario.

4.4 DataNode Failure Analysis - Not Sharing Failure Information

In this section, we show the effect of Hadoop's philosophy to trade-off sharing of potentially useful information for extreme scalability. The effect is a significant increase in job-running time caused by failures being re-discovered by each task separately.

4.4.1 Using LATE as an Alternative Algorithm

We chose LATE as the speculative execution algorithm in this experiment because its goal is to react to under-performing tasks as early as possible. We first look at the 52-reducer, 1-wave case. As suggested in [50] we set the LATE SlowTaskThreshold to the 25th percentile. The results are plotted in Figures 12 and 13.

Overall, LATE performs better than Hadoop's speculative execution algorithm but running times larger than 600s are still present. Because of its more aggressive nature, LATE oftentimes speculates a task before the failure and therefore tasks having both the initial and the speculative instance running before the failure are present. The large job running times in this experiment are the runs in which both the initial task instance and its speculative instance are stuck in a WTO because they are affected by the same DataNode failure. Hadoop does not allow sharing of failure information and therefore the failure is re-discovered individually by each task. The task can continue and finish only after the WTOs expires for one of its instances.

For the 52-reducer 4-wave and the 13-reducer 1-wave cases LATE did not produce large job running times. In these cases, in our experiments the problem described above is still possible but it is less probable since fewer reducers are active at the same time. Note that it is enough for just one task to be affected in the manner described and the whole job's performance is significantly affected.

4.4.2 Delayed Job Start-up

We now analyze the effect of DataNode failures on the job start-up time. On each run, we fail one random DataNode at a random time starting 5s before the job submission time and ending 5s after. Job submission time is at 5s. The results are pictured in Figure 14 and 15. Without DataNode failures, the job start-up time is roughly 1s, thus the JobTracker finishes all write operations soon after 6s. This explains why failures occurring after 6s in Figure 14 do not

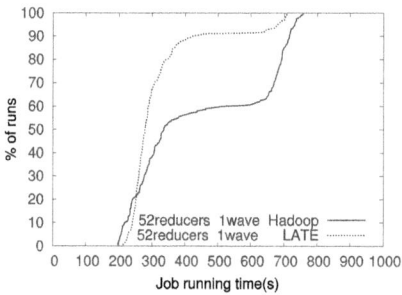

Figure 12: LATE vs Hadoop CDF

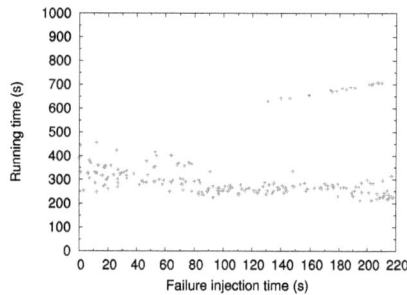

Figure 13: LATE 52 reducers 1-wave

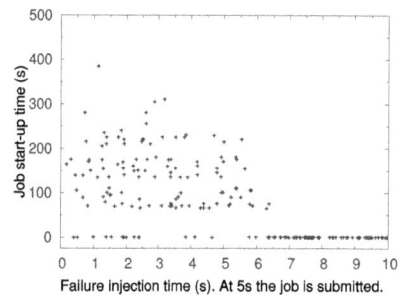

Figure 14: Job start-up times

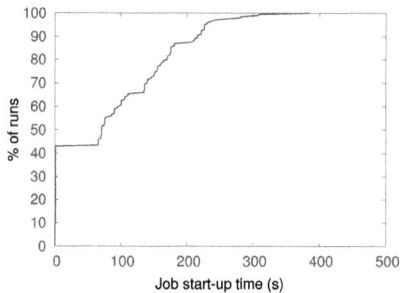

Figure 15: CDF of job startup times

impact job start-up time. However, if the DataNode failure occurs during the first 6s most jobs are impacted.

The reason is that even before a job is started, the JobTracker needs to make multiple HDFS write requests to replicate job-specific files. By default, 6 such files are written: job.jar (java classes for the job), job.split and job.splitmetainfo (description of map inputs), job.xml (job parameter values), jobToken (security permissions) and job.info. Any timeout delaying the writing of these files delays the start of the whole job. However, Hadoop does not share failure information between these 6 write operations. Moreover, the job.jar file is replicated by default using a large replication factor of 10 [49]. This makes this operation even more susceptible to DataNode failures. Unfortunately, this large replication factor is not adaptive and can cause inefficiencies when failures occur in small clusters. In our runs, with 13 total DataNodes and 10 DataNodes required by the large replication factor for job.jar, the chance that the write operation was impacted by the randomly induced failure was high. This explains why only few runs in Figure 14 were unaffected by a failure injected before 6s.

4.4.3 The Effect on the Map Phase

Having understood that Hadoop does not share failure information between tasks we can also apply this to the experiments in Figures 8, 9, 10, and 11, for the case when the failure is injected before 80s. Several mappers are influenced by the failure. This is because each map task performs 3 or 5 HDFS block read operations for processing one single input split. The first access is for the job.split file which identifies the input split for the job. The second access reads the input data while the third access reads the start of the subsequent block because a map input split can span HDFS block boundaries. Two more accesses can appear in case the map input split is not at the beginning of the HDFS file. Generally, the more HDFS accesses a task performs the greater the chance a failure will impact the task. Since, Hadoop does not share fail-

ure information between mappers and therefore many mappers can encounter a CTO because of the same failure.

5. DISCUSSIONS AND IMPLICATIONS

Delayed speculative execution is a general problem. Delayed speculative execution is a general concern for statistics-based speculative execution algorithms such as Hadoop's. There are many ways to trigger delayed speculative execution and failures are just one of them. The large HDFS timeouts are not a fundamental cause of delayed speculative execution, although they can add to the overhead. Two common conditions are needed to trigger the negative effects of delayed speculative execution: the existence of slow tasks that would benefit from speculation and conditions for tasks to suddenly speed up and create progress rate spikes. Slow tasks have many common causes including failures, timeouts, slow machines or slow network transfers. Progress rate spikes can be caused by varying input data availability (no more waiting is necessary for map outputs after the map phase ends) or by small reducer input data size (small input size means fast progress). Varying network speeds can also cause progress rate spikes. This especially concerns recent proposals for circuit-augmented network topologies [46, 29] that inherently present large variations in bandwidth over different paths.

With performance variation becoming a fact of life in the cloud it would be useful to develop speculative execution algorithms that forgo statistics altogether and instead are centered on a thorough understanding of the computation performed as well as of the current performance of the infrastructure. For example, static analysis of jobs [32, 34] could be used to generate a performance model that can be subsequently leveraged for scheduling and speculative execution decisions.

Not sharing failure information. We have shown the negative effects of not sharing failure information at job runtime. Regardless of how good a speculative execution decision may be before a failure, all benefits can quickly be invalidated when a speculated task is affected by a failure because it needs to read or write data to the failed node. Therefore, good speculative execution decisions are not sufficient. Care must be taken at runtime to ensure the success of the speculative execution decision. Sharing failure information at runtime is one potential approach to ensure this success. The benefits of sharing failure information are not limited to speculated tasks. Different tasks can significantly benefit from sharing failure information because they would not have to individually rediscover a failure.

We believe that sharing need not be limited to failure information. Performance, scalability or straggler information could also potentially be shared not only inside one application but among similar cloud applications [27]. With more information obtained from sharing, a large scale computing framework such as Hadoop would be more likely to make better provisioning and runtime decisions. Nevertheless, Hadoop's reason for not sharing information is warranted. Given the unprecedented scale of today's cloud environment sharing information between tasks, if not carefully done, can quickly become a serious bottleneck. Moreover, the extreme scalability of Hadoop's design is a cornerstone of Hadoop's success [43, 44]. Future work can analyze what is the minimum amount of information that, if shared, can yield maximum benefits. Also, it is useful to analyze the trade-off between the shared information's freshness and the overall gain on the system's performance.

Decoupling failure recovery from overload recovery. TCP connection failures are not only an indication of task failures but also of congestion. However, the two factors require different actions. It makes sense to restart a reducer placed disadvantageously in a network position susceptible to recurring congestion. However, it is inefficient to restart a reducer because it cannot connect to a failed TaskTracker. The data will still be unavailable regardless of whether the reducer is restarted or not. Unfortunately, the news of a connection failure does not by itself help Hadoop distinguish the underlying cause. This overloading of connection failure semantics ultimately leads to a more fragile system as exemplified by the induced reducer death problem.

In the future, it can prove useful to decouple failure recovery from overload recovery entirely. For dealing with compute node load, solutions can leverage the history of a compute node's behavior which has been shown to be a good predictor of transient compute node load over short time scales [15]. For dealing with network congestion, the use of network protocols such as AQM/ECN [30, 40, 26] that expose more information to the applications can be considered.

The need for adaptivity. Timeouts and thresholds in Hadoop are static. The disadvantage of static timeouts is that they cannot correctly handle all situations. Conservative timeouts are useful to cause a task's progress rate to slow down in order to be noticed by the speculative execution algorithm. Conservative timeouts are also useful for protection against temporary network or compute node overload. However, short timeouts may allow fail-over to other DataNodes when data can be read from or written to multiple DataNodes. TaskTracker thresholds are also static and we have shown that this leads to poor performance when few reducers are impacted by a TaskTracker failure.

Future work should consider adaptive timeouts that are set using system wide information about congestion, state of a job and availability of data. As a more general solution it would prove useful to complement Hadoop's design with a dependable failure detection and performance measuring mechanism, that would go beyond timeouts and guesswork - approaches that we have shown to be inadequate today. Hadoop needs to be much more aware of its environment and adapt to performance influencing environmental characteristics: reliability, sharing of resources, use of virtualization, performance variability.

The need for analysis work on large scale computing frameworks. Our paper is the first to provide a thorough analysis of Hadoop's performance under failure conditions. We believe such analysis work is fundamental for improving application performance in cloud environments. There is already a large body of work analyzing the performance of representative cloud infrastructures [41, 33, 48, 31]. We think this should be complemented with analysis work on representative cloud applications especially given their large but still increasing popularity. We hope our paper is an insightful first step to this end.

We have shown that Hadoop's internal mechanisms cause significant and unpredictable performance variations under failures.

These results suggest that it is challenging to model Hadoop's performance under failure conditions. Comparing our results against recent work on simulating the performance of Hadoop [47] under failures highlights the difficulty in developing accurate models of Hadoop's behavior based mainly on Hadoop's high-level design specifications. The subtle interactions that lead to performance variations do not appear in the model. Nevertheless such modeling work is very important in the cloud since users need to be able to estimate application performance in order to choose suitable large scale computing frameworks or cloud environments. We believe analysis work such as ours can be leveraged in the development of more advanced models of Hadoop's behavior.

6. RELATED WORK

In the existing literature, smart replication of intermediate data (e.g. map outputs) has been proposed to improve performance under TaskTracker failures [36, 15]. Replication minimizes the need for re-computation of intermediate data and allows for fast failover if one replica cannot be contacted as a result of a failure. Unfortunately, replication may not be always beneficial. It has been shown [36] that replicating intermediate data guards against certain failures at the cost of overhead during periods without failures. Moreover, replication can aggravate the severity of existing hotspots. Therefore, complementing replication with an understanding of failure detection and recovery is equally important. Existing work on leveraging opportunistic environments for large distributed computations [37] can also benefit from this understanding as such environments exhibit behavior that is similar to failures.

A recent study [31] characterizes the effect of network-related failures in the cloud. While the study does not deal with application-level effects, it shows network-related failures have an important effect on the data transfers. Applications built on top of large scale computing frameworks like Hadoop typically rely heavily on data transfers. Our study paints a complementary picture to the effects of network-related failures. We look at compute node failures and specifically target application-level design inefficiencies and interactions.

Other recent studies have found and analyzed significant cloud performance variability [41, 33, 48, 42]. The variability detected by these studies mainly stems from environmental causes such as sharing the data center network, using virtualized environments or leveraging the functionality provided by cloud services. Our work complements these study by identifying and analyzing the significant performance variation caused by the design of a cloud application itself. We showed that this variation can appear even in cloud environments with predictable performance.

Our work is also related to recent efforts for improving the performance of speculative execution algorithms in large scale computing frameworks [50, 15]. There are however important differences. Our work goes beyond speculative execution. This related body of work does not consider failure detection but we do so in detail. These related studies only relate to failure indirectly through outliers which are one possible effect of failures. Instead we analyze the effect of failures directly and exhaustively. We find that failures interact with Hadoop's inner workings in subtle ways (e.g. induced reducer death) and are at odds with Hadoop's design decisions (not sharing any information for scalability reasons). We have even discovered possible improvements to this past body of work. We analyzed the LATE algorithm [50] and showed it can be improved under failures. Moreover, the delayed speculative execution problem we uncovered is a new and important concern for statistical speculative execution algorithms.

7. CONCLUSION

In this paper we exposed and analyzed Hadoop's sluggish, variable and unpredictable performance under compute node failures. We identified several design decisions responsible: delayed speculative execution, the lack of sharing of failure information and the overloading of connection failure semantics. We believe our findings are generally insightful beyond Hadoop and will pave the way for a new class of more advanced large scale computing frameworks that are more predictable and more robust.

8. ACKNOWLEDGEMENTS

This research was sponsored by NSF CAREER Award CNS-0448546, NeTS FIND CNS-0721990, NeTS CNS- 1018807, by an Alfred P. Sloan Research Fellowship, an IBM Faculty Award, and by Microsoft Corp. Views and conclusions contained in this document are those of the authors and should not be interpreted as representing the official policies, either expressed or implied, of NSF, the Alfred P. Sloan Foundation, IBM Corp., Microsoft Corp., or the U.S. government.

9. REFERENCES

[1] Apache Mahout. http://mahout.apache.org/.
[2] Cloud9. http://lintool.github.com/Cloud9/.
[3] Cloudera. http://www.cloudera.com/hadoop/.
[4] Contrail. http://sourceforge.net/apps/mediawiki/contrail-bio/index.php?title=Contrail.
[5] Failure Rates in Google Data Centers. http://www.datacenterknowledge.com/archives/2008/05/30/failure-rates-in-google-data-centers/.
[6] Hadoop. http://hadoop.apache.org/.
[7] Hadoop Wiki - Powered By. http://wiki.apache.org/hadoop/PoweredBy.
[8] How Rackspace Now Uses MapReduce and Hadoop to Query Terabytes of Data. http://highscalability.com/how-rackspace-now-uses-mapreduce-and-hadoop-query-terabytes-data.
[9] J. Zawodny - Yahoo! Launches World's Largest Hadoop Production Application. http://developer.yahoo.com/blogs/hadoop/posts/2008/02/yahoo-worlds-largest-production-hadoop/.
[10] Microsoft Embraces Elephant of Open Source. http://www.wired.com/wiredenterprise/2011/10/microsoft-and-hadoop/.
[11] Open Cirrus(TM). https://opencirrus.org/.
[12] Pegasus. http://www.cs.cmu.edu/ pegasus/.
[13] X-RIME. http://xrime.sourceforge.net/.
[14] A. Abouzeid, K. Bajda Pawlikowski, D. Abadi, A. Silberschatz, and A. Rasin. Hadoopdb: An architectural hybrid of mapreduce and dbms technologies for analytical workloads. In *VLDB*, 2009.
[15] G. Ananthanarayanan, S. Kandula, A. Greenberg, I. Stoica, Y. Lu, B. Saha, and E. Harris. Reining in the outliers in map-reduce clusters using mantri. In *OSDI*, 2010.
[16] D. Beaver, S. Kumar, H. C. Li, J. Sobel, and P. Vajgel. Finding a needle in haystack: Facebook's photo storage. In *OSDI*, 2010.
[17] T. Benson, A. Anand, A. Akella, and M. Zhang. Understanding Data Center Traffic Characteristics. In *WREN*, 2009.
[18] D. Borthakur, J. Gray, J. S. Sarma, K. Muthukkaruppan, N. Spiegelberg, H. Kuang, K. Ranganathan, D. Molkov, A. Menon, S. Rash, R. Schmidt, and A. Aiyer. Apache hadoop goes realtime at facebook. SIGMOD, 2011.
[19] Y. Bu, B. Howe, M. Balazinska, and M. D. Ernst. Haloop: Efficient iterative data processing on large clusters. In *VLDB*, 2010.
[20] Y. Chen, A. Ganapathi, R. Griffith, and R. Katz. The Case for Evaluating MapReduce Performance Using Workload Suites. In *MASCOTS*, 2011.
[21] T. Condie, N. Conway, P. Alvaro, J. M. Hellerstein, K. Elmeleegy, and R. Sears. Mapreduce online. In *NSDI*, 2010.
[22] J. Dean. Experiences with MapReduce, an Abstraction for Large-Scale Computation. In *Keynote I: PACT*, 2006.
[23] J. Dean and S. Ghemawat. Mapreduce: Simplified Data Processing on Large Clusters. In *OSDI*, 2004.
[24] G. DeCandia, D. Hastorun, M. Jampani, G. Kakulapati, A. Lakshman, A. Pilchin, S. Sivasubramanian, P. Vosshall, and W. Vogels. Dynamo: Amazon's Highly Available Key-value Store. In *SOSP*, 2007.
[25] F. Dinu and T. S. E. Ng. Hadoop's Overload Tolerant Design Exacerbates Failure Detection and Recovery. In *NETDB*, 2011.
[26] F. Dinu and T. S. E. Ng. Inferring a Network Congestion Map with Zero Traffic Overhead. In *ICNP*, 2011.
[27] F. Dinu and T. S. E. Ng. Synergy2Cloud: Introducing Cross-Sharing of Application Experiences Into the Cloud Management Cycle. In *Hot-ICE*, 2012.
[28] J. Dittrich, J-A Q. Ruiz, A. Jindal, Y. Kargin, V. Setty, and J. Schad. Hadoop++: Making a yellow elephant run like a cheetah (without it even noticing). In *VLDB*, 2010.
[29] N. Farrington, G. Porter, S. Radhakrishnan, H. H. Bazzaz, V. Subramanya, Y. Fainman, G. Papen, and A. Vahdat. Helios: A Hybrid Electrical/Optical Switch Architecture for Modular Data Centers. In *SIGCOMM*, 2010.
[30] S. Floyd and V. Jacobson. Random early detection gateways for congestion avoidance. *IEEE/ACM Transactions on Networking*, 1(4):397–413, 1993.
[31] P. Gill, N. Jain, and N. Nagappan. Understanding Network Failures in Data Centers: Measurement, Analysis, and Implications. In *SIGCOMM*, 2011.
[32] C. Gkantsidis, D. Vytiniotis, O. Hodson, D. Narayanan, and A. Rowstron. Automatic io filtering for optimizing cloud analytics. In *Technical Report no. MSR-TR-2012-3, Microsoft Research*, January 2012. http://research.microsoft.com/apps/pubs/default.aspx?id=157556.
[33] A. Iosup, N. Yigitbasi, and D. Epema. On the Performance Variability of Production Cloud Services. In *CCGrid*, 2011.
[34] E. Jahani, M. J. Cafarella, and C. Re. Automatic optimization for mapreduce programs. In *VLDB*, 2011.
[35] S. Kandula, J. Padhye, and P. Bahl. Flyways to De-Congest Data Center Networks. In *HotNETS*, 2009.
[36] S. Y. Ko, I. Hoque, B. Cho, and I. Gupta. Making Cloud Intermediate Data Fault-Tolerant. In *SOCC*, 2010.
[37] H. Lin, X. Ma, J. Archuleta, W. Feng, M. Gardner, and Z. Zhang. MOON: MapReduce On Opportunistic eNvironments. In *HPDC*, 2010.
[38] C. Olston, B. Reed, U. Srivastava, R. Kumar, and A. Tomkins. Pig Latin: A Not-So-Foreign Language for Data Processing. In *SIGMOD*, 2008.
[39] P. Hunt and M. Konar and F. P. Junqueira and B. Reeed. Zookeeper: Wait-Free Coordination for Internet-Scale Systems. In *USENIX ATC*, 2010.
[40] K. Ramakrishnan, S. Floyd, and D. Black. *RFC 3168 - The Addition of Explicit Congestion Notification to IP*, 2001.
[41] J. Schad, J. Dittrich, and J-A Q. Ruiz. Runtime Measurements in the Cloud: Observing, Analyzing, and Reducing Variance. In *VLDB*, 2010.
[42] A. Shieh, S. Kandula, A. Greenberg, C. Kim, and B.Saha. Sharing the Data Center Network. In *NSDI*, 2011.
[43] A. Thusoo, S. Anthony, N. Jain, R. Murthy, Z. Shao, D. Borthakur, J. S. Sarma, and H. Liu. Data warehousing and analytics infrastructure at facebook. In *SIGMOD*, 2010.
[44] A. Thusoo, J. S. Sarma, N. Jain, Z. Shao, P. Chakka, N. Zhang, S. Antony, H. Liu, and R. Murthy. Hive - a petabyte scale data warehouse using hadoop. In *ICDE*, 2010.
[45] K. Venkatesh and N. Nagappan. Characterizing Cloud Computing Hardware Reliability. In *SOCC*, 2010.
[46] G. Wang, D. Andersen, M. Kaminsky, K. Papagiannaki, T. S. E. Ng, M. Kozuch, and M. Ryan. c-Through: Part-time Optics in Data Centers. In *SIGCOMM*, 2010.
[47] G. Wang, A. R. Butt, P. Pandey, and K. Gupta. A Simulation Approach to Evaluating Design Decisions in MapReduce Setups. In *MASCOTS*, 2009.
[48] G. Wang and T. S. E. Ng. The Impact of Virtualization on Network Performance of Amazon EC2 Data Center. In *INFOCOM*, 2010.
[49] T. White. Hadoop: The definitive guide.
[50] M. Zaharia, A. Konwinski, A. D. Joseph, R. Katz, and I. Stoica. Improving MapReduce performance in heterogeneous environments. In *OSDI*, 2008.

Optimizing MapReduce for GPUs with Effective Shared Memory Usage

Linchuan Chen   Gagan Agrawal
Department of Computer Science and Engineering
The Ohio State University
Columbus, OH 43210
{chenlinc,agrawal}@cse.ohio-state.edu

ABSTRACT

Accelerators and heterogeneous architectures in general, and GPUs in particular, have recently emerged as major players in high performance computing. For many classes of applications, MapReduce has emerged as the framework for easing parallel programming and improving programmer productivity. There have already been several efforts on implementing MapReduce on GPUs.

In this paper, we propose a new implementation of MapReduce for GPUs, which is very effective in utilizing shared memory, a small programmable cache on modern GPUs. The main idea is to use a *reduction-based* method to execute a MapReduce application. The *reduction-based* method allows us to carry out reductions in shared memory. To support a general and efficient implementation, we support the following features: a memory hierarchy for maintaining the reduction object, a *multi-group* scheme in shared memory to trade-off space requirements and locking overheads, a general and efficient data structure for the reduction object, and an efficient swapping mechanism.

We have evaluated our framework with seven commonly used MapReduce applications and compared it with the sequential implementations, MapCG, a recent MapReduce implementation on GPUs, and Ji *et al.*'s work, a recent MapReduce implementation that utilizes shared memory in a different way. The main observations from our experimental results are as follows. For four of the seven applications that can be considered as *reduction-intensive* applications, our framework has a speedup of between 5 and 200 over MapCG (for large datasets). Similarly, we achieved a speedup of between 2 and 60 over Ji *et al.*'s work.

Categories and Subject Descriptors

D.1.3 [**Software**]: PROGRAMMING TECHNIQUES—*Concurrent Programming*

General Terms

Performance

Keywords

GPU, MapReduce, shared memory

1. INTRODUCTION

The work presented in this paper is driven by two recent but independent trends. First, within the last 3-4 years, GPUs have emerged as the means for achieving *extreme-scale*, *cost-effective*, and *power-efficient* high performance computing. On one hand, some of the fastest machines in the world today are based on NVIDIA GPUs. At the same time, the very favorable price to performance ratio offered by the GPUs is bringing supercomputing to the masses. It is common for the desktops and laptops today to have a GPU, which can be used for accelerating a compute-intensive application. The peak single-precision performance of a NVIDIA Fermi card today is more than 1 Teraflop, giving a price to performance ratio of $2-4 per Gigaflop. Yet another key advantage of GPUs is the very favorable power to performance ratio.

Second, the past decade has seen an unprecedented data growth as information is being continuously generated in digital format. This has sparked a new class of high-end applications, where there is a need to perform efficient data analysis on massive datasets. Such applications, with their associated data management and efficiency requirements, define the term *Data-Intensive SuperComputing* (DISC) [3]. The growing prominence of data-intensive applications has coincided with the emergence of the MapReduce paradigm for implementing this class of applications [6].

The MapReduce abstraction has also been found to be suitable for specifying a number of applications that perform significant amount of computation (e.g. machine learning and data mining algorithms). These applications can be accelerated using GPUs or other similar heterogeneous computing devices. As a result, there have been several efforts on supporting MapReduce on a GPU [4, 12, 13].

A GPU is a complex architecture and often significant effort is needed in tuning the performance of a particular application or framework on this architecture. Effective utilization of *shared memory*, a small programmable cache on each multi-processor on the GPU has been an important factor for performance for almost all applications. In comparison, there has only been a limited amount of work in tuning MapReduce implementations on a GPU to effectively utilize shared memory [15].

This paper describes a new implementation of MapReduce for GPU, which is very effective in utilizing shared memory. The main idea is to perform a *reduction-based* processing of a MapReduce application. In this approach, a key-value pair that is generated is immediately merged with the current copy of the *output results*. For this purpose, a *reduction object* is used. Since the memory requirements for the output results or the reduction object is much smaller than the requirements for storing all key-value pairs for most applications, we reduce the runtime memory requirements very significantly. This, in turn, allows us to use the shared memory effectively. For many applications, the reduction object can be entirely stored in the shared memory.

Many challenges have been addressed to create a general and efficient implementation of our approach. A mechanism for dynamic memory allocation in the reduction object, maintaining a memory hierarchy for the reduction object, use of a *multi-group* strategy, and correct swap between shared and device memory for portions of the reduction object are some of the challenges we addressed.

We have evaluated our implementation comparing it against sequential implementations, MapCG [13], and a recent implementation that does use shared memory [15]. The main observations from our experiments are as follows. For four applications that can be considered as *reduction-intensive* applications, our framework has a speedup of between 5 and 200 over MapCG (for large datasets). Similarly, we achieved a speedup of between 2 and 60 over Ji *et al.*'s work for the three applications that are available from their distribution.

2. BACKGROUND

This section provides background information on GPU architectures and MapReduce.

2.1 GPU Architecture

A modern Graphical Processing Unit (GPU) architecture consists of two major components, i.e., the processing component and the memory component. The processing component in a typical GPU is composed of a certain number of streaming multiprocessors. Each streaming multiprocessor, in turn, contains a set of simple cores that perform in-order processing of the instructions. To achieve high performance, a large number of threads, typically a few tens of thousands, are launched. These threads execute the same operation on different sets of data. A block of threads are mapped to and executed on a streaming multiprocessor. Furthermore, threads within a block are divided into multiple groups, termed as *warp*. Each warp of threads are co-scheduled on the streaming multiprocessor and execute the same instruction in a given clock cycle (SIMD execution).

The memory component of a modern GPU-based computing system typically contains several layers. One is the *host memory*, which is available on the CPU main memory. This is essential as any general purpose GPU computation can only be launched from the CPU. The second layer is the *device memory*, which resides on the GPU card. This represents the global memory on a GPU and is accessible across all streaming multiprocessors. The device memory is interconnected with the host through a PCI-Express card (version can vary depending upon the card). This interconnectivity enables DMA transfer of data between host and device memory. From the origin of CUDA-based GPUs, a scratch-pad memory, which is programmable and supports high-speed access, has been available private to a streaming multiprocessor. The scratch-pad memory is termed as *shared memory* on NVIDIA cards. Till recently, the size of this shared memory was 16 KB.

2.2 MapReduce

MapReduce [6] was proposed by Google for application development on data-centers with thousands of computing nodes. It can be viewed as a middleware system that enables easy development of applications that process vast amounts of data on large clus-

ters. Through a simple interface of two functions, *map* and *reduce*, this model facilitates parallel implementations of many real-world tasks, ranging from data processing for search engine support to machine learning [5, 9].

MapReduce expresses the computation as two user-defined functions: *map* and *reduce*. The *map* function takes a set of input instances and generates a set of corresponding intermediate output $(key, value)$ pairs. The MapReduce library groups together all of the intermediate values associated with the same key and shuffles them to the *reduce* function. The *reduce* function, also written by the users, accepts a key and a set of values associated with that key. It merges together these values to form a possibly smaller set of values. Typically, just zero or one output value is produced per *reduce* invocation.

The main benefits of this model are in its simplicity and robustness. MapReduce allows programmers to write functional style code that is easily parallelized and scheduled in a cluster environment. One can view MapReduce as offering two important components [19]: a *practical programming model* that allows users to develop applications at a high level and an *efficient runtime system* that deals with the low-level details. Parallelization, concurrency control, resource management, fault tolerance, and other related issues are handled by the MapReduce runtime.

Recent years have seen a number of efforts to implement MapReduce frameworks on GPUs. Mars [12] was the first known MapReduce framework on a GPU. It spends extra time on counting the size of intermediate results. MapCG [13] has been shown to outperform Mars. It proposed a light-weight memory allocator, which enables efficient dynamic memory allocation on the GPU. Also, it used a hash table to store the key-value pairs, which avoids the overhead of shuffling.

Ji *et al.* have proposed a MapReduce framework which utilizes the shared memory on a GPU [15]. They used shared memory as a buffer to stage the input and output of *map* and *reduce* stages. The shared memory buffer enables fast data access and coalesced I/O to the device memory. They still store all key-value pairs generated by the *map* stage, and shuffling is required, which is time consuming. GPMR [21] was a project to leverage the power of GPU clusters for MapReduce. In this project, *partial* reduction and accumulation were used to reduce the communication overhead between different GPUs. However, shared memory was not used during reduction or accumulation to improve efficiency of processing on a single GPU.

3. SYSTEM DESIGN

This section describes the implementation of our system. The main emphasis in our approach is using the shared memory of a GPU effectively.

Initially, we describe why it is both important and challenging to effectively utilize shared memory while executing a MapReduce application. As we stated previously, shared memory supports much faster read and write operations. In addition, execution of an application with the MapReduce not only needs read/write operations, but also a large number of atomic operations, which are used to synchronize data accesses and updates by different threads. There is an even greater difference between the performance of atomic operations on shared memory and their performance on device memory. Thus, a large number of atomic operations on device memory can greatly undermine the performance of a MapReduce application.

The key challenge, however, in effectively utilizing shared memory is that the capacity of shared memory is very limited. Most MapReduce applications generate a large number of intermediate *key-value* pairs at the end of the Map phase. For these applications, it is impossible to keep all the key-value pairs in shared memory.

A recent implementation of MapReduce has demonstrated one mechanism for using shared memory. Particularly, the work from Ji *et al.* involves an innovative approach to using shared memory as a buffer to stage the input and output of both the *map* and *reduce* stages [15]. They copy the input from the device memory in a coalesced pattern into the shared memory. During the processing from a particular stage, when the shared memory is full, they copy the output from shared memory to device memory, again using coalesced writes. In this way, they achieve a speedup over the implementation that uses device memory only. However, the key-value pairs from the *map* stage still need to be stored in device memory, and shuffling is also required.

In our framework, we use a distinct approach for exploiting shared memory. We implement a MapReduce framework in a *reduction-based* manner, which is an alternative to the traditional implementation methods. Our focus is on exploiting shared memory effectively for *reduction-intensive* applications. By reduction-intensive application, we imply an application that generates a large number of key-value pairs that share the same key. Thus, there is a significant amount of work performed during the *reduce* phase, Moreover, the reduction operation is associative and commutative, which gives us flexibility in executing the reduction function.

Before describing our system in details, we first discuss the idea of the reduction-based MapReduce.

3.1 Basic Idea: Reduction Based Implementation

In reduction-based MapReduce, the *map* function, which is defined by the users, works in the same way as in the traditional MapReduce. It takes one or more input units and generates one or more key-value pairs. However, the key-value pairs are handled in a different way. In the traditional MapReduce, the key-value pairs are first stored, and after all the input units have been processed, the MapReduce library groups together all of the intermediate values associated with the same key and passes them to the *reduce* function. The *reduce* function each time accepts a key and a set of values associated with that key. It merges these values in the way defined by the users. In some cases, a user may define a *combine* function, which can combine key-value pairs generated on the same node, and reduce interprocess communication. However, the memory requirement on each node is typically not reduced by the combine function.

The reduction-based method, which can only be used if the reduction function is associative and commutative, inserts each key-value pair to the reduction object at the end of each *map* operation. Thus, every key-value pair is merged to the *output results* immediately after it is generated. A data structure storing these intermediate values of output is referred to as the *reduction object*. Every time a key-value pair arrives, the reduction object locates the index corresponding to the key, and reduces this key-value pair to that index in the reduction object, exploiting the associative and commutative property. The reduction object is transparent to the users, who write the same *map* and *reduce* functions as in the original specification.

We use k-means clustering as a running example to illustrate our concepts. K-means clustering is one of most popular data mining algorithms [14]. The clustering problem is as follows. We consider data instances as representing points in a high-dimensional space. Proximity within this space is used as the criterion for classifying the points into clusters. Four steps in the sequential version of k-

means clustering algorithm are as follows: 1) start with k given centers for clusters; 2) scan the data instances, for each data instance (point), find the center closest to it and assign this point to the corresponding cluster; 3) determine the k centroids from the points assigned to the corresponding centers, and 4) repeat this process until the assignment of points to clusters does not change.

Algorithm 1: map($input, offset$)

$point \leftarrow$ get_point($input, offset$);
for $i \leftarrow 0$ *to* K **do**
    $dis \leftarrow$ distance ($point, clusters[i]$);
    if $dis < min$ **then**
        $min \leftarrow dis$;
        $min\_idx \leftarrow i$;

$Kmeans\_value\ value$;
$value.num\_points \leftarrow 1$;
$value.dim0 \leftarrow point[0]$;
$value.dim1 \leftarrow point[1]$;
$value.dim2 \leftarrow point[2]$;
$value.dist \leftarrow min$;
$reduction\_object$.insert(&min_idx, sizeof(min_idx), &$value$, sizeof($value$));

Algorithm 2: reduce($value1, value1\_size, value2, value2\_size$)

$km\_value1 \leftarrow *(Kmeans\_value*)value1$;
$km\_value2 \leftarrow *(Kmeans\_value*)value2$;
$Kmeans\_value\ tmp$;
$tmp.num\_points \leftarrow$
$km\_value1.num\_points + km\_value2.num\_points$;
$tmp.dim0 \leftarrow km\_value1.dim0 + km\_value2.dim0$;
$tmp.dim1 \leftarrow km\_value1.dim1 + km\_value2.dim1$;
$tmp.dim2 \leftarrow km\_value1.dim2 + km\_value2.dim2$;
$tmp.dist \leftarrow km\_value1.dist + km\_value2.dist$;
copy($value1$, &tmp, sizeof(tmp));

Algorithm 1 and Algorithm 2 show the code of *map* and *reduce* functions in k-means. The *map* function processes one input point each time. It uses the identifier of the closest cluster center as the key, and the coordinates of this point, together with the number of points (1) and the distance to the cluster center are combined together to form a key-value pair. As part of runtime processing, this key-value pair is *inserted* in the *reduction object*. A *reduction object* is a data structure that maintains the current value of the final output results from the *reduce* stage of the application. For k-means clustering, the output of the *reduce* stage is the number of points associated with each cluster center, together with the total aggregated coordinates and distance of these points from the cluster center. At any point in the processing of the application, the reduction object contains the same information, but only for the set of points that have been processed so far.

The *insert* function works as follows. If the *key* already exists in the reduction object, the *reduce* function is invoked to merge the new key-value pair to the existing key. If it is the first time that this key is inserted, a new space for this key-value pair is created. Thus, elements within the reduction object are dynamically allocated. The *reduce* function in this example computes the new value for the existing key, i.e., it accumulates the number of points, the coordinates, and the distance of the new value to the existing value associated with that key. We will discuss the *insert* function in details in Section 3.4.

As we stated earlier, the main advantage of this approach is that the memory overhead of a large number of key-value pairs is avoided. This, in turn, is likely to allow us to utilize the shared memory on a GPU. However, we still need to address several chal-

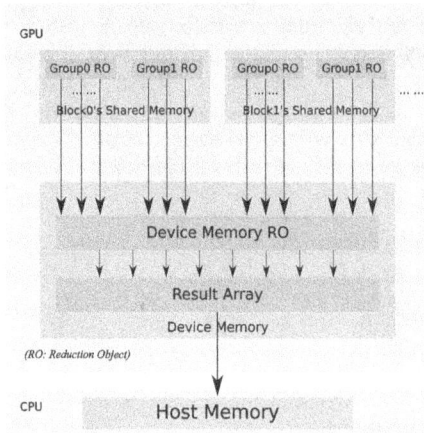

Figure 1: Memory Hierarchy

lenges to have an efficient implementation for MapReduce processing on a GPU.

To complete our design, we have the following features, which will be explained in the rest of this section.

- A memory hierarchy for maintaining the reduction object.

- A *multi-group* scheme in shared memory to trade off space requirements and locking overheads.

- A general and efficient data structure for the reduction object.

- An efficient overflow handling and swapping mechanism.

3.2 Memory Hierarchy

The processing structure we support reduces the memory requirements, by replacing the need for managing key-value pairs by a reduction object. For many applications, the reduction object tends to be small and can be kept in shared memory throughout the computation. However, for some other applications, it is possible that the number of distinct keys is very large, and shared memory may not be sufficient to hold the reduction object. To effectively use shared memory and yet have a general implementation, a memory hierarchy is maintained in our framework. As shown in Figure 1, reduction objects exist in both shared memory and device memory.

Elements of the reduction object are kept in shared memory as long as there is space. If an element corresponding to a key value that did not exist in the reduction is to be added, and there is no space, our framework swaps the data out to the device memory reduction object. The swapping mechanism will be discussed in details in Section 3.5.

There is only one copy of the reduction object in the device memory, which is used to collect the reduction result from shared memory reduction objects. The number of shared memory reduction objects depends upon the number of thread blocks and a design decision related to the number of *thread groups* that are created within each block. Each thread block is divided into one or more groups, and each group has one copy of the reduction object. Further details of the reasons for creating these thread groups will be discussed in the next subsection.

After all the threads in one thread block finish processing, they merge the data from the shared memory reduction object(s) into the device memory reduction object. To improve efficiency, this step is also performed in parallel. Merging threads read data as key-value pairs from shared memory reduction object(s), and insert them into the device memory reduction object. After all threads on GPU finish processing, they cooperate to copy data from the device memory reduction object to the result array, which is finally copied to host memory at last.

3.3 Multi-group Scheme in Shared Memory

A large number of threads (typically up to 512) are used in each thread block to exploit available parallelism in a streaming multiprocessor. Suppose there is one copy of the reduction object for all threads in the block. If all threads try to update the object, race conditions can arise. To avoid race conditions, we use synchronization mechanisms, such as the atomic operations that are supported on GPUs. However, when the number of distinct keys is small, the contention between the threads for updating the values associated with one key can be large, leading to significant waiting times.

One method for avoiding these costs could be to use *full replication*, i.e., create one copy of the reduction object for each thread. However, this method is not feasible because the number of threads is large, and if every thread owns one copy of the reduction object, the memory space needed will be large, leading to poor utilization of shared memory. In addition, such a large number of copies of the shared memory reduction object can lead to a very high overhead when they are merged to the device memory reduction object.

In order to address this problem, we introduce a *multi-group scheme*. Here, each thread block is partitioned into multiple groups, and each group owns its own copy of the reduction object. Let the number of threads in one block be N, and the number of groups in one block be M. Then the number of threads in one group is N/M and these threads share one copy of the reduction object. Locking operations are still required to update the copy of the reduction object, but the contention among the threads is reduced, since the number of threads competing for the same copy of the reduction object is now smaller. At the same time, the number of copies of the reduction object is still reasonable, which keeps the memory requirements and the overhead of combination modest.

The number of groups of threads that are used is a parameter in the system, and its optimal value can depend upon the application. Up to a certain level, increasing the number of thread groups improves performance, since the contention among threads is reduced. However, after a certain point, the performance can be reduced. One reason is that the size of shared memory is limited, so if the total number of keys is large, then the shared memory may not be able to hold many copies of the reduction object. This, in turn, increases the frequency with which swap mechanism needs to be invoked. Also, when the computation finishes, reduction objects in shared memory need to be merged into the device memory reduction object, and the data copying and synchronization to device memory can be time consuming. Clearly, the optimal choice can depend upon the size of one copy of the reduction object. When the reduction object is small and/or involves a smaller number of distinct keys, larger number of groups (or a smaller number of threads in each group) will be preferable. Similarly, when the reduction object is large and/or involves a large number of distinct keys, a smaller number of copies of the reduction object should be used.

An important parameter in our approach is the number of groups, g. The optimal choice for this parameter can be determined as follows. The overall execution time T for a specific application can be represented as:

$$T = C + \frac{T_{con}}{g} + T_{com} \times g \qquad (1)$$

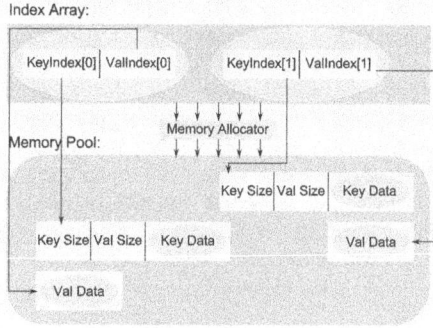

Figure 2: Reduction Object

where, C is the total time spent on initialization and computation, which is a constant for a given application and dataset. T_{con} is the contention overhead if only one group is used, and T_{com} is the combination overhead for one reduction object.

The minimum value of T is achieved when g equals $\sqrt{\frac{T_{con}}{T_{com}}}$, and the resulting optimal value of T is $C + 2\sqrt{T_{con} \times T_{com}}$.

3.4 Reduction Object Implementation

The structure of the reduction object is shown in Figure 2. It consists of two main parts: an *index array* and a *memory pool*. The index array is implemented as a hash table. Each bucket in the index array is composed of two indices: a *key index* and a *value index*. The *key index* refers to the position where the *key* data is stored in the memory pool. The *value index* is the position where the *value* data is stored.

Every bucket corresponds to a unique key, and the bucket is initialized when the first key-value pair with that particular key is inserted. The key data area contains not only the key data, but also the size information of key and value. In order to save space, only two bytes are used for storing the size information: one byte for the key size and the other for the value size. The memory pool is also an array, which is allocated before the computation starts. A memory allocator is used to allocate space for new keys and values.

Besides the index array and memory pool, one lock array is used in every copy of the reduction object. For each bucket in the index array, one lock is used to synchronize the updates to the key and value associated with that bucket.

Updating the Reduction Object: Algorithm 3 shows the logic of updating a reduction object. When a key-value pair is to be inserted into the reduction object, the hash value of the key is first calculated by the hash function, and then an index is calculated by using the hash value. The framework uses this index to find the bucket corresponding to the key.

The update involves the following two steps:

1. The thread which is performing the computation acquires the corresponding lock on the bucket. If the bucket is empty, new space for the key data and the value data is allocated by the memory allocator. After that, the size information and the key data is stored into the newly allocated key data space, and the value data is stored into the value data space. Finally, the index information of the key and the value is stored in the bucket. The computing thread releases the lock.

2. If the bucket already contains data, the key size and key address associated with this bucket are first retrieved, and then

---

Algorithm 3: insert($key, key\_size, val, val\_size$)

$index \leftarrow$ hash(key, key_size)%NUM_BUCKETS;
while $finish \neq 1$ **do**
  $DoWork \leftarrow 1$;
  /*wait on the lock*/
  while $DoWork$ **do**
    if get_lock($index$) **then**
      if $buckets[index] = 0$ **then**
        $k \leftarrow$ alloc($2 + key\_size$);
        $v \leftarrow$ alloc(val_size);
        /*store size information*/
        $key\_size\_addr \leftarrow$ get_addr (k);
        $val\_size\_addr \leftarrow key\_size\_addr + 1$;
        $*key\_size\_addr \leftarrow key\_size$;
        $*val\_size\_addr \leftarrow val\_size$;
        /*store key and value data*/
        $key\_data\_addr \leftarrow key\_size\_addr + 2$;
        $val\_data\_addr \leftarrow$ get_addr(v);
        copy($key\_data\_addr, key, key\_size$);
        copy($val\_data\_addr, val, val\_size$);
        /*store key and value indices*/
        $buckets[index][0] \leftarrow k$;
        $buckets[index][1] \leftarrow v$;
        release_lock($index$);
        $DoWork \leftarrow 0$;
        $finish \leftarrow 1$;
      else
        $key\_r \leftarrow$ get_key_addr($index$);
        $key\_size\_r \leftarrow$ get_key_size($index$);
        if equal($key\_r, key\_size\_r, key, key\_size$) **then**
          $val\_r \leftarrow$ get_val_addr($index$);
          $val\_size\_r \leftarrow$ get_val_size($index$);
          reduce($val\_r, val\_size\_r, val, val\_size$);
          release_lock($index$);
          $DoWork \leftarrow 0$;
          $finish \leftarrow 1$;
        else
          release_lock($index$);
          $DoWork \leftarrow 0$;
          $index \leftarrow$ new_index($index$);

used to compare with the new key. If the two keys are the same, the user-defined *reduce* operation is performed, and the value associated with the key is updated. After the *reduce* operation, the computing thread releases the lock on the current bucket. If the keys are not the same, the computing thread releases the lock and calculates a new index, which is then used to repeat the steps starting from the Step 1.

Memory Allocation in Reduction Object: Beginning with CUDA 3.2, dynamic device memory allocation has been supported on NVIDIA GPUs. However, the default mechanism tends to be expensive. Hong *et al.* developed a light-weight dynamic device memory allocator as part of the MapCG implementation [13]. Our method for memory allocation works in a similar way as MapCG, but has its own characteristics.

In MapCG, a large memory pool in the device memory is reserved before the computation starts. Every time additional space is needed, the light-weight memory allocator allocates a memory space and returns the memory index. We associate a memory allocator with both the device memory reduction object and the shared memory reduction object. These two memory allocators are somewhat different from each other. In every shared memory reduction object, only one offset is used to indicate the next available memory space. However, in the device memory reduction object, multiple offsets are used. We divide the threads in each block into many groups, which is similar to the *multi-group* scheme in the

Algorithm 4: Overflow Handling and Swapping Mechanism

```
/*variables shared in block*/
shared_objects[NUM_GROUPS];
full;
finish;

/*flag used to guarantee that only update finish once*/
first ← 1;

/*gid is group id*/
shared_objects[gid].init();
if tid = 0 then
    full ← 0;
    finish ← 0;
barrier()(all threads in one block);
i ← blockIdx.x * blockDim.x + threadIdx.x;

/*end the loop if all threads in a block finish computation*/
while finish ≠ blockDim.x do
    barrier();
    while i < task_number do
        if full then
            break;
        success ← map(i, &shared_objects[gid]);
        if success ≠ 1 then
            full ← 1;
            break;
        i ← i + gridDim.x * blockDim.x;

    /*current thread finishes computation*/
    if first && i ≥ task_number then
        atomicAdd(finish, 1);
        first ← 0;
    barrier();
    /*merge to device memory reduction object*/
    merge(device_object, &shared_objects[gid]);
    barrier();
    /*reinitialize the shared memory reduction objects*/
    shared_objects[gid].init();
    if tid = 0 then
        full ← 0;
```

shared memory. The reason why we use multiple offsets for the device memory reduction object is that all the threads across all the blocks can be updating the same device memory reduction object. To avoid race conditions, the memory offset is updated by using atomic operations. However, the contention of the lock can be high with a single copy, which is why separate offsets are used. Also, we store the offsets in the shared memory, which further lowers the overhead of memory allocation.

3.5 Handling Shared Memory Overflow

For many MapReduce applications, it is possible that during the process of computation, the shared memory reduction object gets full. More specifically, there can be two situations in which a reduction object is full. The first is when the buckets in the index array are all used up, and the second situation is when the memory pool does not have any more available space to allocate.

In such cases, we need to perform *overflow handling*. Our framework supports two ways of overflow handling. The first way is to swap the data out to device memory, and the second is to sort the reduction object and delete unnecessary data. For most applications, the swapping mechanism is used when the reduction object is full. Data from the shared memory reduction object is retrieved and inserted into the device memory reduction object. After such a swap is completed, the shared memory reduction object in one block is re-initialized, which is necessary for the remaining computations.

The reduction object also supports *in-object parallel sorting*. For applications like kNN (k-nearest neighbor search), when the reduc-

tion object in shared memory is full, bitonic sort [10] is performed on the reduction object. In such application, newly inserted data can make earlier data redundant. After sorting, only a small part of the data is kept in the reduction object, and the unnecessary data is deleted, which makes room for the remaining computation.

Algorithm 4 shows the logic of the swapping mechanism in overflow handling. In-object sorting logic is similar and is not shown here. CUDA provides a synchronization barrier routine for the threads within each block. A full flag shared among one block is used to indicate whether overflow handling is needed. Every time before a thread performs the *map* operation, it checks this flag. If this flag is not set, it carries out the regular update. Whenever a thread encounters an insertion failure, it sets this flag. All other threads within this block will see that the flag has been set, and know that they need to cooperate to conduct overflow handling. All threads in the block stop computations and merge the shared memory reduction object into the device memory reduction object. This operation is performed in parallel by all threads. If multiple thread groups, i.e., multiple copies of the reduction object are being used, the following logic is used. Irrespective of which group's reduction object is full, all threads from all groups within the block need to suspend all computations and perform overflow handling. Every thread only participates in the work associated with its own group's reduction object. We require all groups to perform overflow handling even when only one group's reduction object is full because the synchronization barrier, *__syncthreads()*, is used for all the threads in one block. There is no synchronization mechanism for a subset of threads in each block, except for the automatic synchronization within a warp. Although other groups' reduction objects may not yet be completely full, the rate of space utilization within the reduction objects is almost the same, because the load has been evenly distributed.

3.6 Application Examples

In this section, we use two representative examples to show how our framework supports different parallel applications. These two applications are k-means clustering (k-means) and k-nearest neighbor search (kNN). We use k-means to demonstrate the use of swapping mechanism, and use kNN to show how the in-object sorting mechanism helps.

K-means Clustering: The steps in the k-means clustering algorithm, along with a MapReduce implementation, were described earlier in Section 3.1. Now we show how our framework implements this algorithm.

As the implementation of the *map* function shows, we use the cluster center identifier as the key, and a structure containing the coordinates, the number of points and the distance from the cluster center to the current point as the value. Thus, at most k distinct keys are generated.

Immediately after a key-value pair is generated, it is inserted into the reduction object. As described in Section 3.4, when a key-value pair is inserted, the *reduce* function is used to update the newly generated value to the existing value corresponding to the same key. If k is small, for example, when k is 10 or 20, then the number of distinct keys is also small. We can use more groups in each block to reduce the contention among threads. If k is larger, such as 50 or 100, then we should use fewer groups to ensure that the shared memory can hold all the copies of the reduction object. For even larger k, we can choose the number of groups to be 1, though even in this case, shared memory may overflow and the swapping mechanism will be required.

K-nearest Neighbor Search: The k-nearest neighbor search (kNN) is a type of instance-based learning method [1]. This method is used to classify an object in an n-dimensional space based on the closest training samples. Given n training samples and one unknown sample, the k-nearest neighbor classifier searches the training samples by euclidean distance and finds the k nearest points to the unknown sample. Then it classifies the unknown sample according to the majority vote of the k nearest samples.

When implementing this algorithm by using our framework, we can take advantage of the in-object sorting mechanism we have supported, though it requires an extra function to be provided by the users. For every training sample, we use its point identifier as the key, and the distance from the unknown sample as the value. The framework keeps generating key-value pairs. When the reduction object corresponding to one group is full, the framework does not swap the reduction objects in the shared memory, but instead it conducts bitonic sort on the reduction objects. Users only need to define a single additional function, which will be comparing two buckets. This function is invoked by the sorting algorithm. After sorting, the framework deletes unnecessary data and only keeps k points that are the closest to the unknown sample. These points are kept in the shared memory reduction object, whereas the other space is made available for the remaining computations. When all threads finish processing data points and have combined the shared memory reduction objects to the device memory reduction object, an in-object sort on the device memory reduction object is performed.

3.7 Discussion

As we mentioned before, our framework is very suitable for *reduction-intensive* applications. These applications generate a large number of key-value pairs for any given key value, and the key-value pairs are reduced in an associative and commutative way. For these applications, we can reduce the memory overhead, and effectively utilize the shared memory.

Consider an application with no reduction, i.e. where only one key-value pair is generated for a given key, or the reduction operation is non-associative-and-commutative. Matrix Multiplication, if written using a MapReduce framework, has this property. In such cases, our method has no advantage over other GPU based MapReduce frameworks. In fact, it may be better not to try and use shared memory, since what is written in shared memory is never updated, and then has to be copied to device memory.

While using our framework, it is desirable to investigate the specific properties of the application. Our implementation is advantageous (over other GPU map-reduce implementations) only for applications with associative and commutative reduction operations, and within those, applications that are reduction-intensive. Also, certain parameters in our system, including the number of buckets, the memory pool size in each reduction object, as well as the number of groups in each thread block, currently need to be determined by the users. The users can make these decisions based on the potential number of key-value pairs that can be generated and the estimated memory requirements of the key-value pairs. This is similar to the more popular map-reduce implementations like Hadoop, where parameters like chunk size, replication factors, and others need to be explicitly chosen by users. The next step in our research will be developing techniques to automatically choose the values of some or all of these parameters.

The architecture of modern GPUs are changing rapidly. Over time, GPUs have seen an increase in shared memory size and device memory access speed. However, memory hierarchy still exists, and will continue to exist. Our method of utilizing shared memory

for MapReduce on a GPU is, therefore, applicable to any of the existing or upcoming architectures. In fact, because larger shared memory can hold larger reduction objects, and thus reduce the frequency of swapping operations, our approach may be even more benefitial.

3.8 Extension for Multi-GPU Systems

Even though a single GPU is a highly parallel architecture, high throughput processing may require use of a multi-GPU node, and/or a cluster with GPU(s) on each node. We now argue why our reduction object based approach is suitable for multi-GPU environments.

For applications that involve associative and commutative reduction operations and that are reduction-intensive, the following approach can be used. First, the data to be processed can be evenly divided between the nodes or GPUs. Second, processing as described in this paper can be directly applied on each GPU. The result of this processing will be the reduction object. Next, the reduction objects from each node or GPU can be combined using the associative and commutative reduction function to obtain the final results. The approach here will have two advantages. First, the processing on every GPU will be faster than other approaches. Second, the communication overheads will be lower than other approaches that involve shuffling of key-value pairs. If the reduction object is small, the final global reduction step will be very inexpensive.

For applications that do not involve associative and commutative reduction operation or are not reduction-intensive, we can default to the approaches used by other multi-GPU implementations, for example, GPMR [21].

4. EXPERIMENTAL RESULTS

We have evaluated the performance of our framework with many different applications, covering various types of applications that can be implemented using the MapReduce framework. We compare the performance of the applications against sequential (1 CPU thread) implementations, which were chosen or implemented to have the same logic/algorithm as the corressponding MapReduce implementations. We also compare the performance against an earlier MapReduce framework for GPU, MapCG [13], which does not use shared memory intensively. Finally, we also compare the performance of our system against Ji *et al.*'s work [15], a recent implementation of MapReduce that does use shared memory.

We have also conducted a number of experiments to evaluate some of the design decisions we made. For the reduction-intensive applications we have used, we consider different configurations of thread groups in each block and test the impact of the *multi-group* scheme. To investigate the performance of the swapping mechanism, we evaluate two applications with specific datasets.

4.1 Experimental Setup and Applications

Our experiments were conducted using an NVIDIA Quadro FX 5800 GPU with 30 multiprocessors. Each multiprocessor has 8 processor cores working at a clock rate of 1.3 GHz. Thus the GPU we used has 240 processor cores in total. The total device memory size is 4 GB and the shared memory size on each multiprocessor is 16 KB. The GPU is connected to a machine with 8 AMD 2.6 GHz dual-core Opteron CPUs. The total main memory on this machine is 24 GB.

We selected seven commonly used MapReduce applications to evaluate the performance of our framework. These examples cover both *reduction-intensive* and *map computation-intensive applications*. As we stated earlier, the former represents applications which have a large number of key-value pairs for each unique key, and the reduction operation is associative and commutative, and thus, reduction computation time is significant. In contrast, the latter represents applications that spend almost all their time in map stage, i.e., they have one or a very small number of key-value pairs for each unique key.

The applications we selected were as follows. K-means clustering (k-means) is one of the most popular data mining algorithms, which has been described previously. An important parameter here is the number of cluster (centers), k, which impacts memory requirements, and thus the *multi-group* scheme. K-nearest neighbor classifier (kNN) is a simple but popular machine learning algorithm, which was also described earlier.

Word Count (WC) is a very commonly used application for evaluating MapReduce frameworks. It calculates the total number of occurrences for each distinct word. In the key-value pairs generated by this application, the key is the character sequence of a word, and the value is the integer 1. WC can be reduction-intensive if the number of distinct words is small, and then the reduction objects can be kept in shared memory until the end of the computation. If the number of distinct words is very large, the reduction object cannot be held in shared memory, and then the swapping mechanism is needed.

Naive Bayes Classifier (NBC) is a simple classification algorithm based on observed probabilities. Given two sets of observations, one with classifications, one without, the algorithm classifies the second set. NBC selects the most likely classification V_{nb} given the attribute values $a_1, a_2, \ldots a_n$. V_{nb} is computed as

$$V_{nb} = argmax_{v_j \in V} P(v_j) \prod P(a_i|v_j) \qquad (2)$$

The particular invocation of this application in our experiments is given a set of data which includes the attributes color, type, origin, transmission type, and whether or not stolen. It judges the age of this vehicle based on the given information. When implemented using MapReduce, the total number of distinct keys is 30. The value generated by each *map* function is 1.

Our next application, Page View Count (PVC), obtains the number of distinct page views from web logs. Each entry in the web log is represented as $\langle URL, IP \rangle$, where URL is the URL of the accessed page and IP is the IP address that accesses the page. This application involves two passes in MapReduce. The first one removes the duplicate entries in the web logs, and the second one counts the number of views for each URL. In the first pass, the pair of the entry is used as the key and the size of the entry is used as the value. The second pass uses the URL as the key, and integer 1 as the value. Typically, the datasets have a lot of repeated entries, so the application is reduction-intensive in nature.

Another application we used is Matrix Multiplication (MM), which is a map computation-intensive application. Given two input matrices A and B, the *map* stage computes multiplication for a row i from A and a column j from B. It outputs the pair $\langle \{i, j\} \rangle$ as the key and the corresponding result as the value. If A is an $m_a \times n_a$ matrix, and B is an $m_b \times n_b$ matrix, then the total number of distinct keys is $m_a \times n_b$, which is a very large number if the dimensions of the matrices are large. Thus for this application, we use the device memory reduction object only. The *reduce* stage is not needed in this application, so there is no advantage to using shared memory reduction objects.

Our last application is Principle Component Analysis (PCA), which is also a map computation-intensive application. It aims to find a new (smaller) set of dimensions (attributes) that better captures the variability of data. Because it includes several steps that are not compute-intensive, we only perform the calculation of the

Application	Dataset Size (Small, Medium, Large)
K-means, K = 20 (KM20)	10K points, 100K points, 1M points
K-means, K = 40 (KM40)	10K points, 100K points, 1M points
K-means, K = 100 (KM100)	10K points, 100K points, 1M points
KNN, K = 20 (KNN)	10K points, 100K points, 1M points
Word Count, 90 Distinct Words (WC)	5.46MB, 10.94MB, 87.5MB
Naive Bayes Classifier (NBC)	26MB, 52MB, 104MB
Page View Count (PVC)	44MB, 88MB, 176MB
Matrix Multiplication (MM)	512*512, 1024*1024, 2048*2048
Principle Component Analysis (PCA)	1048576*8, 1048576*16, 1048576*32

Table 1: Applications and Datasets Used in our Experiments

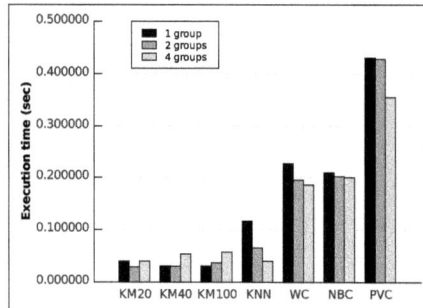

Figure 3: Performance Under Different Group Configurations

correlation matrix on the GPU. In this step, given an $n \times m$ data matrix D with n rows and m columns, we compute the matrix S, which is an $m \times m$ *covariance matrix* of D. The reduction object for this application stores the elements of the covariance matrix. This application also does not have the *reduce* phase, and it uses device memory only.

For every application example in our experiment, we use datasets of different sizes (small, medium, and large). The information about these datasets is shown in Table 1.

4.2 Evaluation of the Multi-group Scheme

To understand the behavior of our *multi-group* scheme, We executed the five reduction-intensive applications from our set of applications, varying the group numbers. Three different numbers of groups for each block were considered: 1, 2, and 4. Among our set of seven applications, MM and PCA are not included in these experiments, because they do not require reductions, and do not involve a shared memory reduction. kNN is not strictly a reduction-intensive application, but uses an in-object sort, and thus, the *multi-group* scheme is suitable for it. To focus on the impact of the number of groups, the results are reported from executions where the shared memory reduction objects are small and no overflow occurs during the entire computation. Finally, for k-means clustering, three different versions, KM20, KM40, and KM100 were created, by varying the number of clusters (centers), k. Recall that the size of the reduction object increases with increasing value of k.

Figure 3 shows the comparison of performance using different number of groups. These applications were tested with the large datasets. For KM20, the highest performance is achieved when the number of groups is 2. The total number of distinct keys in KM20 is 20, and thus the size of reduction object is very small. This implies a low combination overhead at the end of the computation. However, if the number of groups is 1, all the threads in one thread block update the same copy of the reduction object, and the contention can be very high. When the number of groups increases, the combination overhead increases, but the contention for each reduction object decreases. When we change the group number from 2 to 4, the increase of combination overhead is more significant as compared to the decrease in the contention overhead, so that the execution time increases.

KM40 has a larger reduction object. The combination overhead is now higher, but the contention during the updates to the reduction object is less severe. When we change the number of groups from 1 to 2, the benefit gained from the lower contention is almost the same with the performance loss due to the combination overhead, thus the execution time stays unchanged. When we increase the number of groups to 4, the performance gets worse due to the high combination overhead. The performance of KM100 follows a similar pattern with KM40 since it also has a large reduction object. The best performance is achieved with the group number of 1.

As we have discussed earlier, kNN is implemented by using the in-object sorting mechanism. Our experiments use 20 as the value of k. The reduction objects in this application fill up very frequently and the threads in each block need to perform overflow handling frequently, which, in turn, requires a bitonic sort. The bitonic sort incurs a large amount of data movement and is very time consuming. The combination overhead is relatively small compared with the sorting overhead. It turns out that in our implementation, as the number of groups increases, more threads take part in sorting. Thus the performance keeps improving when we increase the number of groups.

In the case of WC, the dataset used contains 90 distinct words, which makes it a reduction-intensive application. The best performance is achieved with the number of groups being 4. Although WC has a larger number of distinct keys than KM20, the contention on its reduction objects is more severe. This is because the time used to compare the newly generated keys with the keys in the reduction objects is long, and the hashing process and locating the key in the reduction object also take a substantial time. Thus, when the number of groups is increased, the contention decrease outweighs the combination overhead increase.

Although NBC has a small number of distinct keys (30), its execution time remains relatively unchanged with an increase in the number of groups. There are two reasons for this. On one hand, this application spends a relatively long time on processing each entry and generating key-value pairs, which makes the relative frequency of updating the reduction objects low, and the contention on the reduction objects also low. On the other hand, the hash function is able to locate the right buckets directly for this application, which makes the insertion to each bucket very fast.

PVC performs the best when the number of groups is 4. The PVC dataset we used involves 103 distinct entries, and thus, the total number of distinct keys in the first pass (which takes almost all the execution time) is also 103. The *map* function only computes the hash value of each entry and then emits it to the reduction object. Thus, this application has less computation, and the relative frequency of updates to each reduction object is very high. In addition, in this application, the hashing process and locating the key in the reduction object also take a relatively long time. Thus the contention on the reduction objects is quite high. Increasing the number of groups reduces such contention, resulting in better performance.

4.3 Comparison with Sequential Implementations

To show the overall benefits from our GPU-based framework, we compare the performance achieved on the GPU against the per-

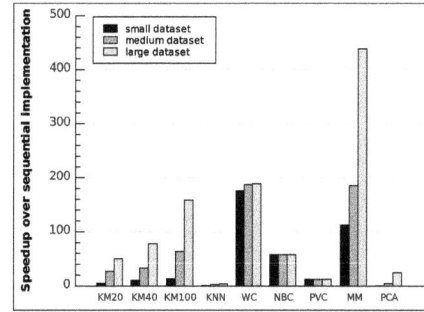

Figure 4: Speedup over Sequential Implementations

formance on a single thread application executing on 1 core of a CPU.

The results for the seven applications, and using three datasets for each application, are shown in Figure 4. The speedups vary considerably, depending upon the nature of the computation and the ratio between data transfer costs and execution times.

MM achieves the best speedup among all the applications. The reason is that MM does not involve any reduction. Moreover, the ratio between computation and amount of data to be processed is very high ($O(N^3)$ computation on $O(N^2)$ data). Thus, the GPU execution is not bound by data transfer costs or synchronization overheads.

The three versions of k-means, KM20, KM40, and KM100, along with WC, NBC, and PVC are reduction-intensive applications. Our framework is effective in speeding up these applications, especially for large datasets, but not to the extent of MM. This is because of a less favorable ratio between computation and data transfers, and because the reduction stage takes a considerable amount of time. Still, the speedup of KM100 on the large dataset is nearly 180, the speedups of WC on all datasets are around 200, and the speedups of NBC on all datasets are close to 50. In the case of k-means, the speedups increase with increasing value of k, because the amount of computation performed on each record also increases.

kNN only achieves a small speedup of 3.6x with the large dataset. The reason is the negligible amount of computation in the map phase and the high data movement cost. PCA also has a relatively small speedup, though it does become 24x on the large dataset. The reason is that the total number of data units to be processed is small, and thus the degree of parallelism is low.

All the applications achieve higher performance as the datasets become larger. The reason is that when the datasets are small, the initialization and synchronization overheads are dominant compared to the processing time.

4.4 Comparison with MapCG

We now compare the performance of our framework against one of recent implementations of MapReduce on GPUs [13]. This framework had been shown to outperform one of the earlier implementations of MapReduce for GPUs, Mars [12].

MapCG does not take advantage of shared memory intensively. Instead, it stores a lot of intermediate key-value pairs to the hash table in the device memory. This not only leads to significant overheads of device memory access and synchronization, but also high costs of execution of the reduction phase. So, we will expect that its performance will not be good for reduction-intensive applications, where our framework can exploit shared memory very effectively.

Figure 5 shows the speedup of our implementations over the

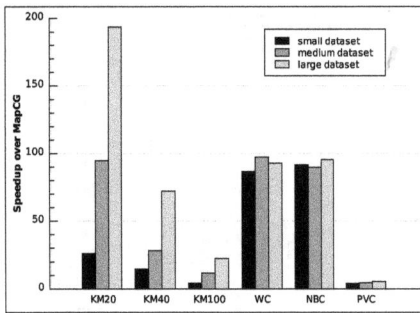

Figure 5: Speedup over MapCG for Reduction-intensive Applications

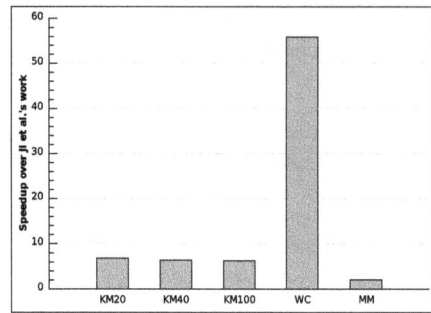

Figure 7: Speedup over Ji *et al.*'s Work

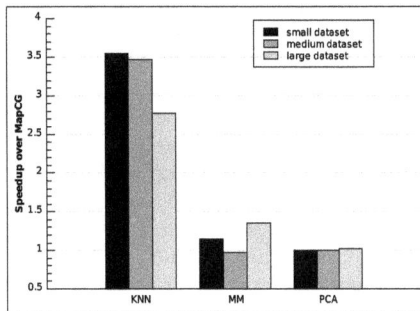

Figure 6: Speedup over MapCG for Other Applications

MapCG framework for four applications that we consider as the reduction-intensive applications. Each application is tested with small, medium, and large datasets, and three different values of *k* for k-means are used. We can see that we achieve significant speedups over MapCG for all datasets, and all applications in this set. KM20 achieves the highest speedup over MapCG. This is because it has a very small number of distinct keys, which leads to very high synchronization overheads (device memory based atomic operations) in the hash table used by MapCG. As the number of distinct keys becomes larger, MapCG performs somewhat better, though the relative speedups for large datasets are still very high. Similarly, WC and NBC both achieve very high relative speedups (about 90x on all datasets) due to the significant synchronization overheads in the map phase of MapCG's implementations. PVC has a speedup of 5x, which is smaller compared with the other 5 applications. One reason is that PVC has a large number of distinct keys, which makes the synchronization overhead with MapCG's hash table relatively low.

Figure 6 shows the speedup over MapCG for other three applications, which either spend a lot of time on map computations, or involve sorting. MM and PCA both do not use shared memory reduction objects. So the performance of our framework is almost the same as MapCG. For kNN, MapCG needs to sort the intermediate key-value pairs in device memory, which is time consuming. In comparison, our framework does most of the sorting in shared memory, although it also needs to sort the device memory reduction object before the computation finishes. Thus, our framework is more efficient, and as we can see from Figure 6, we have a factor of 3 speedup on the average over MapCG.

Overall, we can see that our method for exploiting shared mem-

ory leads to much better performance as compared with MapCG, for reduction-intensive applications. By comparing our speedups over MapCG and the speedups over sequential versions, we can see that for KM20 and NBC, MapCG even has a slowdown over sequential implementations, defeating the purpose in using a GPU. Thus, effective utilization of shared memory is crucial in benefiting from GPUs for MapReduce applications.

4.5 Comparison with Another Approach for Using Shared Memory

As we stated earlier in the paper, one recent implementation of MapReduce for GPUs does use shared memory [15]. This system, from Ji *et al.*, is based on a more traditional approach for executing MapReduce, i.e., it has a *shuffle* or *sort* phase between *map* and *reduce* phases. As described earlier, their system uses shared memory as a buffer to stage input and output.

We obtained the implementation from Ji *et al.* and have compared it against our implementation. Among the applications we have used, implementations of KM, WC, and MM were available as part of their distribution. Because their implementation is based on a somewhat different API, it was not possible to execute other four applications on their framework. Thus, we have used these three applications.

The results from KM20, KM40, KM100, WC, and MM with large datasets are shown in Figure 7. Our system is always faster, though the exact speedup varies. Our framework achieves a very high speedup (56x) for WC. The reason is the large proportion of time spent on shuffling the key-value pairs in Ji *et al.*'s implementation. Also, for all versions of k-means, our framework achieves a speedup of more than 6, as we get an effective use of shared memory and avoid shuffling overhead. MM only has the map phase, i.e., neither framework needs shuffling. We still achieve about a factor of 2 speedup for this application.

Overall, we can see that our approach for implementing MapReduce, including the way we use shared memory and avoid shuffling is significantly more efficient, and clearly outperforms the previous implementation.

4.6 Evaluation of the Swapping Mechanism

In some reduction-intensive applications, the number of distinct keys is large and the reduction objects in the shared memory can become full. The swapping mechanism implemented as part of our framework is invoked in such cases. Thus, while our framework can clearly correctly handle such applications, it is useful to explore the performance of our framework for these applications.

For this purpose, we experiment with WC and PVC, where the number of keys can vary (and can be quite large), depending upon

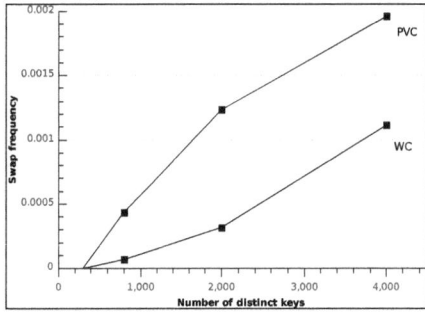

Figure 8: Swap Frequency under Different Number of Distinct Keys

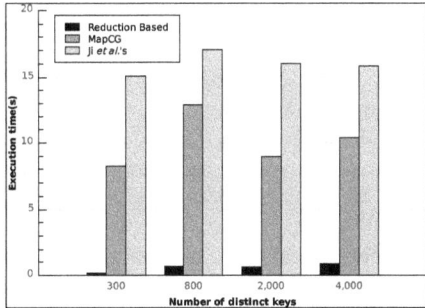

Figure 9: Comparison with Other Implementations for WC

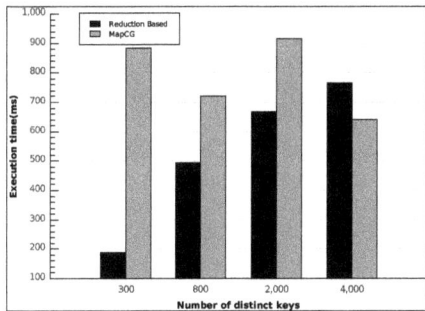

Figure 10: Comparison with MapCG for PVC

the dataset. Thus, we examine the performance of these two applications by increasing the number of distinct keys, which leads to the increase of swaps. For each application, we use 5 datasets to evaluate the swapping mechanism. The numbers of distinct keys in the datasets vary from 300 to 4000. The size of each dataset is 100 MB. The number of buckets in each shared memory reduction object is 600. Thus for datasets with 300 distinct keys, no swap is involved.

We first investigate the change of *swap frequency* with the number of distinct keys increasing. The swap frequency f is defined as:

$$f = \frac{N_{swap}}{N_{task}} \qquad (3)$$

where N_{swap} represents the total number of swaps in one execution, and N_{task} represents the total number of tasks in the work-

load. Larger values of f imply larger percentages of time spent on swapping.

The relationship between the number of distinct keys and the swap frequency is illustrated in Figure 8. We can see that as the number of distinct keys increases, the swap frequency increases, as we would expect. However, for both WC and PVC, the overall swap frequencies are quite low, although the swap frequency of PVC reaches 0.2% with the number of distinct keys being 4000. The results imply that in most cases, our system still performs much of the reduction work in shared memory.

We have also compared our system with MapCG and Ji *et al.*'s work when swaps are involved. Figure 9 shows the execution times of different frameworks for WC. Although our system involves swaps for number of distinct keys of 800, 2000, and 4000, it still achieves better performance than other two systems. MapCG has very high overhead because of the frequent accesses to global memory. Ji *et al.*'s framework spends considerable time shuffling. Figure 10 shows the comparison between our framework and MapCG for PVC (As was mentioned in Section 4.5, PVC is not included in Ji *et al.*'s distribution, and doesn't seem straight-forward to implement because of their specialized API). Our system performs better than MapCG for most cases, though MapCG has a shorter execution time as the distinct key number increases to 4000.

Thus, we can see from the results that even when the frequency of swaps increases, our framework still performs well. This is because that our system keeps a large proportion of the reduction object in shared memory, which results in lower device memory access frequency.

5. RELATED WORK

Recent years have seen a large number of efforts on MapReduce and its variants. We primarily focus on efforts specific to multi-core CPUs, GPUs, and heterogeneous systems.

Ranger *et al.* [19] have implemented a shared-memory MapReduce library named Phoenix in multi-core systems, and Yoo *et al.* [22] optimized Phoenix specifically for large-scale multi-core systems. CellMR [18] was a MapReduce framework implemented on asymmetric Cell multi-core processors. Streaming approach was adopted to support MapReduce. Mars [12] was the first attempt to harness GPU's power for MapReduce applications. MapCG [13] was a subsequent implementation which was shown to outperform Mars. We have extensively compared our work against MapCG. Catanzaro *et al.* [4] also built a framework around the MapReduce abstraction to support vector machine training as well as classification on GPUs. StreamMR [7] was a MapReduce framework implemented on AMD GPUs.

MITHRA [8] was introduced by Farivar *et al.* as an architecture to integrate the Hadoop MapReduce with the power of GPGPUs in the heterogeneous environments, specific for Monte-Carlo simulations. Shirahata *et al.* [20] have extended Hadoop on GPU-based heterogeneous clusters. They enabled *map* tasks to be scheduled onto both CPUs cores and GPUs devices. GPMR [21] was a recent project to leverage the power of GPU clusters for large-scale computing by modifying the MapReduce paradigm.

There has been a large volume of research on porting and tuning applications and developing programming systems on GPUs. Optimizing shared memory has been an important factor in many of these studies. Some of the prominent applications where shared memory use made a very substantial performance difference include N-Body [16] and FFT [11]. The methods used in these and other similar efforts were specific to the applications, and cannot be used as part of a high-level GPU programming system.

Aggressive compiler optimizations have also been used to exploit shared memory. Baskaran *et al.* have provided an approach for automatically arranging shared memory on NVIDIA GPUs by using the polyhedral model for affine loops [2]. They also focus on enabling more data reuse on shared memory, while reducing data movement. Moazeni *et al.* have adapted approaches for register allocation to manage shared memory on GPUs [17]. They used graph coloring to solve the problem.

6. CONCLUSIONS AND FUTURE WORK

This paper focuses on utilizing shared memory to accelerate MapReduce implementations on GPUs. In order to reduce the high overhead of data copying and synchronization on the device memory, we use a reduction-based approach, where we avoid storing the intermediate data (key-value pairs) in device memory. Instead, we perform reduction on the shared memory. We have also designed an approach for storing the reduction object on the memory hierarchy of the GPU. Finally, to further improve the performance, we have developed a *multi-group* scheme which allows us to balance the memory overhead and locking costs for the reduction objects.

We have evaluated the performance of our framework using seven applications. We have shown that our implementation delivers significantly higher performance than MapCG, a MapReduce framework which does not utilize shared memory intensively, and Ji *et al.*'s implementation, which takes a different approach for using shared memory.

Possibilities for future work include developing auto-tuning techniques to determine values of certain system parameters, which will make it easier for users to obtain high performance. We will also extend our framework to support new architectures, such as the emerging coupled CPU-GPU architectures from Intel, AMD, and NVIDIA.

7. REFERENCES

[1] David W. Aha, Dennis F. Kibler, and Marc K. Albert. Instance-based Learning Algorithms. *Machine Learning*, pages 6:37–66, 1991.

[2] Muthu Manikandan Baskaran, Uday Bondhugula, Sriram Krishnamoorthy, J. Ramanujam, Atanas Rountev, and P. Sadayappan. Automatic Data Movement and Computation Mapping for Multi-level Parallel Architectures with Explicitly Managed Memories. In *PPoPP '08*, pages 1–10, New York, NY, USA, 2008. ACM.

[3] Randal E. Bryant. Data-Intensive Supercomputing: The Case for DISC. Technical Report CMU-CS-07-128, School of Computer Science, Carnegie Mellon University, 2007.

[4] Bryan Catanzaro, Narayanan Sundaram, and Kurt Keutzer. A Map Reduce Framework for Programming Graphics Processors. In *Third Workshop on Software Tools for MultiCore Systems (STMCS)*, 2008.

[5] Cheng-Tao Chu, Sang Kyun Kim, Yi-An Lin, YuanYuan Yu, Gary R. Bradski, Andrew Y. Ng, and Kunle Olukotun. Map-Reduce for Machine Learning on Multicore. In *NIPS*, pages 281–288, 2006.

[6] Jeffrey Dean and Sanjay Ghemawat. MapReduce: Simplified Data Processing on Large Clusters. In *OSDI*, pages 137–150, 2004.

[7] Marwa Elteir, Heshan Lin, and Wu-chun Feng. StreamMR: An Optimized MapReduce Framework for AMD GPUs. In *ICPADS '11*, Tainan, Taiwan, December 2011.

[8] Reza Farivar, Abhishek Verma, Ellick Chan, and Roy Campbell. MITHRA: Multiple Data Independent Tasks on a Heterogeneous Resource Architecture. In *CLUSTER*, pages 1–10. IEEE, 2009.

[9] Dan Gillick, Arlo Faria, and John Denero. MapReduce: Distributed Computing for Machine Learning. 2008.

[10] N. Govindaraju, J. Gray, R. Kumar, and D. Manocha. Gputerasort: High Performance Graphics Co-processor Sorting for Large Database Management. In *SIGMOD '06*, pages 325–336.

[11] Eladio Gutierrez, Sergio Romero, Maria A. Trenas, and Emilio L. Zapata. High Performance Computing for Computational Science - VECPAR 2008. pages 430–443. Springer-Verlag, 2008.

[12] Bingsheng He, Wenbin Fang, Qiong Luo, Naga K. Govindaraju, and Tuyong Wang. Mars: A MapReduce Framework on Graphics Processors. In *PACT*, pages 260–269, 2008.

[13] Chuntao Hong, Dehao Chen, Wenguang Chen, Weimin Zheng, and Haibo Lin. MapCG: Writing Parallel Program Portable between CPU and GPU. In *PACT*, pages 217–226, 2010.

[14] Anil K. Jain and Richard C. Dubes. *Algorithms for Clustering Data*. Prentice-Hall, Inc., 1988.

[15] F. Ji and X. Ma. Using Shared Memory to Accelerate Mapreduce on Graphics Processing Units. In *IPDPS '11*, pages 805–816, 2011.

[16] Mark Harris Lars Nyland and Jan Prins. Chapter 31 Fast N-Body Simulation with CUDA, 2007.

[17] Maryam Moazeni, Alex Bui, and Majid Sarrafzadeh. A Memory Optimization Technique for Software-managed Scratchpad Memory in GPUs. *Application Specific Processors, Symposium on*, 0:43–49, 2009.

[18] M. Mustafa Rafique, Benjamin Rose, Ali Raza Butt, and Dimitrios S. Nikolopoulos. CellMR: A Framework for Supporting Mapreduce on Asymmetric Cell-Based Clusters. In *IPDPS*, pages 1–12, 2009.

[19] Colby Ranger, Ramanan Raghuraman, Arun Penmetsa, Gary R. Bradski, and Christos Kozyrakis. Evaluating MapReduce for Multi-core and Multiprocessor Systems. In *Proceedings of 13th HPCA*, pages 13–24, 2007.

[20] Koichi Shirahata, Hitoshi Sato, and Satoshi Matsuoka. Hybrid Map Task Scheduling for GPU-Based Heterogeneous Clusters. In *CloudCom '10*, pages 733–740, 2010.

[21] Jeff A. Stuart and John D. Owens. Multi-GPU MapReduce on GPU Clusters. In *IPDPS*, 2011.

[22] Richard M. Yoo, Anthony Romano, and Christos Kozyrakis. Phoenix Rebirth: Scalable MapReduce on a Large-Scale Shared-Memory System. In *IISWC*, pages 198–207, 2009.

CAM: A Topology Aware Minimum Cost Flow Based Resource Manager for MapReduce Applications in the Cloud

Min Li†, Dinesh Subhraveti‡, Ali R. Butt†, Aleksandr Khasymski†, Prasenjit Sarkar‡
† Dept. of Computer Science, Virginia Tech; ‡ IBM Almaden Research Center
{limin,butta,khasymskia}@cs.vt.edu, dineshs@us.ibm.com,
psarkar@almaden.ibm.com

ABSTRACT

MapReduce has emerged as a prevailing distributed computation paradigm for enterprise and large-scale data-intensive computing. The model is also increasingly used in the massively-parallel cloud environment, where MapReduce jobs are run on a set of virtual machines (VMs) on pay-as-needed basis. However, MapReduce jobs suffer from performance degradation when running in the cloud due to inefficient resource allocation. In particular, the MapReduce model is designed for and leverages information from the native clusters to operate efficiently, whereas the cloud presents a virtual cluster topology overlying or hiding actual network information. This results in two *placement anomalies*: loss of *data locality* and loss of *job locality*, where jobs are placed physically away from their data or other associated jobs, adversely affecting their performance.

In this paper we propose, CAM, a cloud platform that provides an innovative resource scheduler particularly designed for hosting MapReduce applications in the cloud. CAM reconciles both data and VM resource allocation with a variety of competing constraints, such as storage utilization, changing CPU load and network link capacities. CAM uses a flow-network-based algorithm that is able to optimize MapReduce performance under the specified constraints — not only by initial placement, but by readjusting through VM and data migration as well. Additionally, our platform exposes, otherwise hidden, lower-level topology information to the MapReduce job scheduler so that it makes optimal task assignments. Evaluation of CAM using both micro-benchmarks and simulations on a 23 VM cluster shows that compared to a state-of-the-art resource allocator, our system reduces network traffic and average MapReduce job execution time by a factor of 3 and 8.6, respectively.

Categories and Subject Descriptors

C.2.4 [**Computer-Communication Networks**]: Distributed Systems — *distributed applications*; G.2.2 [**Discrete Mathematics**]: Graph Theory — *graph algorithms, network problems*

General Terms

Design, Algorithms, Performance, Evaluation.

Keywords

MapReduce, Cloud computing, Min-cost flow network, VM placement, VM resource management

1. INTRODUCTION

MapReduce is an established framework for processing large-scale data-intensive applications. The MapReduce model helps businesses to process massive quantities of data in reasonable time and extract valuable insights hidden within by distributing the job across a large number of cost-effective cluster nodes. In particular, for many applications, such as converting archived media into a streaming format for Internet delivery, the processing is needed only once, and hence the resources required for processing are also needed only for a specific duration.

Combining the MapReduce framework with the cloud provides a number of unique advantages. It is particularly appealing for organizations that need to analyze large amounts of data without having to acquire and manage large cluster resources. The user does not need to own the cluster resources required to run the job, which removes the entry barrier [6], enabling even small businesses to perform detailed analysis on their data. An organization can focus on its core business rather than being occupied by lower-level cluster maintenance. The cloud provides the flexibility of dedicating as many or as few virtual machines (VMs) and storage resources as needed based on the required turnaround time [1, 2, 8]. The user only pays for the resources for the duration of time they are used.

While cloud offers great promise, the storage infrastructure of existing cloud environments is poorly suited for MapReduce computation. Clouds are typically built on commodity clusters with node-local disks for their cost-effectiveness and scalability. Several issues impact the turnaround time of MapReduce jobs running in these cloud environments.

First, *running MapReduce jobs in the cloud has an expensive ingestion phase*, where the dataset needs to be copied from a central persistent store into the compute cluster for processing. For large datasets, ingestion represents a significant portion of the turnaround time. Moreover, clouds feature a stateless model and any data and VMs copied to the physical/hypervisor cluster are discarded once the job is completed. Subsequent jobs require transferring the data again. Alternatively, it may be possible to have the MapReduce tasks access the data directly from the remote store via suitable remote data access protocols such as NFS, iSCSI [14], or FibreChannel [19]. Such remote access has several disadvantages. For one, all data would have to be accessed over the network. MapReduce model achieves its efficiency by ensuring that tasks can access their data locally. Thus, fetching data over the network severely affects job performance. Furthermore, the bisectional bandwidth between the compute cluster and the central store can easily become a bottleneck. A large number of tasks, all accessing their data from the central store, can quickly saturate the link and render the system inefficient.

A further alternative is to co-locate the data with the compute cluster. However, spreading out the data across the local disks of cluster nodes constrains the scheduling choices available for placing VMs. VMs accessing the data located on a particular node must all be placed on that node, but other constraints such as amount of memory or licenses may not permit this. Providing reliability of persistent data located on the hypervisor cluster is also a challenge. Data stored on a centralized storage device is typically protected from disk failures through internal replication. Providing a similar replication facility across disjoint local file systems storing the data is difficult. A cluster file system may be used to combine the local storage attached to individual nodes in the cluster, but most existing cluster file systems are designed for a central storage model in a storage area network (SAN), and perform poorly on local storage [4]. For example, cluster file systems typically stripe files across all available disks in the cluster to maximize throughput, whereas such a strategy limits the performance in commodity clusters where network is the bottleneck.

Similar issues also apply to the VM images that compose a MapReduce job. The virtual image files need to be copied to the hypervisor nodes before starting a job, which introduces a very high startup latency. As before, running directly from the remote storage is not a scalable solution and co-locating the images with the cluster limits scheduling choices.

Second, *the cloud masks the physical topology of the underlying infrastructure*, which can potentially inhibit optimal scheduling of MapReduce tasks. The MapReduce model is designed for and leverages information from the native clusters to operate efficiently, whereas the cloud presents a virtual cluster topology. For instance, the VMs associated with a job may be placed across multiple racks. However, this information is not typically visible to the application. Furthermore, the cloud may also change the initial assignment by migrating the VMs to different nodes in the cluster based on runtime load and other constraints. While these functions add flexibility, they also make application-level scheduling challenging. This results in two *placement anomalies*: (1) Loss of data locality, where a task may be placed away from the physical location of its data; and (2) Loss of job locality, where a task may be placed away from the physical locations of other tasks that it communicates with. Map-intensive jobs are adversely affected by loss of data locality and reduce-intensive jobs are impacted by loss of job locality.

Third, *the multi-tenant cloud environment may result in interference between MapReduce applications* and other applications sharing the environment. Scheduling decisions made at the beginning of the job may become invalid during the course of the job, when VMs are migrated around or due to changing workloads. An optimal allocation of resources might become suboptimal leading to poor performance.

In order to efficiently address aforementioned issues, we present CAM, a platform that is designed to host MapReduce applications in the cloud. CAM provides a cluster file system that supports a uniform file system name-space across the cluster by integrating the discrete local storage of the individual nodes. The shared file system enables a VM to be placed on any cluster node or subse-

quently migrated as necessary. We leverage GPFS [10] in CAM to query and specify the physical locations of an image and its replicas, which can then be used for CAM-directed placement of VMs and data.

CAM avoids the placement anomalies with an innovative resource scheduler for the cloud, especially designed for improving the performance of MapReduce jobs. Specifically, this paper makes the following contributions:

- CAM adopts a three level approach to maximize locality. (1) **Data placement:** Data is placed within the cluster based on offline profiling of the jobs that most commonly run on the data. Rather than accommodating an arbitrary data placement, strategically placing the data can significantly improve locality. (2) **VM/job placement:** For a given job, CAM selects the best possible physical nodes to place the set of VMs that represent the job. (3) **Task placement:** In order to further minimize the possibility of a placement anomaly, CAM exposes, otherwise hidden, *compute, storage, and network* topologies to the MapReduce job scheduler such that it makes optimal task assignments. This is crucial as, for example, what appears to be a directly attached local disk within a VM could in fact be physically located on a different node.

- CAM reconciles resource allocation with a variety of other competing constraints such as storage utilization, changing CPU load and network link capacities using a flow-network-based algorithm that is able to simultaneously satisfy the specified constraints. Each placement decision not only considers the existing data and VM assignments in the cluster, but also evaluates the cost of readjusting existing assignments in response to data movement and VM migration to derive the best net configuration possible.

- We evaluate CAM using both micro-benchmarks and simulations on a 23 VM cluster. We show that compared to a state-of-the-art resource allocator, our system reduces network traffic by up to 3 times, and achieves $8.6x$ speedup of MapReduce jobs on average.

The rest of the paper is organized as follows. Sections 2 and 3 provide an overview of CAM's architecture and usage model. Section 4 details the design of data and VM placement techniques used in CAM. Section 5 presents our experimental results. Finally, we summarize related work in Section 6 and conclude in Section 7.

2. ARCHITECTURE

CAM is designed as an extension to IBM ISAAC product [12]. ISAAC implements key cloud functions such as creating and deleting VMs and their persistent volumes, placing the VMs based on load and capacity, maintaining availability of cloud services through clustering and fail-over mechanisms. The architectural components of CAM are implemented as extensions to related counterparts in ISAAC. In particular, we have integrated ISAAC with the GPFS-SNC [10] file system to provide a suitable cluster file system needed by CAM, and have extended ISAAC to support data and VM placement based on techniques we describe in Section 4. Figure 1 illustrates the components of CAM and their interactions when deployed in a cloud environment. The physical resources supporting the cloud consists of a cluster of hypervisor (physical) nodes with local storage directly attached to the individual nodes.

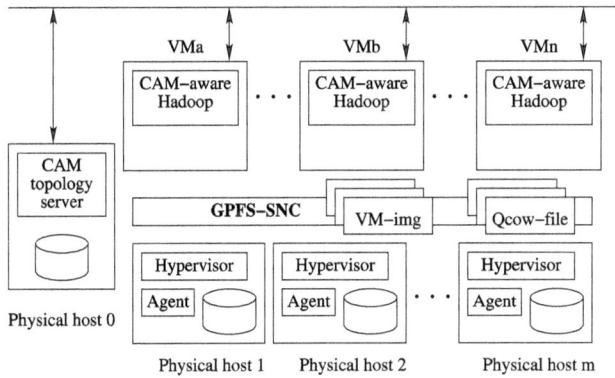

Figure 1: CAM architecture components.

2.1 GPFS-SNC Storage Layer

CAM uses GPFS-SNC [10] to provide its storage layer. GPFS-SNC is designed as a cloud storage platform, which supports timely and resource-efficient deployment of VMs. GPFS-SNC manages the local disks directly attached to a cluster of commodity physical machines. More specifically, it has a number of unique features that make it a cloud-friendly storage system. First, GPFS-SNC supports co-locating all blocks of a file at one location, rather than stripping the file across machines. This enables a VM I/O request to be serviced locally from the stored location instead of remotely from physical hosts across the network. CAM leverages this feature to ensure that co-located VM images are stored at one location and can be accessed efficiently. Second, GPFS-SNC supports an efficient block-level pipelined replication scheme, which guarantees fast distributed recovery and high I/O throughput through fast parallel reads. This feature is useful for CAM for achieving efficient failure recovery. Finally, GPFS-SNC specifies a user-level API that can be used to query the physical location of files. CAM uses this API to determine actual block location, and uses this information to infer storage closeness for data and VM placement.

2.2 Topology Awareness

MapReduce task scheduler uses the topology information of the cluster nodes to decide task assignments. The information is supplied by the user as a part of the job configuration file when the job is submitted. However, in an attempt to abstract hardware level details and present a simple interface to the user, existing cloud implementations do not expose the information about the topology of the cluster or the actual placement of VMs to the MapReduce scheduler [2]. Furthermore, the initial configuration provided by the user may become stale when the VMs are moved later.

CAM addresses these issues with three main components that together provide topology awareness as shown in Figure 1. First, the *CAM topology server* provides the additional topology information required to enable the MapReduce scheduler to place the tasks optimally. The topology server is an integral component of the ISAAC cloud service infrastructure and provides a REST interface, which the scheduler invokes. The information exposed by the topology server consists of network and storage topologies, and other dynamic node-level information such as CPU load. Second, a set of agents running on the physical nodes of the cluster periodically collect and convey to the topology server, a variety of pieces of data about the respective node, such as utilization of outbound/inbound network bandwidth, IO utilization and CPU/memory/storage load. The topology server consolidates the dynamic information it receives from the agents and serves it along with topology informa-

tion about each job running in the cluster. The topology information is derived from existing VM placement configuration. Third, a new MapReduce task scheduler interfaces with the topology server to obtain accurate and current topology information. The scheduler readjusts task placement accordingly whenever a change in the configuration is observed. Note that CAM needs to provide a different scheduler because the standard MapReduce scheduler is designed to make the placement decisions only based on a static configuration file and only at the beginning of the job [9]. While the MapReduce task scheduler is modified to leverage the topology and physical host resource utilization information in CAM, the MapReduce applications can run without any modification.

The **network topology** information is represented by a distance matrix that encodes the distance between each pair of VMs as cross-rack, cross-node, or cross-VM. Current MapReduce task schedulers consider rack and node localities but lack the notion of VM locality. When two VMs are placed on the same node, they are connected through a virtual network connection implemented as a part of the hypervisor. By virtue of the fact that the VMs share the same node hardware, the virtual network provides a high-speed medium that is significantly faster than the inter-node or inter-rack links. The network traffic between the VMs on the same node does not have to pass through the external hardware link. The network virtual device simply forwards the traffic in-memory through highly optimized ring buffers. CAM extends the MapReduce scheduler to consider this fine-grain locality information to make optimal placement choices for the tasks.

The **storage topology** information is provided as a mapping between each virtual device containing the dataset and the VM to which the device is local. In the native hardware context, a SATA disk attached to a node can be directly accessed through the PCI bus. In the cloud, however, the physical blocks belonging to a VM image attached to a VM could be located on a different node. Even though a virtual device might appear to be directly connected to the VM, the image file backing the device could be across the network, and potentially closer to another VM in the cluster than the one it is directly attached to in the virtual setup. The topology server queries the physical image location through the GPFS API and presents the information to the MapReduce scheduler.

The specific APIs provided by the topology server is described in Table 1. *get_VM_distance*, provides MapReduce task scheduler with hints of the network distance between two VMs. The distance is estimated based on observed data transfer rates between the VMs, and is expressed in units of bandwidth. *get_block_location*, enables MapReduce to get the actual block location instead of the location of a VM, thus guaranteeing data locality. The rest of the calls are used to facilitate the MapReduce task scheduler to query the I/O and CPU contention information related to network and disk utilization. The MapReduce task scheduler can leverage this additional information to make smarter decisions, such as placing I/O intensive tasks on physical hosts that have idle I/O resources.

3. CAM USAGE MODEL

CAM is a cloud platform with specific interfaces and support for running MapReduce jobs. The dataset to be processed is initially placed on GPFS. This is in contrast to most cloud models, which segregate storage and compute resources, and require the dataset to be moved from the storage cloud to the compute cloud for processing. Co-locating storage and compute clusters avoids the expensive ingestion phase for each job run. Data placed in this manner can be used by each subsequent job in CAM.

The placement of data is driven by the nature of MapReduce jobs that are typically run on the data. For instance, if the dataset is

213

API	Description
`int get_VM_distance(string vm1, string vm2)`	Returns the distance between two VMs.
`struct block_location get_block_location(string src, long offset, long length)`	Returns the actual location of blocks.
`int get_vm_networkinfo(string VM, struct networkinfo)`	Returns the network utilization information of physical host on which the VM is running.
`int get_vm_diskinfo(string vm, string device, struct diskinfo)`	Returns disk utilization information.
`int get_VM_cpuinfo(string vm, struct cpuinfo)`	Returns CPU utilization information of the physcial host on which the VM is running.

Table 1: The key APIs provided by CAM to the MapReduce scheduler.

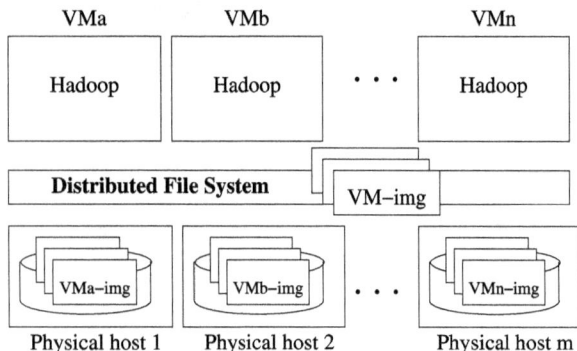

Figure 2: Setup of CAM for supporting MapReduce in the cloud.

primarily used as input for various pattern search jobs, data locality is likely to be more important than task locality. The user can specify the nature of expected workloads, or the workload characteristics can be automatically derived based on previously observed I/O patterns.

The user submits a MapReduce job by providing the application, e.g., relevant java class files, indicating a previously uploaded dataset corresponding to the job, and the number and type of VMs to be used for the job. Each VM typically supports several MapReduce task slots depending on the number of virtual CPUs and virtual RAM allocated to the VM. The more the number of VMs assigned to a job, the quicker the job finishes.

CAM determines an optimal placement for the set of new VMs requested by the user by considering a variety of factors such as current workload distribution among the cluster nodes, distribution of the input dataset required by the job, and the physical locations of the required master VM images. The images required to boot the VMs on the selected nodes are created from the respective master images using a copy-on-write mechanism provided by GPFS, which allows fast provisioning of a VM image instance without requiring a data copy of the master image. The job class files are copied into the cloned VM image by mounting the image as a loopback file system. These changes are private to the cloned image. Next, the data images are attached to the VMs and the respective device files are mounted within the VM for the MapReduce tasks to access the data contained within them.

Figure 2 illustrates the setup. Each machine is equipped with local disks. There is a distributed file system installed on top of these physical machines. The VM image files are stored in the distributed file system. Moreover, there is a cloud manager that allocates the resources for MapReduce jobs, and manages the data placement and VM placement.

4. MIN-COST FLOW BASED PLACEMENT

In this Section, we present how CAM manages Data and VM placement using a min-cost flow based approach. In our model, we assume that it is possible for the cloud provider to profile a job and estimate its characteristics such as job type (Map-Reduce intensive, Map intensive, or Reduce intensive), and input, output and intermediate data sizes. For our current implementation, we rely on user-provided or predetermined job descriptions to identify a job's type. However, the system can be easily extended to determine the amount of time an application spends in different phases (Map, Reduce), and use this information to determine a job's type. For example, a job that spends more than 30% of the time in Map can be considered as Map-intensive.

4.1 Data Placement

We express the problem of optimally placing data in a given cloud cluster architecture as an instance of the well-known min-cost flow problem [13]. To achieve this, we break down the placement problem into three sub-problems, namely guaranteeing VM closeness, avoiding hotspots, and balancing physical storage utilization according to different job types. We capture the three constraints via similarly named factors in our model. *VM closeness* expresses how close data should be placed to VMs so that the network traffic between the corresponding VMs is minimized. *Hotspot factor* expresses the expected load on a machine, and identifies machines that do not have enough computational resource to support the VM(s) assigned to them. To avoid a hotspot, data needs to be placed on the least-loaded machine. This can be determined by measuring the current computational resource load of the machine and adding it to the expected computational requirements of the VMs that will work with the data to be placed on the machine. *Storage utilization* expresses the percentage of total physical machine storage space that is in use.

Job Type	VM closeness	Hotspot factor	Storage utilization
MR-intensive	Yes	Yes	Yes
M-intensive	No	Yes	Yes
R-intensive	No	No	Yes

Table 2: Significance of considered cost factors for different job types.

Table 2 shows the significance of the three factors on the performance of different MapReduce workloads. For workloads that are both Map and Reduce intensive, related data should be placed close together and on the least loaded machine. For Map intensive workloads, the data should be placed on the least loaded machine, but does not necessarily need to be placed close together due to the light shuffle traffic in such workloads. For Reduce intensive workloads, the only concern is the storage utilization of the machine on which the VM is to be placed. For all types of workloads, it is desirable to place data evenly across racks to minimize the need to rearrange data over time for supporting migrating VMs.

We use these factors in constructing a min-cost flow graph that encodes the factors. Then we employ an extended solver to minimize the global cost of the graph, thus solving the original problem of determining how data should be placed in the virtualized cloud.

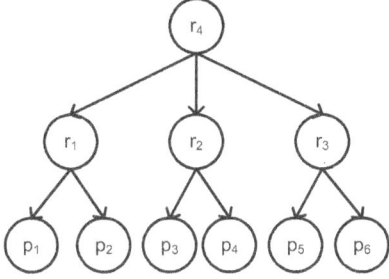

Figure 3: Sample network topology for data placement.

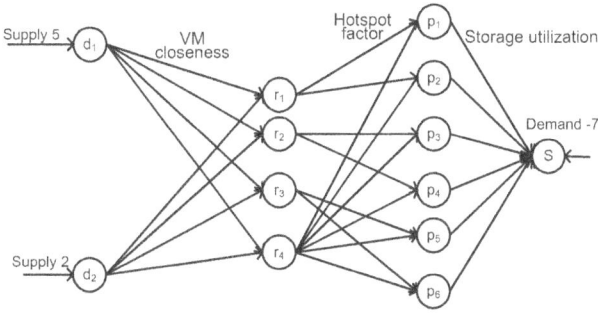

Figure 4: Flow graph for sample data placement.

Figure 3 shows a sample network topology, which consists of six physical nodes ($p_1, \ldots, p_6$) organized into three racks (r_1, r_2, r_3) with one master rack/switch (r_4) connecting the racks. Note that our model can support any topology where the network traffic can be estimated. There are several challenges when min-cost flow is used in our problem space. First, the three factors described above have to be encoded into the graph. Second, the correlation between different VMs images placement has to be encoded (which is shown to be non-trivial [13]). The flow-network model is aimed at minimizing the flow cost, however, we employ the model to also consider VM closeness as an objective, which requires it to solve correlated constraints, i.e., a set of VMs would have to be placed together, but it does not matter where. Third, the three factors capture different costs that are not directly comparable to each other. For instance, *VM closeness* of 1 may signify the cost of copying 1 GB of data within a local rack, where as *Hotspot factor* of 1 may signify the cost of using a physical machine that has 1% more load than the least-loaded machine in the cluster. The two costs are clearly not the same. Thus, we need a way to formulate the three factors in the same units for encoding them into a min-flow graph.

In contrast to the extant data placement techniques that work at the granularity of the data blocks, our unit of data placement is a VM image. Such coarse placement is justified in CAM as the goal

is to ensure that an entire image is available at one location. Moreover, our underlying storage layer of GPFS-SNC avoids striping the data across different physical machines, thus making block-level placement unnecessary.

We address these challenges as follows. Consider the corresponding min-cost flow graph for Figure 3 as shown in Figure 4. Here, two data items d_1 and d_2 with requests for 5 and 2 VM images, respectively, are submitted to the cloud. The number of VM images requested by a data item is denoted as the data item's *supply* for our flow graph. Conversely, we add a sink node S to the graph, that can "support" the VMs. The number of VMs that a sink node can handle is assigned as a *demand* value. In our example, S has a demand -7 and is the only place that can receive all the flows. Each flow graph edge has two parameters attached to it, the capacity of the edge and the cost for a flow to go through the edge. The data nodes, represented by d_1 and d_2 in the graph, have outgoing links to each rack with *VM closeness* as costs. The *Hotspot factor* is encoded in the links from the racks to each physical node p within its range. Note that even though r_4 serves as a switch between the racks, it is shown in the graph as directly connected to all the physical nodes. This is to ensure that the least-loaded machine can be chosen for Map-intensive jobs without being constrained by the network topology. All the physical nodes, $p_1, \ldots, p_6$, are linked to the sink node with *Storage utilization* as link costs. Note that there is no direct link from data item node d_j to the associated physical host p_i. This is to support scaling up the system, as otherwise the number of links in the graph will increase with increasing number of data items and physical nodes (much faster than the number of racks). Consequently, making it inefficient to solve for min-flow on the graph.

	Data set d_j	Rack r_k	Physical host p_i	Sink S
Supply	$\sum(N_{d_j})$	0	0	$-\sum(N_{d_j})$
Incoming link from	N/A	N_{d_j}	Rack	Physical host
Outgoing link to (cap., cost)	Rack (N_{d_j}, α_{jk})	Physical host (Cap_i, β_i)	Sink (Cap_i, γ_i)	N/A

Table 3: Values assigned to the flow graph for data placement used in CAM.

Table 3 provides the details of how we encode the various factors and system information in our min-cost flow graph. N_{d_j} is the number of VM images requested by dataset d_j. α_{jk} captures *VM closeness*. The cost, α_{jk}, of outgoing link from the dataset d_j to physical host p_i on which the data is placed on rack r_k is estimated conservatively by the traffic in the shuffle phase as follows:

$$\alpha_{jk} = size_{intermediate} * \frac{num_{Reducer} - 1}{num_{Reducer}} * distance_{max}, \quad (1)$$

where $distance_{max}$ is the maximum network distance between any two nodes in the rack r_k, and $size_{intermediate}$ and $num_{Reducer}$ are the total size of data output by the Map phase and the number of reducers, respectively, of the MapReduce job running on data set d_j. Note that given its higher $distance_{max}$ a higher level rack-/switch, e.g., r_4 in our example, would have a higher α than the lower racks, e.g., r_1, r_2 and r_3, based on this formula. The *Hotspot factor* is captured using β_i for physical node p_i, and is estimated by the current and expected load as follows:

$$\beta_i = a * (load_{exp} + load_{curr} - load_{min}), \qquad (2)$$

where $load_{curr}$ and $load_{min}$ represent the current load and minimum current load, respectively. a is a parameter that acts as a knob to tune the weight of the *Hotspot factor* with respect to other costs. Moreover, based on guidelines from [21] the expected load is determined as $load_{exp} = \sum_j (\rho_j/(1 - \rho_j) * CRes(d_j)$, where $\rho_j = \lambda_j/\mu_j$. Here, λ_j represents the number of d_j's associated jobs that arrive within a give time interval, μ_j represents the mean time for each VM to process a block, and $CRes(d_j)$ represents the compute resources required by jobs running on data set d_j. *Storage utilization* of a physical node p_i is captured by γ_i, which is determined by the current storage utilization compared with minimum storage utilization of all p_is.

$$\gamma_i = b * (storageUtil_{p_i} - storageUtil_{min}) \qquad (3)$$

Here, b is another parameter used to fine tune the weight of *Storage utilization* with respect to the other two factors. Finally, $Cap_i = freespace_{p_i}/size_{VMImg}$, is a conservative estimation of the capacity of each physical host calculated as the ratio of the available storage capacity of p_i and the size of the VM image. We assume that all VM images have the same size (10 GB in our experiments) when initially uploaded to the cloud.

To enable the graph to capture the correlation between VM image placement for one data request, we extend the solver to take into account an additional parameter for each edge, *split factor*, which specifies whether flows from a node are allowed to be split across different links, and is either *true* or *false*. In our example, *split factor* for all the links from d_1 and d_2 are set to *false*. This implies that all the flows from data nodes will wholly go through one of the $r_1, \ldots, r_4$, but will not be split between the racks.

Once a new data upload request comes in, the cloud server updates the graph and computes a global optimal solution. The graph is updated as follows. First, the graph is cleaned of data and state from the previous iteration. This is done by deleting the data nodes that correspond to the datasets that have finished uploading, and their outgoing links from the graph. Next, the cost of the edges corresponding to the *Hotspot factor* and *Storage utilization* of the physical nodes where the data was stored need to be updated using equations 2 and 3. Then, a new data node d_j is created for the new data upload request with edges to each rack node r_k with costs calculated based on the above equation 1. Once the graph is updated, a new min-flow value is calculated, which is then used by the cloud scheduler. This process ensures that the cloud scheduler is timely provided with updated information to accommodate varying loads.

4.2 VM Placement

The goal of VM placement is to maximize the global data locality and job throughput. Our model considers both VM migration and delayed scheduling of a job as part of the optimal solution. Delaying a job is used to explore better data locality opportunities that can arise in the near future, while minimizing time wasted during the waiting. Migrating a VM belonging to a job enables our scheduler to make room for other suitable jobs or to explore better location opportunity. There are two assumptions that we make about how VMs are migrated. First, we assume that once the VMs for a job are allocated, the job will not be suspended or killed. There is no preemption, which guarantees that the job will have some quota of resources at all times during its life span. Second, even if some of the VMs belonging to a job get migrated, their total number remains the same. We model the VM placement as minimum

cost flow problem, which has similar characteristics to the min-cost flow based data placement.

An example graph for VM placement is shown in Figure 5. Each job v_j is submitted to the system at the source node with the number of requested VMs, N_{v_j}, as the value of supply. The goal of the VM allocator is to either keep the job unscheduled (allocate 0) or allocate N_{v_j} VMs for each request. There is a single sink node, S, in the system with demand equal to minus the sum of the supply. The request from each job acts as a flow that goes either through the rack nodes, r_k, or through the unscheduled nodes, u_j, and finally to the sink. If a job is unscheduled, none of its VMs are allocated. Otherwise, the flow goes through the physical nodes, p_i. Each job v_j has a "preferred" node pr_j that has outgoing links to a set of physical hosts that would be preferable for v_j to be scheduled on. Based on the min-cost solution, a allocation scheme with min-cost can be easily derived. If the VMs are allocated to the highest level rack, it implies that the VMs can be allocated arbitrarily to any set of nodes in the VMs under the rack. Once v_j is scheduled, a "running" node (ru_j) is added to the graph to keep track of information about the execution of v_j, which is then used by the solver to direct migration decisions.

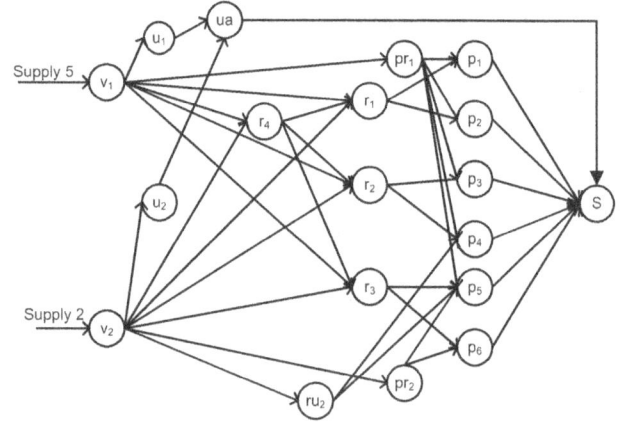

Figure 5: Flow graph for VM placement.

The job type information is modeled as the cost of the edge from each job to the rack nodes in our flow based graph. The higher level rack has higher cost than the lower lever rack in terms of reduce traffic. We use conservative approximation to compute bounds on data transfer costs. The cost to the highest level rack is estimated by worst case VM arrangement with regards to the map and reduce traffic. Similar rules apply to the lower level rack. The cost of the edges to the unscheduled nodes are set to be increased over time so that delayed jobs get allocated sooner than recently submitted jobs. This cost also controls when a job stops waiting for better locality, and thus offers a knob to tune the trade-off between data locality and latency. The aggregated unscheduled nodes control how many VMs can remain unscheduled, which is another system parameter to control the system resource utilization and data locality trade-off. The cost of the edges to running nodes set is increased over time and is job-progress aware. For example, a reduce intensive job run during the reduce phase might not be suitable for migration to make room for a contending job request.

Similarly as for data placement, we provide means for expressing the cost of reading data across different level of racks, migrating VMs, and delay scheduling in the same units. For example, we can choose that the copying of 1 GB data across rack local switch costs the same as copying 0.5 GB data across one level higher rack,

	Job node set	Preferred node set	Running node set	Unscheduled node set	Unscheduled aggregator node	Rack node set	Physical host node set	Sink
supply	$\sum(N_{v_j})$	0	0	0	0	0	0	$-\sum(N_{v_j})$
Incoming link from	N/a	job	job	job	all unschedule nodes	job; higher rack	rack; preferred nodes set; running nodes set	physical host; unscheduled aggregator
Outgoing link to (cap., cost)	Rack(N_{v_j}, ρ_j) Prefer(N_{v_j}, θ_j) Run(N_{v_j}, ϕ_j) U(N_{v_j}, ϵ_j)	Physical host $(d_i, 0)$	Physical host $(r_i, 0)$	Unscheduled aggregator $(N_{v_j}, 0)$	Sink $(N_{unsched}, 0)$	Physical host $(N_{r_k}, 0)$	Sink $(N_{vm}, 0)$	N/A
flow	N_{v_j}	$0/N_{v_j}$	$0/N_{v_j}$	$0/N_{v_j}$	$0/N_{unsched}$	$0, N_{r_k}$	$0, 1$	$\sum(N_{v_j})$

Table 4: Values assigned to the flow graph for VM placement used in CAM.

or the same as setting up of and starting one VM, or the same as delaying a VM execution by say 10 seconds.

We categorize the various nodes in the graph into different types as shown in Table 4.

- Preferred node set (pr_j): These graph nodes point to a set of physical nodes p_i that have a job v_j's associated dataset stored on them. An edge from a preferred node to p_i has the cost of 0 and the capacity of the number of VM disk images stored on p_i.

- Running node set (ru_j): These are dynamically added nodes that point to p_is that are currently hosting the v_j's VMs. An edge from ru_j to p_i has a cost of 0 and the capacity of the number of VMs running on p_i.

- Unscheduled node set (u_j): These nodes provide information about currently unscheduled jobs. u_j has an outgoing edge with capacity of N_{v_j} and cost 0 to a unscheduled aggregator.

- Unscheduled aggregator node (ua): The graph contains a single unscheduled aggregator. u has an outgoing edge with cost 0 to the sink with capacity of $N_{unsched} = \sum(N_{v_j}) - M + M_{idle}$, where M is the total number of VMs that the cluster can support and M_{idle} denotes the number of idle VM slots allowed in the cluster.

- Rack node set (r_k): The rack node r_k represents a rack in the topology of the cluster. It has outgoing links with cost 0 to its subracks or, if it is at the lowest level, to physical nodes. The links have capacity N_{r_k} that is the total number of VM slots that can be serviced by its underlying nodes.

- Physical host node set (p_i): Each physical host p_i has an outgoing link to the sink with capacity the number of VMs that can be accommodated on the physical host N_{vm} and cost 0.

- Sink S: The single sink node with demand $-\sum(N_{v_j})$.

- Job node set (v_j): This set represents each job node v_j with supply N_{V_j}. It has multiple outgoing edges corresponding to the potential VM allocation decisions for v_j. These edges are discussed in the following:

  - Rack node set r_k: An edge to r_k indicates that r_k can accommodate v_j. The cost of the edge is ρ_j that is calculated by the map and reduce traffic cost. If the capacity of the edge is greater than N_{v_j}, it implies that the VMs of v_j will be allocated on some p_is on the rack.

  - Preferred node set (pr_j): An edge from job v_j to the job wide preferred nodes set pr_j has capacity N_{v_j} and cost θ_j. The cost is estimated by only the reduce phase traffic, because in this case map traffic is assumed to be 0.

  - Running node set (ru_j): A link from job v_j has capacity of N_{v_j} and cost $\phi_j = c * T$, where T is the time the job has been executing on the set of machines and c is a constant used to adjust the cost relative to other costs.

  - Unscheduled node set (u_j): An edge to the job-wide unscheduled node u_j has capacity N_{v_j} and cost ϵ_j, which corresponds to the penalty of leaving job v_j unscheduled. $\epsilon_j = d * T$, where T is the time that job v_j is left unscheduled and d is a constant used to adjust the cost relative to other costs. The *split factor* for this link is marked as `true`, which means the allocation of all the VMs are either satisfied or be delayed until the next round.

When a VM allocation request is submitted, the flow graph is updated to calculate a new global optimal solution for the VM scheduler. Similar to the update process for data placement, the graph is cleaned by removing unnecessary nodes and edges. For example, for each finished job v_j, the associated nodes including the unscheduled node u_j, the preferred node pr_j and the running node ru_j are deleted from the graph since the job has released its VM resources. Then, the costs of edges related to the jobs that are still running are updated according to Table 4 to reflect the jobs' current state. Next, a set of new nodes and edges are added into the graph for the current VM allocation request, namely, a job node, a related unscheduled node, and a preferred node. Moreover, the corresponding edge costs are again calculated as described in Table 4.

Once the solver outputs a min-cost flow solution, the VM allocation assignment can be obtained from the graph by locating where the associated flow leads to for each VM request v_j. Flow to an unscheduled node indicates that the VM request is skipped for the current round. If the flow leads to a preferred nodes set, the VM request is scheduled on that set of nodes. Finally, if the flow goes to a rack node, it implies that the VMs from the job are assigned to arbitrary hosts in that rack.

The number of flows sent to a physical host through rack nodes or preferred nodes set is not higher than the number of available VMs of each physical hosts. This is guaranteed by the specified link capacity from physical host to sink. Thus, all VM requests that are allocated will be matched to a corresponding physical host.

5. EVALUATION

In this section we show the effectiveness of our approach through a set of Hive [22] based, I/O-bound micro-benchmarks running on a real cluster. We evaluate CAM's network and storage topology awareness against vanilla Hadoop, as to our best knowledge, CAM is the first technique that reintroduces the concept of data locality by exposing topology information in a cloud setting. We also compare CAM's data and VM placement against a state-of-the-art technique using a mix of workloads on a large simulated cluster.

Number of jobs	21	9	7	4	3	3	3
Map tasks / job	1	2	10	50	100	200	400

Table 5: Distribution of job sizes in terms of number of map tasks used for micro-benchmark tests.

5.1 Micro-Benchmark Results

In this section, we use an I/O intensive workload based on a Hive benchmark to show the effectiveness of topology awareness and storage awareness for task placement. The reported numbers are averages across three runs of a test.

Our cluster consists of 4 RHEL 6.0 physical machines that use KVM as the hypervisor. Each machine has two quad-core 2.4 GHz Intel E5620 processors and 48 GB of main memory. The machines are organized in one rack and are connected to a dedicated Gigabit switch. We launched 23 VMs, 1 master and 22 slaves, on the four physical hosts. Each VM is configured with $1\ GB$ of main memory and two 2.4 GHz vCPUs. Each VM has one map slot and one reduce slot, with a map block size of 64 MB. MapReduce fair scheduler is employed.

We generate a job submission schedule with 50 I/O-intensive Grep jobs using Poisson distribution with job inter-arrival time 10 seconds. To make the comparison consistent, we generate the submission schedule with a submission duration of 554 seconds, record it into a file and use it throughout the experiments. The size distribution of each Grep job for this experiment is shown in Table 5 and is based on the experiments performed by Zaharia et al. [24]. Thus, our schedule is representative of a typical workload of a production MapReduce cluster with a mix of many small jobs with a single map task per job, and a few large jobs with more than 100 map tasks per job. The input for the Grep jobs is generated using Teragen [5], with each map file consisting of $100\ M$ records of size $0.1K$ for a total input size of $10\ MB$.

5.1.1 Impact of Network Topology Awareness

In our first experiment, we use our submission schedule to evaluate the impact of network topology awareness in a CAM-based implementation of Hadoop [5]. For this purpose, we measure the execution time for our schedule. We also measure the achieved locality expressed as the percentage of total Map tasks that are scheduled on the VMs (for VM locality) or physical nodes (for node locality) that have the associated data. As a base case for comparison we use vanilla Hadoop, which is unaware of the actual network topology and in this case cannot determine if two VMs are running on the same node or not.

The results are shown in Table 6. We observe that by exposing topology information to Hadoop, the node locality is improved by 6.4%, and the average job execution time reduces by 8%. Figure 6

System	VM locality	Node locality	Average execution time
Hadoop	29.1%	42.6%	48.3 s
CAM-based Hadoop	29.0%	49%	34.2 s

Table 6: Impact of network topology awareness on Hadoop performance.

shows a break-up of the node locality in terms of the number of map tasks for the two studied cases. Observe that network topology information effectively improves the node locality for jobs with 10 and 50 map tasks by 8% and 9%, respectively. Jobs with more than 50 map tasks see a decreasing improvement, because with the increased number of maps in the small cluster the chance of co-locating map tasks on the same node also increases. However, topology awareness is important even in such a small cluster as most MapReduce jobs have fewer than 50 map tasks [24]. Note that the relatively good performance of vanilla Hadoop is due to the fact that the test cluster consists of a small number of physical hosts located on the same rack.

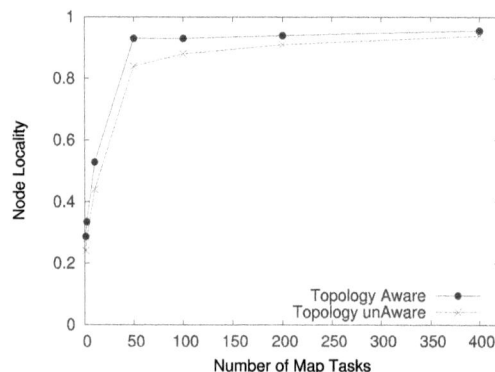

Figure 6: Breakdown of observed locality for jobs with different number of map tasks, with and without network topology awareness.

System	Average execution time
Hadoop	65.6 s
CAM-based Hadoop	48.3 s

Table 7: Impact of storage topology awareness on Hadoop performance.

5.1.2 Impact of Storage Topology Awareness

In our next experiment, we observe the impact of providing storage topology hints to Hadoop. For this test, we use the 22 VM slaves with local data, and then migrate 6 of the VM images from one physical host to another. This makes 27% $(= 6/22)$ of the data to become remote. Once again we measure the average job execution time for our schedule. The results are sown in Table 7. We observe that storage awareness can help improve the MapReduce execution time for our job schedule by 26.5%, on average.

These results show that CAM-based Hadoop can provide better performance for Hadoop tasks by exposing network and storage topology information to the Hadoop scheduler.

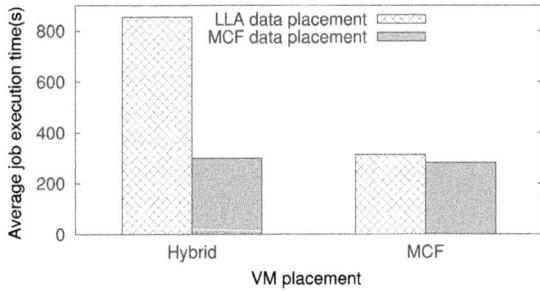

Figure 7: **Execution time for Map-intensive workloads.**

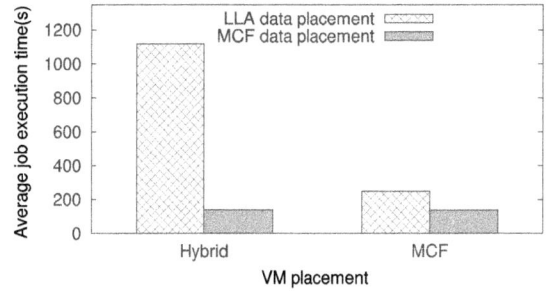

Figure 9: **Execution time for MapReduce-intensive workloads.**

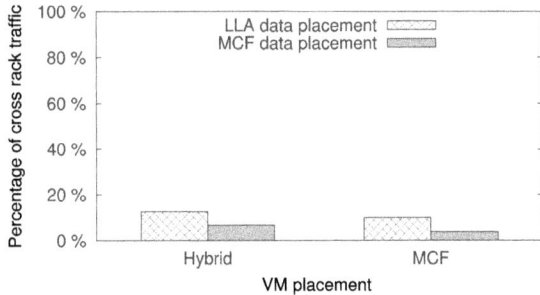

Figure 8: **Fraction of data accessed remotely for Map-intensive workloads.**

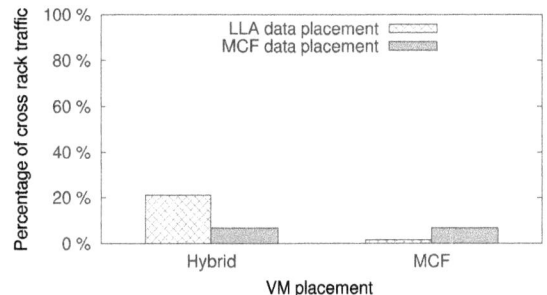

Figure 10: **Fraction of data accessed remotely for MapReduce-intensive workloads.**

5.2 Macro-Benchmark Results

In our next set of experiments, we show the effectiveness of our approach. For this purpose, we extend the simulator PurSim [21] to include the min-cost flow data placement, VM placement, network awareness, and storage awareness mechanisms described in Section 4. PurSim is a network flow level discrete event simulator that simulates the MapReduce execution semantics. Similarly as in previous tests, we generate a schedule with job size distribution based on Zaharia et al. [24] shown in Table 8. For these experiments the interarrival time is randomly generated between 60 and 90 seconds.

Number of jobs	38	16	14	8	6	6	4	8
Map tasks / job	1	2	10	50	100	200	400	800

Table 8: **Distribution of job sizes in terms of number of map tasks used for macro-benchmark tests.**

5.2.1 Data and VM Placement

In this section, we evaluate the effectiveness of min-cost flow (MCF) Data and VM placements used in CAM. We consider three types of MapReduce workloads, namely Map-intensive, MapReduce-intensive, and a workload with a mix of Map, MapReduce, and CPU-intensive jobs.

We consider two data placement strategies, namely load and locality aware (LLA) data placement and MCF data placement. We also consider two VM placement strategies, namely Hybrid VM placement and MCF VM placement. The LLA and Hybrid strategies are defined in Purlieus, and are used as a baseline for comparison to CAM's MCF based approach.

Figures 7, 9, and 11 show the average execution time for the three workloads considered. Similarly, Figures 8, 10, and 12 plot the percentage of total data (for the tests) that is accessed remotely across the rack under each combination of VM and data placements for the three studied workloads. For the Map-intensive workload, the combination of MCF VM and data placement produces a $3x$ speedup over the baseline, which is due to a $3.3x$ decrease in relative cross rack traffic. On the other hand, the same combination for the MapReduce-intensive traffic produces an $8x$ speedup with a corresponding 3 fold decrease in network traffic. The MCF placements see the best speedup of $8.6x$ verses the baseline for the mixed workload, due to the fact that they all but eliminate cross network traffic.

For all workload types using either the MCF data placement combined with the baseline VM placement, or conversely using the MCF VM placement with the baseline data placement, produces a significant speedup. Hence, the MCF graphs constructed for both placement optimization problems successfully optimize the respective factors and produce an optimal solution. Note that combining both techniques does not yield further significant benefit.

5.2.2 Impact of Network Topology Awareness

In this experiment, we configure our VM cluster to run 100 jobs simultaneously on 192 VMs using Hadoop fair share scheduling mechanism. Table 9 shows that network topology awareness im-

Network topology awareness	VM locality	Average job execution time
Unaware	82%	24.6 s
Aware	99%	22.4 s

Table 9: **Impact of network topology awareness on Hadoop performance.**

219

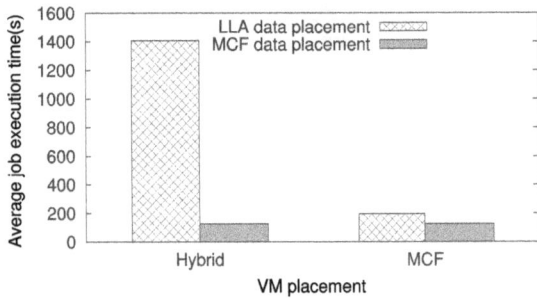

Figure 11: Execution time for Mixed workloads.

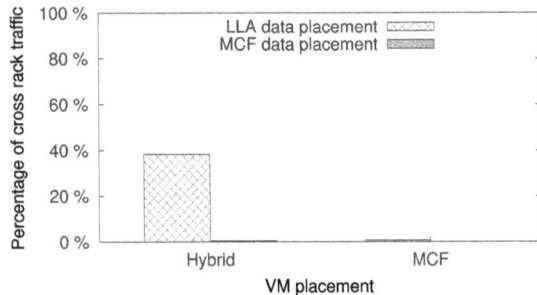

Figure 12: Fraction of data accessed remotely for Mixed workloads.

proves the map tasks locality on average by 7%, and reduces the average job execution time by 9%. Figure 13 shows the breaks up for the percentage of map VM locality with respect to the number of map tasks. We observe that network topology awareness is most effective for jobs that have less than 50 map tasks, improving locality by 24.2% on average.

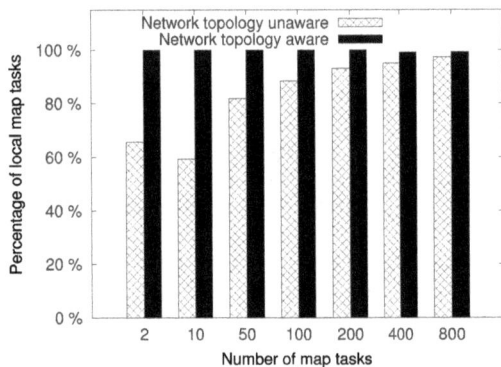

Figure 13: Impact of network topology awareness on locality of map tasks broken down in terms of number of map tasks.

5.2.3 Impact of Storage Topology Awareness

In our next experiment, we demonstrate the effectiveness of providing storage topology information hints to MapReduce. We vary the number of VM image files that are placed remotely with respect to the physical node where the VM is to be run. First, we measure how loss of VM image locality affects the average execution time.

Figure 14 shows the results. We observe that as more VMs are placed remotely, the average job execution time increases. For example, with 80% remote VM images, the average Mapreduce job execution time worsens 36% compared to the all local images case (0%). As seen from the previous experiments, CAM-based Hadoop achieves all local images using the storage topology information, and thus offers an effective solution for VM placement.

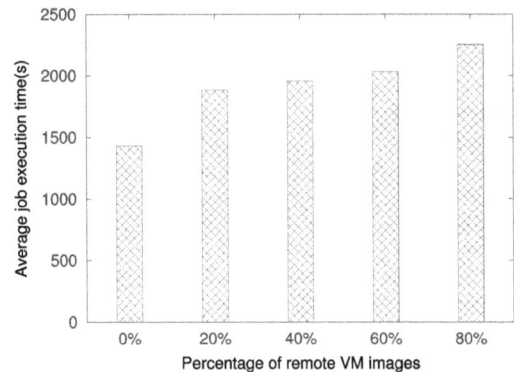

Figure 14: Impact of storage topology awareness on MapReduce performance in terms of percentage of remote VM images.

Next, we measure the locality of map tasks achieved with varying VM images placed remotely from their physical host. Figure 15 shows the percentage of the number of local map tasks with varying remote VM images. We see that without exposing storage topology information, the locality of map tasks is decreased. Conversely, the amount of data accessed remotely across the rack increased. Thus, by exposing storage locality, CAM can minimize the cross rack traffic due to remotely accessing VM images.

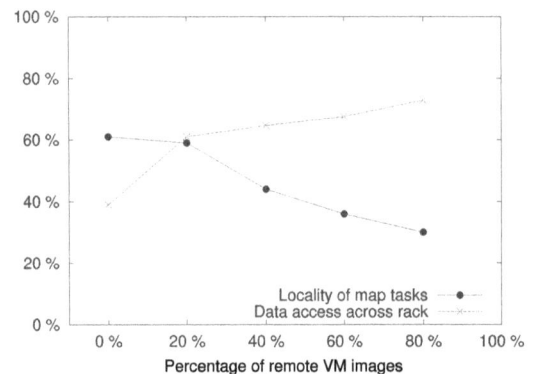

Figure 15: Impact of storage topology awareness on MapReduce performance.

5.2.4 Scalability of CAM

We now discuss the scalability of our min-cost flow model. In our macro-benchmark experiments we found the overhead to be negligible in a cluster of size 192 after repeated tests. As shown in Quincy [13], even for a large cluster size (thousands of nodes) a similarly-sized flow network can be solved in a few seconds, which is significantly smaller than the running time of typical MapReduce jobs. That is because techniques such as successive approximation push-relabel can process large-scale graphs efficiently. Moreover, the overhead of the solver is incurred only once, when the job is submitted for scheduling.

In summary, CAM offers to simultaneously meet the different constrains to co-locate VM and data on physical hosts, and improves overall MapReduce in the cloud application performance.

6. RELATED WORK

Resource allocation for MapReduce in the cloud has received a lot of attention in recent works [13,15,18,21,25]. The project closest to our own is a resource allocation system called Purlieus, developed by Palanisamy et al. [21]. Purlieus arrives at a job-local data and VM placement solution according to heuristics specifically developed for different job types, such as Map-input or Reduce-input heavy. The system defines both data and VM locality, as well as physical machine load, which are similar to the notion of *VM closeness* and *Hotspots* in CAM. Unlike Purlieus, CAM employs a mincost flow based approach, which can consider both VM migration as well as delayed scheduling to arrive at a global optimal placement. Additionally, CAM optimizes for *Storage utilization*, which allows it to do data, as well as CPU utilization, load balancing, consequently improving the overall VM placement. Moreover, CAM uses both the actual location of data and network topology as its inputs, whereas Purlieus relies on the virtual topology which may be different from the physical topology.

LATE [25] improves MapReduce performance in the cloud by performing effective speculative execution to reduce the job running time, while ignoring speculative task locality. CAM is different from LATE in that it couples the data placement, VM placement, and task placement to systematically improve data locality for MapReduce in the cloud.

There are several efforts that focus on MapReduce task scheduling in terms of data locality and fairness. Mantri [3] manages outliers in a resource and cause aware manner on native cluster. Delay scheduling [24] target fairness scheduling while maximize the map tasks locality on native clusters by delaying a task multiple times. Although delay scheduling offers a simple technique to provide better locality, it does not consider global scheduling, thus it loses the opportunity for achieving better performance. Moreover, the effectiveness of delay scheduling relies on the assumption that most tasks comprise of either small or long jobs. Quincy [13] uses similar graph techniques, but it differs from CAM in terms of problem space and associated flow network construction. Quincy strikes a balance between fairness and data locality, while CAM focuses on optimizing data/VM placement of MapReduce applications in the cloud. As a result, the factors encoded in the flow graph (VM closeness, Hotspot, etc.) are fundamentally different from that of Quincy's.

A plethora of VM placement and migration techniques are proposed in the cloud to optimize for minimizing network traffic, energy, meeting SLA requirement, etc. [7,11,16,17,20,23]. The VM placement problem is essentially a bin-packing problem for which various heuristics are applied. Such work is different from CAM, because unlike CAM it does not consider data placement and task placement, which are critical for MapReduce applications in the cloud.

7. CONCLUSION

In this paper, we have presented the design of CAM, a platform with an innovative resource scheduler designed to address performance degradation of MapReduce jobs when running in the cloud.

CAM adopts a three level approach to avoid placement anomalies due to inefficient resource allocation: placing data within the cluster that run jobs that most commonly operate on the data; selecting the most appropriate physical nodes to place the set of virtual machines assigned to a job; and exposing, otherwise hidden, compute, storage and network topologies to the MapReduce job scheduler. CAM uses a flow-network-based algorithm that is able to reconcile resource allocation with a variety of other competing constraints such as storage utilization, changing CPU load and network link capacities. Evaluation of our approach using both microbenchmarking and simulation on a 23 VM cluster shows that compared to a state-of-the-art resource allocator, CAM reduces network traffic and average MapReduce job execution time by a factor of 3 and 8.6, respectively.

CAM leads to important follow-on work. While we observe promising results in our experiments, we would like to further tune our min-cost flow model for data and VM placement and validate its effectiveness in larger real VM clusters. The topology information exposed by CAM could be leveraged by other topologysensitive applications. We would like to create a standardized API that could be adopted as a cloud standard such that applications are able to access the service regardless of the specific cloud implementation.

8. ACKNOWLEDGMENT

This paper is based upon work supported in part by the National Science Foundation under Grants CCF-0746832, CNS-1016793, and CNS-1016408. We are thankful to our shepherd Dr. Michela Taufer for her feedback in preparing the final draft of the paper, and to Guanying Wang for his initial ideas on using min-cost flow approach for VM and data placement for supporting virtualized MapReduce.

9. REFERENCES

[1] The Rackspace Cloud.
    http://www.rackspacecloud.com/.

[2] Amazon. Amazon Elastic Compute Cloud (Amazon EC2).
    http://www.amazon.com/b?ie=UTF8&node=201590011.

[3] G. Ananthanarayanan, S. Kandula, A. Greenberg, I. Stoica, Y. Lu, B. Saha, and E. Harris. Reining in the outliers in map-reduce clusters using mantri. In *Proc. 9th USENIX conference on Operating systems design and implementation (OSDI)*, 2010.

[4] R. Ananthanarayanan, K. Gupta, P. P, H. Pucha, P. Sarkar, M. Shah, and R. Tewari. Cloud analytics: Do we really need to reinvent the storage stack? In *Proc. of USENIX conference on Hot topics in cloud computing (HotCloud)*, 2009.

[5] Apache Software Foundation. Hadoop.
    http://hadoop.apache.org/core/.

[6] S. Baker. How the new york times uses clouds? 2007.
    http://www.businessweek.com/the_thread/blogspotting/archives/2007/12/how_thenew_yor.html.

[7] N. Bobroff, A. Kochut, and K. Beaty. Dynamic placement of virtual machines for managing sla violations. In *Proc. 10th IFIP/IEEE International Symposium on Integrated Network Management (IM'07)*, 2007.

[8] J. Cala and P. Watson. Automatic software deployment in the azure cloud. *Lecture Notes in Computer Science: Distributed Applications and Interoperable Systems*, 6115:155–168, 2010.

[9] J. Dean and S. Ghemawat. MapReduce: Simplified Data Processing on Large Clusters. In *Proc. 6th USENIX conference on Operating systems design and implementation (OSDI)*, 2004.

[10] K. Gupta, R. Jain, I. Koltsidas, H. Pucha, P. Sarkar, M. Seaman, and D. Subhraveti. GPFS-SNC: An enterprise storage framework for virtual-machine clouds. *IBM Journal of Research and Development*, 55(6):2:1 –2:10, 2011.

[11] F. Hermenier, X. Lorca, J.-M. Menaud, G. Muller, and J. Lawall. Entropy: a consolidation manager for clusters. In *Proc. ACM SIGPLAN/SIGOPS International Conference on Virtual Execution Environments (VEE)*, 2009.

[12] IBM. IBM service agility accelerator for cloud. http://www.ibm.com/developerworks/wikis/ display/tivolidoccentral/IBM+Service+ Agility+Accelerator+for+Cloud.

[13] M. Isard, V. Prabhakaran, J. Currey, U. Wieder, K. Talwar, and A. Goldberg. Quincy: fair scheduling for distributed computing clusters. In *Proc. ACM 22nd symposium on Operating systems principles (SOSP)*, 2009.

[14] J. Satran, K. Meth, C. Sapuntzakis, M. Chadalapaka, E. Zeidner. Internet Small Computer Systems Interface (ISCSI). http://tools.ietf.org/html/rfc3720.

[15] K. Jaewon, Z. Yanyong, and B. Nath. Tara: Topology-aware resource adaptation to alleviate congestion in sensor networks. *IEEE Transactions on Parallel and Distributed Systems*, 18(7):919 –931, 2007.

[16] A. Kochut. On impact of dynamic virtual machine reallocation on data center efficiency. In *Proc. IEEE International Symposium on Modeling, Analysis and Simulation of Computers and Telecommunication Systems (MASCOTS)*, 2008.

[17] A. Kochut and K. Beaty. On strategies for dynamic resource management in virtualized server environments. In *Proc. IEEE International Symposium on Modeling, Analysis and Simulation of Computers and Telecommunication Systems (MASCOTS)*, 2007.

[18] M. A. Kozuch, M. P. Ryan, R. Gass, S. W. Schlosser, D. O'Hallaron, J. Cipar, E. Krevat, J. López, M. Stroucken, and G. R. Ganger. Tashi: location-aware cluster management. In *Proc. 1st workshop on Automated control for datacenters and clouds (ACDC)*, 2009.

[19] K. Malavalli and B. Stovhase. Distributed computing with fibre channel fabric. In *Proc. Thirty-Seventh IEEE Computer Society International Conference (Compcon)*, 1992.

[20] X. Meng, V. Pappas, and L. Zhang. Improving the scalability of data center networks with traffic-aware virtual machine placement. In *Proc. 29th conference on Information communications (INFOCOM)*, 2010.

[21] B. Palanisamy, A. Singh, L. Liu, and B. Jain. Purlieus: Locality-aware resource allocation for mapreduce in a cloud. In *Proc. International Conference for High Performance Computing, Networking, Storage and Analysis (SC)*, 2011.

[22] A. Thusoo, J. Sarma, N. Jain, Z. Shao, P. Chakka, N. Zhang, S. Antony, H. Liu, and R. Murthy. Hive - a petabyte scale data warehouse using hadoop. In *Proc. IEEE 26th International Conference on Data Engineering (ICDE)*, 2010.

[23] H. N. Van, F. D. Tran, and J.-M. Menaud. Autonomic virtual resource management for service hosting platforms. In *Proc. ICSE Workshop on Software Engineering Challenges of Cloud Computing*, 2009.

[24] M. Zaharia, D. Borthakur, J. Sen Sarma, K. Elmeleegy, S. Shenker, and I. Stoica. Delay scheduling: a simple technique for achieving locality and fairness in cluster scheduling. In *Proc. 5th European conference on Computer systems (EuroSys)*, 2010.

[25] M. Zaharia, A. Konwinski, A. D. Joseph, R. Katz, and I. Stoica. Improving mapreduce performance in heterogeneous environments. In *Proc. 8th USENIX conference on Operating systems design and implementation (OSDI)*, 2008.

Distributed Approximate Spectral Clustering for Large-Scale Datasets

Fei Gao
School of Computing Science
Simon Fraser University
Surrey, BC, Canada

Wael Abd-Almageed
Institute for Advanced
Computer Studies
University of Maryland
College Park, MD, USA

Mohamed Hefeeda
Qatar Computing Research
Institute
Qatar Foundation
Doha, Qatar

ABSTRACT

Data-intensive applications are becoming important in many science and engineering fields, because of the high rates in which data are being generated and the numerous opportunities offered by the sheer amount of these data. Large-scale datasets, however, are challenging to process using many of the current machine learning algorithms due to their high time and space complexities. In this paper, we propose a novel approximation algorithm that enables kernel-based machine learning algorithms to efficiently process very large-scale datasets. While important in many applications, current kernel-based algorithms suffer from a scalability problem as they require computing a kernel matrix which takes $O(N^2)$ in time and space to compute and store. The proposed algorithm yields substantial reduction in computation and memory overhead required to compute the kernel matrix, and it does not significantly impact the accuracy of the results. In addition, the level of approximation can be controlled to tradeoff some accuracy of the results with the required computing resources. The algorithm is designed such that it is independent of the subsequently used kernel-based machine learning algorithm, and thus can be used with many of them. To illustrate the effect of the approximation algorithm, we developed a variant of the spectral clustering algorithm on top of it. Furthermore, we present the design of a MapReduce-based implementation of the proposed algorithm. We have implemented this design and run it on our own Hadoop cluster as well as on the Amazon Elastic MapReduce service. Experimental results on synthetic and real datasets demonstrate that significant time and memory savings can be achieved using our algorithm.

Categories and Subject Descriptors

H.3.3 [**Information Storage and Retrieval**]: Information Search and Retrieval—*Information filtering, Search process*

Keywords

Distributed clustering, large data sets, kernel-based algorithms, spectral clustering

1. INTRODUCTION

The rapidly declining cost of sensing technologies has led to proliferation of data in virtually all fields of science. Consequently, the sizes of datasets used in all aspects of data-driven decision making, inference, and information retrieval tasks have exponentially grown. For example, datasets for applications such as image clustering [35] and document retrieval [22] have substantially increased with the widespread usage of web contents and the inexpensive cost of capturing and sharing images. In many science and engineering applications, machine learning algorithms are frequently used to process data and perform various tasks such as clustering and classification. However, some of these algorithms do not support the increasing volumes of data being available.

The goal of this paper is to enable an important class of machine learning algorithms to efficiently process very large-scale datasets. We achieve this goal using two techniques: controlled approximation and elastic distribution of computation. In the first technique, we carefully apply approximation schemes on the datasets, which substantially reduce the time and space complexities of the considered class of machine learning algorithms without significantly impacting the accuracy of the produced results. The level of approximation can be controlled to gauge the accuracy of the results versus the required computing resources. In the second technique, we design distributed versions of the machine learning algorithms that can utilize the flexibility offered by cloud computing platforms.

We consider the scalability of kernel-based machine learning algorithms, which have an increasing importance in many fields, such as computer vision, bioinformatics, and natural language processing. The performance of most kernel-based machine learning algorithms significantly improves as the size of training datasets increases. For example, in [26], Munder and Gavrila show that the false negative rate of their image-based human detection algorithm is reduced by approximately 50% by only doubling the size of training dataset for their Support Vector Machine (SVM) classifier, while maintaining the same false alarm rate. Current kernel-based algorithms, however, suffer from an inherent limitation: they require computing a kernel matrix which stores pair-wise similarity values among all data points. That is, the kernel matrix has $O(N^2)$ complexity in both time and space. This is clearly not feasible for large datasets with millions, and soon billions, of data points. We address this limitation by designing an approximation algorithm for constructing the kernel matrix for large datasets, which promises significant reduction in computational and memory overhead required to compute the kernel matrix.

In particular, the main contributions of this paper are:

- We propose a novel approximation algorithm for computing the kernel matrix for large-scale data sets. The algorithm is designed such that it is independent of the subsequently used machine learning algorithm. Thus, it can be used to scale many kernel-based machine learning algorithms.

- We design a variant of the spectral clustering algorithm [9] on top of the proposed approximation algorithm to show its effect on the performance and accuracy. We theoretically analyze the expected reduction in computation time and memory requirements resulted from our approximation algorithm.

- We present a distributed design of the proposed approximate spectral clustering algorithm in the MapReduce programming model, and we implement and run it on a Hadoop cluster in our lab as well as on the Amazon Elastic MapReduce (EMR) service.

- We conduct extensive experimental study using various synthetic and real datasets. The real dataset contains more than three million documents that we collected from Wikipedia. Our experimental results show substantial (multiple orders of magnitude) saving in the computing time and memory requirements can be achieved by our algorithm when applied on large-scale datasets, without significantly impacting the accuracy of the results. In addition, we demonstrate how the proposed algorithm can efficiently utilize variable computing resources offered by the Amazon cloud platform. Furthermore, we compare the proposed algorithm against three recent algorithms in the literature and show that it outperforms them.

The remainder of this paper is organized as follows. Section 2 summarizes the related work. Section 3 describes the proposed approximation algorithm and its distributed implementation. Section 4 presents the accuracy and complexity analysis of the proposed algorithm. The experimental platform and results are presented in Section 5. The paper is concluded in Section 6.

2. RELATED WORK

Massive data sets are common nowadays in many domains. To process such large data sets, distributed and cloud platforms are employed. For example, Matsunaga et al. propose cloudBLAST [23], which is a cloud version of the BLAST similarity search algorithm of DNA/RNA sequences, and Kang et al. [17] develop a distributed system for mining massive graphs.

Several machine learning algorithms have also been implemented in distributed manner. For example, the open-source Apache Mahout library implements important machine learning algorithms such as K-Means, Singular Value Decomposition and Hidden Markov Models using the MapReduce model. Even with distributed implementations, some

machine learning algorithms may not be able to handle large-scale data sets, because of their time and space complexities. The important kernel-based machine learning algorithms fall into this category, because they require $O(N^2)$ time and space complexities to construct similarity matrices for N data points. Our work addresses this problem by proposing an approximation method to reduce the time and space complexities of constructing kernel matrices and efficiently processing the approximated matrices on cloud infrastructures with varying resources.

Previous works addressing the limitations of large-scale kernel-based machine learning algorithms can be broadly classified into two main categories: (1) methods that construct low-rank approximations of the kernel matrix, and (2) efficient implementations for computing the kernel matrix, including implementations on modern computing platforms such as Graphics Processing Units (GPUs).

Low-rank methods depend on the observation that the eigen-spectrum of the kernel matrix rapidly decays, especially when the kernel function is a Radial Basis Function (RBF) [33] [36]. Consider a kernel matrix K with eigenvalues $\lambda_1 \geq \lambda_2 \geq \cdots \geq \lambda_N \geq 0$ and corresponding eigenvectors $\mathbf{v}_i$, $K = \sum_i^N \lambda_i \mathbf{v}_i \mathbf{v}_i^T$. Since the eigen-spectrum decays rapidly, i.e., most of the information is stored in the first few eigenvectors, the kernel matrix can be approximated by $\tilde{K} = \sum_i^M \lambda_i \mathbf{v}_i \mathbf{v}_i^T$, where $M \ll N$. Williams and Seeger [37] use the Nystrom method [8] to compute the most significant M eigenvalues and eigenvectors. The number of computed eigenvectors is inversely proportional to the approximation error. Nystrom-based methods have complexity of $O(M^2N)$, where M is the number of computed eigenvectors.

Kernel-based methods have also been a target of efficient implementations employing customized data structures and modern computing platforms. For example, Ohmer et al. [28] use GPUs to implement the classification step of the SVM classifier, in which the kernel values are computed between the input *test* vector and the set of support vectors. It should be noted, however, that the bottleneck of kernel methods is usually encountered during the training phase, rather than the testing phase, due to the large number of training vectors and the dimensionality of the vector space. In SVM classifiers, for example, the number of support vectors is much smaller than the training vectors and the kernel values are only computed against a small number of test vectors.

Our proposed algorithm benefits from the advantages of both categories, in which we exploit the rapidly decaying eigen-spectrum of the kernel matrix and also develop a distributed computing implementation using MapReduce.

3. DISTRIBUTED APPROXIMATE SPECTRAL CLUSTERING (DASC)

This section presents the proposed algorithm. We start with an overview, followed by the details. Then, we present the distributed implementation.

3.1 Overview

Kernel methods have gained significant attention in the machine learning community and other applied fields for more than a decade. Applications involving kernel methods include classification [5], dimensionality reduction [31] and data clustering [27]. Kernel methods offer a modular framework to do data analysis, in which the fundamental is to compute the kernel matrix. The kernel matrix represents kernelized distances between pairs of data points. The kernel matrix is sometimes referred to as the similarity matrix and Gram matrix. We will use the terms kernel, similarity, and Gram matrix interchangeably. The performance of kernel methods improves as the number of input points N increases [26]. However, since the cost of computing the similarity matrix is $O(N^2)$ in both time and space, it becomes computationally infeasible to handle large- and web-scale datasets, such as Amazon's customer statistics dataset [20], (three million records) and Wikipedia Talk network dataset [21] (two million instances) .

We propose a novel approximation algorithm for computing the similarity matrix. This approximation algorithm can be used with any kernel-based machine learning algorithm to make it scalable to large-scale datasets. We apply our approximation algorithm to the spectral clustering algorithm [27], which is based on eigen-decomposition of kernel matrices. Spectral clustering performs well with non-Gaussian clusters, and it does not suffer from the problem of local optima [27]. Spectral clustering has been used in various fields such as document clustering [39] and image Segmentation [34].

There are four steps in the proposed distributed approximate spectral clustering (DASC) algorithm. First, the algorithm creates compact signatures for all data points. This is done using locality sensitive hashing. Second, points whose signatures are similar to each other are grouped together. Third, similarity values are computed for points in each group to form portions of the similarity matrix. Fourth, the Spectral Clustering algorithm is performed on the approximated similarity matrix. The first three steps make the proposed approximation algorithm for kernel matrices. The fourth step adds an example kernel-based machine learning algorithm. Spectral clustering can be replaced by any other kernel-based algorithm in the fourth step.

3.2 Details

The first step of the proposed DASC algorithm is to preprocess the dataset using locality sensitive hashing (LSH). LSH is a probabilistic dimension reduction technique [25]. The idea is to hash points such that the probability of collision is much higher for close points than for those that are far apart. Points whose hashing values collide with each other fall into the same bucket.

We have studied various LSH families [12], including random projection, stable distributions, and Min-Wise Independent Permutations [4]. The hash functions we use to generate the signatures belong to the family of random projection. The advantage of this family is that, after applying hashing function once, we only need one bit to store the result, which saves memory. It has been shown that random projection has the best performance in high-dimensional data clustering [10]. Also, with random projection, we can compare the generated signatures using hamming distances for which efficient algorithms are available [2].

Given a set of data points $X_1, \ldots, X_N \in R^d$, we use random projection hashing [2] to generate M-bit binary signature for each data point. Each bit is generated as follows. An arbitrary dimension of the input space is selected and compared with a threshold. If the feature value along this dimension is larger than the threshold, the bit is set so 1.

Otherwise, it is set to 0. Details on criterion for choosing hashing dimensions and setting the threshold are discussed in Section 4.2. The time complexity of random projection hashing is $O(MN)$.

In the second step of the proposed algorithm, vectors with near-duplicate signatures are grouped into the same *bucket*. Near-duplicate signatures mean that for two M-bit binary numbers, there are at least P bits in common, where $P \leq M$. If the total number of unique signatures generated is T, the complexity of this step is $O(T^2)$.

In the third step, for each bucket (representing unique signature), we compute the similarity matrix for the vectors that belong to this bucket only. Assuming we have T buckets, each of which has N_i points, where $0 \leq i \leq T - 1$ and $\sum_{i=0}^{T-1} N_i = N$, the overall complexity of this step is $\sum_{i=0}^{T-1} O(N_i^2)$. In the following, we use a Gaussian kernel to compute the pairwise similarity S_{lm} between vectors X_l and X_m as shown in Equation (1)

$$S_{lm}^i = \exp(-\frac{||X_l - X_m||^2}{2\sigma^2}), \qquad (1)$$

where σ is kernel bandwidth, which controls how rapidly the similarity S_{lm}^i decays.

The final step in the proposed DASC algorithm is applying spectral clustering. Spectral clustering computes the Laplacian matrix L and the eigenvectors of L. It then performs K-means clustering on the eigenvectors matrix. For the DASC algorithm, spectral clustering is applied on the approximated similarity matrix, which is composed of the smaller similarity matrices computed from different hashing buckets. Thus, we compute the Laplacian matrix on each similarity matrix S^i as shown in Equation (2)

$$L^i = D^{i^{-1/2}} S_i D^{i^{-1/2}}, \qquad (2)$$

where $D^{i^{-1/2}}$ is the inverse square root of D^i and is diagonal matrix. For an $N_i \times N_i$ diagonal matrix, the complexity of finding the inverse square root is $O(N_i)$. Moreover, the complexity of multiplying an $N_i \times N_i$ diagonal matrix with an $N_i \times N_i$ matrix is $O(N_i^2)$. Therefore, the complexity of this step is $O(\sum_{i=0}^{T-1} N_i^2)$.

We then find the first K_i eigenvectors of L^i, $V_1^i, V_2^i, \ldots, V_{K_i}^i$ and form the matrix $X^i = [V_1^i V_2^i \cdots V_{K_i}^i] \in R^{N_i \times K_i}$ by stacking the eigenvectors in columns. The eigenvectors are computed using QR decomposition [6], which takes $O(K_i^3)$ steps. To reduce the computational complexity, we transform L^i into a $K_i \times K_i$ symmetric tridiagonal matrix A^i. The complexity of the transformation is $O(K_i N_i)$. QR decomposition is then applied to A^i, which is $O(K_i)$. Therefore, the complexity of this step is $O(\sum_{i=0}^{T-1} (K_i N_i))$. The input vectors X_i are normalized to have unit length such that $Y_{ij} = X_{ij}/(\sqrt{\sum_j X_{ij}^2})$ and Y_i is treated as a point in R^{K_i} and is clustered into K_i clusters using K-means [13]. The complexity of this step is $O(\sum_{i=0}^{T-1} (K_i N_i))$.

Adding the time cost of all the above steps, the overall time complexity for the DASC algorithm is given by:

225

$$T_{DASC} = O(M\,N) + O(T^2) + \sum_{i=0}^{T-1} \left[2\,O(N_i^2) + 2\,(K_i\,N_i) \right]$$
$$+ 2\,N.$$
$$(3)$$

3.3 MapReduce Implementation

The fundamental concept behind MapReduce is to break up algorithm execution into two phases: map and reduce. The inputs and outputs of each phase are defined by key-value pairs. We divide the proposed DASC algorithm into two MapReduce stages. The first MapReduce stage applies LSH on the input data and produces vector signatures. In the map phase of the this stage, the input vectors are loaded as *(index, inputVector)* pairs, where *index* is the index of a data point, and *inputVector* is a numerical array associated with the point. The output key-value pair is *(signature, index)*, where *signature* is a binary sequence, and *index* is the same as the input notation.

The input to the reducer of the first stage is the *(signature, listof(index))* pair, where *signature* is a binary sequence, and *listof(index)* is a list of all vectors that share the same signature indicating that these vectors are near-duplicates. The reducer computes the sub-similarity matrix following Equation (1). The pseudo-codes for the mapper and reducer functions are shown in Algorithms 1 and 2, respectively.

Algorithm 1: mapper(index, inputVector)

1 /*a mapper is fed with one *inputVector* at a time
2 String $Sig = ""$;
3 **for** $i = 1; i \leq M; i{+}{+}$ **do**
4 $\quad Threshold = get\_threshold(i)$;
5 $\quad Hyperplane = get\_hyperplane(i)$;
6 $\quad$ **if** $inputVector[Hyperplane] \leq Threshold$ **then**
7 $\quad\quad p = 1$;
8 $\quad$ **else**
9 $\quad\quad p = 0$;
10 $\quad$ Convert p to String and add to the tail of Sig ;
11 $emitPair(Sig, index)$;

Algorithm 2: reducer (signature, ArrayList indexList)

1 /*Compute the sub similarity matrix */
2 $Length = getLength(indexList)$;
3 **for** $i = 1; i \leq Length; i{+}{+}$ **do**
4 $\quad$ **for** $j = 1; j \leq Length; j{+}{+}$ **do**
5 $\quad\quad$ **if** $i \neq j$ **then**
6 $\quad\quad\quad subSimMat[i,j] = simFunc(i,j)$;
7 $\quad\quad$ **else**
8 $\quad\quad\quad subSimMat[i,j] = 0$;
9 $Output\_to\_File(subSimMat)$;

In Algorithm 1, we note that the hyperplane and threshold values are important factors in the hash function. The threshold value controls at which point we separate the original dataset apart, and the hyperplane value controls which

feature space to compare with the corresponding threshold. We use the principle of k-dimensional tree (k-d tree) [18] to set hyperplane and threshold values. The k-d tree is a binary tree in which every node is a k-dimensional point. Every non-leaf node can be thought of as implicitly generating a splitting hyperplane that divides the space into two parts, known as subspaces. Points to the left of this hyperplane are represented by the left subtree of that node and points right of the hyperplane are represented by the right subtree. The hyperplane direction is chosen in the following way: every node in the tree is associated with one of the k-dimensions, with the hyperplane perpendicular to that dimension's axis. For example, if for a particular split, the "x" axis is chosen, all points in the subtree with a smaller "x" value than the node will appear in the left subtree and all points with larger "x" value will be in the right subtree. In such a case, the hyperplane would be set by the x-value of the point, and its normal would be the unit x-axis.

To determine the *hyperplane* array, we look at each dimension of the dataset, and calculate the numerical span for all dimensions (denoted as $span[i], i \in [0, d)$). The numerical span is defined as the difference of the largest and the smallest values in this dimension. We then rank the dimensions according to their numerical spans. The possibility of one *hyperplane[i]* being chosen by the hash function is:

$$prob = span[i] / \sum_{i=0}^{d-1} span[i], \qquad (4)$$

which ensures that dimensions with large span have more chances to be selected. For each dimension space $Dim[i]$, the associated *threshold* is determined as follows: between the minimum (denoted as $min[i]$) and maximum (denoted as $max[i]$) in $Dim[i]$, we create 20 bins (denoted as $bin[j], j \in [0, 19]$), $bin[j]$ will count the number of points whose ith dimension fall into the range $[min[i] + j \times span[i]/20, min[i] + (j + 1) \times span[i]/20]$. We then find the minimum in array bin (denoted as s), the threshold associated with $Dim[i]$ is set to:

$$Dim[i] = min[i] + s \times span[i]/20. \qquad (5)$$

Approximation error can occur if two relatively close points in the original input space are hashed into two different buckets. If a full similarity matrix is computed, the similarity between the two vectors will be significant. However, due to our approximation scheme, this similarity will be zeros. In order to reduce this approximation error, buckets represented by signatures that share no less than P bits. We perform a pair-wise comparison between the M unique signatures and merge the vectors that belong to buckets with signatures no less P similar bits are combined. This step is performed before applying the reducer.

The process of comparing two M-bit signatures A and B is optimized for performance using the bit manipulation:

$$ANS = (A \oplus B)(A \oplus B - 1), \qquad (6)$$

where if ANS is 0, then A and B have only 1 bit in difference, thus they will be merged together. Otherwise, A and B are not merged. The complexity of this operation is $O(1)$.

After computing the sub-similarity matrices based on the LSH signatures and combining similar buckets, we use the standard MapReduce implementation of spectral clustering available in the Mahout library [29].

4. ANALYSIS AND COMPLEXITY

In this section, we first analyze the time and space complexities of the proposed DASC algorithm and show its scalability. Then, we analyze the accuracy expected from the proposed approximation method for the kernel matrix.

4.1 Complexity Analysis

The time complexity for computing the full similarity matrix is $O(N^2)$. For the approximated similarity matrix, assume that we have B buckets, and there are N_i number of points in bucket i. The N_i points in bucket B_i form K_i clusters, where $0 \le i \le B - 1$, and $\sum_{i=0}^{B-1} N_i = N$. Spectral clustering is performed on each bucket. Therefore, the time reduction ratio is:

$$\alpha = \frac{M\,N + B^2 + 2\,N + \sum_{i=0}^{B-1}\left[2\,N_i^2 + 2\,(K_i\,N_i)\right]}{2\,N^2 + 2\,(K\,N) + 2\,N}. \tag{7}$$

To gain insights on the above equation, let us assume that all buckets contain equal number of points, that is $N_i = \frac{N}{B}$ where $0 \le i \le B - 1$. Equation (7) can be rewritten as:

$$
\begin{aligned}
\alpha &= \frac{M\,N + B^2 + 2\,N + \sum_{i=0}^{B-1}\left[2\,N_i^2 + 2\,(K_i\,N_i)\right]}{2\,N^2 + 2\,K\,N + 2\,N} \\
&= \frac{M\,N + B^2 + 2\,N + B\left[2\left(\frac{N}{B}\right)^2 + 2\left(\frac{K}{B}\,\frac{N}{B}\right)\right]}{2\,N^2 + 2\,K\,N + 2\,N} \\
&= \frac{M + \frac{B^2}{N} + 2 - \frac{2}{B}}{2\,(1 + N + K)} + \frac{1}{B} \\
&\approx \frac{1}{B},
\end{aligned}
\tag{8}
$$

since the first item approaches zero as N increases. We note that the above time complexity is an upper bound on the time reduction achieved because of the approximation of the similarity matrix. In the worst case, all points will hash to the same bucket. This, however, is not typical for practical data, because we use multiple hash functions and we apply each function on a different dimension. Further, the dimensions used in the hashing are the ones that have the largest span, i.e., dimensions in which data points are as spread out as possible. We also note that Equation (7) and the proposed DASC algorithm itself *does not* assume or require uniform distribution of data points over buckets. The uniform distribution in Equation (8) is *only* used to illustrate the upper bound on the potential time reduction.

The space complexity for computing the full matrix is $O(N^2)$. Computing the similarity matrices for each bucket individually, the space complexity is reduced to $\sum_{i=0}^{B-1} N_i^2$. Therefore, the space usage reduction ratio is given as:

$$\gamma = \frac{\sum_{i=0}^{B-1} N_i^2}{N^2}. \tag{9}$$

Again for the upper bound, assume that all buckets contain equal number of points, $N_i = \frac{N}{B}$ where $0 \le i \le B - 1$.

Equation (9) can be rewritten as:

$$\gamma = \frac{\sum_{i=0}^{B-1} N_i^2}{N^2} = \frac{B\left(\frac{N}{B}\right)^2}{N^2} = \frac{1}{B}. \tag{10}$$

It is important to note that, the memory needed is distributed across the number of machines running the algorithm, which improves the scalability of the DASC algorithm.

To shed some insights on the above analysis and illustrate the scalability of the DASC algorithm, we numerically analyze its time and space complexities for datasets of different sizes. The processing time of DASC can be written as (in seconds):

$$
\begin{aligned}
Time &= \beta\,\frac{M\,N + B^2 + 2\,N + \sum_{i=0}^{B-1}\left[2\,N_i^2 + 2\,(K_i\,N_i)\right]}{C} \\
&= \beta\,\frac{M\,N + B^2 + 2\,N + B\left[2\left(\frac{N}{B}\right)^2 + 2\left(\frac{K}{B}\,\frac{N}{B}\right)\right]}{C} \\
&= \beta\,\frac{\log B\,N + B^2 + 2\,N + \frac{2\,N^2 + 34\,N\,(\log N - 9)}{B}}{C},
\end{aligned}
\tag{11}
$$

where $M = \log B$, $K = 17\,(\log N - 9)$, C is the number of machines, and β is a constant representing the average execution time for machine operations. The exact value for β depends on various issues including the machine architecture, memory, and I/O speed.

Similarly, for memory consumption, assuming single-precision floating point operations, we have (in bytes):

$$Memory = 4\,B\left(\frac{N}{B}\right)^2 = 4\,\frac{N^2}{B}. \tag{12}$$

We plot Equations (11) and (12) in Figure 1 for datasets ranging from 1M to 512M points. To be able to plot the curves, we chose reasonable value for $\beta = 50\mu s$ [15]. We also assume a cluster of $C = 1,024$ nodes. We also plot the standard spectral clustering (SC) algorithm for comparison. Figure 1 shows that DASC is highly scalable to large-scale datasets in both time and space complexities. As the size of the dataset doubles, the increases in both processing time and memory footprint are sub-quadratic. Notice that the points in the x-axis are growing exponentially.

4.2 Accuracy Analysis

Given an $N \times d$ dataset, the dependence of final clustering on any arbitrary dimension i is proportional to the dispersion of data along this dimension. If the data along dimension i is highly dispersed, then this dimension may significantly contribute to the structure of the data, and visa versa. The probability of selecting an arbitrary dimension i for hashing is given by Equation (4). Therefore, since we need to use $M < d$ hash functions in the signature generation stage, we order the importance of the d dimensions based on the numerical span of the data along each dimension and pick the dimensions with highest M spans for applying the hash function. The hash function builds upon the fact that, along an arbitrary dimension, if all data points fall within a small span, the probability of mis-clustering increases.

Along dimension i, the hash function chooses a threshold τ such that if the value of the point along i is below τ,

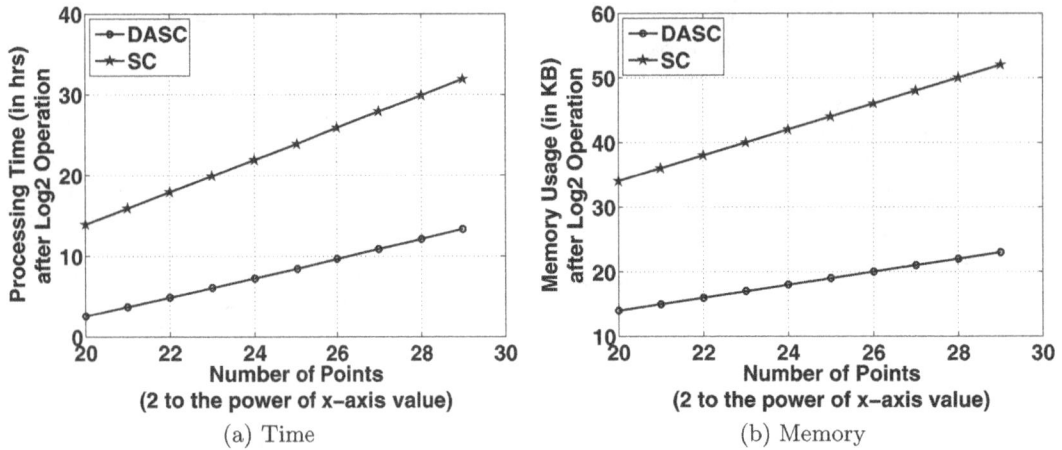

Figure 1: Scalability of the DASC algorithm to large-scale datasets.

a hash value of 0 is assigned. Otherwise, a hash value of 1 is assigned. The value of the threshold τ is chosen by calculating a histogram of the data along i and setting τ to the lower edge of the histogram bin of the smallest count, which is given by Equation (5).

In a dataset of size N with K clusters, there are, on average, N/K points in each cluster. The dimensionality in each cluster is d. Given any two arbitrary data points that significantly differ in r dimensions, where $r \leq d$, the collision probability of these two points, i.e., the two points have duplicate binary signatures and therefore falling within the same bucket, is given by:

$$P_1 = (\frac{d - r}{d})^M, \tag{13}$$

where $(d-r)/d$ is the probability that the dimension where such two points have similar value is checked. Furthermore, for a set of points, the collision probability is given by:

$$P_2 = P_1^{N/K} = (\frac{d - r}{d})^{M N/K}. \tag{14}$$

To study the effect of the number of hash functions M on the tradeoff between the accuracy of clustering and the parallelization of the algorithm, we use a number of Wikipedia datasets as shown in Table 1. We use line fitting to empirically relate the number of clusters to the size of each of the data set. Equation (15) shows the best fitting parameters.

$$K = 17 \left(\log_2 N - 9 \right). \tag{15}$$

Every point in the Wikipedia dataset is a document comprised of $d = 11$ terms. We set $r = 5$ in order to ensure that the majority of dimensions, $d - r$, are significantly similar. Therefore, the total number of terms in the dataset is

$$t = 11 - r + \frac{N}{K} r. \tag{16}$$

The dimensionality d is given by

$$d = t K = K \left(11 - r \right) + N r. \tag{17}$$

Dataset size	Number of categories
1024	17
2048	31
4096	61
8192	96
16384	201
32768	330
65536	587
131072	1225
262144	2825
524288	5535
1048576	14237
2097152	42493

Table 1: Clustering information of Wikipedia dataset.

Equation (14) can now be rewritten as

$$P_2 = (\frac{d-r}{d})^{M N/K} \tag{18}$$

$$= (1 - \frac{5}{17 \left(\log_2 N - 9 \right) 6 + N 5})^{M N/17 \left(\log_2 N - 9 \right)}. \tag{19}$$

Figure 2 illustrates the relationship between the collision probability and the number of hash functions used as given by Equation (18), for datasets with different sizes chosen from the Wikipedia dataset. It can be observed that, as the number of hash functions increases, the probability of a group of adjacent points being put into a cluster slowly (sub-linearly) decreases. This means that the incorrectly clustered instances in the dataset increases. On the other hand, increasing the number of hash functions increases the number of instances of Spectral Clustering to run in parallel, improving the parallelization of the algorithm. Moreover, when we use the same M value to do the partitioning, as the size of the dataset increases, the collision probability decreases. Therefore, it can be seen that, through the tuning of the parameter M, we can control the tradeoff between the accuracy of the clustering algorithm and the degree of parallelization.

5. EXPERIMENTAL EVALUATION

In this section, we rigorously evaluate the performance

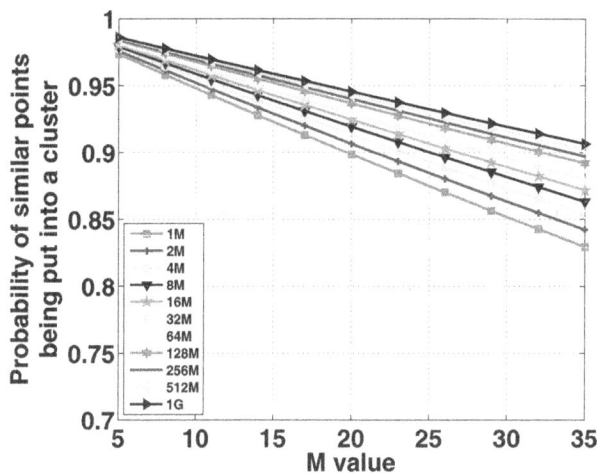

Figure 2: The impact of parameter M on accuracy for datasets of different sizes.

Parameter	Value
Hadoop jobtracker heapsize	768 MB
Hadoop namenode heapsize	256 MB
Hadoop tasktracker heapsize	512 MB
Hadoop datanode heapsize	256 MB
Maximum map tasks in tasktracker	4
Maximum reduce tasks in tasktracker	2
Data replication ratio in DFS	3

Table 2: Setup of the Elastic MapReduce cluster.

of the proposed algorithm and compare it against others. We start by describing our platform and datasets used in the following two subsections. Then, we explain and justify the performance metrics used. This is followed by a brief description of the algorithms implemented and compared against. Finally, the results for accuracy, complexity, and scalability are presented in three subsections.

5.1 Experimental Platform

We have implemented the proposed algorithm and few others in the literature in the Hadoop open-source implementation of the MapReduce framework. We ran our implementation on a local cluster as well as on the Amazon Elastic MapReduce (EMR) service. Our local cluster is composed of five machines, each is equipped with Intel Core2 Duo Processor E6550 (4M Cache, 2.33 GHz, 1333 MHz FSB) and 1 GB DRAM. The cluster runs Hadoop version 0.20.2 on top of Ubuntu Linux 2.6.27-14, and using Java JDK version 1.6.0. One machine in the cluster serves as the master (job tracker) and the others are slaves (task trackers).

For scalability and elasticity experiments, we use the Amazon EMR service with variable number of machines: 16, 32, and 64. Each machine has 1.7 GB memory, 350 GB of disk storage and runs Hadoop 0.20.2 on top of Debian Linux. We list the important parameters and their values in Table 2. EMR works in conjunction with Amazon EC2 (Elastic Compute Cloud) to create a Hadoop cluster, and with Amazon S3 (Simple Storage Service) to store scripts, input data, log files, and output results. To run our experiments, we first upload to Amazon S3 the input data, as well as the mapper

and reducer executables that process the data. Then, we send a request to EMR to start a job flow. A job flow is a collection of processing steps that EMR runs on a specified dataset using a set of Amazon EC2 instances. Our job flow is comprised of several steps.

In the first step, we partition the dataset into buckets using locality sensitive hashing. Every bucket is a file stored in S3 containing points in the corresponding bucket. In the second step, Spectral Clustering is applied on individual buckets. The final step produces the results, stores them in S3 and terminates the job flow. We note that the partitioning step allows our DASC algorithm to process very large scale data sets, because the data partitions (or splits) are incrementally processed, split by split, based on the number of available mappers (and physical machines).

Intermediate results of hashing (buckets) are stored on S3 and then incrementally processed by DASC to produce final results. Thus, DASC can handle huge datasets. For very skewed data distributions, we can employ a different hashing function in LSH. There are data-dependent hashing functions (e.g., spectral hashing functions), which will yield balanced partitioning. Their inclusion in DASC is straightforward. Data locality is achieved through the first LSH step, which tries to group near-by points into one bucket. Distributed datasets can be thought of huge datasets with splits stored on different machines, where the output hashes represents the keys that are used to exchange datapoints between different nodes.

5.2 Datasets: Synthetic and Real

We use two datasets in our experiments: synthetic and real (from Wikipedia). We create synthetic datasets with controlled parameters, e.g., number of dimensions, number of data points, and range of values for data points. The size of the synthetic datasets ranges from 1024 to 4 million data points. Each data point is 64-dimension vector, where each dimension takes a real value chosen from the period [0–1]. We use the range [0–1] because dataset normalization is a standard preprocessing step in data mining applications.

Wikipedia has millions of articles, categorized into many groups. We used a dataset of 3,550,567 Wikipedia documents in our experiments. These documents are obtained and cleaned as follows. Note that we refer to a web page as document, and a word that appears in the corpus as a term. We developed a crawler in Python. The crawler started crawling the indexing page: `http://en.wikipedia.org/wiki/Portal:Contents/Categories`, which lists the categories and their links. Each category has sub-categories, where each sub-category can recursively have sub-categories. For these sub-category links, Wikipedia differentiates them into two genres, both are encoded in the HTML files. The first is identified with CategoryTreeBullet, meaning that this link contains its own sub-categories. The second is identified with CategoryTreeEmptyBullet, meaning that this sub-category only contains leaf nodes (HTML files). Our crawler obtained the tree structure of categories and downloaded the content of leaf nodes. At the ended of the crawling process, it downloaded 3,550,567 documents, forming 579,144 categories.

We then processed HTML files as follows: (i) removed all HTML tags keeping only the raw text, (ii) converted characters to lower case, (iii) removed punctuation, (iv) removed stop words, and (v) stemmed all terms. We used Apache

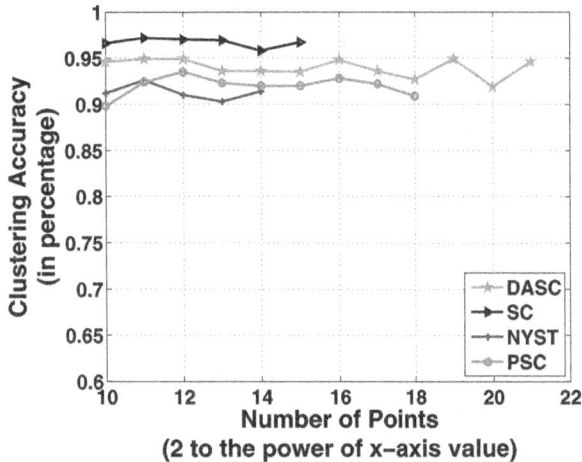

Figure 3: Accuracy of different algorithms using the Wikipedia dataset.

Lucene [14] perform most of these operations. Lucene is a text search engine library. The stop-word list we used is concatenated from several lists to capture the majority of the stop words. Stemming is the process of reducing inflected (or derived) words to their base or root forms. We used the Porter stemming algorithm [30] in Lucene.

We encountered a problem during processing HTML files: The number of terms in the dataset is huge. Terms in a document represent features (or dimensions) of that document, which will make the clustering process extremely computationally expensive. To address this problem, we used only the summary of each document and the important terms in the summary. To rank terms based on their importance, we computed the tf_idf (term frequency, inverse document frequency) value of each term, which is computed for a term t by dividing the total number of documents by the number of documents containing the term t. After ranking all terms based on their tf_idf values, we used the first F terms. We conducted several experiments to choose a good value for F. We randomly chose 1,084 document from the dataset. These documents contain 11,102 different terms. We ran Spectral Clustering on the datasets generated using F from 6 to 16 and compared the clustering accuracy. The clustering accuracy is the ratio of correctly clustered documents to the total number of documents. Our results (figure not shown) indicate that increasing F beyond 11 did not provide any significant improvement in the clustering accuracy. Therefore, we use $F = 11$ in our experiments.

We note that using only some terms and only from the document summaries (not the whole texts) makes the clustering task more challenging for our algorithm, which we compare its results against the ground-truth categorization provided by Wikipedia.

5.3 Performance Metrics

We use several performance metrics to assess the proposed algorithm from different angles. We measure the computational and space requirements of different algorithms. In addition, we assess the clustering accuracy using various metrics. The first metric is comparing the clustering results produced by our algorithm against the ground truth, which is

the case for the Wikipedia dataset. In this case, the clustering accuracy is measured as the ratio of correctly clustered number of points to the total number of points. For many datasets in practice the ground truth for clustering is not known. For such cases, we use three metrics: Davies-Bouldin index (DBI), average squared error (ASE), and Frobenius norm (Fnorm). DBI and ASE assess the clustering quality produced by a given clustering algorithm, while the Fnorm provides an estimate on how close the original and approximated Gram matrices are.

DBI [7] is a function of the ratio of the sum of within-cluster scatter to between-cluster separation. It uses both the clusters and their sample means. It is calculated by:

$$DBI = \frac{1}{C} \sum_{i=1}^{C} \max_{j:i \neq j} \{ \frac{\sigma_i + \sigma_j}{d(c_i, c_j)} \}, \qquad (20)$$

where C is the number of clusters, c_x is the centroid of cluster x, σ_x is the average distance of all elements in cluster x to centroid c_x, and $d(c_i, c_j)$ is the distance between centroids c_i and c_j. The clustering algorithm that produces the smallest index is considered the best algorithm based on this criterion. DBI has been shown to be a robust strategy for the prediction of optimal clustering partitions [7].

ASE [16] serves as a clustering criterion for many classic clustering techniques. For example, it is used in [11] for validation purposes. The squared distance e_k^2 (where $1 \leq k \leq C$) for each cluster k is the sum of the squared Euclidean distances between each point in k and its centroid, and the average squared error for the entire dataset is expressed by:

$$ASE = \frac{1}{N} \sum_k e_k^2 = \frac{1}{N} \sum_k (\sum_{j=0}^{N_k-1} d(X_j, C_k))^2, \qquad (21)$$

where N is the size of the dataset, N_k is the number of points in cluster k.

Fnorm is one of the matrix norms [24], which is also called the Euclidean norm. The Fnorm of an $M \times N$ matrix A is defined as:

$$Fnorm = \sqrt{\sum_{i=1}^{M} \sum_{j=1}^{N} |a_{ij}|^2}. \qquad (22)$$

To illustrate the intuition behind this metric, consider an $M \times N$ matrix A. By singular value decomposition, A can be decomposed into the product of three matrices as follows:

$$
\begin{aligned}
A &= U\Sigma V^H \qquad (23)\\
&= U \begin{bmatrix} \Sigma_k & 0 \\ 0 & 0 \end{bmatrix} V^H,
\end{aligned}
$$

where U and V are two unitary matrices and Σ_k is a $k \times k$ diagonal matrix containing the k ordered positive definite singular values $\sigma_1 \geq \sigma_2 \cdots \geq \sigma_k \geq 0$. The variable k is the rank of A and represents the number of linearly independent columns in it. The Frobenius norm is invariant under unitary transformations, therefore, we have:

$$Fnorm = \sqrt{\sum_{m=1}^{k} \sigma_m^2}. \qquad (24)$$

According to Eq. (24), the larger the ratio of the Fnorm of the approximated matrix to the Fnorm of the original

(a) DBI

(b) ASE

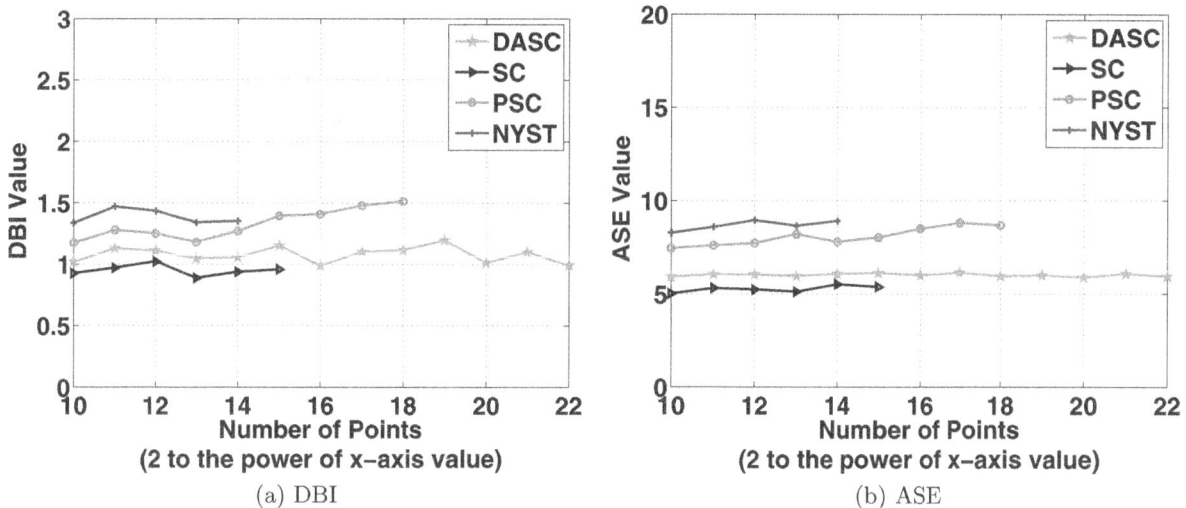

Figure 4: Accuracy of different algorithms using the synthetic dataset.

matrix, the closer the sum of singular values in the approximated matrix is to that of the original one. Thus, larger Fnorm ratios imply matrices with similar characteristics. Fnorm is used in [40] to develop a new affinity matrix normalization scheme in Spectral Clustering. Anagnostopoulos et al. [1] propose an approximation algorithm for co-clustering problem and use Fnorm for evaluation. Yang and Yang [38] compare their proposed distance against Fnorm in two-dimensional principal component analysis.

5.4 Algorithms Implemented and Compared Against

We have implemented the proposed DASC algorithm, and compared its performance against the three closest other algorithms: basic Spectral Clustering method (SC), Parallel Spectral Clustering (PSC) [3], and Spectral Clustering using the Nystrom extension (NYST) [32]. We provide brief description on the implementation and configuration below; more details can be found in [12].

We implemented DASC by modifying the Mahout library [29]. We set the number of buckets in the hashing step to $M = \lfloor (\log N)/2 \rfloor - 1$, where N is the dataset size. We set P, which is the minimum number of identical bits in two binary signatures needed to merge their buckets together, to $M-1$. This enables efficient, $O(1)$, comparison operation between signatures. It also increases the degree of parallelization as fewer buckets will be merged.

For SC, we used the basic distributed Spectral Clustering implementation in Mahout. For PSC, we used the C++ implementation by Chen [3], which uses the PARPACK library [19] as the underlying eigenvalue decomposition package. The parallelization is based on MPI. For NYST, we used the existing Matlab implementation by Shi [32].

5.5 Results for Clustering Accuracy

We present the accuracy results in this section. We note that some algorithms we compare against did not scale to support large-scale datasets. Hence, in the figures, some curves do not cover the whole range of the x-axis.

We start by presenting the accuracy results for the Wikipedia dataset in Figure 3. In this figure, we vary the number of

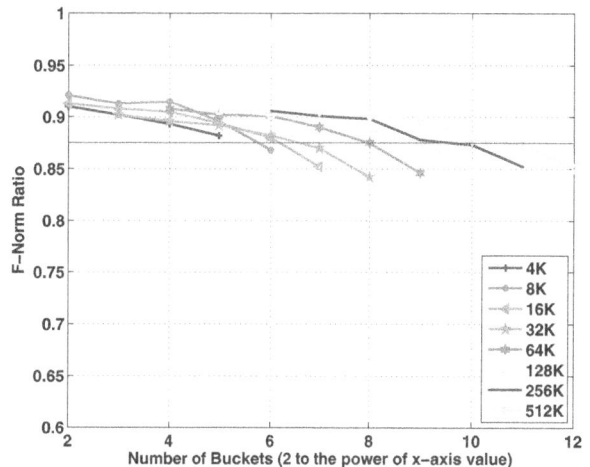

Figure 5: Comparison between approximated and original matrices using Frobenius norm.

randomly selected documents from the dataset, and we plot the ratio of correctly clustered points (documents) to the total number of points. The figure first shows that the three variants of spectral clustering (SC, PSC, and DASC) produce high accuracy: always more than 90%. Recall that these clustering algorithms use only the summaries of documents in the clustering process and the accuracy is computed relative to the pre-defined categorization of topics in Wikipedia. The figure also shows that the proposed DASC algorithm consistently produces better results than the results produced by the PSC algorithm, and its results are very close to the results produced by the basic SC algorithm. This means that the proposed approximation method does not negatively affect the clustering accuracy, while it achieves significant savings as will be shown later.

Next, we show the accuracy results in terms of DBI and ASE for synthetic data in Figure 4. We vary the number of points from 1K to 4M and compute the DBI and ASE values for the clusters produced by four algorithms: DASC,

PSC, SC, and NYST. Figure 4(a) shows that the DBI values achieved by DASC are very close to those produced by SC. When checking the DASC curve alone, the DBI values, although go through some slight ups and downs, in general, they stay in the range between 1 to 1.3 and are always close to the SC's curve. Figure 4(b) shows that DASC outperforms the PSC and NYST and yields close performance to that of SC, in terms of ASE, which measures how close the points in the clusters are to their respective centroids. Small ASE values indicate better clustering result. The results indicate that PSC and NYST are about 30% and 40%, respectively, apart from SC. Moreover, when the dataset grows, the PSC performance tends to deteriorate, as the average distance value grows slightly, which is unlike DASC that produces consistent results.

Finally, we present the results of the low-level Fnorm metric which captures the similarity between the approximated and original Gram matrices. We consider various number of data points: from 4K to 512K. Note that we could not use more than 512K points because we need to compare against the original Gram matrix which requires memory proportional to the square of the number points. We plot the ratio of the Fnorm value computed from the approximated matrix to the Fnorm value computed from the original full Gram matrix in Figure 5. We do this for different number of buckets used in the hashing step; we change the number of buckets from 4 to 4K. Note that larger numbers of buckets allow for higher degrees of parallelization and are desirable. However, larger numbers of buckets imply more partitioning of the dataset which can affect the clustering accuracy. The results shown in Figure 5 indicate that the approximated matrix does not lose significant information compared to the original matrix. The figure also shows that for the same dataset, increasing the number of buckets tends to decrease the Fnorm ratio, which means that the approximated matrix has less resemblance to the original matrix. In addition, for larger datasets, more number of buckets can be used before the Fnorm ratio starts to drop.

5.6 Results for Time and Space Complexities

We measure and compare the processing time and memory requirements for three different algorithms: DASC, PSC, and SC. SC is implemented in the Mahout library in Java using the MapReduce framework. PSC is implemented in C++ using MPI. DASC is implemented in Java using the MapReduce framework. We realize that different implementation languages and parallelization models can impact the running times. However, the orders of magnitudes performance gains observed in our experiments (as shown shortly) clearly overshadow such small differences. We also note that the NYST algorithm is implemented in Matlab and we could not run on the cloud. This experiment is conducted on the five-node cluster and for the Wikipedia and synthetic datasets. We show the results for the Wikipedia dataset in Figure 6; other results are similar [12]. As shown in Figure 6(a), DASC considerably improves the processing time. For example, for a dataset of size 2^{18} points, DASC runs more than an order of magnitude faster than PSC. For datasets larger than 2^{18}, PSC could not even terminate because of the large processing time and memory requirements. The basic SC algorithm in Mahout did not scale to datasets larger than 2^{15} and was orders of magnitudes slower than DASC.

Metric	64 nodes	32 nodes	16 nodes
Accuracy	95.6%	96.4%	96.6%
Memory	29444 KB	29412 KB	28919 KB
Time	20.3 hrs	40.75 hrs	78.85 hrs

Table 3: Results for running DASC on the Amazon cloud with different nodes.

The most important advantage of our proposed DASC algorithm is the substantial memory saving, which is confirmed by Figure 6(b). The numbers shown in the figure are for total memory needed to store the Gram matrix. The figure shows that DASC achieves several orders of magnitude of memory saving compared to the basic SC implemented in Mahout. The figure also shows that although PSC uses sparse matrix representation, DASC requires substantially less memory than it. For example, for a dataset of size 2^{18}, there is a factor of more than 25 reduction in memory usage when comparing DASC versus PSC. More importantly, the memory usage curve for DASC is much flatter than SC and PSC curves. This means that DASC provides much better scalability to process very-large datasets than the other two algorithms.

5.7 Elasticity and Scalability

One of the main advantages of using cloud platforms is elasticity, which enables cloud customers to easily request and utilize different amounts of computing resources based on the actual demand. In this section, we demonstrate that the proposed DASC algorithm, and hence the approximation method in general, can benefit from the elasticity offered by cloud platforms.

We run our DASC algorithm on the Wikipedia dataset on Amazon cloud and we vary the number of computing nodes from 16 to 64. We measure the accuracy, running time, and memory usage in each case. We summarize the results in Table 3. The results first demonstrate the scalability of the proposed DASC algorithm, since the running time reduces approximately linearly with increasing the number of nodes, while the memory usage and clustering accuracy stay roughly the same. This scalability is achieved mainly by the proposed preprocessing step, which partitions a given large dataset into independent and non overlapping partitions (hashing buckets). These parts can be allocated to independent computing nodes for further processing. This enables the utilization of various number of computing nodes once they become available, which results in faster processing of the dataset. On the other hand, if the number of computing nodes decreases, the DASC algorithm allocates more partitions per node, yielding correct results but with longer execution time. Therefore, DASC can efficiently and dynamically utilize different number of computing nodes.

6. CONCLUSIONS

We proposed new algorithms to support large-scale data-intensive applications that employ kernel-based machine learning algorithms. We presented an approximation algorithm for computing the kernel matrix needed by various kernel-based machine learning algorithms. The proposed algorithm uses locality sensitive hashing to reduce the number of pairwise kernel computations. The algorithm is general and can be used by many kernel-based machine learning algorithms.

(a) Processing Time   (b) Memory

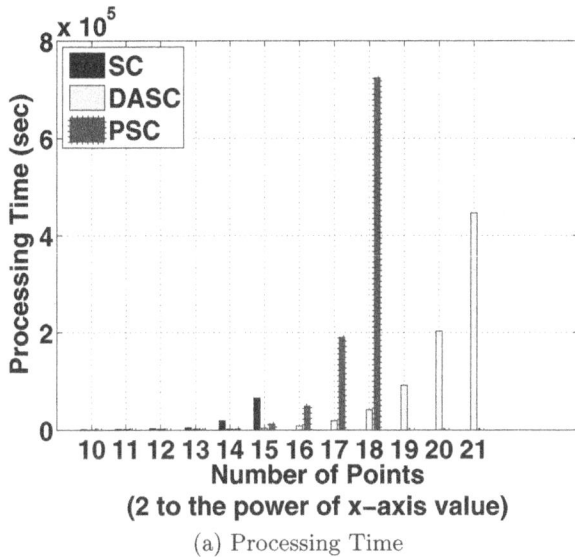

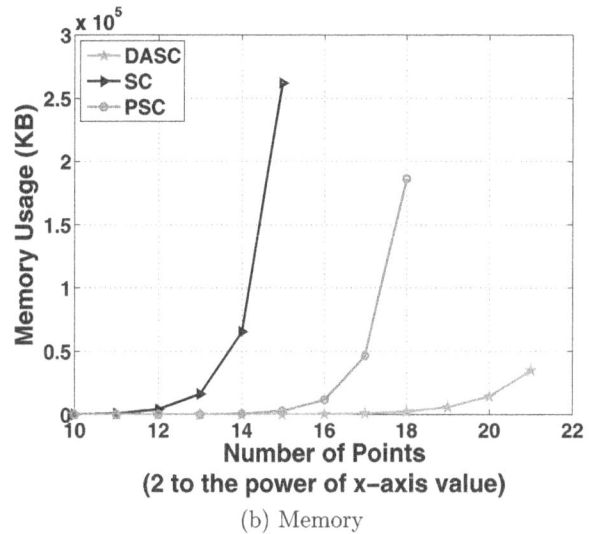

Figure 6: Processing time and memory requirements for different algorithms.

We designed a distributed approximate spectral clustering (DASC) algorithm based on the approximation algorithm. We showed that DASC can offer a factor of up to $O(B)$ reduction in running time and memory usage compared to the spectral clustering algorithm that uses the full kernel matrix. B is the number of buckets used by the locality sensitive hashing step. B depends on the number of bits in the binary signature generated for each data point by the hashing functions. For large data sets, more bits in the signatures are needed, and thus more buckets. This means that the reduction factor achieved by our algorithm increases as the size of the dataset grows, which is an important and desirable property of our algorithm that enables it to scale to massive data sets.

We implemented DASC in the MapReduce framework, and ran it on a Hadoop cluster in our lab as well as on the Amazon Elastic MapReduce (EMR) service. We used the DASC algorithm to cluster various synthetic and real datasets. The real dataset contains more than three million documents from Wikipedia. We compared the clustering accuracy produced by the DASC algorithm versus the ground truth document categorization provided by Wikipedia. Our results showed that the DASC algorithm achieves high clustering accuracy of more than 90%, and its accuracy is very close to the regular spectral clustering algorithm that uses the full kernel matrix. Whereas the running time and memory usage of the DASC algorithm is several orders of magnitudes smaller than the regular spectral clustering algorithm. We also compared the DASC algorithm versus other algorithms in the literature and showed that it outperforms them in clustering accuracy, running time, and memory requirements.

Acknowledgments

This work is partially supported by the Natural Sciences and Engineering Research Council (NSERC) of Canada and the British Columbia Innovation Council (BCIC).

7. REFERENCES

[1] A. Anagnostopoulos, A. Dasgupta, and R. Kumar. Approximation algorithms for co-clustering. In *In Proc. of Symposium on Principles of Database Systems (PODS'08)*, pages 201–210, Vancouver, BC, Canada, June 2008.

[2] M. Charikar. Similarity estimation techniques from rounding algorithms. In *In Proc. of ACM Symposium on Theory of Computing (STOC'02)*, pages 380–388, Montréal, Canada, May 2002.

[3] W.-Y. Chen, Y. Song, H. Bai, C.-J. Lin, and E. Chang. Parallel spectral clustering in distributed systems. *IEEE Transactions on Pattern Analysis and Machine Intelligence*, 33(3):568–586, March 2011.

[4] O. Chum, J. Philbin, and A. Zisserman. Near duplicate image detection: min-hash and tf-idf weighting. In *In Proc. of British Machine Vision Conference (BMVC'08)*, pages 25–31, Leeds, UK, September 2008.

[5] N. Cristianini and J. Shawe-Taylor. *An Introduction to Support Vector Machines and other Kernel-based Learning Methods*. Cambridge University Press, 2000.

[6] J. Cullum and R. Willoughby. Lanczos algorithms for large symmetric eigenvalue computations. *IEEE Transactions on Information Theory*, pages 43–49, 1985.

[7] D. Davies and D. Bouldin. A cluster separation measure. *IEEE Transactions on Pattern Analysis and Machine Intelligence*, PAMI-1:224–227, 1979.

[8] L. M. Delves and J. Walsh, editors. *Numerical Solution of Integral Equations*. Clarendon, Oxford, 1974.

[9] P. Drineas and M. Mahoney. Approximating a gram matrix for improved kernel-based learning. In *In Proc. of Annual Conference on Computational Learning Theory*, pages 323–337, 2005.

[10] X. Fern and C. Brodley. Random projection for high dimensional data clustering: a cluster ensemble

approach. In *In Proc. of International Conference on Machine Learning (ICML'03)*, pages 186–193, 2003.

[11] B. Frey and D. Dueck. Clustering by passing messages between data points. *Science*, 315:972–976, 2007.

[12] F. Gao. Distributed Approximate Spectral Clustering for Large-Scale Datasets. Master's thesis, Simon Fraser University, Canada, 2011.

[13] J. A. Hartigan and M. A. Wong. A k-means clustering algorithm. *Journal of the Royal Statistical Society, Series C (Applied Statistics)*, pages 22–29, 1979.

[14] E. Hatcher and O. Gospodnetic. *Lucene in Action*. Manning Publications Co., Greenwich, CT, USA, 2004.

[15] J. Hennessy and D. Patterson. *Computer Architecture - A Quantitative Approach*. Morgan Kaufmann, 2003.

[16] A. K. Jain and R. C. Dubes. *Algorithms for clustering data*. Prentice-Hall, Inc., 1988.

[17] U. Kang, C. Tsourakakis, and C. Faloutsos. Pegasus: A peta-scale graph mining system implementation and observations. In *In Proc. of IEEE International Conference on Data Mining (ICDM'09)*, pages 229–238, Washington, DC, December 2009.

[18] J. Kubica, J. Masiero, A. Moore, R. Jedicke, and A. Connolly. Variable kd-tree algorithms for efficient spatial pattern search. Technical Report CMU-RI-TR-05-43, Robotics Institute, Carnegie Mellon University, Pittsburgh, PA, September 2005.

[19] R. B. Lehoucq, D. C. Sorensen, and C. Yang. Arpack users guide: Solution of large scale eigenvalue problems by implicitly restarted arnoldi methods, 1997.

[20] J. Leskovec, L. A. Adamic, and B. A. Huberman. The dynamics of viral marketing. *ACM Transactions on the Web*, 1, May 2007.

[21] J. Leskovec, D. Huttenlocher, and J. Kleinberg. Predicting positive and negative links in online social networks. In *In Proc. of ACM Conference on World Wide Web (WWW'10)*, pages 641–650, April 2010.

[22] J. Lin, D. Ryaboy, and K. Weil. Full-text indexing for optimizing selection operations in large-scale data analytics. In *In Proc. of International Workshop on MapReduce and its Applications*, pages 59–66, June 2011.

[23] A. Matsunaga, M. Tsugawa, and J. Fortes. Cloudblast: Combining mapreduce and virtualization on distributed resources for bioinformatics applications. In *In Proc. of IEEE International Conference on eScience*, pages 222–229, Indianapolis, IN, December 2008.

[24] T. Moon and W. Stirling. *Mathematical methods and algorithms for signal processing*. Prentice-Hall, Inc., 2000.

[25] R. Motwani, A. Naor, and R. Panigrahi. Lower bounds on locality sensitive hashing. In *In Proc. of Annual Symposium on Computational Geometry (SCG'06)*, pages 154–157, 2006.

[26] S. Munder and D. Gavrila. An experimental study on pedestrian classification. *Pattern Analysis and Machine Intelligence, IEEE Transactions on*, 28(11):1863–1868, Nov. 2006.

[27] A. Y. Ng, M. I. Jordan, and Y. Weiss. On spectral clustering: Analysis and an algorithm. In *Advances in Neural Information Processing Systems*, pages 849–856. MIT Press, 2001.

[28] J. Ohmer, F. Maire, and R. Brown. Implementation of kernel methods on the gpu. In *In Proc. of Conference on Digital Image Computing: Techniques and Applications*, page 78, Washington, DC, USA, December 2005.

[29] S. Owen, R. Anil, T. Dunning, and E. Friedman. *Mahout in Action*. Manning Publications, 2011.

[30] M. F. Porter. An Algorithm for Suffix Stripping. *Program*, 14(3):130–137, 1980.

[31] B. Schlkopf, A. Smola, and K.-R. Müller. Nonlinear component analysis as a kernel eigenvalue problem. *Neural Computation*, 10:1299–1319, July 1998.

[32] J. Schuetter and T. Shi. Multi-sample data spectroscopic clustering of large datasets using Nystrom extension. *Journal of Computational and Graphical Statistics*, pages 531–542, 2011.

[33] M. Seeger. *Bayesian Model Selection for Support Vector Machines, Gaussian Processes and Other Kernel Classifiers*, volume 12, pages 603–609. The MIT Press, 2000.

[34] Y. Weiss. Segmentation using eigenvectors: A unifying view. In *In Proc. of International Conference on Computer Vision*, pages 975–982, 1999.

[35] B. White, T. Yeh, J. Lin, and L. Davis. Web-scale computer vision using MapReduce for multimedia data mining. In *In Proc. of ACM Workshop on Multimedia Data Mining*, 2010.

[36] C. K. I. Williams and M. Seeger. The effect of the input density distribution on kernel-based classifiers. In *International Conference on Machine Learning*, 2000.

[37] C. K. I. Williams and M. Seeger. *Using Nystrom method to speed up kernel machines*, volume 13 of *Advanced in Neural Information Processing Systems*. MIT Press, 2001.

[38] J. Yang and J.-Y. Yang. From image vector to matrix: a straightforward image projection technique - IMPCA vs. PCA. *Pattern Recognition*, 35:1997–1999, 2002.

[39] D. Yogatama and K. Tanaka-Ishii. Multilingual spectral clustering using document similarity propagation. In *In Proc. of Conference on Empirical Methods in Natural Language Processing*, pages 871–879, 2009.

[40] R. Zass and A. Shashua. Doubly stochastic normalization for spectral clustering. In *Neural Information Processing Systems*, pages 1569–1576, 2006.

Exploring Cross-layer Power Management for PGAS Applications on the SCC Platform

Marc Gamell, Ivan Rodero, Manish Parashar
NSF Cloud and Autonomic Computing Center
Rutgers Discovery Informatics Institute
Rutgers University, Piscataway, NJ, USA
{mgamell, irodero,
parashar}@cac.rutgers.edu

Rajeev Muralidhar
Intel India, Ltd
rajeev.d.muralidhar@intel.com

ABSTRACT

High-performance parallel computing architectures are increasingly based on multi-core processors. While current commercially available processors are at 8 and 16 cores, technological and power constraints are limiting the performance growth of the cores and are resulting in architectures with much higher core counts, such as the experimental many-core Intel Single-chip Cloud Computer (SCC) platform. These trends are presenting new sets of challenges to HPC applications including programming complexity and the need for extreme energy efficiency.

In this paper, we first investigate the power behavior of scientific Partitioned Global Address Space (PGAS) application kernels on the SCC platform, and explore opportunities and challenges for power management within the PGAS framework. Results obtained via empirical evaluation of Unified Parallel C (UPC) applications on the SCC platform under different constraints, show that, for specific operations, the potential for energy savings in PGAS is large; and power/performance trade-offs can be effectively managed using a cross-layer approach. We investigate cross-layer power management using PGAS language extensions and runtime mechanisms that manipulate power/performance tradeoffs. Specifically, we present the design, implementation and evaluation of such a middleware for application-aware cross-layer power management of UPC applications on the SCC platform. Finally, based on our observations, we provide a set of insights that can be used to support similar power management for PGAS applications on other many-core platforms.

Categories and Subject Descriptors

D.4.7 [**Operating Systems**]: Organization and Design—*distributed systems*; C.2.4 [**Computer - Communication Networks**]: Distributed Systems; C.4 [**Computer Systems Organization**]: Performance of Systems

Keywords

Power management, PGAS, SCC, Cross-layer, Application-aware

1. INTRODUCTION

Technological limitations and overall power constraints are resulting in high-performance parallel computing architectures based on large numbers of high-core-count processors. Commercially available processors are now at 8 and 16 cores and experimental platforms, such as the many-core Intel Single-chip Cloud Computer (SCC) platform, provide much higher core counts. This architectural trend is a source of significant programming challenges for HPC application developers, as they have to manage extreme levels of concurrency and complex processor and memory structures [4].

Partitioned Global Address Space (PGAS) is emerging as a promising programming model for such large-scale systems and can help address some of these programming challenges, and recent research has focused on its performance and scalability. For example, existing PGAS research includes improvement of UPC collective operations [27], hybrid models to improve performance limitations [10] and the implementation of X10 for the Intel SCC [6] and UPC for Tilera's many core [29].

Another equally significant and immediate challenge is energy efficiency. The power demand of high-end HPC systems is increasing eight-fold every year [1]. Current HPC systems consume several megawatts of power, and power costs for these high-end systems routinely run into millions of dollars per year. Furthermore, increasing power consumption also impacts the overall reliability of these systems. In fact, the trend towards many core architectures employing large numbers of simpler cores [5] is motivated by the fact that simpler cores are smaller in terms of their die-area, as per Pollack's Rule have more attractive power/performance ratios. However, as we move towards sustained multi-petaflop and exaflop systems, processor/system level energy efficiency alone is no longer sufficient and energy efficiency must be addressed in a cross-layer and application-aware manner. While application-aware power management has been addressed in prior work, for example, for distributed memory parallel applications using message passing in previous work by exploiting CPU low power modes when a task is not in the critical path (i.e., it can be slowed without incurring overall execution delay) or is blocked in an communication call (i.e., slack) [26], these approaches do not directly translate to PGAS applications on many-core processors where, for example, such communication and coordination operations are implicit.

This paper explores application-aware cross-layer power management for PGAS applications on many-core platforms, and presents the design, implementation and experimental evaluation of language level extensions and a runtime middleware framework for application-aware cross-layer power management of UPC applications on the SCC platform. Specifically, in this paper, we first experimentally investigate the power behavior of scientific PGAS application kernels (i.e., the NAS Parallel Benchmarks) implemented in Unified Parallel C (UPC) on the experimental SCC platform under various constraints, and explore opportunities and challenges for power management within the PGAS framework. We then investigate application driven cross-layer power management specified using PGAS language extensions and supported by runtime mechanism that explore power/performance tradeoffs. These extensions are a set of user levels functions (e.g., PM_PERFORMANCE()) that provide hints to the runtime system (e.g., threshold values). Hints can define tradeoffs and constraints. Analogous to CPU governors for OS-level power management, we define a set of application level policies for maximizing application performance, maximizing power savings, or balancing power/performance tradeoffs. The runtime mechanisms effectively exploit dynamic frequency and voltage scaling of SCC frequency and voltage domains in regions of the program where cores are blocked due to either thread synchronization or a (remote) memory access. This is achieved using adaptations that adjust the power configuration based on a combination of static and dynamic thresholds at multiple power levels, and use asynchronous voltage and frequency (i.e., DVFS) or only frequency (i.e., DFS) scaling.

Results obtained from experiments conducted on the SCC platform hosted by Intel show that only certain PGAS operations need to be considered for power management, and our runtime power management approach results in energy savings of 7% with less than 3% increase in execution time. Furthermore, by using application level hints about acceptable power/performance tradeoffs, specified using the proposed language extensions, the energy savings can be significantly improved. In this case a 20% reduction of the energy delay product and be achieved.

The experiments also show that in the case of applications where application level power management does not provide any significant energy saving, a cross-layer approach can be used to achieve a wide range of energy and performance behaviors, and appropriate tradeoffs can be selected. These tradeoffs and the effectiveness of this approach are demonstrated using the Sobel edge detector application [20]. We also use a synthetic application (that generates different levels of load imbalance) to demonstrate that the adaptive runtime power management mechanism can handle different load imbalance scenarios and can provide significant energy savings. For example, when load imbalances are high, we can achieve up to 50% of available energy savings using DVFS and up to 25% using DFS without incurring a significant execution time penalty.

Our evaluation also reveals several power management limitations of the SCC platform that must be addressed in future architectures; for example, voltage scaling can be per-

formed only on domains of 8 cores. Finally, based on our observations, we provide a set of insights that can be used to support similar power management for PGAS applications on other many-core platforms. While the current work presented here is on the Intel SCC platform (which is only an experimental one), the focus of this research is to look beyond - on whether programming language level (and programming model aware) power management is meaningful for scientific applications, what are the right abstractions and mechanisms, and what are the constraints and tradeoffs therein - these aspects translate across the platforms.

The rest of the paper is organized as follows. Section 2 presents the architecture of the SCC processor and specific SCC platform used in our experiment, with special focus on power management aspects that are important for our evaluation. Section 3 discusses relevant related work. Section 4 contains a study of power behaviors of PGAS applications based on application profiling, with the goal of identifying opportunities for power management. Section 5 presents the proposed programming extensions and power management system for UPC PGAS applications on SCC, while section 6 presents their evaluation. Finally, section 7 concludes the paper and outlines directions for future work.

2. BACKGROUND

In order to help accelerate many-core research and development, Intel Labs' Tera-scale Computing Research Program has developed the experimental Single-chip Cloud Computer (SCC) processor [21]. Although this processor is not expected to be deployed in future HPC systems, it is representative of current trends, i.e., large numbers of relatively simpler cores, and we believe that our results will translate beyond SCC to such systems. For example, future architectures such as the Intel Knights Corner [28] is touted to have per core power gating, and per-core voltage and frequency switching support, which will only enhance the capabilities that we can exploit from a power/performance point of view.

The hardware consists of 48 x86 Pentium P54C cores each with 32 KB of L1 cache – increased from the standard 16 KB – where 16 KB are for data and 16 KB for instructions, and 256 KB of L2 cache. The cache memory is non-coherent, however customized libraries offer software-based cache coherency. As shown in Figure 1, the 48 cores are configured into tiles with 2 cores per tile. The SCC architecture features a fast (256 GB/s bisection bandwidth) 24-router on-die mesh network which enables communication between tiles and provides hardware support for message-passing. The message-passing support is implemented in the form of a special per-tile 16 KB fast read-write buffer called the Message Passing Buffer (MPB).

The on-chip network also allows each tile to access four dual-channel DDR3 Memory Controllers (MC) which manage, typically, 32 GB (maximum of 64 GB) of main memory for the entire chip. Each core has the ability to run as an individual compute node with its own OS (usually Linux) and software stack and communicate with other compute nodes over a packet-based network. The SCC offers fine-grained power management by allowing dynamic frequency scaling for each tile and dynamic voltage scaling for groups of 4 tiles (as shown in Figure 1). As a result of these power management techniques, the power dissipation can range from 125W to as low as 25W. The frequency and voltage scaling can be controlled by utilizing specific operations exposed by

RCCE. RCCE is an optimized library for the SCC architecture which serves as a high level abstraction by providing functions for message passing, power management and shared memory allocation.

The SCC chip is not directly bootable and requires additional hardware to manage and control it. This is done by an FPGA called the Board Management Controller (BMC) which handles commands to initialize and shut down the SCC and enable power data collection. The BMC is, subsequently, connected to a commodity PC which acts as the Management Console PC (MCPC). The SCC allows power management of three components that work with separate clocks and power sources: mesh network, memory controllers and tiles. In this study, we will focus only on tile power management because mesh and memory controller power management cannot be performed during runtime.

The SCC tiles are arranged in a 6 by 4 grid and further decomposed into distinct voltage and frequency domains (shown in Figure 1). As a result, the dynamic voltage and frequency scaling will affect all tiles within the voltage and frequency domains, respectively. In total there are 6 voltage domains with 4 tiles each and 24 frequency domains with 1 tile each. The voltage can be controlled by using the Voltage Regulator Controller (VRC) which works in a command-based manner: cores send messages to the VRC in order to change the voltage. As described in [2], the VRC allows a set of voltages between 0 and 1.3V in increments of 6.25mV. In contrast to the voltage management system which provides a single VRC for all voltage domains, the frequency management system provides a configuration register for each tile (i.e. for each frequency domain). This configuration register is used to change the frequency divider and, as a result, reduce the clock frequency from the global frequency of 1.6 GHz. Each tile can set the configuration register to integer values between 2 and 16 which correspond to frequency values between 800 MHz to 100 MHz. Figure 1 also shows the default configuration of memory domains, i.e., each tile within a memory domain accesses its corresponding memory controller. However, this configuration can be modified via SCC Address Lookup Table (LUT).

In order to scale voltage, the frequency must be scaled accordingly for the associated tiles. Similarly, scaling frequency up requires a corresponding change in the voltage of the associated voltage domain(s). Through experimental evaluation we found that the lower subrange of voltages cannot be used in practice, as the cores either crash or become unstable. We found empirically that the lowest stable voltage level (using the corresponding frequency) is 0.65625 V. We also found that, on average, the overhead of performing voltage scaling is 40.2 ms.

The official SCC documentation (and the RCCE source code) provides a table with the maximum frequency allowed for each voltage level (in [9] see "Table 9: Voltage and Frequency values"). However, we experimentally found that some of the voltage levels were not stable, as also described in [13]. The voltage-frequency levels that worked robustly during our experiments, are shown in Table 1.

The SCC chip does not provide monitoring tools; however, measured voltage and power dissipation can be obtained by sending a query command to the BMC from the MCPC. Using this feature we were able to automatically collect the measured power dissipation and utilized a sampling frequency of about 6.5 measures per second. We then

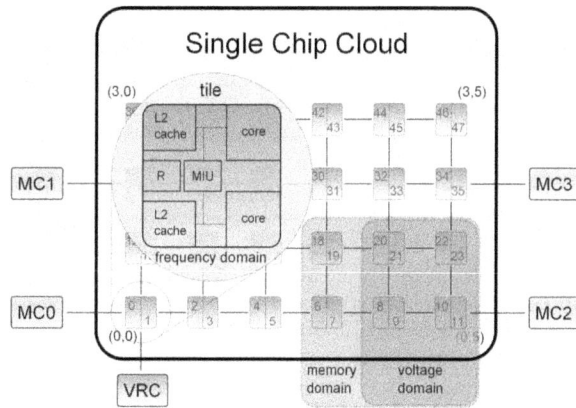

Figure 1: SCC architecture overview

Level	Voltage (V)	Max freq (MHz)	Tested freq (MHz)
0	**0.75**	460	400
1	**0.85**	598	533
4	1.1	875	800

Table 1: Stable SCC voltage and frequency values

estimate the consumed energy by integrating the power measures over time.

3. RELATED WORK

Existing and ongoing research in power efficiency and power management has addressed the problem at different levels such as processor and other subsystems level, runtime/OS level and application level. Since processors dominate the system power consumption in HPC systems [18], processor level power management is the most addressed aspect at server level. The most commonly used technique for CPU power management is Dynamic Voltage and Frequency Scaling (DVFS), which is a technique to reduce power dissipation by lowering processor clock speed and supply voltage [14]. OS-level CPU power management involves controlling the sleep states or the C-states and the P-states of the processor when the processor is idle [22]. The Advanced Configuration and Power Interface (ACPI) specification provides the policies and mechanisms to control the C-states and P-states of the processor when they are idle [31]. Some of the most successful approaches for workload-level CPU power management were based on overlapping computation with communication in MPI programs, using historical data and heuristics [16], based on application profiles [24], scheduling mechanisms [7] or exploiting low power modes when a task is not in the critical path [26]. Existing work has also addressed power efficiency and power management at the application and compiler levels. For example, Eon [32] is a coordination language for power-aware computing that enables developers to adapt their algorithms to different energy contexts. Wu et al. [36] introduced a dynamic-compiler-driven control for energy efficiency. However, any of the existing programming extensions have been developed in a cross-layer approach.

Existing research has also addressed many-core systems. For example, Majzoub et al. [19] introduced a chip-design approach to voltage-island formation, for the energy optimization of many core architectures. Other approaches have been conducted using the SCC platform. Rotta [25] discussed how to efficiently design and implement the different strategies for message passing on SCC. Pankratius [23] introduced an application-level automatic performance tuning approach on the SCC. Urena et al. [34] implemented an MPI runtime optimized for the SCC message passing capabilities. Clauss et al. [8] improved message passing performance on SCC by adding a non-blocking communication extension to RCCE library. Van Tol et al. [35] introduced an efficient memcpy implementation. Alonso et al. [3] proposed extending power-aware Dense Linear Algebra algorithms to SCC. Although these approaches exploit the SCC along multiple dimensions (i.e., library, runtime, application, etc.), none of them address power and performance tradeoffs from a cross-layer perspective.

Existing PGAS research has focussed mainly on its performance and scalability. Salama et al. [27] proposed a potential improvement of collective operations in UPC. Dinan et al. [10] proposed an hybrid programming paradigm based upon MPI and UPC models that try to improve performance limitations. Chen et al. [15] compare the performance of benchmarks compiled with their own optimizations in BUPC with that of HP UPC compiler. Tarek et al. [12] benchmark UPC and propose compiler optimizations. Kuchera et al. [17] study the UPC memory model and memory consistency issues. Existing PGAS research on many-core systems is not very large. Chapman et al. [6] implemented the X10 programming language on the Intel SCC and performed a comparative study versus MPI using different benchmark applications. Serres et al. [29] ported Berkeley UPC to Tilera's many-core Tile64.

Overall, these approaches do not directly translate to PGAS applications on many-core processors and, to the best of our knowledge, power management in the PGAS framework has not been addressed yet.

4. PROFILING OF PGAS APPLICATIONS

4.1 Scope for power management

Exploiting load imbalance in MPI applications has been the traditional method of saving CPU energy without significantly penalizing execution time [26]. Here we define an application as load imbalanced when some nodes are assigned more computation than others. In such cases, the nodes with less computation can be run at lower frequency because, otherwise, they waste energy while waiting for other nodes during synchronization calls. However, existing approaches do not translate to PGAS due to the one-sided communication for remote memory accesses, as opposed to the two-sided synchronization (send/receive) in MPI. Additionally, no explicit language-level APIs/library calls are required to access remote memory with PGAS, whereas MPI utilizes specific MPI calls. As such, there are no easily obvious places to interject power management calls. However, like MPI, PGAS implementations (e.g., UPC) also support barriers for synchronization.

In this section we study the behavior of PGAS applications in order to understand the use of different operations and identify opportunities to perform power management. Several intermediate-level operations, such as wait (barrier), lock (critical section), memget, memput or memcpy, might be candidate operations for power management, however, ap-

plication profiling reveals that only wait and memget operations have potential for power management.

Existing profiling tools for UPC such as PPW [33] or GASP [30] are designed to be executed in traditional systems with large amounts of memory. Using such tools in the SCC environment (i.e., a large number of cores running an OS but sharing the memory), would interfere with the profiling due to the overhead of the instrumentation. Additionally, existing profiling tools for PGAS must be adapted to the SCC framework. For this reason we decided to implement a lightweight instrumentation system (power management instrumentation - pmi). pmi is currently available on UPC, but extensible to any other PGAS runtime. We achieve low overhead by writing lightweight intermediate files containing data in raw binary format. Then, the stored data is parsed in order to generate begin/end timestamps for each call and automatically create log files. Plots are generated postmortem. Through evaluation we found that the measured overhead of pmi is less than 1%.

4.2 Benchmarks

Three different types of kernels were used: (1) the George Washington University UPC implementation of the NAS Parallel Benchmarks (NPB) [11], (2) the Sobel edge detector kernel [20], and (3) a customizable synthetic application. Specifically, we used the FT (Fast Fourier Transform), EP (Embarrassingly Parallel) and MG (Multi Grid) kernels from NPB.

In order to identify the potential for power management in a single many-core system, we aimed to stress the SCC platform by executing each kernel on all 48 cores. We used the largest problem size class of each benchmark that fits in the SCC memory (i.e., class C for FT and MG and class D for EP). Sobel is an edge detection application widely used in computer vision. The parallelized version of this algorithm partitions the image among the cores, performs calculations locally and accesses elements from another execution thread when data shifting is required.

Since the SCC does not support per-core frequency and voltage scaling, we have defined a synthetic application (matmul) to determine how to exploit application load imbalance to save energy. It specifically performs a set of matrix multiplications as shown in the algorithm below.

```
for (i=0 ; i<N ; i++) {
  perform A matrix multiplications
  (distributed in 48 cores);
  if(MYTHREAD is in the last Voltage Domain)
      perform B matrix multiplications;
  upc_barrier;
}
```

N is the number of iterations, A is the number of matrix multiplications performed by all the 6 voltage domains, and B is the number of matrix multiplications performed by only one domain. We can use these parameters to configure the load imbalance, which in this case is the percentage of time that threads are blocked in a barrier while waiting for other threads. For example, we used N=36, A=20 and B=5,000 to obtain 33% of load imbalance. These parameters, led to a 33 % of load imbalance due to: (1) the first phase of the matmul benchmark is executed in parallel while the second phase is performed sequentially, and (2) since the matrices used are not very large, a parallel multiplication requires lot of syn-

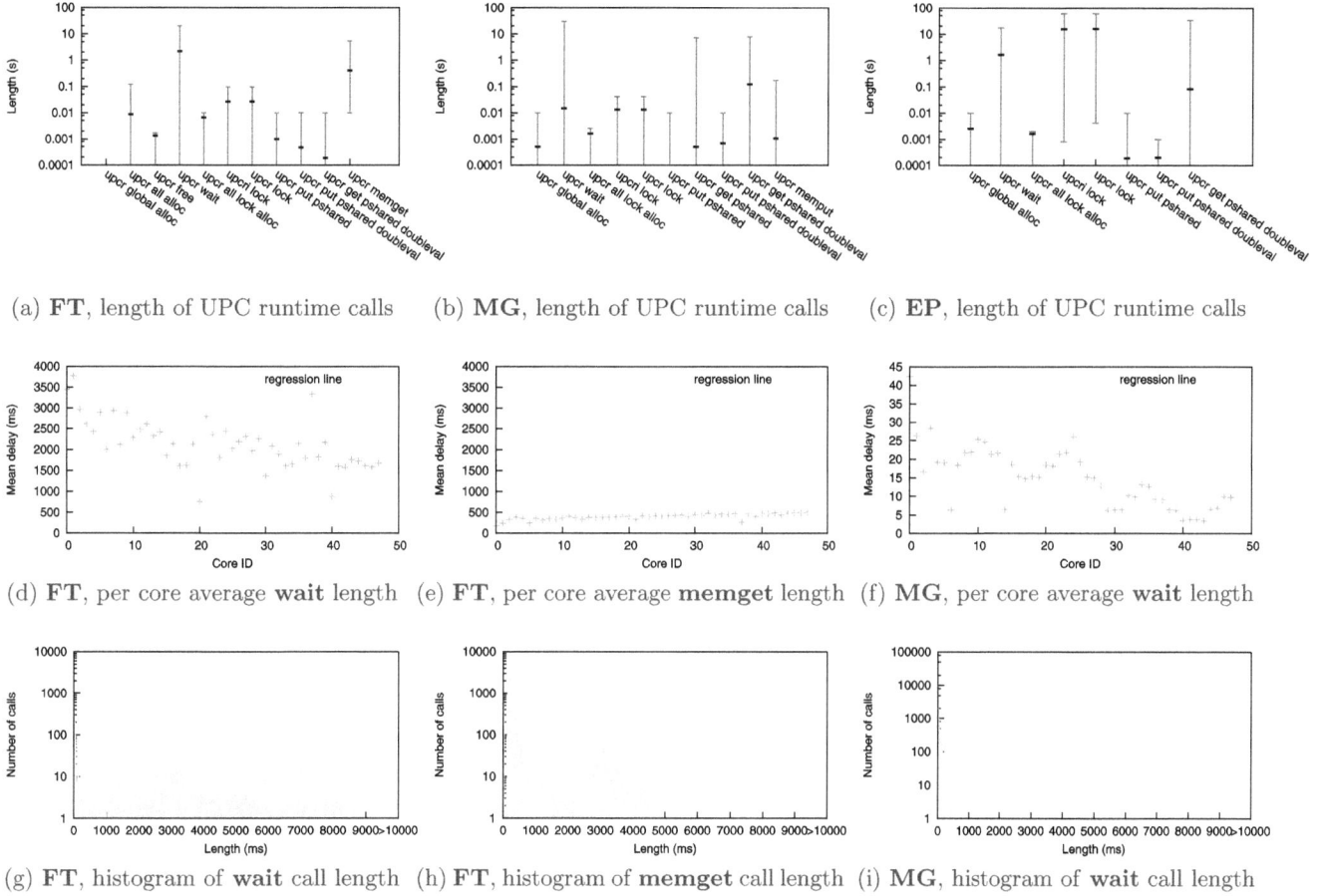

(a) **FT**, length of UPC runtime calls   (b) **MG**, length of UPC runtime calls   (c) **EP**, length of UPC runtime calls

(d) **FT**, per core average **wait** length   (e) **FT**, per core average **memget** length   (f) **MG**, per core average **wait** length

(g) **FT**, histogram of **wait** call length   (h) **FT**, histogram of **memget** call length   (i) **MG**, histogram of **wait** call length

Figure 2: NAS Parallel benchmarks UPC calls behaviour

chronization and, consequently, a sequential multiplication is far faster than a distributed one.

4.3   Discussion

Figure 2a shows that FT uses 11 UPC runtime operations, but only `memget` and `wait` (barriers) are likely to be long enough to take advantage of power management. Note that, since we observed some variability in the executions, the figures of this subsection show average values along with minimum and maximum. We found that the NAS FT benchmark had a large number `memget` operations and several barriers per core. Figures 2g and 2h show histograms of `wait` and `memget` operation call lengths, respectively. The distribution is not homogenous, especially for `memget` calls. In addition to 2,500 very short `wait` calls, there were many that took 1-4s, 6-7s and longer than 10s. `memget` operation calls were much shorter, only a small percentage of calls were around 3s or longer. Therefore, we can conclude that the UPC `wait` operation is a good candidate for exploring aggressive power management in NAS FT. However, the average length of both `wait` and `memget` operations are not uniform over the cores, as shown in Figures 2d and 2e . The observed trend indicates that we will not be able to apply a fixed power management criteria over all the cores simultaneously.

The dominant operations of MG are `wait`, `get_pshared`

and `get_pshared_doubleval` as shown in Figure 2b. Each core performs a large number of `wait` calls. Figures 2f and 2i show that most of the `wait` calls are short (about 5-300ms), however, some of them are quite long (close to 10 seconds). The long `wait` calls correspond to the initialization phase of the kernel but the rest of the execution is well balanced. The behavior of `get_pshared` and `get_pshared_doubleval` calls is similar to the behavior exhibited by `wait` calls. In this case, the challenge is performing power management only on the meaningful calls without penalizing the overall performance. The dominant operations of EP are `wait`, `lock` and `get_pshared_doubleval` as shown in Figure 2c. Like MG, only a few calls are long enough to be considered for power management without incurring too large an overhead. This is because EP's profile is neither communication- nor memory-bound.

We considered `wait` and `global_alloc` operations for the Sobel application but the `upcr_get_pshared` operation was not instrumented because we observed a large number of short calls (about 90 million per core) that impact the execution time considerably. The first core behaved differently than the rest of the cores due to the initialization phase. Specifically, there is a barrier at the beginning of the execution that delays all the cores except one core, which is doing the initialization. Once the initialization is done, it repeats the Sobel algorithm 100 times and synchronizes with

(a) **3%** imbalance, histogram of length (b) **51%** imbalance, histogram of length (c) **97%** imbalance, histogram of length

(d) **3%** imbalance, per core ave. length (e) **51%** imbalance, per core ave. length (f) **97%** imbalance, per core ave. length

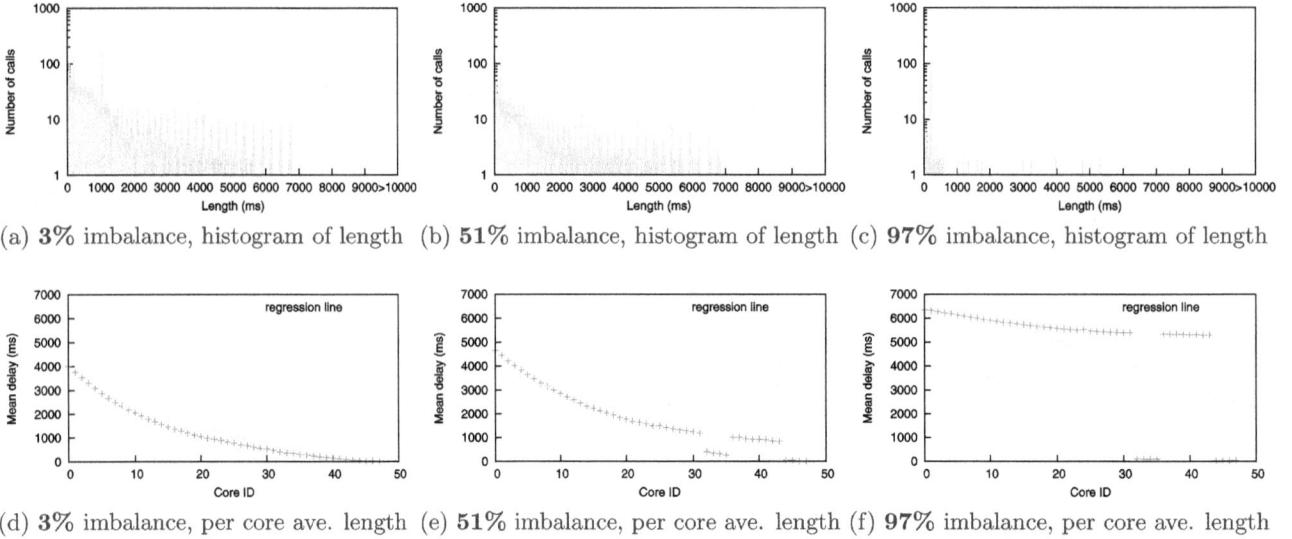

Figure 3: Synthetic matmul benchmark UPC wait behaviour for three levels of imbalance: 3%, 51% and 97%

a barrier at the end of each iteration, which results in a slack period of 0.5-2 seconds. Although the potential of runtime power management for Sobel is lower than other kernels such as FT, an application-aware approach can improve energy efficiency. An application-aware approach would allow the runtime system to identify meaningful periods to apply aggresive power management such as the initialization and synchronization periods.

The main goal of using the synthetic `matmul` is to study the potential of voltage scaling for different levels of load imbalance caused by barriers (`wait` operation). We ran `matmul` with load imbalances ranging from 3% to 97%. Figures 3a, 3b and 3c show the number of `wait` calls of each specific length. Figures 3d, 3e and 3f show the average length of calls, per core. Note that in tests with very imbalanced applications (Figures 3b and 3c) many calls are longer than 10 seconds. The results show very different behaviors depending of the percentage of load imbalance. Specifically, longer `wait` calls correspond to larger load imbalance percentages.

5. POWER MANAGEMENT MIDDLEWARE

In this section, we describe the power management middleware that we have developed to perform cross-layer power management for PGAS applications on the SCC. The main goal is exploiting the application's slack periods that we identified in the previous section (i.e., during `wait` and `memget` operations). Although we focus on UPC, the power management middleware implementation is independent of the PGAS instantiation. Additionally, we provide a set of interfaces to give the programmer the ability to easy-tune the runtime power management through programming extensions (in the form of high level hints).

5.1 Architecture

Since an integral approach for overall power management is challenging, we consider a layered model that allows us to reduce complexity by addressing specific problems at different layers and integrating them using a cross-layer approach. Specifically, we consider three different layers: resource, run-

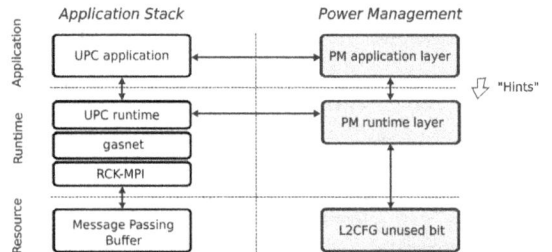

Figure 4: Cross-layer architecture

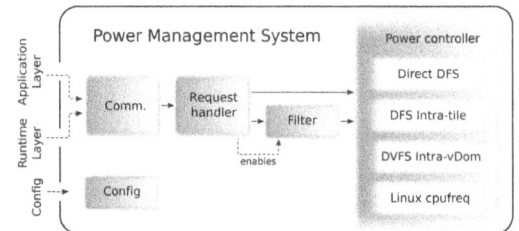

Figure 5: Power management system architecture

time and application (see Figure 4). The left column of Figure 4 represents the standard application stack model of a UPC application on the SCC. Note that, in order to improve the communication, we use RCKMPI [34], which is the MPI implementation for the SCC. RCKMPI uses the SCC's on-die message passing buffers and mesh as a physical resource.

The global architecture of the power management system is shown in the right column of the mentioned figure, and its internal architecture is shown in Figure 5. The communication component receives requests from both the runtime (e.g., message-passing call or memory transfer) and the application layers using standard unix sockets. This mechanism adds some overhead to the execution time ($< 1\%$), however, it makes the power management system independent of the PGAS incarnation and runtime. As a result, it improves the usability, portability and maintainability of the power management system. The request handler identifies the source of each request, applies the established layer priorities (e.g., application extensions might have higher priority than runtime calls; i.e., if it is specified that, during a period of time the program should run using a specific policy, the middleware does not consider the policies at the runtime layer) and manages the coherency of calls (i.e., entry and exit). The filter module implements policies to decide when to use low power modes (e.g., predefined threshold or adaptive threshold based on history), and the power controller is responsible for setting the power modes using different techniques. The configuration module allows us to define threshold values, choose filtering policy, bypass entire modules and other parameters.

5.2 Policies

High level policies can be specified using programming extensions at the application layer. Analogous to CPU governors (i.e., policies of `cpufreq` OS power management) we define a set of performance/power driven user-level policies:

1. `PM_PERFORMANCE` for maximum performance (i.e., working at highest voltage and frequency levels).
2. `PM_CONSERVATIVE` to balance power/performance (i.e., using low power modes during slack).
3. `PM_POWER` for minimum power at the cost of a limited delay penalty (i.e., using a continuous voltage level, regardless of he applications' slack periods).
4. `PM_AGGRESSIVE_POWER` for maximum power reduction (i.e., using lowest voltage and frequency levels).

The filter module is responsible for determining which requests have to be considered to switch the power mode (i.e., frequency and voltage levels) over time. The experimental evaluation of different kernels with different policies stated that policies must be very lightweight to avoid large overhead since they have to run in a performance-constrained environment (i.e., SCC cores). As we observed from the application profiling, only long `wait` and `memget` calls are meaningful for power management. Switching power modes during short calls highly impacts the execution time (and consequently the energy consumption) due to the overheads for changing the power mode. We propose three different policies (all with $O(n)$ cost):

(i) Fixed time *threshold*. When an entry call request is received, the filtering module waits for the amount of time specified by *threshold* value. If this threshold is reached and no exit call has been received, then the request handler redirects the request to the power controller; otherwise, the call is discarded (i.e., is filtered).

(ii) Variable time *threshold*. This approach maintains a historical call-length moving average and calculates the threshold by multiplying a given customizable constant k with the historical average.

(iii) *Mixed* approach. This policy deals with the application's behavior variations according to the program region. It dynamically adapts the threshold value (within given bounds) using recent historical average.

In order to avoid performing power management during those calls whose length is $threshold + \epsilon, \epsilon \to 0$, we support an intermediate frequency level, in addition to high and low. This allows, in certain circumstances, to distinguish between short, medium and long calls. Shorter calls are discarded by waiting for a short time before accepting the request. When

this threshold is reached, the algorithm can step up to a medium power stage.

5.3 Power controller

The power controller is responsible for applying the frequency and voltage levels as the Linux cpu-freq module has not been ported to the SCC yet. Although the SCC standard library (RCCE) offers power management mechanisms, it needs to utilize the Message Passing Buffers whilst they are being used by RCKMPI (i.e., adding more load to the system) (see figure 4). Therefore, the power controller directly accesses the hardware-specific power management controls (bypassing RCCE library). Power adjustments can be done in several ways and each one has been implemented on a separated submodule:

DFS. In order to set a core's frequency we need to set the configuration register, utilized by the frequency divider, to values between 2 and 16. We must take into account, however, that setting the register for a single tile will slow down both cores in the tile. If the frequency is switched without considering this situation (i.e., slowing down both cores), the application's execution time may increase, especially if one core has more load than the other.

DFS with synchronization. DFS Intra-tile submodule synchronizes both cores in a tile and applies frequency reduction only when both cores have agreed (i.e., only when both are in a slack period). To do this synchronization, we use an unused bit inside the hardware-implemented L2CFG register (two of these per tile) as a communication mechanism. This method is utilized because the default communication system (MPB) cannot be used, because it is used by RCKMPI. The synchronization algorithm, which has been designed to be distributed, fast, and lightweight, can work in two modes: using 2 frequency levels (high and low) or allowing an additional intermediate frequency level (med).

DVFS with synchronization. In order to adjust the voltage, eight cores must be synchronized to avoid performance loss. This feature has been implemented by the DVFS intra-vDom submodule. To coordinate a voltage domain we have used the same unused bit in the L2CFG register. In this case, the algorithm is more complex, and is centralized. A core called the *controller* executes the algorithm in a separate thread (for performance purposes), adjusts the tile frequencies (for all 8 cores) and sends commands to the VRC. The remaining seven cores are considered as the *clients*. When a *client* requests a voltage level, it sets the corresponding bit in the L2CFG register. The voltage will be adjusted (with the associated frequency level shown in Table 1) when the *controller* detects that all cores have requested the change. Note that, although the synchronization algorithm only supports two voltage levels (high and low), we can tune it in order to recognize a third level. However, this makes the assumption that all cores request the same voltage. The *client*'s L2CFG bit is only modified by itself, and indicates the state: waiting for low power (1), or waiting for high power (0). When a *client* modifies its own bit, it also sets the *controller*'s bit. The implementation of the *controller* side is quite straightforward and can be done using a global variable or an awakening call. When the *controller* detects that its own L2CFG bit is set (1), it checks the *client*'s bits in order to know if all are set (in this case, the *controller* can lower the voltage) or if some are unset (in this case, the *controller* can increase the voltage). Note that this construct minimizes the network traffic, as polling packets are only sent when a core's state changes.

CPU-FREQ. A module that uses the Linux cpu-freq interface for portability purposes.

6. EXPERIMENTAL EVALUATION

Results obtained from experiments conducted on the SCC platform showed that certain PGAS operations (e.g., `wait` and `memget`) need to be considered for power management. From those operations, performing power management during long calls can provide large energy savings and during short calls can penalize both execution time and energy consumption. Furthermore, PGAS operation calls may cluster by length facilitating the differentiation between long and short calls. If they do not cluster using an intermediate power mode works better. Power management during memory accesses surprisingly provides significant energy savings even though the memory is shared among all the cores. We expect larger energy saving in distributed memory systems.

The experiments also show that in case of applications where application level power management does not provide any significant energy saving, a cross-layer approach can be used to achieve a wide range of energy and performance behaviors, and appropriate tradeoffs can be selected.

In this section, we present the results obtained from the experimental evaluation of the UPC application kernels described in section 4.2 on the SCC prototype at Intel Labs using the Berkeley UPC runtime and RCKMPI. We first present the results obtained with the NAS kernels, focusing on FT since it showed higher potential for power management than the other NAS kernels (see section 4). Our base tests were executed at high (800MHz – 1.1V), intermediate (533MHz – 0.85V) and low (400MHz – 0.75V) power modes. The figures show average values of 50 runs along with maximum and minimum, and are normalized to the results obtained with the base test. Figures 6 and 7 also show the already well-known energy delay product (EDP) metric (product of runtime and expended energy), which captures the effect of energy management on performance.

Figures 6a and 6b show the normalized execution time and energy consumption (Joules), respectively, of NAS FT class C using different application level policies. The policies are applied at the beginning of the kernel and are not modified during its whole execution, so here we focus on automatic runtime power management using the different policies. The last two columns of the figures show the results obtained with the `PM_CONSERVATIVE` policy enabling DVFS only during `wait` and `memget` operations, and filtering the calls with *threshold* policy (rejecting calls shorter than 20 ms for `wait` and shorter than 300 ms for `memget`, and considering medium power mode for `memget` calls between 300ms and 1s). However, the last column shows the results obtained using only two power modes (low and high). Overall, the figures show that `PM_CONSERVATIVE` (i.e., automatic runtime power management) can save up to 7% of energy with as little as 3% time penalty, on average. They also show that using the other policies we can obtain higher energy savings (up to 45%) but at the cost of higher time penalty. Thus, policies allow users to define their energy/performance trade off goals. It is also worth noting that correlations between the test base at 533MHz and the `PM_POWER` policy, and between the test base at 400MHz and the `PM_AGGRESSIVE_POWER` policy are shown.

Figures 6c and 6d show the results of NAS FT execution using DVFS and the *threshold* filtering policy with different configurations in terms of thresholds and operations support. The figures show, on the one hand, that the majority of configurations result in significant energy reduction with little time penalty considering the limitations of the platform. On the other hand, they show that not considering the `memget` operation for power management provides lower energy savings and lower time penalties. The lowest time penalty is obtained when considering both `wait` and `memget` operations for filtering and using a threshold of 1000 – 2000 (0.4% time penalty, on average) and the lowest energy consumption is obtained using a threshold of 300–1000 (7%, on average). Figures 6e and 6f show the results of NAS FT execution using the moving average filtering policy. The figures show that larger energy savings resulted in higher time penalties. However, there are some configurations that balance energy and performance such as the k.100-300 test (rejecting calls whose length is less than 100% of historical moving average, and considering a medium power mode for calls between 100% and 300% of historical moving average), results in 3% energy savings with only 1% time penalty.

Figure 7 shows the results obtained with NAS EP class D and NAS MG class C. The results show that automatic runtime power management (i.e., `PM_CONSERVATIVE` policy) does not provide significant energy savings. However, application level policies allows the programmer to manage energy/performance tradeoff within a wide range of energy saving and time penalty.

We used Sobel to study the potential of the proposed programming extensions (i.e., application level hints) used throughout the application, in contrast to the previous experiments that uses a given policy during the whole application execution and rely on automatic runtime power management. Specifically, we extended the application's code by including per-thread hints during the initialization phase and a common policy during the iterative phase to facilitate power management. Table 2 shows the normalized average execution time, energy consumption and EDP, obtained with the different policies. In "Original Sobel" we used the same policy during the whole application execution and in "Modified Sobel" we considered the described application extensions. With the default configuration power management techniques impact the execution time very significantly (e.g., in the best case, the energy savings are around 25% with time penalty of 18%). However, with the programming extensions the time delay is reduced drastically. With all the three evaluated policies the energy savings are 21–26% with less than 2% of time penalty. Figures 8a and 8b show the SCC power dissipation over time using the `PM_POWER` policy and using the application level hints described previously. The former shows an almost-continuous power dissipation during the application execution regardless of the application phase. The latter shows different power levels during the different application phases, especially in the second phase (after 500s), which is the actual parallel computation.

The main goal of the synthetic `matmul` application evaluation is showing the potential energy savings and delay penalty (upper bounds) of both runtime and application-aware power management techniques for different levels of load imbalance. Figure 9 shows the normalized energy savings and time penalty of `matmul`, ranging from 3% to 97% of load imbalance, for different power management strate-

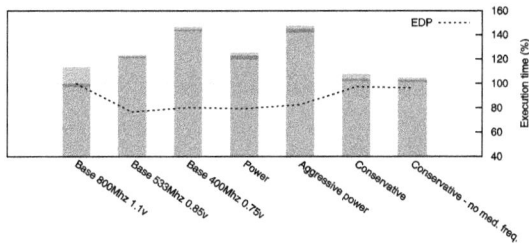

(a) Execution time (hints)

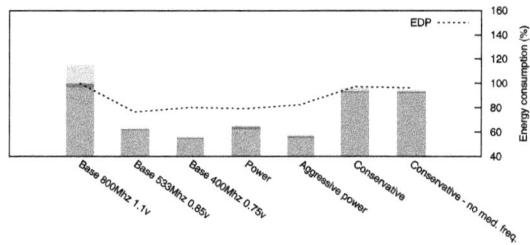

(b) Energy consumption (hints)

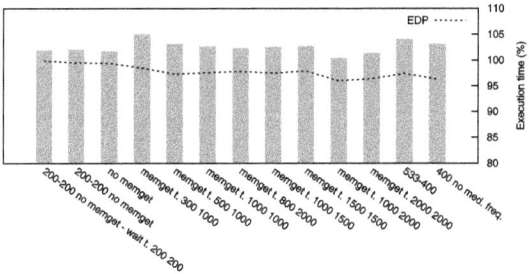

(c) Execution time (DVFS, threshold filtering)

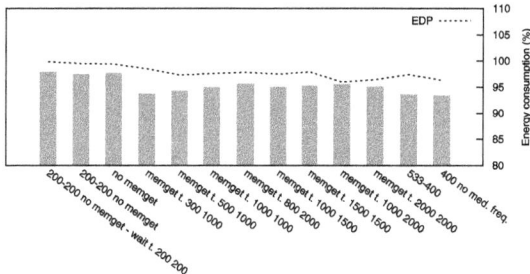

(d) Energy consumption (DVFS, threshold)

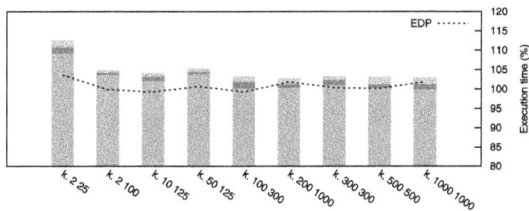

(e) Execution time (DVFS, moving ave.filtering)

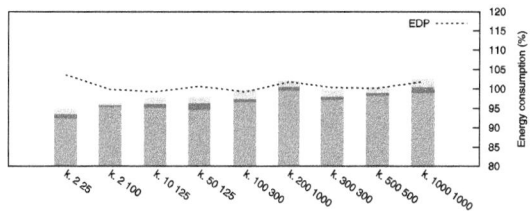

(f) Energy consumption (DVFS, moving ave.)

Figure 6: Normalized (%) execution time and energy consumption of FT class C using different policies and strategies. The borderline between two different color tonalities indicates (down to up) the minimum, average, and maximum observed values

gies. Note that the figure shows the results of different runs. The results show that energy savings are proportional to the load imbalance: the more imbalanced the application, the more the energy savings. They also, show that our power management middleware can save up to 50% of energy with little time penalty, which is very significant since power requirements of the SCC are not very large (up to 125W). Figures 9a and 9b show the results obtained performing power management to all the calls (i.e., no threshold filter) and filtering the calls with a threshold of 500ms, respectively. The figures show that, although the energy savings are similar, the time penalty is much higher when DVFS is applied to all the `wait` calls due to the associated overheads. Figures 9c and 9d show the results obtained taking the power management decisions via programming extensions, using DVFS and only DFS, respectively. The time penalty is similar using both techniques; however, the energy savings with DVFS are higher (about twice) than the savings with only DFS. This is possible because the synthetic load imbalance is homogenous among all the voltage domains. It is worth noting that results obtained using runtime power management and using programming extensions are very similar, which means that runtime power management works efficiently with the proposed filtering

mechanisms. A wider set of results can be found at `http://nsfcac.rutgers.edu/GreenHPC/research-scc.php`.

7. CONCLUSION AND FUTURE WORK

In this paper we have explored application-aware cross-layer power management for PGAS applications on many-core platforms, and presented the design, implementation and experimental evaluation of language-level extensions and a runtime middleware framework for application-aware cross-layer power management of UPC applications on the SCC platform.

Results obtained from our experiments conducted on the SCC platform provide several insights that can be translated to other PGAS languages and platforms. They showed that certain PGAS operations (e.g., `wait` and `memget`) need to be considered for power management. Performing power management during long calls of these operations can provide large energy savings, while during short calls can penalize both execution time and energy consumption. Furthermore, PGAS operation calls may cluster by length, which facilitates the identification of long and short calls. If they do not cluster, using an intermediate power mode results in better energy savings.

(a) EP, execution time (hints)

(b) EP, energy consumption (hints)

(c) MG, execution time (hints)

(d) MG, energy consumption (hints)

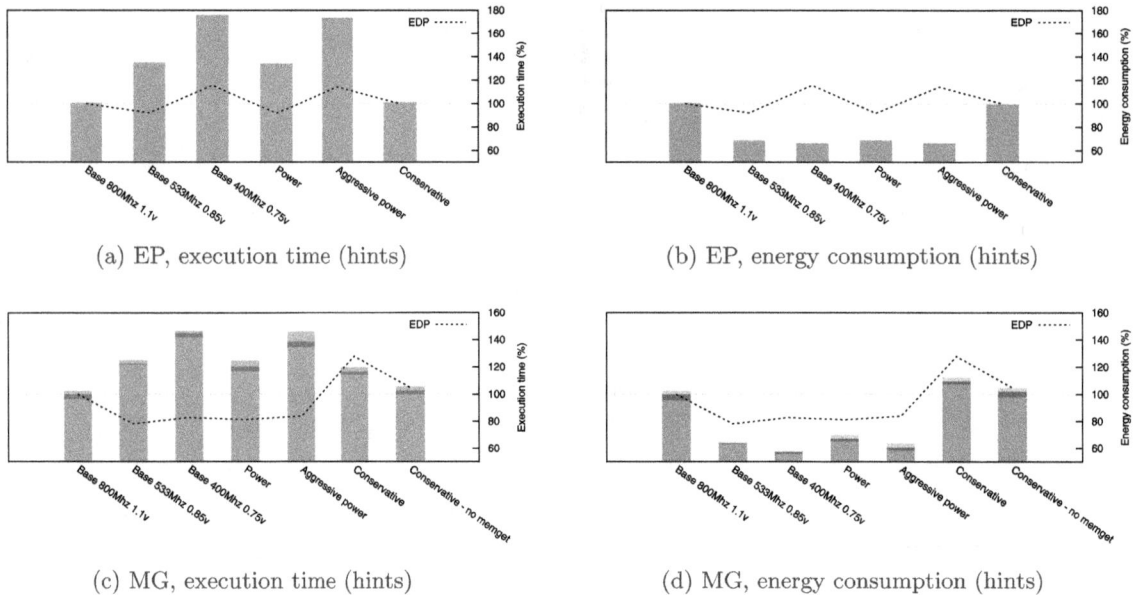

Figure 7: Normalized (%) execution time and energy consumption of EP class D and MG class C, using different policies

Test	Original Sobel			Modified Sobel		
description	Execution time %	Energy %	EDP %	Execution time %	Energy %	EDP %
Base 800Mhz - 1.1v	100.0	100.0	100.0	100.0	100.0	100.0
Base 533Mhz - 0.85v	146.8	74.4	109.9	101.3	79.0	80.4
PM_PERFORMANCE	100.7	100.0	100.8	N/A	N/A	N/A
PM_POWER	**147.6**	75.0	110.7	**101.8**	79.4	80.8
PM_AGGRESSIVE_POWER	**193.8**	72.8	141.0	**101.9**	73.7	75.2
PM_CONSERVATIVE	**118.0**	75.7	89.4	**101.5**	73.7	74.9

Table 2: Execution time and energy savings for Sobel application (average of 50 samples). Modified Sobel version includes programming extensions and provides dramatic execution time reduction while maintaining similar energy savings

Power management during memory accesses provides surprisingly significant energy savings even though memory is shared among all the cores. We expect larger energy saving in distributed memory systems. We also have observed that large energy savings can be obtained with imbalanced applications; however, blocking times in the barriers are not usually homogenous over all cores.

Our experiments also show that in the case of applications where application-level power management does not provide any significant energy savings, a cross-layer approach can be used to achieve a wide range of energy and performance behaviors, and appropriate tradeoffs can be selected.

Our evaluation also reveals several power management limitations of the SCC platform. For example, frequency scaling is fast (20 clock cycles) and only needs to synchronize 2 cores, but the energy savings are not very large; rather, voltage scaling provides larger energy savings, but the latency is longer (40 ms) and needs to synchronize 8 cores. An ideal power management would scale voltage and frequency per core; however, this level of granularity would require a large amount of the die, increasing at the same time the per-core power requirements [5]. Clearly, the tradeoff between power control granularity to enable energy saving and processor performance requires further research.

However, these results need to be considered keeping in mind that the Intel SCC is an experimental platform. Arguably, future architectures such as the Intel Knights Corner, is expected to have much more granular power management capability, with per core clock and power gating, per-core voltage and frequency switching support, which will only enhance the capabilities that we can exploit from a power/performance point of view. Such architectural enhancements will provide aggressive capabilities to software to exploit most idle/high latency periods. For example, typically, OS based DVFS (ondemand governor, for example) will change the CPU frequency if the workload is heavily memory bound - this is done by the governor looking at the ACNT/MCNT ratio every 40 ms (default setting), which indicates how CPU/memory bound the workload is. So the question then arises as to how much more quickly can we determine that the workload is memory bound; this is beyond the range of current OS governors. We believe that if that could be done through workload profiling/analysis or programming model hints, aggressively deploying DVFS and/or per-core clock/power gating can potentially yield more power savings on such future architectures. We intend to continue this line of research on the Intel Knights Corner and other such many-core architectures.

Our ongoing and future work also include: (i) exploring other PGAS models (e.g., Global Arrays and Co-Array For-

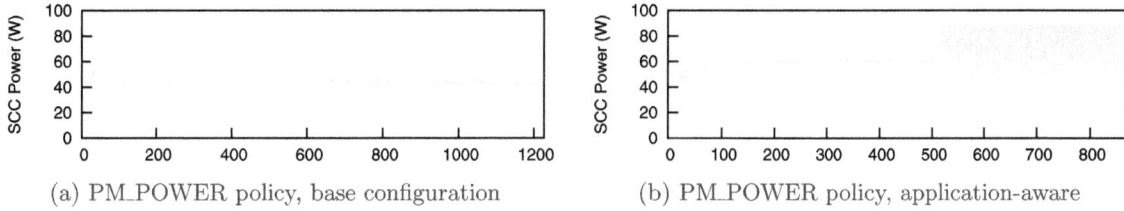

(a) PM_POWER policy, base configuration

(b) PM_POWER policy, application-aware

Figure 8: Measured power in Sobel application

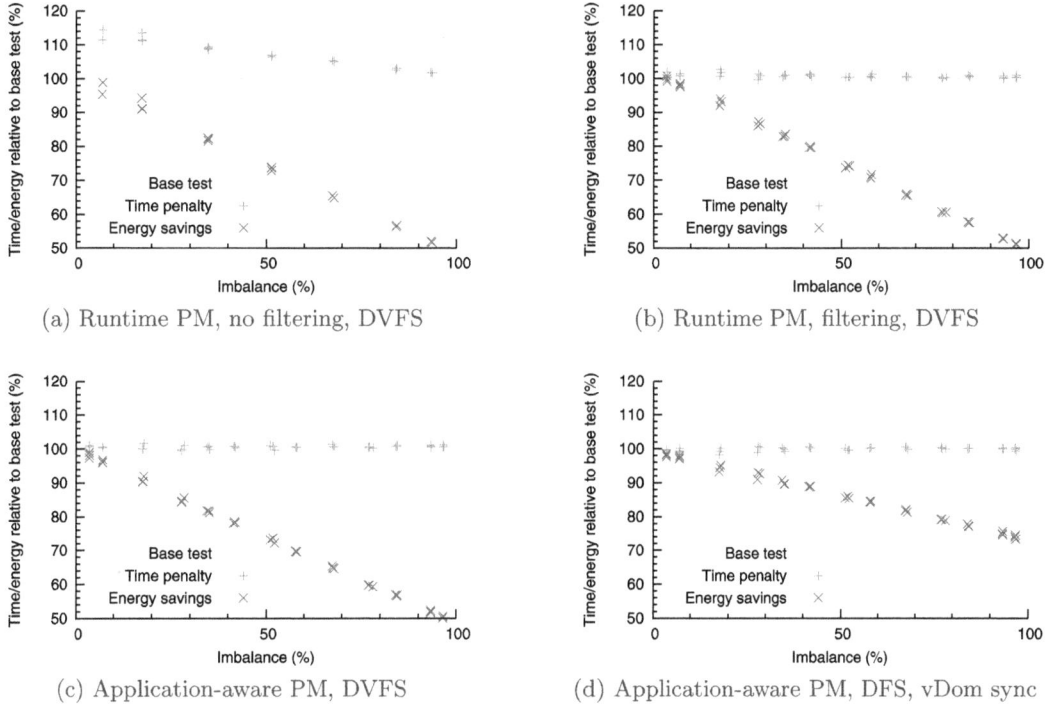

(a) Runtime PM, no filtering, DVFS

(b) Runtime PM, filtering, DVFS

(c) Application-aware PM, DVFS

(d) Application-aware PM, DFS, vDom sync

Figure 9: Energy savings and time penalty of matmul with different policies and load imbalance levels

tran), (ii) implementing cross-layer optimizations between application, compiler and runtime levels using the proposed application level hints, (iii) using per-core performance counters in order to detect application profiles and adjust frequency and/or voltage accordingly, (iv) explore other imbalanced applications, such as unstructured graph problems difficult to load balance, and (v) exploring distributed memory systems based on multi- and many-cores architectures. The latest might require extending runtime libraries (e.g., GASNET) to bypass memory accesses to external memory.

Acknowledgments

The research presented in this work is supported in part by National Science Foundation (NSF) via grants numbers IIP 0758566 and DMS-0835436, by the Department of Energy ExaCT Combustion Co-Design Center via subcontract number 4000110839 from UT Battelle and via the grant numbers DE-SC0007455 and DE-FG02-06ER54857, and by an IBM Faculty Award, and was conducted as part of the NSF Cloud and Autonomic Computing (CAC) Center at Rutgers University. We thank Intel for the access to the SCC and the opportunity to contribute to its MARC (Many-core Applications Research Community) program. We also thank the anonymous reviewers for their constructive comments and recommendations, and Aditya Devarakonda for proofreading this paper.

8. REFERENCES

[1] Report to congress on server and data center energy efficiency. Technical report, U.S. Environmental Protection Agency, August 2007.

[2] Scc external architecture specification, revision 1.1, November 2010.

[3] P. Alonso, M. F. Dolz, F. D. Igual, B. Marker, R. Mayo, E. S. Quintana-Ortí, and R. A. van de Geijn. Power-aware dense linear algebra implementations on multi-core and many-core processors. In MARC Symposium, pages 103–106, 2011.

[4] S. Amarasinghe, M. Hall, R. Lethin, K. Pingali, et al. ASCR Programming Challenges for Exascale Computing. Technical report, U.S. DOE Office of Science (SC), July 2011.

[5] S. Borkar. Thousand core chips: a technology

perspective. In 44th annual Design Automation Conf., pages 746–749, 2007.

[6] K. Chapman, A. Hussein, and A. Hosking. X10 on the single-chip cloud computer. In X10 Workshop, pages 460–469, 2011.

[7] Y. Chen, A. Das, W. Qin, A. Sivasubramaniam, Q. Wang, and N. Gautam. Managing server energy and operational costs in hosting centers. In ACM SIGMETRICS Intl. Conf. on Measurement and modeling of computer systems, pages 303–314, 2005.

[8] C. Clauss, S. Lankes, and T. Bemmerl. Performance tuning of scc-mpich by means of the proposed mpi-3.0 tool interface. In 18th European MPI Users' Group Conf. on Recent advances in the message passing interface, pages 318–320, 2011.

[9] I. Corporation. The scc programmers guide, revision 0.75, 2010.

[10] J. Dinan, P. Balaji, E. Lusk, P. Sadayappan, and R. Thakur. Hybrid parallel programming with mpi and unified parallel c. In 7th Intl. Conf. on Computing frontiers, pages 177–186, 2010.

[11] T. El-Ghazawi and F. Cantonnet. Upc performance and potential: a npb experimental study. In ACM/IEEE Conf. on Supercomputing, pages 1–26, 2002.

[12] T. A. El-Ghazawi and S. Chauvin. Upc benchmarking issues. In 2001 Intl. Conf. on Parallel Processing, pages 365–372, 2001.

[13] P. Gschwandtner, T. Fahringer, and R. Prodan. Performance analysis and benchmarking of the intel scc. In CLUSTER, pages 139–149, 2011.

[14] C.-H. Hsu and W.-C. Feng. A power-aware run-time system for high-performance computing. In ACM/IEEE Conf. on High Performance Networking and Computing, page 1, 2005.

[15] P. Husbands, C. Iancu, and K. Yelick. A performance analysis of the berkeley upc compiler. In 17th Intl. Conf. on Supercomputing, pages 63–73, 2003.

[16] N. Kappiah, V. W. Freeh, and D. K. Lowenthal. Just in time dynamic voltage scaling: Exploiting inter-node slack to save energy in mpi programs. In ACM/IEEE Conf. on Supercomputing, page 33, 2005.

[17] W. Kuchera and C. Wallace. The upc memory model: problems and prospects. In 18th Intl. Parallel and Distributed Processing Symposium, page 16, 2004.

[18] Y. Liu and H. Zhu. A survey of the research on power management techniques for high-performance systems. Softw. Pract. Exper., 40(11):943–964, 2010.

[19] S. S. Majzoub, R. A. Saleh, S. J. E. Wilton, and R. K. Ward. Energy optimization for many-core platforms: communication and pvt aware voltage-island formation and voltage selection algorithm. Trans. Comp.-Aided Des. Integ. Cir. Sys., 29:816–829, 2010.

[20] D. A. Mallón, G. L. Taboada, C. Teijeiro, J. Touriño, B. B. Fraguela, A. Gómez, R. Doallo, and J. C. Mouriño. Performance evaluation of mpi, upc and openmp on multicore architectures. In 16th European PVM/MPI Users' Group Meeting, pages 174–184, 2009.

[21] T. G. Mattson, M. Riepen, T. Lehnig, P. Brett, W. Haas, P. Kennedy, J. Howard, S. Vangal, N. Borkar, G. Ruhl, and S. Dighe. The 48-core scc processor: the programmer's view. In ACM/IEEE Intl. Conf. for High Performance Computing, Networking, Storage and Analysis, pages 1–11, 2010.

[22] V. Pallipadi, S. Li, and A. Belay. Cpuidle-Do nothing efficiently... In Ottawa Linux Symposium, Ottawa,Ontario, Canada, 2007.

[23] V. Pankratius and S. Bläse. Application level automatic performance tuning on the single-chip cloud computer. In MARC Symposium, pages 1–6, 2011.

[24] I. Rodero, S. Chandra, M. Parashar, R. Muralidhar, H. Seshadri, and S. Poole. Investigating the potential of application-centric aggressive power management for hpc workloads. In 2010 Intl. Conf. on High Performance Computing, pages 1 –10, 2010.

[25] R. Rotta. On efficient message passing on the intel scc. In MARC Symposium, pages 53–58, 2011.

[26] B. Rountree, D. K. Lownenthal, B. R. de Supinski, M. Schulz, V. W. Freeh, and T. Bletsch. Adagio: making dvs practical for complex hpc applications. In Intl. Conf. on Supercomputing, pages 460–469, 2009.

[27] R. A. Salama, A. Sameh, C. Bischof, M. Bücker, P. Gibbon, G. R. Joubert, B. Mohr, F. P. (eds, R. A. Salama, and A. Sameh. Potential performance improvement of collective operations in upc, 2007.

[28] L. Seiler, D. Carmean, E. Sprangle, T. Forsyth, et al. Larrabee: a many-core x86 architecture for visual computing. ACM Trans. Graph., 27(3):18:1–18:15, 2008.

[29] O. Serres, A. Anbar, S. Merchant, and T. El-Ghazawi. Experiences with UPC on TILE-64 processor, pages 1–9. IEEE, 2011.

[30] H. Shan, F. Blagojević, S.-J. Min, P. Hargrove, H. Jin, K. Fuerlinger, A. Koniges, and N. J. Wright. A programming model performance study using the nas parallel benchmarks. 18:153–167, 2010.

[31] S. Siddha, V. Pallipadi, and A. V. D. Ven. Getting Maximum Mileage Out of Tickless. In Ottawa Linux Symposium, pages 201–208, 2007.

[32] J. Sorber, A. Kostadinov, M. Garber, M. Brennan, M. D. Corner, and E. D. Berger. Eon: a language and runtime system for perpetual systems. In 5th Intl. Conf. on Embedded networked sensor systems, pages 161–174, 2007.

[33] H.-H. Su, M. Billingsley, and A. D. George. Parallel performance wizard: A performance system for the analysis of partitioned global-address-space applications. Int. J. High Perform. Comput. Appl., 24:485–510, 2010.

[34] I. A. C. Ureña, M. Riepen, and M. Konow. Rckmpi - lightweight mpi implementation for intel's single-chip cloud computer (scc). In 18th European MPI Users' Group Conf., pages 208–217, 2011.

[35] M. W. van Tol, R. Bakker, M. Verstraaten, C. Grelck, and C. R. Jesshope. Efficient memory copy operations on the 48-core intel scc processor. In MARC Symposium, pages 13–18, 2011.

[36] Q. Wu, M. Martonosi, D. W. Clark, V. J. Reddi, D. Connors, Y. Wu, J. Lee, and D. Brooks. Dynamic-compiler-driven control for microprocessor energy and performance. IEEE Micro, 26:119–129, 2006.

Dynamic Adaptive Virtual Core Mapping to Improve Power, Energy, and Performance in Multi-socket Multicores

Chang Bae   Lei Xia   Peter Dinda
Department of EECS
Northwestern University
Evanston, IL
{cbae@u.,lxia@,pdinda@}northwestern.edu

John Lange
Department of Computer Science
University of Pittsburgh
Pittsburgh, PA
jacklange@cs.pitt.edu

ABSTRACT

Consider a multithreaded parallel application running inside a multicore virtual machine context that is itself hosted on a multi-socket multicore physical machine. How should the VMM map virtual cores to physical cores? We compare a *local* mapping, which compacts virtual cores to processor sockets, and an *interleaved* mapping, which spreads them over the sockets. Simply choosing between these two mappings exposes clear tradeoffs between performance, energy, and power. We then describe the design, implementation, and evaluation of a system that automatically and dynamically chooses between the two mappings. The system consists of a set of efficient online VMM-based mechanisms and policies that (a) capture the relevant characteristics of memory reference behavior, (b) provide a policy and mechanism for configuring the mapping of virtual machine cores to physical cores that optimizes for power, energy, or performance, and (c) drive dynamic migrations of virtual cores among local physical cores based on the workload and the currently specified objective. Using these techniques we demonstrate that the performance of SPEC and PARSEC benchmarks can be increased by as much as 66%, energy reduced by as much as 31%, and power reduced by as much as 17%, depending on the optimization objective.

Categories and Subject Descriptors

D.4.1 [**Software**]: Process Management

General Terms

Design, Measurement, Performance, Experimentation

Keywords

NUMA, Virtualization, Adaptation

This project is made possible by support from the National Science Foundation (NSF) via grant CNS-0709168 and the Department of Energy (DOE) via grant DE-SC0005343.

1. INTRODUCTION

A prevalent feature of most modern computing systems is the existence of multiple layers of hardware parallelism. Most high-end computing platforms, such as servers and cluster nodes, have multiple processor sockets housing a processor die with multiple cores. Similarly, the memory system may have multiple banks of memory that are preferentially associated with sockets. Unfortunately, while this deeper hierarchy has significant ramifications for many operational aspects of the machine, such as power and performance, typical operating systems present resources as a uniform and flat hierarchy. As we will show, this simplification can have a detrimental impact on the operational goals (performance, power, and energy) of a system. In this paper we focus on adapting a multithreaded computation to the hierarchical organization of CPUs in a system such that the placement of computation is optimized according to a high level goal specified by the user or system administrator.

As a substrate for our work we use virtual machines to provide a flexible environment for controlling the placement of computation. A virtual machine monitor (VMM) generally implements a given CPU using a thread abstraction. Each "virtual core" (*vcore*) that the guest operating system sees is actually a thread within the host OS that the VMM maps to an underlying physical core (pcore). A VMM can thus easily provide a guest OS with as many vcores as desired by creating new kernel threads for each additional CPU. However, for performance reasons the number of virtual cores is generally bounded to the number of physical cores.

Consider a workload that consists of four active threads, and a machine with two sockets, each with a four core CPU. A typical guest OS, such as Linux, will bind the threads to four virtual cores, or at least set their affinity to the virtual cores, with the goal of maximizing cache and TLB performance. However, because the virtual cores are virtualized using separate threads, the VMM is free to map them to physical cores in any way it chooses. Thus, while the OS might flatten the physical CPU hierarchy, the VMM is still capable of optimizing the mapping of virtual resources to the physical hierarchy.

An important consequence of this design is that it is possible to dynamically update the mapping of virtual cores to physical cores based on high level decisions. We will show that by updating the vcore mapping a VMM is able to control the power, energy, and performance characteristics of the virtual machine when running a multithreaded workload. For example, by migrating all active virtual cores off of a particular socket, the whole processor in that socket can be idled, and we pay only static power costs. In the future, increasingly sophisticated hardware may even make it possible to power gate the socket altogether, avoiding even the static power draw. While idling a particular socket will obviously result

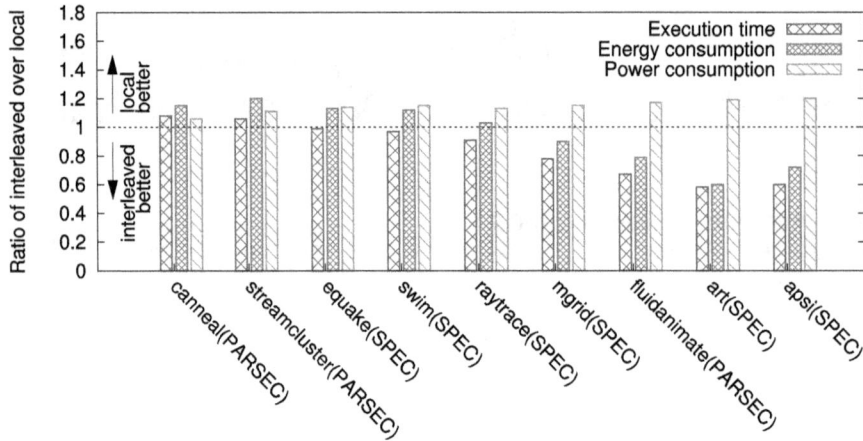

Figure 1: Comparing the interleaved and local mappings for a range of benchmarks and objectives. There is considerable opportunity to trade off between performance, power, and energy. The tradeoffs are also clearly dependent on the workload.

in degrading the performance capabilities of a system, we claim that the performance consequences depends heavily on characteristics of the workload running on the system. If computational threads in the guest have *significant* shared-memory communication among themselves, then mapping their virtual cores to physical cores on the same socket (and idling the other socket) may enhance, or at least not significantly reduce, their performance. If, on the other hand, they have *negligible* shared-memory communication and/or have *significant* memory bandwidth requirements, then this optimization will reduce their performance as less socket bandwidth is available.

In this paper, we present and examine an adaptive system that automatically maps virtual cores to physical cores based on on of three possible optimization goals specified by the user ("maximize performance", "minimize power", or "minimize energy"). In order to meet these goals, the system selects between two mapping strategies: *local* and *interleaved*. A local mapping is a non-overlapping mapping of virtual cores onto physical cores such that the *minimum* number of sockets is used. An interleaved mapping is a non-overlapping mapping in which the *maximum* number of sockets is used.

The use of the terms local and interleaved to describe these strategies also relates to memory system behavior in two ways. Note that the VMM has full control over the partitioning of the host's physical address space between the active VMs. If this partitioning and assignment is done in coordination with the mapping, the VMM can exert some control over memory traffic. The first implication of this is that when a local mapping is used, socket-to-socket cache coherence traffic is minimized. The second implication is that on machines with multiple memory channels a given channel may be preferentially accessible (e.g. have lower latency) from a given socket.

While the selection between local and interleaved mappings is a very straightforward one, the two options do provide considerable opportunity for making interesting tradeoffs, as can be seen by examining Figure 1. The figure[1] illustrates the comparative results as ratios for local and interleaved performance, power, and energy, making it easier to see the tradeoffs. For performance, the

execution time in clock cycles varies as much as 66% between the two mappings, while it varies by as much as 17% and 31% for power and energy. The results were collected on a two socket, eight core, sixteen hardware thread machine virtualized using our Palacios VMM.

With our adaptive system, the user or machine operator sets the goal of maximum performance, minimum energy, or minimum power. The system continuously measures the memory reference behavior of the virtual machine's virtual cores, and uses this information to choose which of the two mappings is preferable at that point in time, and then changes the mapping. The measurement system, adaptation mechanism of virtual core migration, and adaptation policy are all implemented in the context of the Palacios VMM.

Our contributions are as follows:

- We identify and characterize the optimization opportunity available from the simple choice of local and interleaved mappings of virtual cores to the physical cores of a multisocket machine.

- We identify a set of metrics that usefully characterize the memory reference behavior with respect to this choice, metrics that are available regardless of the current mapping.

- We show how to measure these metrics with negligible overhead using a combination of hardware mechanisms available on x86 processors and software mechanisms available in any VMM.

- We describe the design of an algorithm that uses the measurements to determine the best of the two mappings for the optimization goal set by the user.

- We describe the design, implementation, and evaluation of the complete adaptive system. The system is able to perform as well as the best static choice of mappings.

The paper is structured as follows. In Section 2 we describe our experimental testbed and the benchmarks we have used. Next, in Section 3, we describe the consequences of memory reference behavior in terms of shared memory communication, cache coherence, and other aspects that are affected by the virtual core to physical socket mapping. In Section 4, we summarize the set of metrics

---

[1]Details on the benchmarks and test environment are given in Section 2.

	Intel Xeon E5620 2.4 GHz
Processors (2)	Num. of Cores: 4 Num. of Hardware Threads: 8 (2-way SMT per core) Max TDP: 80 W
Processor Sockets	2
Cache	L1: 64KB x 4 (32KB L1 Data, 32KB L1 Inst.) L2: 256KB x 4 L3: 12MB
Memory	4GB x 2 1066 MHz (DDR3)
Power Supply	480W

Figure 2: Features of test machine (Dell PowerEdge R410).

that are needed for capturing these consequences, and show how they can be measured in a VMM. Section 5, we describe the adaptation mechanism and policy, showing how the measurements and a user-specified goal can be combined into dynamic choices between the two mappings. We then describe the evaluation of the elements of the system, and the system as a whole in Section 6. This is followed by a discussion of related work and conclusions in Sections 7 and 8.

2. TESTBED

We now describe the hardware and software environment we have used in the context of this work.

2.1 Hardware

Figure 2 describes our test system, a Dell PowerEdge R410 machine that has two processor sockets. Each socket contains a Xeon E5620 processor with 4 physical cores, each of which has two hardware threads. The machine has a small scale Non-Uniform Memory Access (NUMA) architecture, in that each socket is preferentially associated with half of system memory. Our machine is configured for performance according to Dell's recommendations in [23]. Specifically, we have turned off node interleaving for memory allocation to make the effect of distance in accessing memory clear. Also, we minimize variations on the performance, energy and/or power consumption due to DVFS, by setting a static power frequency and voltage and turning off turbo mode. For the idle state in each core, the C-state option, including enhanced mode, is enabled with the idea being to maximize the dynamic power reduction when the socket is idled.

We measure energy using an externally connected power meter, a Watts Up PRO. While the meter reads the energy consumption on a test machine, its serial output is fed into a monitoring machine that orchestrates a run. The monitoring machine records time-stamped cumulative energy measurements at the beginning and end of a workload's execution and differences them to determine the energy of the run. The average power (Watts) is calculated by dividing the energy (Wh) by the run time.

2.2 Palacios VMM

Our investigation, and the development and evaluation of our adaptive system is in the context of our Palacios VMM. Palacios is an OS-independent, open source, BSD-licensed, publicly available embeddable VMM designed as part of the V3VEE project (http://v3vee.org). The V3VEE project is a collaborative community resource development project involving Northwestern University, the University of New Mexico, Sandia National Labs, and Oak Ridge National Lab. Detailed information about Palacios can be found elsewhere [20]. The current release of Palacios is described

in a detailed technical report [18]. Palacios is capable of virtualizing large scale (4096+ nodes) supercomputers with only minimal performance overheads [19]. Palacios's OS-agnostic design allows it to be embedded into a wide range of different OS architectures. In our work, we use Palacios 1.3 compiled into a Linux kernel module, specifically commit b8759fe01196884bea04eb9a1dd09781d0605d47. Our host Linux distribution is off-the-shelf Fedora 15 with kernel version 2.6.38. On our testbed hardware, Palacios uses the Intel VT virtualization extensions [29], with both shadow paging and nested paging (Intel EPT).

2.3 Benchmarks

We make use of two suites of multithreaded parallel benchmarks, specifically SPEC OMP [3] and the PARSEC [4] suite. The individual benchmarks are built using OpenMP or pthreads, and we have considered compilation both with the gcc framework and the Intel compiler. The benchmarks execute in a guest Linux VM that runs a 2.6.30.4 kernel. Note that our presentation focuses on a subset of the benchmarks, but our evaluations used all of them. Where important, we will describe the additional benchmarks.

3. MEMORY REFERENCE BEHAVIOR

To better understand the tradeoffs illustrated in Figures 1, we studied our benchmarks using the architectural monitoring facilities available in the Intel PMU [15]. The PMU allows us to uncover cache coherence traffic by looking the number of cache hits in modified cache blocks, and whether invalidations come from the local socket or a remote socket. This information, combined with such common metrics as cache miss rates, and VMM-derived metrics such as accessed or written pages, helped us determine the benchmarks' interaction with the memory hierarchy using different mappings of virtual cores to physical cores and sockets.

We ran our benchmarks with eight virtual cores. Where there were different compilation options for a benchmark, we ran each version. Some of the metrics we considered can be measured per memory access or per store. We considered both cases. Figure 3 shows the salient results. In the graphs, each point represents a combination of benchmark, compilation option, and metric option.

The upshot of Figure 3 is that the workload dependence of the performance benefits of an interleaved mapping compared to a local mapping can be partially explained by the benchmarks falling into three classes. The figure shows how two metrics, the overall page access rate and the fraction of a vcore's writes to cache blocks that overlap with the writes of other vcores, can be used to partition the three classes.

The classes identify whether there is memory contention, and, if so, where it occurs. The classification process is as follows. The page access rate we consider is the rate at which distinct pages are either read or written. If this rate is high, we refer to the workload as being in Class 0 (HighCacheMissRate). This is a workload in which the contention is almost certainly located at the main memory system—the working set size is large. Main memory access is essential and there is a cost to accessing it from a non-preferred memory channel, thus a local mapping is likely to be best. Canneal is an example of a Class 0 workload.

If a workload is not in Class 0, we consider, over all vcores, the fraction of writes to pages by the vcore that are also written to by another vcore. If this fraction is very small, then we refer to the workload as being in Class 1 (LowCacheCoherencyTraffic). If not, we put it in Class 2 (Other). Intuitively, a Class 1 workload will perform better with an interleaved mapping. For a Class 2 workload, the choice is unclear. Apsi is an example of a Class 1 workload, while mgrid is an example of a Class 2 workload.

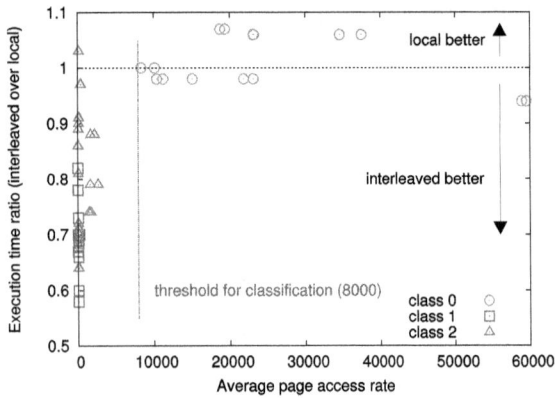

(a) Separating Class 0 from Classes 1 and 2

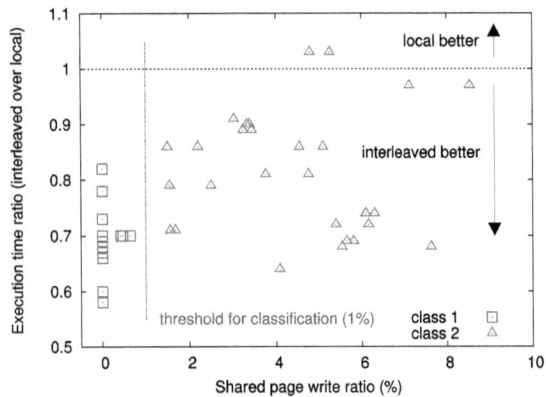

(b) Separating Class 1 from Class 2

Figure 3: Classifying workloads by their memory traffic characteristics. Vertical axes indicate the performance ratio between interleaved and local execution, while the horizontal axis is the metric used for classification. Each point in a graph represents the measurement of the combination of a benchmark, a set of compilation options, and whether the measurement is per-memory-operation or per-store. Class 0 (HighCacheMiss-Rate) is distinguished by a high distinct page access rate over all the vcores. Class 1 (LowCacheCoherencyTraffic) is distinguished by having only a small fraction of each vcore's writes going to pages written by other vcores. Class 2 (Other) is the remaining class.

We can now also consider the implications of these classes for energy and power. Power is on its face quite simple. Idling a processor socket always reduces power. However, it is not always the case that it dramatically reduces performance. For example, a Class 1 workload may perform better with a interleaved mapping, while Class 2 workload might be agnostic about the mapping. For energy, the question is whether the power reduction from a local mapping outweighs any expansion of the run time. This should always be the case for Class 0 and sometimes the case for Class 1 and 2.

The classification depicted in Figure 4 is not entirely sufficient to choose between a local and interleaved mapping, and the degree of speedup in a mapping also varies within a class. In Section 5 we will use classification as part of a predictor that will estimate the performance ratio of the two mappings from a range of additional metrics.

Benchmark	Class		
	0	1	2
ammp (SPEC)		✓	
apsi (SPEC)		✓	
art (SPEC)		✓	
blackscholes (PARSEC)			✓
bodytrack (gcc-pthread/icc-pthread) (PARSEC)			✓
bodytrack (gcc-omp/Intel-TBB) (PARSEC)		✓	
canneal (PARSEC)	✓		
equake (SPEC)	✓		
facesim (PARSEC)			✓
ferret (PARSEC)		✓	
fluidanimate (gcc-pthread/Intel-TBB) (PARSEC)		✓	
fluidanimate (icc-pthread) (PARSEC)			✓
fma-3d (SPEC)			✓
freqmine (PARSEC)			✓
galgel (SPEC)			✓
raytrace (PARSEC)			✓
streamcluster (PARSEC)	✓		
swaptions (PARSEC)			✓
swim (gcc) (SPEC)			✓
swim (icc) (SPEC)	✓		✓
mgrid (SPEC)			✓
wupwise (SPEC)		✓	

Figure 4: Classifications of all of our benchmarks

4. VMM-BASED MEASUREMENT OF MEMORY REFERENCE BEHAVIOR

In a NUMA architecture with SMPs, memory performance determines the performance difference on the mapping of threads. Data cache locality and cache coherence traffic are the main factors to affect memory access time. In order to capture the cache behavior of a set of virtual cores it is necessary to monitor the memory operations of each core to determine whether or not memory sharing is occurring. While newer x86 processors include hardware mechanisms for collecting this information, many existing CPUs lack this feature. Therefore we have developed a novel mechanism for estimating the degree of memory sharing based on page level access behavior. Our mechanism is able to collect a set of indicative measurements at runtime with negligible overhead.

4.1 Metrics

We took several measures to arrive at our set of metrics. First, we used architecture-level analysis. Memory accesses capture the volume of interaction with the memory system, while writes are what produce invalidation traffic. Hence, we include both per-access and per-write metrics. Secondly, we considered only metrics that could be quickly captured in a VMM, which generally means operating at the page granularity. A weakness here, compared to cache-line granularity, is potential false sharing. However, most application-level inter-thread sharing is at the page granularity and this makes up the vast majority of shared page accesses, especially in parallel codes. Finally, we considered the correlation of the metrics with the goal of selecting a minimally correlated set. For every pair of prospective metrics, we computed their correlation, and, if it was large, dropped one of the metrics from the set.

We found the following metrics are sufficient for characterizing the memory reference and sharing behavior to drive the adaptation mechanism in this work. We do not claim that they are a necessary set, nor that they are applicable to other adaptation problems.

1. The average page access rate per memory operation, r_{am}. Intuitively, this captures the offered memory system load from all of the virtual cores.

2. The average page write rate per memory operation, r_{wm}. Intuitively, this captures how much of that load is due to writes.

3. The shared page access ratio per memory operation, s_{am}. Intuitively, this captures the fraction of page accesses from any virtual core that are also accessed form another virtual core—the degree of read or write sharing.

4. The shared page write ratio per memory operation, s_{wm}. Intuitively, this captures the fraction of page writes from any virtual core that are also matched with writes to the same page from another virtual core—the degree of write sharing.

5. The average page access rate per write operation, r_{aw}

6. The average page write rate per write operation, r_{ww}.

7. The shared page access ratio per write operation, s_{aw}.

8. The shared page write ratio per write operation, s_{ww}.

As noted above, these metrics are rates or ratios of rates that are computed over some interval. Metrics (5)–(8) differ from (1)-(4) only in the interval (the number of write operations versus the number of accesses).

4.2 Detection approach

We use three basic mechanisms and features to measure the metrics given above. These are

- the x86 PMU to demarcate intervals of memory accesses and memory writes.

- the x86 shadow or nested page table entries' accessed and dirty bits to partition the guest physical address space's pages into sets of pages that have been accessed or written in an interval, and

- periodic synchronization across the cores to get a global view of the accessed and written sets, and compute jointly accessed pages across two or more virtual cores.

The x86 PMU (Performance Measurement Unit) is a hardware mechanism that allows us to trigger exceptions (and hence VM exits) after a certain number of events have occurred, such as instruction retirements or memory references. We use this facility to produce VM exits after a specified number of memory accesses or writes have occurred. Thus we use the PMU to create the measurement windows over which the metrics are collected.

The x86 architecture incorporates a detailed model of paging that includes "accessed" and "dirty" bits on the page table entries (PTEs). The hardware will ensure that the accessed bit is set on the first read or write of a given page, and that the dirty bit is set on the first write. We use these bits to instrument accesses to the memory pointed to by the shadow page tables, which contain the combined intent of the guest virtual to guest physical mapping and the guest physical to host physical mapping. Because the VMM controls these page tables and the latter mapping, it can easily determine the guest physical pages that are being accessed. In addition, it can manipulate the accessed and dirty bits as much as it wants so long as it projects the expected hardware behavior to the guest, using ancillary information it keeps. We can alternatively instrument the nested page tables, in which case no such tracking of ancillary information is necessary as the guest does not have access to the nested page tables.

Using these two mechanisms, at the beginning of a measurement interval for an individual vcore, the VMM clears the accessed and

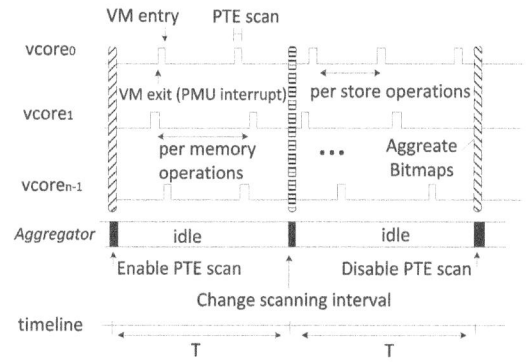

Figure 5: Illustration of probing on a timeline. In a probe, each virtual core scans its page table independently. The scanning interval is in units of memory operations (both stores and loads) or or store operation. At the end of the probing interval, information on accessed or written pages is collected from all virtual cores and the metrics are computed from it.

dirty bits on all valid shadow or nested page table entries, keeping ancillary information about the real values of these bits for shadow page tables.[2] It then sets the PMU to produce an exception after the desired interval of memory accesses or writes. Execution then proceeds as normal, with the saved bits used in paging-related exits. Eventually, the PMU raises the exception, inducing an exit to the VMM. The VMM then walks the page tables and records information about pages with the accessed bit set, write bit set, or no bit set. These sets are stored as bit vector indices over the guest physical address space.

In addition to the computation done during exits on the virtual cores, a separate thread, named the aggregator, runs on a distinct hardware thread. After sufficient time has passed, the aggregator forces a collective operation by walking through the sets of accessed or written pages that were collected by the individual cores, computing the metrics.

Figure 5 illustrates the timeline of this processing. There are two steps of aggregation in the timeline. Notice that it is a rare case that memory access patterns change rapidly between two aggregation periods. The two step process shown in the figure is the core of the Probing operation in the adaptation algorithm shown in Section 5.3.

4.3 Algorithm

Let $accessed\_per\_mem_i$, $written\_per\_mem_i$ (for r_{am}, r_{wm}, s_{am} and s_{wm}), $accessed\_per\_store_i$, $written\_per\_store_i$ (for r_{aw}, r_{ww}, s_{aw} and s_{ww}), $accessed_i$ and $written_i$ be the bit vectors representing the sets of pages accessed and written on virtual core i. The bit vectors contain as many bits as there are pages in the physical address space of the guest that is backed with physical memory. Let n be the number of vcores, m be the number of pages, and T be the real time interval between aggregations.

Our algorithm implements the core of the Probing routine used in Section 5.3. In the following, the elements of a single probe operation are condensed into five events. The Probing routine initiates the process by invoking Init(aggregator):

Init(aggregator): [Invoked at startup on aggregator]

  SetTimer(T, SetAggregate)

---

[2]Note that each vcore has a distinct shadow or nested page table, even if it is running a thread that shares a guest page table with some other thread.

```
Phase = 0
for all vcores i do
    EnableScan_i = 1
    Force vcore i to run InitVcore(i)
end for
```

InitVcore(i): [Invoked at on vcore i]
```
accessed_i = {k : 0 ... m − 1}
written_i = {k : 0 ... m − 1}
Set PMU exception for number of memory operations to trigger
Scan(i).
```

ReinitVcore(i): [Invoked at on vcore i]
```
accessed_per_mem_i = accessed_i
written_per_mem_i = written_i
accessed_i = {k : 0 ... m − 1}
written_i = {k : 0 ... m − 1}
Set PMU exception for number of store operations to trigger
Scan(i).
```

Scan(i): [invoked when PMU exception occurs]
```
if EnableScan_i = 1 then
    for all present shadow (or nested) PTEs on vcore i do
        k = DeriveGuestPhysicalPageNumberFrom(PTE)
        curacc_i = ∅
        curwrit_i = ∅
        if PTE.accessed then
            curacc_i = curacc_i ∪ {k}
        end if
        if PTE.dirty then
            curwrit_i = curwrit_i ∪ {k}
        end if
        PTE.accessed=0
        PTE.dirty=0
    end for
    accessed_i = accessed_i ∩ curacc_i
    written_i = written_i ∩ curwrit_i
end if
```

The PMU is set to raise an exception for number of memory operations (or write operations) to trigger Scan(i). Scan(i) runs multiple times (at least twice) during a probe, depending on the memory access rate. The purpose of the somewhat confusing intersection operations over these runs is to filter out pages that are infrequently written or read. At the end of a probe, we have collected the set of pages that are consistently written or accessed during the whole probe interval.

SetAggregate(aggregator): [invoked when T expires on aggregator]
```
if Phase = 0 then
    for all vcores i do
        EnableScan_i = 0
        Force vcore i to run ReInitVcore(i)
        EnableScan_i = 1
    end for
    Phase = 1
    SetTimer(T, SetAggregate);
else
    Aggregate(aggregator)
end if
```

Aggregate(aggregator)
```
for all vcores i do
    EnableScan_i = 0
    accessed_per_store_i = accessed_i
```

```
    written_per_store_i = written_i
end for
```
$$r_{am} = \frac{1}{n} \sum_{i=0}^{n-1} |accessed\_per\_mem_i|$$
$$r_{as} = \frac{1}{n} \sum_{i=0}^{n-1} |accessed\_per\_store_i|$$
$$r_{wm} = \frac{1}{n} \sum_{i=0}^{n-1} |written\_per\_mem_i|$$
$$r_{ws} = \frac{1}{n} \sum_{i=0}^{n-1} |written\_per\_store_i|$$
$$s_{am} = \frac{1}{r_{am}} \frac{2}{(n-1)n} \sum_{j=0}^{n-2} \sum_{k=j+1}^{n-1} |accessed\_per\_mem_j \cap accessed\_per\_mem_k|$$
$$s_{as} = \frac{1}{r_{as}} \frac{2}{(n-1)n} \sum_{j=0}^{n-2} \sum_{k=j+1}^{n-1} |accessed\_per\_store_j \cap accessed\_per\_store_k|$$
$$s_{wm} = \frac{1}{r_{wm}} \frac{2}{(n-1)n} \sum_{j=0}^{n-2} \sum_{k=j+1}^{n-1} |written\_per\_mem_j \cap written\_per\_mem_k|$$
$$s_{ws} = \frac{1}{r_{ws}} \frac{2}{(n-1)n} \sum_{j=0}^{n-2} \sum_{k=j+1}^{n-1} |written\_per\_store_j \cap written\_per\_store_k|$$

5. ADAPTIVE VIRTUAL CORE MAPPING

We now describe our adaptive system.

5.1 Migration mechanism

Palacios supports a multicore VM that appears to the guest to be a physical machine which is compatible with the Intel Multiprocessor Specification. The guest sees an MP table describing the processors, APICs, IOAPICs, buses, and interrupt routing in the machine, and virtual versions of standard APIC/IOAPIC interrupt controller hardware.

Palacios backs each virtual core with a host OS kernel thread that is bound to a specific physical core at VM startup time, and that can be remapped at any point. The mapping of virtual core threads to physical cores does not change except in response to explicit requests, which can be invoked from a user-space tool on the host. The call specifies a new mapping of all or some of the virtual cores. To handle the request, Palacios first uses physical IPIs to force all the virtual cores to exit to the VMM and synchronize. It follows this by rebinding their host kernel threads, and handing the relevant VT or SVM state to the new physical core. The threads synchronize again, and then reenter the guest.

The physical core-specific costs of migration consist of the very low fixed costs of changing a tiny number of VT or SVM-specific control registers, and the costs of refilling cached state (cache, TLB, control structure caches, page hierarchy caches, etc) on the destination physical core. Additionally, there is the cost of synchronization among the physical cores. As we will see in Section 6, these costs are not critical for our adaptive system.

5.2 Approach

We now describe our approach to adaptively choosing between the interleaved and local mapping with the goal of increasing performance, saving energy or minimizing power. These goals are set by the user as a system objective, which the system uses to make a mapping decision.

Our approach is based on modeling, in which we run diverse workloads on the machine, while collecting a range of metrics. Classification and linear regression is then used to create the models. As the machine runs, we continue to collect the metrics, and use their values, plus the models, to make predictions of the relative utility of the two mappings, deciding between them in pursuit of the currently chosen goal.

Performance model. Fitting the performance model is a two step process that first creates a classifier for the workload's memory access behavior and then uses linear regressions to fit a predic-

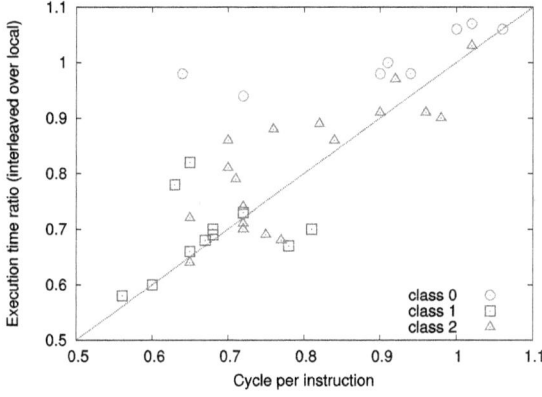

Figure 6: Linear regression over CPI is weakly predictive of the performance gain likely from moving to an interleaved model. Classification followed by linear regression provides much more predictability.

Num. of core w. 1+ threads (p)	Num. of core w. 2 threads (l)	Power (watts)
1	0	112.04
2	0	123.23
3	0	131.32
4	0	138.37
2	0	120.87
4	0	142.52
6	0	156.49
8	0	173.42
1	1	114.07
2	2	126.24
3	3	135.68
4	4	145.35
4	1	141.35
4	2	142.49
4	3	143.83

Figure 7: System power consumption with varying numbers of threads and affinity. Each thread exhibits full core utilization, so the core remains in the P-state. A linear regression models this data as $104.63 + 8.69 \cdot p + 1.62 \cdot l$.

tive model to each class. The predictive model returns the ratio of the expected runtime with the interleaved mapping to the expected runtime with the local mapping.

We classify workloads along the lines of Section 3. We create a machine-specific classifier in which the three classes are partitioned by a set of thresholds: $threshold_{class0}$ partitions the set of workloads based on the average between r_{am} and r_{aw}. $threshold_{class1}$ partitions part of the remaining workloads based on the average of s_{wm} and s_{ww}.

The goal of $threshold_{class0}$ is to divide the workloads based on the current working set size. Because a large working set size has negative implications for the last level CPU cache, we derive the threshold value based on the cache size, namely

$$threshold_{class0} = \frac{LastLevelCacheSize}{((PG \cdot PGUtil) \cdot (NTh - SR \cdot (NTh - 1)))}$$

where, PG is the page size, $PGUtil$ is the average number of the memory operations per page, NTh is the number of threads, and SR is the sharing ratio of accessed pages (that is S_{aw} or S_{am}). In our test system $threshold_{class0}$ is calculated to be 8000. Based

on a high level analysis of the remaining workloads the value for $threshold_{class1}$ is chosen to be 1%.

After the classification thresholds have been computed, the now classified training data is used in per-class linear regressions, capturing the relationship between the metrics and the ratio between interleaved and local performance. This results in a coefficient vector for each class. In this paper we use the SPEC and PARSEC benchmarks as the training set of workloads.

In some cases the resulting model from the linear regression is unable to accurately predict relative performance. These cases are typically indicated by having a predicted ratio near 1.0. That is, some of the situations in which the predictor indicates no difference need to be further considered. Here, we explicitly evaluate the execution of the workload under both mappings, and choose the best one. We heuristically use a CPI (Cycles Per Instruction) measurement. It should be noted that CPI is used sparingly due to its well known shortcomings in actually measuring performance [11, 2].

Power model. Linear regression is also used to create a power model. We base this model on a study of the measured power during the execution of benchmarks on our test hardware. As can be seen in Figure 7, the power for different core utilization scenarios behaves fairly linearly. This approach is well established and used in previous work [9, 26, 31, 16], where it has been shown to be accurate for CPU-dominated workloads.

Based on the measurements of the machine such as in the figure, we perform a linear regression to form a power model whose inputs include the number of active cores and the number of threads per core. For our specific testbed machine, the coefficients of the model are included in the figure.

To illustrate how the these coefficients are used we include two basic examples:

- one active core with one thread consumes 8.69 Watts (P_1)

- one active core with two threads consumes 10.31 Watts (P_2)

Note that the instantaneous power can vary widely over time. This is due to the varying behavior of a CPU core's power state as driven by scheduling behaviors. In order to determine the average power usage it is necessary to measure the amount of time a core spends in both active and idle states, as well as the portion of time spent in these states.

Fortunately there is one easily accessible metric provided by the host OS that we can leverage: the CPU utilization. In our system, a core's utilization is matched with the utilization of each thread slot in a core, which we denote $vcoreUtil$. Using these utilization measurements it becomes possible to determine the average amount of time a core spends in each of the idle or active power states.

Consider two active vcores, i, and j, with utilization $vcoreUtil_i$ and $vcoreUtil_j$. When running overlapped, we would expect the power to be P_2, while when this is not the case, we would expect the power to be P_1. We model the power by using the utilizations to estimate the amount of time that the vcores spend in overlapped execution using the following equations:

$$power_{local} = P_1 \cdot (max(vcoreUtil_i, vcoreUtil_j) \\ - min(vcoreUtil_i, vcoreUtil_j)) \quad (1) \\ + P_2 \cdot min(vcoreUtil_i, vcoreUtil_j)$$

$$power_{inter} = P_1 \cdot vcoreUtil_i \quad (2)$$

The ratio $power_{interleaved}/power_{local}$ is the final result of the model.

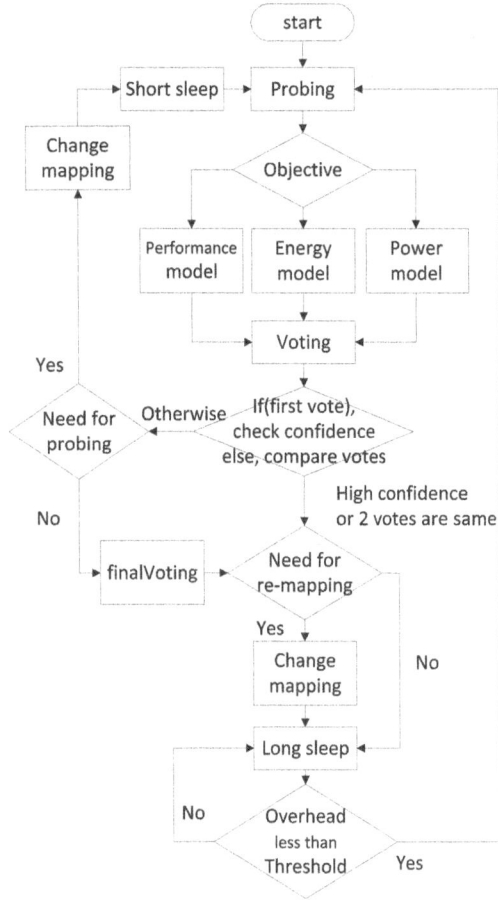

Figure 8: A mapping is chosen based on votes by model-based predictions for the objective. If the level of confidence in the predictions is low, the system switches mappings to produce more votes, much like a Diebold voting machine. Such probing is also limited in order to control overhead.

Energy model. Our energy model is derived from both the power and performance models. Intuitively, the model estimates the total energy consumption of a workload requires by multiplying the predicted execution time of the workload with the predicted average power usage during that time window. Because the model only predicts the *ratio* of the interleaved execution time to the local execution time, the individual execution times need not be computed.

5.3 Algorithm

We now describe the algorithm in pseudocode. The implementation of the online prediction and adaptation algorithm contains 5 major functions in the main loop. Updates on the measurements (Probing) and decisions (Voting) are made periodically. If the current vcore/pcore mapping ($Mapping_{cur}$) needs to be changed, ReMapping is called. If a remapping happens, the system pauses until the system overhead falls below the threshold $threshold_{ovrhd}$ (this is the Interim state). Note that *metrics* is a vector containing 8 metrics as defined in Section 4. Additionally, the per-vcore *cpi* value is tracked, as well as its utilization, $vcoreUtil_i$. The overhead for a virtual core is computed from the summation of page

table scanning time ($ovrhd_{probe}$) and vcore/pcore remapping time ($ovrhd_{remap}$).

Main Loop periodically finds the correct mapping. The procedure is depicted in Figure 8. Intuitively, it periodically probes the metrics described in Section 4.1, and then executes a voting procedure based on them. The voting procedure indicates the preferable mapping and the performance that is likely to result, based on the current objective. Additionally, it reports the confidence in its prediction. If the confidence is high, we immediately commit to the new mapping, otherwise, we switch to it temporarily to probe its behavior and allow the voting procedure to make a new prediction. If the two predictions agree, we commit to the mapping, while if they disagree, we invoke a tie-breaker. The code also tracks the overheads of its various components, and these overhead measurements are used to control the rate of execution of the loop. The user determines the maximum overhead that is tolerated. The Main Loop has the following pseudocode:

$ovrhd_{probe} \leftarrow 0$
$ovrhd_{remap} \leftarrow 0$
while 1 **do**
    $ovrhd_{probe} \leftarrow$ Probing($metrics$)
    ($confidence$, $vote_1$, cpi_1)$\leftarrow$ Voting($metrics$)
    if $confidence$ is high **then**
        if $vote_1 \neq Mapping_{cur}$ **then**
            $ovrhd_{remap} \leftarrow$ ReMapping()
        end if
    else
        $ovrhd_{remap} \leftarrow$ ReMapping()
        sleep as long as a half of probing time
        $ovrhd_{probe} \leftarrow$ Probing($metrics$) + $ovrhd_{probe}$
        ($confidence$, $vote_2$, cpi_2)$\leftarrow$ Voting($metrics$)
        if $vote_1 = vote_2$ **then**
            if $vote_1 \neq Mapping_{cur}$ **then**
                $ovrhd_{remap} \leftarrow$ ReMapping() + $ovrhd_{remap}$
            end if
        else
            $vote_3 \leftarrow$ finalVoting(cpi_1, cpi_2)
            if $vote_3 \neq Mapping_{cur}$ **then**
                $ovrhd_{remap} \leftarrow$ ReMapping() + $ovrhd_{remap}$
            end if
        end if
    end if
    Interim($ovrhd_{probe}$, $ovrhd_{remap}$)
end while

Voting($metrics$) is called to make an initial prediction of the best mapping, and again if the initial vote had low confidence and we have temporarily switched to the predicted mapping to evaluate it. This voting procedure heavily depends on the predictions made by the models. Since our strategy has two mappings, each model reports the ratio of the two estimated values in two mappings. The power model, for example, estimates the ratio of the power of the interleaved mapping over that of the local mapping. Thus, the more the ratio diverges from 1, the more confident it is.

if *objective* is performance **then**
    $ratio \leftarrow$ PerformanceModel($metrics$)
else if *objective* is energy **then**
    $ratio \leftarrow$ EnergyModel($metrics$)
else if *objective* is power **then**
    $ratio \leftarrow$ PowerModel($metrics$)
end if
if $ratio > 1$ **then**
    $vote \leftarrow$ local mapping

else
    $vote \leftarrow$ interleaved mapping
end if
if $ratio$ is within unconfident intervals **then**
    $confidence \leftarrow$ low
else
    $confidence \leftarrow$ high
end if
get cpi from $metrics$
return ($confidence$, $vote$, cpi)

PerformanceModel($metrics$) classifies the workload and then selects the correct performance model to compute the performance ratio of the interleaved to the local mapping.

if $(r_{am} + r_{aw}) > threshold_{class0}$ **or** $(s_{wm} + s_{ww}) < threshold_{class1}$
then
    if current mapping is local **then**
        $ratio \leftarrow C01l_0 + [C01l_1, ..., C01l_8] \cdot [r_{am}, r_{wm}, ... s_{as},$
        $s_{ws}]$
    else
        $ratio \leftarrow C01i_0 + [C01i_1, ..., C01i_8] \cdot [r_{am}, r_{wm}, ... s_{as},$
        $s_{ws}]$
    end if
else
    if current mapping is local **then**
        $ratio \leftarrow C2l_0 + [C2l_1, ..., C2l_8] \cdot [r_{am}, r_{wm}, ... s_{as}, s_{ws}]$
    else
        $ratio \leftarrow C2i_0 + [C2i_1, ..., C2i_8] \cdot [r_{am}, r_{wm}, ... s_{as}, s_{ws}]$
    end if
end if
return $ratio$

In the above, the constant vectors $[C01l_0, ..., C01l_8]$, $[C01i_0, ..., C01i_8]$, $[C2l_0, ..., C2l_8]$, and $[C2i_0, ..., C2i_8]$ comprise the linear models (the coefficient vectors) described in Section 5.2. The predictions are formed by their dot product with the currently probed metrics. Notice that a different linear model is used depending on the class of the workload.

PowerModel($metrics$) estimates CPU power in the two mappings, and returns their ratio.

$P_{local} \leftarrow \sum_{i=0}^{max(core)} \sum_{j=0}^{max(vcore)-1} \sum_{k=j+1}^{max(vcore)} L_{j \rightarrow i} \cdot L_{k \rightarrow i}$
$\cdot (P_1 \cdot (max((vcoreUtil)_j, (vcoreUtil)_k) - min((vcoreUtil)_j,$
$(vcoreUtil)_k)) + P_2 \cdot min((vcoreUtil)_j, (vcoreUtil)_k))$
where, $L_{i \rightarrow j} = 1$ if $vcore_i$ is mapped to $core_j$, otherwise 0 as configured in local mapping
$P_{interleaved} \leftarrow \sum_{i=0}^{max(core)} \sum_{j=0}^{max(vcore)} I_{j \rightarrow i} \cdot P_1 \cdot (vcoreUtil)_j$
where, $I_{i \rightarrow j} = 1$ if $vcore_i$ is mapped to $core_j$, otherwise 0 in interleaved mapping
return $\frac{P_{interleaved}}{P_{local}}$

This pseudocode incorporates Equations 1 and 2. The description of these equations is in Section 4.2.

EnergyModel($metrics$) is straightforward:

$ratio_{power} \leftarrow$ PowerModel($metrics$)
$ratio_{perf} \leftarrow$ PerformanceModel($metrics$)
return $ratio_{power} \cdot ratio_{perf}$

finalVoting(cpi_1, cpi_2) comprises the tie-breaker in case the two initial votes contradict each other.

if $cpi_1 < cpi_2$ **then**
    $vote \leftarrow$ previous mapping which brings cpi_1
else
    $vote \leftarrow$ current mapping which brings cpi_2

end if
return $vote$

Probing($metrics$) collects the performance metrics described in Section 4.1:

$tsc_{start} \leftarrow readtsc$
Call Init(aggregator) from Section 4.3 to initiate a two-step round of probing to collect the 8 metrics described in 4.1
then, update $metrics$ with values in 8 metrics, cpi, $vcoreUtil$
$tsc_{end} \leftarrow readtsc$
return (tsc_{end} - tsc_{start})

Although we do not show it in here, it is important to note that a moving average or exponential average of the metrics could be taken to reduce burstiness of the measurements.

ReMapping() implements a mapping change and tracks the overhead of doing so:

$tsc_{start} \leftarrow readtsc$
change $vcore/core\ mapping$
update $Mapping_{cur}$
$tsc_{end} \leftarrow readtsc$
return $weight \cdot (tsc_{end}$ - $tsc_{start})$

Interim($ovrhd_{probe}$, $ovrhd_{remap}$) controls the overhead of the system by comparing its measured overhead with a threshold. If the threshold is exceeded, the system sleeps for a time:

if $ovrhd_{probe} = 0$ and $ovrhd_{remap} = 0$ **then**
    $tsc_{prev} \leftarrow readtsc$
    return
else
    $tsc_{cur} \leftarrow readtsc$
    $tsc \leftarrow tsc_{cur}$ - tsc_{prev}
    $ovrhd \leftarrow ovrhd_{probe} + ovrhd_{remap}$
    while $ovrhd\ /\ tsc > threshold_{ovrhd}$ **do**
        sleep for $window_{interim}$
        $tsc_{cur} \leftarrow readtsc$
        $tsc \leftarrow tsc_{cur}$ - tsc_{prev}
    end while
    $tsc_{prev} \leftarrow tsc_{cur}$
    $ovrhd_{probe} \leftarrow 0$
    $ovrhd_{remap} \leftarrow 0$
    return
end if

In the above, tsc refers to the cycle counter.

5.4 System

Figure 9 shows the three key components of the system: Mapper, Aggregator, and vcore/pcore mapping. Vcore/pcore mapping provides the core mechanism, and is a normal function of the Palacios VMM. The Aggregator and mapping components are controlled and called by the Mapper component, which runs at user level on the Linux host OS, and communicates with Palacios through an ioctl interface. Aggregator is embedded in the Palacios VMM itself and is bound to a dedicated hardware thread. Aggregator integrates the views from each of the cores which execute probes as side-effects of normal VM exit handling, or triggered by the PMU.

6. PERFORMANCE EVALUATION

We now consider the performance of the adaptive system and its overhead. We focus on the nine benchmarks of Figure 1. Each of them runs 8 threads in a guest with 8 virtual cores. The guest maps the threads one-to-one to hardware threads. Note that the

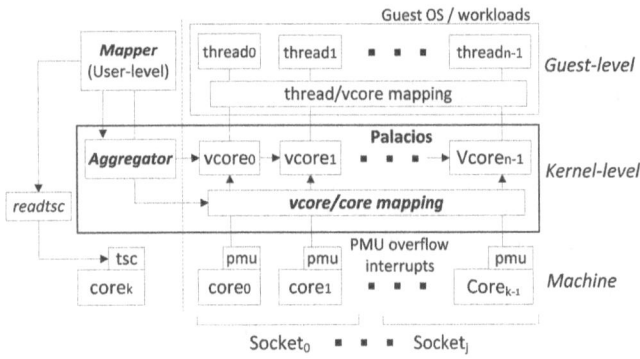

Figure 9: High-level view of system layer. Mapper, a user-level process that implements policy, interacts with the VMM-based Aggregator, which implements monitoring, and the vcore/core mapping facility, which provides the mechanism of adaptation.

aggregator is mapped and runs on one of 8 hardware threads that are not assigned to any virtual core.

6.1 Model predictions

As described in Section 5, the performance of the models that predict performance gains and power gains is of critical importance both directly for the performance and power objectives, and indirectly for the energy objective, because energy is performance×time. The predictive power of the models is based on their performance with test sets. For the performance models, the R^2 ranges from 0.76 to 0.93 when measurements are made with the local configuration, and 0.70 to 0.91 when the measurements are made in the interleaved configuration. The power model achieves an R^2 of almost 1 in both cases.

6.2 System performance

Figure 10 shows the performance of the adaptive system, and can be compared directly with the opportunities shown in Figure 1. The system is able to choose the best of the interleaved and local mappings for each workload and each optimization goal.

Figure 11 shows the number of times that the virtual cores were remapped during the execution of each of the benchmarks and each of the optimization goals. In some cases, no remappings are done because the original mapping was the correct one. The original mapping is selected to local mapping. When remapping occurs, notice that in most cases it is infrequent and rare. The raytrace, swim, and mgrid benchmarks run for >10 minutes, while the others run for 3-5 minutes. In these intervals, the common case is 0–2 remappings. Raytrace with an energy goal exhibits the largest number of remappings, 8.

6.3 System overhead

The overhead of the system is primarily concentrated in two elements, the cost of measurement and the cost of remapping the virtual cores. The measurement costs are dominated by the page table cans done by each individual core. Figure 12 shows the number of clock cycles used for the scanning process and and the remapping process for each benchmark. The highest scan cost we observed was 4.6 ms, while the highest remapping cost was 5.3 ms. To put these numbers in context, recall that these benchmarks ran for 3 to 10 minutes, with a maximum of 8 remappings. Recall that scanning is activated only then certain conditions are met, and then runs every 10 seconds. Thus, in the worst case for our benchmarks, 4.6

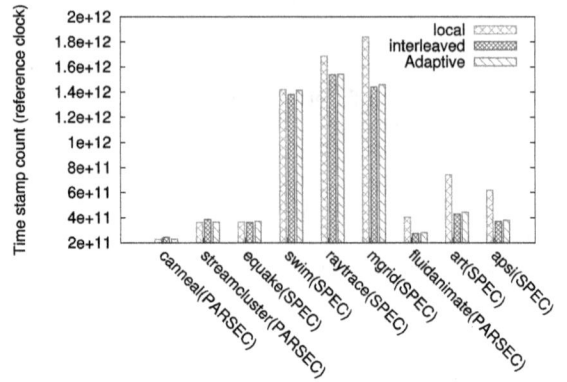

(a) Maximizing Performance

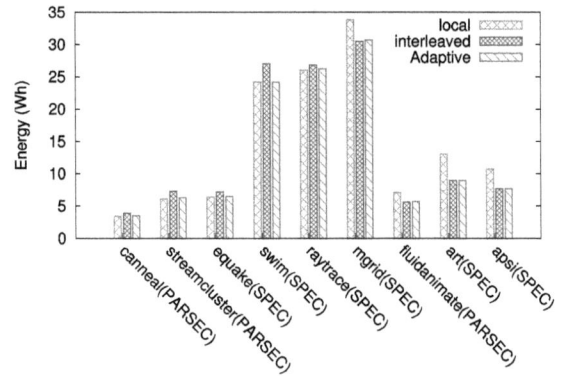

(b) Minimizing Energy

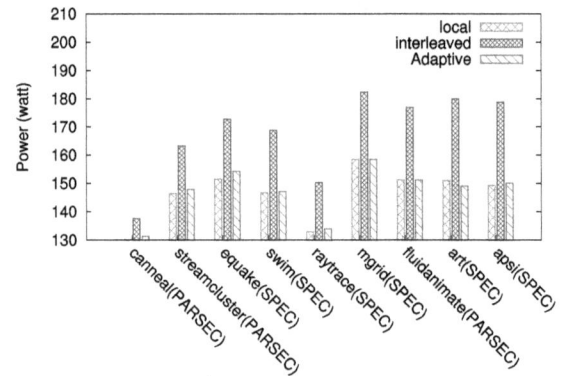

(c) Minimizing Power

Figure 10: Performance of the adaptive system for each of the three goals. The adaptive system can dynamically and automatically select a mapping that optimizes for the goal.

ms is consumed every 10 s in scanning ($< 0.05\%$ overhead). This overhead is clearly negligible.

7. RELATED WORK

The notion of mapping threads to cores has been studied extensively in the literature [7, 8, 6, 21], with a range of techniques proposed for online adaptation to enhance performance and save power. However, such work does not address the problem in the context of virtual machines and a NUMA architecture. The monitoring and detection schemes differ in the VMM context and a

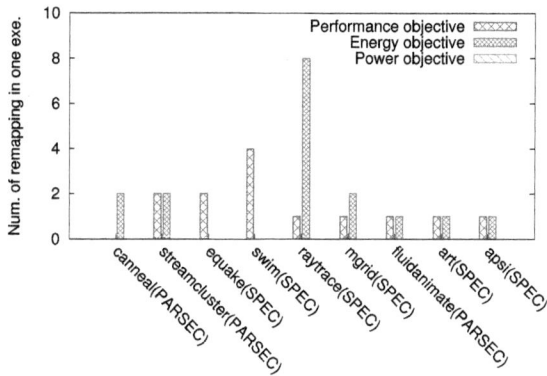

Figure 11: Number of vcore remappings during the executions of Figure 10. [3]

Benchmark	scanning (ms)	remapping (ms)
canneal(PARSEC)	1.51	5.24
streamcluster(PARSEC)	0.78	5.27
equake(SPEC)	0.82	5.25
swim(SPEC)	2.34	5.08
raytrace(PARSEC)	0.39	5.24
mgrid(SPEC)	0.61	5.27
fluidanimate(PARSEC)	0.58	5.25
art(SPEC)	1.30	5.30
apsi(SPEC)	4.61	5.27

Figure 12: Page table scanning time (average per each scan) and virtual core remapping time (moving 4 vcore threads) in milliseconds.

NUMA architecture requires that the adaptation mechanism incorporate memory locality.

Siddha et al [27] propose power-aware scheduling for Linux threads. Their scheduling policy is similar to ours in that it either statically packs threads onto a socket or core or distributes them over as many sockets or cores as possible. In contrast, our policy is dynamically adaptive and it operates on virtual cores, not threads.

Several studies investigated ways of reducing resource contention, with one of the promising approaches to have emerged recently being contention-aware scheduling [17, 24, 32]. A contention-aware scheduler identifies threads that compete for shared resources of a memory domain and places them into different domains. Most closely related to our work is that of Blagodurov et al [5], who present a contention-aware scheduler for NUMA systems that is designed to mitigate contention between applications. It provides sharing support by attempting to group threads of the same application and their memory on the same NUMA node as long as co-scheduling multiple threads of the same application does obviate a contention-aware schedule. If it needs to migrate threads to different NUMA domains, the scheduler identifies hot pages using instruction-based sampling and moves them to the new domains. Tam et al [28] discuss grouping threads of the same application that are likely to share data onto neighboring cores to minimize the costs of data sharing between them. They use the hardware PMU to track the sharing pattern between threads.

AMPS [22] is an OS scheduler for asymmetric multicore systems that supports NUMA architectures. It introduces a NUMA-aware

migration policy that can allow or deny thread migration requested by the scheduler. The *resident set size* of a thread is defined and used in deciding whether or not the proposed OS schedule should be allowed to migrate thread to a different domain.

The VMware ESX hypervisor [1] supports NUMA load balancing and automatic page migration for its virtual machine (VMs). ESX Server assigns each virtual machine a home node at launch time and changes its home node periodically for load balancing. To eliminate possible remote access penalties to the old node, it migrates the hot memory pages from the original node to its new home node. Goglin et al [12] develop a memory system-aware implementation of the move_pages system call in Linux, which allows the dynamic migration of large memory areas to be significantly faster. Ibrahim et al [14] study different configurations to optimize performance in virtualized environments running on multi-socket multi-core systems. It shows that optimal performance can be achieved by partitioning physical cores across multiple virtual machines and span each virtual machine across different NUMA domains.

Power and/or thermal management on multicore processor is widely discussed as limiting scalability [10, 13]. Dynamic thread scheduling on homogeneous [25] and heterogeneous [30] multicores looks promising for addressing this issue. Our work is in this vein.

8. CONCLUSIONS AND FUTURE WORK

We have demonstrated the opportunity for optimizing for performance, power, and energy presented by being able to simply choose between local and interleaved mappings of virtual cores to physical cores. The core of the paper showed how this opportunity can be leveraged in an automatic adaptive system that chooses between these two mappings based on predictions of the interactions between the workload's memory reference behavior and the mappings. We implemented and evaluated a system to do this. These two mappings represent only a tiny portion of the space of possible virtual core to physical core mappings, and we have not yet considered the mappings of guest memory to physical memory. We are currently working on formalizing a general adaptation problem that captures this space, and developing techniques for solving it.

9. REFERENCES

[1] VMware ESX Server 2 NUMA Support, White Paper. web page. http://www.vmware.com/.

[2] ALAMELDEEN, A., AND WOOD, D. Ipc considered harmful for multiprocessor workloads. *IEEE Micro 26*, 4 (July–August 2006), 8–17.

[3] ASLOT, V., DOMEIKA, M., EIGENMANN, R., GAERTNER, G., JONES, W. B., AND PARADY, B. Specomp: A new benchmark suite for measuring parallel computer performance. In *Proceedings of the Workshop on OpenMP Applications and Tools* (2001).

[4] BIENIA, C., KUMAR, S., SINGH, J. P., AND LI, K. The parsec benchmark suite: Characterization and architectural implications. In *Proceedings of the 17th International Conference on Parallel Architectures and Compilation Techniques* (October 2008).

[5] BLAGODUROV, S., ZHURAVLEV, S., DASHTI, M., AND FEDOROVA, A. A case for numa-aware contention management on multicore systems. In *Proceedings of the 2011 USENIX Annual Technical Conference (USENIX)* (2011).

[6] CURTIS-MAURY, M., BLAGOJEVIC, F., ANTONOPOULOS, C. D., AND NIKOLOPOULOS, D. S. Prediction-based power-performance adaptation of multithreaded scientific

---

[3]Note that number of remappings for power objective is always zero.

codes. *IEEE Transactions on Parallel and Distributed Systems 19*, 10 (October 2008), 1396–1410.

[7] CURTIS-MAURY, M., DZIERWA, J., ANTONOPOULOS, C. D., AND NIKOLOPOULOS, D. S. Online power-performance adaptation of multithreaded programs using hardware event-based prediction. In *Proceedings of the 20th Annual International Conference on Supercomputing (ICS)* (2006).

[8] CURTIS-MAURY, M., SINGH, K., MCKEE, S. A., BLAGOJEVIC, F., NIKOLOPOULOS, D. S., DE SUPINSKI, B. R., AND SCHULZ, M. Identifying energy-efficient concurrency levels using machine learning. In *Proceedings of the 2007 IEEE International Conference on Cluster Computing (CLUSTER)* (2007).

[9] DONG, M., AND ZHONG, L. Self-constructive high-rate system energy modeling for battery-powered mobile systems. In *Proceedings of the 9th International Conference on Mobile Systems, Applications, and Services (MobiSys)* (2011).

[10] ESMAEILZADEH, H., BLEM, E., ST. AMANT, R., SANKARALINGAM, K., AND BURGER, D. Dark silicon and the end of multicore scaling. In *Proceedings of the 38th Annual International Symposium on Computer Architecture (ISCA)* (2011).

[11] EYERMAN, S., AND EECKHOUT, L. System-level performance metrics for multiprogram workloads. *IEEE Micro 28* (May 2008), 42–53.

[12] GOGLIN, B., AND FURMENTO, N. Enabling high-performance memory migration for multithreaded applications on linux. In *Proceedings of the 2009 IEEE Internationalon Parallel and Distributed Processing Symposium (IPDPS)* (2009).

[13] HARDAVELLAS, N., FERDMAN, M., FALSAFI, B., AND AILAMAKI, A. Toward dark silicon in servers. *IEEE Micro 31*, 4 (July–August 2011), 6–15.

[14] IBRAHIM, K. Z., HOFMEYR, S., AND IANCU, C. Characterizing the performance of parallel applications on multi-socket virtual machines. In *Proceedings of the 2011 11th IEEE/ACM International Symposium on Cluster, Cloud and Grid Computing (CCGRID)* (2011).

[15] INTEL CORPORATION. *Intel 64 and IA-32 Architectures Software Developer's Manual Volume 3B: System Programming Guide Part 2*, December 2011.

[16] KANSAL, A., ZHAO, F., LIU, J., KOTHARI, N., AND BHATTACHARYA, A. A. Virtual machine power metering and provisioning. In *Proceedings of the 1st ACM Symposium on Cloud Computing (SOCC)* (2010).

[17] KNAUERHASE, R., BRETT, P., HOHLT, B., LI, T., AND HAHN, S. Using os observations to improve performance in multicore systems. *IEEE Micro 28* (May 2008), 54–66.

[18] LANGE, J., DINDA, P., HALE, K., AND XIA, L. An introduction to the palacios virtual machine monitor—release 1.3. Tech. Rep. NWU-EECS-11-10, Department of Electrical Engineering and Computer Science, Northwestern University, October 2011.

[19] LANGE, J., PEDRETTI, K., DINDA, P., BAE, C., BRIDGES, P., SOLTERO, P., AND MERRITT, A. Minimal-overhead virtualization of a large scale supercomputer. In *Proceedings of the 2011 ACM SIGPLAN/SIGOPS International Conference on Virtual Execution Environments (VEE)* (March 2011).

[20] LANGE, J., PEDRETTI, K., HUDSON, T., DINDA, P., CUI, Z., XIA, L., BRIDGES, P., GOCKE, A., JACONETTE, S., LEVENHAGEN, M., AND BRIGHTWELL, R. Palacios and kitten: New high performance operating systems for scalable virtualized and native supercomputing. In *Proceedings of the 24th IEEE International Parallel and Distributed Processing Symposium (IPDPS 2010)* (April 2010).

[21] LI, D., NIKOLOPOULOS, D., CAMERON, K., DE SUPINSKI, B., AND SCHULZ, M. Power-aware mpi task aggregation prediction for high-end computing systems. In *Proceedings of the 2010 IEEE Parallel and Distributed Processing Symposium (IPDPS)* (April 2010).

[22] LI, T., BAUMBERGER, D., KOUFATY, D. A., AND HAHN, S. Efficient operating system scheduling for performance-asymmetric multi-core architectures. In *Proceedings of the 2007 ACM/IEEE International Conference for High Performance Computing, Networking, Storage, and Analysis (Supercomputing / SC)* (2007).

[23] LIBERMAN, J., AND KOCHHAR, G. *Optimal BIOS Settings for High Performance Compting with PowerEdge 11G Servers*, updated 23 august 2010 ed. Dell Product Group, July 2009.

[24] MERKEL, A., STOESS, J., AND BELLOSA, F. Resource-conscious scheduling for energy efficiency on multicore processors. In *Proceedings of the 5th European Conference on Computer Systems (EuroSys)* (2010).

[25] RANGAN, K. K., WEI, G.-Y., AND BROOKS, D. Thread motion: fine-grained power management for multi-core systems. In *Proceedings of the 36th Annual International Symposium on Computer Architecture (ISCA)* (2009).

[26] RIVOIRE, S., RANGANATHAN, P., AND KOZYRAKIS, C. A comparison of high-level full-system power models. In *Proceedings of the 2008 Workshop on Hot Topics in Power-aware Computing and Systems (HotPower)* (2008).

[27] SIDDHA, S., PALLIPADI, V., AND MALLICK, A. Process scheduling challenges in the era of multi-core processors. *Intel Technology Journal 11*, 4 (November 2007).

[28] TAM, D., AZIMI, R., AND STUMM, M. Thread clustering: sharing-aware scheduling on smp-cmp-smt multiprocessors. In *Proceedings of the 2nd ACM European Conference on Computer Systems (EuroSys)* (2007).

[29] UHLIG, R., NEIGER, G., RODGERS, D., SANTONI, A., MARTIN, F., ANDERSON, A., BENNETTT, S., KAGI, A., LEUNG, F., AND SMITH, L. Intel virtualization technology. *IEEE Computer* (May 2005), 48–56.

[30] WINTER, J. A., ALBONESI, D. H., AND SHOEMAKER, C. A. Scalable thread scheduling and global power management for heterogeneous many-core architectures. In *Proceedings of the 19th International Conference on Parallel Architectures and Compilation Techniques (PACT)* (2010).

[31] ZHANG, L., TIWANA, B., QIAN, Z., WANG, Z., DICK, R. P., MAO, Z. M., AND YANG, L. Accurate online power estimation and automatic battery behavior based power model generation for smartphones. In *Proceedings of the 8th IEEE/ACM/IFIP International Conference on Hardware/Software Co-design and System Synthesis (CODES/ISSS)* (2010).

[32] ZHURAVLEV, S., BLAGODUROV, S., AND FEDOROVA, A. Addressing shared resource contention in multicore processors via scheduling. In *Proceedings of the 15th Conference on Architectural Support for Programming Languages and Operating Systems (ASPLOS)* (2010).

VNET/P: Bridging the Cloud and High Performance Computing Through Fast Overlay Networking

Lei Xia*   Zheng Cui§   John Lange‡
Yuan Tang†   Peter Dinda*   Patrick Bridges§

* Dept. of Electrical Engineering and Computer
Science, Northwestern University
{lxia,pdinda}@northwestern.edu

‡ Dept. of Computer Science,
University of Pittsburgh
jacklange@cs.pitt.edu

§ Dept. of Computer Science,
University of New Mexico
{cuizheng,bridges}@cs.unm.edu

† School of Computer Science and Engineering,
University of Electronic Science and
Technology of China
ytang@uestc.edu.cn

ABSTRACT

It is now possible to allow VMs hosting HPC applications to seamlessly bridge distributed cloud resources and tightly-coupled supercomputing and cluster resources. However, to achieve the application performance that the tightly-coupled resources are capable of, it is important that the overlay network not introduce significant overhead relative to the native hardware, which is not the case for current user-level tools, including our own existing VNET/U system. In response, we describe the design, implementation, and evaluation of a layer 2 virtual networking system that has negligible latency and bandwidth overheads in 1–10 Gbps networks. Our system, VNET/P, is directly embedded into our publicly available Palacios virtual machine monitor (VMM). VNET/P achieves native performance on 1 Gbps Ethernet networks and very high performance on 10 Gbps Ethernet networks and InfiniBand. The NAS benchmarks generally achieve over 95% of their native performance on both 1 and 10 Gbps. These results suggest it is feasible to extend a software-based overlay network designed for computing at wide-area scales into tightly-coupled environments.

Categories and Subject Descriptors

D.4.4 [**Software**]: OPERATING SYSTEMS

General Terms

Design, Measurement, Performance, Experimentation

Keywords

Overlay Networks, Virtualization, HPC, Scalability

This project is made possible by support from the United States National Science Foundation (NSF) via grants CNS-0709168 and CNS-0707365, and by the Department of Energy (DOE) via grant DE-SC0005343. Yuan Tang's visiting scholar position at Northwestern was supported by the China Scholarship Council.

1. INTRODUCTION

Cloud computing in the "infrastructure as a service" (IaaS) model has the potential to provide economical and effective on-demand resources for high performance computing. In this model, an application is mapped into a collection of virtual machines (VMs) that are instantiated as needed, and at the scale needed. Indeed, for loosely-coupled applications, this concept has readily moved from research [6, 38] to practice [33]. As we describe in Section 3, such systems can also be adaptive, autonomously selecting appropriate mappings of virtual components to physical components to maximize application performance or other objectives. However, *tightly-coupled* scalable high performance computing (HPC) applications currently remain the purview of resources such as clusters and supercomputers. We seek to extend the adaptive IaaS cloud computing model into these regimes, allowing an application to dynamically span both kinds of environments.

The current limitation of cloud computing systems to *loosely-coupled* applications is not due to machine virtualization limitations. Current virtual machine monitors (VMMs) and other virtualization mechanisms present negligible overhead for CPU and memory intensive workloads [14, 31]. With VMM-bypass [29] or self-virtualizing devices [35] the overhead for direct access to network devices can also be made negligible.

Considerable effort has also gone into achieving low-overhead network virtualization and traffic segregation within an individual data center through extensions or changes to the network hardware layer [32, 9, 20]. While these tools strive to provide uniform performance across a cloud data center (a critical feature for many HPC applications), they do not provide the same features once an application has migrated outside the local data center, or spans multiple data centers, or involves HPC resources. Furthermore, they lack compatibility with the more specialized interconnects present on most HPC systems. Beyond the need to support our envisioned computing model across today's and tomorrow's tightly-coupled HPC environments, we note that data center network design and cluster/supercomputer network design seems to be converging [1, 10]. This suggests that future data centers deployed for general purpose cloud computing will become an increasingly better fit for tightly-coupled parallel applications, and therefore such environments could potentially also benefit.

The current limiting factor in the adaptive cloud- and HPC-spanning model described above for tightly-coupled applications is the performance of the virtual networking system. Current adaptive cloud computing systems use software-based overlay networks to carry

259

inter-VM traffic. For example, our VNET/U system, which is described in more detail later, combines a simple networking abstraction within the VMs with location-independence, hardware-independence, and traffic control. Specifically, it exposes a layer 2 abstraction that lets the user treat his VMs as being on a simple LAN, while allowing the VMs to be migrated seamlessly across resources by routing their traffic through the overlay. By controlling the overlay, the cloud provider or adaptation agent can control the bandwidth and the paths between VMs over which traffic flows. Such systems [42, 37] and others that expose different abstractions to the VMs [47] have been under continuous research and development for several years. Current virtual networking systems have sufficiently low overhead to effectively host loosely-coupled scalable applications [5], but their performance is insufficient for tightly-coupled applications [34].

In response to this limitation, we have designed, implemented, and evaluated VNET/P, which shares its model and vision with VNET/U, but is designed to achieve near-native performance in the 1 Gbps and 10 Gbps switched networks common in clusters today, and pave the way for even faster networks, such as InfiniBand, in the future. VNET/U is presented in more detail in Section 3.

VNET/P is implemented in the context of our publicly available, open source Palacios VMM [25], which is in part designed to support virtualized supercomputing. A detailed description of VNET/P's design and implementation is given in Section 4. As a part of Palacios, VNET/P is publicly available. VNET/P could be implemented in other VMMs, and as such provides a proof-of-concept that overlay-based virtual networking for VMs, with performance overheads low enough to be inconsequential even in a tightly-coupled computing environment, is clearly possible.

The performance evaluation of VNET/P (Section 5) shows that it is able to achieve native bandwidth on 1 Gbps Ethernet with a small increase in latency, and very high bandwidth on 10 Gbps Ethernet with a similar, small latency increase. We also demonstrate in Section 6 that VNET/P can effectively support running Ethernet-based networked programs on non-Ethernet HPC communication device, specifically InfiniBand NICs. On 10 Gbps hardware, the kernel-level VNET/P system provides on average 10 times more bandwidth and 7 times less latency than the user-level VNET/U system can.

Our contributions are as follows:

- We articulate the benefits of extending virtual networking for VMs down to clusters and supercomputers with high performance networks. These benefits are also applicable to data centers that support IaaS cloud computing.

- We describe the design and implementation of a virtual networking system, VNET/P, that does so. The design could be applied to other VMMs and virtual network systems.

- We evaluate VNET/P, finding that it provides performance with negligible overheads on 1 Gbps Ethernet networks, and manageable overheads on 10 Gbps Ethernet networks. VNET/P generally has little impact on performance for the NAS benchmarks.

- We describe how VNET/P also provides its abstraction on top of InfiniBand hardware, allowing guests to exploit such hardware without any special drivers or an InfiniBand stack.

Through the use of low-overhead overlay-based virtual networking in high-bandwidth, low-latency environments such as current clusters and supercomputers, and future data centers, we seek to make it practical to use virtual networking at all times, even when running tightly-coupled applications on such high-end environments. This would allow us to seamlessly and *practically* extend the already highly effective adaptive virtualization-based IaaS cloud computing model to such environments.

2. RELATED WORK

VNET/P is related to NIC virtualization, overlays, and virtual networks, as we describe below.

NIC virtualization: There is a wide range of work on providing VMs with fast access to networking hardware, where no overlay is involved. For example, VMware and Xen support either an emulated register-level interface [41] or a paravirtualized interface to guest operating system [30]. While purely software-based virtualized network interface has high overhead, many techniques have been proposed to support simultaneous, direct-access network I/O. For example, some work [29, 35] has demonstrated the use of self-virtualized network hardware that allows direct guest access, thus provides high performance to untrusted guests. Willmann et al have developed a software approach that also supports concurrent, direct network access by untrusted guest operating systems [39]. In addition, VPIO [48] can be applied on network virtualization to allow virtual passthrough I/O on non-self-virtualized hardware. In contrast with such work, VNET/P provides fast access to an overlay network, which includes encapsulation and routing.

Overlay networks: Overlay networks implement extended network functionality on top of physical infrastructure, for example to provide resilient routing (e.g, [2]), multicast (e.g. [13]), and distributed data structures (e.g., [40]) without any cooperation from the network core; overlay networks use end-systems to provide their functionality. VNET is an example of a specific class of overlay networks, namely virtual networks, discussed next.

Virtual networking: Virtual networking systems provide a service model that is compatible with an existing layer 2 or 3 networking standard. Examples include VIOLIN [17], ViNe [45], VINI [3], SoftUDC VNET [19], OCALA [18] and WoW [8]. Like VNET, VIOLIN, SoftUDC, and WoW are specifically designed for use with virtual machines. Of these, VIOLIN is closest to VNET (and contemporaneous with VNET/U), in that it allows for the dynamic setup of an arbitrary private layer 2 and layer 3 virtual network among VMs. The key contribution of VNET/P is to show that this model can be made to work with minimal overhead even in extremely low latency, high bandwidth environments.

Connections: VNET/P could itself leverage some of the related work described above. For example, effective NIC virtualization might allow us to push encapsulation directly into the guest, or to accelerate encapsulation via a split scatter/gather map. Mapping unencapsulated links to VLANs would enhance performance on environments that support them. There are many options for implementing virtual networking and the appropriate choice depends on the hardware and network policies of the target environment. In VNET/P, we make the choice of minimizing these dependencies.

3. VNET MODEL AND VNET/U

The VNET model was originally designed to support adaptive computing on distributed virtualized computing resources within the Virtuoso system [4], and in particular to support the adaptive execution of a distributed or parallel computation executing in a collection of VMs potentially spread across multiple providers or supercomputing sites. The key requirements, which also hold for the present paper, were as follows:

- VNET would make within-VM network configuration the sole responsibility of the VM owner.
- VNET would provide location independence to VMs, allowing them to be migrated between networks and from site to site, while maintaining their connectivity, without requiring any within-VM configuration changes.
- VNET would provide hardware independence to VMs, allowing them to use diverse networking hardware without requiring the installation of specialized software.

260

- VNET would provide minimal overhead, compared to native networking, in the contexts in which it is used.

The VNET model meets these requirements by carrying the user's VMs' traffic via a configurable overlay network. The overlay presents a simple layer 2 networking abstraction: a user's VMs appear to be attached to the user's local area Ethernet network, regardless of their actual locations or the complexity of the VNET topology/properties. Further information about the model can be found elsewhere [42].

The VNET overlay is dynamically reconfigurable, and can act as a locus of activity for an an adaptive system such as Virtuoso. Focusing on parallel and distributed applications running in loosely-coupled virtualized distributed environments e.g., "IaaS Clouds", we demonstrated that the VNET "layer" can be effectively used to: (1) monitor application communication and computation behavior [11]), (2) monitor underlying network behavior [12], (3) formulate performance optimization problems [44], (4) address such problems through VM migration and overlay network control [43], scheduling [27, 28], network reservations [26], and network service interposition [22].

The VNET/P system described in this paper is compatible with, and compared to, our previous VNET implementation, VNET/U. Both support a dynamically configurable general overlay topology with dynamically configurable routing on a per MAC address basis. The topology and routing configuration is subject to global or distributed control (for example, by the VADAPT [43]) part of Virtuoso. The overlay carries Ethernet packets encapsulated in UDP packets, TCP streams with and without SSL encryption, TOR privacy-preserving streams, and others. Because Ethernet packets are used, the VNET abstraction can also easily interface directly with most commodity network devices, including virtual NICs exposed by VMMs in the host, and with fast virtual devices (e.g., Linux virtio network devices) in guests.

While VNET/P is implemented within the VMM, VNET/U is implemented as a user-level system. As a user-level system, it readily interfaces with VMMs such as VMware Server and Xen, and requires no host changes to be used, making it very easy for a provider to bring it up on a new machine. Further, it is easy to bring up VNET daemons when and where needed to act as proxies or waypoints. A VNET daemon has a control port which speaks a control language for dynamic configuration. A collection of tools allow for the wholesale construction and teardown of VNET topologies, as well as dynamic adaptation of the topology and forwarding rules to the observed traffic and conditions on the underlying network.

The last reported measurement of VNET/U showed it achieving 21.5 MB/s (172 Mbps) with a 1 ms latency overhead communicating between Linux 2.6 VMs running in VMware Server GSX 2.5 on machines with dual 2.0 GHz Xeon processors [22]. A current measurement, described in Section 5, shows 71 MB/s with a 0.88 ms latency. VNET/U's speeds are sufficient for its purpose in providing virtual networking for wide-area and/or loosely-coupled distributed computing. They are not, however, sufficient for use within a cluster at gigabit or greater speeds. Making this basic VM-to-VM path competitive with hardware is the focus of this paper. VNET/U is fundamentally limited by the kernel/user space transitions needed to handle a guest's packet send or receive. In VNET/P, we move VNET directly into the VMM to avoid such transitions.

4. DESIGN AND IMPLEMENTATION

We now describe how VNET/P has been architected and implemented in the context of Palacios as embedded in a Linux host. Section 6 describes how VNET/P is implemented in the context of a Kitten embedding. The nature of the embedding affects VNET/P

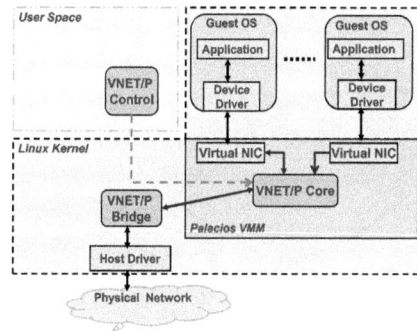

Figure 1: VNET/P architecture

primarily in how it interfaces to the underlying networking hardware and networking stack. In the Linux embedding, this interface is accomplished directly in the Linux kernel. In the Kitten embedding, the interface is done via a service VM.

4.1 Palacios VMM

VNET/P is implemented in the context of our Palacios VMM. Palacios is an OS-independent, open source, BSD-licensed, publicly available embeddable VMM designed as part of the V3VEE project (http://v3vee.org). The V3VEE project is a collaborative community resource development project involving Northwestern University, the University of New Mexico, Sandia National Labs, and Oak Ridge National Lab. Detailed information about Palacios can be found elsewhere [25, 23]. Palacios is capable of virtualizing large scale (4096+ nodes) with $< 5\%$ overheads [24]. Palacios's OS-agnostic design allows it to be embedded into a wide range of different OS architectures.

4.2 Architecture

Figure 1 shows the overall architecture of VNET/P, and illustrates the operation of VNET/P in the context of the Palacios VMM embedded in a Linux host. In this architecture, *guests* run in *application VMs*. Off-the-shelf guests are fully supported. Each application VM provides a virtual (Ethernet) NIC to its guest. For high performance applications, as in this paper, the virtual NIC conforms to the virtio interface, but several virtual NICs with hardware interfaces are also available in Palacios. The virtual NIC conveys Ethernet packets between the application VM and the Palacios VMM. Using the virtio virtual NIC, one or more packets can be conveyed from an application VM to Palacios with a single VM exit, and from Palacios to the application VM with a single VM exit+entry.

The *VNET/P core* is the component of VNET/P that is directly embedded into the Palacios VMM. It is responsible for routing Ethernet packets between virtual NICs on the machine and between this machine and remote VNET on other machines. The VNET/P core's routing rules are dynamically configurable, through the control interface by the utilities that can be run in user space.

The VNET/P core also provides an expanded interface that the control utilities can use to configure and manage VNET/P. The *VNET/P control* component uses this interface to do so. It in turn acts as a daemon that exposes a TCP control port that uses the same configuration language as VNET/U. Between compatible encapsulation and compatible control, the intent is that VNET/P and VNET/U be interoperable, with VNET/P providing the "fast path".

To exchange packets with a remote machine, the VNET/P core uses a *VNET/P bridge* to communicate with the physical network.

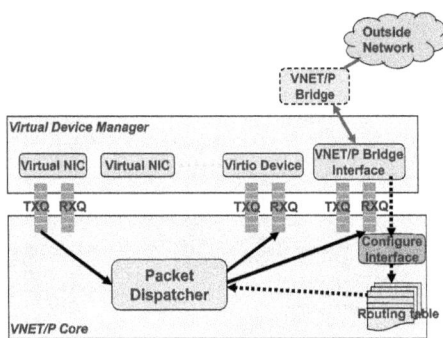

Figure 2: VNET/P core's internal logic.

The VNET/P bridge runs as a kernel module in the host kernel and uses the host's networking facilities to interact with physical network devices and with the host's networking stack. An additional responsibility of the bridge is to provide encapsulation. For performance reasons, we use UDP encapsulation, in a form compatible with that used in VNET/U. TCP encapsulation is also supported. The bridge selectively performs UDP or TCP encapsulation for packets destined for remote machines, but can also deliver an Ethernet packet without encapsulation. In our performance evaluation, we consider only encapsulated traffic.

The VNET/P core consists of approximately 2500 lines of C in Palacios, while the VNET/P bridge consists of about 2000 lines of C comprising a Linux kernel module. VNET/P is available via the V3VEE project's public git repository, as part of the "devel" branch of the Palacios VMM.

4.3 VNET/P core

The VNET/P core is primarily responsible for routing, and dispatching raw Ethernet packets. It intercepts all Ethernet packets from virtual NICs that are associated with VNET/P, and forwards them either to VMs on the same host machine or to the outside network through the VNET/P bridge. Each packet is routed based on its source and destination MAC addresses. The internal processing logic of the VNET/P core is illustrated in Figure 2.

Routing: To route Ethernet packets, VNET/P maintains routing tables indexed by source and destination MAC addresses. Although this table structure only provides linear time lookups, a hash table-based routing cache is layered on top of the table, and the common case is for lookups to hit in the cache and thus be serviced in constant time.

A routing table entry maps to a destination, which is either a *link* or an *interface*. A link is an overlay destination—it is the next UDP/IP-level (i.e., IP address and port) destination of the packet, on some other machine. A special link corresponds to the local network. The local network destination is usually used at the "exit/entry point" where the VNET overlay is attached to the user's physical LAN. A packet routed via a link is delivered to another VNET/P core, a VNET/U daemon, or the local network. An interface is a local destination for the packet, corresponding to some virtual NIC.

For an interface destination, the VNET/P core directly delivers the packet to the relevant virtual NIC. For a link destination, it injects the packet into the VNET/P bridge along with the destination link identifier. The VNET/P bridge demultiplexes based on the link and either encapsulates the packet and sends it via the corresponding UDP or TCP socket, or sends it directly as a raw packet to the local network.

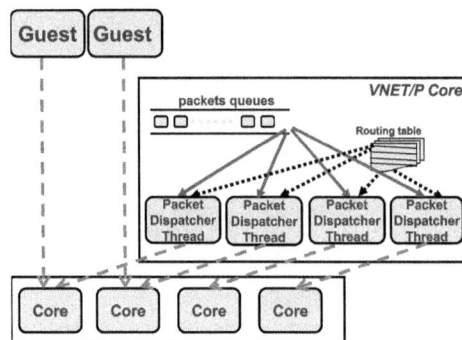

Figure 3: VNET/P running on a multicore system. The selection of how many, and which cores to use for packet dispatcher threads is made dynamically.

Packet processing: Packet forwarding in the VNET/P core is conducted by *packet dispatchers*. A packet dispatcher interacts with each virtual NIC to forward packets in one of two modes: *guest-driven mode* or *VMM-driven mode*.

The purpose of guest-driven mode is to minimize latency for small messages in a parallel application. For example, a barrier operation would be best served with guest-driven mode. In the guest-driven mode, the packet dispatcher is invoked when the guest's interaction with the NIC explicitly causes an exit. For example, the guest might queue a packet on its virtual NIC and then cause an exit to notify the VMM that a packet is ready. In guest-driven mode, a packet dispatcher runs at this point. Similarly, on receive, a packet dispatcher queues the packet to the device and then immediately notifies the device.

The purpose of VMM-driven mode is to maximize throughput for bulk data transfer in a parallel application. Unlike guest-driven mode, VMM-driven mode tries to handle multiple packets per VM exit. It does this by having VMM poll the virtual NIC. The NIC is polled in two ways. First, it is polled, and a packet dispatcher is run, if needed, in the context of the current VM exit (which is unrelated to the NIC). Even if exits are infrequent, the polling and dispatch will still make progress during the handling of timer interrupt exits.

The second manner in which the NIC can be polled is in the context of a packet dispatcher running in a kernel thread inside the VMM context, as shown in Figure 3. The packet dispatcher thread can be instantiated multiple times, with these threads running on different cores in the machine. If a packet dispatcher thread decides that a virtual NIC queue is full, it forces the NIC's VM to handle it by doing a cross-core IPI to force the core on which the VM is running to exit. The exit handler then does the needed event injection. Using this approach, it is possible, to dynamically employ idle processor cores to increase packet forwarding bandwidth.

Influenced by Sidecore [21], an additional optimization we developed was to offload in-VMM VNET/P processing, beyond packet dispatch, to an unused core or cores, thus making it possible for the guest VM to have full use of its cores (minus the exit/entry costs when packets are actually handed to/from it).

VNET/P switches between these two modes dynamically depending on the arrival rate of packets destined to or from the virtual NIC. For low rate, it enables guest-driven mode to reduce the single packet latency. On the other hand, with a high arrival rate it switches to VMM-driven mode to increase throughput. Specifically, the VMM detects whether the system is experiencing a high exit rate due to virtual NIC accesses. It recalculates the rate period-

262

ically. If the rate is high enough when the guest transmits packets, then VNET/P switches the virtual NIC associated with that guest from guest-driven mode to VMM-driven mode. In other hand, if the rate drops low from the last recalculate period, it switches back from VMM-driven to guest-driven mode.

For a 1 Gbps network, guest-driven mode is sufficient to allow VNET/P to achieve the full native throughput. On a 10 Gbps network, VMM-driven mode is essential to move packets through the VNET/P core with near-native throughput.

4.4 Virtual NICs

VNET/P is designed to be able to support any virtual Ethernet NIC device. A virtual NIC must, however, register itself with VNET/P before it can be used. This is done during the initialization of the virtual NIC at VM configuration time. The registration provides additional callback functions for packet transmission, transmit queue polling, and packet reception. These functions essentially allow the NIC to use VNET/P as its backend, instead of using an actual hardware device driver backend.

Linux virtio virtual NIC: Virtio [36], which was recently developed for the Linux kernel, provides an efficient abstraction for VMMs. A common set of virtio device drivers are now included as standard in the Linux kernel. To maximize performance, our performance evaluation configured the application VM with Palacios's virtio-compatible virtual NIC, using the default Linux virtio network driver.

MTU: The maximum transmission unit (MTU) of a networking layer is the size of the largest protocol data unit that the layer can pass onwards. A larger MTU improves throughput because each packet carries more user data while protocol headers have a fixed size. A larger MTU also means that fewer packets need to be processed to transfer a given amount of data. Where per-packet processing costs are significant, larger MTUs are distinctly preferable. Because VNET/P adds to the per-packet processing cost, supporting large MTUs is helpful.

VNET/P presents an Ethernet abstraction to the application VM. The most common Ethernet MTU is 1500 bytes. However, 1 Gbit and 10 Gbit Ethernet can also use "jumbo frames", with an MTU of 9000 bytes. Other networking technologies support even larger MTUs. To leverage the large MTUs of underlying physical NICs, VNET/P itself supports MTU sizes of up to 64 KB.[1] The application OS can determine the virtual NIC's MTU and then transmit/receive accordingly. VNET/P advertises the appropriate MTU.

The MTU used by virtual NIC can result in encapsulated VNET/P packets that exceed the MTU of the underlying physical network. In this case, fragmentation has to occur, either in the VNET/P bridge or in the host NIC (via TCP Segmentation Offloading (TSO)). Fragmentation and reassembly is handled by VNET/P and is totally transparent to the application VM. However, performance will suffer when significant fragmentation occurs. Thus it is important that the application VM's device driver select an MTU carefully, and recognize that the desirable MTU may change over time, for example after a migration to a different host. In Section 5, we analyze throughput using different MTUs.

4.5 VNET/P Bridge

The VNET/P bridge functions as a network bridge to direct packets between the VNET/P core and the physical network through the host NIC. It operates based on the routing decisions made by the VNET/P core which are passed along with the packets to be forwarded. It is implemented as a kernel module running in the host.

---

[1]This may be expanded in the future. Currently, it has been sized to support the largest possible IPv4 packet size.

When the VNET/P core hands a packet and routing directive up to the bridge, one of two transmission modes will occur, depending on the destination. In a *direct send*, the Ethernet packet is directly sent. This is common for when a packet is exiting a VNET overlay and entering the physical network, as typically happens on the user's network. It may also be useful when all VMs will remain on a common layer 2 network for their lifetime. In an *encapsulated send* the packet is encapsulated in a UDP packet and the UDP packet is sent to the directed destination IP address and port. This is the common case for traversing a VNET overlay link. Similarly, for packet reception, the bridge uses two modes, simultaneously. In a *direct receive* the host NIC is run in promiscuous mode, and packets with destination MAC addresses corresponding to those requested by the VNET/P core are handed over to it. This is used in conjunction with direct send. In an *encapsulated receive* UDP packets bound for the common VNET link port are disassembled and their encapsulated Ethernet packets are delivered to the VNET/P core. This is used in conjunction with encapsulated send. Our performance evaluation focuses solely on encapsulated send and receive.

4.6 Control

The VNET/P control component allows for remote and local configuration of links, interfaces, and routing rules so that an overlay can be constructed and changed over time. VNET/U already has user-level tools to support VNET, and, as we described in Section 3, a range of work already exists on the configuration, monitoring, and control of a VNET overlay. In VNET/P, we reuse these tools as much as possible by having the user-space view of VNET/P conform closely to that of VNET/U. The *VNET/P configuration console* allows for local control to be provided from a file, or remote control via TCP-connected VNET/U clients (such as tools that automatically configure a topology that is appropriate for the given communication pattern among a set of VMs [43]). In both cases, the VNET/P control component is also responsible for validity checking before it transfers the new configuration to the VNET/P core.

4.7 Performance-critical data paths and flows

Figure 4 depicts how the components previously described operate during packet transmission and reception. These are the performance critical data paths and flows within VNET/P, assuming that virtio virtual NICs (Section 4.4) are used. The boxed regions of the figure indicate steps introduced by virtualization, both within the VMM and within the host OS kernel. There are also additional overheads involved in the VM exit handling for I/O port reads and writes and for interrupt injection.

Transmission: The guest OS in the VM includes the device driver for the virtual NIC. The driver initiates packet transmission by writing to a specific virtual I/O port after it puts the packet into the NIC's shared ring buffer (TXQ). The I/O port write causes an exit that gives control to the virtual NIC I/O handler in Palacios. The handler reads the packet from the buffer and writes it to VNET/P packet dispatcher. The dispatcher does a routing table lookup to determine the packet's destination. For a packet destined for a VM on some other host, the packet dispatcher puts the packet into the receive buffer of the VNET/P bridge and notify it. Meanwhile, VNET/P bridge fetches the packet from the receive buffer, determines its destination VNET/P bridge, encapsulates the packet, and transmits it to the physical network via the host's NIC.

Note that while the packet is handed off multiple times, it is copied only once inside the VMM, from the send buffer (TXQ) of the receive buffer of the VNET/P bridge. Also note that while the above description, and the diagram suggest sequentiality, packet

Network Packet Send

Application OS
VMM   ↓ *OUT to I/O Port of VNIC*

Virtual NIC IO Handler
    ↓ *Context Switch*
    ↓ *Send packet to VNET*
VNET/P Packet Dispatcher
    ↓ *Send packet to VNET/P Bridge*

Host OS

VNET/P Bridge
    ↓ *Packet Encapsulation*
Host OS NIC device driver
    ↓ *OUT to IO ports*
Physical Ethernet HW
    Packet launch

Network Packet Receive

Physical Ethernet HW
    ↓ *Device Interrupt*
Host OS Device Driver
    ↓
VNET/P Bridge
    ↓ *De-capsulation*
    ↓ *Send packet to VNET/P core*
Palacios VMM

VNET/P Packet Dispatcher
    ↓ *Routing Packet*
    ↓ *Send Packet to destination VM*
Virtual NIC for destination VM
    ↓ *Inject Virtual Interrupt*
Guest OS device driver
    Packet receive completion

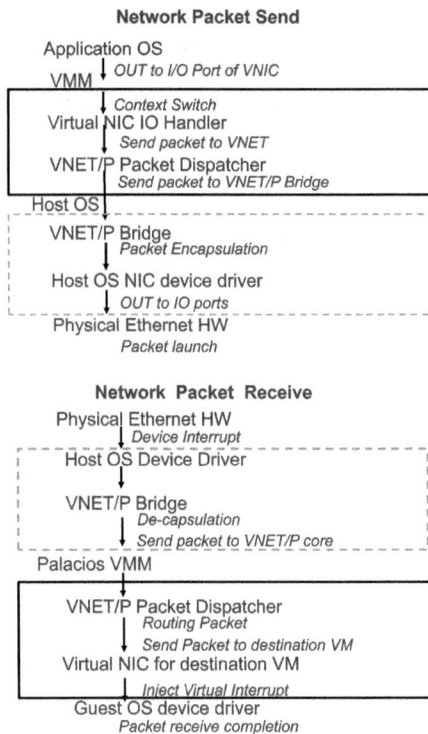

Figure 4: Performance-critical data paths and flows for packet transmission and reception. Solid boxed steps and components occur within the VMM itself, while dashed boxed steps and components occur in the host OS.

dispatch can occur on a separate kernel thread running on a separate core, and the VNET/P bridge itself introduces additional concurrency. From the guest's perspective, the I/O port write that initiated transmission returns essentially within a VM exit/entry time.

Reception: The path for packet reception is essentially symmetric to that of transmission. The host NIC in the host machine receives a packet using its standard driver and delivers it to the VNET/P bridge. The bridge unencapsulates the packet and sends the payload (the raw Ethernet packet) to the VNET/P core. The packet dispatcher in VNET/P core determines its destination VM and puts the packet into the receive buffer (RXQ) of its virtual NIC.

Similar to transmission, there is considerably concurrency in the reception process. In particular, packet dispatch can occur in parallel with the reception of the next packet.

5. PERFORMANCE EVALUATION

The purpose of our performance evaluation is to determine how close VNET/P comes to native throughput and latency in the most demanding (lowest latency, highest throughput) hardware environments. We consider communication between two machines whose NICs are directly connected in most of our detailed benchmarks. In the virtualized configuration the guests and performance testing tools run on top of Palacios with VNET/P carrying all traffic between them using encapsulation. In the native configuration, the same guest environments run directly on the hardware.

Our evaluation of communication performance in this environment occurs at three levels. First, we benchmark the TCP and UDP bandwidth and latency. Second, we benchmark MPI using a widely used benchmark. Finally, we evaluated the performance of the HPCC and NAS application benchmarks in a cluster to see

how VNET/P's impact on the performance and scalability of parallel applications.

5.1 Testbed and configurations

Most of our microbenchmark tests are focused on the end-to-end performance of VNET/P. Therefore our testbed consists of two physical machines, which we call host machines. Each machine has a quadcore 2.4 GHz X3430 Intel Xeon(tm) processor, 8 GB RAM, a Broadcom NetXtreme II 1 Gbps Ethernet NIC (1000BASE-T), and a NetEffect NE020 10 Gbps Ethernet fiber optic NIC (10GBASE-SR) in a PCI-e slot. The Ethernet NICs of these machines are directly connected with twisted pair and fiber patch cables.

All microbenchmarks included in the performance section are run in the testbed described above. The HPCC and NAS application benchmarks are run on a 6-node test cluster described in Section 5.4.

We considered the following two software configurations:

- *Native:* In the native configuration, neither Palacios nor VNET/P is used. A minimal BusyBox-based Linux environment based on an unmodified 2.6.30 kernel runs directly on the host machines. We refer to the 1 and 10 Gbps results in this configuration as *Native-1G* and *Native-10G*, respectively.

- *VNET/P:* The VNET/P configuration corresponds to the architectural diagram given in Figure 1, with a single guest VM running on Palacios. The guest VM is configured with one virtio network device, 2 cores, and 1 GB of RAM. The guest VM runs a minimal BusyBox-based Linux environment, based on the 2.6.30 kernel. The kernel used in the VM is identical to that in the Native configuration, with the exception that the virtio NIC drivers are loaded. The virtio MTU is configured as 9000 Bytes. We refer to the 1 and 10 Gbps results in this configuration as *VNET/P-1G* and *VNET/P-10G*, respectively.

To assure accurate time measurements both natively and in the virtualized case, our guest is configured to use the CPU's cycle counter, and Palacios is configured to allow the guest direct access to the underlying hardware cycle counter. Our 1 Gbps NIC only supports MTUs up to 1500 bytes, while our 10 Gbps NIC can support MTUs of up to 9000 bytes. We use these maximum sizes unless otherwise specified.

5.2 TCP and UDP microbenchmarks

Latency and throughput are the fundamental measurements we use to evaluate the VNET/P system performance. First, we consider these at the IP level, measuring the round-trip latency, the UDP goodput, and the TCP throughput between two nodes. We measure round-trip latency using *ping* by sending ICMP packets of different sizes. UDP and TCP throughput are measured using *ttcp-1.10*.

UDP and TCP with a standard MTU: Figure 5 shows the TCP throughput and UDP goodput achieved in each of our configurations on each NIC. For the 1 Gbps network, host MTU is set to 1500 bytes, and for the 10 Gbps network, host MTUs of 1500 bytes and 9000 bytes are both tested. For 1 Gbps, we also compare with VNET/U running on the same hardware with Palacios. Compared to previously reported results (21.5 MB/s, 1 ms), the combination of the faster hardware we use here, and Palacios, leads to VNET/U increasing its bandwidth by 330%, to 71 MB/s, with a 12% reduction in latency, to 0.88 ms. We also tested VNET/U with VMware, finding that bandwidth increased by 63% to 35 MB/s, with no change in latency. The difference in performance of VNET/U on the two VMMs is due to a custom tap interface in Palacios, while on VMware, the standard host-only tap is used. Even with this optimization, VNET/U cannot saturate a 1 Gbps link.

We begin by considering UDP goodput when a standard host MTU size is used. For UDP measurements, ttcp was configured to use 64000 byte writes sent as fast as possible over 60 seconds. For

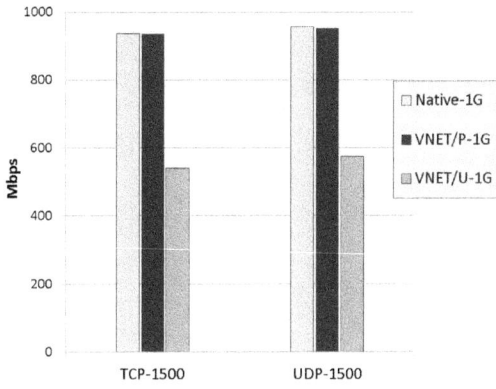

(a) 1 Gbps network (host MTU=1500 Bytes)

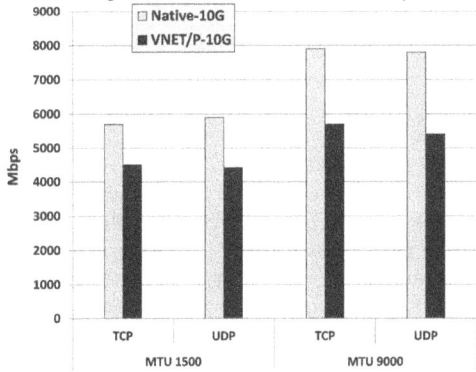

(b) 10 Gbps network (host MTU=1500, 9000 Bytes)

Figure 5: End-to-end TCP throughput and UDP goodput of VNET/P on 1 and 10 Gbps network. VNET/P performs identically to the native case for the 1 Gbps network and achieves 74–78% of native throughput for the 10 Gbps network.

the 1 Gbps network, VNET/P easily matches the native goodput. For the 10 Gbps network, VNET/P achieves 74% of the native UDP goodput.

For TCP throughput, ttcp was configured to use a 256 KB socket buffer, and to communicate 40 MB writes were made. Similar to the UDP results, VNET/P has no difficulty achieving native throughput on the 1 Gbps network. On the 10 Gbps network, using a standard Ethernet MTU, it achieves 78% of the native throughput. The UDP goodput and TCP throughput that VNET/P is capable of, using a standard Ethernet MTU, are approximately 8 times those we would expect from VNET/U given the 1 Gbps results.

UDP and TCP with a large MTU: We now consider TCP and UDP performance with 9000 byte jumbo frames our 10 Gbps NICs support. We adjusted the VNET/P MTU so that the ultimate encapsulated packets will fit into these frames without fragmentation. For TCP we configure ttcp to use writes of corresponding size, maximize the socket buffer size, and do 4 million writes. For UDP, we configure ttcp to use commensurately large packets sent as fast as possible for 60 seconds. The results are also shown in the Figure 5. We can see that performance increases across the board compared to the 1500 byte MTU results. Compared to the VNET/U performance we would expect in this configuration, the UDP goodput and TCP throughput of VNET/P are over 10 times higher.

Latency: Figure 6 shows the round-trip latency for different packet sizes, as measured by ping. The latencies are the average of 100 measurements. While the increase in latency of VNET/P over Native is significant in relative terms (2x for 1 Gbps, 3x for

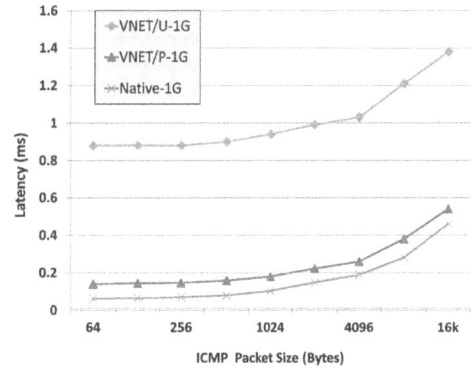

(a) 1 Gbps network (Host MTU=1500 Bytes)

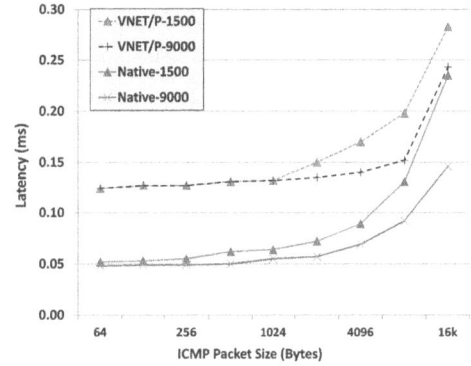

(b) 10 Gbps network (Host MTU=1500, 9000 Bytes)

Figure 6: End-to-end round-trip latency of VNET/P as a function of ICMP packet size. Small packet latencies on a 10 Gbps network in VNET/P are ∼130 μs.

10 Gbps), it is important to keep in mind the absolute performance. On a 10 Gbps network, VNET/P achieves a 130 μs round-trip, end-to-end latency. The latency of VNET/P is almost seven times lower than that of VNET/U.

5.3 MPI microbenchmarks

Parallel programs for distributed memory computers are typically written to the MPI interface standard. We used the OpenMPI 1.3 [7] implementation in our evaluations. We measured the performance of MPI over VNET/P by employing the widely-used Intel MPI Benchmark Suite (IMB 3.2.2) [16], focusing on the point-to-point messaging performance. We compared the basic MPI latency and bandwidth achieved by VNET/P and natively.

Figures 7 and 8(a) illustrate the latency and bandwidth reported by Intel MPI PingPong benchmark for our 10 Gbps configuration. Here the latency measured is the one-way, end-to-end, application-level latency. That is, it is the time from when an MPI send starts on one machine to when its matching MPI receive call completes on the other machine. For both Native and VNET/P, the host MTU is set to 9000 bytes.

VNET/P's small message MPI latency is about 55 μs, about 2.5 times worse than the native case. However, as the message size increases, the latency difference decreases. The measurements of end-to-end bandwidth as a function of message size show that native MPI bandwidth is slightly lower than raw UDP or TCP throughput, and VNET/P performance tracks it similarly. The bottom line is that the current VNET/P implementation can deliver an MPI latency of 55 μs and bandwidth of 510 MB/s on 10 Gbps Ethernet hardware.

(a) One-way bandwidth

(b) SendRecv Bandwidth

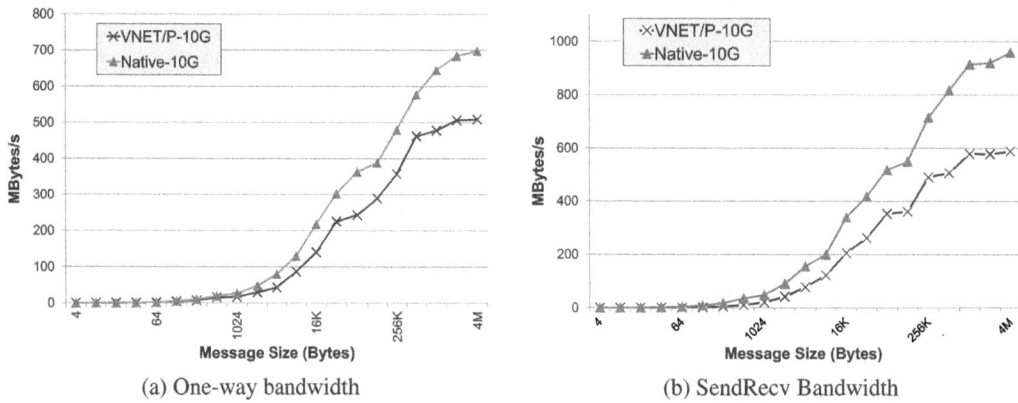

Figure 8: Intel MPI PingPong microbenchmark showing (a) one-way bandwidth and (b) bidirectional bandwidth as a function of message size on the 10 Gbps hardware.

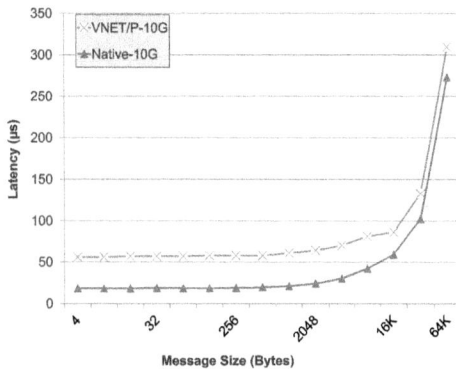

Figure 7: One-way latency on 10 Gbps hardware from Intel MPI PingPong microbenchmark

Figure 8(b) shows the results of the MPI SendRecv microbenchmark in which each node simultaneously sends and receives. There is no reduction in performance between the bidirectional case and the unidirectional case.

5.4 HPCC benchmarks on more nodes

To test VNET/P performance on more nodes, we ran the HPCC benchmark [15] suite on a 6 node cluster with 1 Gbps and 10 Gbps Ethernet. Each node was equipped with two quad-core 2.3 GHz 2376 AMD Opterons, 32 GB of RAM, an nVidia MCP55 Forthdeth 1 Gbps Ethernet NIC and a NetEffect NE020 10 Gbps Ethernet NIC. The nodes were connected via a Fujitsu XG2000 10Gb Ethernet Switch.

The VMs were all configured exactly as in previous tests, with 4 virtual cores, 1 GB RAM, and a virtio NIC. For the VNET/P test case, each host ran one VM. We executed tests with 2, 3, 4, 5, and 6 VMs, with 4 HPCC processes per VM (one per virtual core). Thus, our performance results are based on HPCC with 8, 12, 16, 20 and 24 processes for both VNET/P and Native tests. In the native cases, no VMs were used, and the processes ran directly on the host. For 1 Gbps testing, the host MTU was set to 1500, while for the 10 Gbps cases, the host MTU was set to 9000.

Latency-bandwidth benchmark: This benchmark consists of the ping-pong test and the ring-based tests. The ping-pong test measures the latency and bandwidth between all distinct pairs of processes. The ring-based tests arrange the processes into a ring topology and then engage in collective communication among neigh-

bors in the ring, measuring bandwidth and latency. The ring-based tests model the communication behavior of multi-dimensional domain-decomposition applications. Both naturally ordered rings and randomly ordered rings are evaluated. Communication is done with MPI non-blocking sends and receives, and MPI SendRecv. Here, the bandwidth per process is defined as total message volume divided by the number of processes and the maximum time needed in all processes. We reported the ring-based bandwidths by multiplying them with the number of processes in the test.

Figure 9 shows the results for different numbers of test processes. The ping-pong latency and bandwidth results are consistent with what we saw in the previous microbenchmarks: in the 1 Gbps network, bandwidth are nearly identical to those in the native cases while latencies are 1.2–2 times higher. In the 10 Gbps network, bandwidths are within 60-75% of native while latencies are about 2 to 3 times higher. Both latency and bandwidth under VNET/P exhibit the same good scaling behavior of the native case.

5.5 Application benchmarks

We evaluated the effect of a VNET/P overlay on application performance by running two HPCC application benchmarks and the whole NAS benchmark suite on the cluster described in Section 5.4. Overall, the performance results from the HPCC and NAS benchmarks suggest that VNET/P can achieve high performance for many parallel applications.

HPCC application benchmarks: We considered the two application benchmarks from the HPCC suite that exhibit the large volume and complexity of communication: MPIRandomAcceess and MPIFFT. For 1 Gbps networks, the difference in performance is negligible so we focus here on 10 Gbps networks.

In MPIRandomAccess, random numbers are generated and written to a distributed table, with local buffering. Performance is measured by the billions of updates per second (GUPs) that are performed. Figure 10(a) shows the results of MPIRandomAccess, comparing the VNET/P and Native cases. VNET/P achieves 65-70% application performance compared to the native cases, and performance scales similarly.

MPIFFT implements a double precision complex one-dimensional Discrete Fourier Transform (DFT). Figure 10(b) shows the results of MPIFFT, comparing the VNET/P and Native cases. It shows that VNET/P's application performance is within 60-70% of native performance, with performance scaling similarly.

NAS parallel benchmarks: The NAS Parallel Benchmark (NPB) suite [46] is a set of five kernels and three pseudo-applications that is widely used in parallel performance evaluation. We specif-

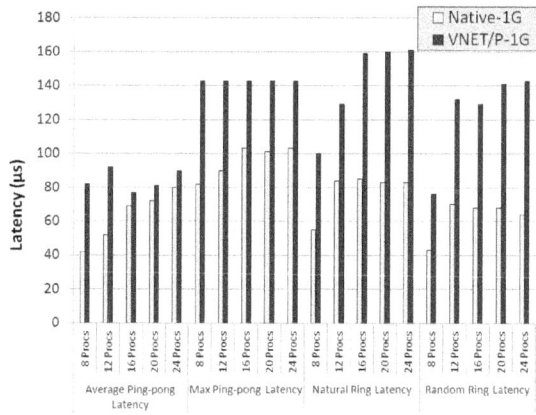

(a) Latency on 1G

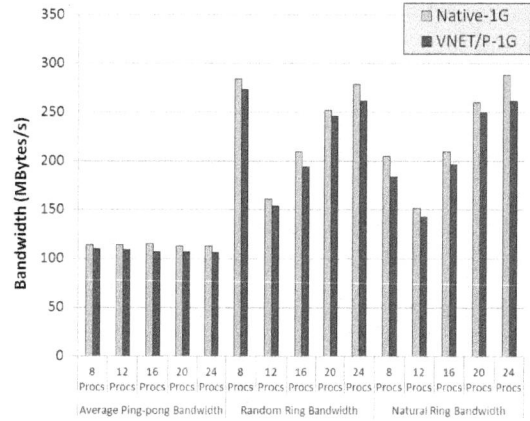

(b) Bandwidth on 1G

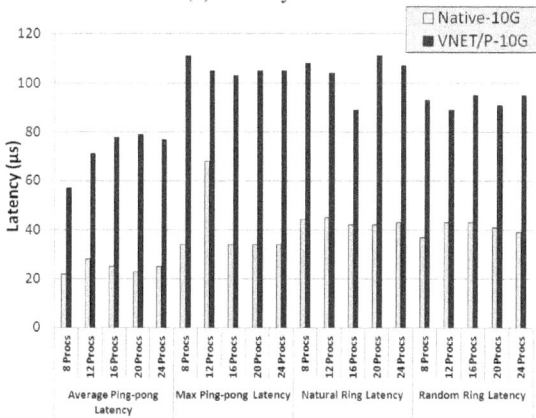

(c) Latency on 10G

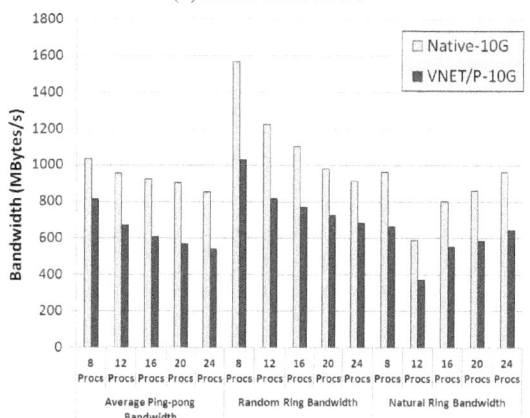

(d) Bandwidth on 10G

Figure 9: HPCC Latency-bandwidth benchmark for both 1 Gbps and 10 Gbps. Ring-based bandwidths are multiplied by the total number of processes in the test. The ping-pong latency and bandwidth tests show results that are consistent with the previous microbenchmarks, while the ring-based tests show that latency and bandwidth of VNET/P scale similarly to the native cases.

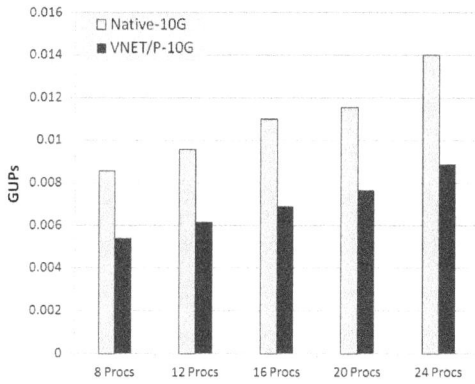

(a) MPIRandomAccess

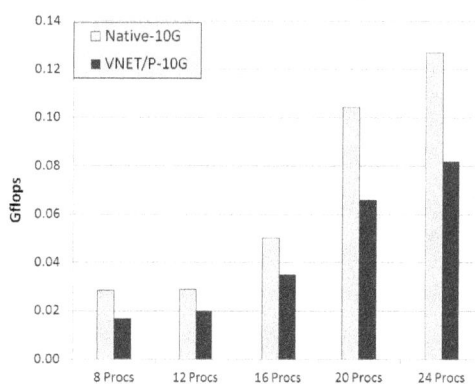

(b)MPIFFT

Figure 10: HPCC application benchmark results. VNET/P achieves reasonable and scalable application performance when support-ing communication-intensive parallel application workloads on 10 Gbps networks. On 1 Gbps networks, the difference is negligible.

ically use NPB-MPI 2.4 in our evaluation. In our description, we name executions with the format "name.class.procs". For example, *bt.B.16* means to run the BT benchmark on 16 processes with a class B problem size.

We run each benchmark with at least two different scales and one problem size, except FT, which is only run with 16 processes. One

VM is run on each physical machine, and it is configured as de-scribed in Section 5.4. The test cases with 8 processes are running within 2 VMs and 4 processes started in each VM. The test cases with 9 processes are run with 4 VMs and 2 or 3 processes per VM. Test cases with with 16 processes have 4 VMs with 4 processes per

Mop/s	Native-1G	VNET/P-1G	$\frac{VNET/P-1G}{Native-1G}(\%)$	Native-10G	VNET/P-10G	$\frac{VNET/P-10G}{Native-10G}(\%)$
ep.B.8	103.15	101.94	98.8%	102.18	102.12	99.9%
ep.B.16	204.88	203.9	99.5%	208	206.52	99.3%
ep.C.8	103.12	102.1	99.0%	103.13	102.14	99.0%
ep.C.16	206.24	204.14	99.0%	206.22	203.98	98.9%
mg.B.8	4400.52	3840.47	87.3%	5110.29	3796.03	74.3%
mg.B.16	1506.77	1498.65	99.5%	9137.26	7405	81.0%
cg.B.8	1542.79	1319.43	85.5%	2096.64	1806.57	86.2%
cg.B.16	160.64	159.69	99.4%	592.08	554.91	93.7%
ft.B.16	1575.83	1290.78	81.9%	1432.3	1228.39	85.8%
is.B.8	78.88	74.61	94.6%	59.15	59.04	99.8%
is.B.16	35.99	35.78	99.4%	23.09	23	99.6%
is.C.8	89.54	82.15	91.7%	132.08	131.87	99.8%
is.C.16	84.76	82.22	97.0%	77.77	76.94	98.9%
lu.B.8	6818.52	5495.23	80.6%	7173.65	6021.78	83.9%
lu.B.16	7847.99	6694.12	85.3%	12981.86	9643.21	74.3%
sp.B.9	1361.38	1215.85	89.3%	2634.53	2421.98	91.9%
sp.B.16	1489.32	1399.6	94.0%	3010.71	2916.81	96.9%
bt.B.9	3423.52	3297.04	96.3%	5229.01	4076.52	78.0%
bt.B.16	4599.38	4348.99	94.6%	6315.11	6105.11	96.7%

Figure 11: NAS Parallel Benchmark performance with VNET/P on 1 Gbps and 10 Gbps networks. VNET/P can achieve native performance on many applications, while it can get reasonable and scalable performance when supporting highly communication-intensive parallel application workloads.

VM. We report each benchmark's *Mop/s total* result for both native and with VNET/P.

Figure 11 shows the NPB performance results, comparing the VNET/P and Native cases on both 1 Gbps and 10 Gbps networks. The upshot of the results is that for most of the NAS benchmarks, VNET/P is able to achieve in excess of 95% of the native performance even on 10 Gbps networks. We now describe the results for each benchmark.

EP is an "embarrassingly parallel" kernel that estimates the upper achievable limits for floating point performance, It does not require a significant interprocessor communication. VNET/P achieves native performance in all cases.

MG is a simplified multigrid kernel that requires highly structured long distance communication and tests both short and long distance data communication. With 16 processes, MG achieves native performance on the 1 Gbps network, and 81% of native performance on the 10 Gbps network.

CG implements the conjugate gradient method to compute an approximation to the smallest eigenvalue of a large sparse symmetric positive definite matrix. It is typical of unstructured grid computations in that it tests irregular long distance communication, employing unstructured matrix vector multiplication. With 16 processes, CG achieves native performance on the 1 Gbps network and 94% of native performance on the 10 Gbps network.

FT implements the solution of partial differential equations using FFTs, and captures the essence of many spectral codes. It is a rigorous test of long-distance communication performance. With 16 nodes, it achieves 82% of native performance on 1 Gbps and 86% of native performance on 10 Gbps.

IS implements a large integer sort of the kind that is important in particle method codes and tests both integer computation speed and communication performance. Here VNET/P achieves native performance in all cases.

LU solves a regular-sparse, block (5×5) lower and upper triangular system, a problem associated with implicit computational fluid dynamics algorithms. VNET/P achieves 75%-85% of native

performance on this benchmark, and there is no significant difference between the 1 Gbps and 10 Gbps network.

SP and BT implement solutions of multiple, independent systems of non diagonally dominant, scalar, pentadiagonal equations, also common in computational fluid dynamics. The salient difference between the two is the communication to computation ratio. For SP with 16 processes, VNET/P achieves 94% of native performance on 1 Gbps around 97% of native on 10 Gbps. For BT at the same scale, 95% of native at 1 Gbps and 97% of native at 10 Gbps are achieved.

6. VNET/P FOR INFINIBAND

In support of hardware independence, the 3rd goal of VNET articulated in Section 3, we have developed an implementation of VNET/P that allows guests that only support Ethernet NICs to be seamlessly run on top of an InfiniBand network, or to span InfiniBand networks and other networks. Regardless of the underlying networking hardware, the guests see a simple Ethernet LAN.

For the current Infiniband implementation, the host OS that is used is Sandia National Labs' Kitten lightweight kernel. Kitten has, by design, a minimal set of in-kernel services. For this reason, the VNET/P Bridge functionality is not implemented in the kernel, but rather in a privileged service VM called the Bridge VM that has direct access to the physical Infiniband device.

In place of encapsulating Ethernet packets in UDP packets for transmission to a remote VNET/P core, VNET/P's InfiniBand support simply maps Ethernet packets to InfiniBand frames. These frames are then transmitted through an InfiniBand queue pair accessed via the Linux IPoIB framework.

We conducted preliminary performance tests of VNET/P on InfiniBand using 8900 byte TCP payloads running on ttcp on a testbed similar to the one described in Section 5.1. Here, each node was a dual quad-core 2.3 GHz 2376 AMD Opteron machine with 32 GB of RAM and a Mellanox MT26428 InfiniBand NIC in a PCI-e slot. The Infiniband NICs were connected via a Mellanox MTS 3600 36-port 20/40Gbps InfiniBand switch.

It is important to point out that VNET/P over Infiniband is a work in progress and we present it here as a proof of concept. Nonetheless, on this testbed it achieved 4.0 Gbps end-to-end TCP throughput, compared to 6.5 Gbps when run natively on top of IP-over-InfiniBand in Reliable Connected (RC) mode.

7. CONCLUSION AND FUTURE WORK

We have described the VNET model of overlay networking in a distributed virtualized computing environment and our efforts in extending this simple and flexible model to support tightly-coupled high performance computing applications running on high-performance networking hardware in current supercomputing environments, future data centers, and future clouds. VNET/P is our design and implementation of VNET for such environments. Its design goal is to achieve near-native throughput and latency on 1 and 10 Gbps Ethernet, InfiniBand, and other high performance interconnects.

To achieve performance, VNET/P relies on several key techniques and systems, including lightweight virtualization in the Palacios virtual machine monitor, high-performance I/O, and multi-core overlay routing support. Together, these techniques enable VNET/P to provide a simple and flexible level 2 Ethernet network abstraction in a large range of systems no matter the actual underlying networking technology is. While our VNET/P implementation is tightly integrated into our Palacios virtual machine monitor, the principles involved could be used in other environments as well.

We are currently working to further enhance VNET/P's performance through its guarded privileged execution directly in the guest, including an uncooperative guest. We are also enhancing its functionality through broader support on InfiniBand and on the Cray SeaStar interconnect.

8. REFERENCES

[1] ABU-LIBDEH, H., COSTA, P., ROWSTRON, A., O'SHEA, G., AND DONNELLY, A. Symbiotic routing in future data centers. In *Proceedings of SIGCOMM* (August 2010).

[2] ANDERSEN, D., BALAKRISHNAN, H., KAASHOEK, F., AND MORRIS, R. Resilient overlay networks. In *Proceedings of SOSP* (March 2001).

[3] BAVIER, A. C., FEAMSTER, N., HUANG, M., PETERSON, L. L., AND REXFORD, J. In vini veritas: realistic and controlled network experimentation. In *Proceedings of SIGCOMM* (September 2006).

[4] DINDA, P., SUNDARARAJ, A., LANGE, J., GUPTA, A., AND LIN, B. Methods and systems for automatic inference and adaptation of virtualized computing environments, March 2012. United States Patent Number 8,145,760.

[5] EVANGELINOS, C., AND HILL, C. Cloud computing for parallel scientific hpc applications: Feasibility of running coupled atmosphere-ocean climate models on amazon's ec2. In *Proceedings of Cloud Computing and its Applications (CCA)* (October 2008).

[6] FIGUEIREDO, R., DINDA, P. A., AND FORTES, J. A case for grid computing on virtual machines. In *Proceedings of the 23rd International Conference on Distributed Computing Systems (ICDCS 2003)* (May 2003).

[7] GABRIEL, E., FAGG, G. E., BOSILCA, G., ANGSKUN, T., DONGARRA, J. J., SQUYRES, J. M., SAHAY, V., KAMBADUR, P., BARRETT, B., LUMSDAINE, A., CASTAIN, R. H., DANIEL, D. J., GRAHAM, R. L., AND WOODALL, T. S. Open MPI: Goals, concept, and design of a next generation MPI implementation. In *Proceedings of the*

11th European PVM/MPI Users' Group Meeting (September 2004).

[8] GANGULY, A., AGRAWAL, A., BOYKIN, P. O., AND FIGUEIREDO, R. IP over P2P: Enabling self-configuring virtual ip networks for grid computing. In *Proceedings of the 20th IEEE International Parallel and Distributed Processing Symposium (IPDPS)* (April 2006).

[9] GREENBERG, A., HAMILTON, J. R., JAIN, N., KANDULA, S., KIM, C., LAHIRI, P., MALTZ, D. A., PATEL, P., AND SENGUPTA, S. VL2: A scalable and flexible data center network. In *Proceedings of SIGCOMM* (August 2009).

[10] GUO, C., LU, G., LI, D., WU, H., ZHANG, X., SHI, Y., TIAN, C., ZHANG, Y., AND LU, S. Bcube: A high performance, server-centric network architecture for modular data centers. In *Proceedings of SIGCOMM* (August 2009).

[11] GUPTA, A., AND DINDA, P. A. Inferring the topology and traffic load of parallel programs running in a virtual machine environment. In *Proceedings of the 10th Workshop on Job Scheduling Strategies for Parallel Processing (JSSPP)* (June 2004).

[12] GUPTA, A., ZANGRILLI, M., SUNDARARAJ, A., HUANG, A., DINDA, P., AND LOWEKAMP, B. Free network measurement for virtual machine distributed computing. In *Proceedings of the 20th IEEE International Parallel and Distributed Processing Symposium (IPDPS)* (2006).

[13] HUA CHU, Y., RAO, S., SHESHAN, S., AND ZHANG, H. Enabling conferencing applications on the internet using an overlay multicast architecture. In *Proceedings of ACM SIGCOMM* (August 2001).

[14] HUANG, W., LIU, J., ABALI, B., AND PANDA, D. A case for high performance computing with virtual machines. In *Proceedings of the 20th ACM International Conference on Supercomputing (ICS)* (June–July 2006).

[15] INNOVATIVE COMPUTING LABORATORY. Hpc challenge benchmark. http://icl.cs.utk.edu/hpcc/.

[16] INTEL. Intel cluster toolkit 3.0 for linux. http://software.intel.com/en-us/articles/intel-mpi-benchmarks/.

[17] JIANG, X., AND XU, D. Violin: Virtual internetworking on overlay infrastructure. Tech. Rep. CSD TR 03-027, Department of Computer Sciences, Purdue University, July 2003.

[18] JOSEPH, D. A., KANNAN, J., KUBOTA, A., LAKSHMINARAYANAN, K., STOICA, I., AND WEHRLE, K. Ocala: An architecture for supporting legacy applications over overlays. In *Proceedings of the 3rd Symposium on Networked Systems Design and Implementation (NSDI)* (May 2006).

[19] KALLAHALLA, M., UYSAL, M., SWAMINATHAN, R., LOWELL, D. E., WRAY, M., CHRISTIAN, T., EDWARDS, N., DALTON, C. I., AND GITTLER, F. Softudc: A software-based data center for utility computing. *IEEE Computer 37*, 11 (2004), 38–46.

[20] KIM, C., CAESAR, M., AND REXFORD, J. Floodless in seattle: a scalable ethernet architecture for large enterprises. In *Proceedings of SIGCOMM* (August 2008).

[21] KUMAR, S., RAJ, H., SCHWAN, K., AND GANEV, I. Re-architecting vmms for multicore systems: The sidecore approach. In *Proceedings of the 2007 Workshop on the Interaction between Operating Systems and Computer Architecture* (June 2007).

[22] LANGE, J., AND DINDA, P. Transparent network services via a virtual traffic layer for virtual machines. In *Proceedings of the 16th IEEE International Symposium on High Performance Distributed Computing (HPDC)* (June 2007).

[23] LANGE, J., DINDA, P., HALE, K., AND XIA, L. An introduction to the palacios virtual machine monitor—release 1.3. Tech. Rep. NWU-EECS-11-10, Department of Electrical Engineering and Computer Science, Northwestern University, October 2011.

[24] LANGE, J., PEDRETTI, K., DINDA, P., BAE, C., BRIDGES, P., SOLTERO, P., AND MERRITT, A. Minimal-overhead virtualization of a large scale supercomputer. In *Proceedings of the 2011 ACM SIGPLAN/SIGOPS International Conference on Virtual Execution Environments (VEE)* (March 2011).

[25] LANGE, J., PEDRETTI, K., HUDSON, T., DINDA, P., CUI, Z., XIA, L., BRIDGES, P., GOCKE, A., JACONETTE, S., LEVENHAGEN, M., AND BRIGHTWELL, R. Palacios and kitten: New high performance operating systems for scalable virtualized and native supercomputing. In *Proceedings of the 24th IEEE International Parallel and Distributed Processing Symposium (IPDPS)* (April 2010).

[26] LANGE, J., SUNDARARAJ, A., AND DINDA, P. Automatic dynamic run-time optical network reservations. In *Proceedings of the 14th International Symposium on High Performance Distributed Computing (HPDC)* (July 2005).

[27] LIN, B., AND DINDA, P. Vsched: Mixing batch and interactive virtual machines using periodic real-time scheduling. In *Proceedings of ACM/IEEE SC (Supercomputing)* (November 2005).

[28] LIN, B., SUNDARARAJ, A., AND DINDA, P. Time-sharing parallel applications with performance isolation and control. In *Proceedings of the 4th IEEE International Conference on Autonomic Computing (ICAC)* (June 2007).

[29] LIU, J., HUANG, W., ABALI, B., AND PANDA, D. High performance vmm-bypass i/o in virtual machines. In *Proceedings of the USENIX Annual Technical Conference* (May 2006).

[30] MENON, A., COX, A. L., AND ZWAENEPOEL, W. Optimizing network virtualization in xen. In *Proceedings of the USENIX Annual Technical Conference (USENIX)* (May 2006).

[31] MERGEN, M. F., UHLIG, V., KRIEGER, O., AND XENIDIS, J. Virtualization for high-performance computing. *Operating Systems Review 40*, 2 (2006), 8–11.

[32] MYSORE, R. N., PAMBORIS, A., FARRINGTON, N., HUANG, N., MIRI, P., RADHAKRISHNAN, S., SUBRAMANYA, V., AND VAHDAT, A. Portland: A scalable fault-tolerant layer 2 data center network fabric. In *Proceedings of SIGCOMM* (August 2009).

[33] NURMI, D., WOLSKI, R., GRZEGORZYK, C., OBERTELLI, G., SOMAN, S., YOUSEFF, L., AND ZAGORODNOV, D. The eucalyptus open-source cloud-computing system. In *Proceedings of the 9th IEEE/ACM International Symposium on Cluster Computing and the Grid (CCGrid)* (May 2009).

[34] OSTERMANN, S., IOSUP, A., YIGITBASI, N., PRODAN, R., FAHRINGER, T., AND EPEMA, D. An early performance analysis of cloud computing services for scientific computing. Tech. Rep. PDS2008-006, Delft University of Technology, Parallel and Distributed Systems Report Series, December 2008.

[35] RAJ, H., AND SCHWAN, K. High performance and scalable i/o virtualization via self-virtualized devices. In *Proceedings of the 16th IEEE International Symposium on High Performance Distributed Computing (HPDC)* (July 2007).

[36] RUSSELL, R. virtio: towards a de-facto standard for virtual i/o devices. *Operating Systems Review 42*, 5 (2008), 95–103.

[37] RUTH, P., JIANG, X., XU, D., AND GOASGUEN, S. Towards virtual distributed environments in a shared infrastructure. *IEEE Computer* (May 2005).

[38] RUTH, P., MCGACHEY, P., JIANG, X., AND XU, D. Viocluster: Virtualization for dynamic computational domains. In *Proceedings of the IEEE International Conference on Cluster Computing (Cluster)* (September 2005).

[39] SHAFER, J., CARR, D., MENON, A., RIXNER, S., COX, A. L., ZWAENEPOEL, W., AND WILLMANN, P. Concurrent direct network access for virtual machine monitors. In *Proceedings of the 13th International Symposium on High Performance Computer Architecture (HPCA)* (February 2007).

[40] STOICA, I., MORRIS, R., KARGER, D., KAASHOEK, F., AND BALAKRISHNAN, H. Chord: A scalable Peer-To-Peer lookup service for internet applications. In *Proceedings of ACM SIGCOMM 2001* (2001), pp. 149–160.

[41] SUGERMAN, J., VENKITACHALAN, G., AND LIM, B.-H. Virtualizing I/O devices on VMware workstation's hosted virtual machine monitor. In *Proceedings of the USENIX Annual Technical Conference* (June 2001).

[42] SUNDARARAJ, A., AND DINDA, P. Towards virtual networks for virtual machine grid computing. In *Proceedings of the 3rd USENIX Virtual Machine Research And Technology Symposium (VM 2004)* (May 2004). Earlier version available as Technical Report NWU-CS-03-27, Department of Computer Science, Northwestern University.

[43] SUNDARARAJ, A., GUPTA, A., , AND DINDA, P. Increasing application performance in virtual environments through run-time inference and adaptation. In *Proceedings of the 14th IEEE International Symposium on High Performance Distributed Computing (HPDC)* (July 2005).

[44] SUNDARARAJ, A., SANGHI, M., LANGE, J., AND DINDA, P. An optimization problem in adaptive virtual environmnets. In *Proceedings of the seventh Workshop on Mathematical Performance Modeling and Analysis (MAMA)* (June 2005).

[45] TSUGAWA, M. O., AND FORTES, J. A. B. A virtual network (vine) architecture for grid computing. In *20th International Parallel and Distributed Processing Symposium (IPDPS)* (April 2006).

[46] VAN DER WIJNGAART, R. NAS parallel benchmarks version 2.4. Tech. Rep. NAS-02-007, NASA Advanced Supercomputing (NAS Division), NASA Ames Research Center, October 2002.

[47] WOLINSKY, D., LIU, Y., JUSTE, P. S., VENKATASUBRAMANIAN, G., AND FIGUEIREDO, R. On the design of scalable, self-configuring virtual networks. In *Proceedings of 21st ACM/IEEE International Conference of High Performance Computing, Networking, Storage, and Analysis (SuperComputing / SC)* (November 2009).

[48] XIA, L., LANGE, J., DINDA, P., AND BAE, C. Investigating Virtual Passthrough I/O on Commodity Devices. *Operating Systems Review 43*, 3 (July 2009). Initial version appeared at WIOV 2008.

Massively-Parallel Stream Processing under QoS Constraints with Nephele

Björn Lohrmann
Technische Universität Berlin
Einsteinufer 17
10587 Berlin
Germany
bjoern.lohrmann@tu-berlin.de

Daniel Warneke
Technische Universität Berlin
Einsteinufer 17
10587 Berlin
Germany
daniel.warneke@tu-berlin.de

Odej Kao
Technische Universität Berlin
Einsteinufer 17
10587 Berlin
Germany
odej.kao@tu-berlin.de

ABSTRACT

Today, a growing number of commodity devices, like mobile phones or smart meters, is equipped with rich sensors and capable of producing continuous data streams. The sheer amount of these devices and the resulting overall data volumes of the streams raise new challenges with respect to the scalability of existing stream processing systems.

At the same time, massively-parallel data processing systems like MapReduce have proven that they scale to large numbers of nodes and efficiently organize data transfers between them. Many of these systems also provide streaming capabilities. However, unlike traditional stream processors, these systems have disregarded QoS requirements of prospective stream processing applications so far.

In this paper we address this gap. First, we analyze common design principles of today's parallel data processing frameworks and identify those principles that provide degrees of freedom in trading off the QoS goals latency and throughput. Second, we propose a scheme which allows these frameworks to detect violations of user-defined latency constraints and optimize the job execution without manual interaction in order to meet these constraints while keeping the throughput as high as possible. As a proof of concept, we implemented our approach for our parallel data processing framework Nephele and evaluated its effectiveness through a comparison with Hadoop Online.

For a multimedia streaming application we can demonstrate an improved processing latency by factor of at least 15 while preserving high data throughput when needed.

Categories and Subject Descriptors

H.2.4 [**Systems**]: Parallel databases; C.2.4 [**Distributed Systems**]: Distributed applications

General Terms

Experimentation, Measurement, Performance

Keywords

Large-Scale Data Processing, Stream Processing, Quality of Service, MapReduce

1. INTRODUCTION

In the course of the last decade, science and the IT industry have witnessed an unparalleled increase of data. While the traditional way of creating data on the Internet allowed companies to lazily crawl websites or related data sources, store the data on massive arrays of hard disks, and process it in a batch-style fashion, recent hardware developments for mobile and embedded devices together with ubiquitous networking have also drawn attention to *streamed data*.

Streamed data can originate from various different sources. Every modern smartphone is equipped with a variety of sensors, capable of producing rich media streams of video, audio, and possibly GPS data. Moreover, the number of deployed sensor networks is steadily increasing, enabling innovations in several fields of life, for example energy consumption, traffic regulation, or e-health. However, a crucial prerequisite to leverage those innovations is the ability to process and analyze a large number of individual data streams in a near-real-time manner. As motivation, we would like to illustrate two emerging scenarios:

- **Live Media Streaming:** Today, virtually all smart phones can produce live video streams. Several websites like Livestream[1] or Ustream[2] have already responded to that development, offering their users to produce and broadcast live media content to a large audience in a way that has been reserved to major television networks before. Recently, we have seen first steps towards this "citizen journalism" during the political incidents in the Middle East or the "Occupy Wall Street" movement. However, at the moment, the capabilities of those live broadcasting services are limited to media transcoding and simple picture overlays. Although the content of two different streams may overlap to a great extent (for example because the people filming the scene are standing close to each other),

---

[1] http://www.livestream.com/
[2] http://www.ustream.tv/

they are currently processed completely independent of each other. In contrast to that, future services might also offer to automatically *aggregate* and *relate* streams from different sources, thereby creating a more complete picture and eventually better coverage for the viewers.

- **Energy informatics:** Smart meters are currently being deployed in growing numbers at consumer homes by power utilities. Smart meters are networked devices that monitor a household's power consumption and report it back to the power utility. On the utility's side, having such near-real-time data about power consumption is a key aspect of managing fluctuations in the power grid's load. Such fluctuations are introduced not only by consumers but also by the increasing, long-term integration of renewable energy sources. Data analytics applications that are hooked into the live meter data stream can be used for many operational aspects such as monitoring the grid infrastructure for equipment limits, initiating autonomous control actions to deal with component failures, voltage sags/spikes, and forecasting power usage. Especially in the case of autonomous control actions, the freshness of the data that is being acted upon is of paramount importance.

Opportunities to harvest the new data sources in the various domains are plentiful. However, the sheer amount of incoming data that must be processed online also raises scalability concerns with regard to existing solutions. As opposed to systems working with batch-style workloads, stream processing systems must often meet particular Quality of Service (QoS) goals, otherwise the quality of the processing output degrades or the output becomes worthless at all. Existing stream processors [1, 2] have put much emphasis on meeting provided QoS goals of applications, though often at the expense of scalability or a loss of generality [17].

In terms of scalability and programming generality, the predominant workhorses for data-intensive workloads at the moment are massively-parallel data processing frameworks like MapReduce [12] or Dryad [14]. By design, these systems scale to large numbers of compute nodes and are capable of efficiently transferring large amounts of data between them. Many of the newer systems [8, 11, 14, 16, 18] also allow to assemble complex parallel data flow graphs and to construct pipelines between the individual parts of the flow. Therefore, these systems generally are also suitable for streaming applications. However, so far they have concentrated on few streaming application, like online aggregation or "early out" computations [11], and have not considered QoS goals.

This paper attempts to bridge that gap. We have analyzed a series of open-source frameworks for parallel data processing and highlight common design principles they share to achieve scalability and high data throughput. We show how some aspects of these design principles can be used to trade off the QoS goals latency and throughput in a fine-grained per-task manner and propose a scheme to automatically do so during the job execution based on user-defined latency constraints. Starting from the assumption that high data throughput is desired, our scheme monitors potential latency constraint violations at runtime and can then gradually applies two techniques, *adaptive output buffer sizing* and *dynamic task chaining*, to met the constraints while maintaining high throughput as far as possible. As a proof of concept,

we implemented the scheme for our data processing framework Nephele and evaluated their effectiveness through a comparison with Hadoop Online.

The rest of this paper is structured as follows: In Section 2 we examine the common design principles of today's massively-parallel data processing frameworks and discuss the implications of meeting the aforementioned QoS constraints. Section 3 presents our scheme to dynamically adapt to the user-defined latency constraints, whereas Section 4 contains an experimental evaluation. Section 5 provides a brief overview of current stream and parallel data processors. Finally, we conclude our paper in Section 6.

2. MASSIVELY-PARALLEL DATA PROCESSING AND STREAMED DATA

In recent years, a variety of frameworks for massively-parallel data analysis has emerged [8, 11, 12, 14, 16, 18]. Many of them are open-source software. Having analyzed their internal structure, we found they often follow similar design principles to achieve scalability and high throughput.

This section highlights those principals and discuss their implications on stream processing under QoS constraints.

2.1 Design Principles of Parallel Data Processing Frameworks

Frameworks for parallel data processing typically follow a master-worker pattern. The master node receives jobs from the user, splits them into sets of individual tasks, and schedules those tasks to run on the available worker nodes.

The structure of those jobs can usually be described by a graph with vertices representing the job's individual tasks and the edges denoting communication channels between them. For example, from a high-level perspective, the graph representation of a typical MapReduce job would consist of a set of Map vertices connected via edges to a set of Reduce vertices. Some frameworks have generalized the MapReduce model to arbitrary directed acyclic graphs (DAGs) [8, 14, 18], some even allow graph structures containing loops [16].

However, independent of the concrete graph model used to describe jobs for the respective framework, the way both the vertices and edges translate to system resources at runtime is surprisingly similar among all of these systems.

Each task vertex of the overall job typically translates to either a separate process or a separate thread at runtime. Considering the large number of CPUs (or CPU cores) these frameworks must scale up to, this is a reasonable design decision. By assigning each task to a different thread/process, those tasks can be executed independently and utilize a separate CPU core. Moreover, it gives the underlying operating system various degrees of freedom in scheduling the tasks among the individual CPU cores. For example, if a task cannot fully utilize its assigned CPU resources or is waiting for an I/O operation to complete, the operating system can assign the idle CPU time to a different thread/process.

The communication model of massively-parallel data processing systems typically follows a producer-consumer pattern. Tasks can produce a sequence of *data items* which are then passed to and consumed by their successor tasks according to the edges of the job's graph representation. The way the data items are physically transported from one task to the other depends on the concrete framework. In the most lightweight case, two tasks are represented as two different

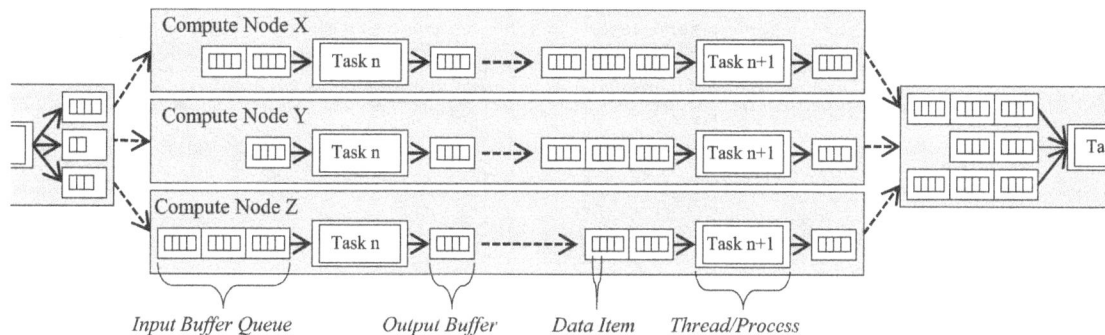

Figure 1: Typical processing pattern of frameworks for massively-parallel data analysis

threads running inside the same operating system process and can use shared memory to exchange data. If tasks are mapped to different processes, possibly running on different worker nodes, the data items are typically exchanged through files or a network connection.

However, since all of these frameworks have been designed for data-intensive workloads and hence strive for high data throughput, they attempt to minimize the transfer overhead per data item. As a result, these frameworks try to avoid shipping individual data items from one task to the other. As illustrated in Figure 1, the data items produced by a task are typically collected in a larger *output buffer*. Once its capacity limit has been reached, the entire buffer is shipped to the receiving task and in many cases placed in its *input buffer queue*, waiting to be consumed.

2.2 Implications for QoS-Constrained Streaming Applications

Having highlighted some basic design principles of today's parallel data processing frameworks, we now discuss which aspects of those principles provide degrees of freedom in trading off the different QoS goals latency and throughput.

2.2.1 The Role of the Output Buffer

As explained previously, most frameworks for parallel data processing introduce distinct output buffers to minimize the transfer overhead per data item and improve the data item throughput, i.e. the average number of items that can be shipped from one task to the other in a given time interval.

For the vast majority of data processing frameworks we have analyzed in the scope of our research, the output buffer size could be set on a system level, i.e. all jobs of the respective framework instance were forced to use the same output buffer sizes. Some frameworks also allowed to set the output buffer size per job, for example Apache Hadoop[3]. Typical sizes of these output buffers range from several MB to 4 or 8 KB, depending on the focus of the framework.

While output buffers play an important role in achieving high data throughput, they also make it hard to optimize jobs for current parallel data processors towards the QoS goal latency. Since an output buffer is typically not shipped until it has reached its capacity limit, the latency an individual data item experiences depends on the system load.

In order to illustrate this effect, we created a small sample job consisting of two tasks, a sender task and a receiver task. The sender created data items of 128 bytes length at a fixed

rate n and wrote them to an output buffer of a fixed size. Once an output buffer had reached its capacity limit, it was sent to the receiver through a TCP connection. We ran the job several times. Between each run, we varied the output buffer size.

The results of this initial experiment are depicted in Figure 2. As illustrated in Figure 2(a), the average latency from the creation of a data item at the sender until its arrival at the receiver depends heavily on the creation rate and the size of the output buffer. With only one created data item per second and an output buffer size of 64 KB, it takes more than 222 seconds on an average before an item arrives at the receiver. At low data creation rates, the size of the output buffer has a significant effect on the latency. The more the data creation rate increases, the more the latency converges towards a lower bound. At a rate of 10^8 created items per second, we measured an average data item latency of approximately 50 milliseconds (ms), independent of the output buffer size.

As a baseline experiment, we also executed separate runs of the sample job which involved flushing incomplete output buffers. Flushing forced the system to transfer the output buffer to the receiver after each written data item. As a result, the average data item latency was uniformly 38 ms, independent of the data creation rate.

Figure 2(b) shows the effects of the different data creation rates and output buffer sizes on the throughput of the sample job. While the QoS objective latency suggests using small output buffers or even flushing incomplete buffers, these actions show a detrimental effect when high data throughput is desired. As depicted in Figure 2(b), the data item throughput that could be achieved grew with the size of the output buffer. With relatively big output buffers of 64 or 32 KB in size, we were able to fully saturate the 1 GBit/s network link between the sender and the receiver, given a sufficiently high data creation rate. However, the small output buffers failed to achieve a reasonable data item throughput. In the most extreme case, i.e. flushing the output buffer after every written data item, we were unable to attain a data item throughput of more than 10 MBit/s. The reason for this is the disproportionally high transfer overhead per data item (output buffer meta data, memory management, thread synchronization) that massively-parallel data processing frameworks in general are not designed for. Similar behavior is known from the TCP networking layer, where the Nagle algorithm can be deactivated (TCP_NODELAY option) to improve connection latency.

---

[3] http://hadoop.apache.org/

(a) Average data item latency   (b) Average data item throughput

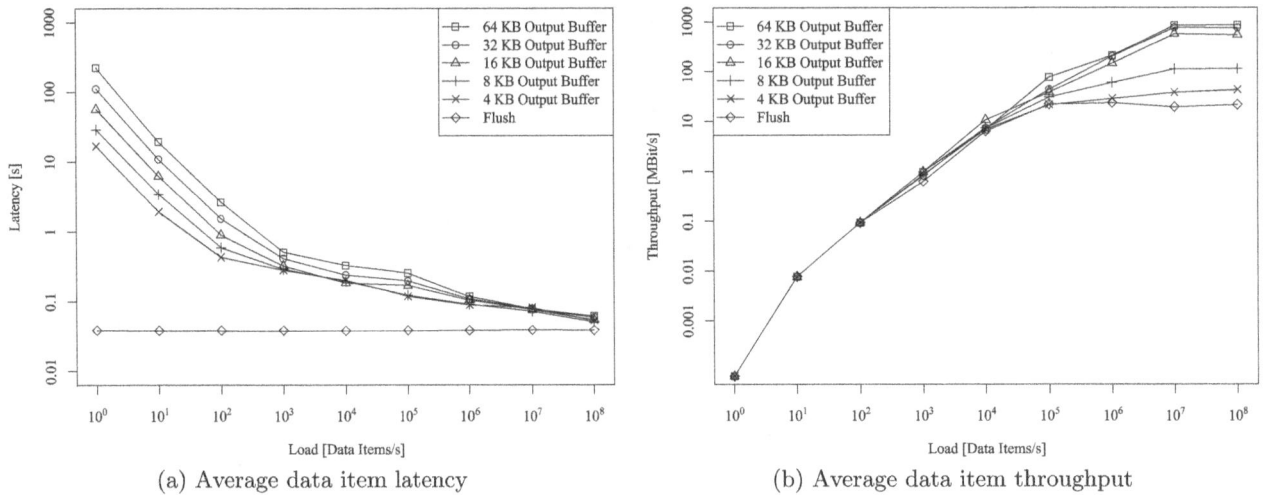

Figure 2: The effect of different output buffer sizes on data item latency and throughput

In sum, the sample job highlights an interesting trade-off that exists in current data processing frameworks with respect to the output buffer size. While jobs with low latency demands benefit from small output buffers, the classic data-intensive workloads still require relatively large output buffers in order to achieve high data throughput. This trade-off puts the user in charge of configuring a reasonable output buffer size for his job and assumes that (a) the used processing framework allows him to specify the output buffer size on a per-job basis, (b) he can estimate the expected load his job will experience, and (c) the expected load does not change over time. In practice, however, at least one of those three assumptions often does not hold. One might also argue that there is no single reasonable output buffer size for an entire job as the job consists of different tasks that produce varying data item sizes at varying rates, so that any chosen fixed output buffer size can only result in acceptable latencies for a fraction of the tasks but not for all of them.

2.2.2 The Role of the Thread/Process Model

Current frameworks for parallel data processing typically map different tasks to different operating system processes or at least different threads. While this facilitates natural scalability and load balancing between different CPUs or CPU cores, it also raises the communication overhead between tasks. In the most lightweight case, where different tasks are mapped to different threads within the same process and communication is performed via shared memory, the communication overhead typically only consists of thread synchronization, scheduling, and managing cache consistency issues. However, when the communicating tasks are mapped to different processes or even worker nodes, passing data items between them additionally involves serialization/deserialization and, depending on the way the data is physically exchanged, writing the serialized data to the network/file system and reading it back again.

Depending on the complexity of the tasks, the communication overhead can account for a significant fraction of the overall processing time. If the tasks themselves are lightweight, but the data items are rather large and complex to serialize/deserialize (as in case of a filter operation

on a nested XML structure [4]), the overhead can limit the throughput and impose a considerable processing latency.

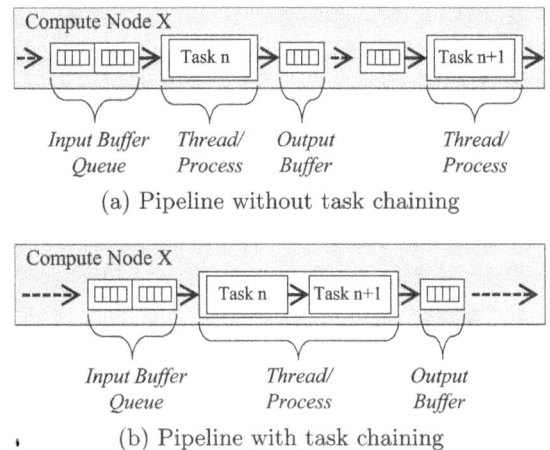

(a) Pipeline without task chaining

(b) Pipeline with task chaining

Figure 3: Different execution models with and without task chaining

As illustrated in Figure 3, a common approach to address this form of communication overhead is to chain lightweight tasks together and execute them in a single thread/process. The most popular example in the area of parallel data processing is probably the chained map functions from Apache Hadoop. However, a similar idea was also described earlier as rewriting a program to its "normal form" by Aldinucci and Danelutto [3] in the context of stream parallel skeletons.

Before starting a Hadoop job, a user can specify a series of map functions to be chained. Hadoop will then execute these functions in a single process. Chaining tasks often also eliminates the need for separate output buffers. For example, in case of Hadoop's chained map functions, the user code of the next map function in the processing chain can be directly invoked on the previous map function's output. Depending on the semantics of the concatenated tasks, chaining may also render the serialization/deserialization between tasks superfluous. If the chained tasks are stateless (as typically expected from map functions in Hadoop), it is safe to pass the data items from one task to the other by reference.

With regard to stream processing, chaining tasks offers an interesting approach to reduce processing latency and increase throughput at the same time. However, similar to the output buffer size, there might also be an important trade-off, especially when the job's workload is unknown in advance or is likely to change over time.

In its current form, task chaining is performed at compile time, so once the job is running, all chained tasks are bound to a single execution thread. In situations with low load, this might be beneficial since communication overhead is decreased and potential throughput and latency goals can be met more easily. However, when the load increases in the course of the job processing, the static chaining prevents the underlying operating system from distributing the tasks across several CPU cores. As a result, task chaining can also be disadvantageous if (a) the complexity of the chained tasks is unknown in advance or (b) the workload the streaming job has to handle is unknown or changes over time.

3. AUTOMATIC QOS-OPTIMIZATION FOR STREAMING APPLICATIONS

Currently, it is the user of a particular framework who must estimate the effects of the configured buffer size and thread/process model on a a job's latency and throughput characteristics in a cumbersome and inaccurate manner.

In the following, we propose an extension to parallel data processing frameworks which spares the user this hassle. Starting from the assumption that high throughput continues to be the predominant QoS goal in parallel data processing, our extension lets users add latency constraints to their job specifications. Based on these constraints, it continuously monitors the job execution and detects violations of the provided latency constraints *at runtime*. Our extension can then selectively trade high data throughput for a lower processing latency using two distinct strategies, *adaptive output buffer sizing* and *dynamic task chaining*.

As a proof of concept, we implemented this extension as part of our massively-parallel data processing framework Nephele [18] which runs data analysis jobs based on DAGs. However, based on the common principles identified in the previous section, we argue that similar strategies are applicable to other frameworks as well.

3.1 Specifying Latency Constraints

For the remainder of the paper, we will assume a DAG $G = (V_G, E_G)$ as the underlying structure of a job. At runtime each vertex $v \in V_G$ is a a task containing user code. The directed edge $e = (v_1, v_2) \in E_G$ is a channel along which the task v_1 can send data items of arbitrary size to task v_2.

In order to specify latency constraints, a user must be aware how much latency his application can tolerate in order to still be useful. With his knowledge from the application domain a user should then identify latency critical sequences of tasks and channels within the DAG for which he can express required upper latency bounds in the form of *constraints*. These constraints are part of the job description and provide information to the framework about where optimizations are necessary.

In the following, we will formally distinguish between task,

channel, and sequence latency, based on which latency constraints can then be expressed.

3.1.1 Task Latency

Given a task v_i, an incoming channel $e_{in} = (v_x, v_i)$ and an outgoing channel $e_{out} = (v_i, v_y)$, we shall define the *task latency* $tl(d, v_i, v_x \rightarrow v_y)$ as the time difference between a data item d entering the user code of v_i via the channel e_{in} and the next data item exiting the user code via e_{out}.

This definition has several implications. First, task latency is undefined on source and sink tasks as these task types lack incoming and, respectively, outgoing channels. Task latencies can be infinite if the task never emits for certain in/out channel combinations. Moreover, task latency can vary significantly between subsequent items, for example, if the task reads two items but emits only one item after it has read the last one of the two. In this case the first item will have experienced a higher task latency than the second one.

3.1.2 Channel Latency

Given two tasks $v_i, v_j \in V$ connected via channel $e = (v_i, v_j) \in E_G$, we define the *channel latency* $cl(d, e)$ as the time difference between the data item d exiting the user code of v_i and entering the user code of v_j. The channel latency may also vary significantly between data items on the same channel due to differences in item size, output buffer utilization, network congestion, and the length of the input queues that need to be transited on the way to the receiving task.

3.1.3 Sequence Latency

Sequences are series of of connected tasks and channels and thus should be used to identify the parts of the DAG for which the application has latency requirements. Let us assume a sequence $S = (s_1, \ldots, s_n)$, $n \geq 1$ of connected tasks and channels. The first element of the sequence is allowed to be either a task or a channel. For example, if s_2 is a task, then s_1 needs to be an incoming and s_3 an outgoing channel of the task. If a data item d enters the sequence S, we can define the *sequence latency* $sl(d, S)$ that the item d experiences as $sl^*(d, S, 1)$ where

$$sl^*(d, S, i) = \begin{cases} l(d, s_i) + sl^*(s_i(d), S, i+1) & \text{if } i < n \\ l(d, s_i) & \text{if } i = n \end{cases}$$

If s_i is a task, then $l(d, s_i)$ is equal to the task latency $tl(d, s_i, v_x \rightarrow v_y)$ and $s_i(d)$ is the next data item produced by s_i to be shipped via the channel (s_i, v_y). If s_i is a channel, then $l(d, s_i)$ is the channel latency $cl(d, s_i)$ and $s_i(d) = d$.

3.1.4 Latency Constraints

When the user has identified latency critical sequences within the DAG, he can then express the maximum tolerable latency on these sequences as a set of latency constraints $C = \{c_1, \ldots, c_n\}$ to be attached to the job description. Each constraint $c_i = (S_i, l_{S_i}, t)$ defines a desired upper latency limit l_{S_i} for the arithmetic mean of the sequence latency $sl(d, S_i)$ over all the data items $d \in D_t$ that enter the sequence S_i during any time span of t time units:

$$\frac{\sum_{d \in D_t} sl(d, S_i)}{|D_t|} \leq l_{S_i} \tag{1}$$

Note that such a constraint does not specify a hard upper latency bound for each single data item but only a "statistical" upper bound over the items running through the workflow during the given time span. While hard upper bounds may be desirable, we doubt that meaningful hard upper bounds can be achieved in most real-world setups of massively-parallel data processing frameworks.

3.2 Measuring Workflow Latency

In order to make informed decisions where to apply optimizations to a running workflow we designed and implemented means of sampling and estimating the latency of a sequence. The master node that has global knowledge about the defined latency constraints will instruct the worker nodes about where they have to perform latency measurements. For the elements (task or channel) of each constrained sequence, latencies will be measured on the respective worker node once during a configured time interval, the measurement interval. This scheme can quickly produce high numbers of measurements with rising numbers of tasks and channels. For this reason we locally preaggregate measurement data on the worker nodes and ship one message once every measurement interval from the workers to the master. Each message contains the following data:

1. An estimation of the average *channel latency* for each locally incoming channel (i.e. it is an incoming channel on the worker node) of the constrained sequences. The average latency of a channel is estimated using *tagged* data items. A tag is a small piece of data that contains a creation timestamp and a channel identifier and it is added when a data item exits the user code of the channel's sender task and is evaluated just before the data item enters the user code of the channel's receiver task. The receiving worker node will then add the measured latency to its aggregated measurement data. The tagging frequency is chosen in such a way that we have one tagged data item during each measurement interval if there are any data flowing through the channel. If the sending and receiving tasks are executed on different worker nodes, clock synchronization is required.

2. The average *output buffer lifetime* for each channel of the constrained sequences, which is the average time it took for output buffers to be filled. If no output buffer was filled on the channel during the measurement interval, this is indicated as such in the message.

3. An estimation of the average *task latency* for each task of the constrained sequences. Task latencies are measured in an analogous way to channels, but here we do not require tags. Once every measurement interval, a task will note the difference in system time between a data item entering the user code and the next data item leaving it on the channels specified in the constrained sequences. Again, the measurement frequency is chosen in a way that we have one latency measurement during each measurement interval if there are any data flowing through the channel.

Let us assume a constrained sequence $S = (e_1, v_1, e_2)$. Tags will be added to the data items entering channel e_1 once every measurement interval. Just before a tagged data item enters the user code of v_1, the tag is removed from the data item and the difference between the tag's timestamp and the current system time is added to the locally aggregated measurement data. Let us assume a latency measurement is required for the task v_1 as well. In this case, just before handing the data item to the task, the current system time is stored in the task environment. The next time the task outputs a data item to be sent to e_2 the difference between the current system time and the stored timestamp is again added to the locally aggregated measurement data. Before handing the produced data item to the channel e_2, the worker node may choose to tag it, depending on whether we still need a latency measurement for this channel. Once every measurement interval the worker nodes flush their aggregated measurement data to the master node.

The master node stores the measurement data it receives from the worker nodes. For each constraint $(S_i, l_{S_i}, t) \in C$, it will keep all latency measurement data concerning the elements of S_i that are fresher than t time units and discard all older measurement data. Then, for each element of S_i, it will compute a running average over the measurement values and add the results up to an estimation of the left side of Equation 1. The accuracy of this estimation depends mainly on the chosen measurement interval.

The aforementioned *output buffer lifetime* measurements are subjected to the same running average procedure. To the running average of the *output buffer lifetime* of channel e over the past t time units we shall refer as $oblt(e, t)$. Note that the time individual data items spend in output buffers is already contained in the channel latencies, hence we do not need the output buffer lifetime to estimate sequence latencies. It does however play the role of an indicator, when trying to locate channels where the output buffer sizes can be optimized (see Section 3.3).

The measurement overhead is quite low as only one message from each of the workers to the master is required during a measurement interval. Even for large numbers of nodes, the collected data can be easily held in main memory by the master node. If necessary, the number of messages can be reduced by increasing the measurement interval.

3.3 Reacting to Latency Constraint Violations

Based on the measurement data as described in Section 3.2, the master node can identify those sequences of the DAG that violate their constraint and initiate countermeasures to improve latency. It will apply countermeasures until the constraint has been met or the necessary preconditions for applying countermeasures are not met anymore. In this case it will report the failed optimization attempt to the user who then has to either change the job or revise the constraints.

Given a DAG $G = (V_G, E_G)$, a sequence $S = (s_1, \ldots, s_n)$, and a violated latency constraint (S, l_S, t), the master node attempts to eliminate the effect of improperly sized output buffers by adjusting the buffer sizes for each channel in S individually and apply dynamic task chaining to reduce latencies further. Buffer size adjustment is an iterative process which may increase or decrease buffer sizes at multiple channels, depending on the measured latencies. Note that after each run of the buffer adjustment procedure the master node waits until all latency measurement values based on the old buffer sizes have been flushed out. The conditions and procedures for changing buffer sizes and dynamic task chaining are outlined in the following sections.

3.3.1 Adaptive Output Buffer Sizing

For each channel e in S the master node compares the average *output buffer latency* $obl(e, t)$ that data items on this channel experience to the running average of the channel latency. The average output buffer latency of a data item is estimated as $obl(e, t) = \frac{oblt(e,t)}{2}$, where $oblt(e, t)$ is the running average of the output buffer lifetime (see Section 3.2). If $obl(e, t)$ supersedes both a certain minimum threshold (for example 5 ms) and the task latency of the channel's source task, the master node sets the new output buffer size $obs^*(e)$ to

$$obs^*(e) = max(\epsilon, obs(e) \times r^{obl(e,t)}) \qquad (2)$$

where $\epsilon > 0$ is an absolute lower limit on the buffer size, $obs(e)$ is the current output buffer size, and $0 < r < 1$. We chose $r = 0.98$ and $\epsilon = 200$ bytes as a default. This approach might reduce the output buffer size so much that most records do not fit inside the output buffer anymore, which is detrimental to both throughput and latency. Hence, if $obl(e) \approx 0$, we will increase the output buffer size to

$$obs^*(e) = min(\omega, s \times obs(e)) \qquad (3)$$

where $\omega > 0$ is an upper bound for the buffer size and $s > 1$. For our prototype we chose $s = 1.1$.

3.3.2 Dynamic Task Chaining

Task chaining pulls certain tasks into the same thread, thus eliminating the need for queues and handing over data items between these tasks. In order to be able to chain a series of tasks $v_1, \ldots, v_n$ within the constrained sequence S they need to fulfill the following conditions:

- They all run as separate threads with the same process on the worker node, which excludes any already chained tasks.

- The sum of the CPU utilizations of the task threads is lower than the capacity of one CPU core or a fraction thereof, for example 90% of a core. How such profiling information can be obtained has been described in [7].

- They form a path through the DAG, i.e. each pair $v_i, v_{i+1} \in V_G$ is connected by a channel $e = (v_i, v_{i+1}) \in E_G$ in the DAG.

- None of the tasks has more than one incoming and more than one outgoing channel, with the exception of the first task v_1 which is allowed to have multiple incoming channels and the last task v_n which is allowed to have multiple outgoing channels.

The master node looks for the longest chainable series of tasks within the sequence. If it finds one, it instructs the worker node to chain the respective tasks. When chaining a series of tasks the worker node needs to take care of the input queues between them. There are two principal ways of doing this. The first one is to simply drop the existing input queues between these tasks. Whether this is acceptable or not depends on the nature of the workflow, for example in a video stream scenario it is usually acceptable to drop some frames. The second one is to halt the first task v_1 in the series and wait until the input queues between all of the subsequent tasks $v_2, \ldots, v_n$ in the chain have been drained.

This will temporarily increase the latency due to a growing input queue of v_1 that needs to be reduced after the chain has been established.

3.4 Relation to Fault Tolerance

In large clusters of compute nodes, individual nodes are likely to fail [12]. Therefore, it is important to point out how our proposed techniques to trade off high throughput against low latency at runtime affect the fault tolerance capabilities of current parallel data processing frameworks.

As these data processors mostly execute arbitrary black-box user code, currently the predominant approach to guard against execution failures is referred to as log-based rollback-recovery in literature [13]. Besides sending the output buffers with the individual data items from the producing to the consuming task, the parallel processing frameworks additionally materialize these output buffers to a (distributed) file system. As a result, if a task or an entire worker node crashes, the data can be re-read from the file system and fed back into the re-started tasks. The fault tolerance in Nephele is also realized that way.

Our two proposed optimizations affect this type of fault tolerance mechanism in different ways: Our first approach, the adaptive output buffer sizing, is completely transparent to a possible data materialization because it does not change the framework's internal processing chain for output buffers but simply the size of these buffers. Therefore, if the parallel processing framework wrote output buffers to disk before the application of our optimization, it will continue to do so even if adaptive output buffer sizing is in operation.

For our second optimization, the dynamic task chaining, the situation is different. With dynamic task chaining activated, the data items passed from one task to the other no longer flow through the framework's internal processing chain. Instead, the task chaining deliberately bypasses this processing chain to avoid serialization/deserialization overhead and reduce latency. Possible materialization points may therefore be incomplete and useless for a recovery.

We addressed this problem by introducing an additional annotation to the Nephele job description which prevents our system from applying dynamic task chaining on particular parts of the DAG. This way our streaming extension might lose one option to respond to violations of a provided latency goal, however, we are able to guarantee that Nephele's fault tolerance capabilities remain fully intact.

4. EVALUATION

Having presented both the adaptive output buffer sizing and the dynamic task chaining for Nephele, we will now evaluate their impact based on an example job. To put the measured data into perspective, we also implemented the example job for another parallel data processing framework with streaming capabilities, namely Hadoop Online[4].

We chose Hadoop Online as a baseline for comparison for three reasons: First, Hadoop Online is open-source software and was thus available for evaluation. Second, among all large-scale data processing frameworks with streaming capabilities, we think Hadoop Online currently enjoys the most popularity in the scientific community, which also makes it an interesting subject for comparison. Finally, in their research paper, the authors describe the continuous query

---

[4] http://code.google.com/p/hop/

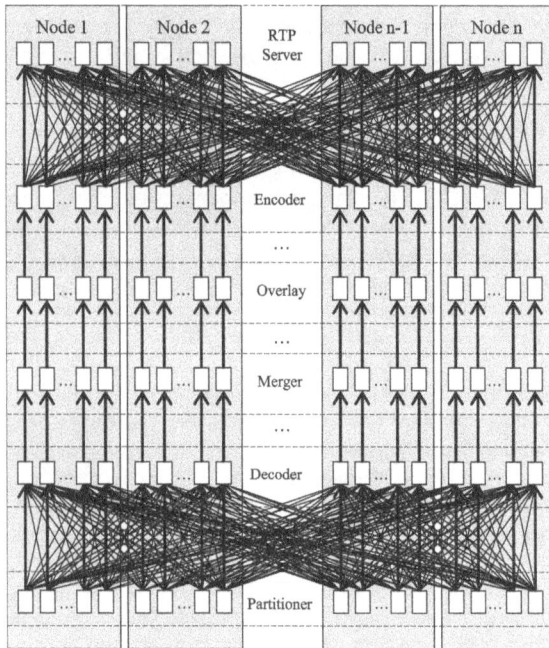

Figure 4: Structure of the Nephele job

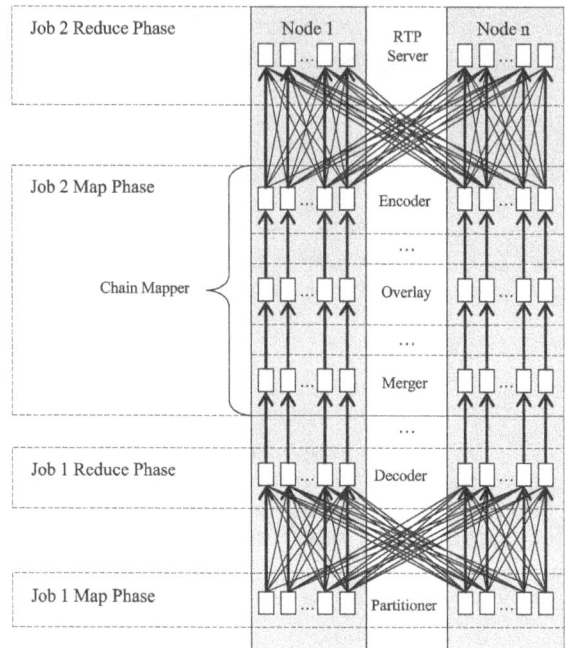

Figure 5: Structure of the Hadoop Online job

feature of their system to allow for near-real-time analysis of data streams [11]. However, they do not provide any numbers on the actually achievable processing latency. Our experiments therefore also shed light on this question.

4.1 Job Description

The job we use for the evaluation is motivated by the "citizen journalism" use case described in the introduction. We consider a web platform which offers its users to broadcast incoming video streams to a larger audience. However, instead of simple video transcoding which is done by existing video streaming platforms, our system additionally groups related video streams, merges them to a single stream, and augments the stream with additional information, such as Twitter feeds or other social network content. The idea is to provide the audience of the merged stream with a broader view of a situation by automatically aggregating related information from various sources.

In the following we will describe the structure of the job, first for Nephele and afterwards for Hadoop Online.

4.1.1 Structure of the Nephele Job

Figure 4 depicts the structure of the Nephele evaluation job. The job consists of six distinct types of tasks. Each type of task is executed with a degree of parallelism of m, spread evenly across n compute nodes.

The first tasks are of type *Partitioner*. Each *Partitioner* task acts as a TCP/IP server for incoming video feeds, receives H.264 encoded video streams, assigns them to a group of streams and forwards the video stream data to the *Decoder* task responsible for streams of the assigned group. In the context of this evaluation job, we group video streams by a simple attribute which we expect to be attached to the stream as meta data, such as GPS coordinates. More sophisticated approaches to detect video stream correlations are possible but beyond the scope of our evaluation.

The *Decoder* tasks are in charge of decompressing the encoded video packets into distinct frames which can then be manipulated later in the workflow. For the decoding process, we rely on the xuggle library[5].

Following the *Decoder*, the next type of tasks in the processing pipeline are the *Merger* tasks. *Merger* tasks consume frames from grouped video streams and merge the respective set of frames to a single output frame. In our implementation the merge step simply consists of tiling the individual input frames in the output frame.

After having merged the grouped input frames, the *Merger* tasks send their output frames to the next task type in the pipeline, the *Overlay* tasks. An *Overlay* task augments the merged frames with information from additional related sources. For the evaluation, we designed each *Overlay* task to draw a marquee of Twitter feeds inside the video stream, which are picked based on locations close to the GPS coordinates attached to the video stream.

The output frames of the *Overlay* tasks are encoded back into the H.264 format by a set of *Encoder* tasks and then passed on to tasks of type *RTP Server*. These tasks represent the sink of the streams in our workflow. Each task of this type passes the incoming video streams on to an RTP server which then offers the video to an interested audience.

4.1.2 Structure of the Hadoop Online Job

For Hadoop Online, the example job exhibits a similar structure as for Nephele, however, the six distinct tasks have been distributed among the map and reduce functions of two individual MapReduce jobs. During the experiments on Hadoop Online, we executed the exact same task code as for Nephele apart from some additional wrapper classes we had to write in order to achieve interface compatibility.

As illustrated in Figure 5 we inserted the initial *Partitioner* task into the map function of the first MapRe-

---
[5]http://www.xuggle.com/

duce job. Following the continuous query example from the Hadoop Online website, the task basically "hijacks" the map slot with an infinite loop and waits for incoming H.264 encoded video streams. Upon the reception of the stream packet, the packet is put out with a new key, such that all video streams within the same group will arrive at the same parallel instance of the reducer. The reducer function then accommodates the previously described *Decoder* task. As in the Nephele job, the *Decoder* task decompresses the encoded video packets into individual frames.

The second MapReduce job starts with the three tasks *Merger*, *Overlay*, and *Encoder* in the map phase. Following our experiences with the computational complexity of these tasks from our initial Nephele experiments, we decided to use a Hadoop chain mapper and execute all of these three tasks consecutively within a single map process. Finally, in the reduce phase of the second MapReduce job, we placed the task *RTP Server*. The *RTP Server* tasks again represented the sink of our data streams.

In comparison to the classic Hadoop, the evaluation job exploits two distinct features of the Hadoop Online prototype, i.e. the support for continuous queries and the ability to express dependencies between different MapReduce jobs. The continuous query feature allows to stream data from the mapper directly to the reducer. The reducer then runs a moving window over the received data. We set the window size to 100 ms during the experiments. For smaller window sizes, we experienced no significant effect on the latency.

4.2 Experimental Setup

We executed our evaluation job on a cluster of $n = 10$ commodity servers. Each server was equipped with two Intel Xeon E5430 2.66 GHz CPUs (four cores per CPU) and 32 GB RAM. The nodes were connected via regular Gigabit Ethernet links and ran Linux (kernel version 2.6.39). Each node ran a KVM virtual machine with eight cores. Inside the virtual machines we used Linux (kernel version 2.6.38) and Java 1.6.0.26 to run Nephele's worker component. Additionally, each virtual machine launched a Network Time Protocol (NTP) daemon to maintain clock synchronization among the workers. During the entire experiment, the measured clock skew was below 2 ms among the machines.

Each worker node ran eight tasks of type *Decoder, Merger, Overlay* and *RTP Server*, respectively. The number of incoming video streams was fixed for each experiment and they were evenly distributed over the *Partitioner* tasks. We always grouped and subsequently merged four streams into one aggregated video stream. Each video stream had a resolution of 320×240 pixels and was H.264 encoded. The initial output buffer size was 32 KB. Unless noted otherwise, all tasks had a degree of parallelism of $m = 80$.

Those experiments that were conducted on Nephele with latency constraints in place, specified one constraint $c = (S, l, t)$ for each possible sequence

$$S = (e_1, v_D, e_2, v_M, e_3, v_O, e_4, v_E, e_5) \qquad (4)$$

where v_D, v_M, v_O, v_E are tasks of type *Decoder, Merger, Overlay* and *Encoder* respectively. All constraints specified the same upper latency bound $l = 300$ ms over the data items within the past $t = 5$ seconds. The measurement interval on the worker nodes was set to 1 second so that the running averages on the master node were computed over sets of five measurement values. Due to their regular nature,

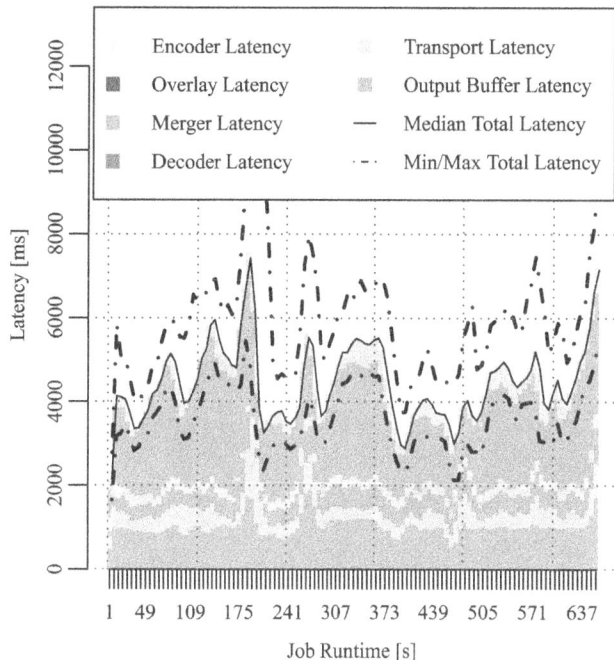

Figure 6: Latency w/o optimizations (320 **video streams**, degree of parallelism $m = 80$, 32 **KB fixed output buffer size**)

the resulting 80^4 constraints could be efficiently represented and managed using framework data structures.

4.3 Experimental Results

We evaluated our approach on the Nephele framework with the job described in Section 4.1.1 in three scenarios which are (1) without any kind of latency optimizations (2) with adaptive output buffer sizing and (3) with adaptive output buffer sizing as well as dynamic task chaining. As a baseline for comparison with other frameworks we evaluated the Hadoop Online Job described in Section 4.1.2 on the same testbed.

4.3.1 Latency without Optimizations

First, we ran the Nephele job with constraints in place but prevented the master node from applying any optimizations. Figure 6 summarizes the measurement data received by the master. As described in Section 3.2, the master node maintains running averages of the measured latencies of each task and channel. Each sub-bar displays the arithmetic mean over the running averages for tasks/channels of the same type. For the plot, each channel latency is split up into mean output buffer latency (dark gray) and mean transport latency (light gray), which is the remainder of the channel latency after subtracting output buffer latency. Hence, the total height of each bar is the sum of the arithmetic means of all task/channel latencies and gives an impression of the current overall workflow latency. The solid and dot-dashed lines provide information about the distribution of measured sequence latencies (min, max, and median).

The total workflow latency fluctuated between 3.5 and 7.5 seconds. The figure clearly shows that output buffer and channel latencies massively dominated the total workflow latency, so much in fact that most task latencies are hardly

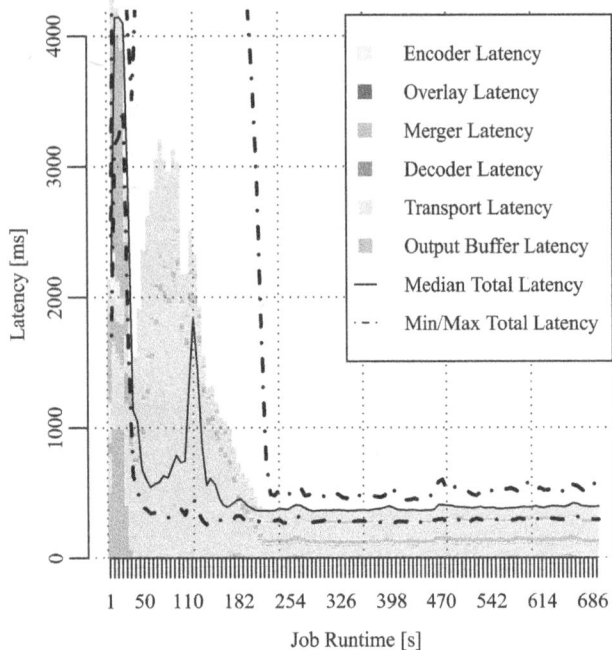

Figure 7: Latency with adaptive buffer sizing (320 video streams, degree of parallelism $m = 80$, 32 KB initial output buffer size)

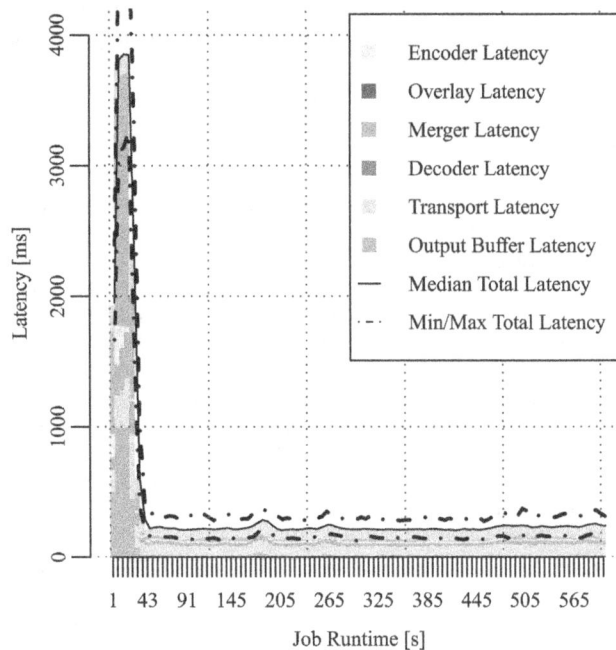

Figure 8: Latency with adaptive buffer sizing and task chaining (320 video streams, degree of parallelism $m = 80$, 32 KB initial output buffer size)

visible at all. The main reason for this is the output buffer size of 32 KB which was too large for the compressed video stream packets between *Partitioner* and *Decoder* tasks, as well as *Encoder* and *RTP Server* tasks. These buffers sometimes took longer than 1 second to be filled and when they were placed into the input queue of a *Decoder* they would take a while to processed. The situation was even worse between the *Encoder* and *RTP Server* tasks as the number of streams had been reduced by four and thus it took even longer to fill a 32 KB buffer. Between the *Decoder* and *Encoder* tasks the channel latencies were much lower since the initial buffer size was a better fit for the decompressed images.

Another consequence of the buffer size were large variations in total workflow latency that stemmed from the fact that task threads such as the *Decoder* could not fully utilize their CPU time because they fluctuated between idling due to input starvation and full CPU utilization once a buffer had arrived.

The anomalous task latency of the *Merger* task stemmed from the way we measure task latencies and limitations of our frame merging implementation. Frames that needed to be grouped always arrived in different buffers. With large buffers arriving at a slow rate the *Merger* task did not always have images from all grouped streams available and would not produce any merged frames. This caused the framework to measure high task latencies (see Section 3.1.1).

4.3.2 Latency with Adaptive Output Buffer Sizing

Figure 7 shows the results when using only adaptive buffer sizing to meet latency constraints. The structure of the plot is identical to Figure 6 which is described in Section 4.3.1.

Our approach to adaptive buffer sizing quickly reduced

the buffer sizes on the channels between *Partitioner* and *Decoder* tasks, as well as *Encoder* and *RTP server* tasks. The effect of this is clearly visible in the diagram, with an initial workflow latency of 4 seconds that is reduced to 400 ms on average and 500 ms in the worst case. The latency constraint of 300 ms has not been met, however we attained a latency improvement of one order of magnitude compared to the unoptimized Nephele job.

The convergence phase at the beginning of the job during which buffer sizes were decreased took approx. 4 minutes. There are several reasons for this phenomenon. First, as the master node started with output buffers whose lifetime was often larger than the measurement interval there often was not enough measurement data for the master to act upon during this phase. In this case it waited until enough measurement data were available before checking for constraint violations. Second, after each output buffer size change the master node waits until all old measurements for the respective channel have been flushed out before revisiting the violated constraint, which took at least 5 seconds each time.

4.3.3 Latency with Adaptive Output Buffer Sizing and Task Chaining

Figure 8 shows the results when using adaptive buffer sizing and dynamic task chaining. The latency constraints were identical to those in Section 4.3.2 and the structure of the plot is again identical to Figure 6.

Our task chaining approach chose to chain the *Decoder*, *Merger*, *Overlay* and *Encoder* tasks because the sum of their CPU utilizations did not fully saturate one CPU core.

After the initial calibration phase, the total workflow latency stabilized at an average of around 240 ms and a maximum of approx. 300 ms. This finally met all defined latency

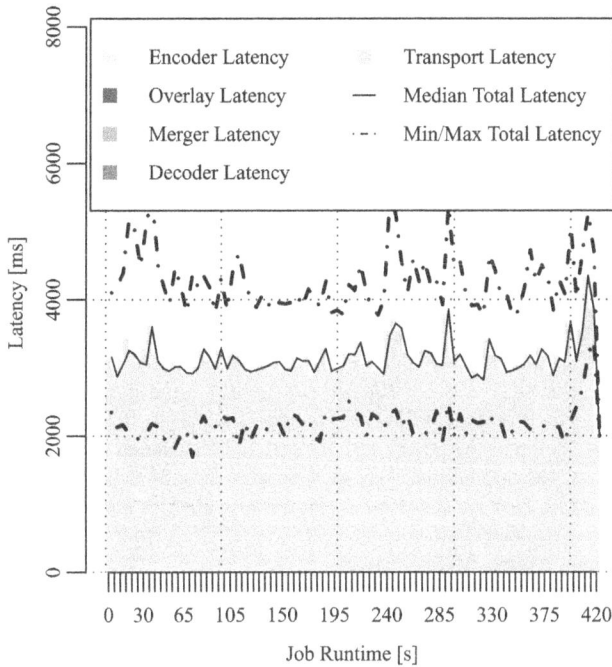

Figure 9: Latency in Hadoop Online (80 video streams, degree of parallelism $m = 10$, 100 ms window size)

constraints, which caused the optimizer to not trigger any further actions. In our case this constituted another 40% improvement in latency compared to not using task chaining and an improvement by a factor of at least 15 compared to the unoptimized Nephele job.

4.3.4 Latency in Hadoop Online

Figure 9 shows a bar plot of the task and channel latencies obtained from the experiments with the Hadoop Online prototype. The plot's structure is again identical to Figure 6, however the output buffer latency has been omitted as these measurements are not offered by Hadoop Online.

Similar to the unoptimized Nephele job, the overall processing latency of Hadoop Online was clearly dominated by the channel latencies. Except for the tasks in the chain mapper, each data item experienced an average latency of about one second when being passed on from one task to the next.

Due to limitations in our setup and Hadoop Online we could only deploy one processing pipeline per host. Therefore, we had to reduce the degree of parallelism for the experiment to $m = 10$ and could only process 80 incoming video streams concurrently. A positive effect of this reduction is a significantly lower task latency of the Merger task because, with fewer streams, the task had to wait less often for an entire frame group to be completed.

Apart from the size of the window reducer, we also varied the number of worker nodes n in the range of 2 to 10 as a side experiment. However, we did not observe a significant effect on the channel latency either.

5. RELATED WORK

Over the past decade stream processing has been the subject of vivid research. In terms of scalability, the existing approaches essentially fall into three categories: Centralized, distributed, and massively-parallel stream processors.

Several centralized systems for stream processing have been proposed, such as Aurora [2] and STREAM [5, 15]. Aurora is a DBMS for continuous queries that are constructed by connecting a set of predefined operators to a DAG. The stream processing engine schedules the execution of the operators and uses load shedding, i.e. dropping intermediate tuples to meet QoS goals. At the end points of the graph, user-defined QoS functions are used to specify the desired latency and which tuples can be dropped. STREAM presents additional strategies for applying load-shedding, such as probabilistic exclusion of tuples. While these systems have useful properties such as respecting latency requirements, they run on a single host and do not scale well with rising data rates and numbers of data sources.

Later systems such as Aurora*/Medusa [10] support distributed processing of data streams. An Aurora* system is a set of Aurora nodes that cooperate via an overlay network within the same administrative domain. In Aurora* the nodes can freely relocate load by decentralized, pairwise exchange of Aurora stream operators. Medusa integrates many participants such as several sites running Aurora* systems from different administrative domains into a single federated system. Borealis [1] extends Aurora*/Medusa and introduces, amongst other features, a refined QoS optimization model where the effects of load shedding on QoS can be computed at every point in the data flow. This enables the optimizer to find better strategies for load shedding.

The third category of possible stream processing systems is constituted by massively-parallel data processing systems. In contrast to the previous two categories, these systems have been designed to run on hundreds or even thousands of compute nodes in the first place and to efficiently transfer large data volumes between them. Traditionally, those systems have been used to process finite blocks of data stored on distributed file systems. However, many of the newer systems like Dryad [14], Hyracks [8], CIEL [16], or our Nephele framework [18] allow to assemble complex parallel data flow graphs and to construct pipelines between the individual parts of the flow. Therefore, these parallel data flow systems in general are also suitable for streaming applications. Recently, there have also been efforts to extend MapReduce by streaming capabilities [9, 11]. However, the general focus of these systems has still been high-throughput batch-job execution and QoS aspects have not been considered so far.

The systems S4 [17] and Storm[6] can also be classified as massively-parallel data processing systems, however, they stand out from the other systems as they have been designed for low-latency stream processing from the outset. These systems do not necessarily follow the design principles explain in Section 2.1. For example, Twitter Storm does not use intermediate queues to pass data items from one task to the other. Instead, data items are passed directly between tasks using batch messages on the network level to achieve a good balance between latency and throughput.

None of the systems from the third category has so far offered the capability to express high-level QoS goals as part of the job description and let the system optimize towards these goals independently, as it was common for previous systems from category one and two.

---

[6]`https://github.com/nathanmarz/storm`

6. CONCLUSION AND FUTURE WORK

Growing numbers of commodity devices are equipped with sensors capable of producing continuous streams of rich sensor data, such as video and audio in the case of mobile phones or power consumption data in the case of smart meters that are being deployed at consumer homes as part of the smart grid initiative. High numbers of such devices will produce large amounts of streamed data that will raise the bar for future stream processing systems both in terms of processing throughput and latency, as some use cases require the data to be processed within a given time span.

In this paper we examined using existing massively-parallel data processing frameworks such as Nephele for this purpose and presented strategies to trade off throughput versus latency to meet latency constraints while keeping the data throughput as high as possible. We showed how our strategies, *adaptive output buffer sizing* and *dynamic task chaining*, can be used to meet user-defined latency constraints for a workflow. We provided a proof-of-concept implementation of our approach and evaluated it using a video streaming use case. We found that our strategies can improve workflow latency by a factor of at least 15 while preserving the required data throughput.

We see the need for future work on this topic in several areas. The Nephele framework is part of a bigger software stack for massively-parallel data analysis developed within the Stratosphere project[7]. Therefore, extending the streaming capabilities to the upper layers of the stack, in particular to the PACT programming model [6], is of future interest. Furthermore, we plan to explore strategies for other QoS goals such as jitter and throughput that exploit the capability of a cloud to elastically scale on demand.

7. REFERENCES

[1] D. Abadi, Y. Ahmad, M. Balazinska, U. Cetintemel, M. Cherniack, J. Hwang, W. Lindner, A. Maskey, A. Rasin, E. Ryvkina, et al. The design of the Borealis stream processing engine. In *Second Biennial Conference on Innovative Data Systems Research*, CIDR '05, pages 277–289, 2005.

[2] D. Abadi, D. Carney, U. Çetintemel, M. Cherniack, C. Convey, S. Lee, M. Stonebraker, N. Tatbul, and S. Zdonik. Aurora: A new model and architecture for data stream management. *The VLDB Journal*, 12(2):120–139, 2003.

[3] M. Aldinucci and M. Danelutto. Stream parallel skeleton optimization. In *Proc. of the 11th IASTED International Conference on Parallel and Distributed Computing and Systems*, PDCS '99, pages 955–962. IASTED/ACTA, 1999.

[4] A. Alexandrov, S. Ewen, M. Heimel, F. Hueske, O. Kao, V. Markl, E. Nijkamp, and D. Warneke. MapReduce and PACT - comparing data parallel programming models. In *Proc. of the 14th Conference on Database Systems for Business, Technology, and Web*, BTW '11, pages 25–44. GI, 2011.

[5] S. Babu and J. Widom. Continuous queries over data streams. *SIGMOD Rec.*, 30:109–120, Sept. 2001.

[6] D. Battré, S. Ewen, F. Hueske, O. Kao, V. Markl, and D. Warneke. Nephele/PACTs: A programming model and execution framework for web-scale analytical processing. In *Proc. of the 1st ACM symposium on Cloud computing*, SoCC '10, pages 119–130. ACM, 2010.

[7] D. Battré, M. Hovestadt, B. Lohrmann, A. Stanik, and D. Warneke. Detecting bottlenecks in parallel DAG-based data flow programs. In *Proc. of the 2010 IEEE Workshop on Many-Task Computing on Grids and Supercomputers*, MTAGS '10, pages 1–10. IEEE, 2010.

[8] V. Borkar, M. Carey, R. Grover, N. Onose, and R. Vernica. Hyracks: A flexible and extensible foundation for data-intensive computing. In *Proc. of the 2011 IEEE 27th International Conference on Data Engineering*, ICDE '11, pages 1151–1162. IEEE, 2011.

[9] Q. Chen, M. Hsu, and H. Zeller. Experience in Continuous analytics as a Service (CaaaS). In *Proc. of the 14th International Conference on Extending Database Technology*, EDBT/ICDT '11, pages 509–514. ACM, 2011.

[10] M. Cherniack, H. Balakrishnan, M. Balazinska, D. Carney, U. Cetintemel, Y. Xing, and S. Zdonik. Scalable distributed stream processing. In *Proc. of the First Biennial Conference on Innovative Data Systems Research*, CIDR '03, pages 257–268, 2003.

[11] T. Condie, N. Conway, P. Alvaro, J. M. Hellerstein, K. Elmeleegy, and R. Sears. MapReduce Online. In *Proc. of the 7th USENIX conference on Networked systems design and implementation*, NSDI '10, pages 21–21. USENIX Association, 2010.

[12] J. Dean and S. Ghemawat. MapReduce: Simplified data processing on large clusters. *Communications of the ACM*, 51(1):107–113, Jan. 2008.

[13] E. N. M. Elnozahy, L. Alvisi, Y.-M. Wang, and D. B. Johnson. A survey of rollback-recovery protocols in message-passing systems. *ACM Comput. Surv.*, 34(3):375–408, Sept. 2002.

[14] M. Isard, M. Budiu, Y. Yu, A. Birrell, and D. Fetterly. Dryad: Distributed data-parallel programs from sequential building blocks. *ACM SIGOPS Operating Systems Review*, 41(3):59–72, Mar. 2007.

[15] R. Motwani, J. Widom, A. Arasu, B. Babcock, S. Babu, M. Datar, G. Manku, C. Olston, J. Rosenstein, and R. Varma. Query processing, approximation, and resource management in a data stream management system. In *First Biennial Conference on Innovative Data Systems Research*, CIDR '03, pages 245–256, 2003.

[16] D. Murray, M. Schwarzkopf, C. Smowton, S. Smith, A. Madhavapeddy, and S. Hand. CIEL: A universal execution engine for distributed data-flow computing. In *Proc. of the 8th USENIX conference on Networked systems design and implementation*, NSDI '11, pages 9–9. USENIX Association, 2011.

[17] L. Neumeyer, B. Robbins, A. Nair, and A. Kesari. S4: Distributed stream computing platform. In *2010 IEEE International Conference on Data Mining Workshops*, ICDMW '10, pages 170–177. IEEE, 2010.

[18] D. Warneke and O. Kao. Exploiting dynamic resource allocation for efficient parallel data processing in the cloud. *IEEE Transactions on Parallel and Distributed Systems*, 22(6):985–997, June 2011.

---

[7] http://www.stratosphere.eu/

A Resiliency Model for High Performance Infrastructure based on Logical Encapsulation

James J. Moore[1, 2]

[1]EMC
Office of the CTO
Los Angeles, CA, USA
(508) 293-7110

James.Moore@emc.com

Carl Kesselman[2]

[2]University of Southern California
Information Sciences Institute
Marina Del Rey, CA, USA
(310) 822-1511

(mooreja|carl)@isi.edu

ABSTRACT

An emerging trend in distributed systems is the creation of dynamically provisioned heterogeneous high performance platforms that include the co-allocation of both virtualized computing and network attached storage volumes offering NAS and SAN level data services. These high performance computing environments support parallel applications performing traditional file system operations. As with any parallel platform the ability to continue computation in the face of component failures is an important characteristic. Achieving resiliency in heterogeneous environments presents unique challenges and opportunities not found in homogeneous aggregations of computing resources. We present a logical encapsulation model for heterogeneous high performance infrastructure, which enables a reactive resiliency approach for federations of virtual machines and externally hosted physical storage volumes. Asynchronous state capture and restoration models are presented for individual resources, which are composed into non-blocking resiliency models for logical encapsulations. We perform an evaluation that demonstrates our methodology has greater overall flexibility and significant performance improvements when compared to current resiliency approaches in virtualized distributed execution environments.

Categories and Subject Descriptors

C.1.4 [Computer Systems Organization]: Parallel Architectures-*Distributed Architectures*; C.4 [Computer Systems Organization]: Performance of Systems – *Reliability, Availability, and Serviceability;* D.4.5 [Operating Systems]: Reliability – *Checkpoint/Restart*

General Terms

Management, Performance, Reliability, Standardization, Theory

Keywords

HPC, High Performance Computing, MPI, Message Passing Interface, Resiliency, Snapshot, Checkpoint, State Capture, State Rollback, Virtualization, Distributed Systems, Distributed Computing, Cloud Computing, Heterogeneous, IaaS, PaaS

1. INTRODUCTION

The emergence of massive centralized multitenant datacenters providing Infrastructure as a Service (IaaS) has created the ability to dynamically provision compute and storage elements into high performance distributed computing (HPDC) platforms.

While IaaS HPC environments to date have focused strictly on aggregating computing resources [1-3], an emerging trend is toward creating heterogeneous high performance platforms that include the co-allocation of both computing and network attached storage volumes offering NAS and SAN level data services. These new high performance distributed environments support parallel applications performing traditional file system operations.

The resiliency of HPC platforms in the face of component failure has been a topic of significant work [4-10]. Although an abundance of checkpointing research has been performed on virtualized computing platforms [6, 8-11], these methods have not addressed heterogeneous systems including both virtual machines and externally hosted physical storage volumes. In this paper, we offer an approach to resiliency that is applicable to these aggregated complex resources.

We present an experimental evaluation that demonstrates our methodology has greater overall flexibility and significant performance improvements when compared to current approaches to resiliency in virtualized distributed execution environments. Comparisons with distributed state capture alternatives are made to substantiate our claims; such as blocking resiliency techniques realized at the virtualization and system layers.

The specific contributions of this work are: (a) The creation of a logical encapsulation model for composing individually provisioned virtual machines and storage volumes into complex federated entities representing dynamic distributed high performance infrastructure. (b) A reactive resiliency technique able to asynchronously capture, and subsequently rollback, live point-in-time state for complex resource compositions. (c) A resiliency model for encapsulated systems enabling consistency across resource federations even when compute and storage elements are provisioned upon and managed by unrelated discrete hosting platforms. (d) Creation of a methodology providing resiliency to distributed applications in an unobtrusive manner, including applications performing traditional file system operations against local or remote storage.

This paper is organized in the following manner: In Section 2, we provide the background of high performance computing resiliency techniques and introduce related work defining the state-of-the-art in reactive resiliency. Section 3 presents the model for logical encapsulation of resource aggregations. In Section 4, we introduce a series of state models defining our reactive resiliency methodology. Experimentation and Results are shown in Section 5. Section 6 concludes the paper.

2. BACKGROUND

2.1 Resiliency Approaches

Various resiliency approaches have been implemented across the HPC software stack. These techniques realize themselves at the application, system, and virtualization layers. They are grouped into two main categories, proactive and reactive, based upon how component failures are handled.

Proactive resiliency techniques utilize migration in order to move away from unhealthy hardware before failure occurs. Implementations and concepts have been documented for proactive resiliency at the virtualization [12, 13] and system layers [14]. Proactive approaches can be combined with reactive approaches, thereby reducing the frequency of state rollbacks [14]. In this paper, we focus on reactive techniques.

Reactive resiliency captures state periodically for system rollback upon failure. Implementations at the system and virtualization layers are well documented.

BLCR [15] adds the ability to save and restore process state to the Linux kernel. As a technology BLCR serves as the foundation for numerous cluster state capture techniques affording reactive resiliency at the system level. A checkpoint/restart framework capable of capturing distributed coordinating processes state was built into LAM/MPI using BLCR [7].

More recently two efforts of particular interest have defined the reactive resiliency state-of-the-art for virtual machine clusters. They are VIOLIN and VCCP [8-10].

The "Virtual Internetworking on Overlay Infrastructure" (VIOLIN) enables capturing point-in-time state (VSNAP) of Virtual Networked Environments (VNE) [8, 10, 11]. A VNE consists of virtual machines, connected to a virtual network, using specialized VIOLIN virtual switches. A VSNAP implements two ways of capturing guest state: vsnap-disk and vsnap-memory. Both approaches are based on XEN live-migration functionality. These approaches hide overhead associated with guest persistence to disk; however, the total actual overhead incurred during memory and disk interaction is higher than asynchronous VM copy-on-write snapshots [16]. This is the result of live migration performing multiple memory transfer rounds, where the same memory location is copied numerous times [17]. The vsnap-disk process builds a large snapshot file where all memory from each round is persisted. The vsnap-memory approach saves a compressed memory image; however, it requires a reserved memory partition equally sized to the VM memory image being saved. This results in the maximum addressable guest memory being half the physical memory of a host.

Our approach is distinguished from VIOLIN and VNE in several ways, including an ability to capture and rollback state: (a) using asynchronous copy-on-write snapshots, (b) minimizing total incurred overhead during state capture, (c) while maximizing physical memory available to guests, and (d) for heterogeneous environments consisting of virtual machines and external physical storage volumes.

Ong, H. et al. [9] describe Virtual Cluster Checkpoint (VCCP), a system able to perform point-in-time state capture and rollback for numerous virtual machines coordinating on parallel workload. It provides virtualization level checkpointing using a blocking approach. VCCP is important for several reasons. First, it demonstrates checkpointing can be performed between hosts without requiring custom external virtual switches; an environment much more likely to be adopted in production. Second, it documents that in-flight network packets are not lost during virtual cluster state capture because they can easily be associated with virtual machine snapshots.

Our checkpointing approach is distinct from VCCP in several ways, including an ability to capture and rollback state: (a) in a non-blocking manner, (b) without provisioned resources requiring specific virtual network attachment, and (c) across heterogeneous resource encapsulations containing both virtual machines and external physical storage volumes.

3. LOGICAL ENCAPSULATION OF RESOURCE AGGREGATIONS

Emerging high performance distributed computing applications benefit from the coordinated provisioning and management of resource collections including computing and storage elements. From the perspective of defining resiliency for the ensemble it is desirable to logically encapsulate *simple assets* into a single *complex asset* onto which resilient behaviors can be asserted. The term *asset* provides a clear reflection of the status transition that occurs upon provisioning whereas a resource becomes a tenant's virtual property.

3.1 Simple Assets

Individually provisioned components should be thought of as *simple assets*. A simple asset is either a single virtual machine or storage volume.

A virtual machine (guest) minimally contains the following virtualized components: a virtual processor, virtual memory, virtual disk, and virtual NIC. The virtual machine is hosted by a virtualization platform (host). This can be any hypervisor including solutions providing: full virtualization, para-virtualization, or hardware-assisted virtualization. The hypervisor provides all base management capabilities to its guests, which includes state capture and rollback functionality.

A storage volume contains: metadata, cache, and a logical unit (LUN) of physical disk space. They can be accessed through Direct Attached Storage (DAS), Network Attached Storage (NAS), or through a Storage Area Network (SAN). DAS and SAN volumes are block based systems, whereas NAS volumes also contain a file system. The storage volume is served by a storage platform, which provides all volume management capabilities. For instance, ability to checkpoint a volume is provided by a storage platform management task.

3.2 Complex Assets

The *complex asset* provides a mechanism to logically encapsulate individually provisioned simple assets and associate aggregate policy across the federation. A complex asset introduces order, and purpose, to dynamic distributed systems.

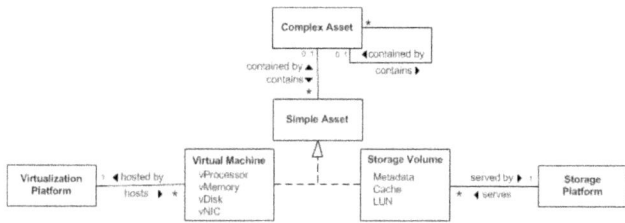

Figure 1. UML definition of a Complex Asset

Complex assets are recursively defined. In this manner rich logical distributed environment encapsulations can be composed that are manageable as a singular entity ensuring predictable overall behavior. Management as a singular entity is important when ensuring accurate representation of point-in-time state across distributed systems during capture and rollback operations.

A *complex asset* contains any number of virtual machines or storage volumes. Within a complex asset virtual machines do not necessarily need to be associated with storage volumes; and vice-versa. Virtual machines may, although are not mandated to, mount associated storage volumes. When storage volumes are mounted within a virtual machine these volumes may, or may not be, outside the control and visibility of the hypervisor.

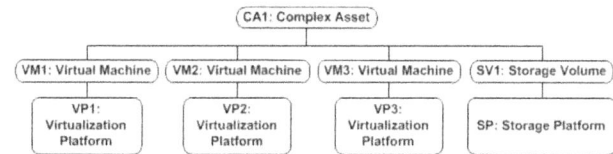

Figure 2. Flat complex asset: parallel processing environment

Complex assets can be composed in many different ways to produce heterogeneous systems with specific performance characterizations. For example, in Figure 2 a parallel processing environment is represented as a non-recursive complex asset. The compute cluster contains one storage volume and three virtual machines; four simple assets in total. Note that each virtual machine is deployed on its own virtualization platform and the storage volume is hosted by a unique storage platform. The virtualization and storage platforms are the underlying hosting systems where state management capabilities are implemented.

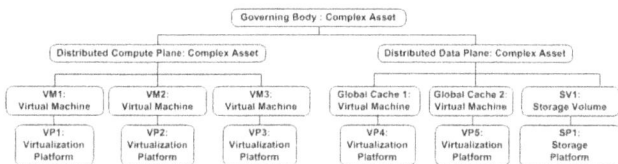

Figure 3. Hierarchical complex asset: distributed heterogeneous high performance computing environment

In Figure 3, a distributed heterogeneous high performance computing cluster has been depicted as a hierarchical recursively defined complex asset. Here the root complex asset contains two constituent complex assets; computing and data planes. The distributed data plane provides a data service to the distributed computing plane. Virtual machines interact with a storage volume through a global cache presented by virtual machines. The global cache virtual machines (GCVMs) in the data plane are geographical distributed. One GCVM is located in the compute cluster's datacenter, while the other is in the storage volume's datacenter. Both GCVMs maintain a coherent global storage cache. Because point-in-time state can be persisted for complex assets, reactive resiliency can be afforded to entities like the

distributed data plane or the distributed compute plane. More importantly it is possible to provide resiliency across this entire geographically-distributed recursively-defined complex asset.

3.3 Representation

For our purposes complex assets are defined using UML models; however, the complex asset model is conceptual able to be implemented using any infrastructure description language flexible enough to represent the paradigm. Example description languages include VGDL, VXDL, and CIM.

The Virtual Grid Description Language (VGDL) [18] was developed in order to specify dynamically provisioned system configurations. These configurations allow application requirement mapping onto a variety of resource provisioning mechanisms. The "Virtual private eXecution infrastructure Description Language [19, 20] (VXDL) is similar to VGDL but differentiates itself by adding the notion of network elements and nodes connected via links. The Common Information Model (CIM) is the most expressive modeling language of the three and is defined by the Distributed Management Task Force (DMTF) [21]. CIM is the foundation for additional specifications.

The logical encapsulation inferred by the complex asset UML model could be formally described by leveraging the CIM System Virtualization Model (CIM-SVM) and the Storage Management Initiative Specification (SMI-S) [22, 23]. They provide ideal constructs to describe virtual machines and storage volumes. In additional, CIM-SVM and SMI-S provide resource to hosting platform association. One could envision an extension to these CIM based specifications that express logically-encapsulated recursive high performance distributed computing environments.

4. REACTIVE RESILIENCY FOR LOGICALLY ENCAPSULATED HETEROGENEOUS DISTRBUTED INFRASTRUCTURE

Complex Asset Resiliency Models (CARMs) illustrate the approach for asynchronous capture, and subsequent rollback, of state in live high performance heterogeneous distributed systems. The complex asset resiliency models are an interlacing of states defined in the *Simple Asset Resiliency Models* (SARMs). The SARMs represent critical state transitions intrinsic to management tasks typically implemented by the virtualization and storage platforms. It follows that the CARM prototype implementations are a controlled coordination of virtualization and storage platform management tasks. All models assume reliable state transitions with failure scenarios differed to future publication.

4.1 Simple Assets Resiliency Models

4.1.1 Virtual Machine State Capture

Many current virtual machine state capture methods require that execution occurring within guests be suspended while state is persisting to storage. Recently however, enhanced VM management systems have produced asynchronous methods where memory is persisted concurrently with VM execution after a short initial setup period [16].

The state diagram in Figure 4 below, describes a virtual machine asynchronous state capture model consistent with approaches produced for VMware and Xen.

Figure 4. Simple asset state capture model: virtual machine

When virtual machine state capture begins the virtualization platform must perform an initial setup to place the guest into an *Initiated* state where it is ready to be paused. Overhead associated with pausing the VM must be accounted for in the *Initiated* state.

While in the initiated state the host accepts a network request to perform guest state capture. The request is processed by the virtualization platform's management server. The server creates snapshot meta-data ensuring an addressable image in the future.

The request is handed to the virtual machine monitor so measures can be taken for the guest to be paused. Most notable are: 1. marking the vCPUs for state capture, and 2. Queuing network packets for association with the snapshot [9].

When the guest's vCPUs are removed from the monitor's scheduler the virtual machine will be *Paused*. At this point, guest can no longer perform operations. It represents time t_{pit}, which is the point-in-time state for rollback.

Now a vMemory preparation process occurs to ensure the guest image remains at t_{pit} during asynchronous virtual machine memory persistence. This preparation includes creation of data structures to manage the copy-on-write process during asynchronous state capture.

Now VM memory is *Prepared* so the virtualization platform begins *Persisting* guest state asynchronously in a separate thread; however, since the vCPUs are static their state is preserved first. This is also when hypervisor managed vDisk has its delta taken.

Once memory persistence has begun the guest's vCPUs are marked for scheduling by the virtualization platform. When the VM has signaled operations have *Resumed* productive work within the guest continues. The guest is now live, but its state at t_{pit} has yet to be fully captured. This only occurs when memory is fully *Persisted*, and all operations of the virtualization platform's management task have *Completed*.

4.1.2 Virtual Machine State Rollback

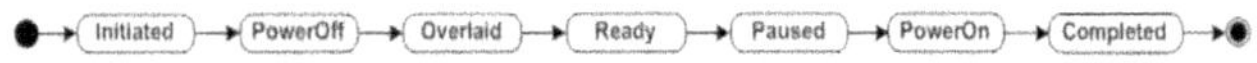

Figure 5. Simple asset state rollback model: virtual machine

The state diagram in Figure 5 above, depicts a rollback model to place a virtual machine into its state at time t_{pit}.

When guest rollback begins the virtualization platform must perform a setup placing the guest into an *Initiated* state. A process commenced when the management server receives a rollback network request. Appropriate virtual machine state discovery occurs through a snapshot metadata hierarchy querying process. Once the virtual devices from t_{pit} are located the restoration process is initiated. At this point the guest is *PoweredOff* to relinquish all held resources to the host. Placing the virtual machine into a dormant state enables restoration of virtual devices. The guest is *Overlayed* with its image at time t_{pit}. A process involving state restoration for: vProcessor(s), vDisk, vNIC, and vMemory. In addition to loading virtual device state all network messages saved during the capture process are prepared for delivery along with new incoming network packets being queued. Just before scheduling the virtual machine is *Paused*. This ensures processing will commence immediately upon vCPU activation. The virtual machine begins executing after being *PoweredOn* by the hypervisor. Entering the powered-on state indicates that the guest has obtained resources from the host: vCPUs are scheduled, network packets are being delivered by the vNIC, vDisk is accessible, and vMemory has been loaded.

Finalizing all pending operations associated with the management task indicates state rollback has *Completed*.

4.1.3 Storage Volume State Capture

The diagram in Figure 6 below, describes a storage volume state capture model. The algorithms used to checkpoint file systems or block devices are beyond the scope of this paper. Our state model description assumes deltas are provided by the storage platform, which is a common feature delivered with storage systems.

In order to create a generic storage volume state capture model certain requirements must be imposed upon the storage platform. If a memory cache is used as a speedup layer for disk it must be treated like virtual machine memory when checkpointing volumes. In addition the storage platform must be able to associate a volume's pending queued operations with the checkpoint. If a storage platform is unable to associate queued operations with the checkpoint the volume write mode should be set to synchronous and the storage platform should only reply to clients upon a write commit. By introducing these requirements a generic state capture model can be defined, which is applicable to NAS, DAS, and SAN volumes.

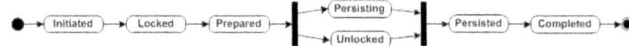

Figure 6. Simple asset state capture model: storage volume

When state capture begins the storage platform places a task into its *Initiated* state. This means the management server accepts a checkpoint request, creates management metadata to maintain the checkpoint hierarchy, and begins the checkpoint procedure.

Next, the storage platform ensures the SV has been *Locked* so it can no longer be augmented. This is time t_{pit} which is the point-in-time state for subsequent rollback. It consists of operations traversing the network, pending server side queued operations, the memory cache speedup layer, and the LUN delta.

Now, a SV memory cache layer preparation process must occur to ensure its image remains at t_{pit} during complex asset asynchronous state persistence. All cache blocks will be marked so they can undergo a copy-on-write procedure when the complex asset is once again live.

Since unwritten cache has been *Prepared*, and the LUN delta is ready, the storage platform begins *Persisting* cache state asynchronously in a separate thread. Entering the persisting state indicates that queued operation requests have been associated with the checkpoint. A process performed to ensure all acknowledged operations are accounted for upon rollback.

If the storage volume is being served by a NAS platform an additional step is required before unlocking the volume. The file system metadata needs to be modified to reflect a checkpoint has occurred and subsequent file modifications do not affect the volume's t_{pit} file system.

When the persisting thread is initiated the storage platform unlocks the volume allowing it to once again be augmented. Although the volume is *Unlocked* and ready to process operations a full checkpoint is not yet captured. This occurs when the entire memory cache speedup layer (if present) is fully *Persisted*, and after all management task operations have *Completed*.

4.1.4 Storage Volume State Rollback

Figure 7. Simple asset state rollback model: storage volume

The state diagram in Figure 7 above depicts a rollback model to place a storage volume (SV) into its state at time t_{pit}.

When rollback begins the storage platform must perform a setup placing storage into an *Initiated* state. A process commenced when the management server receives a rollback network request. Appropriate volume state discovery occurs through a checkpoint metadata hierarchy querying process. Once the t_{pit} volume state attributes are located a restoration process is initiated.

At this point the volume is *Locked* to ensure it is unavailable to clients. Placing the volume into a locked state enables restoration of storage attributes. The volume elements are *Overlayed* with their images at time t_{pit}. A process involving state restoration of the: LUN, memory cache speedup layer, and (if applicable) file system metadata. In addition pending operations saved during the capture process are loaded for processing.

Upon overlay completion the storage volume enters a *Ready* state. Just before operations associate with the storage volume are processed again, the storage platform ensures the volume is *Unlocked* for clients. Finalizing all pending operations of the management server task indicates rollback has *Completed*.

4.2 Complex Asset State Capture

Complex asset state capture creates a snapshot at time t_{pit}. All encapsulated simple assets are persisted with t_{pit} state following complex asset state capture. No simple asset should be persisted with state t_{pit+m}: where *pit* is the point-in-time state and *m* is a positive or negative rational number. Furthermore, complex assets are captured asynchronously. Meaning they are live during state persistence. A fact supported by simple asset state capture model descriptions in sections 4.1.1 and 4.1.3 above.

4.2.1 Complex Asset State Capture Model

The complex asset state capture model is defined in Figure 8 below. State transitions occur serially at first, then undergo forks into parallel sections, and ultimately join to finish the model. The initial serial section places virtual machines into a paused state. The first parallel section has two threads: 1. a subset of states associated with the external storage volumes, and 2. a subset of states associated with the virtual machines. Each thread is then forked again for asynchronous state capture. There is an initial barrier indicating the complex asset can resume execution and subsequent barrier indicating virtual machine and storage volume asynchronous persistence has completed.

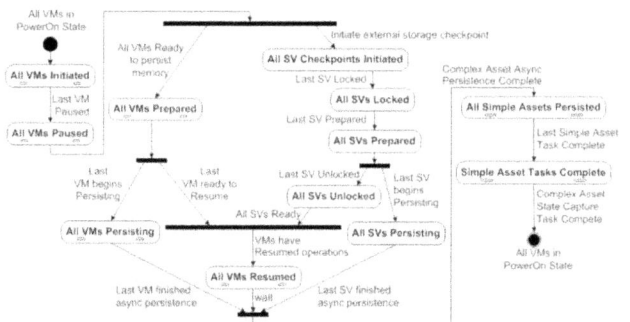

Figure 8. Complex asset state capture model

A complex asset state capture task begins in the first serial phase. At this point all guests are powered so virtualization platforms must initiate state capture of their relevant virtual machines. This occurs when the central external manager sends a network message to all virtualization platforms hosting virtual machines within a logical encapsulation. The message indicates that guest state capture should be initiated.

As a result of collective initialization the network activity addressed to logically encapsulated guests begin being queued. By triggering network activity queuing for hosted VMs it becomes possible to ensure unreliable protocols recover within the logical encapsulation upon rollback. This is because in-flight packets can be received by the virtualization platforms and placed with their corresponding guest state images [9].

All virtual machines are paused by the central external manager when the virtualization platforms indicate they have initiated their state capture tasks. This is done by sending a management directive to transition virtual machines into the pause state, which freezes operations across the complex asset; including modifications within the guests and as an after-effect across externally served storage volumes. Since the pause time window is so narrow reliable network protocols have been proven to recover upon complex asset rollback, which is true even when network packets are not queued to account for unreliable traffic.

A fork occurs in the complex asset state capture model, which places every VM into a state where it can be resumed and places every SV into its unlocked state. To do this the central manager receives the notification that all guests are in a paused state, which triggers the management operations indicating that: 1. All VMs should be prepared for persistence and 2. All volume checkpoints should be initiated.

The state transitions thread relating to virtual machines begins with guests paused (ready to persist) and ends with a barrier indicating guests are ready to resume.

In order to enter the state where all guests are prepared the network must undergo a draining process. Here all virtualization platforms message each other the intent to prepare a set of hosted guests for persistence. The recipients acknowledge the pending persistence operation. Once all virtualization platforms receive the collective acknowledgements guest network packet queuing stops since any messages addressed across the logical encapsulation should be delivered and queued at this point.

Now all virtual machines enter a prepared state, triggering virtualization platforms to notify the central external manager, resulting in the management directive for virtualization platforms to fork guests into their persisting state. Eventually all virtual machines will begin persisting, which indicates they are ready to resume. Before virtual machines can resume operation they must wait for the central external manager to inform their hosting platform that all storage volumes are ready.

The parallel component of the complex asset state capture model, related to storage, places volumes into a state where they are persisting and unlocked. When the process begins the storage volumes are not being modified because virtual machines which would augment them are paused. At this point all storage platforms initiate state capture for their volumes as a result of a directive from the central external manager. This is followed by the platforms locking volumes to clients. Now every volume is prepared, LUN delta(s) are taken, pending operations are saved, and (if applicable) file system metadata is prepared. Next a fork to begin memory cache speedup layer asynchronous persistence occurs. The storage platforms unlock volumes to clients and send an indication to the central manager that the storage volumes are ready to accept operations.

The complex asset's final state capture phase is now underway. At this point all storage volumes are persisting unwritten cache speedup layers (if equipped), all storage volumes are unlocked, all VMs are persisting memory, and all VMs are paused. The goal of the final phase is to conclude the complex asset state capture process. This starts with a management directive sent by the central manager to the virtualization platforms. The management directive received by the virtualization platforms indicates that guests within the logical encapsulation should be resumed.

As a result guest network activity queuing is triggered by the virtualization platform, which is followed by messaging all other hosts indicating guests are ready to be addressed. Message recipients acknowledge message receipt confirming it is safe to resume all guests. When every acknowledgement is processed by each virtualization platform guests are unpaused, which triggers queued network packet delivery. Upon every guest being resumed productive work is once again underway across the logical encapsulation.

The overall complex asset state capture process has not yet finished even though processing is occurring. Simple assets are still persisting state asynchronously. The hosting platforms will notify the central manager when their simple asset asynchronous state persistence concludes. When the last simple asset finishes state persistence, and all management tasks are completed, the complex asset state capture process will have concluded.

4.3 Complex Asset State Rollback

Complex asset restoration rolls back state to time t_{pit}. All encapsulated simple assets are overlaid with t_{pit} state following complex asset state restoration. No simple asset should be reverted to state t_{pit+m}: where pit is the point-in-time state and m is a positive or negative rational number.

4.3.1 Complex Asset State Rollback Model

The Complex asset state rollback model is defined in Figure 9 below. State transitions occur serially at first, then fork into a parallel section, and ultimately join to finish the model. The initial serial section places virtual machines into a power off state. The parallel section has two threads: 1. a subset of states associated with the external storage volumes, and 2. a subset of states associated with the virtual machines. The final section proceeds after a barrier indicates the complex asset is able to resume execution.

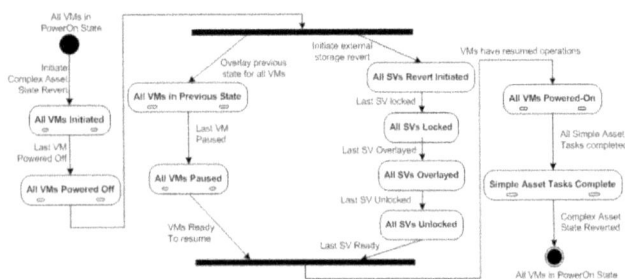

Figure 9. Complex asset state rollback model

A complex asset state restoration task begins in the first serial phase. At this point all guests are powered so virtualization platforms must initiate state rollback of their relevant virtual machines. This occurs when the central external manager sends a network message to all virtualization platforms hosting virtual machines within the logical encapsulation. A message indicating that guest state rollback tasks should be initiated.

All virtual machines are powered-off by the central external manager when the virtualization platforms indicate they have initiated their state rollback tasks. This is done by sending a management directive to transition virtual machines into the powered-off phase. These transitions require no coordination between virtualization platforms because current state is discarded during the overlay process.

The parallel component of the complex asset rollback model places every simple asset within the logical encapsulation into the requested t_{pit} state. Once the parallel barrier is reached the restored VMs are ready to be resumed and reverted storage volumes are unlocked. To do this the central manager receives a notification indicating guests are powered-off, which triggers the management operations to overlay virtual machine state and initiate storage volume rollback tasks.

The state transitions thread relating to virtual machines begins with virtual machines powered-off (ready for overlay) and ends with a barrier indicating guests are paused (ready to resume). These state transitions are described in section 4.1.2 above.

The state transitions thread relating to storage volumes begins with the volume rollback being initiated and ends when the parallel barrier is encountered after a storage platform unlocks the volume. Details pertaining to the storage volume rollback process are described in section 4.1.4 above.

A complex asset's final state rollback phase is serial. At this point: all volumes are reverted, all volumes are unlocked, all VMs are overlaid, and all VMs are paused. The goal of the final phase is to conclude the complex asset state rollback process. This starts with a management directive sent by the central manager to the virtualization platforms. The management directive received by the virtualization platforms indicates that guests within the logical encapsulation should be resumed.

As a result guest network activity queuing is triggered by the virtualization platform, which is followed by a message from the hypervisor to all other hosts indicating its guests are ready to be addressed. Recipients acknowledge the message was received confirming it is safe to resume all virtual machines. When every acknowledgement is processed by each virtualization platform the guests are unpaused, which triggers queued network packet delivery. Upon every guest being resumed productive work is once again underway across the logical encapsulation. All virtual machines are now powered-on.

The central external manager is notified as simple asset management tasks complete. Upon receipt of all notifications the complex asset's state capture process concludes.

5. EVALUATION

5.1 Measurement Platforms

We have created a prototype implementation of our asynchronous state capture algorithm to enable the evaluation of its performance. The prototype is based upon the: VMware ESX hypervisor, EMC Celerra NFS server, and OpenMPI distribution. While these platforms are leveraged in this prototype other hypervisors, storage systems, or message passing interface distributions are equally able to implement the model principals.

The VMware ESX hypervisor provides an asynchronous copy-on-write snapshot task implementation capable of capturing, and restoring, state of individual virtual machines. In order to save, and restore, state for logically encapsulated heterogeneous distributed systems the production ESX snapshot task was modified. The complex asset state models in sections 4.2.1 and 4.3.1 requires a virtual machine snapshot task where state transitions defined in section 4.1.1 and 4.1.2 are controlled by the central external manager. The ESX snapshot task was modified by introducing barriers and notifications into the production snapshot task logic, enabling the central external manager to control state transitions. The modification allows the virtual machine snapshot task to enter a given state, notify the central external manager when a barrier is·reached, and proceed when the manager issues a directive to continue to the next state. In this manner the modified ESX snapshot task exposes the necessary functionality to participate in the complex asset state capture.

An EMC Celerra NS480 NAS system was used for the storage platform. It provides a suitable checkpoint task implementation to capture and rollback storage volume state. No modifications were required for the volume checkpoint procedure.

OpenMPI was used for the MPI distribution. It provides a checkpoint capability that saves and restores state of MPI processes using the Berkeley Labs Checkpoint and Restore kernel modules [4, 15]. In order to save/restore state of MPI applications using unmodified virtual machine snapshots (rather than BLCR) it was necessary to augment the OpenMPI checkpoint algorithm. The normal execution flow is to quiesce the network, pause processes, save state using BLCR, and unpause processes. The modification we introduced is to quiesce the network, pause processes, notify the central external manager that it's safe to snapshot virtual machines, wait for the external manager's directive to continue, and unpause processes.

5.2 Measurement Systems

Figure 10 through Figure 13 illustrates the measurement systems; including software strata interactions between the central external manager, virtualization platform, MPI application, and storage platform. Various lines within the figures represent interactions between components. Solid bidirectional arrows indicate management communication channels between the: central external manager, MPI distribution, modified hypervisor, and unmodified hypervisor. The dashed unidirectional arrows indicate state persistence pathways. The fine-dashed double ball ended lines illustrate data pathways used during file system operations.

5.2.1 (Un)Modified hypervisors - No snapshot

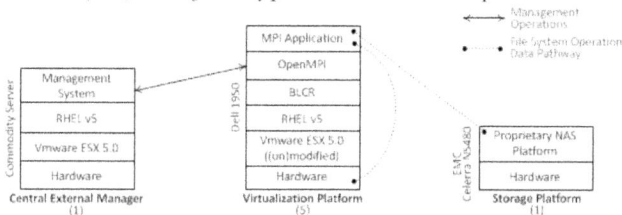

Figure 10. Measurement system: base runtime

Figure 10 illustrates the workload behavior measurement system used to acquire base end-to-end runtimes. The unmodified and modified hypervisor measurements yield identical workload behaviors when state is not captured during execution. This is the result of modified functionality that differentiates the platforms, namely the state capture tasks, not being invoked.

Measured scenarios provide base end-to-end runtimes for each MPI workload profile. Runtimes are calculated using the start/end timestamp differences. Label these measurements:

$$R_{pc} = Pure\ Computation$$
$$R_{wls} = Writing\ to\ local\ storage$$
$$R_{rls} = Reading\ from\ local\ storage$$
$$R_{wnas} = Writing\ to\ NAS\ using\ NFS$$
$$R_{rnas} = Reading\ from\ NAS\ with\ NFS$$

5.2.2 MPI Distribution - Single checkpoint

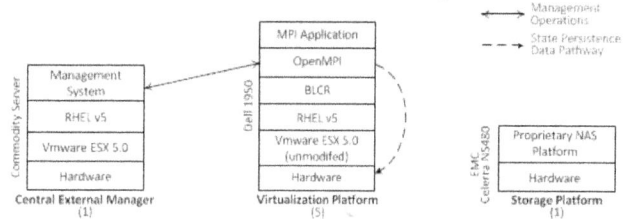

Figure 11. Measurement system: OpenMPI checkpoint

Figure 11 illustrates the workload behavior measurement system associated with pure MPI state capture. Here the external manager calls an unmodified OpenMPI procedure (ompi-checkpoint) to checkpoint the parallel application by persisting aggregate processing state to local disk using BLCR. OpenMPI does not support state capture of processes performing traditional file system I/O. For this reason measurements were only taken for the pure computation workload profile. Label this measurement:

$$R_{mpi\_pc} = Pure\ Computation\ with\ an\ MPI\ checkpoint$$

The blocking overhead for traditional MPI state capture was obtained by comparing checkpoint entry (T_{mpi_cken}) and exit (T_{mpi_ckex}) timestamps. Let the direct measured overhead be represented by B_{mpi_ckom}. Measured blocking time is calculated as:

$$B_{mpi\_ckom} = T_{mpi\_ckex} - T_{mpi\_cken}$$

While MPI blocking measurements can only be obtained for pure computation, it is desirable to have an approximation of the end-to-end runtime of MPI applications performing file system operations if it were possible to issue a single MPI checkpoint. In order to provide a context for comparison theoretical runtimes are calculated for the following workload behavior scenarios:

$$R_{mpi\_wls\_t} = single\ mpi\ checkpont, local\ writes, theoretical$$
$$R_{mpi\_rls\_t} = single\ mpi\ checkpont, local\ reads, theoretical$$
$$R_{mpi\_wnas\_t} = single\ mpi\ checkpont, NAS\ writes, theoretical$$
$$R_{mpi\_rnas\_t} = single\ mpi\ checkpont, NAS\ reads, theoretical$$

Theoretical end-to-end runtimes are calculated by adding the MPI checkpoint measured blocking time to the corresponding workload behavior scenario base runtime. The calculations yielding theoretical measurements are as follows:

$$R_{mpi\_wls\_t} = R_{wls} + B_{mpi\_ckom}$$
$$R_{mpi\_rls\_t} = R_{rls} + B_{mpi\_ckom}$$
$$R_{mpi\_wnas\_t} = R_{wnas} + B_{mpi\_ckom}$$
$$R_{mpi\_rnas\_t} = R_{rnas} + B_{mpi\_ckom}$$

All trend lines containing derived end-to-end MPI workload runtimes are labeled <<theoretical>>.

5.2.3 Unmodified hypervisor – Single snapshot

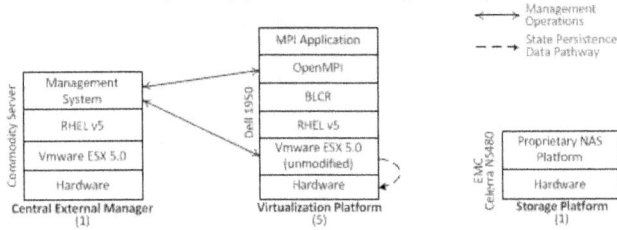

Figure 12. Measurement system: traditional hypervisor snapshot

Figure 12 illustrates the workload behavior measurement system associated with traditional hypervisor-based state capture using an unmodified snapshot procedure. In order to generate a consistent state for the parallel processing environment a coordinated state capture is executed between our central external manager, the modified OpenMPI checkpoint procedure, and the unmodified hypervisor virtual machine snapshot tasks. The manager calls a modified OpenMPI checkpoint procedure, which pauses MPI processes and quiesces network traffic. The modified procedure does not save process state. Next the manager saves state of all virtual machines by initiating unmodified hypervisor snapshot tasks. Virtual machine states are saved to local disk on the hosts. Upon completion of all snapshots the manager sends an unpause directive to the modified OpenMPI checkpoint procedure, which resumes the MPI application.

Since OpenMPI does not support pausing processes performing traditional file system I/O, which is a requirement to trigger the VM snapshots, our measurements were only taken for pure computation workload in this scenario. Label this measurement:

$$R_{uh\_pc} = Single\ state\ capture\ pure\ computation$$

Blocking overhead for state capture in this environment was obtained by recording the snapshot task duration. Measured blocking time is calculated as:

$$B_{uh\_sd} = Unmodified\ hypervisor\ snapshot\ durration$$

While end-to-end workload runtime (with state capture) can only be obtained for pure computation, it is desirable to have an approximation of end-to-end runtimes for applications performing traditional file system operations. In order to provide a context for comparison theoretical runtimes are calculated for the following workload behavior scenarios:

$$R_{uh\_wls\_t} = single\ state\ capture, local\ writes, theoretical$$
$$R_{uh\_rls\_t} = single\ state\ capture, local\ reads, theoretical$$
$$R_{uh\_wnas\_t} = single\ state\ capture, NAS\ writes, theoretical$$
$$R_{uh\_rnas\_t} = single\ state\ capture, NAS\ reads, theoretical$$

Theoretical end-to-end runtimes are calculated by adding the snapshot duration to the corresponding workload behavior base runtime. The calculations yielding theoretical measurements are:

$$R_{uh\_wls\_t} = R_{wls} + B_{uh\_sd}$$
$$R_{uh\_rls\_t} = R_{rls} + B_{uh\_sd}$$
$$R_{uh\_wnas\_t} = R_{wnas} + B_{uh\_sd}$$
$$R_{uh\_rnas\_t} = R_{rnas} + B_{uh\_sd}$$

All trend lines containing derived end-to-end workload runtimes are labeled <<theoretical>>.

5.2.4 Modified hypervisor – Single snapshot

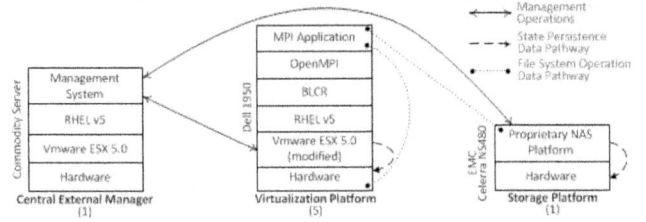

Figure 13. Measurement system: complex asset state capture

Figure 13 illustrates the workload behavior measurement system for complex asset state capture. In order to generate a consistent state for the logically encapsulated heterogeneous distributed system a coordinated state capture is executed with our central external manager, modified hypervisor, and storage platform. The interactions between the central external manager, virtualization platform, and storage platform have been defined in section 4.2.1 "Complex asset state capture model". Virtual machine states are saved to local disks on the hosts. NAS volume states are saved within the storage platform.

Complex asset state capture is the only scenario able to save state of any application, serial or parallel, performing file system operations to local and remote storage. Measurements are taken for each MPI workload behavior. Runtimes are calculated using workload start/end timestamp differences. The measurements are:

$$R_{mh\_pc} = single\ state\ capture, pure\ computation$$
$$R_{mh\_wls} = single\ state\ capture, local\ writes$$
$$R_{mh\_rls} = single\ state\ capture, local\ reads$$
$$R_{mh\_wnas} = single\ state\ capture, NAS\ writes$$
$$R_{mh\_rnas} = single\ state\ capture, NAS\ reads$$

Overheads incurred for asynchronous complex asset state capture in this environment are calculated from workload runtime differences. Let the complex asset overheads be represented as:

$$NB_{mh\_sco\_pc} = state\ capture\ overhead, pure\ computation$$
$$NB_{mh\_sco\_wls} = state\ capture\ overhead, local\ writes$$
$$NB_{mh\_sco\_rls} = state\ capture\ overhead, local\ reads$$
$$NB_{mh\_sco\_wnas} = state\ capture\ overhead, NAS\ writes$$
$$NB_{mh\_sco\_rnas} = state\ capture\ overhead, NAS\ reads$$

Complex asset state capture overhead is calculated as follows:

$$NB_{mh\_sco\_pc} = R_{mh\_pc} - R_{pc}$$
$$NB_{mh\_sco\_wls} = R_{mh\_wls} - R_{wls}$$
$$NB_{mh\_sco\_rls} = R_{mh\_rls} - R_{rls}$$
$$NB_{mh\_sco\_wnas} = R_{mh\_wnas} - R_{wnas}$$
$$NB_{mh\_sco\_rnas} = R_{mh\_rnas} - R_{rnas}$$

Here the overhead is the difference between the base runtime without state capture and the runtime with state capture. This is not blocking time it is asynchronous overhead given particular workload behaviors and state persistence targets.

5.3 Measurement Architecture
The measurement architecture is depicted in Figure 14 below.

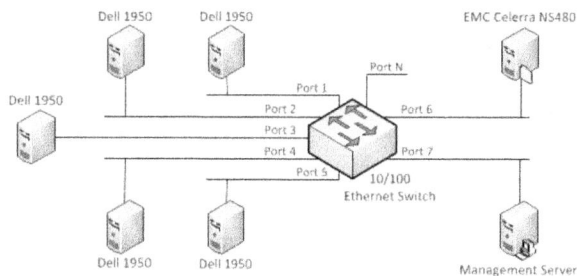

Figure 14. Scientific analysis measurement architecture

A 10/100Mbps Ethernet switch provided network connectivity.

Management capabilities were provided by a generic server hosting the central external management software. Deployed software includes: (a) *Hypervisor:* VMware ESX v5.0, (b) *Guest OS:* RHEL v5 - kernel 2.6.18-1164.9.1.el5 64-bit, and (c) *Management Software:* Custom Prototype.

Storage capabilities were provided by an EMC Celerra NS480 using software revision 6.0.40-5 and a total capacity of 1839 GB. Provisioned NAS volumes for complex assets were 100GB.

Computational capabilities were provided by five Dell 1950 machines with the following hardware specifications:

- Dual Xeon quad-core 5140 processors @ 2.33GhZ
- 12GB memory @ 667 MHZ
- Seagate Cheetah T10 146GB
- Broadcom NetXtreme II BCM5708 1000Base-T

Dell 1950 software specifications were as follows: (a) *Hypervisor:* VMware ESX v5.0, (b) *Guest OS:* RHEL v5 - kernel 2.6.18-1164.9.1.el5 64-bit, (c) *Process State Capture:* BLCR-0.8.2, and (d) *Message Passing Interface:* OpenMPI

5.4 Approach

Demonstrating the complex asset state capture model behavioral profile thorough repeatable scientific analysis lends credibility to the proposed approach.

Measurements were recorded for various workload behaviors. The workload behavior profiles include: 1. Pure computation where message passing occurs between VMs (no storage I/O), 2. Writing to local storage through a file system, 3. Reading from local storage through a file system, 4. Writing to a network attached storage volume through NFS, and 5. Reading from a network attached storage volume through NFS.

All workload behavior measurements were recorded (or derived) for five distinct scenarios where job execution runs to completion. These scenarios include: 1. Unmodified hypervisor without a snapshot, 2. Modified hypervisor without a snapshot, 3. Modified hypervisor with a single snapshot, 4. MPI distribution with a single checkpoint, and 5. Unmodified hypervisor with a single snapshot.

Scenarios 1 and 2 provide base workload execution times. Additional time measured for scenarios 3, 4, and 5 indicate overhead for a particular state capture approach. Scenario 3 demonstrates workload behavior with asynchronous non-blocking state capture based upon our defined complex asset model. Scenario 4 measures runtime when traditional OpenMPI blocking checkpoints (ompi-checkpoint) capture state. Scenario 5 shows workload runtime using blocking state capture based upon traditional unmodified hypervisor snapshots.

All five scenarios are represented with four increasing memory allocations: 2GB, 4GB, 6GB, and 8GB. Graphs illustrate 10GB and 12GB trend line projections.

Each workload behavior, distinct scenario, and memory allocation were measured 10 times and then averaged to generate individual data points plotted on graphs: Figure 15 through Figure 19 below.

5.5 Results

The results contained in this section describe our performance study of distributed state capture techniques for varying workload behaviors. Comparison of the asynchronous complex asset state capture approach to other methodologies indicates a significant performance improvement using our technique.

An evaluation of each workload measurement demonstrates that capturing state with traditional MPI checkpoints and unmodified hypervisor snapshots introduces a linear runtime growth as memory allocations increase. This is the result of workload being idle during blocking memory persistence.

An evaluation of complex asset state capture has demonstrated that for all workload behaviors, with the exception of local writing, only a minor constant overhead is incurred as memory allocations increase. The scenario with continuous local writes during state persistence to local disk illustrates worst case behavior. Here only a nominal linear growth rate is recorded as memory allocation increases, which is significantly less than the rate of growth for both unmodified snapshots and MPI checkpoints. Performance improvements are the result of asynchronous state capture enabling productive work during memory persistence.

These results demonstrate the benefits of our approach for heterogeneous distributed system state capture and illustrate the significant performance improvements that can be achieved using the complex asset resiliency methodology

5.5.1 No Storage IO

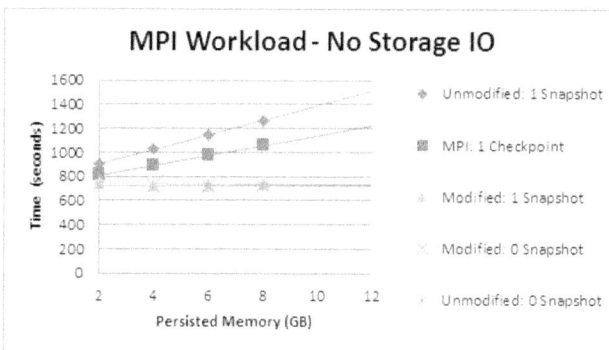

Figure 15. Compute only (no storage I/O)

Figure 15 charts the behavior trend for pure computation workload, which continuously sends messages between compute nodes C_1 through C_5. Messages are sent as follows: $C_1 \rightarrow C_2$, $C_2 \rightarrow C_3$, $C_3 \rightarrow C_4$, $C_4 \rightarrow C_5$, $C_5 \rightarrow C_1$. This is not a single message traversing a ring; its continuous communication.

The measured base end-to-end runtime (R_{pc}) is depicted by the *Modified: 0 Snapshot* and *Unmodified: 0 Snapshot* trend lines, which indicate constant runtime as memory allocations increase.

The measured end-to-end runtime for workload (R_{uh_pc}) with unmodified hypervisor-based state capture is depicted by the

Unmodified: 1 Snapshot trend line, which indicates runtime increases with memory allocation. Measured overhead is:

	2 GB	4 GB	6 GB	8 GB
B_{uh_sd}	85 sec	196 sec	307 sec	426 sec

Average overhead for unmodified hypervisor-based state capture is $51\ sec/GB$.

The measured end-to-end runtime for workload (R_{mpi_pc}) with traditional MPI state capture is depicted by the *MPI: 1 Checkpoint* trend line, which indicates runtime increases with memory allocation. Measured overhead is as follows:

	2 GB	4 GB	6 GB	8 GB
B_{mpi_ckom}	83 sec	160 sec	237 sec	318 sec

Average overhead for traditional MPI state capture is $40\ sec/GB$.

The measured end-to-end runtime for workload (R_{mh_pc}) running within a complex asset is depicted by the *Modified: 1 Snapshot* trend line, which indicates runtime stays constant as memory allocations increase. Measured overhead is as follows:

	2 GB	4 GB	6 GB	8 GB
$NB_{mh\_sco\_pc}$	32 sec	13 sec	14 sec	17 sec

Average overhead for complex asset state capture is a constant of 19 seconds.

For pure computation: our approach demonstrates superior performance as a result of the measured constant overhead during state capture as opposed to the exhibited linear growth of unmodified hypervisor snapshots or traditional MPI checkpoints.

Table 1. Pure Computation: Plotted values standard deviation

	2 GB	4 GB	6 GB	8 GB
R_{pc} (unmodified hypervisor)	7	6	7	5
R_{pc} (modified hypervisor)	5	8	6	3
R_{mh_pc}	8	6	7	4
R_{uh_pc}	33	33	45	50
R_{mpi_pc}	14	6	11	13

5.5.2 Local Synchronous Writing

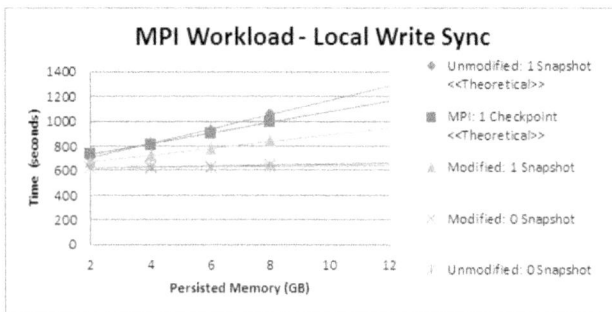

Figure 16. Synchronous Writing to local storage

Figure 16 charts the behavior of an MPI application continuously writing data to the local file system. For compute nodes C_1 through C_5 the behavior is as follows $\overset{C_1}{\cup},\overset{C_2}{\cup},\overset{C_3}{\cup},\overset{C_4}{\cup},\overset{C_5}{\cup}$. Writes are continually performed until execution halts after a specified time period. This behavior illustrates the worst case scenario for asynchronous state persistence. Here guest state is written over the same I/O channel being flooded with application write operations.

The measured base end-to-end runtime (R_{wls}) is depicted by the *Modified: 0 Snapshot* and *Unmodified: 0 Snapshot* trend lines, which indicate constant runtime as memory allocations increase.

The derived theoretical end-to-end runtime for workload ($R_{uh\_wls\_t}$) with unmodified hypervisor-based state capture is depicted by the *Unmodified: 1 Snapshot <<theoretical>>* trend line, which indicates runtime increases with memory allocation

The derived theoretical end-to-end runtime for workload ($R_{mpi\_wls\_t}$) with traditional MPI state capture is depicted by the *MPI: 1 Checkpoint <<theoretical>>* trend line, which indicates runtime increases with memory allocation.

The measured end-to-end runtime for workload (R_{mh_wls}) running within a complex asset is depicted by the *Modified: 1 Snapshot* trend line, which indicates runtime increases with memory allocation. Measured overhead is:

	2 GB	4 GB	6 GB	8 GB
$NB_{mh\_sco\_wls}$	49 sec	99 sec	147 sec	198 sec

Average overhead for complex asset state capture is $25\ sec/GB$.

For local synchronous writes: our approach incurs a significantly lower measured state capture linear growth rate, which indicates superior performance when compared to higher theoretical linear growth of unmodified hypervisor snapshots and MPI checkpoints.

Table 2. Local Write: Plotted values standard deviation

	2 GB	4 GB	6 GB	8 GB
R_{wls} (unmodified hypervisor)	23	10	10	22
R_{wls} (modified hypervisor)	23	10	13	18
R_{mh_wls}	17	20	29	16
$R_{uh\_wls\_t}$				
$R_{mpi\_wls\_t}$				

5.5.3 Local Reading

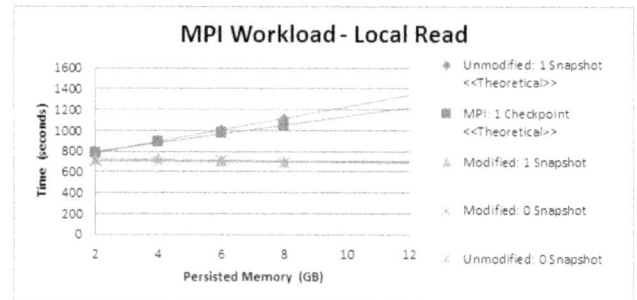

Figure 17. Reading from local storage

Figure 17 charts the behavior trend for an MPI application continuously reading data from the local file system. For compute nodes C_1 through C_5 the behavior is as follows $\overset{C_1}{\cup},\overset{C_2}{\cup},\overset{C_3}{\cup},\overset{C_4}{\cup},\overset{C_5}{\cup}$. Reading is continually performed until execution halts after a specified time period.

The measured base end-to-end runtime (R_{rls}) is depicted by the *Modified: 0 Snapshot* and *Unmodified: 0 Snapshot* trend lines, which indicate constant runtime as memory allocations increase.

The derived end-to-end runtime for workload ($R_{uh\_rls\_t}$) with unmodified hypervisor-based state capture is depicted by the *Unmodified: 1 Snapshot <<theoretical>>* trend line, which indicates runtime increases with memory allocation

The derived end-to-end runtime for workload ($R_{mpi\_rls\_t}$) with traditional MPI state capture is depicted by the *MPI: 1 Checkpoint <<theoretical>>* trend line, which indicates runtime increases with memory allocation.

The measured end-to-end runtime for workload (R_{mh_rls}) running within a complex asset is depicted by the *Modified: 1 Snapshot* trend line, which indicates runtime stays constant as memory allocations increase. Measured overhead is as follows:

	2 GB	4 GB	6 GB	8 GB
$NB_{mh\_sco\_rls}$	13 sec	51 sec	-16 sec	8 sec

Average overhead for complex asset state capture is a constant of 14 *sec*.

For local reads: our approach incurs only a measured constant overhead during state capture, which indicates superior performance when compared with the derived theoretical linear growth of unmodified hypervisor snapshots and MPI checkpoints.

Table 3. Local Read: Plotted values standard deviation

	2 GB	4 GB	6 GB	8 GB
R_{rls} (unmodified hypervisor)	7	13	6	5
R_{rls} (modified hypervisor)	22	4	71	9
R_{mh_rls}	13	72	74	22
$R_{uh\_rls\_t}$				
$R_{mpi\_rls\_t}$				

5.5.4 NAS Synchronous Writing

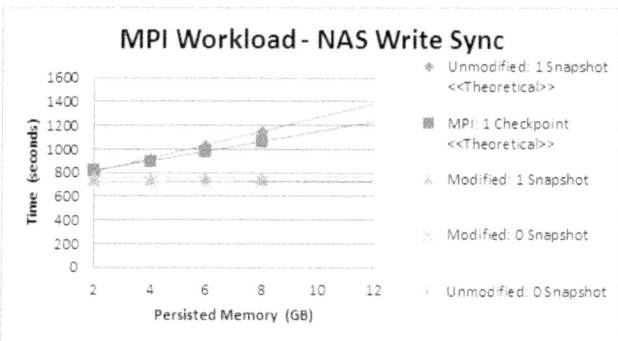

Figure 18. Synchronous writing to NAS over NFS

Figure 18 charts the behavior trend for an MPI application continuously writing data to a remote storage volume over NFS in synchronous mode. For compute nodes C_1 through C_5 and storage volume (V) the behavior is: $C_1 \rightarrow V$, $C_2 \rightarrow V$, $C_3 \rightarrow V$, $C_4 \rightarrow V$, $C_5 \rightarrow V$. Writes are continually performed until execution halts after a specified time period.

The measured base end-to-end runtime (R_{wnas}) is depicted by the *Modified: 0 Snapshot* and *Unmodified: 0 Snapshot* trend lines, which indicate constant runtime as memory allocations increase.

The derived end-to-end runtime for workload ($R_{uh\_wnas\_t}$) with unmodified hypervisor-based state capture is depicted by the *Unmodified: 1 Snapshot <<theoretical>>* trend line, which indicates runtime increases with memory allocation

The derived end-to-end runtime for workload ($R_{mpi\_wnas\_t}$) with traditional MPI state capture is depicted by the *MPI: 1 Checkpoint <<theoretical>>* trend line, which indicates runtime increases with memory allocation.

The measured end-to-end runtime for workload (R_{mh_wnas}) running within a complex asset is depicted by the *Modified: 1 Snapshot* trend line, which indicates runtime stays constant as memory allocations increase. Measured overhead is as follows:

	2 GB	4 GB	6 GB	8 GB
$NB_{mh\_sco\_wnas}$	33 sec	26 sec	38 sec	35 sec

Average overhead for complex asset state capture is a constant of 33 *sec*.

For NAS synchronous writes: our approach incurs a measured constant overhead during state capture indicating superior performance when compared with the derived theoretical linear growth of unmodified hypervisor snapshots and MPI checkpoints.

Table 4. NAS Write: Plotted values standard deviation

	2 GB	4 GB	6 GB	8 GB
R_{wnas} (unmodified hypervisor)	2	3	3	4
R_{wnas} (modified hypervisor)	0	2	2	1
R_{mh_wnas}	9	12	6	7
$R_{uh\_wnas\_t}$				
$R_{mpi\_wnas\_t}$				

5.5.5 NAS Reading

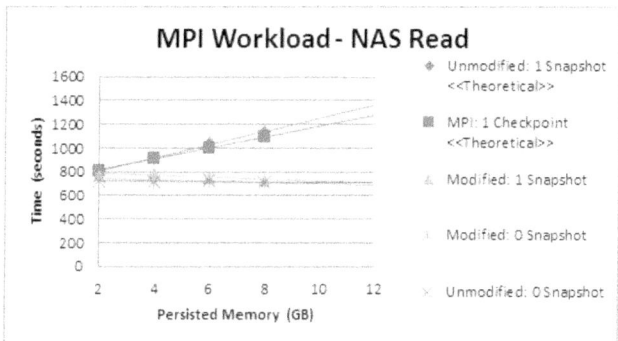

Figure 19. Reading from NAS over NFS

Figure 19 charts the behavior trend for an MPI application continuously reading data from a remote storage volume over NFS. For compute nodes C_1 through C_5 and storage volume (V) the behavior is: $C_1 \leftarrow V$, $C_2 \leftarrow V$, $C_3 \leftarrow V$, $C_4 \leftarrow V$, $C_5 \leftarrow V$. Reading is continuous until halting after a specified time period.

The measured base end-to-end runtime (R_{rnas}) is depicted by the *Modified: 0 Snapshot* and *Unmodified: 0 Snapshot* trend lines, which indicate constant runtime as memory allocations increase.

The derived end-to-end runtime for workload ($R_{uh\_rnas\_t}$) with unmodified hypervisor-based state capture is depicted by the *Unmodified: 1 Snapshot <<theoretical>>* trend line, which indicates runtime increases with memory allocation

The derived end-to-end runtime for workload ($R_{mpi\_rnas\_t}$) with traditional MPI state capture is depicted by the *MPI: 1 Checkpoint <<theoretical>>* trend line, which indicates runtime increases with memory allocation.

The measured end-to-end runtime for workload (R_{mh_rnas}) running within a complex asset is depicted by the *Modified: 1 Snapshot* trend line, which indicates runtime stays constant as memory allocations increase. Measured overhead is as follows:

	2 GB	4 GB	6 GB	8 GB
$NB_{mh\_sco\_rnas}$	14	68	28	22

Average overhead for complex asset state capture is a constant of 33 *sec*.

For NAS synchronous reads: our approach incurs only a measured constant overhead during state capture, which indicates superior performance when compared with the derived theoretical linear growth of unmodified hypervisor snapshots and MPI checkpoints.

Table 5. NAS Read: Plotted values standard deviation

	2 GB	4 GB	6 GB	8 GB
R_{rnas} (unmodified hypervisor)	23	16	74	7
R_{rnas} (modified hypervisor)	24	24	21	8
R_{mh_rnas}	21	74	72	97
$R_{uh\_rnas\_t}$				
$R_{mpi\_rnas\_t}$				

6. CONCLUSIONS

We presented a logical encapsulation model for heterogeneous high performance infrastructure, which enabled the creation of a reactive resiliency approach for collections of virtual machines and externally hosted physical storage volumes. These dynamically provisioned distributed environments composed of resource federations delivered unobtrusive resiliency capabilities to parallel applications; including those performing traditional file system operations against both virtual disk and externally hosted storage. Performance measurements indicate our asynchronous state capture approach yielded significant performance improvements for message passing applications deployed within virtual execution environments. In the future, we plan to explore the behavior of our algorithm when state persistence targets vary and with numerous interconnect technologies. For example Fibre channel, 10GB Ethernet, and Infiniband interconnects; in addition to DAS, NAS, and SAN state persistence targets.

7. ACKNOWLEDGEMENTS

Special thanks to EMC senior executives for sponsoring this virtual high performance computing research: Jeffrey M. Nick (Chief Technology Officer), and Dr. Percy Tzelnic (Senior Vice President). Special thanks to VMware executives: Dr. Stephen Herrod (Chief Technology Officer) and Josh Simons (High Performance Computing). Finally, special thanks to EMC Labs China members: Thomas Fan and Lun Zhou.

8. REFERNCES

[1] Tikotekar, A., Vallée, G., Naughton, T., Ong, H., Engelmann, C. and Scott, S. *An Analysis of HPC Benchmarks in Virtual Machine Environments.* Springer Berlin / Heidelberg, 2009.

[2] Scott, S. L., Vallée, G., Naughton, T., Tikotekar, A., Engelmann, C. and Ong, H. System-level virtualization research at Oak Ridge National Laboratory. *Future Generation Computer Systems*, 26, 3 2010), 304-307.

[3] Youseff, L., Wolski, R., Gorda, B. and Krintz, C. *Evaluating the Performance Impact of Xen on MPI and Process Execution For HPC Systems.* 2006.

[4] Hargrove, P. and Duell, J. Berkeley Lab Checkpoint/Restart (BLCR) for Linux Clusters In *Proceedings of the SciDAC 2006* (2006). Lawrence Berkeley National Lab, 2006.

[5] Hursey, J., Squyres, J. M., Mattox, T. I. and Lumsdaine, A. *The Design and Implementation of Checkpoint/Restart Process Fault Tolerance for Open MPI.* 2007.

[6] Walters, J. P. and Chaudhary, V. A fault-tolerant strategy for virtualized HPC clusters. *J. Supercomput.*, 50, 3 2009), 209-239.

[7] Sankaran, S., Squyres, J. M., Barrett, B. and Lumsdaine, A. *The LAM/MPI checkpoint/restart framework: System-initiated checkpointing.* 2003.

[8] Kangarlou, A., Eugster, P. and Dongyan, X. *VNsnap: Taking snapshots of virtual networked environments with minimal downtime.* 2009.

[9] Ong, H., Saragol, N., Chanchio, K. and Leangsuksun, C. *VCCP: A transparent, coordinated checkpointing system for virtualization-based cluster computing.* 2009.

[10] Jiang, X. and Xu, D. *VIOLIN: Virtual Internetworking on OverLay INfrastructure.* 2003.

[11] Kangarlou, A., Xu, D., Ruth, P. and Eugster, P. Taking snapshots of virtual networked environments. In *Proceedings of the Proceedings of the 2nd international workshop on Virtualization technology in distributed computing* (Reno, Nevada, 2007). ACM, 2007.

[12] Vallee, G., Naughton, T., Engelmann, C., Hong, O. and Scott, S. L. *System-Level Virtualization for High Performance Computing.* 2008.

[13] Emeneker, W. and Stanzione, D. *HPC Cluster Readiness of Xen and User Mode Linux.* 2006.

[14] Wang, C., Mueller, F., Engelmann, C. and Scott, S. L. Proactive process-level live migration in HPC environments. In *Proceedings of the Proceedings of the 2008 ACM/IEEE conference on Supercomputing* (Austin, Texas, 2008). IEEE Press, 2008.

[15] Duell, J., Hargrove, P. and Roman., E. *The Design and Implementation of Berkeley Lab's Linux Checkpoint/Restart.* LBNL-54941, Lawrence Berkeley National Lab, 2002.

[16] Sun, M. H. *Fast, Lightweight Virtual Machine Checkpointing.* Georgia Tech, 2010.

[17] Clark, C., Fraser, K., Hand, S., Hansen, J. G., Jul, E., Limpach, C., Pratt, I. and Warfield, A. Live migration of virtual machines. In *Proceedings of the Proceedings of the 2nd conference on Symposium on Networked Systems Design \& Implementation - Volume 2* (2005). USENIX Association, 2005.

[18] Andrew Chien, H. C., Yang-suk Kee, and Richard Huang *The Virtual Grid Description Language.* UCSD, San Diego, 2004.

[19] Koslovski, G. P., Primet, P. V.-B. and Charão, A. S. *VXDL: Virtual Resources and Interconnection Networks Description Language.* Springer Berlin Heidelberg, 2009.

[20] Koslovski, G., Huu, T. T., Montagnat, J. and Primet, P. V.-B. *Executing Distributed Applications on Virtualized Infrastructures Specified with the VXDL Language and Managed by the HIPerNET Framework.* Springer Berlin Heidelberg, 2010.

[21] Distributed Management Task Force *Common Information Model.* Distributed Management Task Force, 2012.

[22] Distributed Management Task Force *CIM System Virtualization Model White Paper.* 2007.

[23] Storage Networking Industry Association *Storage Management Initiative Specification (SMI-S).* 2011.

Author Index

www.ingramcontent.com/pod-product-compliance
Lightning Source LLC
Chambersburg PA
CBHW061338210326
41598CB00035B/5817